Roberta,

To your
health and
happiness,

Carol

JANE BRODY'S GOOD FOOD BOOK
Living the High-Carbohydrate Way

OTHER BOOKS BY JANE E. BRODY

Secrets of Good Health (with Richard Engquist)
You Can Fight Cancer and Win (with Dr. Arthur I. Holleb)
Jane Brody's Nutrition Book
Jane Brody's The New York Times Guide to Personal Health

JANE BRODY'S GOOD FOOD BOOK

Living the High-Carbohydrate Way

by Jane E. Brody

Illustrations by Ray Skibinski

W·W·NORTON & COMPANY · NEW YORK LONDON

The text of this book is composed in Garamond, with display type set in Garamond and
Lucian. Composition and manufacturing by the Haddon Craftsmen, Inc.
Book design by Margaret M. Wagner.

Library of Congress Cataloging in Publication Data
Brody, Jane E.
Jane Brody's Good food book.
Includes index.
1. High-carbohydrate diet—Recipes.   I. Title.
II. Title: Good food book.
RM 237.59.B76   1985   613.2'8   85-2966

0-393-02210-2

W. W. Norton & Company, Inc., 500 Fifth Avenue, New York, N.Y. 10110
W. W. Norton & Company Ltd., 37 Great Russell Street, London WC1B 3NU

1 2 3 4 5 6 7 8 9 0

CONTENTS

II. A GUIDE TO THE GOOD CARBOHYDRATES

III. EAT YOUR WAY TO GOOD HEALTH AND WEIGHT CONTROL

V. RECIPES I HAVE KNOWN AND LOVED

TABLES

FOREWORD

In my days as a restaurant chef in New York, my life was sheltered. The restaurant kitchen that I oversaw had its rules, and I was comfortable with them. There was a tradition of centuries behind what we did at the old Pavillon, and when we changed something, when we let our creativity loose, it was within certain well-known parameters. Even in the terrible tumult of a busy professional kitchen, amid the clamor of pots hurled across the floor and orders shouted about, one was aware of the shades of the great men of French cooking, Auguste Escoffier foremost among them, quietly hovering and watching, taking care that nothing went awry.

I emerged from that shelter some years ago to take part in an American revolution of sorts. Everywhere in this country people were learning to cook. With James Beard and Julia Child leading the way, cooking had moved from the restaurant kitchen into the home.

In the main, the results have been admirable. As I have made my own contribution to the study of cooking, I have traveled widely, with an open mind and a great sense of enjoyment. So many cooks in this country, professional and amateur, have taken to good food with energy and art. Occasionally, though, I have seen what can go wrong. Once, I judged a contest in which one of the offerings was an eggplant soup that employed 2 cups of cream and 1 cup of butter for a mere 10 cups of broth. I was tempted to take out my whisk and beat the thing into a foam. Then there was the chocolate cake that used 24 ounces of chocolate, 1 pound of butter, 1½ cups of sugar, and 1 quart of cream. It clings to the palate even now.

I have seen excess on the other side, too. One dietetic asparagus soup I was presented with calls for margarine, flour, ½ cup of evaporated skim milk, instant chicken-broth mix, and 6 asparagus. This anemic recipe also tells the bewildered cook to add ¼ bay leaf. Now, what ¼ bay leaf is going to do for that soup (especially when it is seasoned by a chicken-broth mix whose ingredients are largely mysterious) is beyond me.

In the first two instances—the eggplant soup and chocolate cake—I see richness for its own sake, a kind of culinary decadence. In the last instance—the asparagus soup—I see the mindless fashioning of food combinations that are meant to contribute to one's good health but, I believe, can only leave the eater impoverished through the experience.

I know Jane Brody, and I knew as I approached the book at hand that she would not be guilty of excess in either direction. If there were a way to combine an emphasis on modern nutritional wisdom with care and intelligence in cooking, Jane Brody would certainly find it.

In no way did she let me down. The nutrition discussions in the first part of the book are pure Jane Brody and will please anyone who has been a fan of her "Personal Health" column in *The New York Times.* That column has become so successful because of the author's warm and genuine regard for the quality of our lives, a regard that she combines with the skills of a probing journalist. The result of that combination is that her readers bestow on her the gift of their trust.

As in her trustworthy newspaper columns, Jane Brody pulls off a neat trick in this book. Just after she has informed us that practically every evident tendency in American eating is misdirected—too much fat, too much protein, too much sugar, and too much salt—she manages to persuade us that life can still be worth living. The support for that contention is the large collection of recipes that forms Part V of this book.

Those recipes surprised me. I did not expect such adventurousness from a nutrition writer. Nor did I expect myself to feel so comfortable among the recipes. Jane Brody has demonstrated here a sharp eye for good cooking. The dishes can be solidly traditional or bold and innovative, yet sensible. The recipes, for the most part, adhere to my own principles of seasoning: to use seasoning amply but subtly blended so that each dish has its own, new complex flavor.

The recipes are chosen from most of the world's cuisines, showing Jane Brody's delightful willingness to be open to many culinary influences. But, as international as the collection ultimately is, I kept feeling that I was really leafing through a great American cookbook, one destined to take its place alongside such classics as *The Joy of Cooking* or *America Cooks.*

I was pleased to see how similar in many ways the cooking philosophy enunciated in this book is to my own. I especially like the concentration on carbohydrates. The pasta, potatoes, beans, and rice that are central to all of my own cooking are presented here by Jane Brody in their rightful place as the most healthful and satisfying of foods. In my native France, they are the heart of peasant and bourgeoise cooking—and, in some measure, haute cuisine, too. They will not clog the arteries. (If the French guzzled cream the way Americans think they do, one of the world's great cultures would have long ago perished.) Potatoes and rice have kept much of the earth's population alive. In my own home one or the other is served nearly every day, and I make a point of serving it attractively. For instance, I take humble boiled rice and add bits of colorful pepper, then mold it in a demitasse cup for individual servings.

Jane Brody does not take as strong a position as I do on the issue of butter versus margarine. But I was gratified to see that she and I really are not very far apart. I view margarine as a culinary catastrophe that has struck this country. I have watched, appalled, as people slather margarine on their bread, thinking it somehow dietetic when in fact it has just as many calories as butter. True, margarine is lower in cholesterol. But butter, used sparingly and well in cooking, adds very little to one's total dietary cholesterol. Not only that. One tends to be disciplined in the use of butter, whereas margarine seems so innocuous that it may be used with far less restraint. The penalty for this benighted, excessive use of margarine is, of course, food that does not benefit from the silken richness that the smallest bit of butter can impart. Any cook who fails to acknowledge that can't be on my team. Jane Brody, I'm pleased to say, makes the team easily.

While Jane Brody has been searching for ways to wed her nutritional principles to cooking, I have been looking for ways to join my cooking principles to current nutritional thinking. Thus I, too, have been laboring of late to create and find recipes that fit into the contemporary drive toward greater health. The work has been difficult, and so I can well appreciate what Jane Brody has done here. Her new book is a considerable achievement. I leave it with a sense that she and I, having come from such divergent origins, are traveling companions nonetheless.

Pierre Franey

PROLOGUE: WHY YOU SHOULD READ THIS BOOK

One of the most frequent questions I've been asked since the publication of *Jane Brody's Nutrition Book* in 1981 is: "Where can I get a cookbook that follows the nutrition guidelines outlined in your book"—that is, for a diet emphasizing the starchy foods but low in fats and added sugars and moderate in protein? Although there are hundreds of cookbooks—many of them excellent—that cater to such diets as low-calorie, low-sodium, low-fat, low-cholesterol, no-added-sugar, high-fiber, vegetarian, macrobiotic, all-natural-food, etc., none exists that was designed for the ordinary health-conscious American who doesn't need a therapeutic diet or want totally meatless menus, the American who's not interested in fads, rigidity, fanaticism, deprivation, and constant self-denial, or in spending hours a day in the kitchen. Since I am such a person, I decided to write a book that would meet these demands without sacrificing the pleasure of good food and well-orchestrated meals. In the course of my research, I learned a great deal about foods and cooking, food selection and preparation, kitchen equipment and organization, recipe modification, sources for healthful ingredients, and shortcuts for the busy consumer. I have gathered these together here, and now pass them on to you.

In my previous book I set out the overall principles of good nutrition—the relative value of various nutrients and foods, from vitamins and minerals to fast foods and health foods. I recommended there that our diets should lean more heavily on the complex carbohydrates—starchy foods like potatoes, rice, pasta, beans, and bread. This book gives the full story of these health-promoting carbohydrates and shows you how to put such a diet to work for you. It is a practical, everyday guide to eating sensibly that can help you gradually relinquish old unwholesome patterns of food selection and preparation and substitute delicious but healthful new ones. The recipes and menus will help you choose and prepare foods that stimulate your taste buds without undermining your health, expanding your waistline, emptying your pockets, or depriving you of eating pleasure. Even though overweight is the nation's most visible nutrition problem, it is far from its only one. And even if weight is not one of your problems, the approach to eating and the shopping and cooking techniques described here are still critically important to your health and the quality of your continued life.

The book is organized into two main sections. In the first section I discuss basic guidelines to good nutrition and why you should follow them. Since my approach to nutrition emphasizes the health-promoting starchy foods, a large portion of the text is devoted to helping you gain an appreciation for the value of these foods—both throughout human history and for you and your family today. There are chapters on the major starches, such as potatoes and pasta, as well as on fruits, vegetables, nuts, and seeds. There are also chapters on weight control, the nation's number one nutritional problem, and guidelines on restructuring your eating and exercise habits (both at home and when eating out) to help you achieve and maintain a normal body weight for the rest of your life *without dieting.* And there are chapters on how to make healthful home cooking an enjoyable part of your busy life.

The second section of the book is a cookbook, filled with recipes that my family and my friends have tasted and enjoyed. In many cases, the recipes were modified from ones that I once made in less nutritious forms. Others are newly invented or adopted or adapted from well-established cookbooks and cooking magazines. Following the recipes is a menu guide to show you how these recipes can be used in planning nutritious meals for you and your family.

This is a book for people who enjoy eating. It will allow you to eat along with mainstream America, only better—more healthfully, less expensively, and with fewer of your calories turning to body fat. And you won't have to shop in special stores or give up all your favorite foods or become a galley slave to do it. The menus and recipes in the second section of the book are designed to suit most every person and every occasion—young and old; families and single people; two-career households; dinner and holiday guests; weight-watchers and salt-, fat-, cholesterol-, sugar-, and additive-watchers—without leaving you, your family, or your guests feeling hungry or deprived. The chapter on dining out will help you to continue your healthful eating habits away from home, whether you're a brown-bagger or fast-food freak, or you dine often in four-star restaurants, or you frequently find yourself on airplanes at mealtime.

My aim is to help you get more pleasure out of eating while reducing your risk of developing heart disease, cancer, diabetes, high blood pressure, and other life-shortening health problems that currently plague so many millions of Americans. In the bargain, you'll be able to shave dollars off your weekly food budget and excess pounds off your frame without going "on a diet." My husband lost 26 pounds effortlessly and painlessly and has kept them off now for five years by eating according to the principles outlined in this book. In fact, many of the recipes and food preparation tips herein are his.

To be sure, cooking healthfully is not as simple as throwing a steak in the broiler, frozen French fries in the pan, and a can of peas in the pot (not to mention popping a prepared frozen dinner in the microwave). But once you get the hang of it, you'll find that preparing healthful, good-tasting meals that the whole family can enjoy is a lot easier than you now think it is. (If you're a novice in the kitchen, be sure to read Part IV.) Even if you do end up spending more time and thought on selecting and preparing meals, it will be worth it in the end, for you will have gained extra years of wellness and peak energy. To those who say "But I don't have time to cook," my answer is "People make time for the things they consider important." And *how you feed your body is important,* not just to your future but to the quality of your present life as well.

Healthy cooking requires some advance planning, but it can also give you many ready-made and nearly instant nutritious and delicious meals and enable you to make use of practically all leftovers. In my house, we almost never throw out food. Most leftovers are used in a soup or stir-fry; old cheese gets grated into casseroles, breads, and soups along with wilted or leftover vegetables; soured milk, yogurt, or cottage cheese is used to create light and luscious pancakes and baked goods. And our freezer is stocked with home-made "TV dinners" and heat-and-serve lunches, all of them far more nutritious and delicious than what you'd buy in the store.

As in *Jane Brody's Nutrition Book,* the emphasis here is on variety, moderation, and gradual change. Your meals and menus needn't and shouldn't be boring or overly repetitious. You don't have to give up all your favorite foods to eat healthfully. And you don't have to revolutionize your diet overnight. In fact, a gradual change in your cooking and eating habits is far easier, more enjoyable, and much less likely to inspire a counterrevolution that catapults you and your family right back to your old ways. Start slowly. Learn the basic principles, and begin to reorient your thinking away from meals centered on large portions of animal protein; periodically introduce new and healthier dishes into your current eating plan; and gradually reduce your dependence on fats, sugars, and salt.

The menus and recipes in this book were developed in just this way—slowly, over a period of years, as my nutrition consciousness and knowledge grew. Many are derived from old established but unhealthful favorites that I modified to suit the needs of a modern, fast-moving, but health-conscious life style. Some were generously contributed by friends and acquaintances. All have been prepared by me one or more times and eaten and enjoyed by family and friends, among others. Many of the recipes were taste-tested at special "dinner parties" where the sole requirement for attendance was an enjoyment of good eating and a willingness to complete taste questionnaires about each dish. This gave me an opportunity to further modify some dishes before passing them along to you and to discard those that did not meet the criteria of excellence demanded by discerning friends. Finally, Lori Longbotham, a professional cook and food consultant, has evaluated all of the recipes and further tested many of them.

Many of you may be experienced cooks, while others may be less confident in the kitchen. But once you come to appreciate the basic principles of my high-carbohydrate health plan and learn which ingredient substitutions work and under what conditions, you'll be able to make your own modifications in favorite recipes to increase their nutritive value without compromising taste and eating pleasure.

You may now find this hard to believe, but chances are that after a year or two you won't even think to buy a steak or roast for dinner, or feast on half a fried chicken, or breakfast on bacon and eggs. And you won't even miss them! Human tastes and food preferences are far more malleable than most people realize. People like to eat what they're used to eating. For most of us, food selection and preparation are deeply ingrained habits, acquired in childhood and carried over from the way our parents cooked and ate. We are used to certain tastes, certain ways of doing things in the kitchen, certain meal patterns, certain menu favorites. Unfortunately, though comfortable, these eating habits are not always good for us. But fortunately, although habits may be well entrenched, they are not immutable. Old unhealthy habits can be replaced by new and healthier ones—and with no loss of pleasure or choice in the process. This book is designed to show you why and how to make that change. For more details about the basics of good nutrition and specific requirements for people of various ages and life circumstances, consult *Jane Brody's Nutrition Book,* now available as a Bantam paperback as well as in hardcover from W. W. Norton & Company.

The facts presented and recommendations made in this book are based on the best scientific knowledge available by the end of 1984. As new and better information comes to light, it will be included in future editions. Since this is a book intended for use by the general public, no scientific bibliography is included, although references are usually made to the sources of studies. General readers interested in further information might consult the books listed under "For Further Reading" at the end of some chapters.

To be sure, many controversies still remain about the potential benefits and risks of various nutritional guidelines. Science, by its very nature, is constantly evolving and discovering new facts that dispute the old. However, we cannot afford to wait for the day—if that day ever comes—of irrevocable nutritional certainties. All of us make decisions every day on what to eat, and none of us can afford to wait for every *i* to be dotted and *t* to be crossed. We have to choose our foods based on the best information currently at hand.

It's also important to realize that it's never too late to change your diet and other habits to improve your health and your chances of living long and happily. Although it is best to start in youth to prevent some of the most devastating damage caused by poor nutrition, at any time in life that you improve your diet you can benefit from the change.

It's just as easy to get used to and to enjoy eating foods that are good for you as it is to live on the health-robbing, high-fat, high-sugar, high-salt, high-calorie diet most Americans now consume. And when your basic diet is nutritious and health-promoting, you'll be able to indulge occasionally in old not-so-nutritious favorites without compromising your health or your figure. You don't have to become a fanatic or a health-food devotee to eat healthfully. In fact, you can have your cake and eat it too, as long as it's not too much cake too often! Now—read, eat, and enjoy.

Jane E. Brody, March 1985

ACKNOWLEDGMENTS

For more than two years, friends (both old and new) and family (both old and young) have been thrust, willingly or not, into the role of official tasters for the hundreds of recipes in this book (and the hundreds of others that didn't make it into the book). After a while the kids stopped asking me such questions as "Are these *normal* pancakes?" and "Is this a test or is it *regular* food?" I knew I had won converts when, after breakfasting out on so-called normal pancakes, they confessed that mine were much better.

As for friends, all they ever asked was "How soon can I buy this book?" and "Can I get the recipe *before* it comes out?"

Thank you all for your enthusiasm and encouragement, patience and forbearance, not to mention advice and comments. They helped, I hope, to make this *the book* for health-, weight-, and food-conscious Americans—people who want to eat to live at the same time that they live to eat.

While it is not possible to thank by name all who helped to make this book possible, a few deserve special mention:

My agent, Wendy Weil, who provided invaluable guidance and unfailing enthusiasm for the project.

My editor at Norton, Mary E. Cunnane, who dealt calmly and intelligently with an occasionally unwieldy manuscript and an author who some times ran amok.

Manuscript editor Carol Flechner, whose skill is unsurpassed in whipping a 1,500-page manuscript into a case study of editorial clarity in record time. I wish I had a dollar for every embarrassing goof she spared me.

Artist Ray Skibinski and designer Margaret Wagner, whose talents and instincts turned a collection of words into a work of art.

Production manager Andy Marasia, who turned handsprings and performed other miracles that made it possible for this book to be published on time without any sacrifice in quality.

Publicity director Fran Rosencrantz and subsidiary rights director Jeannie Luciano, whose sterling efforts were so crucial to the success of *Jane Brody's Nutrition Book* and who promise to do even more for this one.

Everyone else at Norton, who never wavered in their unqualified support for this project. It is a pleasure to work with you.

My special friends Faith Sullivan, Margaret Shryer, Jo-Ann Friedman, and Susan McGee, who provided shoulders to lean on when the weight of work wore me down as well as deft hands in the kitchen whenever needed.

My boss, Rick Flaste, who never flagged in his faith in me to do two full-time jobs at once and who provided the flexibility to make it possible.

My husband, Richard Engquist, who put up with overstuffed refrigerators, bursting cupboards, and thousands of receipts for food and equipment, not to mention a perpetual smorgasbord of foods to eat and a steady stream of errands to run for missing ingredients.

My sons, Erik and Lorin, who shouldered the bulk of KP with minimal protest over the millions of dishes, pots, pans, and utensils I dirtied while testing up to 12 recipes a day. Sorry, boys, but I don't think I like "regular food" any more!

Jane E. Brody

I. The New Nutrition: Back to the Basics

Introduction

How would you like to eat more potatoes, pasta, bread, rice, and other starchy foods without feeling nutritionally guilty or worrying about putting on unwanted pounds? How would you like to say good-by forever to distorted weight-reduction schemes and feelings of deprivation and self-denial, and instead leave the table satisfied, invigorated—and slender? How would you like to increase your expendable income by saving money on food and medical bills? How would you like to enjoy your later years unmarred by chronic, fun-robbing illness? And how would you like to do it all without sacrificing the enjoyment of food and social dining?

The eating plan outlined in this book will help to make this possible. All that's required is a return to the high-carbohydrate, high-fiber diet that human beings evolved on and that most people of the world still live on. There are no guarantees, of course, but there is the opportunity to improve your odds of living a long, healthy, happy life, and to get more pleasure from your food in the process.

Within this century, the diet of the average American has undergone a radical shift away from plant-based foods such as grains, beans and peas, nuts, potatoes, and other vegetables and fruits and toward foods derived from animals —meat, fish, poultry, eggs, and dairy products. The shift to more costly animal foods has occurred even among the poor, whose dietary habits tend to mimic the middle-class values disseminated through the mass media.

Studies of primates from the most primitive monkey to modern man indicate that we are all opportunistic meat eaters. This means that given the opportunity, we are likely to consume as much animal food as we can, a characteristic that is undoubtedly an evolutionary carry-over to make sure that we ate enough high-quality protein as part of our mostly vegetarian diet. In the wild, the amount of animal protein available for consumption by two- and four-legged primates is limited by infrequent opportunity. During an invasion of locusts, for example, a colony of baboons is likely to turn its back on most plant foods and instead subsist on a diet that is 90 percent animal protein (locusts are a favorite baboon food); but as soon as the swarm of insects moves on, our evolutionary relatives return to their more customary vegetarian menu.

Modern society in an affluent culture like ours imposes no such restrictions. Animal-protein foods are readily and consistently available—from supermarkets and four-star restaurants to fast-food drive-ins and street vendors—and the predominant dietary value suggests that they be served at every meal. Unfortunately, there is considerable evidence that the diet possible in this land of opportunity is doing many of us in even before the Biblical three score and 10.

It's true that in this century, the life expectancy of Americans has increased nearly 30 years. But almost the entire gain has resulted from fewer deaths among infants, children, and postpartum women, made possible by such public-health advances as improved sanitation, immunizations, and antibiotics. Little has been done to extend life beyond middle age. The average middle-aged American today does not live much longer than his or her counterpart did in 1900. Today's 45-year-old American male can look forward to living only four years longer, to age 74, than his age mate did in 1900; and the 45-year-old American female today lives only seven years longer, to age 80, than her counterpart did at the turn of the century. These statistics reflect the fact that older Americans who are now saved from fatal infections by antibiotics and immunizations are instead succumbing to chronic, incurable disease. Even those who survive to 70 or beyond often spend the last decades of their lives plagued by debilitating diseases, many of which are related to our affluent diet.

In a groundbreaking report "Health and Behavior," published with little fanfare in 1982, a prestigious committee of the National Academy of Sciences–National Research Council concluded that at least 50 percent of the deaths from the 10 leading causes of death in the United States today are related to life-style factors. In other words, we are largely wiping out the public-health gains of our younger years by the way we now live, and especially by the way we now eat. Too many Americans think that eating healthfully means stuffing themselves with vitamins and minerals. These are indeed essential nutrients, but they are the *microingredients* of the diet, and, given our abundant and varied food supply, currently their intake represents the least of our nutritional problems. Rather, it is the kinds and amounts of the *macroingredients*—fats, proteins, and carbohydrates—that have the most significant health impact today. A vast body of evidence indicates that the current American diet contains *too much* fat, sugar, protein, and *too little* starch as found in grains, beans, and potatoes.

Studies comparing groups of people nationally and internationally, as well as experiments with laboratory animals, have linked these dietary patterns to a greatly increased risk of developing such killers and cripplers as heart disease, cancer, high blood pressure, stroke, diabetes, osteoporosis, and the most prominent of dietary disorders—obesity.

Based on these findings, public-health experts—including the American Heart Association, the American Cancer Society, the United States Department of Agriculture, and the National Institutes of Health—have issued solemn warnings: Americans must change their culinary ways if they don't want to eat themselves into an early grave or a poor imitation of the Goodyear blimp. And the problem is hardly limited to Americans. It afflicts nearly all affluent "Westernized" societies—England, Germany, France, Sweden, Australia—every country where people eat too high on the hog and let their fingers, rather than their feet, do the walking. It's time for all peoples to return to a diet that more closely resembles what the human body was biochemically designed to handle.

1 ·
DIETARY LESSONS FROM HUMAN EVOLUTION

Most of us have an impression of early man as a successful hunter who, dressed in a loin cloth, went out each day with a club over his shoulder to catch something for supper. Usually, however, early man came back empty-handed because most animals were simply too swift for a man armed with only a club. The real hero of the survival of the human species was not early man but early woman. She spent her days near the base camp gathering fruits, nuts, seeds, tubers, roots, berries, beans, and grains and made meals for the early human family out of complex carbohydrates—starchy foods—and fresh fruits and vegetables, with occasional feasts of meat when her mate was lucky enough to bag a mole or lizard.

Until recently, archaeological evidence had greatly exaggerated the role of meat in the diets of prehumans and prehistoric humans because animal bones are far better preserved in the rocky fossil record than are softer plant materials. Even recently abandoned sites of modern aboriginal tribes show no plant remains, although these tribes are known to eat mostly vegetable foods. However, in the last decade or so, anthropologists and archaeologists have devised some ingenious techniques that clearly reveal the vegetarian emphasis of our progenitors.

For example, microscopic studies of fossilized teeth from early human ancestors who roamed the earth some 4 million years ago indicate that they were primarily fruit eaters, according to Dr. Alan Walker, a Johns Hopkins University anthropologist. The wear patterns on the fossil teeth of the forebears of *Homo sapiens* look exactly like those on the teeth of modern fruit eaters, and there are almost no marks that result from eating meat and bones. Not until the evolution about 1.5 million years ago of *Homo erectus,* the immediate ancestor of our species, was there evidence of a mixed diet of plant and animal foods. But even then, there is reason to believe that animal foods were not the primary fare until quite recently in our evolutionary history. Analyses of fossils of human feces deposited by North American peoples from 300,000 years ago to a few hundred years ago reveal that our human ancestors subsisted primarily on a vegetable diet, consuming over 100 different varieties of plant foods. In rockshelter sites in southwestern Texas that are less than 3,000 years old, evidence indicates that except for grasshoppers, a limited amount of animal protein was eaten by those who dwelled there. The Human Nutrition Program at the University of Michigan has been examining the diets of Stone Age people who inhabited the lower Illinois Valley 5,000 years ago. Studies of their remains show that they consumed seeds, nuts, berries, and roots from hundreds of plant species, many of which still grow in the area and most of which ironically are now considered weeds.

The hunting and eating of mammoths, those now-extinct elephantlike creatures pushed southward by the advancing glaciers of the Ice Age, date back only about 300,000 years. And even then, meat was not the central item in the diet. Plants were. Dairy products did not become a significant part of the diet until the domestication of cattle, about 10,000 years ago. Eggs, too, were a rare luxury, obtained only by robbing birds' nests before fowl were domesticated. In short, if the human species had had to depend on large supplies of animal protein for its survival, it would have died out 2 million years ago.

MODERN TRIBES EAT MOSTLY PLANT FOODS

The hunter-gatherer tribes that today live like our prehistoric human ancestors consume primarily a vegetable diet supplemented with animal foods. An analysis of 58 societies of modern hunter-gatherers, including the !Kung of southern Africa, revealed that one-half emphasize gathering of plant foods, one-third concentrate on fishing, and only one-sixth are primarily hunters. Overall, two-thirds or more of the hunter-gatherer's calories come from plants. Detailed studies of the !Kung by A. S. Truswell, food scientist at the University of London, showed that gathering is a more productive source of food than is hunting. An hour of hunting yields on average about 100 edible calories, whereas an hour of gathering produces 240. Plant foods provide 60 percent to 80 percent of the !Kung diet, and no one goes hungry when the hunt fails. Interestingly, if they escape fatal infections or accidents, these contemporary aborigines live to old ages despite the absence of medical care. They experience no obesity, no middle-aged spread, little dental decay, no high blood pressure, no coronary heart disease, and their blood cholesterol levels are very low (about half that of the average American adult). While no one is suggesting that we return to an aboriginal life style, we certainly could use their eating habits as a model for a healthier diet.

Even among less primitive cultures that have not yet achieved the affluence of twentieth-century America, dietary patterns more closely resemble human evolutionary destiny. In the meals of Mexico, India, Japan, the Middle East, China, Turkey, Greece, and Italy, emphasis is on the starchy foods, using animal protein more as a condiment and as a complement to the protein in plant foods than as the centerpiece of the menu. To be sure, as affluence increases in these and similar countries, so does the consumption of animal foods, especially red meat. And along with it goes an increase in the chronic health problems that now afflict Americans.

A look at our digestive apparatus is also revealing. Our teeth are structured more for grinding, like those of herbivorous cattle, than for tearing meat, like the teeth of carnivorous cats and dogs. And our long and convoluted intestinal tracts are better designed for the slow digestion of fibrous plant foods, rather than the short, straight, fast tract needed by carnivores to process meat and quickly dispose of the resulting toxic wastes. Noted anthropologist Dr. F. Clark Howell of the University of California, Berkeley, points out that our gastrointestinal tract, liver, metabolic enzymes, and kidneys evolved long before our big brains did some 3 million years ago. "We are little different in these respects from modern subhuman primates," he says.

OUR DIET IS OUT OF BALANCE

But while our digestive and metabolic systems have not changed in any substantive way in the last 2 million years, our diet has changed drastically. Compared with our evolutionary ancestors, most people in industrialized countries today are voracious meat eaters. Throughout the world, diets rich in animal foods like red meat, fish, poultry, and eggs have become symbols of affluence.

This is especially so in the United States, where per-capita consumption of animal foods has been rising steadily throughout this century. Even as recently as 1900, Americans were far less dependent on animals to flesh out their diets. In 1900, two-thirds of our protein came not from animals, but from plant foods. Today that statistic is turned completely around: 70 percent of the protein we consume is derived from animals, and only 30 percent comes from plants. The problem with animal-derived protein is the baggage it usually comes with. The most popular animal protein foods are nearly all more fat than protein. About 80 percent of the calories in steak or hamburger are fat calories, not protein; 75 percent of the calories in most hard cheeses come from fat; and even chicken (when eaten with the skin) is 50 percent to 60 percent fat calories.

Most plant proteins, on the other hand, derive the bulk of their calories from complex carbohydrates—starches—which are not linked to any serious health risks. (Exceptions are nuts and seeds, which contain large amounts of fat, though not the artery-clogging saturated fats found in most animal foods.) Although diet is not the only important factor, there is ample evidence that the shift away from a diet rich in complex carbohydrates has seriously undermined our health and limited our longevity. If we're truly interested in improving the quality of life as well as its length, it's time to return to a healthier diet that more closely resembles our biological destiny.

FOR FURTHER READING

Farb, Peter, and George Armelagos. *Consuming Passions: The Anthropology of Eating.* Boston: Houghton Mifflin, 1980.
Sussman, Vic. *The Vegetarian Alternative.* Emmaus, Pa.: Rodale Press, 1978.

2 ·
TOO MUCH PROTEIN, FAT, SUGAR, AND SALT

Portrait of a typical American dinner:

- A generous portion of animal protein—maybe 5 to 8 ounces of red meat or a quarter of a chicken or ½ pound of fish
- Potatoes deep-fried and salted or, if baked, topped with butter and salt
- Vegetables liberally buttered and salted
- A salad doused with a salty, oil-based dressing
- A sugary soft drink
- Pudding, ice cream, cake, or pie for dessert

You don't have to be rich to sit down to such a dinner. Millions of Americans eat it almost every night, thinking they are meeting their nutritional requirement as they satisfy their appetite. But while the diners may not be rich, that meal most certainly is. The amount of protein is double, triple, even quadruple the amount needed in a single meal; the fat content easily adds up to half the total calories; the salt meets the recommended amount for an entire day; and there may be as much as 27 teaspoons of sugar in the drink and dessert.

We are a nation that thrives on excess, and American nutritional habits have long been based on the premise that "if some is good, more must be better." This may be a fine guideline if the commodity in question is money, love, or sex, but it breaks down like cotton candy when it comes to food and nutrients. Doubling your protein intake, for example, is not better for you than sticking to the minimum recommended amount. Just because sugar and fat make foods taste good doesn't mean foods will taste twice as good with twice the amount of these nutrients. And while a sprinkling of salt may enhance the flavor of some foods, ½ teaspoon may disguise the real flavor as well as do you bodily harm.

The previous chapter should have convinced you that we're not biologically destined to eat the way Americans do today. Let's take a closer look at how we got to this sorry nutritional state, what harm it can do, and what we should and can be doing about it.

OUR PASSION FOR PROTEIN

If you remember anything you were taught about good eating habits in school, no doubt you recall the admonitions to eat enough protein. Since protein is an essential nutrient without which we cannot survive, and since the "highest quality" protein foods tend to be the most expensive items in the grocery cart, our dietary gurus wanted to be sure we did not stint on it. And we took them seriously. Encouraged by steadily increasing affluence and our notion that "more must be better," Americans took to protein with such a vengeance that now the average person in this country, rich and poor alike, eats at least two times more protein than is really needed for good nutrition.

STRAINING BUDGET AND BODY. More than two-thirds of the protein we consume comes from animals, especially beef cattle, our favorite prestige food. Most of these animals are prepared for market on feed lots, where they consume large quantities of grain. As much as 8 pounds of grain are needed to produce just 1 pound of meat. (By contrast, for poultry and hogs, the grain-to-meat ratio is only about 2.5 to 1.) Not only is this wasteful of the earth's resources and an unnecessary strain on our budgets, there is also fast-growing evidence that it's not good for us. Excess consumption of protein has been linked to such hazards as a shorter life expectancy, increased risk of developing cancer and heart disease, loss of calcium from our bones, stress on our kidneys, dehydration, and obesity.

Test animals fed high-protein diets die sooner than animals given the same number of calories but with fewer of them coming from protein. Animals that are slightly underfed do even better, and studies dating back over a 50-year period (beginning with the 1935 findings of the late Dr. Clive McCay of Cornell University) have repeatedly shown that the longest-lived animals are those that eat a low-protein diet spare enough in calories to keep them 25 percent to 30 percent slimmer than their littermates. One benefit of a low-protein, low-calorie diet, the animal studies show, is that it boosts the ability of the immune system to defend the body against cancer.

Since our favorite protein foods—meat, cheese, poultry, eggs, and fish—come laden with saturated animal fats and cholesterol, their overconsumption is a risk to the health of our heart and blood vessels, which tend to get clogged up with fatty deposits on such a diet. You'll recall that although we think of these foods as high in protein (and they *are* good sources of high-quality protein), most contain more fat calories than protein. Feed-lot–fattened beef cattle are the fattest of all: their carcasses often have five times more fat than do range-fed cattle, and more than twice as much fat ends up as "marbling" in the meat itself.

But even a lean high-protein diet can promote the development of fat-clogged arteries, according to studies in such animals as pigeons, rabbits, and monkeys. If we ate less total protein and got more of our protein from plant foods such as dried beans, nuts, seeds, potatoes, pasta, rice, and corn, we would significantly reduce the amount of harmful fats and cholesterol we consume.

(See p. 170 for guidelines on how to get good protein from plant foods.) More than two decades of research among 25,000 Seventh-Day Adventists by Dr. Roland Phillips and Dr. David Snowdon of Loma Linda, California, revealed that American vegetarians who eat no animal products or only dairy foods and eggs generally have less cholesterol in their blood and lower blood pressure, and are far less likely to suffer premature heart disease than are meat-eating Americans. Autopsies of hundreds of people whose diets were studied before they died showed that those who consumed lots of legumes (dried peas and beans and peanuts) and vegetables had less clogging of their blood vessels than those whose diets were rich in milk and meat products. And recent studies in both the United States and Italy revealed that soy protein, which is consumed in significant amounts by most vegetarians, actually helps to lower blood cholesterol levels and may actively protect against coronary heart disease.

Both in people and in laboratory rats, diets high in protein have been shown to increase the loss of calcium from bones, possibly contributing to osteoporosis, a thinning of the bones with age that is almost epidemic among older Americans, especially women, and that can ultimately lead to crippling fractures. High-protein diets can also result in high levels of uric acid in the blood, which may lead to gout. Too much protein can further impair kidney function in people who already have kidney disease, which is often undiagnosed until kidney failure is imminent. The kidneys rid the body of the nitrogen part of the protein molecule that is not needed for building or rebuilding body tissues. So much nitrogen is excreted by Americans that it's been suggested (not entirely facetiously) that we could stop producing artificial fertilizer if instead we harvested and used the wasted nitrogen in American toilet bowls.

What is left behind of the protein molecule after your body disposes of unneeded nitrogen simply becomes a source of calories. If you are already consuming enough calories to maintain a normal body weight, you will gain weight eating extra protein. You can get just as fat by eating too many hamburgers or too much chicken as by eating too many doughnuts. The body makes no distinction: extra calories from whatever source get stored as body fat. And while there is a prevailing notion that high-protein reducing diets can make it easier for people to lose unwanted pounds (spawning literally dozens of fad diets during the last 100 years), recent research conducted by Dr. Robert B. Bradfield and Dr. Martin H. Jourdan at the University of California, Berkeley, shows this to be a myth. It had been thought that the process of digesting and metabolizing protein used up about one-third of the calories the protein contributed. However, this turns out to be untrue when a person consumes a mixed diet of protein, fats, and carbohydrates, which you necessarily do when you eat real food.

In the California study, obese women lived on medically controlled formula diets in a special hospital ward for 10 days. The researchers found no caloric advantage to consuming a high-protein diet. In fact, just the opposite may be true. More calories are "wasted" when less protein is consumed. A research team (Drs. Patillo Donald, Grover C. Pitts, and Stephen L. Pohl) at the University of Virginia in Charlottesville showed that rats gained weight faster and put on proportionally more body fat on a high-protein diet than on one with the identical number of calories but with less protein and more carbohydrates.

Other notions about the advantages of high-protein diets also turn out to be more myth than fact. For example, athletes do not need extra protein; their muscles cannot use protein for fuel—only fats and carbohydrates. Excess protein can also cause dangerous dehydration because the kidneys must excrete a lot of water to get rid of unneeded nitrogen. Too much protein may thus impair athletic performance, both by robbing muscles of needed water and by making it necessary to empty the bladder in the midst of a game or race. And large amounts of protein do not make people stronger. The only way to increase body strength is to exercise your muscles against resistance, such as in hitting a tennis ball or lifting weights.

FAT, OUR WORST NUTRITIONAL FAILING

Given our passion for protein, it is interesting to learn that fat is a far more popular nutrient than protein as a constituent of the American diet. Whereas protein contributes about 15 percent of the calories we consume each day, fat is the source of more than 40 percent of our total calories. And whereas most of the protein we eat is a source of essential nutrients, most of the fat we consume is merely empty calories. We could fully satisfy our nutritional requirement for fat by consuming the equivalent of 1 tablespoon of vegetable oil each day. But the average American consumes eight times that amount—the fat equivalent of one stick of butter a day—and in the process packs in a load of extra calories.

Although by weight fat is about equal to protein as a dietary ingredient, when its caloric contribution is considered, it looms far more prominently. Fat supplies two and a quarter times more calories than the same amount of protein. There are 9 calories in a gram of fat compared to 4 calories in a gram of protein. Fat is also more fattening than starch or sugar, each of which yields 4 calories per gram. It is even more fattening than alcohol, which provides 7 calories per gram. Thus, fat is our most fattening nutrient. In fact, fat makes a far greater contribution to the weight problems of Americans than does sugar, which accounts for less than 20 percent of the calories in the typical American diet. Fat is also a leading culprit in our two most deadly diseases: heart disease and cancer.

HARD ON THE HEART. Fat and its sidekick, cholesterol, should concern all Americans, not just those people known to have a "cholesterol problem" or a family history of heart disease. Half of Americans die of heart and blood-vessel diseases, and most of those people do not have very high levels of cholesterol in their blood. Yet autopsies of their blood vessels show large deposits of fatty gunk, which represent the cumulative effect of years of eating too much saturated fat and cholesterol. It is true that the human body manufactures a lot of cholesterol on its own—much more, in fact, than an ordinary person is likely to consume in a day. However, the cholesterol you eat seems to be handled differently. Studies by Dr. Robert W. Mahley, pathologist at the University of California, San Francisco, and director of the Gladstone Foundation Laboratories there, indicate that internally manufactured cholesterol goes into the metabolic pipeline that results in the manufacture of needed hormones, cell membranes, vitamin D, and protective sheaths for nerve fibers. But *dietary* cholesterol seems to follow a different route, entering the general circulation and beating a more direct path to blood vessels. In 1980, Dr. Richard B. Shekelle of Rush–Presbyterian–St. Luke's Medical Center in Chicago analyzed deaths among 1,900 middle-aged American men whose diets were first examined more than 20 years earlier. The analysis showed that those who consumed large amounts of cholesterol had a much greater chance of dying prematurely of a heart attack. And a national study completed in 1983 among 3,806 men by the National Heart, Lung, and Blood Institute showed that reducing cholesterol in the blood can indeed be life-saving. When the men, all of whom faced a high risk of developing heart disease, were treated with a cholesterol-reducing drug and dietary advice, each 1-percent fall in cholesterol produced a 2-percent drop in their rate of coronary heart disease.

Saturated fats (those that are hard at room temperature) increase the amount of cholesterol carried in the general circulation. Fats from animal foods (suet, lard, butterfat, chicken fat, etc.) tend to be highly saturated. Two vegetable fats are also saturated—in fact more so than any animal fats: coconut "oil" and palm "oil" (both are really hard fats), which happen to be two of the most popular fats used in processed foods because they're cheap and don't turn rancid readily. Fats from fish are less saturated than other animal fats. If they weren't, fish oils would solidify in cold water and the fish would lose their flexibility.

Unsaturated fats, which are oils at room temperature, don't have adverse effects on blood cholesterol. In fact, according to recent evidence, both types of unsaturated fats—monounsaturates *and* polyunsaturates—help to lower the amount of cholesterol in the blood. The so-called monounsaturated fats, such as olive oil and peanut oil, are the main fats used in societies like Japan, Greece, and Italy, where the rates of coronary heart disease are very low. Polyunsaturated fats include corn, soybean, safflower, sunflower, and cottonseed oils. These, too, can help counter the cholesterol-raising effects of saturated fats, which is why they are used to make margarine and butter-margarine blends.

One of the most interesting recent discoveries about fat and heart disease has been the finding of a group of substances in fish oil that seems to protect against heart disease. This is probably a main reason why Greenland Eskimos, who live on a very high-fat but "fishy" diet, have such a low rate of heart disease. The substances are collectively called omega-3 long-chain fatty acids: eicosapentaenoic acid and docosahexaenoic acid, or EPA and DHA for short. When consumed frequently, they appear to be even more effective than polyunsaturated vegetable oils in reducing the risk of heart disease. Two factors may account for this finding: (1) they help to lower the level of cholesterol and other harmful fatty substances in the blood; and (2) they reduce the tendency of the blood to form clots. Based on these investigations, heart experts are now urging more frequent consumption of fatty fishes. These include tuna, salmon, sardines, mackerel, sable, whitefish, bluefish, swordfish, pompano, rainbow trout, eel, and herring. In addition, squid and shellfish, which are not high in fat, are also recommended because the fat they do contain has a high proportion of omega-3 fatty acids. Especially desirable are low-cholesterol shellfish like mussels, oysters, and scallops.

A ROLE IN CANCER. In recent years, our high-fat diet has also been singled out as contributing to our high rates of certain cancers, especially cancer of the colon and breast, and probably also the prostate, endometrium (lining of the uterus), ovary, pancreas, and even the lung. Numerous studies throughout the world have shown a direct relationship between diets high in fat and very high rates of cancers of the colon and breast. In Israel, for example, researchers at Tel Aviv University showed that people who live in a kibbutz, where the diet is low in animal fat and high in fruits and vegetables, had only a third the colon-cancer rate as other Israeli residents of the same age and ethnic background. In Israel generally, Jews of European and American origin are more than twice as likely to develop colon cancer as Jews of Asian and African origin, whose traditional diets are much lower in fat. And a recent study by Dr. M. Ward Hinds and colleagues at the Cancer Center of Hawaii in Honolulu revealed that smokers who eat a lot of fats and cholesterol have a greater chance of developing lung cancer than do smokers on a low-fat diet.

How can fats promote cancer? One possibility is that during the metabolism of fats and cholesterol, substances are formed that are cancer-promoting, including some chemicals that mimic the action of sex hormones, which are notorious for their ability to stimulate the growth of cancers. Or dietary fats may simply enhance the cancer-causing potential of other chemicals. Numerous studies have demonstrated that dietary fats and cholesterol can promote the development of tumors in animals pretreated with a cancer-causing chemical. When it comes to cancer, some studies suggest, polyunsaturates may be even more deadly than saturated fats.

THAT'S NOT ALL. Other hazards linked to a high-fat diet include the enhanced development of autoimmune diseases, in which the body's immune system overreacts to the person's own tissues and produces antibodies to destroy them. For example, according to studies by a research team from the University of California, San Francisco, and University of Southern California, animals born with a susceptibility to the autoimmune disease, systemic lupus erythematosus (SLE), were far more likely to develop the disease if they were fed a high-fat diet. Similarly, animals genetically susceptible to diabetes were more likely to develop this blood-sugar disorder on a high-fat diet, researchers at the Upjohn

Company showed. Finally, in three studies by James Iacono and colleagues at the United States Department of Agriculture among men with moderately raised blood pressure, eating less fat in general and less saturated fat in particular was shown to lower blood pressure even though the men's weight remained stable.

Thus, it is not enough merely to switch from saturated butter and lard to polyunsaturated margarine and vegetable oils. All things considered, preventive-medicine specialists recommend that Americans eat significantly less total fat. Actually, all that is needed for nutrition's sake is 1 tablespoon of vegetable oil a day to supply the essential fatty acids that the body cannot make on its own. Also important is the ratio of polyunsaturated fats to saturated fats in the diets. You should end up eating one-third to one-half less fat than you do now (so that fat represents only 20 percent to 30 percent or less of your daily calories), with each type of fat making approximately an equal contribution: one-third saturates, one-third monounsaturates, and one-third polyunsaturates. It is important not to make a fetish out of polyunsaturates, since eating too much of them may increase cancer risk. If you are determined to avoid nearly all saturated fats, it would be best to replace them with monounsaturates, like olive oil. (The tips described on pp. 172–176 will help you achieve this goal without having to resort to calculators and complicated dietary analyses.) One of the simplest ways to reduce your consumption of fats generally and saturated fats in particular is to eat less protein overall and to substitute plant protein for some of the animal protein you now consume.

SUGAR: OUR LIVES ARE TOO SWEET

Sugar in the current American diet is both an abused substance and the subject of abuse. As an abused substance, sugar, which provides none of the 44 nutrients needed to sustain human life, accounts for far too large a share of our daily calories. Currently, one-fifth to one-quarter of our daily caloric intake comes from sugars that are added to foods. If you add that to the two fifths of our calories derived from nonessential fats, you have a grand total of three-fifths or more of our calories that are nutritionally empty. This means we have to get 100 percent of our essential nutrients from just 40 percent of the calories we consume each day—hardly a well-balanced dietary budget.

As the subject of abuse, however, sugar has been dubbed a killer and accused of causing everything from heart disease and diabetes to hyperactivity and hypoglycemia. The fact is that none of these accusations can be supported by sound scientific research. The one disease that is incontrovertibly linked to sugar consumption is tooth decay, and even here it is not the total amount of sugar that matters as much as when and how often sweets are consumed and the consistency of the food itself. Sweets frequently consumed between meals and those that cling readily to the teeth are more likely to promote decay than sweet drinks, for example, or a sweet dessert that is brushed off the teeth after meals.

Honey is more damaging to teeth than ordinary table sugar because it comes equipped with the glue that decay-causing bacteria use to stick to tooth surfaces.

Why, then, should we worry so much about sugar? First, because we are consuming more than 120 pounds a year of a substance for which we have no physiological need. That's a total of more than 600 unnaturally sweetened calories a day. Since these sweet calories count toward the daily total we must consume to maintain a normal body weight, they are taking the place of calories that could supply some of the nutrients we need to survive. From a nutritional standpoint, it matters little how you take your sugar: as sucrose (white table sugar), brown sugar, honey, raw sugar, fructose, or whatever. Only molasses provides the body with a significant number of nutrients in addition to calories. And because sugar, like all foods, uses up vitamins and minerals in the course of being metabolized, it actually results in a net loss of essential nutrients. To make matters worse, most heavily sweetened foods are also high in fat, which adds to their nutritional emptiness.

Second, a very large number of sweet calories can get packed into a very small amount of food, making it easy to eat too many calories before your hunger is satisfied. A 1-ounce candy bar contains about the same amount of sugar (and three times the calories) as a 5-ounce apple, yet the candy bar takes up far less space in your empty stomach. Thus, while ounce for ounce sugar doesn't make you any fatter than protein or starch would, an uncurbed passion for sweets can lead to overeating and problems with weight control.

Third, sugar is a false pick-me-up that soon lets you down lower than you started out. We evolved on a diet that lacked very concentrated sources of sugar, and our metabolic processes are not well designed to handle them. Sugar is a simple carbohydrate that requires little or no processing by your digestive tract to be absorbed into your bloodstream. It's the job of the pancreatic hormone insulin to keep blood sugar at a steady, healthy level. If blood sugar rises, insulin is released to lower it. Perhaps because the pancreas "expects" other foods to come along with the sugar, too much insulin is often released and the blood sugar drops too low within an hour after you've eaten a concentrated sweet. You may end up feeling irritable, hungry, and weak, and have difficulty concentrating on your work.

Fourth, at the same time that insulin processes blood sugar, it also promotes the storage of fat. Thus, every time you eat foods that require a large outpouring of insulin, you fatten yourself up a little bit. So sweet snacks between meals add more than just their caloric contribution. In effect, they make sure that some of those calories get put "on hold" as body fat.

Fifth, it's easy to get hooked on the sweet taste. The more some people have of sweets, the more they want. And they develop a tolerance for extremely sweet foods. This is one reason, incidentally, to stay away from artificially sweetened foods if you're trying to reduce your dependence on sugar. Diet soft drinks and the like merely perpetuate your sweet tooth and make it more likely that you'll succumb to the temptation of a sugar-sweetened, high-calorie food at another time. There is also evidence that saccharin (the main sweetener even in many foods with NutraSweet) can stimulate the appetite and thus make it harder for people concerned about their weight to control overeating.

Finally, while sugar is not a direct *cause* of killer diseases, it can be a health hazard for people already afflicted. For example, 10 million people with diabetes cannot safely consume large amounts of sugar without jeopardizing control of their disease. The same is true of the ½ million people with medically proved hypoglycemia (low blood sugar). Some 20 million Americans are genetically sensitive to carbohydrates and will develop high levels of blood fats called triglycerides on a high-sugar diet. (However, when the diet is high in both fiber and *complex* carbohydrates—starches—triglyceride levels fall dramatically in such people.) Sugar has been shown in monkey studies to enhance the ability of salt to raise blood pressure. And while sugar itself has never been conclusively linked to an increased risk of heart disease, in laboratory animals one type of sugar that is fast growing in popularity—fructose—can cause a significant increase in cholesterol levels and in artery-clogging deposits. In addition, two popular sweeteners, honey and corn syrup, can be life-threatening to infants, who risk developing botulism poisoning because their digestive tracts permit the growth of botulinum spores sometimes found in these sweeteners.

None of the above means that to be healthy you must strike every sweet calorie from your current diet. Sugar plays some useful roles as components of food (for example, as a preservative of processed fruits and as a flavor enhancer) and clearly adds to the pleasure of eating. A few cookies, a piece of candy, or a slice of cake or pie now and then won't jeopardize an otherwise sound diet. In fact, from the standpoint of your health and your weight, it's far better to include a circumspect sweet treat into your daily diet than to deprive yourself for weeks and then indulge in a sweet orgy when your resistance wears thin.

SALT: ITS USE AND ABUSE

Excluding sugar, salt is the nation's leading food additive. The average American consumes 15 pounds of salt a year, or as much as all other food additives combined. Not only is salt our most popular additive, it is also the one we should be worrying most about. Unlike sugar, salt *is* a killer—at least a potential killer for the 20 percent of Americans who are sensitive to the blood-pressure-raising effects of the sodium in salt. Although some dissenting views would absolve salt of a primary role in producing high blood pressure, in the last decade or so an impressive body of evidence has been gathered that points to salt as a major triggering factor in this widespread and sometimes fatal disease. High blood pressure contributes to the top four or five leading causes of death among Americans, some 60 million of whom have abnormally high blood pressure. To be sure, other factors besides salt intake, including heredity and obesity, contribute to a person's risk of developing high blood pressure. But unlike heredity, salt consumption is a factor that is well within our control.

Human beings are born with the ability to taste salt, but our taste for a high-salt diet is an acquired one. Newborns do not particularly like salty foods. But when given them, after a while they acquire a taste for salt, and by early to middle childhood they prefer salted foods to those that are unsalted. A long-term study under the direction of Dr. David L. Yeung, a nutritional scientist at the University of Toronto, showed that children's taste for salt at the age of 4 is determined by how much salt their parents feed them in infancy. A preference for salt does not develop in cultures where salt is not added to foods. In such societies, even the adults do not like salt.

But just as a taste for salty foods can develop, the reverse can occur as well. Researchers from the Monell Chemical Senses Center at the University of Pennsylvania showed that young adults placed on low-sodium diets for five months lost their taste for salty foods. The level of saltiness in canned soups and salted crackers that appealed to them before they started their low-sodium diet was rated as too salty afterward.

Salt is, chemically, a combination of two mineral substances that are essential nutrients—sodium and chloride. But these substances are needed in far smaller quantities than nearly all Americans consume. The biological need is for about 220 milligrams of sodium daily, the equivalent of about 1/10 teaspoon of salt. Sodium helps to sustain cell activities throughout the body and is critical to the transport of water and other substances in and out of cells. For safety's sake, the Food and Nutrition Board of the National Academy of Sciences–National Research Council recommends 1,100 to 3,300 milligrams of sodium daily as a "safe and adequate" amount for adults. (These levels are equivalent to 1/2 and 1 1/2 teaspoons of salt, respectively.) But the average American consumes the sodium equivalent of 2 to 4 teaspoons of salt, and against that salty background, tens of millions develop high blood pressure. In fact, among those who live to age 65 and beyond, half develop high blood pressure.

The harmful effects of salt on blood pressure were first suggested in 1904. Studies among the Japanese, Americans, Eskimos, South Sea Islanders, and others have shown a direct relationship between the level of salt consumption and the incidence of high blood pressure. In fact, in Japan high blood pressure, that nation's leading killer, is more common in the north, where salt intake is highest, than in the south, where it is somewhat lower (but still very high). And when people migrate from a country where salt is rarely consumed to one where daily salt intake is similar to that in the United States, their blood pressure increases proportionately.

The effects of salt on blood pressure can even be seen in newborns. Researchers at Erasmus University Medical School in Rotterdam, the Netherlands, showed that 6-month-old infants had lower blood pressure if they were fed a low-sodium diet (such as they would get if they consumed only breast milk) than if they were fed a normal-sodium diet (as in infant formulas and other foods).

It has also been shown that blood pressure usually drops when people with high blood pressure reduce their salt intake, and that maintaining a very low-sodium diet can actually prevent the development of high blood pressure in people who are susceptible to this disease. Studies that have looked at the relationship between salt intake and blood pressure in societies like ours rarely show any difference in blood-pressure readings between people at the high and low ends of the sodium-consumption curve. But these seemingly confusing results have a logical explanation. Nearly everyone in this country is on a high-salt diet, and above a certain level of salt consumption, it is hard to discern differences in blood pressure that are related to salt intake. In other words, our population is salt-saturated. To demonstrate a direct effect of salt intake on blood pressure, we have to look at groups of people that differ dramatically in their level of salt consumption.

Salt and other sources of sodium enter the American diet in three ways. About one-third of the sodium we eat is naturally present in foods, including dairy products, meats, and seafood. Another third comes from salt added to foods at home and in restaurants during cooking and at the table. And the final third is introduced during food processing. Nearly every one of the 18,000 products that are found in supermarkets today contains some sodium, and in many processed foods the level of sodium is astronomical. For example, one serving of an ordinary canned soup may contain 1,000 to 1,500 milligrams of sodium, the amount you should consume in a day. A single fast-food meal of a special burger, fries, and a shake can contain twice the recommended sodium intake. An ounce of some breakfast cereals contains more sodium than an ounce of cheese or salted peanuts.

If you look at the diet human beings evolved on, you'll find that it was very low in sodium but that it contained ample amounts of another mineral, potassium, that seems to protect against the development of high blood pressure. Potassium is prominent in fresh fruits and vegetables, but with the increased consumption of processed foods, potassium intake has dropped dramatically in this country in recent decades. This is another reason to reduce consumption of heavily processed foods and eat more foods in the form that nature provides.

Even if you now have low blood pressure, you cannot count on it always staying low. Since it is not now possible to predict who will and who will not develop high blood pressure on a high-salt diet, it's best if everyone reduced his or her salt intake by half or more. Such a reduction—to 1,100 milligrams of sodium a day or less—is especially important for people with a family history of high blood pressure, but many others can also benefit. Experts point out that since low-sodium diets are not harmful and may be helpful to millions of Americans, there is no reason not to adopt this approach nationwide.

FOR FURTHER READING

Brody, Jane E. *Jane Brody's Nutrition Book.* New York: Norton, 1981, and Bantam, 1982.

Hausman, Patricia. *Jack Spratt's Legacy: The Science and Politics of Fat and Cholesterol.* New York: Richard Marek, 1981.

Reader's Digest. *Eat Better, Live Better.* Pleasantville, N.Y.: Reader's Digest Association, 1982.

3 ·
A NEW FOCUS ON STARCHY FOODS

By now you may be thinking "But what is there left to eat? If staying healthy means I have to eat less protein and cut way back on fats and sugars, how am I going to fill my belly?" The answer is: with the very same foods your evolutionary ancestors ate—the complex carbohydrates, or starches, like potatoes, rice, pasta, bulgur, kasha, couscous, millet, corn, peas and beans, etc., along with fruits and vegetables. When consumed mainly in their unrefined state, the complex carbohydrates represent the only category of foods that won't undermine your health, even if as many as 80 percent of your calories come from starch. (This presumes that the remainder of your caloric intake provides the protein, fatty acids, and additional vitamins and minerals needed to sustain life.)

Affluence and cultural development seem to induce a kind of dietary snobbery that turns its nose up at so-called peasant foods. As soon as we could afford to, we rejected the coarse, dark breads of our grandparents and substituted lily-white, refined breads that can be rolled into pasty balls and used for fish bait. In the refining process, we removed 26 nutrients from the flour (replacing only 4 of them when the white flour is "enriched") and fed the milling remains to animals that turned them into flesh and fat. We in turn consumed the flesh and fat, taking ever smaller portions of the starchy staples that had sustained thousands of previous generations of *Homo sapiens.* We reasoned that we could afford to eat better, that we were watching our waistlines, and that anyway these foods were "just starch" and could be skipped since they provided few essential nutrients. How wrong we were!

STARCHES ARE NOT FATTENING

The first thing most Americans do when they decide to shed unwanted pounds is to cut out bread, pass up the potatoes and rice, and cross spaghetti dinners off the menu entirely. Instead, they may subsist on steak and salad, cottage cheese and fruit, tuna salad and tomatoes, chicken and green beans, or some such combination of a high-protein animal food and a low-calorie fruit or vegetable. Before long they're feeling tired and listless and bored and may even have trouble falling asleep at night. Studies by Drs. Richard and Judith Wurtman at the Massachusetts Institute of Technology have shown that carbohydrate deprivation depletes the brain of an important transmitter of nerve messages—serotonin. This neurotransmitter acts as a calming factor and sleep inducer. When brain levels drop too low, cravings for carbohydrates are likely to occur. Pretty soon, then, low-carbohydrate dieters are crumbling at the sight of a cookie or piece of bread and salivating at the smell of pizza. Eventually their resolve falters, and they fall off the low-carbohydrate wagon, often with a binge of their favorite missed foods. How much better it would be to avoid deprivation and denial by including carbohydrates in their weight-loss plan. That way they'd never have to "go off the diet" to eat the foods they love.

A high-protein, low-carbohydrate diet can make a laboratory animal fatter faster than a low-protein, high-carbohydrate diet will. A number of recent studies indicate that the body "wastes" more of the calories derived from complex carbohydrates than those that come from protein foods. There are at least two reasons for this caloric waste. (1) Carbohydrates seem to stoke the body furnace, causing more calories to be burned up as heat. This, incidentally, helps to keep you warm, which may explain why some women, many of whom subsist on high-protein diets, are "always cold." (2) Up to a third of carbohydrate calories are not digested and instead are excreted unabsorbed. Thus, some carbohydrate calories you eat don't count as far as your body is concerned. (This is true only of *complex* carbohydrates. Unless you have an enzyme deficiency, sugars are usually fully digested and absorbed.)

Furthermore, foods high in complex carbohydrates are *less fattening* than many of the most popular diet foods. This is because they contain less fat, and fat, you'll recall, is far more fattening than the same amount of starch, sugar, or protein. For example, a 5-ounce steak provides about 550 calories (80 percent of them fat calories). A 5-ounce baked potato, however, has only about 100 calories (0 percent fat, if you don't add any). Even with 2 pats of butter or margarine or 2 tablespoons of sour cream, the potato has less than 200 calories. Other starchy foods are also less fattening than steak. Five ounces of rice have 154 calories; kidney beans, 167 calories; pasta, 210 calories; and even bread (that's six slices of pasty white bread, four of a hearty whole grain bread) has only 390 calories—still fewer than the 5-ounce steak. This is not to say that when you want to lose weight, you should skip the meat and eat only the potatoes, pasta, and bread. But it does suggest that it would be wise to have some of both, with the emphasis on the starch rather than on the fatty protein food. In fact, a spaghetti dinner made with a lean meat and tomato sauce (see, for example, the recipe on p. 364) has fewer calories than just the steak part of a steak dinner and is likely to leave the dieter more satisfied much longer.

It's not the starchy foods themselves that are high in calories, but the fat we're in the habit of putting on them that can turn them into high-calorie foods: the butter and sour cream on potatoes, the cream cheese on bagels, the cream-and-cheese sauce on pasta. But if the starchy foods are eaten without fat or with just small amounts of it, they can be less fattening than the animal-protein foods that are naturally high in fat.

By placing overweight young men on a bread diet, Dr. Olaf Mickelsen, a nutrition researcher at Michigan State University, "proved" that bread was not as fattening as most people think. Whatever else the men ate, they *had* to consume 12 slices of bread a day. They were also advised to keep to a minimum their consumption of high-calorie, low-nutrient foods like beer and doughnuts. After 8 weeks, the men who ate ordinary white bread has lost an average of 13.7 pounds and those who ate a high-fiber bread has lost an average of 19.4 pounds. This is not meant to recommend a diet that emphasizes bread to this extent, but merely to demonstrate that including bread in your diet can help you control your weight.

My husband is a perfect example of what can happen when you reduce your reliance on meats and eat more starches in their stead. If he ate less than a ½ pound of meat at dinner, he said, he would still be hungry. Then he decided to give the high-carbohydrate plan a try. A year later, he was 26 pounds thinner without having gone on a diet and without ever feeling hungry or deprived. He's thinner today at 52 than he was at 32, when we were married. And he feels healthier and more energetic than he has in years. As he put it, "I hadn't realized that in cutting back on meats, I could eat more potatoes, rice, spaghetti, and bread. When I fill up on the starches, I'm satisfied with less meat." And by eating less meat and other animal foods, he consumes less fat and fewer calories.

Today, the ½ pound of flesh my husband used to eat by himself for dinner feeds our four-member family, including two fast-growing teen-aged boys. In the process, we all eat less fat and save money in the bargain. Our 2-ounce portions of animal protein are supplemented by the protein in the starchy foods that are the foundation of our meals. And some dinners contain little or no animal protein because this essential nutrient is instead provided primarily by protein-rich legumes (dried beans and peas). Additional protein contributions come from our vegetables, bread, and milk.

FIBER, THE FILLER-UPPER

One reason my husband is so satisfied by his high-carbohydrate meals before he's consumed too many calories is that the starchy foods come along with a low-calorie belly-filler—fiber. Fiber is plant material that cannot be digested by human beings. It is found in substantial amounts in all unrefined grains (whole wheat, rye, corn, oats, brown rice, etc.), dried beans and peas, and all fruits and vegetables. Refined starches also contain fiber, but much less of it. On average, fibrous foods take longer to eat than meats and dairy products, and thus they slow down the consumption of calories. In other words, although you may spend more time eating, you actually consume fewer calories on a high-fiber diet. Furthermore, fiber takes up space in your stomach and small intestine, where it absorbs water and slows down digestion enough to prolong feelings of satiation. Then it is passed along to the colon, or large intestine, where it acts like a Roto-Rooter, helping you to eliminate solid wastes without stress or strain. In the colon, resident bacteria partially digest some of the fiber, producing gases that may be absorbed by your digestive tract. But most of the fiber is excreted without making any caloric contribution to the consumer. Thus, fiber gives you something for nothing, and eating high-fiber foods as part of your regular meals and snacks can help you to achieve and maintain a normal body weight.

In a fascinating demonstration at the University of Alabama, 10 obese and 10 normal-weight men and women were served two types of diets. One, called a low-energy-density diet, contained lots of bulk from fresh fruits, vegetables, whole grains, and dried beans, but very little fat. The second, the high-energy-density diet, had only a small amount of bulk and larger amounts of fat and simple sugars as meats and desserts. (Thus, for a given volume of food, the high-energy-density diet was richer in calories.) The diets were rated as equally acceptable by the participants, who were each served one of the two diets for a five-day period, then switched to the second diet. They were told to eat as much as they wanted of each diet until they felt satisfied. Although the participants spent about one-third more time eating when they were on the low-energy-density diet, their average daily caloric intake was only one-half the amount they consumed while on the high-energy-density diet. The researchers concluded that switching to a high-bulk diet may help *prevent* as well as treat obesity, and that more efforts should be made to change the patterns of food selection among obese people than to change their actual eating behaviors.

Fiber is perhaps best known for its laxative effect. People who live on high-fiber diets are almost never troubled by constipation. Nor are they likely to develop hemorrhoids, diverticulosis, or a host of other intestinal problems, including cancer of the colon, a leading cancer killer in this country. Fiber aids elimination by adding bulk to the stool and softening it through water absorption, which makes the stool easier to pass. If all Americans ate adequate amounts of dietary fiber, the laxative industry would soon go bankrupt. Instead, on the low-fiber diets most Americans consume, this industry earns well over a quarter of a billion dollars a year.

Adding fiber to the diet actually increases the amount of fat that you excrete, which may help to protect against heart disease as well as assist in weight loss. Fiber also helps to lower blood cholesterol and to maintain blood sugar on a more even keel. Since fluctuating blood-sugar levels in part influence feelings of hunger and irritability and energy level, high-fiber meals also help to keep *you* on a more even keel. In fact, diets rich in fiber and complex carbohydrates are now being routinely prescribed for diabetics, many of whom are then able to reduce or eliminate their dependence on drugs and insulin to control their blood sugar. High-fiber diets may soon become standard fare for ulcer patients as well (see p. 24).

Fiber is not one substance but at least six different kinds of substances, each with its own health effect. The main types of dietary fibers are cellulose and hemicellulose (bran, for example); lignin (a woody substance also in cereal grains); pectins (prominent in vegetables and fruits like apples and grapes); gums (in oats and legumes like chickpeas); and mucilages (in seeds). Pectins, guar gum (in beans), and the fiber in oats and carrots can significantly lower blood cholesterol, whereas bran has no effect on cholesterol levels. Raw carrots, incidentally, may be a far more effective "bulking" agent than bran. Bran absorbs only 5 times its weight in water, whereas carrots can absorb 20 to 30 times their weight. To get the full benefits that fiber can offer, you should eat a variety of plant foods—grains, legumes, fruits, and vegetables—on a regular basis. This doesn't mean that every starch in your diet has to be brown and chewy to be good for you. But whenever circumstances and your tastes allow it, it helps to choose plant foods in their unrefined, high-fiber state.

STARCHES ARE NUTRITIOUS

Fiber is not the only desirable dietary constituent of starchy foods. Most are also good sources of essential nutrients—protein, vitamins, and minerals—especially when eaten in their natural state. The potato is my favorite example. An average-sized potato (about 5 ounces) provides about 5 percent of the calories needed by an average adult in a day. For that 5 percent of calories, here's what you get to help meet your nutritional needs: 6 percent of your protein requirement; 8 percent of your folacin, phosphorus, and magnesium; 10 percent of your iron, niacin, and copper; 15 percent of your iodine; 20 percent of your B_6; 35 percent of your vitamin C; plus some thiamin, riboflavin, and zinc. Thus, the potato is a nutrient bargain, giving you far more in essential nutrients than it contributes in calories.

But potatoes are far from being the only nutritious carbohydrate food. As you will see in subsequent chapters, bread, pasta, rice, corn, oats, and most other high-starch foods also contain reasonable amounts of protein, vitamins, and minerals. And legumes contain more than reasonable amounts—enough protein, in fact, to sustain life. Eaten along with vegetables and fruits, which supply large amounts of certain vitamins and minerals that tend to be in short supply in other foods, starchy foods can just about sustain a healthy human life. In fact, after six months of age, the only nutrient needed from animal foods is vitamin B_{12}.

COMPLEX CARBOHYDRATES ENHANCE HEALTH

Whether you're an athlete, a diabetic, or a heart patient, or you're suffering from high blood pressure or overweight, or you're just a healthy person interested in staying that way, a diet that is high in fiber and complex carbohydrates is apparently your best bet for living long and well. It may even help to protect you against cancer. One by one, leading experts on the nation's serious diseases are recommending a high-carbohydrate diet as the most health-promoting. And because this diet deemphasizes costly meat, convenience foods, and packaged snacks, you can, if you follow it, save 20 percent to 30 percent on grocery bills.

The American Diabetes Association and a number of leading nutritionists now recommend this diet for everyone, regardless of their state of health. As Dr. Marion Nestle, nutritionist and associate dean of the University of California School of Medicine in San Francisco, puts it: "Both normal and therapeutic diets converge on a common theme—a diet that contains a wide variety of unprocessed high-carbohydrate foods in moderate amounts." She explains that the recommended diet includes fruits, vegetables, and whole grains that are relatively low in calories, fat, sugar, salt, and food additives. It also contains relatively large amounts of vitamins, minerals, and dietary fiber.

AN ATHLETIC BOOST. Runners were perhaps the first to discover the benefits of carbohydrates. They found that a high-carbohydrate diet improved performance because, researchers have shown, this diet promotes storage of muscle fuel. It also speeds up the restocking of muscle fuel following exercise. More and more today, professional athletes, many of whom used to down large quantities of red meat on a regular basis, are turning to a high-carbohydrate regimen. Coaches who once encouraged pregame steak dinners are now pushing pasta. And some top athletes, including a number of Olympic Gold Medalists, don't eat any meat or flesh at all. But you don't have to be a world-class athlete to reap the benefits of complex carbohydrates.

COMBATTING HEART DISEASE. For patients already suffering from heart disease as well as those at risk of developing it, a high-fiber, high-carbohydrate diet helps to reduce three coronary risk factors: overweight, high blood cholesterol, and high blood pressure. In a dramatic demonstration of the reversal of such benefits, Dr. Frank M. Sacks of Harvard Medical School and his collaborators showed that adding about 9 ounces of meat a day to the diets of strict vegetarians raised their blood cholesterol levels by 19 percent in just two weeks. Blood pressure also increased significantly during the period of meat-eating. These effects occurred even though the vegetarians did not increase their calorie intake. A high-fiber, high-carbohydrate diet, coupled with daily exercise, has enabled many people to avoid coronary bypass operations. Such a diet can reduce blood cholesterol levels by 30 percent and blood triglyceride levels by 80 percent, at the same time that it permits weight loss without hunger. Preliminary evidence in both animals and human patients strongly suggests that blood vessels also become partly unclogged when this diet is combined with a sensible exercise program. Even those who undergo surgery to replace fat-clogged coronary arteries can benefit from such a diet, since they have to keep the bypasses free of fatty deposits and prevent other coronary arteries from becoming totally clogged.

DOWN WITH DIABETES. Perhaps the most dramatic demonstration of the benefits of a high-fiber, high-carbohydrate diet has involved patients with diabetes. In the not-too-distant past, diabetics were placed on high-protein, high-fat, low-carbohydrate diets designed to reduce their need for insulin as well as to keep their blood sugar from rising precipitously. Unfortunately, these diets encouraged the development of clogged arteries and heart disease, which causes three-fourths of deaths among diabetics.

The new diet, which has been used successfully to treat thousands of diabetic patients, instead emphasizes complex carbohydrates and high-fiber foods and keeps fatty protein foods to a minimum. According to Dr. James W. Anderson, diabetologist at the University of Kentucky in Lexington and author of *Diabetes: A Practical New Guide to Healthy Living* (published by Arco in hardcover and paperback), nearly all patients have been able to reduce greatly and sometimes to eliminate entirely their dependence on drugs and insulin to control their blood sugar. Dr. Anderson reports that dietary fiber increases the number of receptors for insulin; these are sites on cell surfaces that act as locks into which insulin fits like a key, and they enable insulin to clear sugar out of the blood. In adult-onset diabetes, there is often a deficiency of insulin receptors, which interferes with the proper regulation of blood sugar.

A GODSEND FOR YOUR GUT. As for your digestive tract, the aforementioned benefits of a high-fiber diet are legion. You can forget about constipation forever. This diet is also now frequently recommended for people suffering from such disorders of the colon as diverticulosis, Crohn's disease (regional enteritis), hemorrhoids, and the alternating constipation and diarrhea of irritable bowel syndrome. In fact, British studies have indicated that patients with Crohn's disease ate substantially more refined sugar, less dietary fiber, and especially less raw fruit and vegetables *before* they developed their colon disease, suggesting that a high-fiber diet may protect against this common, serious bowel disorder. The high-fiber diet may also prevent ulcers. Researchers in Oslo, Norway, recently showed that ulcer patients placed on the standard bland, low-fiber ulcer diet experienced nearly twice the number of recurrences as those who ate a high-fiber diet for six months. The researchers reasoned that the bulkiness of the high-fiber diet may help protect the lining of the intestine from the caustic effects of stomach acid.

KEEP CANCER AT BAY. The most exciting potential benefit of the high-fiber, high-carbohydrate diet concerns cancer of the colon and possibly other cancers as well. Dietary fiber and starchy foods are thought to reduce the exposure of intestinal tissues to cancer-causing chemicals, as well as take the place of cancer-promoting fats in the diet. Throughout the world, the incidence of colon cancer is very low among people who regularly consume a high-fiber, low-fat diet, but the risk of developing this disease rises as a more Western-type, low-fiber, high-fat diet is adopted. Studies in laboratory animals have shown that dietary fiber protects against the development of colon cancer following exposure to a known cancer-causing chemical. Dr. Walter Troll, professor of environmental medicine at New York University School of Medicine, has identified certain enzymes in such "seed foods" as corn, beans, and rice that protect against the development of fatal skin cancers in laboratory mice. And researchers at the

University of California at San Francisco have found that women who are chronically constipated (and thus undoubtedly consume a low-fiber diet) are much more likely to have abnormal cells in their breasts, which may indicate that they also have an increased risk of developing breast cancer. As with colon cancer, breast cancer throughout the world is associated with high-fat, high-calorie, and, presumably, low-fiber diets.

Although there is no surefire nutritional means to prevent cancer, a prestigious committee of the National Academy of Sciences–National Research Council has advised that cancer risk might be reduced significantly if you eat

- less fat, especially fatty cuts of meat, whole-milk dairy products, cooking oils and fats.
- very little processed meats—anything that is salt-cured, salt-pickled, or smoked, including sausages, frankfurters, salami, bologna, bacon, and ham. These meats contain chemicals that can be converted to potent cancer-causing substances in the body. Most are also very high in fat, deriving as many as 85 percent of their calories from fat.
- whole grains daily, including whole-grain cereals and breads. In addition to fiber, whole grains contain various vitamins that may have an anticancer effect.
- fruits and vegetables daily that are rich in vitamin A (or its precursor, beta-carotene), like carrots, orange-colored melons, sweet potatoes, winter squash, broccoli, spinach, and other dark-green leafy vegetables. Vitamin A seems to protect against cancer development in epithelial tissues, which are the sites where cancers of the lung, breast, colon, bladder, and other organs usually start.
- fruits and vegetables daily that are rich in vitamin C, including citrus fruits, tomatoes, green peppers, strawberries, melons, potatoes, and dark-green vegetables. Vitamin C seems to block the formation of certain cancer-causing chemicals.
- more vegetables in the cabbage family that naturally contain cancer-blocking factors, including cabbage, broccoli, cauliflower, kale, Brussels sprouts, kohlrabi.

The committee also recommended drinking alcohol only in moderation.

CARBOHYDRATES' SIDE EFFECTS

The main drawback of a diet high in fiber and complex carbohydrates is an increase in flatulence. Bacteria that normally reside in the bowel produce gas by digesting some of the carbohydrate that has escaped the human digestive process. For most people, this is a temporary problem that subsides in a few weeks as the body adapts to its new menu. If you increase your consumption of fiber and carbohydrates gradually, you're much less likely to have difficulty with intestinal gas and bloating.

Some high-fiber carbohydrate foods, fruits, or vegetables may cause more problems with gas than others. Beans, for example, are notorious gas producers (see p. 95). But, for the most part, different people react differently to the various foods. In some people, a so-called food intolerance, usually due to the lack of a particular enzyme, creates difficulties in digesting certain carbohydrate foods. Trial and error will usually help you to identify and then avoid those foods that are most disruptive to your digestive tract. For example, after several attacks of severe bloating and abdominal pain, I discovered that I am unable to digest some constituent of soybeans. So I simply stay away from soybeans and foods made from them. Although soybeans are the best source of plant protein, there are many other highly nutritious and good-tasting beans that I can eat (see pp. 104–106).

A less obvious but potentially more serious drawback of increasing the fiber content of your diet concerns its possible interference with the absorption of essential minerals, especially calcium and iron, which are already in short supply in the diets of many Americans. Other nutrients that may be partly blocked by dietary fiber include zinc, magnesium, copper, and vitamin B_6. There is no question that more minerals are excreted on a high-fiber diet, but many factors help to determine how much is lost and what significance the loss has to the individual. For the average American who consumes a mixed diet, scientists at the United States Department of Agriculture report that mineral losses are nutritionally insignificant when fiber content of the diet is increased. The body also seems to adapt to a high-fiber diet by improving its ability to utilize certain nutrients. Vegetarians, for example, make better use of the zinc and iron in their diets than meat eaters do, with or without the addition of fiber, according to studies by Dr. Constance Kies, nutritionist at the University of Nebraska in Lincoln. Dr. Kies has pointed out that "nutrient balances remain positive even at high levels of fiber supplementation" on an otherwise well-balanced diet. Problems arise primarily if an individual's diet starts out with inadequate amounts of the nutrients that are inhibited by fiber. Experts are especially concerned about excess fiber consumption by infants and by the elderly, many of whom are already consuming a diet that is deficient in several essential nutrients. But for athletes, most of whom consume more nutrients than other people because they can eat more food without getting fat, fiber-induced nutrient losses do not seem to be a problem.

FOR FURTHER READING
Anderson, James W., M.D. *Diabetes: A Practical New Guide to Healthy Living.* New York: Arco, 1981.
Burkitt, Denis. *Don't Forget Fiber in Your Diet.* New York: Arco, 1984.
Eyton, Audrey. *The F-Plan Diet.* New York: Bantam, 1984.

II.   A Guide to the Good Carbohydrates

Introduction

Just as meat is nutritionally different from eggs or milk, not all starchy foods are equally nutritious as they come from the earth. And the way you buy and prepare them can make a further difference in how many calories and nutrients they provide for your body. Currently, you may be eating starches in their least desirable form: overly refined and/or with lots of added fat. But just because you now adore French fries sodden with oil and heavily salted does not mean you cannot learn to enjoy a plain baked potato seasoned with a low-fat yogurt-dill sauce. You may be familiar with beans only in pork and beans, a dish high in fat, sugar, and salt, but there are many more nutritious ways to eat and enjoy beans—for instance, in low-fat soups, salads, and casseroles.

Our parents and grandparents knew a lot more about starchy foods than most of us do today. Many people have no idea how to select, store, and prepare some of the most nourishing high-carbohydrate foods. For example, whenever I mention dried beans and peas as a good source of some nutrient, a few people ask, "But how do you eat them?" In this meat-dominated era of convenience foods, not many people know how to cook beans from scratch or why they should bother.

As you've seen in Part I, complex-carbohydrate foods have played a major role in nourishing humankind for thousands of years. Before people lived in one place for long periods and began cultivating crops, starchy foods were gathered, cooked, and eaten in their wild forms. To this day, wild varieties are bred with cultivated ones to develop improved crops that have desirable nutritional and growing characteristics. Breeding specialists often spend several months a year combing the countryside of a crop's original home in search of desirable wild traits that can be bred into our highly cultivated varieties. Thus, what is true of a carbohydrate food's nutritional value today may be improved upon in the near future. Breeders are looking especially to enhance the protein value of starchy foods, so that we'll be able to derive more complete protein from single foods and have to worry less about combining different kinds of plant protein.

In this part, I will discuss in detail—from history to cooking techniques—the leading starchy foods readily available to most Americans. I will also briefly describe some nutritionally valuable starchy foods that are now more obscure or harder to obtain. When you're finished reading this section, you may be struck by the tremendous number of choices available and the wide varieties of ways to eat foods that you may have once regarded as boring starches. I myself am continually discovering delicious new ways to prepare and eat "the same old thing." Chances are that as you become familiar with the characteristics of the starchy foods, you'll be inventing tempting new dishes of your own.

4 ·
PLEASE PASS THE POTATOES

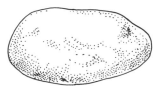

No nourishing human food has had a harder time than the potato in fulfilling its biological destiny. Harvested in its wild form by mountain-dwelling South American Indians before 6000 B.C., the potato became the staple of the Inca empire some 500 years ago. Spanish explorers brought the first potatoes to Europe in the mid-1500s, but the potato's arrival was greeted like—well—a hot potato. According to a report by Robert E. Rhoades in *National Geographic* (May 1982): "When introduced to Europe, the potato was cursed as an evil food. The Scots refused to eat it because it wasn't mentioned in the Bible. Leprosy, consumption, and rickets were attributed to potato eating," and the poet Lord Byron accused the potato of possessing "unwholesome aphrodisiac effects," Rhoades reports. Others said it could cause scrofula and warts. Its nearest relatives, the deadly nightshade and mandrake, with their alkaloid poisons that have hallucinogenic and narcotic effects, did not help the potato win friends.

Yet, if only for its adaptability to a wide range of growing conditions, the potato would eventually assume world-wide importance as a food crop. Potatoes can grow at altitudes up to 14,000 feet, in climates that see little sun or warmth, in soils that would otherwise sustain not much more than a few hardy weeds. About the only place potatoes don't do well is in humid jungles, where they succumb to diseases. The potato is also a high-yielding crop. Because more than one planting is possible in many areas, an acre of potatoes can yield twice as much food as an acre of grain. Potatoes, which are not roots but tubers, or swollen underground stems, are also highly versatile. In addition to the many ways they can be prepared fresh, they can also be dehydrated (permitting lengthy storage), frozen, converted to alcohol, and used as starch, paste, and dye.

In 1744, Frederick the Great of Prussia launched the potato's first public-relations campaign. According to Alvin and Virginia B. Silverstein, authors of *Potatoes* (an award-winning children's science book published by Prentice-Hall), Frederick regarded the potato as a possible answer to periodic famine, not just as the cattle feed it was then used for. He ordered potatoes to be planted in the royal garden and had the royal cooks devise new recipes. Then he invited prestigious citizens to feast on the results, distributing recipes and planting instructions to the people. But the peasants remained unconvinced. So the determined ruler sent soldiers throughout the countryside to distribute seed potatoes and decreed that anyone who refused to grow and eat them would have his nose and ears cut off. The autocratic plan worked, and potatoes soon became basic to the Prussian diet, preventing starvation of both German soldiers and prisoners of war during the Seven Years' War.

The French resistance to potatoes was finally overcome through an interesting ploy devised by Antoine-Auguste Parmentier, who claimed to have survived only on potatoes during his imprisonment in Germany in 1757. He convinced King Louis to allow him to grow potatoes in a field that was protected by day by royal guards. Believing a treasured crop was planted there, nearby peasants started raiding the field at night when the guards left. The potato, prestigiously named *pomme de terre* ("apple of the earth"), soon became a key ingredient in French haute cuisine.

For the Irish, the potato had assumed an even more prominent role. Irish farmers of the late sixteenth century, plagued by continual wars, soon discovered that fields of potatoes were more likely than others to survive the fires and raids of invading soldiers. Sustained by the potato's nutrients, the Irish population exploded until by the mid-1800s it had reached a density greater than that in China today. The typical Irish peasant consumed 9 to 14 pounds of potatoes a day! Then in 1845 a devastating blight struck the Irish potato, and field upon field withered and rotted. The resulting famine caused 1 million deaths and forced another 1 million to 2 million Irishmen to leave their homeland to avoid starvation.

In North America, the potato began to take root after early Irish immigrants introduced it to New England in 1719. But cultivation was slow until the great wave of Irish immigrants arrived more than a century later. By 1900, Americans were eating 200 pounds of fresh potatoes per person each year, securing the potato's place as an American staple. Then, as affluence and consumption of animal foods increased, the potato's popularity plummeted. Rhoades recalls being taught in his college economics class that "the potato is a classic example of an inferior food, something to fill up on only when you can't afford better; as my income rises, I should desire to eat fewer potatoes."

Not surprisingly in light of that societal attitude, by the 1950s, consumption of potatoes in the United States had dropped to half its former level and only began to rise again with the advent of fast-food and frozen French fries. The average American thinks of the potato in such denigrating terms as "just starch," "too fattening," and "filler food." Along with bread, potatoes are likely to be the first food scratched from the menu of the weight-conscious. But, in truth . . .

POTATOES ARE NOT FATTENING

The potato's reputation as a fattening food no doubt stems from how it is commonly served: French-fried in oil that adds some 200 empty calories to a typical serving; baked and slathered with butter or sour cream (a single table-spoon of butter doubles the calories in a medium-sized potato); mashed with butter and milk; boiled and cut up, then doused with mayonnaise in a cold salad. Rarely is the potato eaten without oodles of added fat, although unadulterated or seasoned only with noncaloric spices or low-calorie dressings, it can be delicious as well as nutritious.

The potato itself has fewer calories than many foods people turn to when trying to lose weight. A medium-sized potato weighing 5 ounces that has been baked, boiled, or steamed contains about 100 calories. But ½ cup of creamed cottage cheese has 130 calories; a 3-ounce hamburger, 270; 1 cup of plain yogurt, 120; an 8-ounce glass of orange juice, 110; and a lettuce salad with 2 tablespoons of dressing, 170.

Potatoes are relatively low in calories because they contain almost no fat. Nearly 100 percent of the potato's calories come from carbohydrates (mostly starch) and protein. The potato is 78 percent water by weight, and water has no calories. The potato also contains dietary fiber (especially if eaten with the skin), and thus provides the bulk that dieters need to satisfy their hunger before they've overconsumed calories. Dr. Hans Fisher, chairman of the nutrition department at Rutgers University, proved the potato's value in weight control by placing a dozen students on a 1,000-calorie-a-day potato diet. With belly-filling potatoes included in every meal and snack, the students lost an average of 14 pounds in 8 weeks.

AND THEY'RE NUTRITIOUS

You've already seen that the Irish practically lived on potatoes. With just some dairy products and greens added to a potato diet, potatoes are indeed life-sustaining. To prove a point, a Scandinavian man lived healthfully for 300 days on only potatoes with a small amount of margarine, Rhoades reports. According to nutrition labeling approved by the Food and Drug Administration, a medium (5 ounce) potato contains 3 grams of protein, 22 grams of carbohydrate, 0 grams of fat, and about 100 calories (or 4 percent to 5 percent of the calories needed by the average adult in a day). Table 1 provides a breakdown of what you get for those calories as percentages of the U.S. Recommended Daily Allowances (USRDA) for various essential nutrients.

Table 1	NUTRIENTS IN A POTATO *(5 ounces, 100 calories)*				
Nutrient	*% USRDA*	*Nutrient*	*% USRDA*	*Nutrient*	*% USRDA*
Protein	6	Iron	10	Magnesium	8
Vitamin C	35	Vitamin B$_6$	20	Zinc	4
Thiamin	4	Folacin	8	Copper	10
Riboflavin	2	Phosphorus	8	Iodine	15
Niacin	10				

The vitamin-C content of the potato varies with age; new potatoes have the most, with a 5-ounce potato supplying more than half the USRDA, and those stored six months have only a third the original amount. The potato also contains trace minerals that are essential to human nutrition but for which a USRDA has not yet been established. Among them are manganese, chromium, selenium, and molybdenum. Since the largest concentration of vitamins and minerals is found in and just beneath the skin, potatoes are most nutritious eaten skin and all or at least cooked with the skin on and peeled afterward.

The potato is naturally low in sodium, containing only about 10 milligrams in 5 ounces, at the same time that it supplies about 20 percent of the potassium recommended for daily consumption. Thus, it is an ideal food for preventing and treating high blood pressure. All told, then, the potato is a nutrient bargain, giving you a large percentage of essential nutrients for the number of calories it supplies. The protein in a potato is also high-quality, as vegetable proteins go, because it contains a good balance of essential amino acids. Essential amino acids are the protein building blocks that must be provided together in the diet for the body to be able to make full use of the protein you eat. According to researchers at Michigan State University, on a scale of 0 to 100 (the rating for eggs) the protein of a potato ranks 71—not that far below beef, which ranks 80.

Sweet potatoes and yams are different crops than potatoes with white flesh, but they are also reasonably nutritious. Overall, they contain less protein and more calories than white potatoes (although you may be more inclined to eat a sweet potato without adding any fat). But they (especially the deep-orange ones) are also rich sources of vitamin A as well as being high in vitamin C and potassium. Sweet potatoes have a moist, soft flesh and are traditionally grown in the southern states. The northern sweet potato, or yam, is dry and firm. Either type is more perishable than the white potato.

SOME PROBLEMS WITH POTATOES

Unfortunately, the majority of potatoes eaten in this country are not consumed in their most nutrient-dense, low-calorie form. As recently as 1950 nearly all the potatoes Americans ate were purchased "fresh" and prepared at home. By 1965, 46 percent were processed. And now about 56 percent are processed, usually in a way that adds a large number of empty fat calories that dilute the concentration of nutrients naturally present in the potato. Frozen French fries were one of the first, and remain one of the most popular, convenience foods. Their still-growing use in fast foods helped to pull the potato industry out of the root cellar. But they didn't do much to improve the nutritional balance of the fat-heavy American diet. The extra fat calories in a serving of French fries are equivalent to the calories in 2 tablespoons of butter.

Potato chips, one of the nation's favorite snack foods, sprinkle salt on the fatty nutritional wound. The potato chip is a quick-fried potato slice. The hot oil boils off most of the water, in effect dehydrating the potato and replacing the water with oil. Whereas a 1-ounce bag of chips retains most of the nutrients found in about 3½ ounces of fresh potato, the calorie, fat, and salt content of the chip is vastly greater. A 1-ounce serving of chips (about 16 chips) contains 150 calories—90 of them (60 percent) from fat—and about 220 milligrams of sodium (one-tenth of the daily recommended amount). A 3½-ounce fresh potato has 70 calories, virtually no fat, and about 7 milligrams of sodium.

Processed potatoes are also sold as dehydrated flakes or granules to make instant mashed potatoes. Consumers Union found that instant mashed potatoes have less thiamin, magnesium, and vitamins B_6 and C than a fresh baked potato, but more niacin and iron. However, the instant variety has six times more sodium (before the consumer adds any), five times more fat (when prepared according to package directions), and a third less of nourishing starch. The instant product also has a host of additives used to prepare, stabilize, and preserve it. But while the nutritional value of instant potatoes is not seriously compromised, the taste is. *Consumer Reports* describes instant mashed potatoes as tasting and smelling more like cardboard than a properly cooked potato and as "overly gritty, runny, or salty." Of course, if you bake or boil potatoes at home and then mash them, you're likely to add fat and salt, but you would have more control over what is added. If you use skim milk and diet margarine, you'd be adding fewer fat calories and the fat would be largely unsaturated. You could also add little or no salt and season instead with pepper and/or herbs or lemon juice. Or you could sprinkle the potatoes with grated Parmesan, which adds protein and calcium along with some salt.

Other forms of processed potatoes—for example, instant hash browns, scalloped potatoes, and potatoes au gratin—also are higher in fat and often much higher in salt than a potato ought to be. And you may pay about twice as much for the convenience of the instant product. Canned potatoes are boiled and fat-free but often salty. Dehydrated potatoes may also be found as sliced or diced.

However they are sold or prepared, potatoes may not be the most desirable starchy food for people with diabetes. Recent studies indicate that the body treats them more like a sugar than a starch, resulting in a more rapid rise in blood sugar than would occur after eating other starchy foods. This does not mean diabetics must steer clear of potatoes, but they would be wise to keep in mind the hyperglycemic effect of potatoes and limit the amount eaten at any one time.

You may have heard that potatoes contain a "deadly poison" that is especially hazardous for people with arthritis and other joint diseases. The poison in question is solanine. It is found in and under green patches on potatoes and in eyes that have sprouted. Such areas should be removed before cooking since they result in a bitter taste. In any event, solanine is destroyed in the cooking process. Furthermore, rheumatologists say there is no connection between arthritis and potatoes or any other foods containing solanine-type chemicals.

BUYING AND STORING POTATOES

All is not bleak in potato trends. In the late 1970s, per-capita consumption began increasing for the first time in 60 years. Perhaps the recent promotional campaign of the Potato Board had helped to make the difference. In an award-winning series of ads, the potato was depicted as "99.9% fat-free," "the fat fighter's secret weapon," "I am not 'fattening'!" and "The potato. Something good that's good for you." The ads, of course, emphasized the unadulterated fresh potato, adorned at most with a 35-calorie pat of butter.

Fresh potatoes come in four basic types in this country.

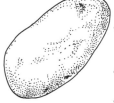

- *Russets* (also called *Idahos,* for their place of origin) are elongated cylinders with, as you might guess, a russet-colored (reddish-brown) skin. They are on the mealy side and thus make excellent potatoes for baking and French-frying.
- *Long whites* are even longer cylinders with a tan, smooth skin. They are firm and good for all-around home use: boiling, frying, mashing, and roasting.
- *Round whites* are also good all-purpose potatoes. Buff-colored and very smooth, they are firm and good boiled, steamed, home-fried, mashed, or roasted.
- *Round reds* are reddish on the outside, firm and white within. They are best for boiling, steaming, and roasting.

So-called "new potatoes" are not a separate variety but rather are young, small potatoes of any variety that are harvested during the first nine months of the year. Their skins are very thin and either off-white or red, and they are superb boiled or steamed, peels on, and eaten either hot (perhaps with fresh chopped parsley or dill) or cold (sliced or cubed in a salad). "Late" potatoes have a corky skin and drier flesh and are best used in dishes that contain added liquids.

In buying potatoes, the U.S. grade is not of much help. Grading is done at the point of shipment and says nothing about how the potatoes are stored thereafter and what shape they are in by the time you buy them. Since four-fifths of the potatoes are harvested in the fall and stored for months before sale, much degradation can take place after the crop has been graded. Instead of a grade, look for potatoes that are firm and fairly smooth. The more "eyes," bumps, and indentations a potato has, the greater the waste when peeled. Avoid potatoes that have sprouted or have wilted or wrinkled skin, cut surfaces, green or dark areas, or worm holes. If you're planning to cook them whole, choose potatoes that are approximately the same size so that they will cook at the same rate.

Potatoes can be purchased loose or prepackaged, usually in 5-pound and 10-pound bags. The bags are less expensive (often one-third the cost of loose potatoes). Buying large quantities of potatoes inexpensively is no bargain, however, unless you can use them up within a week or keep them under ideal storage conditions (in which case they will last for several weeks without significant wastage).

Once you get them home, potatoes are best stored in a cool, humid (but not wet), dark place that's well ventilated (hence, the common use of root cellars in days of yore). They should not be washed before storage. The ideal storage temperature is 40 to 50 degrees Fahrenheit. Potatoes should not be refrigerated; at temperatures below 40 degrees, some of the starch will be converted to sugar, making the potato undesirably sweet and causing it to darken when cooked. (A potato that has gotten too cold and sweet can be brought back to normal by storage for two to three weeks at about 70 degrees.) On the other hand, a potato that is too warm will sprout and shrivel. Prolonged exposure to light develops the solanine (see p. 33), causing potatoes to turn green and take on a bitter flavor (if this should happen, be sure to peel off all the green part before cooking). And a potato that is too wet will rot. Since most American kitchens lack ideal storage conditions, potatoes are best purchased in quantities small enough to get used up within a week.

HOW TO COOK POTATOES

Start by cleaning them in water, rubbing the skin with a vegetable brush, sponge, or dish cloth. If you must peel the potatoes before cooking, use a vegetable parer and take off the thinnest possible layer to preserve the potato's vitamin and mineral content. Peeled potatoes will darken if you let them stand around uncooked. But while soaking them in water will retard the darkening, it will also result in a loss of nutrients. You would be better off protecting their whiteness by tossing them with some lemon juice or ascorbic acid (vitamin C) dissolved in a little water. Still better, don't peel or cut them until just before you're ready to cook them. And best of all, don't peel them at all. With one-third of the potato's nutrients just beneath the skin, the less peeling you do before cooking, the less nutrient loss. And if you eat the skins, all the better, since you get a fiber bonus as well.

YIELDS OF POTATOES
1 pound of potatoes (three medium potatoes) makes any of the following:
3 cups of sliced potatoes.
2½ cups of diced potatoes.
2 cups of mashed potatoes.
2 cups of French fries.
3 servings of potato salad

STEAMING: This is one of the best ways to preserve a potato's nutrients, since few are leached out into the cooking water. You can use a steamer pot (a spaghetti cooker will work as well as one designed for steaming vegetables or Chinese food) or an inexpensive steamer rack that fits into a saucepan. You can even improvise a potato steamer by inserting custard cups or balls of crumpled foil on the bottom of a saucepan and placing the potatoes on these little platforms. The lid should fit tightly. Put water at the bottom of the pan and bring it to a boil; add the potatoes and cover the pot, steaming the potatoes until they are tender when they are pierced with a fork. Depending on their size, whole potatoes usually take 30 to 45 minutes to steam, and cut-up potatoes take 20 to 30 minutes. If the pot lid doesn't fit tightly, check once or twice to make sure the water has not cooked out.

BOILING: Put about 1 inch of water (if desired, add salt to the water to taste) in a saucepan with a thick bottom and tight-fitting lid. Cook the potatoes until they are fork-tender—about 30 to 40 minutes whole, 20 to 25 minutes cut up. Again, if the lid isn't tight, check to be sure the water doesn't boil out. If you are planning to bake bread or make soup in the near future, save the cooking water in the refrigerator and use it in your recipe. That way you'll retrieve any nutrients that cooked out of the potatoes and, if used in bread dough, you'll improve the quality of the bread. Of course, potatoes can also be peeled, cut, and boiled directly in a soup or casserole.

BAKING: Potatoes do not require a specific oven temperature for cooking, making it possible to bake them at the same time you bake or roast other foods at oven temperatures ranging from 325 to 450 degrees Fahrenheit. At 400 degrees, medium-sized potatoes will bake in about 40 to 45 minutes. The lower the temperature, the longer the potatoes take to bake through. You can speed the baking by using "potato nails" (aluminum nails inserted lengthwise through the center of the potato) or standing the potatoes on the spikes of a multi-potato baker. If you're not using nails or spikes, it's a good idea to pierce the potato skin in a few places before baking. This allows steam to escape and keeps the potato from bursting. However, don't wrap the potato in foil unless you want a steamed, rather than baked, flavor. Besides, it takes longer to bake a foil-wrapped potato. Potatoes can be baked directly on the oven rack or on a cookie sheet. Or you can use a stove-top potato baker, which is more fuel-efficient than the oven when the oven is not already in use for some other purpose. Test the potato for doneness by gently squeezing it (be sure to protect your hand with a pot holder) or piercing it with a skewer or fork.

MICROWAVING: This is an ideal method for the harried or hungry cook who can't wait 45 minutes to bake a potato. It has become very popular with single folks and working parents. One single friend says her favorite late supper is a microwave-baked potato topped with yogurt and chives, ready in the five minutes it takes her to change clothes. First wash and dry the potato, and prick it with a fork. Then place it on a double layer of paper toweling in the center of the microwave. For cooking more than one potato, arrange them as if each potato were the spoke of a wheel radiating from the center of the microwave floor. Follow the oven's cooking instructions. A 6-ounce potato will usually take about 4 minutes, with 1 to 2 minutes extra for each additional potato. Be sure to turn the potato over halfway through baking. I do not, however, recommend the microwave for boiling potatoes. It takes considerably longer than baking, and I find it to be more of a hassle than it's worth for the little time you save.

ROASTING: If prepared along with roasted meat, chicken, or turkey, arrange peeled, cut-up potatoes around the edges of the pan about 1½ hours before you expect the meat or bird to be done. To roast potatoes by themselves, boil or steam them first for about 10 minutes, peel them, and then arrange them in a shallow pan. They'll have a better flavor if you brush them with a small amount of melted butter, melted margarine, or vegetable oil. Roast whole potatoes at 400 degrees for about 45 minutes.

FRYING: I regard frying as the least nutritious way to eat potatoes. However, now and again home-made French-fried or home-fried potatoes can be a treat. I've even on occasion made my own potato chips (really "crisps") by slicing potatoes very thin (with a hand slicer or food processor) and frying them in hot oil. For French-frying, the oil should be 375 to 400 degrees, and the ¼-inch strips should be fried in small batches to keep the temperature from dropping drastically. Use a deep fryer or heavy saucepan with about 4 inches of vegetable oil. Frying is easiest if you can put the potatoes into a basket that fits into the pot; but a slotted spoon or small strainer will do for removing the strips, which take about 5 minutes to cook through. Be sure to drain off the excess oil by placing the cooked potatoes on paper towels. You can keep the first batches warm in a 300-degree oven while the rest are cooking.

A personal favorite is home fries made by slicing leftover steamed or boiled new potatoes and frying them in a small amount of oil with sliced onions.

SERVE THEM UP DELICIOUS AND NUTRITIOUS

A potato doesn't have to be seasoned with high-calorie fats or dressings to taste good. Here are some low-calorie suggestions for seasoning baked, boiled, or steamed potatoes:

- low-fat yogurt mixed with chopped chives, fresh dill, parsley, onions, scallions (green onions), horseradish, or green pepper
- dried herbs, either individually or a mixture, either alone or with a little lemon juice
- grated Parmesan or a similar cheese
- freshly ground black pepper with lemon juice or a few drops of sesame oil
- cottage cheese and lemon juice puréed in a blender
- a few drops of soy sauce, if you can handle the salt
- a tablespoon or 2 of stewed tomatoes
- a sprinkle of curry powder
- a few drops of flavored vinegar
- a teaspoon of melted butter or margarine (about 35 calories) or 2 teaspoons of diet margarine with lemon juice or a little Dijon mustard
- a tablespoon of sour cream (26 calories) with or without other seasonings
- defatted gravy or sauce from a stew
- soup broth

Now, just serve and enjoy!

5 ·
WHEAT AND OTHER GRAINS OF TRUTH

If one factor could be said to have made America the land of opportunity, it is its ability to support the growth of wheat and other grains—from the Indian corn of native Americans to the buckwheat of Russian immigrants. Grains provided the nourishment that sustained the pioneers and early settlers of the West, and what wasn't eaten directly by people became feed for their livestock. Unfortunately, as our standard of living rose, grains took a threshing beyond that needed to separate the nutritious kernels from their inedible hulls. The richer we are, the fewer grain foods we eat. A national survey showed that for every 10-percent rise in household income, there was a corresponding 5-percent decline in the purchase of rice, pasta, and corn meal. Much to our nutritional detriment, we now consume far fewer grains directly than did our forebears on this continent. In the 1970s alone, per-capita consumption of bread declined 9 percent among Americans, and that of nonsandwich bread dropped 31 percent. And most of the grains we do eat are consumed in their least nourishing forms—overly refined and/or overwhelmed by fat and sugar.

In the last few years, however, grain foods have begun to make a comeback as millions of Americans with an interest in good health and good-tasting food discover the appetizing versatility of the good grains. Cereal grains now provide about one-fifth of the calories Americans consume, a proportion that could easily be doubled or tripled to the benefit of our bodies and our pocketbooks. For the world's population in general, cereal grains provide the majority of the calories and about half the protein. To Dr. Paul Lachance of Rutgers University, "Cereal grains are the principal crops which have made the continuation of mankind possible."

WHAT ARE GRAINS?

Grains are the seed-bearing fruits of grasses. Each kernel of grain has a "germ" —or seed—as its core, surrounded by a storage packet of starch, the endosperm, that would nourish the young embryo if the seed sprouted. The entire kernel is protected by a layer of bran and usually also by an outermost inedible layer called the hull. The first human consumers of wild grains undoubtedly gnawed on the whole berries, as the kernels are sometimes called. But by the Stone Age, our primitive ancestors were grinding grains into a coarse cereal, or perhaps even into flour, by crushing the berries between two flat rocks. This was the beginning of the milling of wheat and other grains. Although milling greatly expanded the possible uses of grains, it also gradually led to their nutritional degradation and culminated in the production of refined, bleached white flour that is too low in nutrients and fiber to be worthy of the name grain. The vast majority of grain products used in this country are refined—that is, the bran and/or the germ have been removed in the milling process. Even though most refined grains now sold are "enriched" by the addition of four nutrients, what is replaced is only a fraction of the nutritional value that is lost in the refining process.

Indeed, there are far more nourishing and tasty ways to consume grains than as overly refined white bread or delicate pastries (although there can be an occasional place for both in an otherwise wholesome diet). And there are many nutritious grains besides wheat, the overwhelming favorite in this country. Although this book emphasizes "cooking from scratch," I'm not suggesting that you eat only whole berries of grain or grind your own flour. Thanks to the growing interest in more healthful, wholesome, "natural" foods, supermarkets today are usually well stocked with minimally refined nutritious grains and even many convenience foods made from them. Once you fully appreciate the food value of grains and understand how to determine their nutrient content from the package label, you'll have no difficulty selecting grains that are healthful as well as delicious. And you'll be able to expand greatly the variety of your meals by incorporating foods based on grains that are now unfamiliar to your table and taste buds. Among the choices, in addition to wheat, are corn, rice, oats, rye, millet, barley, and buckwheat (technically buckwheat is a fruit, not a grain, since the buckwheat plant is not a grass). Each, in turn, comes in several different forms—as a cereal, a flour, a vegetable, a bread, a pasta, or an ingredient in soups, casseroles, or meat-based dishes. Although grains are now used primarily as side dishes in this country, it's time to return them to the central role they once played in the human diet.

Wheat, the World Champion Grain

Wheat is by far the world's largest and most widely cultivated food crop, and it provides more nourishment for the two-legged inhabitants of this planet than any other single food. Wheat is the source of from 15 percent to 60 percent of the calories and protein in the diets of nearly all countries. If the world's total wheat production were uniformly distributed, it would provide a third of the daily calories and half the protein needed by every man, woman, and child alive today. Wheat and the breads into which it is often made are considered "the staff of life" in most cultures. And in every country wheat is considered too precious a commodity to feed to animals (only the remains of wheat refining

—ironically, the most nutritious part of the wheat berry—find their way into the bellies of livestock). Indeed, as you'll soon see, wheat comes close to being able to sustain life, and for thousands of years it was the mainstay of the human diet. In Berlin around 1800, a mason with a family of five would have spent 44 percent of his income on bread—more than the combined expenditures for animal foods, lodging, lighting, heating, clothing, and sundries. The prestige of meat notwithstanding, the availability of wheat for food was long regarded as a sign of a high stage of civilization, and for centuries countries that had adequate supplies of wheat have been considered nutritionally well off.

The United States is the world's largest producer of wheat, growing 600 million bushels a year that are ground into 20 billion pounds of flour. More than 60 percent of the wheat grown here is exported, making American wheat a major force in our balance of trade as well as a source of sustenance for millions of people in poorer countries.

Wheat is a very adaptable crop. As long as there is adequate rainfall, it will grow over a wide range of temperatures and at altitudes of up to 10,000 feet. In this country, wheat is grown commercially in 41 of the 50 states, and for 11 states it is the primary cash crop. Wheat is also an economical food. Cropland planted to wheat can provide nourishment for more people than the same land would yield if used to produce animal food. Looked at another way, it takes an average of 8 pounds of grain to produce 1 pound of meat; but 8 pounds of wheat supply many times more nutrients than you'd get from 1 pound of meat.

The origins of this "gift of the gods" are somewhat uncertain. The best available evidence points to 10,000 B.C. to 15,000 B.C. in southwestern Asia, the home of a wild grass called einkorn that could well be the ancestor of modern wheat. Another ancestral relative is emmer, a wild wheat-type plant found in the mountains of Syria and Palestine. Certainly, wheat has been cultivated and used for human food for many thousands of years: in Egypt since about 4000 B.C.; in China since at least 2800 B.C.

The ancient Egyptians ground wheat into flour, combined it with liquid, and baked it into bread. They also "discovered" the property of wheat that has made this the most popular grain for bread baking: the ability of wheat dough to rise and form a high loaf when yeast is added as a fermenting agent. The ancient Hebrews also made raised loaves of wheat dough by souring it. Centuries later, scientists showed that an elastic protein called gluten gives wheat the ability to rise.

Although wild wheat was not native to the Western Hemisphere, wheat seeds were brought here by Columbus, Cortez, and European immigrants, who sowed them far and wide and gave birth to the "amber waves of grain" in our national hymn.

NUTRITIONAL WONDERS OF WHEAT

Dr. Donald R. Davis, research scientist at the Clayton Foundation Biochemical Institute of the University of Texas at Austin, points out that "wheat grain contains significant amounts of many more nutrients than is sometimes realized, and does not deserve the scorn sometimes directed indiscriminately at all starchy or carbohydrate-rich foods." In addition to starch the wheat berry contains reasonable amounts of 22 known vitamins and minerals, a high-quality protein, and dietary fiber. The amounts of these nutrients in wheat are in good proportion to its calorie value, making the wheat berry a "nutrient-dense" food. Among its most notable nutritional assets are a good supply of essential amino acids (total protein varies from 7 percent to 20 percent, depending on the type of wheat—see p. 44), magnesium, vitamin B_6, vitamin E, folacin, niacin, pantothenic acid, thiamin, chromium, iron, manganese, and zinc, most of which, Davis says, "are only marginally supplied to significant segments of Western populations." Thus, wheat can help make up for nutritional deficiencies in many Western diets. All told, only 4 of the 44 known essential nutrients naturally obtained from foods are absent from whole wheat: vitamins A, B_{12}, and C, and the mineral iodine. The fat content of wheat is very low—less than 3 percent of its calories come from fat—which enhances its nutritive value. And although wheat protein is not as complete as that in animal foods, its deficiencies—lysine and tryptophan—can be easily corrected by adding a small amount of protein from dairy products, poultry, fish, or meat, or by eating wheat with any legume (peanuts, dried beans or peas, or lentils).

The nutrients of wheat are not evenly distributed throughout the kernel. The bran, a multilayered outer coating, is only 15 percent of the wheat kernel by weight but contains about 20 percent of the protein (including the essential amino acid lysine, which is otherwise relatively deficient in wheat and other grains), 33 percent of the thiamin, 42 percent of the riboflavin, 50 percent of the pantothenic acid, 73 percent of the vitamin B_6, and 86 percent of the niacin. The germ of the wheat, the tiny oval at the bottom of the kernel that is the seed for a new plant, is only 2.5 percent of the kernel by weight but contains 8 percent of the protein, 21 percent of the B_6, 26 percent of the riboflavin, 64 percent of the thiamin, and all of the vitamin E. The germ also contains essential fatty acids. And the bran and the germ are the main sources of dietary fiber. The bulk of the kernel, the endosperm, is 83 percent by weight but contains 72 percent of the protein, 3 percent of the thiamin, 6 percent of the B_6, 12 percent of the niacin, and 43 percent of the pantothenic acid. Most of the endosperm is starch.

Thus, the most nutritious way to eat wheat is to consume the whole berry (intact or ground) or as close to that as possible. Unfortunately, 80 percent of the wheat Americans now consume (a total of 150 pounds per capita each year) is refined—stripped of bran and germ and most of its valuable nutrients.

MILLING, THE RAPE OF THE WHEAT BERRY

The history of wheat is marked by the bad pushing out the good. Wheat was originally eaten as the roasted whole berry (minus the hull, which is removed during threshing) or pounded with stones into small particles that made a porridge when cooked with water. But to expand its uses, wheat had to be milled into a flour or granular product. Small rotary hand mills were used in homes for 2,000 years before the Christian era, and by the time of Christ large bakeries in Italy and Greece used rotary mills driven by water or animals. But these stone mills could not remove the coarse brown-colored bran and germ that "contaminated" the fine, whitish flour that had been prized by the privileged classes for thousands of years. To get rid of these "undesirable" features, stone-ground flour was sieved through fine cloth, a laborious and expensive technique called bolting.

In colonial America, the original mills that served people in nearby villages were grooved stone wheels powered by wind, water, or oxen. They produced a dark, coarse bread like that eaten by European peasants. But in the mid-1700s, following the Roman example, many American mills began bolting their stone-ground flour to make a more expensive, high-status, but low-nutrient product. In addition to the well-to-do, the pioneers prized the white flour because it kept longer: lacking the fat of the wheat germ, it didn't turn rancid during the year between harvests. Then, in the mid-nineteenth century, came the invention that finally brought white flour to the masses: the roller mill which ground the wheat between steam-powered steel rollers. This invention efficiently separated the bran and germ from the endosperm and made fine white flour available widely and cheaply. This flour could be shipped great distances without spoiling and baked into light, desirable loaves. When the larger mills adopted roller mills, most of the small stone mills could no longer compete and white bread spread over the land like dandelion fluff. About 95 percent of the flour used in the United States today is white, and the goodies removed in milling are used to fatten chickens and other animals. The usual white flour purchased in the United States is about 70 percent to 75 percent "extraction," which means that only about three-fourths of the original wheat kernel remains in the flour.

Having already read about how the nutrients are distributed in the wheat berry, it shouldn't surprise you to know that refined flour is missing up to 80 percent of the nutrients found in the original kernel. The content of 22 vitamins and minerals is diminished by 70 percent to 80 percent, and the fiber content is only 7 percent of the original amount. The essential fatty acid, linoleic acid, is cut in half, and although the protein content is only slightly affected, the nutritional value of that protein is greatly reduced because the essential amino acid lysine is lost. What little vitamin E is left after refining is destroyed when the flour is bleached to make it "whiter than white."

When refined white flour or food products made from it are enriched, only 4 nutrients are added: thiamin, riboflavin, niacin, and iron. (Enrichment brings the level of these nutrients back to that of whole wheat except for riboflavin, which is enriched to three times the original level.) But compared to whole wheat, the enriched product remains deficient in 18 vitamins and minerals, fiber, and protein value. Thus, while enriched white flour is better than unenriched, it is a far cry from the original nutritious wheat berry. Table 2 clearly demonstrates the nutritional advantages of whole-wheat flour in comparison to white refined flour, whether enriched or not.

Table 2   NUTRIENT CONTENT OF WHEAT FLOURS *(per cup)*

	Whole wheat	*White unenriched*	*White enriched*
Calories	400	455	455
Protein (g.)	16.0	13.1	13.1
Fat (g.)	2.4	1.3	1.3
Carbohydrate (g.)	85.2	95.1	95.1
Calcium (mg.)	49	20	20
Phosphorus (mg.)	446	109	109
Iron (mg.)	4.0	1.0	3.6*
Potassium (mg.)	444	119	119
Thiamin (mg.)	0.66	0.08	0.55*
Riboflavin (mg.)	0.14	0.06	0.33*
Niacin (mg.)	5.2	1.1	4.4*

SOURCE: USDA Handbook No. 456.
*From added nutrients.

Table 3   NUTRIENTS LOST WHEN WHOLE-WHEAT FLOUR IS REFINED

Nutrient	*% lost*	*Nutrient*	*% lost*	*Nutrient*	*% lost*
Cobalt	88.5	Zinc	77.7	Copper	67.9
Vitamin E	86.3	Thiamin	77.1	Calcium	60.0
Manganese	85.8	Potassium	77.0	Pantothenic acid	50.0
Magnesium	84.7	Iron	75.6	Molybdenum	48.0
Niacin	80.8	Vitamin B_6	71.8	Chromium	40.0
Riboflavin	80.0	Phosphorus	70.9	Selenium	15.9
Sodium	78.3				

SOURCE: Henry A. Schroeder, "Losses of Vitamins and Trace Minerals Resulting from Processing and Preservation of Foods," *American Journal of Clinical Nutrition* 24 (1971).

Davis points out that while whole wheat products can be eaten without concern for their nutritional contribution, refined wheat products may be "compared to refined sugar and fats," which force the consumer to make up for their nutritional deficiencies in the rest of the foods eaten. As a food source for the 20-odd nutrients in whole wheat, refined wheat products are "similar to a mixture of 25 percent whole wheat and 75 percent sugar," he says. Table 3 should make it clear how inadequate "enrichment" of white flour with three B vitamins and iron is in restoring the nutrients lost when whole-wheat flour is denuded in the refining process.

THE MANY KINDS OF WHEAT AND FLOUR

Like potatoes, there are different varieties and types of wheat, each used for different purposes, depending on its particular characteristics. *Spring wheat,* planted in the spring and harvested in the fall, is mostly grown in the colder climates of the northern plains states and Canada. It is generally higher in protein than its seasonal counterpart, *winter wheat.* Winter wheat, grown in milder climates, is planted in the fall and harvested the next summer, resulting in a kernel that is higher in starch. Each may come as a "hard" or "soft" wheat, determined by its ability to form gluten, the protein that helps bread to rise. Because it contains 12 to 14 percent protein and forms a lot of gluten when mixed with liquid, hard spring wheat makes an excellent bread flour. *Durum wheat* is a hard spring wheat grown in North Dakota and Montana that is used almost exclusively to make pasta. *Semolina* is a refined durum flour that is used to make "white" pasta. Whole-wheat pasta is made from the whole durum wheat kernel, including the bran and germ, mixed with other hard and soft flours. Soft winter wheat, with less protein and more starch, is used mainly for flour to make cakes, cookies, and pastries.

BUYING FLOUR. Even with whole-wheat flour and products, the nutrient level can vary depending upon how the flour is milled and processed. You get the most nutrients—and the best flavor—from *stone-ground whole-wheat flour.* If not in the "health food" or regular flour section of your supermarket, you'll find it in health food stores. It is one health food that is worth the extra expense. It is coarsely ground between rotating millstones much like the ones used in centuries past. *Stone-ground graham flour* is whole-wheat flour in which the starchy part of the wheat kernel is finely ground but the bran is left coarse and flaky. Second best is ordinary *whole-wheat flour,* which is less coarse than the stone-ground variety and may contain flour additives (like malted barley flour). You can also buy *whole-wheat pastry flour,* made from soft whole wheat that is finely milled.

When you buy ordinary refined white flour, you get something called *all-purpose flour,* a blend of hard and soft wheat flours suitable for a variety of baked goods, breads, and cakes. It is the least expensive flour on the market and has the longest shelf life. It is often sold *presifted,* which means it's been through a sifter several times before it was packaged. However, if you're making something that should have an especially light "crumb" or where the recipe states "sift before measuring," sift it again. If you do buy white flour (you'll probably want to mix it with whole-wheat or other grain flours to make breads, cakes, cookies, and pancakes), chose an unbleached variety and think about adding some wheat germ to your recipe to enhance its nutritional value. You may notice that the package lists "malted barley flour" among its ingredients. A small amount is added to promote yeast fermentation when the flour is used in bread baking. If a recipe specifies *cake flour* or *pastry flour,* you'll end up with a much lighter product if you use these softer flours rather than all-purpose flour. (If you do use all-purpose flour in a recipe that calls for cake flour, reduce the amount by one-eighth.) Quick breads that are leavened with baking powder and/or baking soda can be made with all-purpose flour, as can most yeast-leavened breads. But some bakers of yeast breads prefer the high-gluten *bread flour* now available in most markets. (See p. 554 for more guidance on bread baking and the handling of dough to control gluten development.) So-called *gluten flour* has been treated to increase its protein content for use in special-purpose breads. It can be combined with a low-gluten flour, such as rye, barley, or triticale, to produce a lighter bread. *Self-rising cake flour* is soft white flour to which salt and a leavening agent have been added. You can easily make your own if you start with ordinary cake flour (add ¼ teaspoon of salt and 1 table-spoon of baking powder to each 3 cups of cake flour). Whichever type of flour you use, if it's not a whole-wheat flour, make sure that it's enriched and, if possible, unbleached. In addition to whitening the flour, bleaching helps to age it to improve its baking characteristics. Unbleached flour, therefore, is aged commercially before you buy it. Sometimes millers add potassium bromate to flour to accelerate aging, resulting in a product call *bromated flour.*

STORING FLOUR. Flour is best stored in a cool, dry place in a container that keeps out moisture and insects. Since whole-wheat flour contains some fat that can go rancid, store it in the refrigerator unless you'll be using it up in a month or two. Stone-ground whole-wheat flour lasts longer than ordinary whole-wheat flour, which is ground by high-speed mills that heat the flour, making it turn rancid sooner. You can also keep flour in the freezer for longer-term storage. Be sure to wrap it in a moisture-proof bag, such as one made of heavy plastic. In the summer, when the heat increases the likelihood of insect infestation and decreases the amount of baking I do, I store most of my flours in the refrigerator or freezer. Even when flour is frozen, it's easy to remove the amount needed at the moment.

BUYING WHEAT BREADS AND CEREALS

Wheat is by far the most popular ingredient of breads, both commercial and homemade, and cereals, both cold and hot. However, the unsuspecting consumer can be easily seduced into buying products that are far removed from wheat's true nutritional value. Some products labeled "100-percent whole wheat" are not that at all. Sure, the whole-wheat flour in them is, as claimed, 100-percent whole wheat, but whole wheat is not the only kind of flour—and perhaps not even the most prominent flour—used in making the products. Then, too, other ingredients may be added, like fats and sugars, that dilute the nutritional value of the wheat. The only way to be sure you're getting your nutritional dollar's worth is to read labels carefully, especially the list of ingredients. (If you're buying unpackaged bread in a bakery, ask the storekeeper what flours were used.) Whether bread or cereal, the first ingredient listed should be whole wheat. If it is stone-ground whole wheat, all the better. This means that at least 51 percent of the flour used is whole-wheat flour; the remaining 49 percent could be refined white flour. If you want a 100-percent whole-wheat product, there should be no other flour listed.

Forget about what the manufacturer calls the product. Just because its brand name says "wheat bread," "bran muffins," "whole-wheat cereal," "wheat berry," "cracked wheat," or any other such designation, it doesn't mean that whole wheat is the only ingredient or even the main one in the product. The phrase "wheat bread" might be used to distinguish the product from one made from oats or rye, or merely to confuse the unwary consumer into thinking that "wheat bread" is synonymous with *whole-*wheat bread. For example, Home Pride *White* Bread is made solely from enriched white flour, and Home Pride *Wheat* Bread is made primarily from enriched white flour; whole-wheat flour is the fifth ingredient listed, after water, corn syrup, and wheat bran. Thomas' Honey Wheat English Muffins are made primarily from enriched white flour with some whole-wheat flour. And Pepperidge Farm markets the following breads, all of which are made primarily from unbleached enriched white flour: Honey Wheat Berry, Honey Bran, Wheat Germ, Cracked Wheat, and Wheat Bread. Oddly enough, the 2-pound loaf called Pepperidge Farm *Family* Wheat is made with stone-ground whole-wheat flour as the main ingredient, but the 1-pound loaf simply called Pepperidge Farm Wheat is made with unbleached enriched white wheat flour as the main ingredient, with stone-ground whole-wheat flour appearing fourth in the list of ingredients.

Some packaged breads that are made solely from whole wheat include Wonder 100% Whole Wheat Bread, Arnold's Stoneground 100% Whole Wheat Bread, Arnold's Dark Wheat Bran'nola (but Original Bran'nola is a combination of whole-wheat and white flours), and Pepperidge Farm's Sprouted Wheat Bread. The latter is a dense, crunchy bread that contains wheat berries, sunflower seeds, and sesame seeds in addition to whole-wheat flour, making it a more substantial sandwich bread and, I think, a more satisfying bread to eat than, say, airy Wonder 100% Whole Wheat, which works well for French toast.

The texture of bread is a less reliable clue to how much whole wheat is added, although in general the coarser the product, the more whole wheat. You should be able to see the wheat berries or cracked wheat in breads that claim to have these ingredients. Color is the least reliable clue. Bread made solely from refined flour can be very dark if molasses is used as the sweetener or caramel or chocolate is added to the dough. Arnold's Pumpernickel Bread, for example, is made from unbleached enriched white flour, malted barley flour, light rye flour, pumpernickel meal, and *caramel* coloring. The last ingredient gives the bread its dark brown color—not whole-wheat flour.

If the bread is made with soy flour, milk (or nonfat milk solids), cheese, sunflower seeds, or egg white, the protein value of the wheat is significantly enhanced. The same would be true if you ate any grain-based bread with a food containing complementary protein from legumes, seeds, or animals.

As for cereals, the best are those made from whole wheat and little else. The less processing, the better. Hot cereals like Wheatena and cold cereals like Shredded Wheat (biscuits or spoon-size) get top billing. Farina, or Cream of Wheat, is prepared from the hulled wheat berry; it contains the germ but not the bran. Other whole-wheat ready-to-eat cereals include Nutri-Grain Wheat, Wheaties, Wheat Chex, Puffed Wheat, Total, and Most. These have nothing but whole wheat as the grain (however, the wheat kernel in puffed wheat has been lightly pearled and heated to high temperatures, which reduces its nutritive value). You may also find whole-wheat flakes made from wheat berries that have been heated and pressed (as in Nutri-Grain). Bran cereals, such as All-Bran, 100% Bran, and Bran Buds, use wheat bran as their base, which is sweetened and flavored. They are higher in dietary fiber than any other cereal. Products like 40% Bran Flakes and Raisin Bran are made from wheat bran and other parts of the wheat kernel. The amount of sugar and salt added to these choices can affect their nutritional value, so be sure to read the nutrition information on the side of the package before you make your selection. Nearly all cereals now show sugar content (under "Carbohydrate Information"), and most also say how much sodium there is in a serving. In any comparison of this sort, Shredded Wheat (unsweetened) is the hands-down winner, with no added sugar or sodium. (For more information on choosing breakfast cereals, see p. 193.)

OTHER WHEATY WONDERS

The "rice" of the Middle East is a granulated wheat called *bulgur,* or cracked wheat. It is parboiled (steamed and dried) wheat that has been cracked into small pieces. It is sold in bulk in specialty food stores and health food stores or in boxes (check the rice or hot-cereal shelves of your supermarket). It can be obtained in three different sizes: the largest for use as a pilaf (like rice), as a stuffing, or in salads; the middle-sized for cereal; and the smallest for the Middle Eastern salad tabbouli (see the recipe on p. 540) and for adding to other recipes, such as those for bread and ground meat. Bulgur has a unique nutty flavor that is delicious by itself or when mixed with rice. However, it is not always a whole-wheat product. Check the granule to see if the dark-brown bran is still present.

Couscous is finely cracked wheat or millet that has been steamed, dried, and refined to some extent. It is the bulgur of North Africa, where it is usually served with meat, vegetables, or fruit (see recipes on pp. 432 and 469).

Wheat berries are commonly sold in health food stores. They are the whole-wheat kernel, pure and unadulterated. They require prolonged cooking (in a heavy saucepan, add 1 cup of wheat berries to 4 cups of boiling water, reduce the heat, cover the pan, and simmer the wheat berries, stirring them occasionally, for 3 hours). But you may find them worth the effort because the yield is a hearty, crunchy, nut-flavored cereal or ingredient for breads and muffins. Once cooked, the berries can be frozen for later use, so you can cook up more than you need for the moment. You can also crack your own wheat berries to make a whole-grain bulgur. Wheat berries can also be sprouted (see p. 110) and the sprouts added to salads, stir-fries, or baked goods.

Wheat germ is just what its name implies: the vitamin- and mineral-rich wheat embryo that is separated out when flour is refined. It is a tasty, nourishing supplement to add to all kinds of recipes—pancakes, meat or vegetable loaves, breads, cookies, casseroles, and breading for fish or chicken, among others. Some people sprinkle it on yogurt or salads, or eat it as a cereal, or add it to other cereals to improve their nutritive value. Because it contains wheat-germ oil, it should be stored in the refrigerator after the jar is opened.

Finally, there are *bran flakes* (sometimes called unprocessed bran), often sold in bags or bulk in health food stores. Since bran by itself resembles fine sawdust in taste and texture, bran flakes are not consumed right from the box. Rather, they are nearly always used as a baking or cooking ingredient to enhance the fiber content of other recipes (see recipes on pp. 586 and 597).

SOME PROBLEMS WITH WHEAT. Whole wheat contains iron and a number of other minerals, the nutritive value of which was long in doubt. Many claimed that these valuable minerals could not be absorbed from wheat because they were linked in an insoluble complex to a substance in wheat bran called phytate. Although phytate is found in many plant foods, it is present in higher concentrations in wheat bran than in most others. However, a study several years ago by scientists at the United States Department of Agriculture showed that even when large amounts of bran were consumed daily for 15 days by 10 volunteers, mineral absorption remained good. For iron, zinc, magnesium, manganese, copper, and calcium, the amount the men consumed was greater than what they excreted over a period of 1 month, indicating that absorption was greater than losses. The men's diets contained 36 grams of bran each day (eaten as bran muffins), which is well into the high-normal range for wheat-fiber intake.

Another "problem" concerns the inability of many people to fully digest the carbohydrate in wheat flour. Dr. Michael D. Levitt and his colleagues at the Veterans Administration Medical Center in Minneapolis found that in virtually everyone about 20 percent of the carbohydrate in white flour (as found in white bread or pasta) and an even larger percentage of that in whole-wheat flour is never absorbed. Instead, the undigested carbohydrate is attacked by bacteria in the large intestine, producing gas and possibly causing loose bowels. For those concerned about calories, this malabsorption may be a hidden blessing, assuming they do not experience serious problems with flatulence or diarrhea.

People who have celiac sprue, an inherited food intolerance to the proteins in wheat and rye (and often other grains), must stay away from all wheat products and other gluten-containing foods.

Corn, the A-maizing Grain

More American than apple pie, more widely grown than any other American crop, and more versatile than the meat it is primarily used to produce—that's corn. It's time to rediscover this native American grain as a direct source of human food, not just as feed for livestock (who turn it into protein, fat, and cholesterol). Save for movie popcorn and chips for dips, canned and frozen kernels of sweet corn, and the occasional corn muffin or the buttered and salted succulent cob of late summer, most Americans are largely unfamiliar with corn-based foods and their potential contribution to our nutritional well-being.

The corn that Christopher Columbus and his men found growing in Cuba in 1492 had already had a long and illustrious history. Thousands of years earlier, the Aztecs and Mayas had domesticated corn from a wild grain. The original plant is lost to antiquity, although modern maize is closely related to a plant called teosinte, which now grows wild in Mexico and Guatemala. Indian corn was found in pre-Inca graves dating back to 3000 B.C. Corn pollen grains that are 80,000 years old were found in the rocks 200 feet below Mexico City, and 5,600-year-old corncobs were found in a cave in New Mexico. Magellan introduced corn to the Philippines in the sixteenth century, and from there it spread to eastern Asia and New Zealand.

In the Western Hemisphere, the popularity of corn quickly spread northward, and by the time Columbus arrived, American Indians had made it the most important human food plant in the West by adapting it to suit growing conditions from near the tip of South America to lower Canada. According to Nobel laureate George W. Beadle, geneticist at the University of Chicago, the Indians' achievement "is perhaps the most remarkable man-made plant transformation of all time, but in the process corn was so altered that it can no longer survive in the wild, for it has no means of disseminating its kernels," which house the seeds of the next generation. The sturdy husk around each ear not only protects the kernels from damage by frost, birds, and insects, but also prevents the seeds from dispersing. Thus, all corn is purposely sown, and in this country more so than anywhere else in the world.

The English colonists fast developed a taste for corn, and there was much fighting among them over cornfields, which the native Indians had taught them to cultivate. One Indian innovation involved planting corn in hills along with beans and winter squash, a highly nutritious combination that made the most efficient use of the land. The beans used the corn stalks for poles, and the squashes grew at their feet, choking off the weeds. The beans provided protein that compensated for corn's deficiencies of the amino acids tryptophan and lysine as well as the vitamins riboflavin and niacin, and the squashes were excellent sources of vitamin A as well as essential fatty acids (in the seeds).

Columbus carried the grain the Indians called "maiz" back to Spain. Within one generation it had spread through southern Europe, and within two generations, around the world. But neither the colonists nor the first European growers of corn fed much, if any, of their corn to animals. A plaque in Truro, Massachusetts, honoring the corn plant quotes the governor of Plymouth Colony as having said: "And sure it was God's good providence that we found this corne, for else we know not how we should have done." Little of the early American corn was eaten fresh. Most was cooked in cakes and breads or dried, ground, and stored for later use as corn meal and flour. Sweet corn, the table corn Americans are most familiar with, was not developed until the 1700s.

Today corn is the nation's number one agricultural commodity, grown on 1 of every 4 acres of cropland. It is produced in every state of the country and throughout the world: from 58 degrees latitude in Canada and Russia to 40 degrees latitude in the Southern Hemisphere; from below sea level in the Caspian plain to altitudes of more than 12,000 feet in the Peruvian Andes; from regions with less than 10 inches of rain a year to the coast of Colombia, with more than 400 inches of rainfall; from the short summers of Canada to the equatorial tropics with its perennial summer. No other crop is distributed over so large an area of the world, and only wheat occupies a larger acreage than corn.

Corn has become the basic food plant of modern American civilization and the most efficient crop we have for capturing the energy of the sun and turning it into food. Unfortunately, 90 percent of the corn we produce is used to feed livestock, making corn by far the leading feed grain. These are the vast stretches of "field corn" you see if you drive out into the countryside: stalks up to 15 feet high with tassles and swollen ears with silken threads near the top. The tassles are the source of pollen, which are carried to each kernel by the silks; to produce a full ear, every kernel must be pollinated. Most of this field corn ends up in feed lots, where our beef cattle put on many pounds—mostly of fat. In addition, substantial portions of the corn we produce are used to make food ingredients (such as nutritionally limited cornstarch and corn syrup), industrial products, feed ingredients, and alcoholic beverages.

MORE NUTRITIOUS WAYS WITH CORN

As with the other complex-carbohydrate foods, there is more to corn than "just starch." The corn kernel consists of an outer hull (mostly roughage) over a layer of hard starch and soft starch. At the center is the nutritious, protein-rich germ that would become the embryo of a new plant. The protein in corn, like wheat, is shy of two essential amino acids: lysine and tryptophan. When combined Mexican-style with a legume (as in a bean enchilada) or with small amounts of animal protein (as in corn pudding or bread), corn protein becomes complete. Corn is also a reasonably good source of B vitamins, vitamins A and C, potassium, and dietary fiber. The vitamin A content varies with the color: the yellower the corn, the more vitamin A it contains. White corn and the corn meal ground from it are nearly devoid of vitamin A. And corn is a low-sodium food —that is, until salt is added in processing, cooking, or at the table.

The nutritive value of a corn-based food depends on the type of corn used, how the grain was processed, and what the corn might have been combined with to produce the finished food. The following are major types of corn:

Dent corn is grown primarily for animal feed and to produce corn meal and corn flour. It is allowed to mature on the stalk and is dried before grinding. Ordinary grinding of corn would not destroy the germ; however, because the germ is rich in oils and spoils more quickly than the rest of the kernel, it is frequently removed. Thus, most *corn meal* and *corn flour* are sold "degermed" or "degerminated" and enriched. It is worth shopping for stone-ground whole corn meal and grits, but be sure to store them in your refrigerator or freezer if you don't use them up in a few weeks.

Popcorn kernels have more hard starch than other types, which helps them to "explode" when heated. No, popcorn was not the invention of Metro-Goldwyn-Mayer. Actually, the Incas cultivated it and used it to decorate bodies for burial, and the Indians who greeted Columbus were wearing necklaces of strung popcorn. The Indians who attended the first Thanksgiving dinner supposedly arrived bearing bowls of popcorn, thus starting a national passion long before there was a nation. According to the Popcorn Institute, Americans gobble 9.6 billion quarts of popcorn each year, or 41 quarts for every man, woman, and child in the country.

Popcorn is an excellent snack food—that is, sans butter and salt. A cup of unadorned popcorn contains only 23 calories—a dieter's delight of munch-minus-calories—and a 3-quart bowl has 276 calories, about the amount in two large cookies. Popcorn is also very high in fiber (be sure to drink plenty of water or some other low-calorie beverage if you don't want to get temporarily constipated after a popcorn orgy). You can keep popcorn calories to the barest minimum by making it in a hot-air popper. Lacking this electrical gadget, brush a heavy saucepan with vegetable oil, add the corn when the saucepan is hot, and keep shaking the covered pan until all the kernels have popped. If you feel you must flavor your popcorn, try sprinkling on some finely crushed herbs or spices or grated Parmesan (added protein is the bonus), or dribble on a small amount of lightly salted melted butter or margarine (but remember, every tablespoon of fat adds 100 calories to the bowl).

Sweet corn has much more sugar than other types and shrivels when dry. It is meant to be eaten in its immature state, while still tender and juicy. If you buy your sweet corn already cut from the cob, there's a good chance that you are missing the nutritious germ. If you eat it from the cob, be sure to chomp off the entire kernel. And if you freeze your own kernels, slice close to the cob to get the full nutritive value of corn. In my view, a freshly picked and properly steamed ear of corn needs no seasoning. And if it isn't freshly picked, it's not worth eating. I steam sweet corn for about five minutes by standing the cobs in an inch of water in a tall pot with a tight cover.

Cream-style corn has the same calories as, but smaller amounts of vitamins and minerals than, plain *corn kernels*. A 3½-ounce serving of either provides between 80 and 90 calories. You can buy canned corn in regular and low-sodium varieties.

FOODS MADE FROM CORN

Among the better-known corn products are corn flakes and puffed corn; corn muffins, fritters, and bread; tortillas; corn grits; corn pudding; corn chips; and corn-meal pancakes. These vary widely in nutrient-to-calorie ratio, depending upon what else they contain. In corn muffins and fritters and some corn-bread recipes, fat looms as a large proportion of total calories, diluting the nutritive value. In corn muffins, for example, fat contributes a third of the calories. Thus, in deciding how to get your nutritional money's worth from corn, it pays to read labels to determine both nutrient content and major ingredients.

CORN CEREALS. Corn was the basis for the very first ready-to-eat breakfast cereal: Kellogg's Corn Flakes. It was devised by Dr. John Harvey Kellogg, who ran a sanitarium in Battle Creek, Michigan. He developed corn flakes as a meat substitute in hopes of improving the digestion and general health of his patients. John's brother, W.K., took an interest in the project, and the two of them launched the American breakfast-cereal industry nearly a century ago. Despite competition from hundreds of camp followers in the next ninety years, corn flakes remains a steady seller.

An ounce of ordinary corn flakes (about 1 cup) has 110 calories, 2 grams of protein, and a negligible amount of fat. But when sugar-coated, as in Kellogg's Sugar Frosted Flakes, the protein content of a 1-ounce serving (about ⅔ cup) is cut in half; and even though total calories remain the same, much of the nutritionally neutral starch has been replaced by less desirable sugar: 11 grams per serving, compared to only 2 grams of sugar in regular corn flakes. The same kind of difference holds for the regular and sweetened varieties of puffed corn, such as unsweetened Kix versus sugar-coated Sugar Corn Pops. Among available cold corn cereals, Nutri-Grain Corn and plain puffed corn (sold in health food stores) give the best nutritive value. They are made from the whole corn kernel—bran, germ, and all—and contain no added sugar (the flavoring of Nutri-Grain comes from malted barley and some salt; plain puffed corn has nothing but corn). Like corn flakes, a 1-ounce serving (about ⅔ cup) of Nutri-Grain contains 110 calories and 2 grams of protein; but the amount of fiber and minerals is greater, the salt content is lower, and, I think, the flavor vastly improved. Other corn-based cold cereals include Corn Chex, made from milled yellow corn and very little sugar (but more salt than Nutri-Grain), and Corn Bran, made from corn flour and high-fiber corn-bran flour but with three times more sugar (6 grams per serving) than nonsugar-coated corn cereals. Like corn flakes, both contain 110 calories and 2 grams of protein per serving.

As for hot corn cereals, whole corn grits are best but hard to get outside of the South or health food stores. To cook whole hominy grits, it's best to use a nonstick saucepan. Gradually add 1 cup of grits to 4 cups of boiling water, stirring the mixture as you go. Add salt as desired, stir until the mixture boils, and then lower the heat to a simmer. Cover the pot, and cook the grits, stirring them occasionally, for 25 to 30 minutes. Let the grits stand 5 minutes before serving. The hominy you buy in cans is made from skinned corn kernels that have lost fiber and some nutrients. Polenta is the Italian version of corn-meal mush: grits cooked in stock. It can be a tasty side dish for dinner, topped with grated cheese. Or it can be refrigerated, sliced, and eaten cold.

CORN BREADS. Corn tortillas, the chief bread of Mexico, are made from masa harina, a flour ground from corn that has been steeped in lime, rinsed, and dried. The flour is mixed with water, shaped into balls, flattened, and baked on a griddle. Tortillas can be baked or fried crisp, as in tacos and tostadas, or stuffed and rolled soft, as in enchiladas. Before frying, they contain almost no fat. Uncooked tortillas can be folded over a filling, then fried or baked into a quesadilla. Cut-up tortillas can be used in Mexican-style casseroles in place of pasta (see the recipe on p. 395). Stale tortillas can be cut up and cooked in a sauce to make chilaquiles. Tortillas dry out quickly and will get moldy in a week. Leftover tortillas should be wrapped in plastic and refrigerated. If not used within a few days, they can be stored in the freezer for weeks and reheated in a slow oven as needed. To reheat, preheat the oven to 250 degrees, sprinkle a little water over the tortillas, wrap them in foil, and place them in the oven for a few minutes until they are soft and hot.

Other types of corn breads are made from more coarsely ground corn meal rather than from corn flour. They are much higher in fat than unfried tortillas and contain leavening, milk, salt, and usually some sweetener. They include skillet corn bread, spoon bread, hush puppies, corn pones, corn sticks, johnnycakes, and corn muffins. When made from whole-grain cornmeal, unsaturated fat (such as vegetable oil rather than butter, lard, or bacon fat), and low-fat milk or buttermilk, these breads can be tasty and nourishing additions to any healthy diet. I sometimes whip up a quick corn bread for breakfast—it bakes while I'm out jogging, and I come home to a most appetizing aroma.

CORN SNACKS. Corn snacks, such as corn chips, taco chips, and nacho chips, are pieces of tortillas that are deep-fried, salted, and otherwise seasoned. Although they represent the least nutritious way to eat corn, they currently claim more than a $800-million share of the American consumer's food budget. You can make your own nutritious corn chips by stacking up soft tortillas, cutting them like a pie into 8 wedge-shaped pieces each, spreading the pieces on a lightly greased or nonstick baking sheet, and baking them at 350 degrees for about 10 minutes or until they are crisp and lightly golden. If desired, you can sprinkle the wedges with dried herbs before baking.

Rice, the World's Leading "Bread"

The American custom of throwing rice after the bride and groom is meant to encourage the fertility of the union. But to the Malays of Southeast Asia, rice is too precious to be tossed about. The Malays believe it possesses an essential life force, and every ceremonial occasion—birth, rites of puberty, marriage, death—is marked by a symbolic meal of rice. To the Malays, as to many Asian peoples, rice is synonymous with food. A meal isn't a meal if it doesn't include rice. Indeed, rice is the staple food of over half the people in the world today.

For many, it is their main source of protein, and for some, it is their only protein. Rice constitutes half the diet for 1.6 billion people and a quarter to half the diet for another 400 million. Yet to most Americans, rice is casually treated as "filler food"—a starchy base that accompanies meat, fish, or poultry, or that gives texture to soups and stews.

Indeed, as most Americans eat it—white and polished—rice leaves something to be desired as a source of nutrients, even if the shiny white kernels are enriched. But rice in its more natural "brown" form (or, if you insist on white rice, as parboiled or converted rice) can be the nourishing base for many meals and types of foods: from appetizers, soups, and cereals to entrées, salads, and desserts. It is also used to make vinegar, wine for drinking and cooking, and beer.

In addition to its unusual versatility, rice offers several dietary and culinary advantages: it is a good source of vitamins, minerals, and protein; it contains practically no fat and very little sodium (that is, until salt is added in cooking); it is highly digestible, making it a suitable food for everyone from infants to the elderly; it is nonallergenic and free of gluten, making it suitable for special diets; it is inexpensive and simple to prepare; it is easy to store; and its blandness allows it to mix well with a wide range of flavors.

Even though rice is the world's third leading grain (after wheat and corn), in this case the United States is the source of but a tiny fraction of world output. We produce less than 2 percent of the 200 million pounds of rice harvested each year, and two-thirds of our harvest is exported to Europe and Africa as well as Asia, where most of the rest is grown. Whereas the average Asian consumes 400 pounds of rice each year, per-capita consumption here is less than 10 pounds, including all the various products into which rice is made.

A PREHISTORIC CROP

Rice is a native of Asia, where it was grown and used for food even before records were kept. Its first formal historical record dates back to 2800 B.C., when a Chinese emperor wrote a ceremonial ordinance for the planting of rice. In fact, the word *rice* in Chinese means "agriculture" or "culture." However, there is evidence that the original home of rice was India, where the wild grass "Newaree" is believed to have given birth to rice. Rice is said to have spread with Buddhism from India to China and throughout most of Asia. Although Alexander the Great returned to Europe with a bounty of rice following his invasion of India, it was centuries before the crop was cultivated there.

Rice arrived on the shores of North America in 1694, when a ship sailing from Madagascar to England was blown off course and forced to land at Charleston, South Carolina. To thank the colonists for their hospitality, the ship's captain gave the governor a handful of rough rice grains, which the colonists used for seed. Today, South Carolina is no longer a major rice-producing area. Six other states—Arkansas, California, Louisiana, Mississippi, Missouri, and Texas—produce more than 99 percent of the nation's rice. Rice thrives in warm, humid areas where there is abundant water, since the plants must be submerged in water for most of their growth period.

THE DIFFERENT FORMS OF RICE

Rice is one case in which the "inventors" of a food don't consume it in its most nutritious form. The Asians insist on eating polished white rice, which has been stripped of its most nourishing outer layers—the bran and germ—leaving behind almost pure starch. Since rice is the main source of calories in the Asian diet, consumption of unenriched polished rice results in widespread vitamin-deficiency disease—notably beriberi, caused by insufficient thiamin. But whereas enrichment of rice with thiamin eliminates this problem in rice-dependent people, as with wheat, the addition of three B vitamins and iron does little to restore what is lost when brown rice is refined and polished. Milling of rice is also extremely wasteful, with only 55 percent of the original weight remaining as whole kernels after milling. Lost is 20 percent as hulls (which must be removed before eating), 10 percent as bran and "polish," and 15 percent as broken kernels. Still, white rice is overwhelmingly the most popular form of rice sold in the United States as well as in the rest of the world. Ninety-nine percent of the rice we eat is white rice.

There are three basic shapes of rice sold in the United States: long grain, medium grain, and short grain. These make more of a difference in cooking characteristics than in nutritive value. In *long-grain rice,* the kernels are four to five times longer than they are wide and, when cooked, the rice grains are separate and fluffy (hardly the way you'd want them if you were eating with chopsticks). Long-grain rice is best for salads, casseroles, and stuffings for fish or poultry, where you would want the kernels to separate. *Medium-grain rice* has a softer, more tender texture when cooked, and *short-grain rice* (sometimes called round rice) tends to stick together after cooking. These work best in stuffings for vegetables (such as sweet peppers or zucchinis), pancakes and croquettes, rice balls, and puddings. It doesn't matter what kind of rice you use in soups, since the rice will separate. *Glutinous,* or *sweet, rice* is a stranger to most Americans. It is a short-grained variety that contains an opaque starch. Thus, the kernel is not translucent as in ordinary white rice. It is popular among Asians in desserts and rice balls. It can also be used to make soft puddings, since it tends to disintegrate when cooked. It is used in this country as a thickener for sauces and gravies and as a tenderizing agent in frozen foods.

Thanks to our imaginative food-processing industry, today Americans can buy rice in bags, boxes, cans, and cartons; cooked or uncooked; wet or dry; and even frozen. But what these packages contain makes a real difference in nutritive value.

Brown rice is the whole unpolished rice grain, with only the outer hull (or husk) and a small portion of the bran removed. Its color comes from the outer layer of nutritious, fiber-rich bran. It has a slightly nutty flavor and chewier texture than white rice, and it is the only form of rice that contains vitamin E and appreciable amounts of dietary fiber. It also has more protein (and better-quality protein) and more phosphorus and potassium than other types of rice. You get more for your money for yet another reason: a cup of dry brown rice cooks up into more rice than ordinary white rice does. (More liquid is needed, and cooking time is longer.) If you and your family are not ready to eat your stir-fried dishes on a bed of brown rice, you might mix brown and white (just start cooking the brown rice first, and stir in the white when there's 15 to 25 minutes' cooking time left, depending on the type of white rice used) or use brown rice as a meat extender or casserole ingredient. An alternative approach is to think of brown rice as a new food added to your dining repertoire, rather than as a "replacement" for white rice. Stick to white rice where it seems most appropriate, but use brown rice at other times. As you become accustomed to the flavor and texture of brown rice, you may find yourself abandoning its paler cousins. In my family, where none of us cared for packaged brown rice, we have found the long-grain brown rice sold in bulk in health food stores to be more to our liking, closer in taste, texture, and color to the white rice we all grew up with.

Regular-milled white rice has been stripped of its husk, bran, polish (a thin skin under the bran), and germ. It comes ready to cook without washing. If the rice has been enriched, washing before cooking merely rinses away some of the added nutrients, which are sprayed on the outside of the kernels. The only rice that needs to be washed is rice that has been coated with talc. Ordinary grocery-store rice is not coated. But if you buy rice in bulk, check the sack from which it comes; if it has been coated with talc, the label will say so. If you do use regular white rice, be sure it is enriched. However, a better choice would be . . .

Parboiled, or converted, white rice. Prior to milling, rice grains can be subjected to a special steam-pressure process that pushes some of the nutrients from the outer portions of the grain into the starchy center. Thus, when the rice is milled, fewer of the goodies in the bran are lost, although the fiber and protein content are lower than in brown rice. Parboiled rice takes a little longer (about 5 to 10 minutes more) to cook than ordinary white rice, but it's worth it. Again, if you buy parboiled (or converted) rice, be sure it's enriched.

Precooked, or instant, rice is the most highly processed and least nourishing form of rice, even when enriched. It is also the most expensive. However, for those who don't have the 20 to 25 minutes needed to cook parboiled rice, it will do in a pinch. I have never found the need for it, since rice will cook while I prepare the rest of the meal and set the table. But I can see its value to the working cook who wants to throw together stir-fried leftovers in the time it takes to boil water for instant rice. As far as I know, brown rice is not available in instant form. (As for packaged rice mixes, you are paying more for the nutritionally questionable seasonings, additives, and salt than for the rice, and you're stuck with how the manufacturer flavors it. Far better—both nutritionally and economically—to make your own seasoned rice from scratch.)

Table 4 can give you some idea of what is lost when brown rice is milled. The bran, polish, and germ are removed and most is fed to livestock.

Table 4	VITAMIN CONTENTS OF RICE AND ITS BY-PRODUCTS				
	(milligrams in 3 ½ ounces)				
Nutrient	*Brown*	*Milled*	*Bran*	*Polish*	*Germ*
Thiamin	0.34	0.07	2.26	1.84	6.5
Riboflavin	0.05	0.03	0.25	0.18	0.5
Niacin	4.7	1.6	29.8	28.2	3.3
Pyridoxine	1.03	0.45	2.5	2.0	1.6
Pantothenic acid	1.5	0.75	2.8	3.3	3.0
Folic acid	0.02	0.016	0.15	0.19	0.43
Biotin	0.012	0.005	0.06	0.057	0.058
Inositol	119	10	463	454	373
Choline	112	59	170	102	300

SOURCE: Stanley F. Brockington and Vincent J. Kelly, in *Rice: Chemistry and Technology,* ed. D. F. Houston (St. Paul, Minn.: American Association of Cereal Chemists, 1972).

FOODS MADE FROM RICE

Rice can be made into breakfast *cereals,* both hot and cold. Cream of Rice is the counterpart to Cream of Wheat, or farina. It is made from granulated, white milled rice, the least nourishing form of the grain. Ready-to-eat rice cereals are also made from white rice. (Manufacturers claim that consumers object to dark specks in cereals made from less refined grains.) However, in making rice flakes, wheat bran is commonly added in amounts up to about 5 percent of the final formula. Probably the best-known rice cereal is Rice Krispies, made solely from milled rice and flavorings. A 1-ounce serving (about 1 cup) supplies 110 calories, 2 grams of protein, 3 grams of sugar, and no fat. By contrast, Kellogg's Frosted Krispies supplies 1 gram of protein and 11 grams of sugar for the same number of calories, and Cocoa Krispies, a sweetened and chocolate-flavored rice cereal, has 1 gram of protein and 13 grams of sugar in a 1-ounce serving. The same is true for Post Cocoa Pebbles, only in addition to lots of sugar Cocoa Pebbles also has 3 grams of highly saturated fat in each serving.

Rice is also puffed from guns or in ovens to make a very light cereal—puffed rice—that is more air than nutrients (but very low in calories, allowing you to fill up on a big bowl of cereal without overeating). Regular-milled white rice is used since the more healthful parboiled rice doesn't store as well. Rice may also be shredded and formed into little pillows (as in Rice Chex), and rice flour may be mixed with other cereal-grain flours to make multigrain flakes.

Rice flour, both white and brown, is finely milled and useful in making noodles, pancakes, breads, cakes, and muffins, usually in combination with wheat flour. However, for people on gluten-free diets, rice flour can be used alone. Nutrient-rich *rice bran* and *rice polish* (you may find them in health food stores) can be used much like wheat bran and wheat germ—as meat extenders and wholesome additions to baked goods.

HOW TO COOK RICE

Rice usually comes packaged with easy-to-follow directions for top-of-the-stove cooking. However, you may buy your rice in bulk or want to vary your techniques and the texture of the resulting product as follows:

TOP-OF-THE-STOVE: For regular-milled white rice, use 2 cups of cooking liquid (water or broth) for each cup of rice. For parboiled and brown rice, use 2½ cups of liquid per 1 cup of rice, or 2¼ cups of liquid if you prefer a drier rice. Optional additions include butter or margarine (up to 1 tablespoon per 1 cup rice) and salt (up to 1 teaspoon per 1 cup rice). Combine the ingredients in a 2- to 3-quart saucepan, bring the mixture to a boil, stir it once or twice, lower the heat to simmer, and cover the pan with a tight-fitting lid. Cook the mixture 15 minutes for regular white rice, 20 to 25 minutes for parboiled rice, and 30 to 45 minutes for brown rice. If all the liquid is not absorbed at the end of this time, cover the pan again and cook the rice a few minutes longer.

If you want a drier rice, fluff the cooked rice with a fork and let it stand, covered, for 5 to 10 minutes after you turn off the heat.

IN THE OVEN: Use boiling liquid in the above proportions. Put the ingredients into an oven-proof pan, stir, cover the pan tightly (you can use foil fitted around the pan), and cook the rice in a preheated 350-degree oven for 25 to 30 minutes for regular white rice, 30 to 40 minutes for parboiled rice, and 1 hour for brown rice.

IN A DOUBLE BOILER: This is especially useful when cooking rice in milk, which tends to boil over and stick. Separate the halves of the double boiler, and put 1 cup of regular white rice in the top half with 3½ cups of milk (up to 1 teaspoon salt is optional). Over a direct flame, heat the rice and milk mixture to boiling while bringing water to a boil in the bottom half of the pot. Then put the top of the double boiler in the bottom, and cook the rice, covered, for about 40 minutes.

IN THE MICROWAVE: Microwave cooking of rice doesn't save cooking time, but does save energy and clean-up time if you cook the rice in a serving dish. Use the same proportions of rice and liquid, but put them into a glass or plastic container with a cover. If you use plastic wrap as a cover, poke a few holes in it to allow the steam to escape. For white rice (regular and parboiled), microwave at maximum power for 5 minutes, then reduce to 50-percent power for the next 15 minutes. Or follow the manufacturer's directions.

YIELDS OF COOKED RICE.
1 cup of regular-milled white rice yields 3 cups of cooked rice.
1 cup of parboiled rice yields 3 to 4 cups of cooked rice.
1 cup of brown rice yields 3 to 4 cups of cooked rice.
1 cup of precooked rice yields 1 to 2 cups of prepared rice.

Cooked rice, white or brown, can be stored in the refrigerator for up to a week (be sure to cover it well to prevent drying and uptake of other flavors). It can also be frozen for months, but be sure to thaw it before reheating.

REHEATING RICE: For each cup of cooked rice, add 2 tablespoons of liquid. Place the rice and liquid in a nonstick saucepan, cover the pan, and heat the rice for 4 to 5 minutes on top of the stove or in the oven. To reheat rice in the microwave, cover the container, and microwave on high for 1 minute for each cup of rice.

WILD RICE, AN ELITE GRAIN

Wild rice is not really rice but the seed of an aquatic grass that is native to America. When thinking rice, wild rice is truly the top of the line. It is harvested by Indians where it grows wild, around the northern Great Lakes (mostly in Minnesota). It is very difficult to grow, but there is now some commercial production in California as well as the Midwest and non-Indian harvesting (a serious threat to the Indians who depend on the wild-rice harvest for their annual income). Although outrageously expensive (from $5 to $10 a pound), it is a delectable treat for special occasions, and, since it expands to about four times its original volume, a little can go a long way (see the recipe on p. 528). The whole grain is cooked (it is never refined). As grains go, wild rice is very nutritious: rich in fiber, protein, B vitamins, and minerals, and very low in fat.

Wild rice comes in various grades, which determine its price. The most expensive is the long-grain "giant" grade, usually served with wild game. The medium-grain "extra fancy" grade is the most popular and is commonly used for salads, stuffings, and side dishes. "Bargain hunters" may choose the equally good-tasting but less expensive short-grain "select" grade. This is most often used where uniform size of the grains doesn't count, such as in pancakes, baked goods, or soups. Or, if you're really short on cash but want the wild-rice flavor, you can buy the short grade premixed with white rice (the percentage of wild rice in these mixtures is quite low) or you can mix it yourself.

TO COOK WILD RICE: Be sure to clean out any debris (put the rice in a bowl, and add water; the debris usually floats to the surface, and the water can then be drained off). For each 4 ounces of rice, use 2¼ cups of liquid (water or broth). Bring the liquid to a boil in a large saucepan, add the rice and any desired seasonings, stir the mixture, and return it to a boil. Lower the heat to simmer, cover the pan, and cook the rice for 45 minutes or until the grains "pop" open. If any liquid remains, uncover the pot and cook the rice over a low heat, stirring to dry the grains.

Cooked wild rice will keep refrigerated for about a week and can be stored in the freezer for months.

Oats: Neigh for Horses, Yeah for Us

The title of this section is not meant to suggest that we should deprive horses of their favorite food—merely that it would be nice if we ate more of this nutritional Cadillac among grains. Although oats are our third leading cereal crop (after wheat and corn) and the fourth most important crop world-wide, their chief use in most countries is to feed our four-legged friends. Less than 5 percent of the world crop of oats is used to feed people—mostly as breakfast cereal. Yet, as a human food, oats are more versatile and nourishing than this statistic would suggest. It's high time more of us were "feeling our oats."

Oats apparently began life as a bothersome weed that grew among crops of the forerunners of modern barley and wheat. They existed in widely separated regions of the world and were generally regarded as a nuisance, getting in the way of the harvest of more desirable grains. The expression "sowing one's wild oats" may have something to do with wide scattering of the seeds of this grain, which ultimately was deliberately sown by early agriculturists, who decided to join 'em since they couldn't really fight 'em.

The origins of oats are a mystery, since they were not mentioned in the Bible or the histories of early Rome. No definite record indicates that oats were known to the ancient Chinese, Hebrews, or Hindus, and the Roman classicists refer to oats only as a weed that was used for medicinal purposes. The first authentic historical record on cultivated oats dates back to the beginning of the Christian era. It indicates that oats were grown by Europeans for grain and forage, especially in Asia Minor.

In the first century A.D., the Roman historian Pliny wrote somewhat disparagingly about the Germanic peoples who ate oats as porridge. (After all, oats were "animal food.") Oat grains were probably carried to Europe from northern Africa and the Near East by the Romans. The seeds adapted readily to the cool, moist climate of the British Isles, where oats eventually became a staple in the diet of Scotland, Ireland, and northern England. Oats also proliferated in northern Germany, Denmark, and Switzerland because they survived well in climates where other grains would have succumbed to the cold.

Oats found their way to the New World via a sea captain who in 1602 planted them on one of the Elizabeth Islands off the southern coast of Massachusetts. The grain became popular among the colonists because it grew well in their coastal areas. But cultivating oats never approached the popularity of cultivating corn, which gave considerably higher yields per acre. Today, nearly half the world's oat crop—more than 4 billion bushels a year—is grown in the United States and Canada.

As food for people, oats found its most hospitable home in Scotland, where every celebration calls for an oat-based food. The Scots turn oats into everything from hot porridge and breads to drinks and desserts. Marlene Ann Bumgarner, author of *The Book of Whole Grains,* said she consulted a Scottish cookbook and found recipes for such dishes as "boose, hodgils, skirlie, mealie pudding, fritters, and oatcakes, all made from oats in one form or another." While I and most Americans are unfamiliar with these dishes, clearly there's more to oats than just oat*meal.* And a look at their nutritional merits should convince you that they're worth experimenting with.

NUTRIENT VIRTUES

The oat grain very closely resembles a kernel of wheat in structure. An outer covering of bran protects the starchy endosperm and the germ that sits at the bottom of the grain. Unlike wheat, however, the nutritious bran and germ are not removed in processing because oats are not refined. Whole-grain oats contain seven B vitamins, vitamin E, and nine minerals, including iron and calcium. In addition, the protein content of oats and the quality of that protein is superior to that of wheat and most other grains. A comparison of the nutrition information on breakfast-cereal boxes is revealing: for the same 110 calories in an ounce of corn or wheat flakes, you get twice the number of grams of protein from oat flakes. But probably the most important nutritional advantage of oats is the soluble fiber (it's what gives oatmeal a gummy texture) that helps to lower cholesterol levels in the blood. The oat bran is apparently a major source of this fiber. When men with abnormally high cholesterol levels were given 100 grams (3½ ounces) of oat bran a day for 10 days as muffins or cooked cereal, their cholesterol levels (and especially the level of artery-damaging LDL cholesterol) dropped significantly. A subsequent study of half that amount of oat bran daily also showed a significant effect on cholesterol levels. Although not a direct nutritional advantage, oats have yet another saving grace: they contain a natural preservative that gives them and products made from them a longer shelf life.

FORMS OF OATS

Grains of oats are enclosed in two tough husks that must be removed before milling. The grains are cleaned and toasted, then hulled and scoured. The resulting whole oat kernels, called *groats,* contain nearly all the original nutritional value of the grain. Oat groats, which are much softer and quicker-cooking than wheat berries, can be used as such and cooked into a porridge or a base for salads or stuffings (see the recipe on p. 525).

TO COOK OAT GROATS: Bring 2 cups of water, stock, or milk to a boil in a heavy saucepan, and stir in 1 cup of oat groats (with salt if desired). Reduce the heat to low, cover the pan, and cook the groats for about 45 minutes. Or, if you are not planning to eat the hot groats right away, cook them for only 15 minutes, then turn off the heat, and let them stand, covered, for about 45 minutes longer. This method eliminates scorching and results in a fluffier groat.

Oat groats can be further processed into granules, flakes, or flour and used as the base for dozens of different dishes. Unlike wheat, rice, and most other grains, oats are not refined before or after processing, so they retain most of their nutrients regardless of the form in which they are eaten.

Oat flour is made by grinding the groats fine; you can make it yourself by grinding rolled oats in a blender or food processor. Oat flour adds a lovely flavor to breads and improves their keeping quality. But because oat flour contains no gluten, which is needed for bread to rise, it must be mixed with gluten-containing flour, such as wheat flour, and the dough should be kneaded well to bake yeast-leavened bread. Try substituting 1 cup of oat flour for 1 of every 5 cups of other flour in your bread recipe. (See the recipe on p. 563.) Oat flour also makes delicious pancakes and muffins. Here no mixing of flours is needed because no yeast is used.

Oat groats are particularly easy to sprout, and *oat sprouts* are a wonderful addition to salads, pita (pocket bread) sandwiches, stir-fried dishes, and soups. They can also be chopped and added to bread dough. Ounce for ounce, sprouted oats are even more nourishing than the grain from whence they came. They contain more protein and B vitamins than the groats, although they are usually consumed in smaller amounts. Try them in salads and on sandwiches.

Steel-cut oats, also known as Scotch oats, are oat groats that have been cut into two or three pieces. Nearly all the nutrients and the crunch of whole groats are retained. But cooking time is considerably longer than for rolled oats. *Old-fashioned rolled oats* are made by steaming and flattening the whole groats with a roller. They take about 15 minutes to cook, if you follow package directions. I prefer to cook them for 1 to 5 minutes, then turn the heat off and let them stand, covered, for 5 to 10 minutes longer (see the recipe on p. 509). *Quick-cooking rolled oats* are made by flattening precut groats. They cook in about 5 minutes. Although many recipes for baked goods call for "quick-cooking" oats, I nearly always use ordinary rolled oats (and add a little extra liquid) with no noticeable difference in the quality of the resulting product. *Instant oats* are made by precooking cut groats and rolling them very thin. Although *instant oatmeal* retains most of the nutrient value of whole and rolled oats, the product is nearly always packaged with salt and sugar. Quick-cooking oats take so little time to prepare that it really pays, both financially and nutritionally, to avoid the instant cereal product. Unless overly doctored with fat and/or sugar, oatmeal—whether from rolled oats or steel-cut—is the nutritional champion of hot breakfast cereals. For example, one serving of cooked oatmeal (from ⅓ cup of uncooked rolled oats) provides 5 grams of protein, 2 grams of fat, and only 10 milligrams of sodium. Unless fortified with soybean flour, no other breakfast cereal, hot or cold, can beat cooked oats for protein value per calorie. In addition to being cooked into a hot breakfast cereal, steel-cut and rolled oats can be used to make breads and rolls, muffins, cookies, pancakes and waffles, dessert "crisps" (such as apple crisp), and granola. (See recipes on pp. 500, 508, 622.)

Ready-to-eat breakfast cereals made from oats are among the most wholesome available and the best buy for your food dollar as well. Among the least adulterated (and, therefore, nutritionally most desirable) oat cereals are Cheerios (originally called Cheeri-Oats and made from oat flour and wheat starch) and Fortified Oat Flakes (these contain soy and wheat flour as well as oat flour). Save for its relatively high salt content (a 1-ounce serving—1¼ cups—of Cheerios has 330 milligrams of sodium before the milk is added), Cheerios would be near the top of my list of nourishing cold cereals. For 110 calories, you get 4 grams of protein and only 1 gram of sugar and 2 grams of fat.

Most *granolas* are made from rolled oats. But if ever there were a nutritionally overrated product, commercial granola is it. Even many of the granolas sold in health food stores have the same nutritional shortcomings as the supermarket varieties. To the nourishing low-fat, unsweet oats, the manufacturer adds fat and sugar. And not just a little fat and sugar. Both these ingredients add empty calories to an otherwise healthful grain. It doesn't matter whether the sweetener is honey, brown sugar, raw sugar, or ordinary white refined sugar. Unless it is molasses, the sweetener has no nutritive value worth mentioning. And the fat commonly used in granola is saturated vegetable fat, such as coconut or palm oil or hydrogenated soybean oil. The nuts and seeds that are often part of the granola formula add further to its fat content.

Granola is also a very dense cereal, so that 1 ounce hardly amounts to a serving that would satisfy more than a mouse. One ounce of Quaker 100% Natural Cereal is only ¼ cup and contains 130 calories, 9 grams of sugar, and 5 grams of fat. If you were eating straight granola for breakfast, chances are you'd eat two to three times the amount designated as "a serving" on the box. Sun Country Granola with Raisins is no better nutritionally speaking. Its main nutritional virtue is its low sodium content—10 milligrams per ¼ cup. The amount of sugar is not indicated on the box, but the ingredients include brown sugar, honey, and raisins, so the sugar content is likely to be similar to—if not higher than—the Quaker product. And Sun Country Granola with Almonds has 10 grams of fat per serving (35 percent of total calories as fat), although it may have less sugar because it has no raisins.

If granola has become a favorite in your house, you would be much better off making your own (see the recipe on p. 508) or, if you buy a commercial brand, using it only as a garnish on other more nutritious cereals rather than as the only cereal in the bowl.

Barley: Too Good for Just Beer and Beast

There was a popular saying in ancient Egypt that translates literally from the hieroglyphics as "Is it wheat or barley?" But its figurative meaning was "Good or bad news?" There is a popular saying in Egypt today—"Like barley, eaten but maligned," pointing to the belief that barley has been unfairly judged. A good look at this grain, its history, and its food value would tend to support the modern saying.

Barley was one of the first domesticated grains. It was cultivated in ancient Egypt between 6000 and 5000 B.C. and used as food for man and feed for beast. Barley grains were among the many treasures found in the tomb of Tutankhamen—the great Egyptian king Tut. Barley was a popular offering to the Egyptian gods. Necklaces of barley were commonly placed on mummies to symbolize resurrection. Barley was used as currency. The Sumerians used it for nearly 2,000 years as their measuring system. Barley was also an ancient medicament.

It was applied to burns, cuts, and bruises. It was used as a remedy for respiratory congestion. And it served as a means of diagnosing pregnancy and determining the sex of an unborn child. The woman's urine was added to wheat and to barley. If the barley grew first, the child was said to be a boy; if the wheat grew first, the woman was expecting a girl; and if neither grew, she wasn't pregnant!

Of course, barley was also an important food for ancient peoples in the Mideast for thousands of years. It was the chief bread grain for the Hebrews, Greeks, and Romans, although it eventually yielded its supremacy to wheat. Barley is still an important food in Asian countries like Japan and China, where records of barley's cultivation date back to 2800 B.C. Recent archaeological evidence indicates that barley was first used in agriculture in western Asia as early as 7000 B.C.

Barley was grown in Europe during the Middle Ages and was brought to America by Dutch and British colonists, mostly for brewing beer. Since, as a crop, barley could not compete with the yields of corn (few grains could!), it was never much used here in bread or as a cereal. Still, barley is a highly adaptable crop—perhaps more so than any other in the world today. It is cultivated in Europe north of the Arctic Circle. Its southern range extends to within a few degrees of the equator, into the high mountains of Ethiopia.

In this country, barley grows best in northern and western states. Although barley is our fifth most important crop, 90 percent of the barley we grow is either fed to animals or fermented to make beer. For most twentieth-century Americans, encounters with barley have been limited to soup and beer. To look at barley's status in this country today, you'd never guess how valued and diverse a crop it was for thousands of years.

THE GRAIN AND ITS NUTRIENTS

Barley grains are protected by two inedible outer husks that cover the embryo (or germ) and by a thin protein-rich layer called the aleurone. This, in turn, houses the starchy endosperm, the bulk of the kernel. When barley is processed for human consumption, the husks, aleurone, and germ are nearly always removed, resulting in a product called "pearled" barley. These white kernels are sold whole for making soups, salads, and side dishes (see recipes on pp. 338, 348, 535). They are also granulated into baby cereals and are ground into flour.

Unfortunately, without the aleurone, much of the nutritional value of barley is lost, including valuable protein, fiber, and B vitamins. It would be far better to buy barley simply hulled into a brown kernel which has most of the aleurone layer intact.

The U.S. Department of Agriculture has analyzed only pearled barley for nutritional content, and the analysis was done only on uncooked barley. However, since it cooks up to about triple its original volume, the following approximations should hold: in 1 cup of cooked barley, you will find about 6 grams of protein (the amount in 6 ounces of milk), less than 1 gram of fat, practically no sodium, and about 230 calories, along with generous amounts of niacin, thiamin, and potassium. Unpearled barley is a rich source of dietary fiber and provides more gut-stimulating bulk to the diet than does whole wheat, according to studies by Patricia Judd, a nutritionist at the Queen Elizabeth College in London.

Barley has also been shown by scientists at the University of Wisconsin to contain an as yet unidentified substance that inhibits the enzyme that controls cholesterol production. The substance, contrary to most expectations, is found in the nonfiber portion of the grain. Chickens fed a barley-based diet had cholesterol levels in their flesh that were 30 percent lower than chickens fed the usual corn-based diet. Laying chickens produced eggs with 25 percent less cholesterol in the yolk when fed barley. For pigs, a barley diet reduced cholesterol in the pork by 40 percent. The Wisconsin scientists noted that atherosclerosis and its common consequence, coronary heart disease, are relatively rare in areas of the world where barley is an important part of the people's diet. Thus, the Egyptians seem to have really been on to something: feed barley to people and lower their cholesterol levels; feed it to animals and get the added advantage of lowering the amount of cholesterol in the animal products people eat.

FORMS OF BARLEY

As already indicated, *whole hulled barley* that is unpearled and brown in color is the most nutritionally desirable form of this grain, if you can get it (try a health food store). Failing that, *pearled barley* can be used to cook whole.

TO COOK WHOLE BARLEY: In a saucepan, add 1 cup of barley to 3 cups of boiling water or broth (use more liquid—up to 4 cups—if you use brown barley), lower the heat to simmer, cover the pan tightly, and cook the barley for 35 to 40 minutes (5 to 10 minutes longer for brown barley). Check the pot after about 30 minutes to see if more liquid is needed. *Pressed barley,* found in Oriental markets, can be similarly prepared.

You may want to try *barley grits,* the whole grain toasted and cracked into half a dozen pieces, as a cereal or meat extender. Grits can be cooked in water or milk. They take about 15 minutes to cook and should be stirred occasionally. You can make your own grits by toasting whole barley in a skillet without fat or water (shake them around often to prevent burning), then cracking them in a blender or food processor.

Unless you grind your own from the whole hulled grain, the *barley flour* you buy most likely will have been made from pearled barley (even the brands commonly found in health food stores). Barley flour needs to be mixed with a gluten-containing flour to make raised yeast breads. However, the Norwegians make a flat loaf that is 100-percent barley bread. When Jesus worked the miracle of the loaves and the fishes, the loaves in question were barley bread. Barley flour is a main ingredient in Tibetan "prayer wheel" bread. It can also be used as a thickening agent.

Whole hulled barley can be sprouted, and the resulting *sprouts* are a delightful and healthful addition to salads (see p. 110 for instructions).

Rye: A Good Grain That Is Losing Ground

To most Americans, rye means bread (you may recall the series of advertisements that claimed "You don't have to be Jewish to love Levy's Jewish Rye"). And, indeed, rye flour as an ingredient in bread dough and crackers is by far the most popular use of this grain world-wide. The Swedes and the Russians, as well as the Jews, are famous for their rye breads (the Swedes make it on the sweet side, the Russians, sour), and rye is a major ingredient in the very substantial German pumpernickel. But there's more to rye than meets the eye of the bread maven.

Like wheat, oats, and barley, rye seems to have originated in southwestern Asia, although it does not have the same long and colorful history as these other grains. There's not a trace of cultivated rye in ancient Egyptian monuments, nor is it mentioned in any ancient writings. Like oats, rye began life on earth as a "noxious weed" in the eyes of ancient farmers, who had difficulty keeping it from becoming mixed with their wheat crop. But because of rye's tolerance of adverse growing conditions (it will grow where it's too wet and too cold for other grains), it eventually won them over. Sometime during the first millennium B.C., rye was introduced to northern Europe, where it quickly established a stronghold because it could withstand a more severe climate than its competitors. For a time, in fact, rye was the main bread grain of Europe, and to this day it remains a popular grain in the colder countries. (Ergot, a mind-altering poison produced by a fungus that has a predilection for rye, is believed to have triggered riots among the peasants of France in 1789 and may have been a precipitating factor in the French Revolution.) Rye was introduced into the northeastern part of our country during colonial times by British and Dutch settlers. It spread south and west, increasing in acreage especially during the years when wheat rust decimated our primary bread grain.

But in recent decades there's been a significant shrinkage in the area of cultivated land throughout the world that is devoted to rye. In Sweden, for example, whereas four times more acreage was given to rye than to wheat at the beginning of the twentieth century, by the mid-1960s the ratio was 1 acre of rye to 6 of wheat. World-wide, acreage given to rye dropped 35 percent between 1961 and 1972, and total production of the grain dropped 11 percent during the same period (though improvements in agricultural practices have resulted in increased yields per acre). Compared to the other major cereal crops, rye ranks eighth in production.

NUTRIENTS IN RYE

In nutrient content, whole rye contains more protein, phosphorus, iron, potassium, and B vitamins than whole wheat. However, it's much harder to find flour and foods made from whole rye than it is to find whole-wheat foods. But it pays to try, since whole-grain rye has twice the protein, three times the calcium and phosphorus, four times the riboflavin, five times the iron and thiamin, six times the niacin, and seven times the potassium as rye from which the bran has been largely removed.

FORMS OF RYE

As with other grains, *whole rye berries* (also called *groats*) can be cooked in liquid and used as a porridge or side dish or sprouted for use in salads, soups, and sandwiches. However, you're not likely to find rye berries outside of a health food store. The berries can be cracked to form *grits* that can be cooked into hot cereal or mixed with other flours into bread dough. Or the berries can be ground more finely into *meal* that can be used in combination with other flours. *Rye flakes,* the rye equivalent of rolled oats, can be cooked into a hot breakfast cereal.

But the most likely way you'll encounter uncooked rye is as a *flour.* Color is your clue to nutritional value: *light* and *medium* rye flours have been sifted (bolted), which removes much of the nutritious bran; *dark* rye flour is unbolted and far more nourishing. The latter flour works best in heavy breads like pumpernickel, but I've used it successfully in all recipes that call for rye flour. When baking yeast breads with rye flour, keep in mind that it is a low-gluten flour and must be mixed with other flours, like wheat, that contain gluten. A reasonable ratio is 1 cup of rye flour for every 2 to 3 cups of wheat flour (see recipes on pp. 568, 572, and 575). Most of the bread that is called "rye bread" in the United States is made with flour that is less than one-third rye flour.

Buckwheat, a Nutrient Giant among the Grains

You've probably eaten, or at least heard of, buckwheat pancakes, but you may not have realized that the flour from which they get their name has nothing to do with wheat and is not even a grain. Buckwheat is a branching plant with heart-shaped leaves and white flowers that are popular with bees, who turn their nectar into buckwheat honey. The buckwheat plant thus looks nothing like the tall, reedy grasses that produce our most popular grains. It is more closely related to rhubarb than to wheat.

The edible part of the plant, for people, is the fruit—a triangular seed that resembles a stout grain. It also cooks like grain, in about the time it takes to prepare rice or bulgur. But it is more nourishing than grains and deserves a wider audience in this country.

Buckwheat is believed to have originated in the mountainous regions of central and western China, where it was cultivated in prehistoric times. It has remained a staple food there, used mainly as a bread grain. But in eastern Europe, where it was introduced by Asian migrants, it is mainly eaten as a porridge or side dish. The Soviet Union remains the world's largest producer of buckwheat and grows about five times more than we do. German and Dutch settlers brought buckwheat to America, first planting it along the Hudson River. It was also adopted in the South, where it became popular for making pancakes. In the early days of our union, buckwheat was a major crop; today it ranks a lowly twelfth in total harvest of cereal crops.

More than half the buckwheat grown here is produced in New York State, especially around the Finger Lakes, where the hardy plant has adapted well to the cool, moist climate. Other states where it is produced commercially include Pennsylvania, West Virginia, Michigan, Ohio, Wisconsin, and Maine. Buckwheat grown in the western states is primarily shipped to Japan, where it is used as the main ingredient in soba, or buckwheat noodles (see the recipe on p. 352). Buckwheat is easy to grow: it is so tough that no chemical pesticides are needed to keep it free from blights and insects; it tolerates poor soil and poor tilling; it will grow in hilly, rocky areas where other crops often fail; it matures fast; and it continues to produce until killed by frost. Still, the main commercial producer of buckwheat in this country (Birkett Mills of Penn Yan, New York) says it must pay farmers a premium to produce enough buckwheat to meet the growing demand for these nutritious kernels. Thus, buckwheat, which used to be a great bargain among grains when you could find it, is now bringing a premium price. Still, it's a lot cheaper than meat and in some ways better for you.

NUTRIENTS IN BUCKWHEAT

Of the grain-type foods, buckwheat has the distinction of being the best source of available protein. The biological value of buckwheat protein to the human body is higher than that of any other plant. It has more than 90 percent of the value of milk solids and more than 80 percent of the value of eggs. Each pound of buckwheat provides the protein equivalent of more than ½ pound of beef. Yet it has no more calories than other grains. A serving of ¾ cup of cooked groats provides 145 calories, 3 grams of protein, and no fat. Buckwheat also contains twice as much B vitamins as wheat and is a rich source of potassium, phosphorus, and iron. Furthermore, buckwheat is always eaten with its fibrous, nutritious outer layer intact. Only the hard outer shell is removed, leaving behind a light brown kernel that can be cooked as such or roasted and then cooked.

FORMS OF BUCKWHEAT

Stripped of its hard outer shell, the buckwheat seed is called a groat. *Buckwheat groats* have a distinctive flavor some people describe as nutlike. But whatever you may call it, they cook up into a flavorful pilaf or porridge and make an excellent stuffing base for fowl and fish. Unroasted buckwheat groats are more commonly used for porridge. Roasting brings out the flavor of the kernels, darkens them, and also gives them a new name: *kasha.* Kasha is the base for a popular dish among eastern European Jews—kasha varnishkas, a combination of kasha pilaf and thick egg noodles that is delicious, nourishing, and satisfying (see the recipe on p. 371).

TO COOK KASHA: In making pilaf or stuffing, the uncooked groats are commonly mixed with a beaten egg and then cooked briefly over high heat for about 2 minutes in a skillet. This keeps the groats from sticking together when cooked further in liquid. The addition of the egg also enhances their food value. If you are on a strict low-cholesterol diet, you can use egg white instead of the whole egg. When dry-roasting, stir constantly to separate the kernels and keep them from burning. Then add 2 cups of boiling liquid (water or broth) for each cup of groats, cover the pot, and cook the kasha over a low heat for about 10 to 15 minutes until the liquid is absorbed.

Roasted groats are eaten whole or cracked into coarse, medium, or fine kasha. *Whole kasha* is best for pilafs, stuffings, and soups. *Coarse kasha* also makes a good pilaf. But for cereal, most people prefer the *medium* or *fine kasha,* and more liquid is used than in making pilaf. *Buckwheat grits,* unroasted groats that are finely cracked, are also used for making hot cereal that has approximately the consistency of Wheatena. Unroasted buckwheat may also be ground into flour, the dark flecks bearing witness to the fact that the whole groat is included along with some of the hull. *Light buckwheat flour* contains about 7 percent of the hull, and *dark buckwheat flour* contains about 17 percent of the hull and is stronger in flavor than its paler relative. Buckwheat flour has no gluten and thus must be used with a gluten-rich flour in baking yeast breads. A reasonable proportion is about ½ cup of buckwheat flour for every 4 cups of wheat flour. In making pancakes, however, buckwheat flour can be used alone. Buckwheat is often the sole flour in the traditional Russian crêpelike pancakes *blinis,* which can be used as a dinner pancake. Delicious fillings can be added at the table by the diner (see the recipe on p. 501).

STORING AND SHOPPING HINTS

Buckwheat flour and buckwheat grits will become rancid more rapidly than most grains, especially in the summer. Unless you can store them in the refrigerator or freezer, it's best to buy no more than you can use up in a month or two.

If you're having difficulty finding buckwheat in its various forms, try a health food store, the gourmet food section of a department store, or any food market that caters to Jewish or Russian clientele. For kasha and groats, look in the section of the market where the rice is kept; if it is not there, try the hot-cereal shelf. Or write to The Birkett Mills, P.O. Box 440A, Penn Yan, New York 14527, and ask about retail outlets in your area. There is also a National Buckwheat Institute at P.O. Box 595, Naples, New York 14512, that may be helpful.

Millet: Not Only for the Birds

If you have a canary or a parakeet or an outdoor bird feeder, chances are you "know" millet, for it is the most popular seed sold to feed small birds. Chances also are that you've never tried to eat the food you feed the birds. But maybe you should, because millet is good food. You don't have to rob the birds' supply, however. Millet as people food is available in health food sections of supermarkets, in health food stores, and in other specialty food shops. Unlike the seed fed to birds, the millet you buy for food has been hulled, so you don't have to contend with the inedible outer layer.

Millet is believed to have originated in Egypt and Arabia, and has been cultivated in Asia Minor and southern Europe since prehistoric times. During the Middle Ages, millet was one of the principal grains produced in Europe, but its popularity gradually declined in favor of blander-tasting grains. Today, although millet is one of the world's most important food plants, its cultivation is restricted mainly to the Eastern Hemisphere, especially to those areas with primitive agricultural practices and dense populations. It is grown extensively in India, where it is the staple grain, as well as in China, Egypt, tropical Africa and South America, the Soviet Union, and Australia. It is also a main food for the Hunzans, the long-lived people of the Himalayas.

In Ethiopia millet flour is used to make the national bread injera, and in India it is made into a flat bread called roti; in northern Africa and India millet is made into porridge, but in the United States most of the millet is used for forage and birdseed. American production of millet is tiny compared to production of such crops as wheat, corn, and oats. Most of our millet is produced in the Dakotas and Colorado, and the seed is used principally to feed poultry.

Different varieties of millet are preferred in different countries. Pearl millet, widely used in India and Egypt, is the most drought-tolerant cereal cultivated anywhere in the world. In general, millet will tolerate sandy soils, hot weather, and scanty rainfall—conditions not usually conducive to the growing of food grains.

NUTRIENTS IN MILLET

The overall nutritive value of millet is comparable to that of other cereal grains, but millet has more protein than rice, sorghum, corn, and oats. However, the biological value of this protein to people has not yet been determined. For pearl millet, this value should be high because, according to scientists at Kansas State University, pearl millet is higher in the amino acid lysine than other cereal grains. Millet is also a good source of B vitamins, phosphorus, iron, manganese, and copper. And it is a useful grain for people who are unable to digest wheat and other gluten-containing grains.

FORMS OF MILLET

You are most likely to find millet as the small, buff-colored kernels called *whole hulled groats.* These can be cooked like rice, although the finished product tends to be drier than rice.

TO COOK MILLET: Add 1 cup of whole millet to 2 cups of boiling water or broth and 1 teaspoon of butter or margarine. Simmer the millet in a covered saucepan for 25 to 30 minutes. (For a stickier consistency, use 2½ cups of water per cup of millet and leave out the fat.)

Cooked whole millet can be used in soups, casseroles, meat loaves, croquettes, salads, soufflés, puddings, stuffings, or as an accompaniment for meat, fish, or chicken (see recipes on pp. 373, 506, and 524).

The *couscous* of North Africa is cracked millet that has been steamed (much like the bulgur of the Mideast). But the couscous sold in boxes in the United States is usually made from durum wheat. You may also find *millet meal,* finely ground and used for baking, or *millet flour,* which is even more finely ground. *Puffed millet* is made from the whole grain heated under pressure and is sold in health food stores as a breakfast cereal. But according to Sheryl and Mel London, authors of *Creative Cooking with Grains and Pasta,* puffed millet can also be used in puddings and breads for extra lightness.

Triticale, a Sum Greater Than Its Parts

Given the long and illustrious histories of all the other grains, triticale, a cross between wheat and rye, is a babe in the field—a mere 200 years old. Since rye was a frequent contaminant of wheat fields, perhaps it was inevitable that the two grains should eventually get to know each other in the Biblical sense. Rye and wheat plants may have fertilized one another on occasion, but, as is often the case among hybrids, the offspring were sterile. The first man-made cross, reported in 1876 to the Edinburgh Botanical Society, resulted in seeds that produced barren plants. This was unfortunate because even early agricultural scientists could see the advantages of combining the desirable characteristics of wheat—a high-yielding grain with superior baking qualities—with the hardiness and quality protein of rye.

Then in 1937, a French scientist discovered that by treating the seedlings of the hybrid plant with colchicine (a derivative of the autumn crocus) he could induce fertility. This paved the way for the development of a new crop. Its name, *triticale* (pronounced trit-i-kay′lee), was derived from the scientific names for wheat *(Triticum)* and rye *(Secale),* and the new grain had a highly desirable nutlike flavor. After numerous crosses and field tests of the resulting offspring, varieties of triticale were found that did indeed exhibit superior qualities. Some, in fact, were better than one might expect from merely combining the properties of the two parents.

Unfortunately, triticale suffered from its own success. It was prematurely hailed as a "superfood" that would solve the problem of world hunger and bring farmers rich returns for their efforts. Neither triticale nor any other supergrain could live up to such hype, and this interesting crop is still not as widely grown in this country as its attributes warrant. Without a Madison Avenue advertising campaign, new foods have trouble gaining a stronghold. But if more Americans at least tried triticale and foods made from it, perhaps its acreage would grow under the pressure of popular demand.

As a man-made grain, triticale proves that everything artificial is not necessarily inferior or less healthful than "natural" alternatives. For triticale is truly better than both wheat and rye in growing characteristics and nutritive value.

NUTRIENTS IN TRITICALE

The average protein content of wheat is 12 percent to 13 percent; that of rye is lower, ranging from 6.5 to 15 percent. But the biological value of rye protein is higher because it contains more of the essential amino acid lysine that is in relatively short supply in most grain proteins. Varieties of triticale have been developed that contain more than 16 percent protein and twice as much lysine as wheat. In fact, laboratory rats raised on a triticale diet grew bigger and faster than those fed wheat or soybeans. The results of growth studies in rats are meaningful to people because rats are believed to require the same amino acids that people do. The biological value of triticale protein is slightly superior to that of soybeans and significantly greater than that of wheat, according to the studies at Texas Tech University.

FORMS OF TRITICALE

Like wheat or rye, *whole triticale berries* can be cooked as pilaf or added to soups.

TO COOK TRITICALE: The berries require overnight soaking followed by about 40 minutes of simmering in boiling water or broth (2¼ cups of liquid for every 1 cup of berries, measured before soaking).

For shorter cooking time, the berries can be *cracked* and, after cooking, used in bread dough for added crunchiness and nutrients. There are also *triticale flakes,* which, like rolled oats, can be cooked into a porridge. But your most likely encounter with this new grain will be as *triticale flour,* which can be used in making bread, muffins, biscuits, pasta, pancakes, cakes, and cookies, among other flour-containing foods.

A word of caution about triticale flour. At first it was thought to be very low in gluten, like one of its parents (rye). It is now known that the gluten is there but is very delicate. If handled too much, it breaks up and the resulting baked product is flat and dense. However, if dough containing triticale flour is handled gently, a light, highly acceptable product can result, even if triticale flour is the only flour used. Even when combining triticale with wheat flour, be sure not to handle the dough too much. Only a few minutes of kneading—just enough to work in the last addition of flour—and one rising are needed. This makes triticale yeast breads almost as fast and easy to make as "quick breads," which don't depend on yeast for leavening.

SHOPPING HINTS: Triticale products are not easily found outside of health food outlets, and often not even there. Arrowhead Mills is the main commercial supplier of triticale products. Write to the company at Box 866, Hereford, Texas 79045, for the names of local distributors, who can then tell you about retail outlets.

Sorghum, a Grain of Many Colors

Until recently, the only way sorghum had entered my house was as a tall, handsome stalk topped by lush clusters of grains in one of several colors. Stalks of sorghum dominate the grain-based "dried flower" arrangement that decorates my dining-room buffet. I was sometimes tempted to "harvest" the grains of sorghum from this fine bouquet (which includes wheat and oats, among other grains) so I could cook and taste them, but I was unsure I'd ever be able to replace them. After reading about sorghum and finally tasting it, I'm almost sorry I never raided my patch or pursued more aggressively my search for a source of the grain.

As a food, sorghum is virtually unknown to Americans, although in amount produced it's our third leading cereal crop (our fifth in total acreage). Except for that saved to sow the next crop, almost all the sorghum we grow ends up in the bellies of animals that provide us with the fatty meats we relish. Sorghum is the major feed grain grown in the Great Plains from South Dakota to Texas. It thrives under the subhumid and semiarid conditions that make farming other crops such a hazard. It can survive drought periods by becoming partially dormant—the farmers say it "waits for rain"—and then growing again when water becomes available. It can also withstand extreme heat better than most crops. It's surprising more has not been done to promote sorghum as "people food" in this country. If it caught on, the farmers no doubt would get a much higher price for their crop than the few cents a pound they now do. If you happen to live near a feed-grain supplier, you may be able to pick up sorghum for as little as 10 cents a pound. Just be sure it has not been treated with pesticides. The milo and kafir types are among American-grown varieties that are used for human food elsewhere.

Sorghum is believed to have originated in Africa, where the grain was domesticated. It was grown in ancient times—a carving depicting the sorghum plant was found in an Assyrian ruin of about 700 B.C.—and probably brought to America by the slave ships from Africa. Today it is a major food grain in most of Africa and India, and is also grown in Asia Minor, Iran, Turkestan, Korea, Japan, Australia, Europe, South and Central America, and the East Indies. World-wide, sorghum is the third largest food grain, and three-fourths of the crop is consumed by people.

It is also a grain of many varieties and names, and several colors—red, pink, yellow, buff, brown, and two-toned. Sorghum is most commonly called "milo," but each variety is likely to have a number of synonyms. For example, the Shallu variety is also called California rice corn, California wheat, chicken corn, Chinese rice corn, Guinea corn, broom corn, Sudan grass, Sorgo, and tall sorghum. The references to corn reflect the botanical similarity of the sorghum plant to the corn plant. But unlike corn, sorghum forms heads with huge clusters of berries—as many as 2,000 grains per stalk.

NUTRIENTS IN SORGHUM

Unlike other grains, sorghum's protein is deficient in only one essential amino acid, lysine. About a decade ago, researchers at Purdue University discovered a popular variety of sorghum prized by the Ethiopians that had about 30 percent more protein than other varieties and an unusually high lysine content. These previously little-known varieties were aptly called in Amharic *Wetet Begunche* ("milk in my mouth") and *Marchuke* ("honey squirts out of it"). With any luck, Americans may one day be able to obtain these high-protein varieties in local food stores rather than from feed suppliers.

The U.S. Department of Agriculture has not analyzed grain sorghum, only the sweet syrup that sorghum is sometimes made into. Suffice it to say that it is comparable to other grains, adequate enough nutritionally to be a dietary staple for more than 300 million people in the world today.

FORMS OF SORGHUM

Outside the United States, sorghum is roasted whole and eaten like popcorn, milled and cooked into porridge or mush, ground into flour to bake flat bread, and brewed into beer. Sorghum may be obtained from Oak Grove Mills, The Blew Family, R.D. 2, Box 255, Pittstown, New Jersey 08867. (Write them first for information on current prices.) The easiest version of sorghum to find here is *sorghum flour* (also called *milo flour*), which can be mail-ordered from Oak Grove Mills. There is no gluten in sorghum, so the flour must be mixed with wheat flour to make yeast breads. For *whole-grain sorghum,* try Oak Grove Mills or a feed store for farm animals. Like rice, it can be cooked in water or stock and served as a side dish or mixed with vegetables.

Amaranth, Golden Grain of the Aztecs

Chances are you've never heard of amaranth. And chances are you'll hear of it again and again and again. After 500 years of obscurity, during which time a relative handful of primitive farmers kept the grain alive, Western agriculturists have recently rediscovered this near-miraculous food plant. As of this writ-

ing, only about two dozen farmers in the United States were growing it commercially (making it hard to get and expensive), but judging from a write-up in 1984 by the National Academy of Sciences and extensive studies in both field and kitchen being done by Rodale Press of Emmaus, Pennsylvania, amaranth may one day be as common a food grain as rye and oats.

Amaranth is at least 5,500 and perhaps as much as 8,000 years old and was a staple of Aztec culture—at least as important as corn and beans. Some 20,000 tons of amaranth grain were sent as an annual tribute to the Aztec emperor Montezuma. The Aztecs believed it gave them supernatural strength, and it was a centerpiece of some gory Aztec ceremonies. Mixed with the blood of human sacrifice, it was formed into huge replicas of Aztec gods and used as the sole food on ceremonial days, a practice that appalled the Spanish conquistadors (who were by no means tame when it came to taking human lives!). As part of Cortez's plan to destroy the Aztec civilization, he decreed an end to the growing of amaranth; anyone caught with the grain was to be put to death. And so, for hundreds of years, a hardy and highly nutritious grain food was for the most part lost to the New World. Interestingly, sometime after Columbus some amaranth seed managed to find its way to Asia, becoming popular among hill tribes in India, Pakistan, Nepal, Tibet, and China, where it is grown to this day. The names for amaranth in India—*rajgira* ("king seed") and *ramdana* ("seed sent by God")—testify to how highly it is prized. In Mexico, Central America, and India, popped amaranth grains are made into popular confections that are sold on the streets.

Like buckwheat, amaranth is a pseudo-cereal grain—it comes from a broadleafed plant, not a grass. It is a vigorous plant that resists drought, heat, and pests, and will grow well in areas that are inhospitable to conventional grains. A single head of the amaranth plant may contain 50,000 tiny, nutritious seeds. Agronomically, amaranth is highly adaptable, and breeding studies are now under way in the United States and elsewhere to develop varieties that will grow almost anywhere—from the tropics to Canada, from sea level to mountaintops, from near-desert to the edges of the rain forest. When you see what amaranth contains, you'll understand better the reason for this interest in developing it further as a food crop for peoples throughout the world.

NUTRIENTS IN AMARANTH

Amaranth exceeds all the common grains as a source of protein. Not only does it contain more total protein than other grains (16 percent as against 12 percent to 14 percent for wheat), but the protein in it is more complete than most other vegetable proteins. Amaranth is especially rich in lysine and in methionine, the amino acid that is deficient in beans. Thus, amaranth will boost the nutritive value of protein from virtually any starchy food. The quality of amaranth protein is so good that it exceeds cow's milk in its ability to sustain life. The germ of the amaranth grain contains as much as 30 percent protein, and the bran is rich in fiber, protein, vitamins, and minerals. It is usually eaten unrefined, so all the nutrients are preserved.

FORMS OF AMARANTH

Currently, amaranth may be obtained as a flour, as whole grain, and as an ingredient in dry cereal and crackers sold in some health food and specialty food stores. Mel London, author of *Breadwinners Too* (Rodale Press, 1984), describes it as having a "slightly peppery taste," and from my own testing of it I would agree—it certainly adds a distinctive but pleasing character to baked goods.

Amaranth *flour* can be used to make breads (it is deficient in gluten and so must be used with a flour like wheat to make yeast-raised breads), biscuits, cakes, crackers, and pancakes. The *seeds* are used to make pilaf, porridge, and breakfast cereals. They can also be popped like corn. The popped grain can be eaten as a snack, a cold cereal, a "breading" on meats and vegetables, or a confection (when mixed with honey or molasses). Both these products can be obtained by mail-order from Walnut Acres (see p. 77).

TO COOK AMARANTH: Amaranth grains can be cooked in liquid or popped dry. To make porridge or pilaf, combine 1 cup of cleaned grains with 3 cups of cold water or broth and salt to taste, if desired, in a medium saucepan (preferably nonstick) with a tight-fitting lid. Bring the amaranth to a boil, cover the saucepan, reduce the heat to low, and simmer the grains for 25 minutes. The cooked grains will keep in the refrigerator for about one week. To pop amaranth grains, use a heavy skillet or a wok. Heat the *ungreased* pan until it is very hot, and then add *1 tablespoon* of the seeds. Stir the seeds continually to prevent them from burning, and remove them from the pan immediately when most of the grains have popped. (They don't all pop, but the unpopped seeds can also be eaten.) Repeat this procedure until you have popped as much grain as you desire; they expand to three or four times their original volume. *Do not try to* *pop more than 1 tablespoon of seeds at a time* or you will end up with a lot of burned, inedible seeds.

Sources of Grains and Grain Products

The following outlets are mail-order sources of various grains that may be hard to obtain locally. You may request a catalogue or simply write for ordering information on the grain you desire. Many outlets also send recipes with your order.

Erewhon Trading Company, 236 Washington Street, Brookline, Massachusetts 02146
Flory Brothers, 841 Flory Mill Road, Lancaster, Pennsylvania 17601
H. Roth & Son, 1577 First Avenue, New York, New York 10028
Shiloh Farms, Box 97, Highway 59, Sulphur Springs, Arkansas 72768
The Vermont Country Store, Weston, Vermont 05161
Walnut Acres, Penns Creek, Pennsylvania 17862

FOR FURTHER READING

Bumgarner, Marlene Anne. *The Book of Whole Grains.* New York: St. Martin's Press, 1976.
London, Mel. *Breadwinners Too.* Emmaus, Pa.: Rodale Press, 1984 (the sequel to Mel London, *Breadwinners* [Emmaus, Pa.: Rodale Press, 1979]).
London, Sheryl, and Mel London. *Creative Cooking with Grains and Pasta.* Emmaus, Pa.: Rodale Press, 1982.

6 ·
PASTA POWER:
A FEATHER IN YOUR CAP

Remember Yankee Doodle Dandy, who went to town on his pony, "put a feather in his cap, and called it macaroni"? If you ever thought about it, the last line probably made no sense to you at all, unless you happened to know that in England in the late 1700s dandified gentlemen gathered at Macaroni Clubs and the word *macaroni* was used to describe things that were elegant to the extreme. The Yankee Doodle ditty was first sung by the British in the days of the American Revolution to make fun of Yankees, who eventually adopted the song themselves and used it to ridicule British dandies. *Macaroni,* meanwhile, became popular slang for anything smart and fashionable.

How appropriate this meaning of macaroni is to describe the current revival of interest in pasta, a food that comes closer to being universally adored than any other single food. And as for the feather in your cap, here, too, there's a double meaning: not only is eating pasta at the height of fashion; but if it is eaten properly, in the low-fat style of its originators, pasta need not add more than the weight of a feather to your frame. In fact, it can help you lose weight.

The history of pasta is long and colorful, and filled with tall tales. The notion that the noodle was invented by the Chinese and brought to Italy by Marco Polo in 1292 is belied by certain historical facts. For one, millennia before the dawn of the Christian era, the Greeks and Romans were routinely making "pastes" out of ground grain and water, and some of these were undoubtedly dried for later use, especially on long journeys. Thus, some version of pasta may have been the very first "convenience food." Thirty miles north of Rome there is a bas-relief on an Etruscan tomb of 400 B.C. that depicts the utensils used to make pasta: a sack of flour, a water jar, a ladle, a table, a rolling pin, a pastry wheel, and a knife. In the early years after the birth of Christ, pasta is mentioned in the writings of Cicero and Horace, and several recipes for pasta dishes are included in a first-century cookbook. And an Arab geographer described spaghetti making in Sicily in the eleventh century. Thus, pasta was being made in what was to become Italy for at least 1,700 years before Marco Polo returned from China.

No doubt, though, this famous traveler brought home some Chinese versions of pasta. Archaeological evidence shows that a type of noodle was the staple of the Shang Dynasty in 1700 B.C., and there are Chinese records, dating back to 5000 B.C., of eating noodles. But while the Chinese may have indeed been the first to invent the noodle, they were not the only such innovators. More likely, pasta in various forms arose independently among many peoples. The Jews, for example, are said to have invented ravioli: they were stuffing pockets of pasta with lamb during the century before Christ. The Greeks are thought to have brought *lasagnon* to Sicily even before that. And Ostrogoth Prince Theodoric is said to have served his *nudel* in Ravenna after the barbarian invasions.

According to food writer Lorraine Latorraca, pasta was popular in England by the Middle Ages, and in 1817 it was considered fit fare for a future king. The prince regent, who later became King George IV, was served "La Timbale Macaroni à la Napolitaine" as a featured banquet entrée. The name may have been fancy, but the dish is familiar to every American child as macaroni and cheese. Thomas Jefferson played a role in introducing pasta to this country. While serving as ambassador to France in the late 1700s, Jefferson traveled to Naples and was so impressed with the pasta he sampled that he ordered crates of "maccarony" sent back to the United States along with a pasta-making machine. According to Karen Green, author of *The Great International Noodle Experience,* the first American pasta factory was opened in Brooklyn, New York, in 1848 by a Frenchman, Antoine Zerega, who harnessed a horse to power the mixing and kneading machines (the poor beast spent the day walking round and round a vertical shaft!). But it was not until the twentieth century that pasta began to make it big in the United States, thanks to the waves of immigrants from various pasta-eating cultures. In addition to the pastas made here by more than 100 regional manufacturers (most of them family businesses started by Italian-Americans), we import pasta from Italy, China, Japan, and Korea.

Still, American consumption of pasta lags behind that of other nations that, incidentally, lack our problems with rampant heart disease and obesity. The average Italian consumes nearly 70 pounds of pasta a year, whereas the average American eats only about 10 pounds a year. (And whereas Americans get fatter every year, pasta-eating Italians do not.) According to the National Pasta Association, however, Americans are eating more pasta today than ever before. In 1949, per-capita pasta consumption was only about 4½ pounds, and since 1977 there's been a 67-percent increase in total pasta consumption and a 59-percent increase in per-capita pasta consumption. This would all be well and good if not for the fact that, as with most other good foods, Americans tend to distort the inherent nutritional virtues of pasta by drowning it in fat- and calorie-laden sauces. There are many ways to eat this most versatile of foods other than having it swim in a sauce of cream, butter, and cheese, as in Fettucine Alfredo. A tomato sauce with clams or squid need not contain more than a few teaspoons of fat for the entire recipe, and a wonderful primavera (vegetable) sauce can be made with not much more fat than that (see recipes on pp. 360 and 368).

There are more varieties of pasta than there are of Heinz products: Heinz makes a mere 57 varieties; but there are at least 80 different shapes, widths, and lengths of pasta—and that doesn't even include the various flours and flavorings from which pastas are made. In addition to refined wheat (the overwhelming favorite), there are pastas made from whole wheat, buckwheat, corn, beans, rice, and yams, and flavored with purées of spinach, beets, carrots, tomatoes, shrimp, nuts, herbs and spices, and even chocolate. You could construct a year-long menu plan, serving pasta every day without repeating yourself once. Different pasta dishes can be served as appetizers, salads, entrées, side dishes, or desserts. And pasta is one dish you never have to wonder whether the kids will eat. I've yet to meet a child who doesn't adore it. Whenever I'm fool enough to ask my sons what they'd like for supper, the answer is invariably "Pasta." Even when they were at that age when mixtures of foods had no appeal and most combination dishes were "deconstructed" so the boys could eat each ingredient separately, pasta dishes nearly always remained intact.

Pasta is easy to digest, making it an ideal food for people of every age (remember pastina, the tiny egg pasta you were probably fed even before you were a toddler?). It is easy to chew. And it is quick and easy to prepare, not much more complicated than knowing how to boil water. In fact, the first meal my children learned to prepare on their own was spaghetti, soon followed by macaroni and cheese (not out of a package). Dried pasta can be stored a long time without any loss of quality, and cooked or fresh pasta can be frozen for later use. If not already mixed with a sauce, leftover pasta can find its way into many different dishes, both hot and cold. And who needs packaged meals or take-out fast food when you've got a leftover pasta dish to reheat for breakfast, lunch, or supper the next day?

PASTA AS A HEALTH FOOD

For a nation of people who grew up thinking of pasta as fattening filler food, short on nutrients and long on calories, the title of this section may come as a surprise. Perhaps our picture of pasta arises from another common American theme: something that tastes so good can't be good for you. Not only is our long-standing notion about pasta untrue, but the opposite *is* true. Properly prepared, pasta is a nourishing food that helps to fill you up *before* you eat more calories than you really need. Meals based on pasta can easily meet the Dietary Goals of the Senate Select Committee on Nutrition and Human Needs, the Dietary Guidelines of the U.S. Departments of Agriculture and Health and Human Services, and the nutritional recommendations of more than a dozen health organizations: eat less fat and cholesterol; eat less sugar and salt; eat more fiber and starches. Pasta has also recently been shown to be an ideal basic food for diabetics because it does not cause blood sugar to rise very much after a meal. Of course, nondiabetics can also benefit from this effect, since rises in blood sugar prompt the release of insulin, which in turn can make you feel sleepy, raise your cholesterol level, and increase the storage of body fat.

PASTA

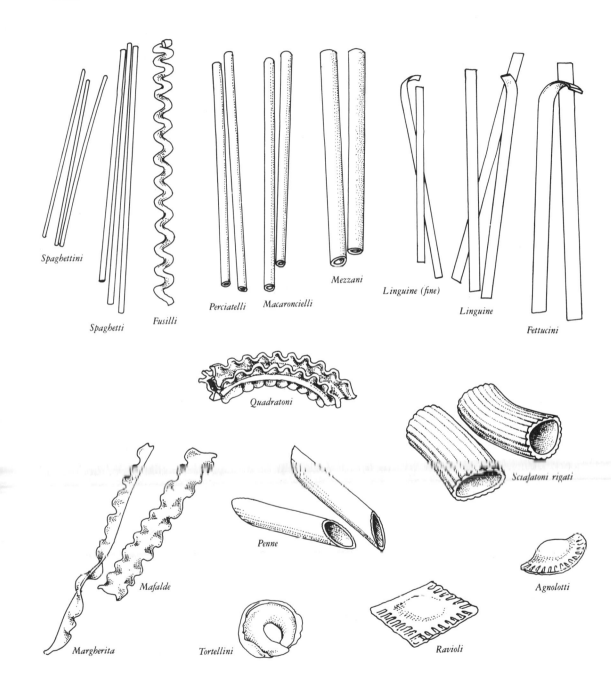

Spaghettini

Spaghetti

Fusilli

Perciatelli

Macaroncielli

Mezzani

Linguine (fine)

Linguine

Fettucini

Quadratoni

Sciafatoni rigati

Mafalde

Penne

Margherita

Tortellini

Ravioli

Agnolotti

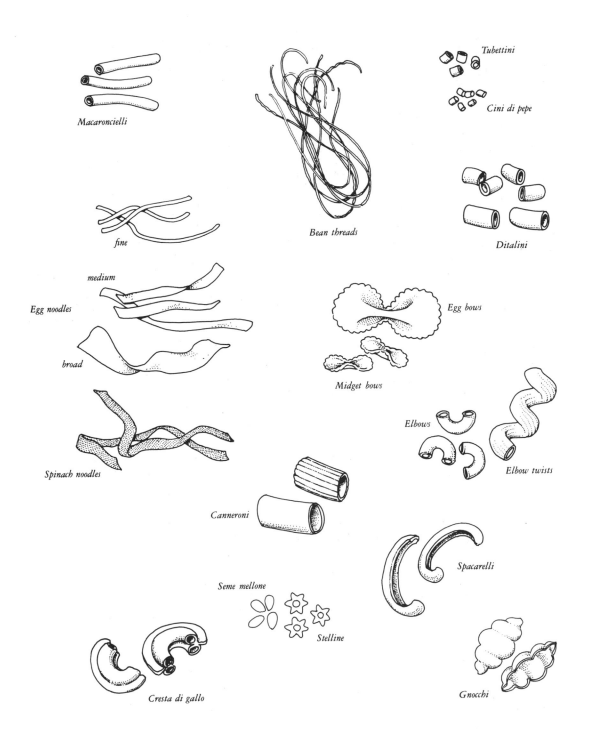

Macaroncielli

fine

medium

Egg noodles

broad

Spinach noodles

Bean threads

Canneroni

Seme mellone

Stelline

Cresta di gallo

Tubettini

Cini di pepe

Ditalini

Egg bows

Midget bows

Elbows

Elbow twists

Spacarelli

Gnocchi

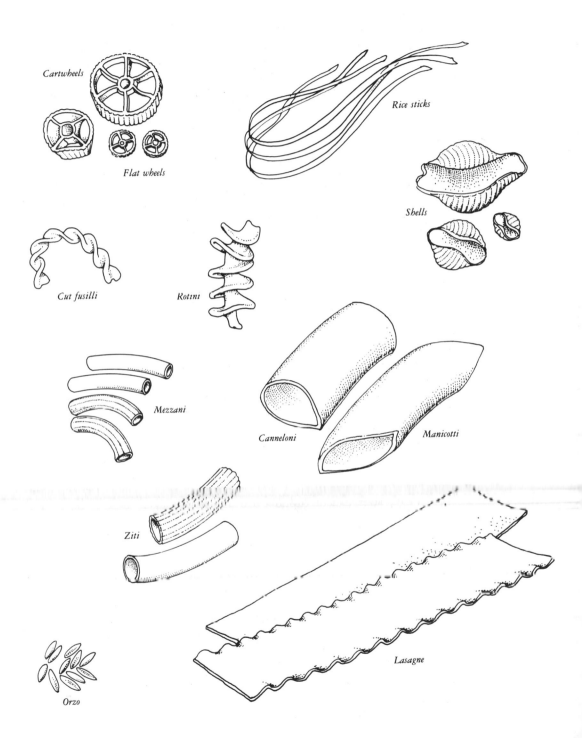

Cartwheels

Flat wheels

Rice sticks

Shells

Cut fusilli

Rotini

Mezzani

Canneloni

Manicotti

Ziti

Lasagne

Orzo

Runners deserve credit for popularizing pasta as excellent muscle fuel. The traditional meal before a race is spaghetti. In fact, all entrants for the New York City Marathon are treated to a pasta supper the night before the race. And the good word about pasta is beginning to spread among athletes in all sports. Even football coaches, who have traditionally fed their teams huge steak dinners before games, have begun to change the pregame menu to—guess what?—pasta.

PASTA IS NOT FATTENING

The aspect of pasta that people worry most about is calories. How nice, then, to discover that a 1-cup serving of cooked spaghetti, which weighs about 5 ounces, has only about 200 calories, less than half the calories in a steak of the same weight. In fact, 10 ounces of cooked spaghetti (a 2-cup serving) still has fewer calories than a 5-ounce steak. And I prepare many sauces—even those with meat, chicken, or fish—that add only about 100 to 150 calories to a generous serving of pasta (see, for example, the recipes on pp. 364, 365, and 369). With a green salad (low-calorie dressing), beverage, and fruit for dessert, you have a very healthful, satisfying meal—fit for a prince—for about the same number of calories as just the steak part of a steak dinner.

What makes a pasta meal fattening—sometimes, that is—are the rich and abundant sauces many Americans choose to go with it or the fact that, in addition to the pasta, we may consume a large, calorie-laden portion of animal protein, which most Italians would regard as a redundancy. Of course, pasta can be served as a first course. But then portions should be dainty, as for any appetizer, and the quantities of the entrée might also be more discreet. Furthermore, according to Carlo Middione, renowned pasta chef and author of *Pasta! Cooking It and Loving It,* Italians do not eat two kinds of starches at the same meal: if pasta is served, bread isn't. But I wouldn't necessarily leave out the bread. You'd be much better off, for instance, if you ate bread than if you ate sausage along with your pasta. Just go easy on the butter, or leave it off altogether, moistening your bread by dipping it in the pasta sauce.

Sheryl and Mel London, authors of *Creative Cooking with Grains and Pasta,* tell about an assignment they had from Alitalia Airlines to produce a documentary film on the foods of Italy. For three seasons, they traveled throughout the Italian countryside, preparing, filming, and eating regional dishes. Despite an abundance of pasta virtually daily, they gained no weight. In fact, both lost a little.

And after years of badmouthing almost every kind of carbohydrate as "too fattening," the major weight-watching organizations have discovered the reverse: filling up on a pasta dish can actually reduce caloric consumption—not just at the meal but also between meals, since this slowly digested food really sticks to the ribs. In fact, among its frozen prepared dinners, Weight Watchers has been pushing lasagne the hardest—"lasagna without guilt" the ads proclaim.

NUTRIENTS IN PASTA

The nutritional value of pasta is determined by what was used to make it. But since the most popular type of pasta is made from refined enriched flour (see Chapter 5, p. 43), it makes sense to emphasize the nutrients in this type even though it puts pasta in a less favorable nutritional light than it needs to be. The improvements in nutrient value possible when different ingredients are used will be described in the next section, "Variety, Thy Name Is Pasta."

If you buy spaghetti or macaroni in a package, the label will suggest that 2 ounces of dry pasta (which cooks up into 5 ounces ready to eat) are 1 serving. That's fine if you are serving a small child or you have a delicate appetite or the pasta dish is not the main part of your meal. As an entrée, however, 3 to 4 ounces of dry pasta are a more likely adult serving (and for teen-aged boys, you may have to figure on 6 ounces per serving). Two ounces of dry pasta (1 cup of cooked spaghetti or 1½ cups of medium-sized macaroni) provide about 210 calories, 8 grams of protein, 1 gram of fat, and 42 grams of carbohydrate (as starch). The amount of sodium depends on whether the product was prepared with salt (many are not and may say so on the label) and on how much salt you add to the cooking water. If no salt is added, a serving would contain less than 10 milligrams of sodium. These values would double if your serving was prepared from 4 ounces of dry pasta (4 servings to the pound). Since pasta made from refined flour is enriched, by law it contains reasonable amounts of iron, riboflavin, niacin, and thiamin. Pasta made from refined flour is not especially high in dietary fiber since the bran and germ of the wheat kernel have been removed. Incidentally, if pasta is made from the "standardized recipe" of enriched white wheat flour and water, the package need not list the ingredients. But if anything else is added to the recipe, all the ingredients must be listed.

The best commercial "white" pasta is made from durum wheat, which is refined and ground into a yellow-white flour called semolina. Most pasta manufacturers who use semolina will proudly say so by listing it on the label. Semolina contains more vitamins and protein than ordinary allpurpose white flour, and that protein has a higher biological value because it has a better distribution of essential amino acids.

Table 5 shows the percentages of the USRDA (the recommended daily intake for adults) a serving (2 ounces dry) of regular pasta would provide. These amounts are not bad since you probably don't eat your pasta straight. Chances are you add a sauce and/or cheese that significantly increases the amount of protein, vitamins, and minerals in the dish. If your sauce is made from vegetables, you also add fiber.

Table 5	NUTRIENTS IN A SERVING OF REGULAR PASTA (2 ounces dry)
Nutrient	*% USRDA*
Protein	10
Thiamin	35
Riboflavin	15
Niacin	20
Iron	10

However, you can get a lot more nutritive value from the pasta alone if you choose one of the many alternatives made with different flours and/or dried vegetable purées.

VARIETY, THY NAME IS PASTA

Pasta comes dried, fresh, or cooked and frozen; white, brown, yellow, green, orange, or pink; in dozens of different shapes and sizes (see the illustration on pp. 81–83); and made from different types of flour. If all the shapes and sizes were available in every color and with each type of flour, you could probably eat a different pasta every day of your life!

Expert cooks recommend the products made from pure *durum wheat semolina* since they cook up firm and slightly chewy (*al dente*—"to the tooth") if not overcooked. But even pasta purists are beginning to recognize the value, both culinary and nutritional, of other types. As a mother whose children could eat pasta straight from the colander, as a cook who tries to keep calories low and nutrients high, and as an eater who adores vegetable sauces that don't necessarily contain much protein, I am especially fond of the new *high-protein pastas* made with soy flour and whey protein in addition to semolina. The resulting product provides about 13 grams of protein in a serving (2 ounces dry), approximately the same amount of protein that you'd get from 2 ounces of cooked meat and a third more than in ordinary enriched pasta. When you use a high-protein pasta, you needn't worry about balancing your meal by adding a high-protein food like meat, fish, or cheese. Just a sprinkle of grated cheese will do. So will a glass of milk with the meal. High-protein pastas are now available nationwide, although regional suppliers differ. Ask your market manager to get some for you if the store doesn't already carry it. Your family may not notice anything different about the taste, but their bodies may appreciate the nutritional boost.

Whole-wheat pastas are also available in many areas, in the health food store if not in the local supermarket. These have a slightly higher protein content, considerably more fiber, and more vitamins and minerals than regular pasta. But the taste and texture are quite different and may take a little getting used to. You might start out by mixing the two. But cook them separately, or add the whole-wheat pasta to the water after the white has cooked a few minutes to keep the whole-wheat pasta from getting too mushy.

Both white and whole-wheat pasta may be available with any of several added ingredients that can improve their nutritive value: powdered purées of spinach, carrots, beets, tomatoes, or Jerusalem artichokes, among other vegetables. The color of the pasta will vary according to the color of the vegetable. You pay a premium price for such products (and most are not available on ordinary supermarket shelves), but they can add variety to your plate and palate as well as some extra nutrients (but not necessarily your money's worth). You may also find pastas prepared with built-in seasonings such as basil, curry, or dill.

A dinner-party favorite of mine is to serve a tricolored pasta dish by combining regular, spinach, and carrot pasta.

By law in this country, anything called a noodle must contain at least 5½ percent egg solids, giving *egg noodles* an added boost of protein, vitamins, and minerals, as well as adding some cholesterol to an otherwise cholesterol-free product. (The amount of cholesterol is not enough for most people to worry about as long as they don't eat egg noodles everyday. But if you are on a special low-cholesterol diet, you should check with your physician.) Thin egg noodles are commonly added to chicken broth, and the wider egg noodles are especially good in sweet pasta recipes like Jewish noodle pudding. *Oriental egg noodles* are the base for one of my most beloved Chinese dishes, lo mein, a mixture of noodles, lots of slivered vegetables, and small amounts of meat, chicken, or seafood (see the recipe on p. 466). Oriental egg noodles taste best when bought fresh, but dried egg noodles will do in a pinch. The fresh kind freeze well, so if you find a supply in an out-of-the-way place, you can safely buy a couple of pounds and divide them into ½-pound packages, seal them in plastic bags, and store them in the freezer for many months. Egg noodles tend to expand more than other types when cooked, so a little can go a long way.

In some parts of the country, stores may carry so-called *light pasta,* which has about a third fewer calories because it contains less starch in a serving. But since pasta is not a high-calorie food to begin with, I can see no reason to pay more to get less food unless your allowable caloric intake is very low.

Health food stores often carry pasta that is not made from wheat, which can be very useful for people with a gluten intolerance. For everyone else, these pastas can add culinary variety. I especially enjoy *buckwheat pasta* made without wheat flour. Wheatless *corn pasta* (sold in health food stores) will do in a pinch, but it has a gummy texture.

In the world of Asian noodles, the variety of ingredients is much greater than in Italian-type pastas, although the shapes and sizes are more limited. Asian noodles are nearly all long strands or threads (symbolizing long life). Except for Oriental egg noodles, none can be called "noodle" in this country because none is made with eggs! Thus, you'll find such names as "imitation noodles" or "alimentary paste" on packages that are obviously noodles by ordinary definition. They may be made with buckwheat flour, as in Japanese *soba;* mung beans (a protein-rich legume), as in Chinese *bean threads* or Japanese *shirataki* (shirataki may also be made from yams or other root plants); rice flour, as in Chinese *rice sticks;* seaweed, as in *cellophane noodles* (also made from mung beans); a mixture of wheat and shrimp paste, as in Southeast Asian *shrimp noodles;* potato starch, as in *potato-starch noodles;* cornstarch, as in Indian *phaluda;* as well as yam noodles (Japanese *saifun*), pea noodles, and wheat noodles, as in Japanese *udon* (also made from corn) or Chinese *won ton* wrappers.

Oriental noodles can also be purchased as instant noodles, precooked and dried and packaged with a packet of dried seasonings (Japanese *ramen,* for example). The noodles are added to boiling water with some cut-up fresh vegetables; then the seasoning is added to made a thick, souplike dish. These noodles can make a wonderful quick lunch especially on a cold winter day. But beware: the packets of seasonings are very salty and may contain MSG, a food additive to which some people are sensitive. When I make these soups, I use at most one-third of the seasoning packet for the whole package of noodles. (An alternative is to add your own seasonings and toss out the packet.) If this is too bland for you, you can always sprinkle a little more seasoning into your bowl, but it's almost impossible to dilute the saltiness if you start by adding the whole packet.

Oriental noodles are not usually available in supermarkets, but you will find them in stores that specialize in Oriental foods and often in greengroceries run by Asians.

In many areas now you can buy *fresh pasta*—that is, pasta that has not been dried. However, this is no guarantee that you'll get a superior product, although it does guarantee a premium price. According to the late food authority James Beard, author of (among other things) *Beard on Pasta,* "So-called fresh pasta that is sold in cardboard trays in supermarkets [is] far inferior to good dried pasta." Also, don't be fooled by the price per pound. Since fresh pasta contains a lot more water than the dried kind, the price for a pound of fresh pasta cannot be directly compared to that of dried pasta. Put another way, a pound of fresh pasta does not go as far as a pound of dried, so cost per pound underestimates the cost per serving of fresh pasta.

But most expensive are the *prepared pasta dishes* that you'll find in cans or in the frozen-food section of your market. These products are certainly time and energy savers for the busy cook or the parent who wants to leave supper or a snack for the kids to heat up themselves. But unless you read the label carefully and its "nutrition information" (including sodium content), it's hard to know whether you're getting your nutritional money's worth. These products are nearly always too salty, and some are higher in fat than a pasta dish needs to be. And, of course, they rarely taste as good as what you can make yourself. You can make your own frozen ready-to-heat-and-eat pasta dishes by preparing a double recipe in your spare time or the next time you make the dish from scratch. Before baking, package family or individual portions in disposable aluminum containers and freeze. Or you can freeze the fully cooked leftovers for shorter reheating time.

For the truly adventurous pasta aficionado, there is also the option of making your own pasta from scratch. *Home-made pasta* represents a considerable investment of time and, sometimes, money, but some cooks find it great fun and well worth the effort. (One of my efficient friends says he can go from flour to dinner in 30 minutes.) Pasta-making machines are now big sellers in kitchen-equipment sections of department stores. They come in various levels of automation, the most automatic being the most expensive. In all likelihood, you'll have to use all-purpose flour in preparing home-made pasta; the semolina flour sold in stores (you're most likely to find it in Italian grocery stores) is too coarse for home equipment. Virtually all pasta cookbooks and all pasta machines include instructions for making your own pasta. I would recommend reading about it before you invest in costly equipment. You may also want to make a batch or two by hand first, by preparing the dough, rolling it out with a long rolling pin, and cutting it into shapes with a knife or rolling blade (the type used to cut pastry strips or pizza will do). If you are in love with the results, then consider automating the process by investing in a pasta-rolling machine or an extruder that rolls and shapes the dough for you or, in the most elaborate types, even mixes and kneads the dough first.

COOKING WITH PASTA

I said earlier that cooking pasta is not much harder than boiling water, and it isn't—if you know how to select the right pasta for a particular dish and you follow some simple basic rules in preparing it.

CHOOSING THE RIGHT SHAPE. Forty percent of the pasta eaten in this country is ordinary white spaghetti. But as you can see from the illustration on pages 81–83, you needn't be limited to those long strands. Choices range from the delicate thin threads of angel's hair (capellini d'angelo) to the broad lasagne, from the tiny pastine to the thick, hearty creste di galli (cocks' comb), from the long, thin tubes called bucati to the giant manicotti waiting to be stuffed. Though the shapes and sizes of pasta can boggle the mind of even the coolest cook, there are just a few basics to consider when deciding which one to use for a particular dish. The following recommendations are derived from Carlo Middione's *Pasta! Cooking It and Loving It* (among other expert sources):

- Fresh pasta is delicate and absorbs sauce more readily than the dried kind, so it works best with a light, nonassertive sauce.
- Pasta that is tubular or has a cuplike space, such as shells, is designed to trap sauces. Use it when you want to eat a lot of the sauce or when the sauce has chopped meat or vegetables in it.
- Rich sauces should be served with a flat pasta or a shape that does not trap too much of the sauce.
- Delicate pastas should be served with delicate sauces. A thin sauce with a seafood base, for example, goes well with thin spaghetti, such as spaghettini or capellini.
- Don't use egg noodles in Italian dishes. They are too soft, sticky, and sweet for that garlic-based cuisine. They work better with meats like chicken and pork, with beef in a light cream sauce, with vegetables like sauerkraut, and in puddings like Jewish noodle pudding.

TO COOK PASTA. No matter how fine the pasta is that you start with, to produce a quality product it must be cooked right. Following the directions on the box can't hurt, except that packages often overestimate the time it takes to cook pasta *al dente*—the best way to eat it unless you have trouble chewing.

The following steps should assure success each time, whether you start with a packaged pasta, loose dried pasta, or fresh pasta:

- Start with a *large pot,* preferably one that is deep rather than wide and that holds at least 2 quarts of water more than the amount you have to use. If the pot has two handles, it will make it easier to drain the pasta. Or, if you do a lot of pasta cooking and steaming of vegetables, you may want to invest in an 8-quart spaghetti cooker—a pot with a deep colanderlike insert (it often also comes with a more shallow steamer basket). Then, when the pasta is done, all you have to do is lift up the colander part and let the water drain back into the pot—no heavy lifting or pouring off of a pot full of boiling water and pasta. This design is especially useful when pasta has to be cooked in two or more batches because you can save the boiling water for the next batch.
- Use *a lot of water*— 4 to 6 quarts per pound of pasta, more if your pot will hold it with room to spare. The pasta should be able to swim in the water. The more water, the less gummy the cooked pasta will be. If you are using the minimum amount of water or if you are cooking fresh pasta or very large pasta like manicotti, add 1 tablespoon of vegetable oil to the water.
- Bring the water to *a hard boil.* If you plan to *add salt* (about 2 teaspoons per pound of pasta), do it when the water is boiling rapidly and you're ready to add the pasta.
- Have the *sauce ready* (and, if possible, the diners) before you cook the pasta, unless you're making a dish that will be served as a cold salad or will be heated or baked and served at another time.
- *Add the pasta in batches* to the boiling water over the space of no more than a minute, stirring after each addition to keep the pieces from sticking together. (Although some cookbooks will tell you to let the water return to a boil after each addition, this method results in uneven cooking, with some pieces getting mushy while others are still too firm.) In cooking long pasta, stand one end of the bunch in the boiling water, and, as it softens, push in the rest. If the boiling stops after you've added the pasta, bring the pot back to a boil as fast as possible. The water will reboil fastest if you cover the pot. But stand by to remove the cover quickly when the boil returns, or you'll have starchy water all over the stove.
- How long the pasta should cook depends on its size and shape, and whether it is fresh or dried (also, James Beard says, on the heat of the day, the amount of water in the pot, the kind of flour used, how much liquid was used in the dough, and how long the pasta has been in the warehouse and on the shelves of the grocery store and your pantry). Fresh pasta cooks very fast—in about 2 to 6 minutes—dried pasta in about 8 to 20 minutes. For some Oriental noodles, all you have to do is pour boiling water on them, then drain. *Stay with your pasta* until it's done, and, for dried pasta, *start testing for doneness* after about 5 minutes (unless your previous experience with that kind of pasta has taught you that it's never done before 15 minutes). Use a long-handled fork or a wooden spoon to remove a strand from the pot, and, after a moment to cool it, taste the strand for doneness.
- When the pasta is done, *drain it immediately* in a colander (some experts

recommend adding 2 cups of cold water to the pot first to stop the cooking). The best kind of colander can be stood firmly in the basin of your sink. Failing that, set a large strainer on top of a pot large enough to hold all the cooking water. Pour the water away from you to avoid a steam burn (or fogged glasses!).

- *Do not rinse* the cooked pasta unless it is to be used in a cold salad, in which case you should rinse it in cold water as soon as it has been drained. When drained, add the cooked pasta to a warm, greased bowl, and toss it with some butter or oil if you cannot immediately add the sauce. Refrigerating cooked pasta without the sauce or salad dressing usually results in a congealed mass. That's okay for use in any number of dishes made from leftover pasta but not ideal for eating sauced pasta the first time around.

- *To reheat* unsauced, cooked pasta, put it in a bowl, pour boiling water over it, stir gently to get all the pieces separated and exposed to the water, and then drain it.

7 ·
FULL O' BEANS?
YOU BET!

What gives you more protein value for your dollar than any other food? What lacks the artery-damaging fats and cholesterol of most high-protein foods?

What keeps indefinitely without preservatives or refrigeration?

What can be made into everything from soup to nuts, from milk to ersatz meat?

What can lower cholesterol levels, control diabetes, and conquer constipation without a physician's prescription?

No doubt you've guessed: beans—specifically the dry beans and peas known as legumes. The fruits of leguminous plants form pods that hang from the stems; inside the pods are the seeds—the beans, peas, lentils, and peanuts that have been helping to sustain human life for thousands of years. In developed countries today, however, beans have a serious image problem. They are widely regarded as the "poor man's meat," eaten primarily by those who cannot afford the more expensive animal sources of protein. That image plus the facts that most dry legumes take a long time to cook from scratch and often leave the diner with a gaseous legacy have regulated beans and peas to the bottom of the American food basket. But given their remarkable value to nutrition, health, the economy, and our pocketbooks, not to mention their extraordinary versatility, legumes deserve to be leading items on American shopping lists.

From East to West, legumes have been an important part of the human diet for at least 4,000 years. They were cultivated in ancient China, Egypt, Central and South America, and Africa. And to this day they serve as a main source of protein and a dietary staple for millions of people throughout the world. Witness Chinese bean curd and bean sprouts, Mexican chili and refried beans, Indian dal, Middle Eastern felafel and hummus, Cuban black beans and rice, not to mention such famous dishes as Italian pasta e fagioli ("pasta fazool") and minestrone soup, British pease porridge, Swedish pea soup, and Brazilian feijoada, and those home-grown favorites Boston baked beans, Senate navy bean soup, and hoppin' John (the black-eyed peas and rice of the American South). Unfortunately, Americans are most familiar with *immature* legumes—green beans and garden peas—which lack the nutritive power of their fully mature counterparts. (Peanuts, which, as their name implies, are used more like nuts than legumes, are discussed in Chapter 9, "Nuts and Seeds.") Dry legumes are allowed to mature and dry on the plant, which dramatically increases their protein content, among other important nutrients. I am reminded of the unfamiliarity of Americans with dry legumes every time I write or speak of their nutritive value. Someone inevitably asks me, "How do you eat them? Dry?"

PROTEIN PLUS . . . PODS FULL OF NUTRIENTS

Dry beans and peas are richer in protein than any other plant foods. Their protein content ranges from about 6 percent to more than 11 percent of their cooked weight. Although most are relatively short of one or two essential amino acids, the deficiencies are easily overcome when beans or peas are eaten together with any grain food or seed or with small amounts of animal protein such as milk, cheese, chicken, or meat. A dish of lentils and rice, a bowl of thick minestrone soup, a bean enchilada, or a peanut-butter sandwich can provide as complete protein as found in a hamburger, an omelet, or a piece of chicken. And one major legume, the soybean, could stand alone as the sole source of protein for people past early childhood. If you're tired of watching your food budget grow out of proportion to your income, look to beans and peas as an economical source of quality protein. Legumes are the least expensive way to fulfill your protein needs, cheaper by far than even eggs and poultry. They are also among the healthiest sources of protein. Among other benefits, bean protein has been shown to reduce the cholesterol level in the blood, the opposite effect of its animal-derived competitors.

The legumes are rich sources of B vitamins, including thiamin, niacin, B_6, and folacin. This is so even though some B vitamins, which are water-soluble, are lost in the cooking process. A serving of cooked dry beans can supply as much as 40 percent of the daily recommended amounts of thiamin and B_6. On a per-serving basis, cooked black-eyed peas are a match for the folacin content of liver or wheat germ, and large lima beans, black-eyed peas, and pink beans outdo the B_6 content of nutritional yeast or wheat germ.

Iron is also a prominent nutrient in cooked legumes. One cup of lentils, for example, contains 42 percent of the RDA for iron for an adult male and 23 percent of the RDA for iron for an adult female. However, all of this iron cannot be absorbed directly from beans. To increase the body's ability to absorb the iron in legumes, they should be consumed along with a food rich in vitamin C such as broccoli, tomatoes, green or red peppers, or citrus fruit or juice. Those bone-building minerals, calcium and phosphorus, are also plentiful in cooked beans and peas. And sodium, which raises blood pressure, is very low, while its protective counterpart, potassium, is in good supply.

Beans and peas are also very low in fat (an exception, soybeans, is discussed below), and what fat they have is polyunsaturated and protective against heart and blood-vessel disease. A cup of cooked kidney beans has less than 1 gram of fat (4 percent of total calories), a cup of split peas has only 2 percent fat calories, and a cup of lentils has but a trace of fat. In most red meat, however, more than 60 percent of the calories are fat calories, and in hard cheese more than 70 percent of the calories come from fat and most of that fat is cholesterol-raising saturated fat. Of course, as plant foods, legumes contain no cholesterol, whereas all animal sources of protein do.

Instead of fat, the protein in beans and peas comes packaged with complex carbohydrates: starches, complex sugars, and dietary fiber. Beans and peas supply more fiber than almost any food except cereal bran—on average, 6 to 8 grams per serving. They are a great help to anyone interested in natural methods of improving bowel function as well as in deriving other known benefits of dietary fiber (see pp. 20–22). The starches in beans are also nutritional wonders. They have less of an effect on blood-sugar levels than any other carbohydrate-rich food and have been shown to improve dramatically the control of blood sugar in diabetics. On diets containing substantial amounts of beans, many adult-onset diabetics have been able to reduce greatly or to eliminate entirely their dependence on insulin and other medications to control blood sugar. This benefit to blood sugar has been attributed in part to the fact that legumes are digested slowly, which should also mean that they have a high satiety value, delaying the return of hunger and the overconsumption of calories by people concerned about their weight.

Furthermore, in terms of calories, beans and peas compare favorably to their animal-protein counterparts. A cup of cooked lentils supplies 212 calories, kidney beans, 218, and split peas, 230. A 3-ounce hamburger has 243, and 1½ ounces of Cheddar has 170. The meat contains about a third more protein, but the cooked beans and peas supply a far more satisfying 7½ ounces of food for fewer calories. And unlike meat, which is fully digestible, not all of the calories in beans and peas are absorbed by the body. If you compare nutrients in the uncooked foods (see Table 6), you can see how much more of your nutritional money's worth you get from beans. Keep in mind that the pound of beef costs about four times more than a pound of dry beans.

Table 6	NUTRIENT COMPARISON OF BEANS AND BEEF					
	(amounts in 1 pound uncooked)					
	Kidney beans	Boneless chuck			Kidney beans	Boneless chuck
Calories	1,556	1,597	Iron (mg.)		31	11
Protein (g.)	102	74	Potassium (mg.)		4,463	1,176
Fat (g.)	7	142	Thiamin (mg.)		2.30	0.32
Carbohydrates (g.)	209	0	Riboflavin (mg.)		0.90	0.66
Calcium (mg.)	499	41	Niacin (mg.)		10.4	17.6
Phosphorus (mg.)	1,842	671				

SOME PROBLEMS WITH BEANS

And Esau came from the field, and he was faint: And Esau said to Jacob, Feed me. . . .
And Jacob said, Sell me this day thy birthright. And Esau said, Behold I am at the
point to die: And what profit shall this birthright do to me? . . . And he sold his
birthright unto Jacob. Then Jacob gave Esau bread and pottage of lentiles; and he did eat
and drink, and rose up, and went his way.
—Genesis 25:19–34

Few Americans would sell anything for a bowl of lentils, let alone something as precious as a birthright. Aside from their poor-man's image, legumes have three deterrents to potential diners: they produce intestinal gas; they may interfere with the absorption of some nutrients; and they take a long time to cook. If beans and peas were perfect foods, humankind may never have turned to meats with such a vengeance and we'd all be healthier for it. Let's look at these problems one by one and see what can be done to minimize them.

"THE MUSICAL FRUIT." You may call it gas, indigestion, bloating, or by its proper medical term, *flatulence.* But whatever term you use, this infamous effect of beans is discomforting and sometimes embarrassing. Interestingly, it may be more of a problem for people who eat beans infrequently. In regular consumers of dry beans and peas, the body often adapts to minimize the problem of flatulence.

The effect has been traced to complex sugars in legumes—raffinose, stachyose, and verbacose—which are not broken down by human digestive enzymes. Instead, these sugars arrive intact in the large intestine, where bacteria ferment them, producing primarily two odorless gases, carbon dioxide and hydrogen, and a tiny percentage of some highly odoriferous ones, including hydrogen sulfide (the rotten-egg odor). In some people, the gas causes abdominal bloating, discomfort, and possibly even diarrhea. The effect is highly individual, so don't assume that because someone you know is severely affected you will have the same reaction. And don't assume that because you react vigorously when you first start eating beans you'll continue to have a problem. In a study at the University of California, Berkeley, bean eaters reported greater tolerance and less discomfort by the end of a three-week period of bean eating.

According to at least one expert, Dr. Joseph Rackis of the United States Department of Agriculture's Northern Regional Research Center in Peoria, Illinois, beans and gas are not necessarily inseparable. He has devised a means of preparing beans that he says washes out most of the indigestible sugars and reduces the flatulence problem by about 60 percent. Here is his technique:

1. Using 9 cups of water for every 1 cup of beans, soak the beans for 4 to 5 hours or overnight. Then discard the water.
2. Add fresh water (the same amount as before), and cook the beans for ½ hour. Again, throw out the water.
3. If the beans are not yet soft, add still more water (the same amount as before), and cook the beans until they are done. Discard the cooking water.

I tried this method several times with various types of beans, and it helped considerably. But unless beans give you serious trouble, I'm not sure it's worth the effort. While the method may wash out the troublesome sugars, it will also cause a loss of up to half the water-soluble vitamins and about 10 percent of the protein. However, you'll still be left with a food that packs a hefty nutritional whollop. An alternative is to add a small amount of sodium bicarbonate (baking soda) to the soaking water. This helps to leach out the troublesome sugars, although it also destroys some thiamin. (In the future, beans may be "deflated" by radiation treatment, which reduces the troublesome sugars by half, according to studies in Bombay, India.)

You'll have less of a problem if you eat only small amounts of beans at any one time and don't mix them with other gaseous vegetables such as cabbage. Or you can stick to the types of beans least likely to produce gas, including lentils, black-eyed peas, lima beans, chickpeas, and white beans. Although soybeans are the most gaseous when eaten as whole beans, the flatulence problem is generally absent from many soy products. In tofu, or soybean curd, for example, many of the indigestible sugars wash out with the whey when the curds are formed. In tempeh, a fermented soybean product, the sugars are used up in the process of forming the product and thus are usually not a problem in the finished food. Foods made from soy-protein concentrates, like textured vegetable protein (TVP), also have little or no sugars in them.

Another gas-producing factor in beans is uncooked starch, which the body cannot digest. Thus, thorough cooking of all legumes is important (see cooking instructions on p. 102). Cooked beans should not require chewing; you should be able to mash them with your tongue against the roof of your mouth.

ANTINUTRIENT EFFECTS. Nutrition scientists have long believed that substances in beans—especially in soybeans—can bind up essential nutrients such as iron and zinc, and prevent their absorption by the body. However, recent studies by the Department of Agriculture among adults and children fed soy protein for 6 months showed little effect on the absorption of iron and zinc. In fact, in some of the volunteers, the amounts of these nutrients in the blood actually rose on the soy-supplemented diet. In another study conducted at the University of Kansas Medical Center, absorption of dietary iron was significantly increased when soy protein or whole soybeans were eaten along with vitamin C (the amount found in about 6 ounces of orange juice).

Other antinutrients in soybeans, which can inhibit protein digestion and affect blood clotting, are destroyed when the beans or bean products are thoroughly cooked. All soy products should be cooked, including soy powder and soybean sprouts, although these need less cooking than soy flour or grits.

COOKING PROBLEMS. Dry legumes are not foods you can start to think about when you come home from work and everyone is clamoring for dinner. These foods take time to prepare: time to soak and time to cook. This can mean as much as an overnight soak plus an hour or two of cooking. So the time to think about making beans is anywhere from three hours to one day before you plan to eat them. (There are exceptions: lentils, split peas, and black-eyed peas do not need soaking, and they cook quickly—in about ½ hour, just a little longer than it would take to cook converted rice; and all beans are amenable to an hour-long "quick soak" [see p. 103].) The easy way out is to buy already-cooked beans and peas in cans or frozen packages. Canned beans are not as high in sodium as many other canned vegetables. However, it's still a good idea to drain and rinse them before adding them to your meal. Commercially prepared beans cost more, but they save time and energy (both yours and your stove's). I always keep a few cans of kidney beans and chickpeas on hand for use in salads, soups, dips, and casseroles that I want to make in a hurry. An alternative is to cook up a large batch of beans when you have the time and freeze the drained beans in meal-sized portions. Cooked beans, tightly covered, will keep for up to five days in the refrigerator.

Soy, the Queen of Beans

The soybean may be the single most important food produced in the world today. It is certainly the most versatile. But its potential as a nourishing and delicious food far exceeds its current role. Though soybeans, dubbed the "cow of China," are a main source of protein for millions of people in Asia, in much of the rest of the world they are fed to livestock. The United States is the leading producer of soybeans—our largest crop in terms of dollars—but 55 percent of what we grow is exported, and nearly all the rest is used as a source of vegetable oil and feed for animals that we raise for food.

Soybeans produce more protein per acre than any other plant or animal, and they do it without the addition of nitrogen fertilizer (as legumes, they can manufacture their own from atmospheric nitrogen). The amount of land it takes to produce beef for 1 person could yield enough soy protein to feed 15 or 20 people. If even one-third of our annual soybean crop went into people food, it could supply the protein needs for the entire country. Unfortunately, only about 3 percent of the soybeans we grow are used to produce foods made from the whole protein-rich bean. However, in recent years there's been a tremendous growth in this country in the market for such soy products as tofu (soybean curd), soy flour (used to boost the protein content of grain-based foods like breads and pasta), and TVP (a high-protein, low-fat, low-cost meat extender). In fact, several major food companies are said to be ready to pounce on tofu as a national supermarket item as soon as health food enthusiasts establish it as a popular food. One commercial tofu product, an ice-creamlike dessert called Tofutti, has so tickled the taste buds of cholesterol- and calorie-watchers nationwide that it was featured in the "Living" section of *Time* magazine.

SOY PROTEIN, THE MEAT OF THE EAST

Among the widely grown beans, the soybean is the best source of protein. By weight, 40 percent of the dry bean and 11 percent of the cooked bean is protein.

A poached egg, by comparison, is 13 percent protein, American cheese is 23 percent protein, and a hamburger is 22 percent protein. One cup of cooked soybeans can provide about 20 grams of protein, a third of the recommended daily intake for an adult male, at only two-thirds the calories in a hamburger with the same protein value. The protein in soy is also better balanced than that in other beans and peas. In fact, it is nearly as good as milk protein in its ability to support the growth of laboratory rats, and studies have shown that human adults can fulfill their protein needs indefinitely using soy as their only protein source. (This is not a recommendation, merely an illustration of the life-sustaining ability of soy.) Under ordinary circumstances, soy protein would be consumed along with such foods as grains, rice, corn, seeds, dairy products, or eggs that supply adequate amounts of the two essential amino acids, methionine and cystine, that are in relatively short supply in soybeans.

Soy protein has recently been shown to reduce significantly blood-cholesterol levels in people who are genetically predisposed to high cholesterol and premature heart disease. Dr. C. R. Sirtori and collaborators at the University of Milan found that a diet rich in soy protein is considerably more effective in lowering cholesterol than is the traditional low-fat "prudent" diet. Even when 500 milligrams of cholesterol—the equivalent of two large egg yolks—were added to the soy diet, blood cholesterol levels did not rise, the study showed. Other researchers found that a menu of equal proportions of beef and soy protein was almost as helpful in lowering cholesterol as the soy alone. And a study of hamsters suggested that when soy protein is substituted for the protein in cows' milk, the formation of gallstones may be prevented. In the National School Lunch Program, the addition of soy protein to foods has been approved for experimental purposes as a meat substitute. While the government is clearly most concerned about saving money on food for schoolchildren, it may inadvertently help to save their health at the same time.

SOY OIL, A BOON TO BLOOD VESSELS

The dry soybean is 5 percent fat by weight and 34 percent by calories, about the same as a sirloin steak trimmed of all its fat and half that of hard cheese or hamburger. But the fat in soybeans is different from that in meat and other animal foods. It is highly unsaturated and actually helps to lower cholesterol levels in the blood. By contrast, more than half the fat in meat and cheese is saturated and raises blood cholesterol. Furthermore, as a vegetable oil, the fat in soybeans contains no dietary cholesterol, which is present in all animal fat.

About 80 percent of commercial salad dressings, margarines, and mayonnaise are made from soybean oil (extracted from the bean, with the protein-rich residue mainly used to feed livestock). Many cooking and salad oils are all or part soybean oil as well. When you buy soybean margarine, choose those that list "liquid soybean oil" as the first ingredient, since they will be the least saturated. Likewise with vegetable shortenings and oil—if the first ingredient is partially hydrogenated soybean oil, choose an alternative made mainly with liquid oil.

In terms of calories, however, it matters little where your fat comes from: all fats supply between 100 and 120 calories per tablespoon. So don't get carried away with soybean oil any more than you would with butter or lard.

A SELECTION OF SUPER SOY FOODS

The whole bean is but one way to consume soy protein and probably not the most popular way at that. There are *soy grits* (which can be cooked as a cereal or a side dish, or used for stuffings), *soy flakes* (dry-roasted soybeans that have been flattened and cut, and can be cooked as a cereal), *soy flour* (ground defatted soybeans commonly used to boost the nutritional value of pasta, breads, pancakes, and other foods that will be thoroughly cooked), *soy powder* (heat-treated and useful as a protein boost in foods that will be minimally cooked), *soy milk* (a drink made from cooked soybeans that is especially useful for children with milk allergies), *soy nuts* (deep-fried or roasted beans that can be eaten as snacks and contain even more protein than peanuts), *tofu* (curdled soy milk that is formed into bland-tasting soft cakes and can be used in place of meat or chicken in soups, stir-fries, and other dishes), *tempeh* (fermented soybeans that form a cake slightly more flavorful than tofu), *bean sprouts* (crunchy additions to salads, bread dough, and stir-fried dishes), and *textured vegetable protein* (or TVP, a protein extract of soybeans that can be formulated into flakes or fashioned into ersatz meats like imitation bacon bits).

TOFU, FAST TRACK TO SOY NUTRITION. Here's a food that gives you nearly all the pluses of soybeans without the minuses. It is fast and easy to prepare (you can even just slice and eat it), very easy to digest, lacks the gaseous legacy of whole beans, but still provides all the protein at a low-cal cost. Its only drawbacks are that it is perishable unless frozen and may still be hard to get in some parts of the country. But its extraordinary versatility and nutritional wonders make it worth looking for. It can be used in salads, salad dressings, hors d'oeuvres, dips, soups, sandwiches, sauces, stir fries, casseroles, quiches, stuffings, burgers, stews, and scrambles, and it can be fashioned into dishes that resemble sour cream, ice cream, mayonnaise, or frosting, turning them into nutrient-rich foods without the saturated fats such foods ordinarily contain (see the index for tofu recipes).

Tofu is made from curdled soy milk in a manner resembling the production of cheese. Soaked soybeans are puréed and then cooked and filtered through cloth. The resulting milk is curdled with a coagulant—typically, magnesium chloride—and the curds are pressed into soft cakes, allowing the whey to drain off. The result is a bland-tasting, custardlike, smooth white block that is high in protein (about 10 grams in a 4-ounce serving), low in calories (about 80 per serving), low in fat (5 grams), free of cholesterol (0 milligrams), and low in sodium (less than 10 milligrams). The precise amounts of nutrients vary from manufacturer to manufacturer and according to how much of the whey has been pressed out: the firmer the cake, the higher the nutrient content because there is less water per ounce. Although more than half the calories in tofu come from fat, the total amount—45 fat calories in 4 ounces—is low and the fat itself is polyunsaturated and therefore not harmful to blood vessels. Tofu also contains iron and calcium, although the amount of calcium can vary widely depending upon whether calcium salts are used to precipitate the curd. Thus, tofu compares very favorably with cottage cheese, which has a lot more sodium and a lot less iron than the soybean product.

Tofu's only nutritional shortcoming is that it lacks the dietary fiber found in the whole soybean. But, to its credit, it also lacks the indigestible sugars that cause intestinal gas (most of these wash out with the whey). The nutrition information in Table 7 was provided by the New England Soy Dairy, Inc., of Greenfield, Massachusetts, which manufactures tofu for sale in northeastern markets.

Table 7	NUTRIENTS IN TOFU			% USRDA	
	Medium tofu	Firm tofu		Medium tofu	Firm tofu
Serving size	4 ounces	4 ounces	Protein	15	25
Calories	90	150	Vitamin A	0	0
Protein (g.)	10	16	Vitamin C	0	0
Carbohydrate (g.)	1	3	Thiamin	4	6
Fat (g.)	6	8	Riboflavin	2	2
Cholesterol (mg./100 g.)	0	0	Niacin	0	0
Sodium (mg./100 g.)	Less than 10.0	6.7	Calcium	4	6
			Iron	15	20
			Phosphorus	15	20

Tofu is also inexpensive, normally selling for less than $1 a pound. It is available in health food stores, Oriental food stores, and a growing number of supermarkets throughout the country (check in the produce department, frozen-food section, or deli counter, or ask the manager). It may be sold unpackaged and floating in water, packaged in water, or vacuum-packed. Unless it is vacuum-packed, tofu is highly perishable and should be kept refrigerated and covered with water that is changed daily. If you buy it packaged in water, slit the package, drain off the water, and replace the water daily. It is best used within a few days to a week, depending upon how fresh it was when you bought it. (Packages are often dated.) If not to be used quickly, tofu can be frozen. This changes the texture to one that is spongier and chewier after defrosting, but the tofu is still useful for many dishes.

Tofu is very bland and readily picks up the flavors of whatever it is cooked with, so it can be made to taste like almost anything you may choose. But beware of recipes that use lots of soy sauce to flavor it, since this salty sauce quickly makes it high in sodium. Stir-frying is okay if little oil is used, but deep-fried tofu has far more fat than a nutritious food should. Although tofu can be substituted for cheese in many dishes, bear in mind that it does not melt.

TEMPEH, A TREAT FROM INDONESIA. Another ancient soy food that incorporates the benefits but not the disadvantages of the whole dry bean is tempeh, an Indonesian bean cake made from cultured soybeans. The dehulled soybeans are split and fermented by a mold, which forms the beans into a solid, off-white cake with a slightly crunchy texture. It is a third higher in protein than the original bean: A 4-ounce serving contains about 20 grams of protein, one-third of the recommended daily amount for an adult. It is also a good source of riboflavin, niacin, and iron. But, contrary to popular claims, it is not a good source of vitamin B_{12} for people (it does contain a lot of the vitamin, but not in a form that humans can absorb). Like tofu, tempeh is very versatile and can be broiled, fried, used in soups, sandwiches, casseroles, stuffings, and so forth (see the recipe on p. 495). It is more flavorful than tofu but still a relatively bland food, and, like tofu, it cooks quickly—in 5 or 10 minutes. Also like tofu, it is perishable and should be refrigerated and used within a week of purchase. It can also be stored frozen for many months. Unfortunately, you're not likely to find tempeh anywhere but in a health food store or in a food outlet that caters to vegetarians. It also costs a lot more than tofu—about $3 a pound—but given its high protein content, it is not an expensive source of protein.

SOYBEAN SPROUTS: GROWING NUTRIENTS. Although soybeans themselves contain no vitamins A or C, when the beans sprout to start a new plant, these vitamins are formed in the edible sprout. Bean sprouts also have less fat and fewer calories than the whole bean, but they remain very rich sources of nearly complete protein (equal to that of the original bean) at a very low calorie cost. In 48 calories worth of sprouts (1 cup), you have as much protein as that in 1 egg, which has 80 calories. And a cup of sprouts certainly takes longer to eat and fills your belly more than 1 egg. Unlike other sprouts, soybean sprouts should be cooked or blanched (cooked for a minute in boiling water) before eating to destroy antinutrients in the soybean.

SOY FLOUR: A PROTEIN BOOST. Soy flour, made from defatted ground soybeans, can turn many a grain-based recipe into a high-protein food. It contains 40 percent to 60 percent protein, depending upon how much oil is removed when the bean is processed. If just 5 percent of the wheat flour in a bread recipe is replaced by soy flour, the protein content of the bread will be increased by 19 percent. Similarly with pasta, the addition of soy flour can nearly double the food's protein value. To boot, the protein in soy complements that of wheat, meaning that the resulting vegetable protein is as complete as that derived from meat or any other animal food. You can also replace some wheat flour with soy in recipes for cookies, muffins, and sweet breads, enhancing the nutritive value of these snack foods. However, soy flour contains no gluten, so in baking yeast-leavened breads, it must be combined with a high-gluten flour like wheat. Soy flour should be stored in a cool, dry place to prevent rancidity.

TEXTURED VEGETABLE PROTEIN. Textured vegetable protein (TVP) is, as its name implies, a very concentrated protein source—70 percent to 90 percent protein, far more than any animal food. It is usually sold in granular form, to be added to main dishes as a protein boost. In consumer taste tests, up to a quarter of the meat in ground-meat dishes can be replaced by TVP without tasters noticing the difference. However, your body and your pocketbook may notice and be glad of it. Isolated soy protein can also be fashioned into ersatz meats, including soy sausages, franks, ham cubes, bacon, chicken cubes and patties, and so forth. (The production of natural bacon, incidentally, requires 10 times as much cropland as the same amount of imitation bacon made from soybeans.) These products were designed primarily for vegetarians who want to give up the substance but not the form of meat. They are also used in some institutional settings to save money and reduce waste. Unfortunately, most of these imitation meats are highly salted, and some are made with significantly more fat than the soybean itself contains. Check the label or query the company before you buy.

FOR MORE RECIPES

This book contains a number of soy-based recipes. But cooks who wish to put more emphasis on soybeans and the products made from them might want to purchase one or more specialty cookbooks. Here are some worth considering:

Clarke, Christina. *Cook with Tofu.* New York: Avon, 1981.
Cusumano, Camille. *Tofu, Tempeh, and Other Soy Delights.* Emmaus, Pa.: Rodale Press, 1984.
Hagler, Louise. *Tofu Cookery.* Summertown, Tenn.: The Book Publishing Co., 1982.
Norton, Reggi, and Martha Wagner. *The Soy of Cooking.* Eugene, Ore.: White Crane, 1980. (For purchase, write to P.O. Box 3081, Eugene, Oregon 97403 *or* P.O. Box 56230, Washington, D.C. 20011.)
van Gundy Jones, Dorothea. *The Soybean Cookbook.* New York: Arco, 1963.

In addition, you might consult a vegetarian cookbook, especially one of these:

Katzen, Mollie. *The Moosewood Cookbook.* Berkeley, Calif.: Ten Speed Press, 1977.
———. *The Enchanted Broccoli Forest.* Berkeley, Calif.: Ten Speed Press, 1982.
Robertson, Laurel, Carol Flinders, and Bronwen Godfrey. *Laurel's Kitchen.* Berkeley, Calif.: Nigiri Press, 1976; New York: Bantam, 1982.

HOW TO COOK BEANS

Beans expand greatly when cooked. One cup of dried beans (about ½ pound) will become 2½ to 3½ cups of cooked beans, depending on the variety. Once you decide how much to cook, look over the beans and pick out any debris or shriveled beans that may have escaped factory inspection. Then wash and drain them. Now you're ready to begin.

SOAKING METHODS. Soaking is not essential if you have hours in which to cook the beans. But it is more economical and, I think, results in a better product. All dry beans and peas except lentils, split peas, and black-eyed peas should be soaked before cooking. This shortens the cooking time, leaches out some of the indigestible sugars, and improves the flavor, texture, and appearance of the beans. There are two methods: one cheap but slow; the other fast but slightly more expensive because you use the stove.

TRADITIONAL METHOD: In a large pot, add 6 cups of cold water to each pound of dry beans. Let the beans stand at room temperature overnight or for about 6 to 8 hours. Do not refrigerate the beans unless you will be soaking the beans for much longer than that. Drain and rinse the beans, and you're ready to cook them.

QUICK METHOD: Add 6 to 8 cups of hot water for each pound of dry beans, heat the water to boiling, and cook the beans for 2 minutes. Then cover the pot, and let the beans stand for 1 hour. Drain, rinse, and cook the beans.

COOKING METHODS. Put the soaked beans into *a large pot* or Dutch oven. Add 6 cups of fresh water for each pound of beans. You may want to add seasonings and some fat to the cooking water at this point, or you can cook the beans in broth. But don't add salt at this point, or it will delay the softening of the beans. The fat, such as 1 teaspoon of cooking oil, will help to prevent foaming. Bring the pot to a boil, cover it with the lid tilted slightly to allow steam to escape, reduce the heat to a simmer, and cook the beans until they are tender. For most beans this will take about 1 hour, but some require as much as 2 hours and soybeans may take 3 hours or longer. Simmer the beans gently if you don't want the skins to burst. The time will depend on the size and dryness of the bean, the altitude, and the hardness of the water (beans take longer to cook at high altitudes and in hard water). If your water is hard, you can add up to ¼ teaspoon of baking soda to the cooking water (no more because it destroys thiamin and may change the flavor). Don't add acidic ingredients (such as lemon juice, vinegar, or tomatoes) to the cooking water until the beans are almost done (acid slows down the softening process).

Beans can also be cooked quickly in the *pressure cooker.* Follow the manufacturer's guidelines, or see suggested cooking times and tips, below. At 15 pounds of pressure, most beans are done in 10 to 35 minutes.

Another option is a *slow cooker:* at low heat, beans will take 10 to 12 hours; at high heat, about 5 to 6 hours. Again, check the manufacturer's instructions.

QUICK GUIDE TO BEAN COOKERY

Table 8 shows the cooking requirements of and yields from 1 cup of dry beans or peas. Except for lentils, split peas, and black-eyed peas, all should be presoaked, as indicated above. The chart refers to top-of-the-stove cooking in an ordinary pot with a lid. By using a *pressure cooker* at 15 pounds of pressure, you can reduce cooking times to 10 to 35 minutes after the gauge begins to jiggle, the exact time depending upon the bean: black-eyed peas, 10 minutes; lentils, pea beans, and Great Northern beans, 20 minutes; small lima beans, 25 minutes; large lima beans and navy beans, 30 minutes; soybeans, 35 minutes. The amount of water used depends on the size of your pot (2 cups for a 4-quart cooker, 2½ cups for a 6-quart cooker), but the pot should not be filled more than one-third full of water because expansion and foam could clog the vent. For best results, follow the instructions in the cookbook that came with your pressure cooker.

Table 8   COOKING REQUIREMENTS OF AND YIELDS FROM BEANS AND PEAS *(1 cup dry)*

Bean or pea	Cooking time (in hours)	Minimum water (in cups)	Yield (cups)
Black beans	1½	4	2
Black-eyed peas	1	3	2
Chickpeas (garbanzos)	3	4	4
Great Northern beans	2	3½	2
Kidney beans	1½	3	2
Lentils	1	3	2¼
Lima beans	1½	2	1¼
Navy beans	1½	3	2
Pinto beans	2½	3	2
Soybeans	3 or more	3	2
Split peas	1	3	2¼

SOURCE: Laurel Robertson, Carol Flinders, and Bronwen Godfrey, *Laurel's Kitchen* (New York: Bantam, 1982).

A Glossary of Great Legumes

There are more kinds of beans and peas grown in the world that are suitable for human consumption than I could begin to tell you about. So I'll stick to those that are available in my local markets and hopefully in yours as well. Since most beans are known by more than one name, to reduce confusion I'll try to provide the pseudonyms. Although all beans have basically the same texture, their taste varies (even before you add seasonings) as well as their color, size, and shape. Combining different legumes in soups or salads can result in an infinite variety of dishes. Just be sure to pay attention to differences in cooking times. It is usually best to cook each type of bean separately and then combine the cooked beans. All dry beans should be stored in closed containers (plastic bags are fine) in a cool, dry place. They keep for years but are best used within 6 to 9 months of purchase. The following are among the most popular varieties of beans and peas.

ADZUKIS   You may not have heard of these Japanese favorites (also spelled *adukis*), but chances are you will. They are small red beans with a high-quality protein that, in addition to being eaten as beans, can be processed into a sweetened paste used in everything from soups to pastries. The dry beans are often sold in health food stores.

BLACK BEANS Oval-shaped, small, and black-skinned, these beans are also known as *turtle beans*. They are a staple in their native South America as well as in Central America and Cuba. They are grown in the American South and are most popularly used to make black bean soup, which is puréed, and black beans and rice.

BLACK-EYED PEAS Also called *cowpeas*, these quick-cooking beans and their kissin' cousins *yellow-eyed beans* are small, oval, and creamy white, with either a black or a yellow spot. In the American South, they are the basis for the very popular hoppin' John, a "soul food" made with rice and typically served on New Year's Eve.

BROAD BEANS Pseudonyms for these large beans include *horse beans, English beans, Windsor beans,* and *fava beans.* They range in color from white to brown. They can be purchased fresh, dried, or precooked in cans.

CHICKPEAS Also known in their diverse native tongues as *garbanzos* (Spanish) or *ceci* (Italian), chickpeas are round, tan, and very hard. They are widely used in Mediterranean countries in stews, soups, salads, and spreads. The Middle Eastern dip hummus is based on a paste of cooked chickpeas, and the balls or patties of felafel are made from ground chickpeas. They are commonly sold precooked in cans, and the smart cook will keep a few cans on hand for a protein boost to salads and hors d'oeuvres. They are good enough to eat like candy, if you can afford to be a nibbler.

CRANBERRY BEANS Also known as *Roman beans,* these have reddish streaks on a buff-colored bean, making them very attractive in dishes like salads and succotash.

FLAGEOLETS Green or white, these small, kidney-shaped beans are imported from France, where they are often served with meats and as an ingredient of cassoulet, a stew of meat or game. When it comes to price, flageolets are the Rolls Royce of beans.

KIDNEY BEANS These large beans, so named for their kidney shape and deep red color, are probably the most popular legumes eaten in this country. They are best known in chili, with or without carne (meat), and are also favored in soups and salads. Like chickpeas, smart cooks will keep a few cans on hand for instant high-protein additions to various dishes.

LENTILS If I have a favorite legume, lentils are it. These small, flat seeds that look like tiny buttons come brown or red. They cook quickly without soaking, form a nutritious base for soups, salads (hot or cold), purées, casseroles, or may be simply combined with rice to produce a hearty, high-protein meal.

LIMA BEANS These are sold fresh as well as dried, large as well as small. The small fresh beans, also known as *Fordhooks* or *butter beans,* are often served as a cooked vegetable, plain or mixed with corn in a creamy vegetable dish called succotash. The dried beans are used in soups and casseroles. Large lima beans have a strong taste, and some cooks suggest that they be skinned before use in a soup or purée.

MUNG BEANS You may buy them whole—small, round beans that are usually green, but also yellow, black, or gold—but they are mostly sold as sprouts (you can sprout them yourself [see p. 110]) or as mung-bean threads, an Oriental pasta made from mung-bean flour.

PINTO BEANS AND PINK BEANS These are pink in color and dotted with brown (the pinto bean) or brown-red (the pink bean). (There is also a *small red bean* that has no dots.) Pinto beans and pink beans are smaller than kidney beans though similar in flavor, and the three can be interchanged in most recipes.

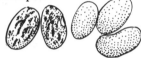

SOYBEANS Small, hard, and tan, these are the world's leading beans because of their high protein content as well as their oil. They can also be transformed into a wide variety of nutritious foods (see pp. 99–102). Most Americans know them best in their least nourishing form: the salty sauce called soy, shoyu, or tamari. Soybeans are sometimes cooked and eaten whole in soups and stews (their very long cooking time discourages many cooks) but are more often consumed as a processed food: flour, bean curd, milk, sauce, and so forth.

SPLIT PEAS Very small and flat on one side, split peas do not need soaking and they cook quickly, like lentils. *Green* split peas are most often eaten as the basis of a hearty soup or thick purée with pork or ham. The *yellow* ones are used in British pease porridge, Swedish pea soup, and a variety of soups that also contain pork products.

WHITE BEANS There are several types: *Great Northern beans, cannelli beans, navy* or *Yankee beans, pea beans* or *pigeon peas,* and *marrow beans.* The smaller navy and pea beans are favored in baked-bean recipes because they hold their shape well. Pea or navy beans are used in pork and beans, navy bean soup, and Boston baked beans. Great Northern beans are popular in cassoulets and in so-called New York baked beans. Cannellini beans are larger, kidney-shaped (they may be called *white kidney beans*), and popular in Italian dishes.

WHOLE PEAS These look like fresh garden peas that have been dried as is. They come in green and yellow, and can be used as a vegetable or as an ingredient in soups and casseroles.

8 ·
SPROUTS: A HOME-GROWN NUTRIENT GARDEN

The sprouts of beans, grains, and seeds (hereafter collectively referred to as seeds), long a nutritious staple in Oriental diets, have in the last decade or so become popular components of Western diets as well. The sprouts of mung beans and alfalfa seeds, at least, are now common items in the produce sections of supermarkets. Sprouts have three major dietary advantages: they are rich in essential nutrients; they are low in calories; and they are inexpensive, especially if you grow your own (see Table 9, p. 111).

Every seed contains the embryo of a future plant and the nutrients needed to nourish its growth. When the seed germinates, it releases these nutrients into the resulting sprout. In the course of sprouting, the seed uses up some of its stored carbohydrate and fat, adds water, and manufacturers some vitamins. Thus, you wind up with a reduced-calorie food that is still rich in protein and may contain even more micronutrients than the original seed. Sprouts are rich in most vitamins and minerals, including vitamin C, and in protein. Sprouts also have dietary fiber, and that along with their high water content means they help to fill you up before you've overconsumed calories. Furthermore, bean sprouts are easier to digest than the bean from whence they came, giving you whole-bean nutrition without the gaseous legacy. But, as with many foods that first became popular with the health food act, sprouts are not the miracle foods they are often touted to be. However, they can be a wholesome addition to your regular diet, included in salads, sandwiches, soups, stir-fries, casseroles, and even chopped up into bread dough or muffin batter for a crunchy, nutritious kick.

Almost any bean, pea, grain, or seed can be sprouted simply at home—you don't need a green thumb or even any soil or sunlight to do it successfully. And you can grow them any time of the year, even when there are 2 feet of snow outside your window. The bean sprouts you find in cans are mung-bean sprouts (look for them in the Oriental foods section of your market). They are usually salted (so rinse and drain them) and can be used if fresh or home-sprouted beans are not available. Mung bean, soybean, and alfalfa sprouts are commonly sold fresh (without added salt) in greengrocers and in the produce sections of supermarkets, as well as in many health food stores. However, it is considerably cheaper to grow your own, and you can obtain a much greater variety of sprouts in your own kitchen than you're likely to find in any market.

Each type of sprout will give you a tiny plant with its own unique flavor and texture. Mung bean and soybean sprouts are mild and crunchy; alfalfa sprouts also are mild but more tender. Wheat-berry sprouts are sweet (an excellent addition to bread dough), whereas cress, radish, and mustard sprouts have a decidedly peppery "bite." Buckwheat sprouts are wonderful in salads, thanks to their attractive shape and delicate, almost nutty flavor. You might alternate them with lentil, barley, and chickpea sprouts for an interesting variety of flavors and shapes.

The small seeds—alfalfa, mustard, radish, millet, and clover—form sprouts with tiny leaves that are excellent in salads. They are rich in vitamins C and K and in many minerals. Sprouts from the grains—barley, oats, rye, and wheat—are rich in vitamin E and protein. They are used in salads and in baking. Dried and ground into a powder, they can be added to flour to enhance its nutritive value. The tender beans like mung and lentil are excellent in salads, soups, and stir-fries; and mung-bean sprouts are rich in vitamins A and C, calcium, phosphorus, and iron. The sprouts of soybeans, chickpeas, and garden peas are the most nourishing of all, rich in vitamins A, B complex, C, and E, and with healthy supplies of calcium, phosphorus, and iron. They are especially good in salads and casseroles.

Most sprouts can be eaten either raw or cooked. However, barley and soybean sprouts and sprouts of the "tough" beans like kidney, lima, navy, pinto, and other hard-shelled beans should be cooked before they're eaten. Sprouts need only a few minutes of cooking at most, and so are usually added near the end of the cooking process. Sprouts of the tough beans are best steamed for about 10 minutes before they are added to recipes.

A WORD OF WARNING: As with all foods, sprouts should be eaten in moderation, since like other vegetables they may contain natural substances that are toxic when consumed in excess. Alfalfa sprouts in particular may be hazardous when overeaten. Dr. M. Rene Malinow, a specialist in cardiovascular diseases at the Oregon Regional Primate Center in Beaverton, was studying the ability of alfalfa sprouts to lower cholesterol levels in the blood. He fed dried alfalfa sprouts to monkeys in amounts that made up to 40 percent of their diet, and he himself consumed them in large quantities. After eating the fresh-weight equivalent of 27 ounces of alfalfa sprouts every day for five months, he became ill with an autoimmune form of anemia. His monkeys, too, got sick, developing symptoms virtually identical to the autoimmune disease systemic lupus erythematosus (SLE or lupus). Dr. Malinow identified a substance in the sprouts that could mistakenly become part of human protein and trigger an immunological attack against the body's own protein tissue. The researcher concluded that the amounts of alfalfa sprouts a person might ordinarily consume should not be harmful, but he does suggest that people with lupus would be wise to avoid eating sprouts altogether.

HOW TO GROW YOUR OWN SPROUTS

In growing your own sprouts, it's important to start with beans or seeds that were intended for human consumption. Don't purchase garden seeds, since these are usually treated with poisonous fungicides. Try your supermarket for dried beans and peas, a health food or natural foods store for sprouting seeds. If no other source can be found, there are mail-order houses that supply beans and seeds for sprouting. They include Walnut Acres, Penns Creek, Pennsylvania 17862, and Diamond K Enterprises, RR1, Box 30, St. Charles, Minnesota 55972.

When deciding how many beans or seeds to sprout, keep in mind that a small amount can expand greatly. Depending upon how large you decide to grow them, the sprouts you end up with may be anywhere from two to ten times the volume of beans or seeds you began with. In general, begin with about ¼ cup of the dry bean or seed (for small seeds start with about 2 tablespoons, and for lentils start with ½ cup), and use a quart-size container to hold them (a 1-quart canning jar or old mayonnaise jar is excellent because of its wide mouth). Small seeds can be sprouted in a tray, such as a rust-proof baking pan. You can also sprout mixtures of seeds that take the same amount of time to grow (for example, alfalfa, millet, radish, and mustard).

Again depending on how big you grow them, sprouts can take from a day or two (for tiny alfalfa sprouts) to a week (for long mung-bean and wheat sprouts). In general, figure on three to five days to obtain sprouts that are a decent size. Sprouts are generally grown in the dark, resulting in a white sprout that lacks chlorophyll. To "green" them, put the sprouting jar in daylight on the last growing day.

Once finished growing, sprouts should be stored in the refrigerator in airtight containers, such as closed plastic bags, along with a damp paper towel or cloth to keep them moist but not wet. You can also store them in the sprouting jar, properly covered. Sprouts are best eaten within two to three days, but most will last a week in the refrigerator. Just be sure they are not sitting in water, or they'll turn sour and rot. You can also store sprouts in the freezer for several months, although when defrosted they will not be crisp. Or they can be dried in a dehydrator or slow oven and ground into flour.

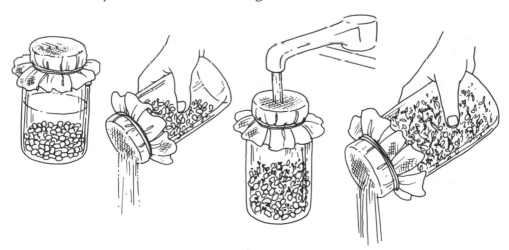

Sprouting at Home

1. Rinse a measured amount of beans or seeds thoroughly in a colander or strainer. Pick out all shriveled, broken, or discolored ones.

2. Place the rinsed beans in a clean glass jar, and, with a string, strong rubberband, or the metal ring of a canning jar secure a stainless-steel or plastic mesh screen or a layer or two of cheesecloth or a nylon stocking to the top of the jar. Add lukewarm water (four times more water than the amount of beans), and let the beans soak, unrefrigerated, overnight or for at least 8 hours in summer, 12 hours in winter. Remove any debris or seeds that may float to the top.

3. Drain the beans thoroughly through the screen by inverting the jar. To maximize drainage, it's a good idea to keep the jar upside down at an angle in a bowl while the sprouts are growing (or, if you drain it well enough yourself, simply turn the jar on its side). Place the jar in a dark place, such as under the kitchen sink.

4. Twice each day rinse the sprouting beans by running cold water over the cheesecloth, swishing the sprouts around, and then draining off the water as in step 3. Four or more rinsings a day are recommended if you are sprouting chickpeas or soybeans.

5. When sprouts are the desired length (grow them to be at least as long as the original bean or seed, and longer for the tougher beans like soybeans), pour them into a bowl and rinse them in water to remove loose hulls. You can skip this step if you wish, since the hulls are nutritious and edible, although less tender than the sprouts themselves. Store the drained sprouts in the refrigerator in an airtight container.

6. If you are sprouting small seeds such as alfalfa, mustard, or barley, you can use a tray lined with moistened cheesecloth. After washing, soaking, and draining the seeds as in steps 1 and 2, spread them over the cheesecloth and cover them with a second layer of moistened cheesecloth. Sprinkle the cheesecloth now and then to keep the seeds moist. On the last day, remove the upper layer of cheesecloth and place the tray in the light if you want the sprouts to green.

SPROUTING: A NUTRIENT BARGAIN

Jeff Breakey, publisher of *The Sproutletter* (P.O. Box 62, Ashland, Oregon 97520), grew 28 different kinds of sprouts and kept track of the costs to produce a pound of each, including the costs of the original seeds. He found, for example, that alfalfa sprouts cost a mere 33.1 cents a pound to grow. That adds up to 10 cups of sprouts at just over 3 cents a cup. The cheapest sprouts were those grown from unhulled buckwheat, rye, and soybeans, each of which cost only 13 cents per pound of sprouts. As can be seen in Table 9, Breakey's experiment dramatically demonstrates the wide range of seeds that can be sprouted into nutritious foods.

Table 9   THE COST OF GROWING SPROUTS

Seed	1 pound sprouts (in cups)	Cost per pound (in cents)
Adzuki bean	4.5	23
Alfalfa	10.2	33
Almond	3.3	170
Barley	3.1	18
Black-eyed pea	3.9	25
Buckwheat (hulled)	6.3	24
Buckwheat (unhulled)	13.4	13
Chinese cabbage	6.7	47
Corn	3.0	15
Fenugreek	6.2	27
Garbanzo (chickpea)	3.1	51
Lentil	4.7	20
Mung bean	6.4	28
Mustard	7.1	29
Oat	2.9	33
Pea	3.5	29
Peanut	3.0	76
Pinto bean	3.4	25
Popcorn	3.2	27
Pumpkin	3.0	203
Radish	7.4	51
Red clover	9.1	52
Rye	3.6	13
Sesame	3.6	48
Soybean	3.4	13
Sunflower (hulled)	3.9	56
Sunflower (unhulled)	12.3	24
Wheat	3.4	13

9 ·
NUTS AND SEEDS:
PROTEIN AT A PRICE

"Nuts to you" is not exactly a kind remark, but offered in a nutritional context, it could be taken as a wholesome gift. Nuts and seeds are on a par with dried beans and peas as having more protein than any other vegetable foods (only soybeans have more). And when nuts and seeds are combined with beans or grains, the result can be a nutritionally complete protein as good as that from any animal source. But, unlike grains and beans, nuts and seeds provide protein at a high-calorie price because they are very high in fat, albeit unsaturated fat that does not harm blood vessels.

The high-energy value of nuts, seeds, and the spreads made from them makes them ideal foods for filling the bellies of growing children and the bottomless pits of adolescents. So, mothers, you can stop fretting about your youngster who will eat only peanut-butter and jelly sandwiches for lunch. Save for the lack of variety, the nutritional value is just fine, providing protein, vitamins, and minerals besides the calories that most children need.

But even if you must be careful about your caloric intake, nuts and seeds can be valuable assets in your diet when eaten in moderation. In addition to balancing the protein in other vegetable foods, they can be portable nourishing snacks and emergency rations that need no refrigeration. Nuts (and raisins) are traditional high-energy foods taken along on hikes, camping trips, and canoe trips. When I travel on business, a peanut-butter sandwich on whole-wheat pita is my constant companion, ready to sustain me when I'm caught with no time for a regular meal or when a plane is delayed or the airline dishes up something inedible. I can eat a peanut-butter sandwich while driving, walking, or sitting on a train. And it will remain fresh in my briefcase for at least two days.

WHAT'S A NUT?

Nuts are the dried fruits of trees. Most are enclosed in hard shells. Strictly speaking, peanuts are legumes, not nuts. They are discussed in this chapter rather than with their true botanical relatives, the beans and peas, because people treat them like nuts and they are more like nuts than beans in their nutrient composition. (Peanuts grow underground on plants, not trees, and are called "groundnuts" in many cultures.) Also, strictly speaking, some of the foods we call nuts, such as Brazil nuts and cashews, are really seeds found inside fruits. And the coconut is a drupe, a fruit with a hard kernel, like the cherry or plum. Nuts were an important part of the human diet long before the advent of agriculture.

Seeds were as well. Seeds—sunflower, sesame, pumpkin, squash, and the like —come from the fruits of plants and, like grains, contain the embryo and food supply for creating the next generation. Most seeds have shells or hulls that are softer than nuts. In some cases, as with pumpkin and sesame seeds, the shells or hulls can be eaten, providing roughage as well as some nutrients.

Save for the spread made from peanuts, the traditional dietary role of nuts and seeds in America has been as snack foods or as an ingredient in snacks and desserts, such as candy, cookies, and cakes. Even when eaten "plain," more often than not their nutritional value is undermined by the addition of oils, salt, and even sugar. (On a recent flight, I was offered a packet of oil-roasted peanuts coated with honey and salt. When I asked the flight attendant if she had any plain, unadulterated peanuts, she confessed, "I don't like these either, but they're very popular with most passengers.")

It's time to revise the image and the role of nuts and seeds in the American diet. They are too good to be relegated to nibbles at cocktail parties, movies, and ball games. Used with respect for their caloric content, they can do much to add texture, variety, and nutritional balance to many a meal.

NUTRIENTS IN NUTS AND SEEDS

The *protein* content of most nuts and seeds ranges from 10 percent to 25 percent by weight. But, when considered as a percentage of calories, the apparent nutritional value is somewhat lower. Peanuts, for example, are 26 percent protein and 48 percent fat by weight. When the protein content is figured as a percentage of total calories, the protein value of peanuts drops to 18 percent. Similarly, walnuts are 15 percent protein and 64 percent fat by weight. Calculated as a percentage of calories, the protein content drops to 9 percent. Chestnuts, on the other hand, are considerably lower in fat and relatively high in carbohydrates, which provide fewer calories than fat. Thus, the chestnut by weight has only 3 percent protein and 1.5 percent fat, but as a percentage of calories, the protein value rises to 6 percent.

The story for seeds is similar. Sunflower seeds, with 24 percent protein and 47 percent fat by weight, are 17 percent protein as a percentage of total calories. Sesame seeds, 18 percent protein and 49 percent fat by weight, become 13 percent protein from a caloric perspective.

Still, the protein value of nuts and seeds remains high. The body can actually make better use of the protein in nuts and seeds than the protein in most beans because nuts and seeds have a better balance of essential amino acids. And when nuts or seeds are combined with other protein-containing plant foods, such as the bread in a peanut-butter sandwich, the result is complete protein comparable to that in a steak. A sandwich made from 2 tablespoons of peanut butter provides 20 percent of the recommended daily allowance for protein for an adult.

As for the *fats* in nuts and seeds, these are mostly unsaturated fats—either polyunsaturates or monounsaturates, which help to lower blood cholesterol levels. Of course, as plant foods, nuts and seeds contain no cholesterol. Peanuts contain more monounsaturates than other nuts, which have mostly polyunsaturated fats. An exception is *coconut.* Coconut is very high in saturated fats (and calories)—more so than even red meat—and in experimental animals it has a more damaging effect on blood vessels than butter or lard. Coconut oil (really fat, since it is hard at room temperature) is widely used in processed foods and is one of the reasons why it is usually healthier to prepare foods from scratch. From a health perspective, coconut is definitely a "sometime" food to be used in small quantities as a flavoring or garnish. In general, the higher the oil content of a nut and the higher the percentage of polyunsaturates, the quicker the nut will turn rancid during storage. As already mentioned, chestnuts are much lower in fat than other nuts, and their high carbohydrate content makes them suitable for use as a vegetable rather than merely as a garnish or complement to the protein in other foods.

Nuts and seeds are also good sources of *dietary fiber,* especially when eaten with their skins or hulls, as well as such important *vitamins* and *minerals* as thiamin, riboflavin, vitamin E, calcium, phosphorus, and potassium. Seeds are rich in iron, potassium, and phosphorus. An ounce of sesame seeds contains about 4 milligrams of iron, nearly three times the iron content of beef liver. And pumpkin, squash, and sunflower seeds have even more iron than sesame seeds. Including such high sources of iron in your diet is especially important if you're going to be eating less red meat, traditionally a main source of iron in the American diet. And nuts and seeds are naturally low in sodium, a nutritional advantage that is often eradicated by a heavy-handed salter in the processing plant.

But do keep in mind the *calories.* An ounce of walnuts (about 7 large nuts) has 185 calories, the amount in a 3-ounce well-done burger. An ounce of cashews (14 large nuts or 18 medium-sized ones) has 159 calories, whereas an ounce of peanuts (10 jumbo nuts) has 105 calories. And seeds are no better: an ounce of sunflower seeds supplies 159 calories, and an ounce of sesame seeds has 164 calories.

BUYING AND STORING NUTS

Nuts are sold in many different forms: raw or roasted in the shell or unshelled; whole, halved, chopped, slivered, or ground; dry-roasted or oil-roasted; with skins or without; unflavored or salted, smoked, sugared, or spiced; loose or packaged in bags, cans, or jars.

Nuts should be purchased in a store where the turnover of merchandise is high—your best assurance that what you get won't be stale or rancid. If you're buying nuts as a snack food, nuts in their shells will help to keep your consumption moderate. They also cost less than shelled nuts, even after figuring what you pay for the weight of the shells. Except for peanuts, look for nuts that don't rattle in their shells—a sign of freshness. The shells should not have cracks or holes in them or signs of mold. Shelled nuts that are vacuum-packed in cans or jars generally keep better than nuts packaged in cellophane bags. Buy only the amount you can expect to use up in a couple of months.

Once you get them home, nuts can be stored in a cool, dry place for several months. They keep better in the refrigerator in a tightly tied plastic bag or in a jar with a tight-fitting lid. When frozen (again, in a tightly closed container), nuts will keep for a year or longer, depending on the type of nut.

The closer to its original form, the longer a nut will keep. Thus, nuts in the shells last longer than those that are shelled; nuts in their skins outlive those that are skinned; and nuts that are whole last longer than chopped nuts. It is best to chop or grind nuts just before you plan to use them.

As with nuts, seeds can be bought either with or without shells, with or without salt, fresh or dried, raw or toasted, and whole or ground into a paste or flour. Again, if you're planning to snack on them, buy them in their shells so you can't easily "mainline" them. If you carve up a pumpkin in the fall or cook a winter squash, save the seeds and toast them for a snack that doubles your money's worth (place seeds on a cookie sheet and bake them for 20 minutes in an oven preheated to 325 degrees). And if you have room against your house or fence to plant a few sunflowers, you'll have a thing of beauty to admire in late summer and a nourishing, delicious treat to harvest in the fall. (But don't plant the double-centered type; the seeds of this plant are more for show than for eating.) True to their name, they turn their lovely large heads toward the sun. Sunflowers were first cultivated for their seeds by American Indians, and they remain an extremely popular crop in the Soviet Union, where sunflower seeds are the national snack. You can also make or buy sunflower butter, a spread made from ground seeds. Its protein is comparable to that in peanut butter, but it has more fat; it also has better spreadability and a unique flavor and color. Sesame seeds are more nutritious with their hulls intact (the package will say "unhulled"); either way, they can be eaten or used in cooking raw or toasted. They, too, can be purchased as a paste or spread, better known as tahini in Middle Eastern circles. Tahini is an ingredient in such appetizers as hummus and baba ghanoush, as well as in salad dressings (see recipes on pp. 292, 293, 645). The Chinese also use sesame-seed paste (a different flavor entirely from the Middle Eastern version and not interchangeable with it in recipes). It is perhaps best known in cold sesame noodles (see the recipe on p. 302).

MERE PEANUTS, YOU SAY?

For more than 2,000 years, peanuts have been grown in South America, where early Spanish and Portuguese explorers found them and carried them back to the Old World. However, fossil evidence indicates that the peanut is far more ancient than that. A 100,000-year-old fossilized peanut was found in China, so it's hard to say on which side of the world the peanut first emerged. It is enough to know that today the peanut is a very popular food in widely diverse cultures: from China (witness spicy chicken with peanuts) and Indonesia to North Africa, South America, and North America, where, during the Civil War, peanuts were an important source of energy and nutrition for the Confederate soldiers.

Peanuts have been a favorite American snack since 1870, and peanut butter, practically synonymous with food for modern American children, was developed by a St. Louis physician in 1890 and introduced as a health food at the World's Fair in St. Louis in 1904. Amazingly, though, peanut butter was *not* among the 300 uses found for the peanut plant by George Washington Carver, the turn-of-the-century agricultural chemist and educator who tried to make peanuts a substitute crop for southern farmers whose cotton had succumbed to the boll weevil.

PEANUT PRODUCTS. Americans consume more than 4 million pounds of peanuts a day, 52 percent in the form of peanut butter, 23 percent as salted peanuts, and 21 percent in candies. That adds up to 6 pounds of peanuts per person a year. Unfortunately, the way most people eat peanuts leaves something to be desired nutritionally. Even the *peanut butter* most people eat undermines the peanut's nutrition virtues. Most American peanut butter—whether smooth or chunky—is sugared, salted, and laced with hydrogenated (saturated) vegetable oil. By law, peanut butter must contain at least 90 percent peanuts, and no artificial flavors, artificial sweeteners, color additives, vitamins, or chemical preservatives can be added. But salt, sugar, honey, and corn syrup are fair game. So is hydrogenated oil, used in most commercial peanut butter to produce a more uniform product that doesn't separate during storage. And if the product is called "peanut spread," all bets are off, since there is no legal definition of its contents.

However, many supermarkets now carry "natural" peanut butter—that is, 100-percent ground peanuts. Sometimes it's called "old-fashioned" peanut butter, a reference to the days before hydrogenation and homogenization kept the oil from separating out. But even natural peanut butter may be salted or sugared, so check the label before you buy. If you cannot find it in your supermarket, try a health food store, or buy peanuts (roasted and skinned) and grind your own in a blender or food processor. The addition of 1 tablespoon of oil for each ½ pound of peanuts may make the blending easier. As the large pieces rise to the top, turn off the machine and push them down. Then blend some more. If you store natural peanut butter in the refrigerator, it will greatly delay separation of the oil. If you prefer room-temperature butter (it spreads much more easily), just stir in any oil that has risen to the top before you use it. Personally, I keep my fresh-ground peanut butter in the pantry and find that it gets used up long before much of the oil has had a chance to separate.

If you're wondering how you will ever get your kids (or yourself) to eat the natural stuff after having become accustomed to sugared and salted peanut butter, I'll tell you how I did it. Start by mixing the commercially flavored butter with the natural kind in a ratio of 2 to 1. Chances are no one will even notice the change. Over the course of the next jar or two, gradually increase the proportion of natural butter until you're at about 3 times more natural than flavored. Then abandon the flavored stuff altogether.

Peanut butter is an appealing, high-protein spread that can be eaten at breakfast, at lunch, or for a midday or bedtime snack. Just keep in mind the calories: 190 in the 2 tablespoons that would be the least you'd be likely to put on a sandwich. For the sake of comparison, 2 slices of bologna have about 170 calories; 2 slices of American cheese, 210 calories; 2 slices of boiled ham, 130 calories; and ½ cup of tuna salad, 175 calories.

As a cooking ingredient, peanut butter can be a nutritious addition to cookie recipes as well as the basis of cake icing. Peanut butter is also good in sauces for chicken, pasta, meat, and can even be used to make soup (see, for example, recipes on pp. 319, 337, and 359).

Peanuts can also be eaten whole or in halves as snack nuts or as ingredients in cooking and baking. Here, your best nutritional buys are *roasted peanuts in their shells, dry-roasted unsalted peanuts,* or *shelled raw peanuts.* Be sure the unshelled peanuts have not been salt-treated. Roasting in oil, the usual method used for shelled cocktail peanuts, only adds fat to an already fatty snack. However, raw peanuts should not be eaten unless they are first roasted or cooked because they contain an antinutrient that can interfere with the body's ability to use essential nutrients. This substance will be destroyed if, in preparing the food, the peanuts are cooked for at least a few minutes at a high temperature. If you're snacking on roasted peanuts, eat the outer red skin for increased fiber and minerals.

As you can see from Table 10, despite the high fat content of peanuts, they more than hold their own when measured against other popular nibble foods. For the number of calories, you get considerably more protein when you snack on peanuts than on the other choices listed, except for unbuttered popcorn.

Table 10	HOW SNACK PEANUTS STACK UP				
Snack (1 ounce)	*Protein (g.)*	*Fat (g.)*	*Carbohydrates (g.)*	*Sodium (mg.)*	*Calories*
Salted peanuts	7	15	5	220 or more	170
Dry-roasted peanuts without salt	7	15	5	Less than 10	160
Popcorn (1 cup, about ⅓ ounce)					
with oil and salt	1	2	5	175	41
plain	1	0	5	Trace	23
Corn puffs (cheese-flavored)	2	10	15	260	160
Corn chips	2	10	16	180	160
Potato chips	2	10	14	260	150
Pretzels	3	1	22	475	110

Some Nuts and Seeds Worth Knowing

There are many more edible nuts and seeds than are described here. Rather than overwhelm you with an exhaustive list, I chose those that you are most likely to encounter as snacks or recipe ingredients.

ALMONDS For snacking and cooking, you'll find only the sweet version of this versatile nut (bitter almonds are used to make almond-flavored extract). Almonds are oval, small, and flat, and their tan shell is relatively easy to crack. They are also easily blanched (stripped of their outer brown skin): cover the nuts with boiling water for 3 to 5 minutes, then drain and peel off the skins with your fingers. Almonds can be used whole (for example, added to stir-fried Oriental dishes), sliced or slivered (such as in trout amandine), chopped (into cookies and breads), or ground into a paste (for marzipan, macaroons, and pastry). One ounce of shelled almonds—about 22 nuts—has 170 calories.

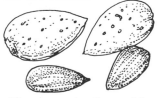

BRAZIL NUTS These nuts (really seeds) are chalk-white and housed in very hard dark-brown, three-sided shells. They are oily and turn rancid faster than most nuts. They are most commonly found in snack nut mixtures. One ounce of shelled nuts—6 to 8 kernels—has 185 calories.

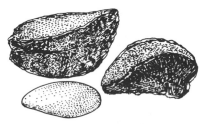

CASHEWS Also seeds, cashews are actually toxic because the raw nuts contain prussic acid. They are only sold shelled since their shells con-

tain a poison, and they are always processed to get rid of the prussic acid. You can buy them "raw" (but treated) or roasted, with or without salt. They are best used in quick-cooking dishes rather than in baking because they soften too much under prolonged heating. They are among the more expensive nuts that snackers covet. One ounce of cashews—14 large or 18 medium nuts—has 159 calories.

CHESTNUTS "Roasting on an open fire" is no doubt how most Americans have heard of chestnuts, though few have ever eaten them that way. Chestnuts are a buff-colored shriveled-looking nutmeat housed in a soft brown shell. Unlike most other nuts and seeds, they are low in fat and high in starch, and thus much lower in calories than other nuts. This greatly enhances their kitchen utility, since they can be eaten puréed as a vegetable, used as stuffing for fowl, or ground into a flour for making puddings, sauces, and cakes. One cup (nearly 6 ounces) of shelled chestnuts has 310 calories, and an ounce has about 54 calories.

COCONUTS Botanically, coconuts are drupes, not nuts. Large and hard and filled with a sweet "milk" (a misnomer for coconut water), they grow on palm trees and are encased in a fibrous husk. You find them fresh year round stripped of the husk but still in their hard brown shell. Inside the shell, which requires a hammer or other blunt object to crack it, is moist white meat covered with a brown skin. The white meat can be eaten fresh or dried. It can be grated or squeezed to yield a fatty liquid called coconut cream. The fat in coconut is highly saturated and very damaging to blood vessels, so keep your consumption low. When buying a whole coconut, shake it and choose one in which you can hear the water sloshing about. Uncracked, it will keep a few months. Shredded fresh coconut should be stored in the refrigerator and used within several days; you can also freeze it, but expect some loss of texture. Dried shredded coconut is a popular ingredient in granolas (see the recipe on p. 508) and nut-and-fruit snack mixtures, as well as in baked goods and puddings (see the recipe on p. 634). About 1½ ounces of fresh coconut meat— a piece $2 \times 2 \times \frac{1}{2}$ inch—has 156 calories; 1 ounce of dried coconut has 187; 1 cup of coconut cream (the liquid squeezed from grated coconut) has 802 calories; 1 cup of coconut milk (a combination of coconut cream and coconut water) has 605 calories; and 1 cup of coconut water, which is rich in potassium, has 53 calories.

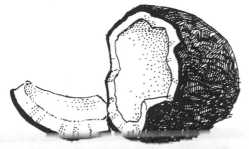

FILBERTS, AKA HAZELNUTS These are the same nuts, differing only in size (hazelnuts are smaller). They are excellent in baking. One ounce of filberts—about 20 nuts—has 180 calories.

GINKGO NUTS These are probably not familiar to you. Oriental in origin, they grow on female ginkgo trees, now a popular street and park tree in the United States. In fall, you may see people of Asian descent gathering ginkgo nuts from under such trees, which are not hard to find: the putrid odor from the fruit surrounding the nuts gives them away. *Be sure to wear gloves* if you decide to collect ginkgo nuts since the flesh contains a serious irritant, and keep the gloves on until you've thoroughly removed the odoriferous outer flesh. You can also buy ready-to-use canned ginkgo nuts (they may be called *ginan*) in Oriental markets and include them in stir-fries or soups. The nut is sweet, white, and crisp. Calorie information is not available.

MACADAMIA NUTS Really seeds that were brought here from Australia, these small tan nuts are now grown in Hawaii and California. They are *very* expensive, high in fat, low in protein. Unless you love a challenge, it's best to buy them shelled since the shells are very hard to crack. They are used primarily as a snack food. One ounce—about 15 halves—has 200 calories.

PEANUTS Since peanuts are discussed at length in the text (see pp. 115–117), they will get only passing reference here. Botanically, they are not nuts or seeds but legumes, relatives of beans and peas. The two most popular varieties are *Virginia* peanuts—large and oval—and *Spanish* peanuts— small and round. One ounce of roasted peanuts —about 10 jumbo Virginia peanuts—has 105 calories.

PECANS As a product of the American South, pecans have achieved a well-deserved national reputation among bakers (pecan pie, coffee cake, cookies) and snackers. The soft two-lobed nut is encased in an oblong brown shell. You can buy pecans with or without shells, whole, halved, or chopped. They are high in fat, turn rancid quickly, and so are best stored in the freezer for periods beyond six months. One ounce of shelled nuts—about 10 nuts (20 halves)—has 195 calories.

PINE NUTS These are also known as *pignoli* (in cooking), *pignolias,* and *Indian nuts.* Their name is derived from the fact that they come from pine cones. They vary in size, from about ⅓ inch to 2 inches, and in shape, from elongated to round. The pine nuts you're most likely to encounter resemble orzo pasta and are sold shelled; the nuts called Indian nuts are rounder and are usually sold in their shells. Both are very expensive—$8 to $9 a pound in most places. Fortunately, only small quantities are needed for most recipes. Pine nuts are the best nut to use in making the basil-flavored sauce pesto, a favorite on pasta and a good seasoning for meats, poultry, soups, and vegetables (see recipes on pp. 392 and 528). Pine nuts are also used in a number of Middle Eastern dishes. They are soft nuts that turn rancid easily, so store them in the freezer. One ounce of pine nuts contains 156 calories.

PISTACHIO NUTS A Middle Eastern import that is now grown in California, the small, round pistachio nut has green flesh and a beige shell that is often treated with a red vegetable dye. The white pistachio nuts have been blanched. They come with or without salt, and their hard shells are usually partly opened. These nuts have a very distinct flavor and are popular for making ice cream and pâtés. One ounce of pistachio nuts has about 168 calories.

PUMPKIN AND SQUASH SEEDS These can be eaten raw or toasted, shell and all. You can buy them in or out of their shells, or gather them from your own pumpkin or squash. Store them in the refrigerator, or freeze them for longer storage. One ounce of seeds has about 156 calories.

SESAME SEEDS Tiny, oval, and off-white, these prized seeds are also known by their African name, benne. They are sold with or without their brownish-gray hull (they are more nutritious if unhulled), and the seeds can be used as is or toasted. They are excellent toppings for breads and rolls, salads, and stir-fries (see, for example, recipes on pp. 394, 538, and 578). When ground into a paste, they are used for sauces and spreads. They are also the basis for that favorite high-calorie candy, halvah. Sesame seeds contain up to 55 percent oil by weight. One tablespoon (⅓ ounce) provides 55 calories.

SUNFLOWER SEEDS These seeds are best known in this country as bird food, but they are excellent nourishment for people as well. Like pumpkin seeds, these can be eaten raw, toasted, or cooked, but they should be shelled. The shell is hard and black, enclosing a small, elongated tan seed. Sunflower seeds are a popular ingredient in granola and are wonderful in home-made breads (see the recipe on p. 576), but most of the national crop is used to make sunflower seed oil, a highly unsaturated cooking and salad oil. The seeds are best stored in the refrigerator. One ounce of hulled seeds has about 159 calories.

WALNUTS The most popular type of walnut consumed is the so-called English or Persian walnut, an off-white, two-lobed nutmeat with a tan skin enclosed in a tan shell. Though a native of the Old World, most walnuts are now grown in California. They can be eaten raw or used in cooking and baking. I keep a bag of shelled walnuts in the freezer, chopping them as needed, for making breads, muffins, and other dishes (see, for example, recipes on pp. 591 and 602). One ounce of shelled walnuts—about 7 nuts—has 185 calories.

WATER CHESTNUTS These are fruits of a water plant, and, unlike nuts, they are low in fat and very low in calories (they contain mostly water and starch). They are crunchy favorites in Oriental dishes of all kinds and can be eaten raw or cooked. They come in cans with their brown skin already peeled, and, if you're lucky, you may be able to buy them fresh in an Oriental market, usually in the spring. The flavor of fresh water chestnuts is extraordinary—sweeter than the canned and in need of no added seasoning. An ounce of water chestnuts provides about 17 calories.

10 ·
VEGETABLES AND FRUITS: LOW-CALORIE FEASTS

"Eat your vegetables!" Chances are you heard those words a million times before you left your teen years. Of course, you might have been one of those kids who actually *liked* vegetables. But if you were like most children, vegetables were the last food on the plate you ate, and, more often than not, you waited until you were too full to eat all of them. (One of my aunts used to bribe her carnivorous young son by refusing to give him any meat until he had eaten all his vegetables.)

Why is it that so many parents are so insistent on getting vegetables into their children? Because vegetables are nutritional dynamite: storehouses of vitamins and minerals and dietary fiber (it may have been called roughage in your house), yet low in calories. Most are also cheap compared to meats and give you something to chew and fill up on without destroying the household budget. The same is true of fruits, most of which are sweet storehouses of nutrients at a caloric and dollar cost much below the low-nutrient desserts they compete with. To my mind, no gooey pastry, sugary pie, or other dessert confection has ever been devised that approaches the soul-satisfying, taste-bud–stimulating delectability of a perfectly ripe peach, pear, pineapple, melon, or mango, not to mention a crisp apple, juicy orange, soothing banana, or sugar-sweet grape. And to think, you can enjoy all that savory goodness without damaging your figure or blood vessels. You even get a built-in thirst quencher, since most fruits are 80 percent to 95 percent water, which helps to fill you up before you overstuff yourself on calories.

When families lived on or near farms earlier in the century, consumption of fruits and vegetables year round was very high: fresh in season, home-canned the rest of the year. Modern rural families—and many urban and suburban gardeners—do the same, except now most home-preserved fruits and vegetables are frozen rather than canned.

Still today, even those who live in cities and who have no more soil than a flowerpot will hold have better access throughout the year to a wider variety of fruits and vegetables than did our farming forebears. Thanks to modern methods of refrigeration and transportation, fresh foods can be nationally distributed at relatively low cost and fast enough to minimize the loss of nutrients between field and market. Whether you live in Maine, Minnesota, or Montana, you should be able to get fresh fruits and vegetables from California, Florida, Hawaii, Mexico, and Central and South America all year. Failing that, your supermarket will carry an extensive line of canned and frozen produce. Of course, the smaller the town, the less fresh produce you can expect to find off-season since the high perishability of fresh produce demands a high turnover and steady consumer demand. However, nearly all markets stock year round such produce as bananas, oranges, apples, potatoes, onions, lettuce, celery, carrots, and those cardboardlike things we now call tomatoes. It stands to reason, though, that the more fresh produce Americans buy, the more stores will carry. You can help start a "Produce Power" movement in your town by mobilizing shoppers to start demanding—and buying—more fresh foods.

Preliminary figures from the U.S. Department of Agriculture indicate that Americans are catching on to the glories of fresh vegetables. Per-capita consumption of fresh vegetables has been rising slowly but steadily in recent years, from about 96 pounds per person in 1970 to 105 pounds in 1981 to 148 pounds in 1983. Today we are eating more fresh vegetables than we have at any time in the last 30 years, when processed vegetables first took the lead. The greatest increase has occurred in consumption of lettuce, which cannot be processed. Of course, consumption of processed vegetables has also increased, but (excluding potatoes) as many fresh as processed vegetables are being consumed and total vegetable consumption is now higher than it has ever been since the Department of Agriculture began keeping records. The recent trend to include salad bars in fast-food restaurants may push the fresh-vegetable market to new heights before this decade is out.

The consumption patterns for fruit have been similar. Total consumption is up to more than 143 pounds per person each year. But the most dramatic rise has occurred in processed fruits, especially processed citrus fruits (thanks to the presqueezed-orange-juice industry). After a steady downhill trend for 30 years, in 1970 consumption of fresh fruit began a gradual upward climb. By 1983, it had reached 92 pounds per person, up from a low of 77 pounds in 1970.

NUTRIENTS IN FRUITS AND VEGETABLES

Fruits and vegetables have what is called in the nutritional trade a high "nutrient density"—that is, for the number of calories they supply, most contain a disproportionately large amount of essential vitamins and minerals. In other words, they help greatly to make the calories you consume count toward good nutrition by providing more than their caloric share of the nutrients you need. It is a great mystery of American nutritional habits that as we eat more and more of the vitamin- and mineral-packed vegetables and fruits, we are also taking more vitamin and mineral supplements. Yet anyone who eats at least four servings a day of fruits and vegetables (easy to do if you have juice or fruit in the morning, salad and a vegetable at lunch or supper, and a piece of fruit for a snack or dessert) is probably getting more than the recommended daily amount of several important vitamins, especially vitamins A and C, as well as minerals like potassium and phosphorus. Many fruits and vegetables also contain significant amounts of calcium, iron, magnesium, and B vitamins, and nearly all are good sources of fiber. Like whole grains and beans, they are natural laxatives, having the added virtue of providing much of the water needed to keep the bowels in good working order. By now, it should not surprise you to learn that a number of vegetables, such as potatoes and broccoli, also contain some protein, which in the course of a day can make a small but significant contribution to your total protein consumption.

If you are interested in good nutrition as well as great food, you should consume at least four servings a day of vegetables and fruits. A serving would be any of the following: ½ cup of cut-up vegetables or fruits; ½ medium-sized grapefruit or melon; 1 orange; 1 medium potato; 1 bowl of salad; 1 wedge of lettuce. Mind you, though, four is the *minimum* number of recommended daily servings. A really well-constructed, wholesome, low-calorie, high-carbohydrate, high-fiber diet will go beyond the minimum. Besides, fruits and vegetables are too delicious to limit to a mere four servings a day. However many vegetables and fruits you eat each day, be sure to include these important sources of *vitamins* among your selections:

- One good *vitamin C* source, like an orange or grapefruit (or the juice from them), a sweet pepper, two tomatoes, a serving of Brussels sprouts or cauliflower, or such dark-green vegetables as kale, broccoli, watercress, collards, or turnip greens. Strawberries, melons, pineapple, cabbage, spinach, Swiss chard, asparagus, and squashes contain fair amounts of vitamin C, and eating two or more servings of these a day could meet the requirement for this vitamin. Vitamin C is soluble in water and readily destroyed by prolonged cooking or high temperatures, so it is best to eat at least one good vitamin-C source fresh and the others minimally cooked. However, if properly refrigerated, prepared orange juice suffers no significant loss of vitamin C even after several days.
- One dark-green or deep-yellow fruit or vegetable, which provides *vitamin A.* These would include carrots, beets, broccoli, winter squash or pumpkin, dark-green leafy vegetables (for example, spinach, watercress, kale, collards, turnip and mustard greens, or Swiss chard), asparagus, tomatoes, yellow corn, cantaloupe, blueberries, pink grapefruit, oranges and tangerines, mangoes, nectarines, peaches, papaya, and plums. Since vitamin A is not a water-soluble vitamin, it is not lost when these vegetables and fruits are cooked or processed.

As for *minerals,* you can obtain significant amounts of some important ones in the following fruits and vegetables. Where a food is listed as "raw," you will get the same nutritive value if you cook 3½ ounces of the raw food. (This, however, will usually come out to a larger serving than 3½ ounces since moisture is likely to be added in the cooking process.) Not included are foods like dried apples that contain the stated amounts of nutrients in a 3½-ounce serving but are not likely to be consumed in so large a serving.

- *Calcium:* Asparagus, beet greens, bok choy (spoon cabbage, an Oriental vegetable now popular here), broccoli (raw), cauliflower, collards, dandelion greens, curly endive (chicory) and escarole, dried figs, kale, kohlrabi, leaf and romaine lettuce, lima beans (fresh or dried), mustard greens, okra, parsley, rhubarb, spinach, turnip greens, and watercress. Each of these contains about 100 or more milligrams of calcium in a 3½-ounce serving.
- *Potassium:* Apricots, avocados, bananas, beets and beet greens, broccoli, Brussels sprouts, raw cabbage, carrots, cauliflower, celery, Swiss chard, chicory, collards, corn kernels, garden cress, dandelion greens, eggplant, curly endive and escarole, guavas, kale, kohlrabi, kumquats (raw), leaf and romaine lettuce, lima beans (fresh or dried), raw mushrooms, melons (except watermelon), mustard greens, onions, oranges, orange juice, papaya, parsley, parsnips, raw peaches, raw green peppers, plantain, Damson plums, pomegranate, potatoes, pumpkin, red radishes, black raspberries, rhubarb, salsify, spinach, raw summer squash, winter squash, sweet potatoes, tomatoes, turnip greens, watercress, and yams. Each of these contains about 200 or more milligrams of potassium in a 3½-ounce serving.
- *Iron:* Beet greens, Swiss chard, dandelion greens, dates, Jerusalem artichokes (raw), Boston and bibb lettuce, lima beans (fresh or dried), mustard greens, parsley, green peas, raisins, scallion tops, and spinach. Each of these contains about 2 or more milligrams of iron in a 3½-ounce serving.

When it comes to *dietary fiber,* these are especially rich in fiber when consumed in normal amounts: apples, beets, berries, broccoli, cabbage, carrots, cauliflower, corn, cranberries, dates, eggplant, figs, grapes, kale, lettuce, mangoes, okra, onions, peppers, prunes, raisins, rhubarb, spinach, and sprouts.

Of course, the above lists contain just the nutrient highlights in fruits and vegetables. Many others nutrients are provided in significant amounts by the various fruits and vegetables. (See pp. 133–163 for further details.)

MAXIMIZING THE NUTRIENTS YOU CONSUME

Regardless of how rich in nutrients a fruit or vegetable may be when first picked, those that reach your palate can be a far nutritional cry from the original. How many of the nutrients originally in fruits and vegetables you actually get to consume is determined by a number of factors: when the fruits and vegetables were picked, how and how long they have been stored, when and how they were prepared for cooking, how they are cooked, and how they are held after cooking. Improperly handled, a high-nutrient vegetable can wind up having the nutrient content of a dishrag. On the other hand, eating foods raw is no guarantee that they will have the most nutrients possible. The nutrients in some vegetables, such as carrots, become more available to the body *after* cooking. Because of the time of picking, length of storage, and method of home preparation, some fresh foods have fewer nutrients than their frozen counterparts. The following tips should help you get your nutritional money's worth from the fruits and vegetables you buy.

HOW TO BUY. Fresh and frozen fruits and vegetables have more nutrients than the same foods in a can. Canning requires high temperatures and liquid that destroys or leaches out some vital nutrients, especially vitamin C. Canned foods may retain only half or less of the nutrients originally in the food, and more is lost during storage in the cans. Besides, most canned vegetables and fruits are nowhere near as good as the fresh originals. Almost by definition, canning overcooks nearly all vegetables. What comes out of the can often requires little or no chewing! Some vegetables, like broccoli, are not canned because they cannot structurally survive the temperatures and cooking times needed for safe canning. Others that do retain some structure lose all texture and taste.

To my mind, canned asparagus, for example, is not even the same vegetable as fresh asparagus properly steamed and dished up *al dente*—a delicacy without butter or salt. My sons, having been raised mainly on fresh vegetables and some frozen ones off-season, refuse to eat the things called vegetables that are served in the school cafeteria. They object not only to the mushy texture of these foods but to the fact that "they all taste the same."

Furthermore, most canned vegetables are heavily salted, giving a sameness to the flavor whether you open a can of green beans or carrots. The recent push for reducing sodium intake has prompted several major producers to market a line of low-sodium canned vegetables. However, in most markets they cost more than the ones to which salt has been added, and the texture problem remains, salt or not.

As for canned fruits, most come packed in a sugary syrup. When I was a child, the syrups were so sweet (the producers call it "heavy") that the fruit within was almost like candy. The addition of all that sugar adds hundreds of empty calories to a can, diluting the natural nutrient density of the fruit within. In recent years, thanks to consumer concern about excessive sugar and calorie intake, a lot of canned fruits are packed in "light" (i.e., less sweet) syrup or are even water- or juice-packed, the nutritionally preferable choice. But, as with vegetables, the texture of the fruit is greatly modified by the cooking needed to can safely.

If you can't easily get fresh fruits and vegetables in the variety you'd like year round, frozen versions are nutritionally and usually gastronomically preferable to canned. Frozen vegetables need only be blanched (dipped in boiling water for a minute or 2) before packaging, so their texture and flavor remain closer to the original. They are also packaged with little or no added salt. You can steam them for a few minutes or add them directly to your recipe, thereby preserving most of the nutrients. If you can afford the added cost, boil-in-the-bag frozen vegetables are preferred for their nutrient content. When my children were infants and learning to eat finger foods, I used to steam frozen mixed vegetables for 2 minutes and then spread them on their feeding tables to be eaten as snacks. In those days even lima beans and green peas went down with relish!

When buying frozen vegetables, avoid those packaged in rich sauces. The sauces are usually high in fat and salt, and add unnecessary calories to an otherwise low-calorie food. If you want variety in your flavors, try different herbs and seasonings that contain little or no fat or salt.

Frozen fruits usually contain some sugar, but less than those in cans. Check the label before you buy. You can also freeze your own when special fruits, like berries, are in season. Spread the clean, dry berries on a tray, and freeze them; when they are hard, pour them into a plastic freezer bag and seal it.

But buying fresh vegetables and fruit is no guarantee of high nutrient content. If the food was picked unripe or has been stored for weeks or has been kept unrefrigerated in the market, it may have suffered severe losses of some nutrients. Then storage in your refrigerator leads to further losses. (See pp. 133–149 and 151–163 for guidelines on picking and storing individual vegetables and fruits.) By the time you eat it, you probably would have been better off with the frozen version that was picked ripe, when nutrient content is highest, and processed soon after picking.

In general, it is best to shop often for fresh produce and, if available, to pick fruits and vegetables that have been ripened on the plant. Avoid wilted or shriveled-looking produce as well as produce with bruises or spoiled spots. Buy no more than you'll be able to use in the next few days. If you can't shop often, from a nutritional perspective you may be better off buying frozen fruits and vegetables.

HOW TO STORE. Whether fresh, frozen, or canned, all foods lose vitamins and minerals during storage. To minimize losses, keep canned foods at about 65 degrees Fahrenheit (or cooler), and maintain frozen foods at 0 degrees or below. Prolonged freezer storage is not recommended. Try to use frozen produce within a couple of months—certainly within 6 or 8 months—for the sake of quality as well as nutrient content.

As for fresh produce, green leafy vegetables like salad greens, spinach, and broccoli should be refrigerated in the vegetable crisper or in moisture-proof bags. They keep their nutrients best when the temperature is cold (near freezing) and the humidity high. Foods like green peas that come in pods should be kept in their shells until ready to use or, if shelled, enclosed in plastic bags. Carrots, sweet potatoes, potatoes, and other roots and tubers keep their vitamins best if they are kept cool and moist enough to prevent withering. Fruits that are picked unripe, including tomatoes, should not be ripened in the sun, since the heat and light increase their nutrient losses.

HOW TO COOK. Except for those that will be peeled before eating, wash all fresh vegetables and fruits before eating or adding to your recipe. But avoid prolonged soaking of fresh vegetables. Rinse them quickly, drain or dry them, and then refrigerate them.

If your schedule permits, don't cut up fruits and vegetables until just before you plan to cook them, since the more they are exposed to air, the greater the nutrient losses. If you must prepare foods for cooking in advance, seal them in plastic bags and refrigerate them.

Fruits, especially those high in vitamin C, are best eaten raw. If you get bored with just "plain old fruit," cut up several different kinds into a colorful fruit salad (be sure, though, to seal the bowl with plastic wrap and refrigerate it if the salad is not immediately devoured). I always keep a fresh-fruit salad in the refrigerator; all that changes with the seasons are the ingredients. It is a wonderful snack or dessert; an instant breakfast or lunch with yogurt or cottage cheese, cereal, or cheese and bread; or the irresistible topping for Brody's Mile-High Pancakes (see the recipe on p. 510).

Vegetables retain more of their nutrients if they are microwaved, pressure-cooked, or steamed than if they are boiled in water. Cook vegetables only until they are tender-crisp; and if you do boil them, use as little water as possible. Then save the cooking water to make soup or gravy or to add to stews or bread dough. If cooked vegetables are not eaten right away, enclose them in a well-covered container, and refrigerate them. You may also freeze them for future use.

OTHER BENEFITS OF FRUITS AND VEGETABLES

As if their high nutrient content were not justification enough to make fruits and vegetables a major part of your daily diet, you have the added enticement of their ability to counter the three main diseases that beset Americans—heart disease, cancer, and obesity—as well as one of the peskiest of common health problems—constipation.

CARDIOVASCULAR DISEASE. Studies dating back to 1961 have demonstrated the ability of pectin, a soluble fiber in many fruits and some vegetables, to lower the level of cholesterol in the blood. Pectin is the substance that enables jellies and jams to thicken. It is especially prominent in such fruits as apples, grapefruit, grapes, berries, and plums. Carrots, too, have a cholesterol-lowering factor; when subjects in one study (conducted at Western General Hospital in Edinburgh) ate 7 ounces of carrots at breakfast each day, their cholesterol levels dropped 11 percent. Similar benefits were noted by researchers at the University of Minnesota when "leafy" vegetables like broccoli, cabbage, lettuce, and celery were added to a diet otherwise high in heart-damaging fats and cholesterol. The vegetables and vegetable fibers seem to work by reducing the amount of cholesterol the body absorbs from food and by increasing the amount of fats and cholesterol the body excretes.

Eating lots of fruits and vegetables may also help to protect against strokes that result from tiny clots that lodge in blood vessels in the brain. Researchers at the University of Bergen in Norway followed 16,713 people since 1967. Consumption of fruits and vegetables was found to be lowest among the 438 people who died of strokes in the next 11½ years. In this country, a steady decline in stroke-caused deaths has coincided with an increased consumption of fresh fruits and vegetables.

CANCER. Two major categories of vegetable foods contain substances that help protect against the development of cancer. One group is the dark-green and deep-yellow vegetables and fruits that are rich in carotene. Carotene is the chemical precursor of vitamin A, which helps to prevent cancerous changes in skin and lining tissues. Cancers that arise in such tissues include lung and breast cancer, the leading cancer killers in this country, as well as cancers of the bladder and digestive tract. A study of nearly 2,000 employees of the Western Electric Company in Chicago showed that even among cigarette smokers, the risk of lung cancer was lower if large amounts of carotene-containing foods were a part of the regular diet. For vegetables and fruits rich in carotene, see the list under vitamin A on page 124.

The second category of protective vegetables is those in the cabbage family. In addition to the various forms of cabbage, these vegetables include broccoli, cauliflower, Brussels sprouts, kale, turnip greens, and kohlrabi. They contain substances called indoles that act as cancer-blocking agents, preventing cancer-causing chemicals from damaging cells. People who eat lots of these vegetables have a reduced risk of developing cancers of the stomach and large intestine.

OVERWEIGHT. Here the evidence is more indirect. Eating lots of produce can protect against overconsumption of calories because fruits and vegetables are filling and, on an ounce-for-ounce basis, much lower in calories than all other foods. In other words, you can fill up on fruits and vegetables without overdosing on calories. As a group, vegetarians are leaner than meat eaters largely because low-calorie fruits and vegetables take the place of some fatty, high-calorie animal foods. The appetite-satisfying effects of fruits and vegetables result from their high water content and dietary fiber, something totally lacking in animal foods. According to studies at Yale University, there is also some evidence that the main sugar in fruits, fructose, may help to suppress appetite and reduce the amount of calories consumed at the next meal. Fruits and vegetables also require a fair amount of chewing, which helps to satisfy the "feeding drive" common to all animals. For the calories in a 1½-ounce piece of sweet chocolate you can eat a whole pound of carrots, and a 3½-ounce burger (without the roll) has as many calories as 1 pound of apples (3 medium-sized apples).

If I want to be sure that I don't eat too much when dining out, I start with a big salad (dressing on the side) and then I'm usually satisfied with an appetizer for my main course. If I should order a full entrée, I get to take most of it home in a "people" bag.

CONSTIPATION. The laxative effect of fruits and vegetables is practically legendary, thanks to their high fiber content as well as the water most of them contain. Perhaps this benefit is at the root of the maxim "An apple a day keeps the doctor away." Certainly, apples and their compatriots will help to keep you away from artificial stimulants of your gut, which ultimately damage the natural muscle action of the intestinal walls. The fiber in these foods softens the stool, making it easier to pass and protecting against the development of hemorrhoids, diverticulosis, and other bowel disorders.

COMMON CONCERNS ABOUT FRESH PRODUCE

Many people question the way modern fruits and vegetables are produced, treated, ripened, stored, and shipped. Some have rejected supermarket fare and instead buy their fruits and vegetables from "organic" farmers, health food stores, and food co-ops. They are worried about the pesticides and fertilizer used in producing the food, and the waxes, colorings, and gases applied after the food is harvested. There are few simple answers to these concerns. But one fact is clear: paying a premium price for organically grown produce is no guarantee that the food is actually free of pesticide residues. In fact, in a number of studies in different parts of the country, some so-called organically grown fruits and vegetables had higher pesticide residues than the same foods purchased in a nearby supermarket. There is also no evidence that foods fertilized only with organic fertilizer are any more nutritious than the same foods grown in the usual way. The nutrient content of a food has much more to do with its genes, the climate, when it was picked, and how it was shipped and stored than with the type of fertilizer used or soil on which it was grown.

It is true, however, that most fruits and vegetables are washed before being shipped to market and that small amounts of fumigants may be added to the wash water to help clean them or to protect against decay. In a few foods, color additives or fixatives are used, such as in some Florida oranges which, when ripe, are still greenish in color. On some mushrooms, a bisulfite solution is used to prevent darkening. The possible hazards of these treatments are ill defined. It is known, however, that some people may be severely allergic to sodium bisulfite and that the use of color additives has been questioned because they are a possible cancer risk. If you are planning to use orange peel in cooking, try to buy California oranges (they are naturally orange) or Florida oranges that are greenish rather than bright orange.

As for waxes, these are often used on apples, cucumbers, turnips, and rutabagas, as well as on cherries, summer squash, tomatoes, and peppers from some areas. The wax serves three purposes: it results in a more attractive product; it keeps the food from drying out; and it protects against decay. The wax used may be derived from plants, petroleum, or other sources. The Food and Drug Administration considers them safe and edible; other nutrition experts do not. The consumer is hard put to remove the wax from fruits and vegetables that are eaten with their skin intact. You might try hot, soapy water, scrubbing the fruits and vegetables lightly with a vegetable brush. You can often tell a food has been waxed by its shiny appearance. But it is easy to be fooled. By law consumers are supposed to be told when a food is waxed. However, foods shipped in bulk containers to retail outlets (as are virtually all fruits and vegetables) need not be individually labeled. Rather, the bulk container indicating that the contents have been waxed is supposed to be in plain view in the market. I have yet to see one such container or label in any market, nor do I know of any retail establishment that has been penalized for ignoring this law.

The gases used to promote ripening of fruits that are picked green mimic the gases naturally produced by fruits to ripen themselves. The most common one is ethylene gas, used commercially to ripen honeydew melons, tomatoes, and bananas. If you put unripe fruit in a bag along with an apple, the ethylene gas exuded by the apple would speed the ripening of the other fruit. A different gas is used to slow ripening and deterioration of some apples and pears that are held off-season in controlled-atmosphere storage. There is no known hazard associated with any of these gases. However, fruits ripened after picking usually have less vitamin C than those ripened on the vine or tree.

Another health concern stems from a natural ingredient in some vegetables. This is oxalic acid, found in spinach, Swiss chard, sorrel, parsley, beet greens, and rhubarb. Oxalic acid can bind some of the calcium and iron in these vegetables, making the nutrients unavailable for absorption through the digestive tract. Thus, don't count on such vegetables as your main source of calcium and iron.

HOW TO GET KIDS TO EAT VEGETABLES

There seems to be a national conspiracy among children between the ages of about 4 and 14 to thwart parents' best efforts to teach them the principles of sound nutrition. Nowhere is this more evident than in the almost universal refusal to eat most of the vegetables that are supposed to be so good for growing bodies. The particular "hates" are often highly individual and quirky. One won't eat anything green, another refuses all red and orange vegetables. Still another adores the mushrooms and onions most kids despise but won't touch a pea, carrot, or green bean, the most popular vegetables among the youngest generation.

My own children are no different: both eat cooked carrots, and neither will touch cooked celery; but when it comes to raw vegetables and dip, one will eat only carrot sticks and the other only celery sticks. As a child, I loved spinach and beets, two of the least favorite vegetables among people under 18, but I wouldn't eat peas, carrots, or broccoli. But all is not lost even if your youngster categorically refuses to taste anything that resembles a vegetable, raw or cooked. Here are some tips for helping children discover the wonders of great vegetables and getting around those who simply have no sense of vegetable adventure. Just remember, you can only lead a horse to water . . . Fortunately, tastes do eventually mature, and few people reach adulthood disliking all the vegetables they despised as children.

First, as early in life as possible, get the kids involved in vegetable and salad preparation. They're more likely to eat something they helped to make. Shelling peas and tearing lettuce can be done, albeit messily, by a 2 year old, and even younger children can add cherry tomatoes to the salad. By 4, most children can safely handle a paring knife and can learn to trim and snap beans, slice cucumbers and zucchini, and scrape carrots. (For cutting hard vegetables, like carrots, however, it's best to wait a few more years.)

Second, serve raw or crunchy steamed vegetables and dip as a first course. It's great for staving off hunger pangs, and children love the act of dipping. They can even prepare the dip themselves, such as my son's favorite: 1 tablespoon of mayonnaise, 2 tablespoons of plain yogurt, and 1 teaspoon of ketchup.

Third, don't serve mushy, overcooked vegetables. Fresh vegetables that are steamed or boiled *al dente* or minimally cooked frozen vegetables are much more appealing. And if the children hate onions or mushrooms, leave them out of their servings. Even though it may be easy to pick out the disliked ingredient, its mere presence on the plate is enough to turn many children off to the main item.

Fourth, serve very small portions of iffy vegetables, asking only that the child taste a teaspoonful of a new vegetable. And introduce only one new food at a time.

Fifth, think of enticing ways to serve vegetables, perhaps giving them a catchy name (broccoli, for example, might be called "baby tree") or arranging them on the plate in a design or figure. If you apply some of the same ingenuity to vegetables that many parents bring to birthday cakes, who knows, the kids may eat the vegetables and snub the cake!

Sixth, sometimes it pays to forget about trying to get kids to like what's good for them and just sneak it in, not necessarily behind their backs but just so the vegetable is not recognizable. I grate zucchini and cabbage into tomato sauce, meat loaf, breads, and omelets. You can do the same with carrots. When making soup, I first cook the vegetables the children dislike and purée them with the broth. Then I cook the vegetables they will eat and add them to the purée.

Seventh, if all else fails, serve fruit. Most children like several different kinds of fruit, and many fruits have the same nutrients as vegetables. Oranges, apples, bananas, grapes, melons, and dried fruits are favorites among most children.

Feasting on Fresh Fruits and Vegetables

While it is not possible in a book like this to list every vegetable and fruit (and no doubt I've left out someone's offbeat favorite), the following descriptions include the best-known vegetables and fruits plus a few that you'd do well to get to know if you don't already. As with nuts, I'm not adhering to strict botanical definitions but rather classifying foods according to the way people commonly eat them. Technically, a vegetable is any part of a plant that is not involved in sexual reproduction. Foods containing seeds are really fruits because they are part of the sexual rather than the vegetative part of the plant. However, here I treat tomatoes, cucumbers, squashes, peppers, avocados, peas, and beans as vegetables, though botanically they are fruits, and I discuss rhubarb, which is really a vegetable, under fruits because that is how it is generally used. (Dried beans and peas are described in Chapter 7.) Wherever possible, both sections provide information on nutrient value, buying and storing tips, and some serving suggestions for each food.

The hardest part about writing these sections was to resist running down to the local greengrocery every few minutes to sample the wares. Just reading and thinking about the various vegetables and fruits whetted my appetite. See if it doesn't whet yours.

VEGETABLES: A WIDE VARIETY OF NUTRIENTS

ARTICHOKE. Artichokes have been a delicacy in Europe for 400 years but did not become popular here until this century. The edible part of the globe artichoke is the unripe head, a layered cluster of fleshy bracts, or modified leaves, that grow at the base of flowers. (The Jerusalem artichoke, an edible tuber, is discussed on p. 140.) Artichokes are most often served as an appetizer, with each bract individually dipped in dressing and then scraped across the lower front teeth to remove the edible flesh. Artichoke hearts, the soft center of the head, are sold in cans or jars and are often used in salads and antipastos. *Choose* tight, heavy, plump heads with thick, green, fresh-looking scales. Allow 1 artichoke per person. Uncooked, unwashed heads can be stored in the refrigerator for a few days wrapped in a damp towel and enclosed in a plastic bag. To eat a globe artichoke, the head must be boiled vigorously for 30 to 40 minutes in a pot with the lid on. (To prevent discoloration, do not use aluminum or cast-iron pots.) Avoid fatty dressings to obtain optimum nutritional value from this low-calorie vegetable, which contains potassium, calcium, phosphorus, and fiber. Canned artichoke hearts are often salty and thus high in sodium.

ASPARAGUS. These prized spears, native to the Mediterranean, were cultivated by the Greeks and Romans for 200 years before the birth of Christ but did not appear in American gardens until the late 1700s. They are seasonally available between mid-February and July, though often obtainable in large metropolitan areas at premium prices for longer periods. *Choose* spears that are round, straight, and of uniform thickness (so that cooking time will be similar for all the spears in a bunch), with tight pointed tips that have not begun to flower. Stalks that are flat or angular are usually tough. Although best used soon after purchase, asparagus, wrapped in a damp towel and enclosed in a plastic bag, can be stored for a few days in the refrigerator. Asparagus are best when steamed until just tender (you may have to peel the bottom of the stalks or trim off about an inch at the tough end of the stalks); they can be laid flat on a steamer rack or stood upright in a tall pot in about an inch of water. Cook them for 4 to 7 minutes, or until they reach peak green color (the color dulls when they are overcooked). Asparagus

gus spears are excellent as a hot vegetable or served cold in salads and vegetable-and-dip platters. Asparagus are very low in fat and calories (12 calories in 4 medium stalks), are a source of vitamins A and C, niacin, potassium, and some iron, and have a natural diuretic effect. One pound will yield about 3 servings.

AVOCADO. A Central American native, the avocado (sometimes called an alligator pear) is a fruit that is popular in tropical and subtropical regions of the Americas. Although highly touted by health food enthusiasts, it is actually a high-fat, high-calorie food. The avocado is 16 percent fat by weight, 88 percent fat by calories. The fat, however, is unsaturated vegetable oil and thus is not damaging to blood vessels. One whole avocado (weighing about 10 ounces with the pit and skin) supplies about 300 calories. Avocados are available year round in most parts of the United States. *Choose* fruits that are heavy and without dark, sunken, or bruised spots. Although commonly sold hard and unripe, they will ripen at room temperature (best in a paper bag). A ripe avocado yields somewhat to gentle pressure but is not soft and mushy. Avocados are nearly always eaten raw, usually peeled and sliced or cut in half and stuffed with a salad. The buttery flesh can also be mashed into a guacamole and served as an appetizer or dip (see the recipe on p. 294). When the cut flesh is exposed to air, it discolors rapidly unless squirted with lemon juice or coated with salad oil. In addition to unsaturated fat, avocados contain protein (about 2 grams in 3½ ounces), potassium, vitamins A and C, and niacin. One medium avocado yields about 1½ cups of cubes.

BEANS.   Botanically speaking, green beans are no different from dry beans. They are simply immature bean pods, far less rich in protein and carbohydrates than the mature versions that are sold dried. And because they are mostly water and fiber, they are also considerably lower in calories. One cup of cooked pods has only 31 calories, compared to 210 in a cup of cooked kidney beans, for example. Yellow varieties of green beans, called wax beans, are also available, as are flat green pods commonly called Italian green beans. The green varieties are often referred to as snap or string beans, although most cultivars are bred to eliminate the tough strings in the seams of the beans. The Chinese produce a variety known as long or asparagus beans, which are of a firmer texture and often appear slightly shriveled before cooking. Fresh green beans are usually available year round, but wax beans are sold seasonally, mid- to late summer. *Choose* slender, smooth, slightly velvety pods without apparent bulging seeds (these indicate older, tougher beans) and with a bright green color. (Snapping, incidentally, is not a sign of freshness.) Beans will keep for several days in the refrigerator in a plastic bag. For maximum nutrients and flavor, they are best cooked by steaming until tender-crisp, about 5 to 8 minutes, depending on their initial tenderness. They can also be cooked directly in soups or stews. Try steamed, chilled beans in salads or on cold vegetable platters (see, for example, recipes on pp. 536 and 537). Green and wax beans with kidney beans make a colorful and nutritious three-bean salad. Both green and yellow snap beans contain vitamin A and potassium as well as some protein, iron, calcium, and vitamin C. A pound of beans makes about 4 servings.

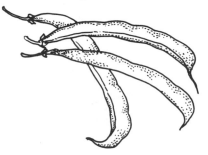

BEETS. Although grown in Roman times, when they were appreciated more for their greens than their roots, beets as we commonly know them originated in Germany and were initially preferred in their yellow form. Unlike most vegetables, in which starch is the primary carbohydrate, beets contain most of their carbohydrate as sugar (and thus are sometimes called sugar beets). *Choose* firm, smooth beets with a deep red color, slender main root, and, if available, fresh-looking tops. To prevent nutrient loss from the roots, beet tops should be removed right after purchase. But leave an inch or 2 of stem to prevent nutrient loss and "bleeding" of color when cooking the roots. The tops, which keep refrigerated only a day or 2, can be boiled or steamed to yield a vegetable rich in vitamin A, iron, and potassium (however, they are also higher in sodium than most vegetables). Beet roots are much less perishable—they can usually be kept for about 2 weeks in the refrigerator—and take far longer to cook. To save time, I usually prepare them in a pressure cooker, although they can also be boiled until fork-tender (about 45 to 60 minutes, depending on size) or baked (325 degrees for an hour or more). *Do not peel* beets until after they are cooked. Serve hot or cold, whole, sliced, or diced. Raw beets can also be shredded or grated for a tasty and colorful addition to salads. Beets, which are noted for their laxative value, are rich in potassium but are otherwise not especially good sources of essential nutrients. One cup of cooked beets supplies 54 calories, twice that in a cup of cooked beet greens. Don't panic: their red pigment may color the stool and/or urine for a day or 2. Plan on about 2 pounds to serve 4 to 6 people.

BROCCOLI. Broccoli was first cultivated by the early Romans but was not introduced here until this century, where it has since become a popular addition to dinner plates and cold vegetable platters. It is sold year round, with peak availability occurring from fall to spring. *Choose* crisp, uniformly green heads with tight clusters that have not begun to flower and stems that are not too thick. Uncooked broccoli will keep for a few days in plastic in the refrigerator. Steaming the flowerets and thinly sliced stalks to tender crispness (about 5 minutes) is by far the best way to prepare broccoli. The green leaves can also be steamed. (Many cooks suggest peeling the stalks. I never do. If they are woody, I discard them or use them when making broth.) Broccoli flowerets can also be eaten raw, although they are more gas-producing this way (try blanching them in boiling water for 1 minute to reduce gassiness). Here is a versatile vegetable that will give you more than your money's worth in nutrients at a very low caloric price. As a member of the cabbage family, it is noted for its anticancer properties, but it has twice the nutrient value of Savoy cabbage. Broccoli is very rich in vitamins A and C, and is a good source of potassium, iron, calcium, and niacin. As vegetables go, it is also rich in protein, containing about 5 grams of protein per cup. And it is a good source of dietary fiber and low in calories (about 40 per cup). A bunch of 2 large or 3 medium stalks weighing 1¼ to 1½ pounds will serve 4.

BRUSSELS SPROUTS. Another cabbage-family vegetable with anticancer properties, Brussels sprouts were, as you might guess, first grown in Brussels in the 1200s. Tight heads that resemble miniature cabbages grow along a stalk.

In the fall you may find them sold as such, though the sprouts are usually removed from the stalk before going to market and are packed into berry boxes. *Choose* firm, compact, bright green sprouts, and use them as soon as possible. They are tastiest when steamed or parboiled for 5 to 10 minutes (overcooking results in a mushy, bitter-tasting vegetable). Brussels sprouts are a good source of vitamins A and C, potassium, iron, and protein. There are about 50 calories in a cup of cooked sprouts. One box will serve 3 or 4.

CABBAGE. As one of the oldest cultivated vegetables (originating in Europe and Asia) cabbage comes in a large number of varieties: green, red, Savoy, bok choy, Chinese, and celery cabbage, as well as such relatives (described separately) as broccoli, Brussels sprouts, cauliflower, collard greens, and kohlrabi. Cabbage was highly regarded by the Romans, and Cato applauded its "physic" and medicinal values. Americans, however, often spurn it for its gas-producing property, the result of its high-fiber content. To reduce gassiness, parboil the cabbage for 5

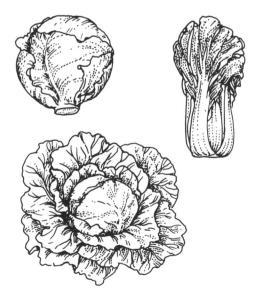

minutes, discard the water, rinse the cabbage, and cook it further in fresh water. *Choose* head cabbages that are firm and heavy in relation to their size and free of yellowing leaves, splits, or soft spots. Loose heads like bok choy should have crisp, green leaves. Tight cabbage heads will store refrigerated for up to 2 weeks; looser varieties should be used within a few days. Cabbage can be eaten raw—shredded, it is the essential ingredient in coleslaw (see the recipe on p. 541) —or cooked by steaming, boiling, or braising (see the recipe on p. 516). It gives you more than your money's worth in nutrients. Raw cabbage is high in vitamin C and potassium (cooking reduces these nutrients) and is very low in calories (a cup of shredded cabbage has 17 calories when raw, 29 after cooking compacts it). Bok choy is very rich in vitamin A. One pound of cabbage will shred into 4 to 5 cups raw, 2½ to 3 cups cooked.

CARROTS. Before the sixteenth century, when cultivation produced better varieties, wild carrots were used by the Greeks and Romans mainly for "medicinal" purposes. The edible part of the plant is an elongated, fleshy root that is orange or yellow-orange in color. The color is due to a pigment, beta-carotene, that is the parent chemical to vitamin A and a substance noted for its cancer-preventing properties. The fiber in carrots can also lower cholesterol levels in the blood. *Choose* carrots that are firm, smooth, evenly shaped, and with a strong orange color. Avoid those that are flabby, shriveled, rough, or cracked. The freshest carrots come with fresh-looking greens attached, but these should be removed right after purchase to prevent drainage on the roots. Some people use the tops when cooking broth. (In summer, I feed them to the caterpillars of parsley swallowtail butterflies to keep them off my patch of parsley.) Although small, slender carrots have long been preferred, the large, thick California varieties now widely available are often sweeter. Wrapped in plastic, they keep well for weeks in the refrigerator (unrefrigerated carrots wilt quickly). Carrots can be eaten raw (scrubbed or scraped, whole, sliced, or shredded), or they can be cut up and cooked by steaming, boiling, stir-frying, or as part of a soup, stew, or casserole. Carrots are very rich in vitamin A—one carrot supplies more than the daily recommended amount. (*Warning:* Overconsumption of carrot juice will result in a yellowish tinge to the skin which, though harmless in itself, can be confused with jaundice.) Carrots are also a good source of potassium. One 3-ounce raw carrot has about 30 calories; a cup of sliced, cooked carrots has 48. One pound will serve 3 or 4 or yield about 3 cups grated, 3½ to 4 cups sliced or diced.

CAULIFLOWER. Cauliflower, like broccoli, is another cabbage-family vegetable with cancer-preventing value. It can be eaten raw or cooked, stalks as well as flowerets. Although most commonly found as a creamy white head, purplish or greenish varieties are now also available. *Choose* clean, firm, compact heads with fresh-looking, green leaves, avoiding bruised heads and those with open flower clusters. Cauliflower, tightly wrapped in plastic and placed in the refrigerator, will keep for about a week. To prevent discoloration, avoid cooking it in an aluminum pot. Milk added to the cooking liquid will sweeten the vegetable. Like its relatives, it is high in vitamin C and potassium, and also contains a reasonable amount of protein and iron. One head, about 1½ pounds, will serve 4.

CELERY. This humble vegetable was used like laurel to crown the heads of athletes in ancient Greece and served as funeral wreaths in Plutarch's time. However, it did not become a table vegetable until the Middle Ages. It is a very low-calorie vegetable with many uses. In fact, every part of the plant except the roots is used for culinary purposes: stalks, leaves, and seeds. *Choose* bunches with crisp green or greenish-white outer stalks and fresh green leaves. Rinse the celery, wrap it in plastic, and refrigerate it for up to 2 weeks. Individual stalks can also be kept crisp in the refrigerator by standing them in about an inch of water. Celery can be eaten raw or cooked (a quick sauté or braising is all that is needed); chopped or sliced, it is a popular flavorful addition to soups and stews. Celeriac, also called knob celery or celery root and resembling a turnip with a strong celery flavor, is not the root of the common celery plant but rather a different variety of celery. It should be peeled before eating, raw or cooked. Celery has only 20 calories per cup of diced pieces and is a good source of potassium, but it is relatively high in sodium (151 milligrams per cup). One large stalk, diced, yields about ¾ cup.

CHARD. This vegetable, commonly called Swiss chard, is really a beet that is grown for its leaves and can be substituted for spinach in most dishes—even salad if the chard is young (see recipes on pp. 382 and 531). It is cooked like spinach, whole or chopped. Be sure to keep the stems, which are the tastiest part. *Choose* crisp bunches with large, dark-green leaves and white stems (some markets sell a reddish variety with red stems that looks like beet greens). Keep chard refrigerated in plastic, and use the veget-

able within a few days. Before cooking them, wash the leaves well to remove grit and sand. Like spinach, chard can be steamed in a saucepan using just the water that clings to the leaves. Swiss chard is very high in vitamin A and a good source of potassium, iron, calcium (however, not all the calcium in chard can be absorbed), and protein. It is also fairly high in sodium—125 milligrams per cup of cooked leaves and stalks—and should be cooked without salt to prevent discoloration and excessive saltiness. One pound equals approximately 2 cups of cooked whole leaves or 1 cup of chopped.

COLLARD GREENS.   Best known as a "soul food" among the blacks of the American South (the vegetable may have been brought to this continent by African slaves), collard greens are a dense source of essential nutrients, particularly calcium. As a relative of cabbage, they are also cancer-preventives and can be used as wrappers in place of cabbage leaves in recipes like stuffed cabbage. They are available year round, espe-

cially in markets that have a large black clientele. (See pp. 518 and 528 for simple, tasty collard recipes.) *Choose* bunches of crisp, green leaves with tender stems, and use them as soon as possible, washing them well before cooking. Collard greens are very high in vitamins A and C, potassium, calcium, iron, niacin, and protein, and are low in sodium and calories. Collards are an excellent source of calcium—the best vegetable source, in fact, since the greens are free of the binding oxalic acid found in most other calcium-rich greens. Cup for cup, they are on a par with milk as a calcium source.

CORN.   Sweet corn, whether eaten on the cob or off, is an all-American vegetable that is lower in starch and higher in sugar than the corn used as a grain. Still, it is a calorically dense vegetable, made all the more so by the smear of butter that ordinarily accompanies it. Fresh sweet corn is a summer crop in most of the country (to my taste, the winter corn from California and Florida is not worth bothering with). Corn is best cooked soon after picking, and to preserve its natural sweetness it must be kept cold between the field and

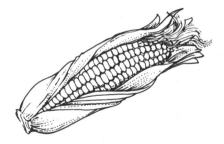

the pot. *Choose* cold cobs (unless they were just picked) still in their fresh-looking green husks and with tassles that are free of decay and worm injury. Refrigerate the cobs in their husks until you are ready to cook them (within a few days). Husk just before cooking (clingy silks can be removed by wiping the cob downward with a damp cloth). Cobs with small, shiny kernels are generally sweeter and more tender than those with large, deep-yellow, dull kernels. Corn is easiest to prepare (and, I think, tastes best) when steamed: stand the husked ears in a tall pot with

an inch or 2 of water, cover the pot, and steam the corn for about 5 minutes (longer for older ears). Some people prefer to boil corn in a large pot of water to which a teaspoon of sugar has been added (do not, however, salt the water since this toughens the kernels). Corn is a source of vitamin A (in yellow kernels only), potassium, niacin, and protein. A medium-sized ear provides about 70 calories; a cup of kernels, 137. Corn is also high in fiber and thus is a natural laxative. Six ears will yield about 3 cups of kernels. Figure on 1 or 2 ears per person.

CUCUMBERS. Cucumbers, eaten as an unripe fruit, are Asian natives that were popular in the Middle East in Biblical times. As a relative of melons, they are very high in water, giving them refreshing properties that no doubt prompted the description "cool as a cucumber." To some, however, they are hard to digest; seedless, or "burbless," cucumbers have been bred to reduce this problem. Both types are available year round, but the smaller pickling (kirby) cucumbers with knobby skins are often seasonal. *Choose* fruits that are green and slender (fat, yellowing ones are old) and free of soft spots or shriveled skin. Ordinary cucumbers are usually waxed to prevent rotting (kirbies are not); either peel them before eating or try to remove the wax by scrubbing the vegetables with a vegetable brush under hot, soapy water. Cucumbers are nearly always eaten raw, with or without the skin, although they can be julienned and sautéed or stir-fried. Raw seeded cucumbers can be puréed into a refreshing cold soup, and may be the basis for the summer delight gazpacho (see recipes on pp. 326 and 327). Although very low in calories (45 in a whole large cucumber, 16 in a cup of slices), cucumbers are not especially nutritious. They are moderate sources of vitamin A, iron, potassium, and fiber.

EGGPLANT. This underappreciated food is a relative of the potato and probably originated in India in ancient times. However, it didn't appear in Europe until the fourteenth century and in the Americas until the seventeenth century. Thomas Jefferson first brought it to the United States from France. The edible part of the plant is a large pear-shaped fruit that is a berry. Most eggplants, also known by their French name *aubergine,* are deep purple, although yellowish white cultivars are sometimes available. The purple ones are marketed year round in most areas. *Choose* fruits that are firm, heavy, free of scars, and deeply colored (if purple). Small, slender eggplants have smaller seeds and are sweeter and more tender, but the larger ones are more practical for dishes in which the eggplant is peeled and/or sliced. Eggplants can be stored at room temperature or in the refrigerator for a week or so. They should always be cooked to eliminate

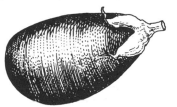

any toxic solanine that may be in the fruit, but the cooked peel can be eaten. They can be broiled or baked whole, or cut up and fried, sautéed, baked, steamed, or stewed. Note that frying adds a lot of fat calories, since eggplants soak up oil like a sponge. Eggplant is the basis of some of my favorite dishes, among them the vegetable stew ratatouille (see the recipe on p. 520), the appetizer and dip baba ghanoush (see the recipe on p. 293), and the entrée eggplant Parmesan. All freeze very well. Oddly shaped eggplants make delightful centerpieces that can be eaten after the party. (Shortly after Watergate, I found one with a "nose" that looked just like former President Nixon.) The eggplant's main nutritional virtue is its high fiber content. It also contains a fair amount of potassium, iron, and protein. A cup of diced eggplant cooked without fat has only 38 calories. One pound of raw eggplant yields about 2½ cups diced, 1¾ cups after cooking.

ENDIVE. This name is applied to three related plants: curly-headed *chicory* or *curly endive,* which has ragged, "scratchy" leaves; the more smoothly curled head of *escarole;* and the smooth, tightly packed, sausage-shaped heads of *Belgian endive.* The latter is by far the most expensive and least available. Chicory and escarole are usually sold year round and can add variety to winter salads. *Choose* crisp heads of chicory and escarole that don't have wilted or yellow leaves. Belgian endive should be firm and tight with light-colored leaves. Wrap Belgian endive in plastic, and store it in the refrigerator. Use it as soon as possible—within a couple of days. Chicory and escarole are usually eaten raw, although they can be cooked briefly in soups or as a vegetable. Belgian endive can be served raw in a salad or braised as a vegetable. Chicory and escarole are very high in vitamin A and contain some potassium and iron. They are very low in calories—only 10 per cup of cut-up leaves.

FENNEL. A licorice-flavored, sweet-smelling relative of parsley and carrots, fennel was widely used in ancient Greece and was mentioned in a papyrus dated 1500 B.C. For many centuries, it was best known for its reputed medicinal properties. Today it is used as both a vegetable (the fleshy stalks) and a seasoning (the feathery leaves and the dried fruit, called seeds). *Choose* white, round stalks with leaves if possible. Wrap the fennel in plastic, and store it in the refrigerator. The stalks can be eaten raw or cooked (steamed or simmered for 5 to 10 minutes if cut up, 10 to 15 minutes if left whole). Fennel leaves are rich in vitamin A.

JERUSALEM ARTICHOKE. This vegetable, also called a *sunchoke,* is neither from Jerusalem (it is an American native) nor does it bear any resemblance to a globe artichoke. Rather, it looks like a knobby root or potato. Actually, it is a tuber of a plant related to the sunflower and was widely cultivated by American Indians. Sunchokes have a sweet, nutty flavor similar to that of an artichoke. They can be boiled or steamed like potatoes (to avoid blackening, do not use an aluminum pan), sautéed, or peeled, sliced, and eaten raw. *Choose* those that are small, firm, and without pink discoloration. Wrap them in plastic, and store them in the refrigerator, where they will keep for about a week. Sunchokes contain a type of sugar, inulin, that can be safely consumed by diabetics. They are a source of calcium, iron, and magnesium.

KALE. My first Christmas in my Victorian row house was spent searching for the source of a pungent odor that seemed to be emanating from under the furniture or radiators. I thought a small animal had died and was decaying somewhere. I never found a carcass, but I did eventually realize that the smell came from something my Polish neighbor was cooking—kale. Having been put off by the odor, it was years before I dared to taste the vegetable and discover what I'd been missing. Kale is delicious and extremely nourishing, and to my taste superior to spinach as a cooked vegetable (see the recipe on p. 522). Kale is a member of the cabbage family and thus

is a cancer preventive. *Choose* crisp, broad, dark-colored leaves (dark green or purplish). Store it in the refrigerator, and use it within 2 or 3 days. Before cooking (the leaves are usually boiled), remove the stringy stalks (use a few when preparing broth) and wash the leaves well. Kale is very rich in vitamins A and C, potassium, and calcium (although absorption is inhibited by oxalic acid), and is a good source of protein and iron. It provides only 43 calories per cup of cooked vegetable.

KOHLRABI. The odd name of this plant reflects its true nature: it is a member of the cabbage family (*kohl* is German for "cabbage"); it resembles a turnip (*rab* means "turnip"). The usual edible portion is a bulbous stem with a mild, sweet taste when cooked. If you find it with the leaves still attached, these, too, can be cooked like other greens. Choose small bulbs (under 3 inches in diameter—larger ones tend to be woody) that have tender skin and are firm and light green or purple. They may be stored in the refrigerator for several days, longer in a cool cellar. The peeled bulbs can be shredded raw into a slaw. Or the bulbs can be steamed or boiled whole (for 15 to 25 minutes), cubed or sliced (for 5 to 10 minutes), or julienned (for 5 minutes). The cooked vegetable can be served as such or dressed and cooled as a salad or appetizer (see recipes on pp. 522 and 544). You might also try it sautéed, mashed, or as an ingredient in a stew. Kohlrabi is rich in potassium and vitamin C and contains some protein. There are about 40 calories in a cup of cooked diced vegetable.

LEEKS. The emperor Nero is said to have eaten leek soup every day to improve his speaking voice. Whether this vegetable, which resembles an overgrown scallion, has this virtue is doubtful, but it does add much flavor to soups and stews of several nationalities. It is perhaps best known for its use in vichyssoise, a cold puréed potato and leek soup, which turned the leek into a prestigious vegetable on this side of the Atlantic (see the recipe on p. 329). The taste is milder and more subtle than that of an onion, its close relative. Choose young, small leeks (avoid oversized bulbs—they're tough and old) with crisp, dark-green tops. They may be wrapped in plastic and stored in the refrigerator for up to a week. When ready to use, wash them very thoroughly, removing and washing each leaf individually to get rid of the grit and dirt in which they are grown. Depending on the size of the pieces, leeks cook in 10 to 25 minutes, simmered in water or braised. Leeks are fairly rich in dietary fiber, low in calories, and are said to possess diuretic properties.

LETTUCE. Lettuce is the hands-down winner as America's most popular cold vegetable. In fact, to many people lettuce is synonymous with salad. Although there is a large number of interesting types of lettuce, the overwhelming favorite here is the firm-headed *iceberg*, the least nutritious (and least flavorful, according to some) of the choices. Iceberg's main virtues are that it costs less, is easier to shred, and keeps longer than other kinds of lettuce. Other lettuces include *romaine* (or *cos*), the cylinder of long, broad, crisp, slightly bitter leaves that is the heart of a Caesar salad; the butterheads *Boston*, *buttercrunch*, and *bibb*, with their soft, loose, tender, whitish-green leaves and subtle flavor; and the loose-leaf lettuces (*oakleaf*, *redleaf*, and *greenleaf*),

large loose heads of crisp, delicately flavored, somewhat curly leaves. Looser-headed lettuces are far more perishable than iceberg or romaine. Choose lettuce that is crisp and free of yellow, wilted, or dry leaves. Wash the lettuce, and spin or pat it dry before storing it in a lettuce bag or in plastic in the refrigerator. Use butterheads and loose-leaf lettuces within a few days, tighter-head lettuces within a week. To prevent wilting, do not add dressing to salads containing lettuce until just before serving them. Though nearly always eaten raw, lettuce can also be braised or added to soups at the end of the cooking. Wilted or discolored outer leaves can be used in making broth. All lettuce is high in fiber. Romaine and loose-leaf lettuces have more vitamin A and calcium than iceberg, and the butterheads have more iron than iceberg.

MUSHROOMS.   Few, if any, foods are more prized by adults and despised by children than is the mushroom. Although there are scores of edible varieties of this umbrella-shaped fungus, only one is cultivated here: a species of *Agaricus* with white- to buff-colored caps and brown gills. Connoisseurs consider it the least interesting of the edible mushrooms. More tasty varieties that are commercially available include a small, slender Japanese mushroom called the *enoki-dake* or enok, which is sold fresh and canned, and several types of dried fungi, mostly Oriental, among them the *tree ear* (mo-er) which contains a natural blood-thinning substance that may provide protection against heart attack. Wild-food enthusiasts would be wise to refrain from eating

wild mushrooms without the counsel of a well-established expert, since it is very easy to mistake a highly poisonous fungus for one that is edible. The main culinary virtue of mushrooms is their subtle flavor and unusual "meaty" texture. Choose clean, white, well-shaped mushrooms that do not have gills showing. Some brown flecking on the surface is okay, but avoid mushrooms with dark discolorations. When buying packaged mushrooms, check the label and avoid those that have been coated with the preservative sodium bisulfite (it changes their flavor, and some people have severe allergic reactions to this chemical). Mushrooms should be stored in a paper bag or open container in the refrigerator and used within 2 days. Do not peel commercial mushrooms. Just before use, wipe them with a damp cloth rather than washing them in water since they absorb water readily. (However, those preserved with sodium bisulfite should be washed under hot running water.) Nutritionally, mushrooms are very low in calories (20 per cup of sliced or diced raw mushrooms) and are fairly high in potassium and niacin. One pound of mushrooms will yield about 6 cups of raw slices or 4 cups of chopped pieces, but will reduce to about a third that amount when cooked.

MUSTARD GREENS.   Here is another "soul food" that has cancer-preventing properties. It is a relative of the cabbage, with dark-green leaves and a taste-bud–tingling pungency, and is delicious as a side dish and an ingredient in stir-fries and soups. Choose small, young, crisp leaves with deep-green color and no insect holes, flabby stems, or seed heads. Store them in the refrigerator in a plastic bag for up to 3 days. Wash them well, and remove tough stems before cooking them. Mustard greens are low in calories (32 per cup of boiled leaves), very rich in vitamin A, and a good source of vitamin C, potassium, and calcium. They also contain a fair amount of protein and iron.

OKRA. A contribution of slaves from West Africa, this pod-shaped vegetable is the quintessential ingredient in gumbos (the word *gumbo* is also African). When cut, it exudes a mucilaginous "fiber" that has thickening properties. If the pods are steamed or simmered whole for about 7 to 10 minutes, they will not be sticky. *Choose* young pods less than 4 inches long with tips that bend easily. Store okra in plastic in the refrigerator, and use the vegetable within 3 days. In addition to its high fiber content, okra supplies a fair amount of vitamin A, potassium, calcium, niacin, and protein.

ONIONS. These are hands-down winners as the single most important and versatile ingredient in cooking, regardless of nationality. They can be eaten raw or cooked; whole, chopped, sliced, or grated; stuffed, boiled, baked, sautéed, deep-fried, or even barbecued. In one or more of their various forms, onions are a valued flavoring agent in most cuisines, and have been so since ancient times. They enhance the flavor of foods by irritating the membranes of the nose and mouth. A native of central Asia, the onion became an object of worship in Egypt and was consumed in large amounts by the ancient Greeks and Romans as well. So-called dry onions are not dehydrated but rather the usual form of mature globe onion with a dry outer skin, as distinguished from immature *green onions,* or *scallions,* which have no outer skin on their bulbs and are sold with their edible green leaves attached. Dry onions have the additional virtues of being inexpensive and storing well without refrigeration. Popular varieties include yellow, Spanish, Bermuda, red, white and pearl. *Chives* are members of the onion family, too, but only the leaves, not the bulbs, are used, mainly as a seasoning or garnish. *Shallots,* a relative of garlic and onion,

taste like a mild subtle onion. The Spanish, Bermuda, and red Italian onions are milder than yellow onions and are often eaten raw in salads and on sandwiches. Spanish and Bermuda onions are excellent stir-fried or sautéed with other ingredients, but red onions take on a disagreeable color when cooked. All types are available year round. *Choose* onions that have their protective skin, are well shaped and are heavy for their size. Avoid those with soft or discolored spots and sprouts. Store dry onions in a cool, dry, dark place that is well ventilated. You may want to refrigerate them in summer. Green onions and chives should have crisp, green tops and should be stored in the refrigerator and used within a few days. Wrap the unused portion of a peeled or cut onion in plastic, and refrigerate it; use it within a few days. Onions will be less likely to irritate your eyes if you place them in the freezer for ½ hour before cutting them. Already-chopped onions can be stored in the freezer. Onions should never be cooked over a high heat since it makes them bitter. To remove the smell of onion from your hands and cooking equipment, rub them with lemon juice (or salt, if your equipment is aluminum, cast iron, or carbon-steel). Other than potassium, some protein, and a fair amount of fiber, onions don't offer much nutritionally. A cup of chopped raw onion has 65 calories; a cup of cooked slices, 61. Green onions have about half the number of calories and, if the tops are consumed, a lot of vitamin A as well as potassium and vitamin C. One bunch of scallions (about 6 bulbs) will yield about ¾ cup of minced or sliced scallions. One large onion (about 7 ounces) will yield 1 cup of sliced, diced, or chopped onion.

PARSLEY.   The ancient Romans used this plant mainly for medicinal purposes. To modern cooks, this herb's primary function is as a seasoning or a garnish, and it is mostly used dried as parsley flakes. The fresh herb, however, has a far superior flavor. Two forms are popular: curly-leaf parsley, which is easy to chop and makes a lovely garnish; and Italian flat-leafed parsley, which has a stronger flavor. (So-called Chinese parsley is not parsley but rather fresh coriander; it is also called cilantro.) *Choose* crisp, fresh-looking bunches with bright-green leaves. If you're stuck with wilted parsley, refresh it by trimming the ends of the stems and standing it in cold water. Nutritionally speaking, our limited perspective on parsley is a shame, for the plant is a rich source of essential nutrients at an extremely low caloric price. One cup of chopped parsley has a mere 26 calories and a day's supply of vitamins A and C, a lot of potassium and iron, and some protein in the bargain. It is also a natural breath freshener. (See pp. 405 and 540 for recipes that use parsley with a generous hand.)

PARSNIPS.   Passions run high about this vegetable: some (I, for instance) love it, others hate it, and there are few on the fence. Parsnips are carrot-shaped, white-fleshed root vegetables, the sweetness of which is enhanced by cold. They are most popular as soup and stew ingredients, but also make an excellent side dish when steamed, sautéed, or baked. They cook faster than carrots and taste best when just tender, not mushy. *Choose* firm, smoothly shaped roots that are not too large. Store them in plastic in the refrigerator for up to several weeks. Parsnips contain a lot of potassium and some protein, iron, and calcium. There are 102 calories in a cup of cooked, diced parsnips.

PEAS.   Fresh garden peas were a childhood treat, albeit rare. I loved to help shell them, tossing a few into my mouth raw as they popped from their protective casing. Like their dried relatives, *garden peas* are legumes, but they are eaten when immature and sweet. Thus, they contain three times more protein than most vegetables, although not nearly as much as mature dry peas. They can also produce flatulence when consumed in too large a quantity. Peas are a native of Italy. From there they traveled northwest to England and west to the New World with the first American settlers. In addition to peas that are shelled before eating, American consumers can sometimes obtain fresh *snow peas* (almost pea-less pods that are an Oriental specialty) and the newest and most delectable cultivar, *sugar snap peas,* both of which are eaten shells and all, raw as well as cooked. Fresh peas are available in late spring and summer. *Choose* pods that are cold (when warm, their sugar turns to starch), uniformly green, and not too fat (large peas are old and tough). Store them in the refrigerator, and use them within a few days. Shell peas can be cooked in their shells or shelled first and then steamed or boiled, or they can be cooked directly in a soup or stew. Snow peas and sugar snaps take but a minute or 2 of steaming or cooking. They are best when eaten tender-crisp. Peas are a good source of vitamin A, potassium, protein, phosphorus, and iron. Snow peas are lower in protein, since their seeds are very small. One cup of green peas has 122 calories. Figure on 2 pounds of garden peas in the pod to feed 4 people (1 pound yields about 1 cup of peas). For snow peas and sugar snaps, 1 pound is enough for 4.

to wash the cutting surface, knife, and gloves with soapy water *before* you take the gloves off. Peppers are available year round, although they are usually more plentiful in late summer and fall. *Choose* firm, thick-fleshed vegetables with a glossy sheen and without soft spots or wrinkled skin. Refrigerate them, and use them within several days. Peppers are very low in calories (22 in a cup of strips) and very rich in vitamin C (on a par with orange juice). They are also a good source of vitamin A and potassium. Chili peppers are very high in vitamins A and C, but, of course, they are rarely eaten in large quantities.

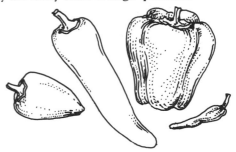

PEPPERS. Peppers are a vegetable with a "borrowed" name. Christopher Columbus was in search of the peppercorns of India when he landed in America and misnamed the plants he found growing here "peppers" and their users "Indians." The sweet bell peppers, frying peppers, banana peppers, and hot chili peppers are totally unrelated to the plant that produces the spice—peppercorn. But they bear their name with the distinction accorded the more costly spice. These American peppers, all of the genus *Capsicum*, come in many varieties. Bell peppers, usually sold green, also are available in their more mature and sweeter red version as well as in yellow and creamy white. The Italian *frying* peppers come in lime-green, reddish-green, and yellow. The *hot* peppers (their fire is due to a chemical called capsaicin) are now used worldwide; among their 200 varieties are cayenne, jalapeño, serrano, chili, pequin, hot cherry, and the Japanese santaka. These can be used directly (finely chopped and in small amounts) to flavor a dish, or dried hot peppers can be cooked in oil to make a hot-flavored oil for cooking and seasoning. When cutting hot peppers, avoid touching the inner flesh and seeds. It's best to wear rubber gloves and, after completing the cutting,

RADISHES. Radishes are tangy roots. Although Americans are most familiar with the little round or oval red table radishes, there are a number of different forms, including the white *icicle* radish and the Japanese *daikon* used in stir-fries and soups as well as shredded raw (see the recipe on p. 392). The red ones are popular as garnishes (unfortunately, more people admire than eat them) and as crunchy additions to salads. Choose smooth, crisp, well-formed roots without black spots. If bought with the tops still attached, the greens should be fresh and have a bright color (however, remove the tops right after purchase to reduce drain on the roots). Store radishes in the refrigerator for up to 2 weeks. Radishes contain potassium and some iron but not much else in the way of essential nutrients. However, they also have very few calories—20 in a cup of sliced radishes.

RUTABAGA. Even though it is a relative of the turnip and often confused with it, the rutabaga is a different plant, a yellow-fleshed edible root of the popular Italian vegetable broccoli di rape. Its popularity in Scandinavia earned it the European name of "swede." It is delicious in soups and stews, as well as boiled or steamed and sliced or mashed as a side dish (see recipes on pp. 432 and 529). Rutabagas are available year round. *Choose* smooth, uncracked, heavy roots. They are nearly always sold waxed and will keep for months in a cool place. The wax is no problem since the root is peeled before cooking. Rutabagas are a good source of potassium, vitamin A, and niacin, and contain a fair amount of calcium. There are 60 calories in a cup of cooked cubes.

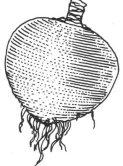

SPINACH. A Persian native introduced by the Moors into Europe around A.D. 1000, spinach was not widely cultivated until after the eighteenth century. Popeye notwithstanding, spinach is not all that it's cracked up to be. But before the youngsters of the world rejoice, it must be said that as vegetables go, spinach has considerable nutritional virtues. It is very high in vitamin A, dietary fiber, potassium, and iron; it contains a fair amount of vitamin C and more protein than most vegetables (5.4 grams in a cup of cooked leaves); and it is low in calories—41 per cup of cooked leaves. But it also has some nutritional detractions, such as a chemical called oxalic acid which can bind minerals like calcium and iron and make them unavailable for absorption by the body (this, however, is usually not a problem in an otherwise well-balanced diet). Spinach can be eaten raw (a spinach salad with mushrooms and red onions is colorful, nutritious, and tasty) as

well as cooked. Chopped, shredded, or whole, it cooks very quickly and can be added at the last minute to a soup or stir-fry. It is available year round, loose or in cellophane packages. *Choose* crisp leaves with a good green color and fresh odor. Most spinach is very sandy and should be washed thoroughly in a sink full of water. However, do not soak spinach, or you'll lose nutrients. Remove tough stems before cooking. Store spinach in the refrigerator in a plastic bag, and use it within a few days. Note that 1 pound of fresh spinach will cook down to just 1 cup, serving 2, or less if chopped and squeezed dry.

SQUASH, SUMMER. These prolific, tender, versatile vegetables are harvested when immature. Although they have no outstanding nutritive virtues beyond being very low in calories, they are popular because they are inexpensive, plentiful, and lend themselves to use in many different dishes. *Zucchini,* the best known of the summer squashes, is believed to have originated in South Africa. Others include *yellow straightneck* (a yellow version of the green zucchini), *yellow crookneck* (like the straightneck but with a hooked neck), *pattypan,* with a shape like a flying saucer and a more succulent flavor than the others, and *chayote,* a hairy pear-shaped native of Mexico with a crunchy texture and neutral flavor. Zucchini and its yellow counterparts can be eaten raw or cooked. Zucchini can be grated and added to tomato sauce or, after the water is squeezed from the pulp, used in baking sweet breads. Overgrown zucchinis should be sliced in half lengthwise and seeded before cooking. They are wonderful stuffed, sprinkled with grated Parmesan, and baked. Zucchinis also make a refreshing cold summer soup. (See recipes on pp. 331,

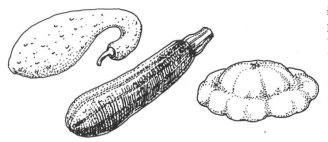

399, 485, among others). Small young zucchinis are delicious sliced thin in salads. Or zucchini sticks can be part of a cold vegetable platter. Zucchinis are in markets year round, but other summer squashes are usually only seasonally available. *Choose* squashes that are on the small side (unless you plan to stuff them), crisp, and free of soft spots and wrinkled skin. Pattypan squash should have a diameter of less than 4 inches and a pale green skin (the skin turns white and hard as it ages). Store summer squash in the refrigerator, and use it within a week. Summer squash, with its high water content, is very low in calories—25 per cup of slices or cubes. It is a good source of potassium, vitamins A and C, and niacin. One pound yields about 3 cups of slices, serving 4.

SQUASH, WINTER. Winter squashes, including pumpkins and gourds, are American plants that spread eastward in the mid-1800s. I always serve these fall vegetables at Thanksgiving dinner as an expression of my gratitude for their rich flavor, high nutrient content, long storage capability, variety, and versatility. I stuff them for a main course or use them in breads, stews, soups, cookies, muffins, puddings, and as side dishes (see, for example, recipes on pp. 324, 401, and 530). And I toast their seeds for nutritious nibbling. Popular varieties include *acorn, butternut, buttercup, Hubbard, pumpkin, turban,* and the newest addition, *spaghetti* (really a gourd). After baking or boiling, the inner strands of spaghetti squash can be pulled apart to resemble spaghetti—delicious sprinkled with Parmesan or tossed with spaghetti sauce (see the recipe on p. 448). My Halloween pumpkin invariably winds up in breads, muffins, cookies, stews, and soup as well as Thanksgiving pie. Pumpkins sustained many an American colonist. As one put it

in 1683: "We had pumpkins in the morning and pumpkins at noon. If it were not for pumpkins, we'd be undone soon." Cooked and puréed, winter squash stores well in the freezer for year-round use. Winter squashes are most readily available in the fall and early winter, although they sometimes can be found well into the spring. Pumpkin and winter squash can be used interchangeably in nearly all recipes. *Choose* firm squashes that are heavy for their size. Make sure they have no soft or discolored spots. Slight variations in skin color are not important. Stored in a cool place, winter squash will keep for months after harvest. These are starchy vegetables with a low water content. Baked, they have about 130 calories per cup; boiled, about 90. They are very rich in vitamin A and potassium, and are a fairly good source of niacin, iron, and protein.

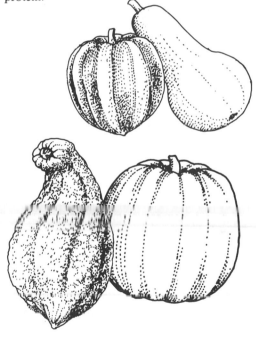

TOMATOES. Here is another American native, a relative of the potato and, like its cousin, indigenous to Peru. Tomatoes were at first thought to be the forbidden fruits of Eden and were aptly called "love apples." The hard, tiny fruits of the tomato's wild ancestors bear little

resemblance to the luscious, modern beefsteak, a model of agricultural engineering. Unfortunately, the tomato's extraordinary popularity and modern genetic ingenuity have also brought us the hard, tasteless semblance of a tomato that was designed more for shipping than for eating. (A critique of the ills of modern agriculture from the consumer's perspective was aptly entitled "Hard Tomatoes, Hard Times.") There has recently been developed a square tomato ideal for packing (but do cartons eat?). My family treats tomatoes like nectarines, watermelons, and other seasonal fruits. We eat lots of fresh tomatoes every summer and fall; and when the juicy, vine-ripened ones are no longer available, we forget about tomatoes until next year. Sometimes we're able to get decent *cherry* tomatoes during the winter, but these are occasional treats. When the bumper tomato crop is in during late August and early September, I make large amounts of tomato sauce that I freeze or can (see the recipe on p. 644). Italian *plum* tomatoes, which are less juicy than the round slicing types, are best for sauces. Otherwise, I use canned tomatoes for winter and spring cooking (Redpack tomatoes in purée are my favorite and often a "best buy"). Fresh tomatoes are available year round, but if you take my advice, you'll wait for the vine-ripened summer and fall varieties. In some areas, low-acid yellow tomatoes may be available. *Choose* plump, unblemished fruits with a distinct tomato smell. Once a pink color has begun to develop, tomatoes can be further ripened off the vine; place them with a ripe apple in a paper bag punched with a few holes, or put them in indirect light (but not in sunlight). Keep ripe tomatoes in the refrigerator, and use them within a week. Tomatoes are low in calories (1 medium tomato

has about 25 calories, a pound of tomatoes only 91); rich in vitamin A, potassium, and niacin; and a reasonably good source of vitamin C, iron, and protein. One medium tomato, chopped, equals about ½ cup. One pound of tomatoes, peeled and seeded, yields about 1½ cups of tomato pulp.

TURNIPS. Like rutabagas, turnips are root vegetables that are often snubbed as peasant fare. But the snobs are missing something good. Turnip greens are a slightly sweet, highly nutritious vegetable, a cabbage relative that has cancer-preventing properties. Turnip roots, which can be eaten raw as well as cooked, are excellent in soups and stews (see recipes on pp. 432, 531, and 532). The roots have a white and purple skin that is peeled before eating the white flesh. Roots are available year round, and the greens may also be. *Choose* small, firm, smooth roots free of cracks and scars; leaves should be crisp and fresh-looking. Refrigerate the leaves, and use them within a day or 2. Roots will keep in the refrigerator for a week or longer. Turnip greens are very rich in vitamins A and C and in calcium, and contain reasonable amounts of iron and protein. The roots are sources of potassium. There are 29 calories in a cup of cooked greens, and 36 calories in a cup of cubed, cooked roots. One pound of turnip roots yields about 4 cups diced.

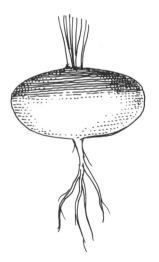

WATERCRESS. My first activity upon arriving in rural Minnesota every summer is to stop at a roadside stream and pick watercress. This vegetable-with-a-bite is a zesty ingredient in salads, stir-fries, and soups, and an attractive garnish on serving platters and dinner plates. Cold watercress soup is an ideal antidote to summer heat and humidity (see page 330). Watercress is also reputed to have diuretic properties. It is usually available all year, sold in bunches held in ice water. *Choose* crisp, tender leaves of uniform green color. Store watercress in a plastic bag in the refrigerator, and use the cress within a day or 2. Or if stood with the stem ends in a glass of water and covered with a plastic bag, it should keep for a week. At only 7 calories per cup, watercress is a dieter's delight that provides lots of vitamin A as well as some vitamin C.

Garlic: A Clove for All Seasons

You can guess what Gilroy's chief product is by sniffing the August air 10 miles from town. Humorist Will Rogers called this agricultural community nestled in California's productive Santa Clara Valley "the only town in America where you can marinate a steak just by hanging it out on a clothesline." The reason is garlic, 150 million pounds of which are produced on 14,000 acres within 90 miles of Gilroy. That's 90 percent of the nation's garlic production. It's not the crop that makes Gilroy smell like a thousand Italian restaurants. Fresh heads of garlic hide their pungent odor very well. Rather, it's the processing plants that turn millions of pounds of fresh garlic into 33 different kinds of powder, flakes, and salts.

Garlic, a bulb that is first cousin to the onion, originated in central Asia, has been cultivated in Egypt and Syria since Biblical times, and was extremely popular with the ancient Greeks and Romans. Although it has long been a dominant flavoring in the cuisines of China, Italy, France, the Middle East, Greece, Spain, and India, Americans didn't discover its culinary potential until well into this century (probably because our Anglo-Saxon ancestors turned their noses up at it). Unfortunately, however, many Americans who cook with garlic have never used "the real thing," relying instead on the artificial-tasting products that emerge from Gilroy's processing plants. A sprinkle of garlic powder on a slice from the corner pizzeria may not do much culinary damage, but relying on dehydrated versions of this extraordinary vegetable is a vast disservice to most made-from-scratch dishes, be they soups, salads, sauces, sautées, stews, or stir-fries. If you haven't already, it's time to discover fresh garlic, not only for its gastronomic qualities, which cannot be duplicated in a bottle of dried seasoning, but also for the various health benefits it is now known to bestow.

Actually, the health value of garlic was suspected in ancient times. What the ancients lacked in scientific expertise they more than made up for with a rich imagination. For example, the Codex Ebers, an Egyptian papyrus from around 1550

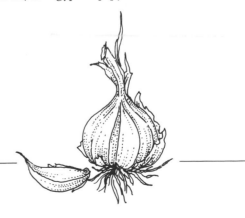

B.C., suggested 22 different garlic-based formulas to cure ailments from body weakness and headaches to tumors of the throat. Other papyruses recommended garlic as a test of a woman's fertility: if a clove of garlic placed in a woman's womb before bed did not result in garlic breath by morning, she was said to be infertile. The Romans touted garlic as a source of power for laborers and gladiators, and the Roman naturalist Pliny proposed 61 garlicky cures for everything from hemorrhoids to snake bites. Hippocrates, the father of medicine, bestowed it with laxative and diuretic properties, and Mohammed used it to treat scorpion stings. Perhaps the most famous claim for garlic, particularly among enthusiasts of the occult, is its purported ability to keep vampires at bay: cover all doors, windows, cracks, and crevices with clusters of garlic heads and wear a bunch around your neck and the bloodthirsty creatures will steer clear of your jugular. And to kill a vampire, stuff his mouth with garlic before driving a wooden stake through his heart.

While few of us need to worry about vampires, other threats to our health and well-being do fall within garlic's therapeutic powers, according to recent scientific evidence. There is a distinct association between the extravagant use of garlic and protection against heart disease. The cholesterol-lowering ability of garlic was first reported in twentieth-century scientific literature in 1949. But not until three decades later was this claim retested using modern scientific study techniques. In 1978 Indian researchers conducted a study of 88 people, 20 of them healthy and 68 with coronary heart disease and high levels of fat (cholesterol and triglycerides) in their blood. Every day for 6 to 10 months, the volunteers consumed fresh garlic oil in an amount equivalent to about an ounce of whole garlic (about half a head of fresh cloves). On average, there was a 17-percent drop in serum cholesterol levels and a 20-percent drop in triglyceride levels. In another study, garlic consumed along with a high-fat meal protected against the cholesterol-raising effects of fat.

In addition, chemical analysis has shown that garlic and onion both contain substances that can inhibit the clumping of blood cells. Such clumping is the start of clots, which are a major factor in heart attacks and strokes. Garlic may also help to lower blood pressure. The Chinese and Japanese have used it to treat high blood pressure for centuries, and the Japanese food and drug administration officially recognizes garlic as a treatment for this condition. At the least, garlic, which has almost no sodium, is a taste-bud–stimulating alternative to salt, which can raise blood pressure in sensitive individuals. The Japanese also have reported evidence that garlic may be effective in treating stomach ulcers, that it enhances the absorption of the B vitamin thiamin, and that it helps to rid the body of toxic wastes.

Garlic may also help to combat diabetes, cancer, and infections. A study in rabbits showed that garlic juice was almost as effective as the drug tolbutamide in lowering blood-sugar levels. Garlic extract protected mice against death from injected cancer cells. A component of garlic juice, allicin, has been shown to have antibiotic properties; indeed, during World War I, garlic reportedly was used successfully to prevent infection and gangrene as a result of battle wounds, and it has been used by millions of Europeans who say it prevents and treats traveler's diarrhea. At the University of Indiana, extracts of garlic were shown to slow or stop the growth of several medically important fungi and molds, including *Candida,* a fungus that is a frequent cause of vaginal infections. And Chinese researchers recently showed that garlic alone could be used to cure a life-threatening fungal form of meningitis, an infection of the lining of the brain and spinal cord. The researchers suggested that garlic was able to stimulate the body's immunological defenses against the invading organisms.

A word of warning to those tempted by "kyolic" and other odorless garlic pills and capsules sold in health food stores. The therapeutic potency of these products has not been adequately tested. Virtually all the evidence for health benefits of garlic is based on fresh garlic or extracts of fresh garlic, with the odoriferous chemicals intact. If you want garlic's health benefits, at the present time you'll have to put up with the reek. To reduce garlic's social liability, convince your friends and relatives to eat it as well: if people have garlic on their breath, they won't notice garlic breath in others.

Fresh heads of garlic are available year round. If possible, buy heads that are sold loose rather than boxed; it's hard to tell if the head is fresh in a box. *Choose* heads that are plump, firm, dry, and free of soft spots or shriveled cloves. Store garlic in a cool, dark, dry, well-ventilated spot rather than in the refrigerator, where it is likely to sprout. Don't peel cloves until you are ready to use them. Unpeeled, a head of garlic should stay reasonably fresh for weeks, and individual unpeeled cloves should last about a week. They can also be frozen indefinitely if unpeeled and enclosed in a plastic bag or container. *To peel* garlic expeditiously, place the clove on its side on a flat surface, cover it with the flat side of a knife blade, and gently pound the blade with your fist.

This loosens the skin, which should come off very easily. The clove is then ready for crushing, mincing, or using whole. The flavor of garlic is better if it is minced with a knife rather than forced through a garlic press, but the latter can serve the purpose for the sake of expedience.

The pungency of garlic is determined by how finely it is cut and how long it is cooked. The smaller the pieces, the "hotter" the flavor; the longer the cooking time, the milder and less fragrant a legacy. You might try using fresh garlic in almost any course except dessert. It is excellent in salad dressings, pasta sauces, stews, and marinades, as well as on vegetables, bread, poultry, and roasts. I use garlic in many dishes (for some recipes in which it is especially prominent, see pp. 317, 436, and 466). Use lemon juice or salt to rid your hands, utensils, and counter top of garlic odor. For your breath, you might try eating parsley—lots of it; the chlorophyll it contains is said to act as nature's mouthwash.

FRUITS: SWEET AND SWELL FOR YOU

APPLES.   Even before Eve supposedly assured the survival of the species by turning on Adam with a bite of an apple, this fruit was prized by human ancestors. Cultivation of apples is believed to date back to the beginning of the Stone Age. By the fourth century A.D., the Romans could list 37 different varieties of apples. Today, there are more than 7,000 varieties in the United States alone. Your local market, however, is likely to offer only a handful of the most popular varieties: *McIntosh, Red Delicious, Golden Delicious, Winesap, Granny Smith, Rome Beauty, Cortland,* and perhaps *Jonathan, Northern Spy,* and *Idared.* If you live on the East Coast, you may be able to find the *Macoun* (an improvement over the McIntosh) and the *Empire,* a premier product of 25 years of breeding by the New York State Agricultural Experiment Station in Geneva, New York. Some varieties are most desirable as eating apples, others are best as cooking or baking apples, and a few, like Jonathan and Granny Smith,

can serve as all three. Apples are so versatile a food that whole books on apple cookery have been written. They can be a part of any meal— breakfast, lunch, dinner, and snacks—and any course—appetizer, salad, soup, entrée, dessert, or beverage. Among other uses, I slice them into salads, chop them into breakfast cereal (both hot and cold), sliver them into pancakes, grate them into breads, and, of course, chomp on them whole (see, for example, recipes on pp. 410, 426, and 509). They are a durable snack that transports well in briefcase and car, and a deli-

cious, nourishing way to stave off between-meal hunger. Apples are available year round; their supply is lowest in summer, but other wonderful fruits are plentiful then. For *eating,* try McIntosh, Granny Smith, Stayman, Macoun, Empire, Winesap, Northern Spy, Baldwin, Gravenstein, and Wealthy, as well as the tiny Lady apples. Red and Golden Delicious are also popular eating apples, but in my view they often look better than they taste and I find other varieties far superior. For *sauce,* try McIntosh, Cortland, Jonathan, Macoun, Golden Delicious, Rhode Island Greening, Northern Spy, Idared, Rome, and crab apples (the latter must have added sugar). For *pies,* Rome, Cortland, Granny Smith, Rhode Island Greening, and Gravenstein are highly suitable. And for *baking* whole, try York Imperial, Rome Beauty, and Cortland. *Choose* fruits that are firm and free of blemishes, soft spots, and wrinkled skin. Unless you're buying from a farmer's market, apples may be sold coated with wax; before eating, try to wash off the wax by scrubbing the fruit lightly with a vegetable brush under hot, soapy water. Apples are best stored in the refrigerator, although they are more durable at room temperature than most noncitrus fruits and they have a better flavor when not too cold. At room temperature, McIntosh and Cortlands will keep about 2 weeks; Empire, Red and Golden Delicious, and Northern Spy, about 3 weeks; and Idared and Rome Beauty, about 4 weeks. If stored in the refrigerator right after purchase, many apples will keep until spring, but it is best to purchase them through the year as needed and to let distributors do the storing. Apples produce a gas, ethylene, which hastens ripening; placing an apple in a bag with unripe bananas, for example, will soon result in ripe bananas. By the same token, fruits in a bowl near apples may become overripe. Cut apples darken on exposure to air unless coated with lemon or other citrus juice or vinegar. If used in cooking or a fruit salad, prepare them at the last minute. Apples contain some potassium and vitamin A, but their principle nutritional virtue is their fiber content, much of it as healthful pectin. A medium-sized apple (3 to a pound) has 80 calories. A pound of apples yields about 3 cups of slices.

APRICOTS. A native of China, this fragile fruit that Alexander the Great is believed to have introduced to the Greeks and Romans had become a rarity in American markets but now seems to be making a comeback. Nearly all apricots sold here originate in California and must be picked unripe for shipment. They will ripen at room temperature, but they may shrivel before that happens. Place unripe fruit in a paper bag with holes for circulation, and keep the bag out of the sun. In most of the country, fresh apricots are available only in June and July. *Choose* firm, unblemished, unwrinkled fruits, preferably those that are already ripe (they should yield to gentle pressure) and yellow-orange in color. Store ripe fruit in the refrigerator, and use it within a few days. Apricots are very rich in vitamin A and are a good source of potassium. There are only 55 calories in 3 apricots (12 to the pound).

BANANAS. Botanically, bananas are a berry and the plant they come from is an herb. Native to tropical Asia and Africa, bananas today are probably the most universally enjoyed of all fruits. Although available in North America for only a century, they now outsell our native apple. Twelve billion bananas are consumed annually by Americans. Bananas are often the first and last fruit a person eats: they are easily digested by infants, the elderly, and the ailing. Although imported from South and Central America and the Caribbean, they are never expensive and can be found any time of year in virtually every market that sells produce. In addition to the common yellow banana that is about 8 to 12 inches long, there are red full-sized bananas and red or yellow small bananas, perhaps 4 inches long, each with a characteristic flavor. A close relative of the banana, the *plantain,* should be cooked before eating. Plantains are larger ʳhan bananas and are sold both green or yellow-green for cooking as a starchy vegetable, or yellow-brown or brown and soft to the touch for preparation as a sweet side dish, snack, or dessert. A West Indian friend got our family hooked on sliced ripe plantains that are dipped in flour and fried in a small amount of oil or butter. Ripe plantains can also be baked, sliced and unflavored, on a lightly greased cookie sheet for a lower-calorie treat. Bananas and plantains are available year round. Food purists may complain that bananas are never allowed to mature naturally on the plant; but if they were, they would not resemble the delicious, tender fruit we know as the banana. For peak flavor and small seeds, bananas must be picked green; they ripen during shipment, in the market, or at home. Even in the tropics, bananas are ripened off the plant. However, thin green bananas or those with dull-gray skins may never ripen properly, and those already separated from the bunch may ripen too quickly. *Choose* firm, plump bananas still in a bunch. If you want to eat them right away, buy those that are uniformly yellow (small brown specks indicate peak ripeness). Ripen green bananas uncovered or in a perforated paper bag at room temperature (60 to 70 degrees is best). Despite the old advertising jingle by Chiquita Banana, bananas that are fully ripe *can be refrigerated* to delay further ripening. Although the cold will darken their skins, the flavor and texture hold up for a few days. Even if your bananas get overripe, do not discard them; mash them for use in banana bread (see the recipe on p. 585) or banana-bran muffins. For an interesting hot-weather treat, try a frozen ripe banana (freeze it with the skin on); or for a special dessert, peel a ripe banana, insert an ice cream stick at one end, dip the banana in melted chocolate, and freeze the banana. Once peeled and sliced, bananas darken unless coated with citrus juice; they should be added to fruit salads just before serving. Bananas are a very rich source of potassium and contain some vitamin A, niacin, iron, and protein. One medium banana (3 to a pound) supplies about 100 calories. Three medium bananas mash down to about 1 cup.

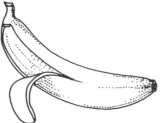

BLUEBERRIES. Though few Americans have access to wild blueberries (they are tiny, tart, and distinctly flavored and grow in such chilly climates as Maine and northern Minnesota), the larger, sweeter cultivated blueberries are now widely available from July through September. To me, they're synonymous with summer, and I can go through a pint in two or three days. I eat them with cereal and milk; yogurt; in fresh-fruit salad; in pancakes, muffins, cobblers, and fresh-fruit tarts; and out of hand like candy (see recipes on pp. 599 and 620). Blueberries can also be made into pies and jams. They are nearly always sold in perforated cardboard boxes covered with plastic and require some care in selection. *Choose* berries that appear plump, unwrinkled, uniformly blue in color, and nearly free of leaves and stems. The boxes should not be stained or have any evidence of mold (check for mold by looking through the holes at the bottom of the box). When you get them home, pick them over and remove any that are squashed, rotting, or moldy, but do not wash the berries until you are ready to use them. Berries will keep in their original container in the refrigerator for up to a week. They can also be frozen on cookie sheets and then transferred to plastic containers for frozen storage, though when defrosted the texture of the berries will be softer. Blueberries contain a fair amount of iron plus some potassium and vitamins A and C. They are high in fiber, an excellent natural laxative. A cup of blueberries supplies 90 calories.

CANTALOUPE. What we call cantaloupe in the United States is really a *musk melon* or *netted melon* (the true cantaloupe has a smooth, pale-green shell); both are believed to be natives of Asia. (See entries below for related melons and watermelon.) Cantaloupe is at its peak in June through October, a nourishing, low-calorie, deliciously refreshing snack as well as an appetizer or dessert or part of a meal. Half a cantaloupe with a dollop of cottage cheese makes a cool, nutri-

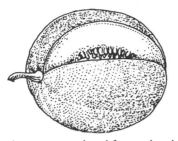

tious summer breakfast or lunch. Although purists claim that the only good melons are locally grown and allowed to ripen on the vine, in recent years the California and Central American cantaloupes, which are picked before full maturity, have been excellent by the time I cut into them. The trick is to pick a ripe, sweet melon or wait until the one you buy has reached its peak ripeness. *Choose* a well-rounded melon with a depressed smooth scar at the stem end and slight softness when pressed at the bottom end. The skin should be uniformly creamy yellow or tan (green areas may be underripe), with a netting that stands out. Most important is the aroma: unless the melon is very cold (in which case don't buy it since you can't tell if it's any good), it should have a sweet odor like a melon you'd want to eat. Avoid those with dented or soft spots or an overripe odor. Underripe melons will ripen at home in a few days out of the sun or, for faster ripening, in a perforated paper bag. However, after picking they do not get sweeter, only softer and juicier. Once ripe, melons should be refrigerated and eaten within a few days. To contain the odor, wrap the cut melons in plastic, and do not remove the seeds until you are ready to eat the melons since the seeds keep the flesh from drying out. Cantaloupes are very rich in vitamins A and C and potassium, and contain a fair amount of niacin and iron. Half of a 5-inch melon provides the day's requirement for vitamins A and C and has only 82 calories—a sweet bargain for any diet.

CHERRIES. Cherries, relatives of plums and peaches, grow wild in western Asia, Europe, and North Africa, and were cultivated in colonial America. Hundreds of varieties exist, but only a handful of the varieties of sweet cherries are available here on the fresh market—primarily the purplish-red *Bing* and the yellow-red *Royal Ann. Sour* cherries, which are used mainly for pies and preserves, are paler-red in color. Sour cherries generally come in first, in June, followed by the peak of the sweet-cherry season in mid-June and July. Cherries should be bought ripe; they will only rot, not ripen, at home. *Choose* plump, firm, highly colored fruit free of bruises or soft spots. The fruit should be glossy and the stems fresh-looking. If the store permits, taste one before you buy. Store cherries in a plastic bag in the refrigerator, and use them within a few days, washing them as you eat. Add them to fruit salads at the last minute to avoid having the red color "run" (the pits can be removed by slicing the cherries in half or by using a cherry pitter that rams a rod through the center of the fruit). Sour cherries can be canned for year-round use, but cherries don't freeze well. Sour cherries are high in vitamin A and contain a fair amount of potassium. There are 60 calories in a cup. Sweet cherries, with 82 calories per cup, contain potassium.

CRANBERRIES. These get my vote for the most underappreciated fruit in America. Their long association with Thanksgiving turkey puts them in a far-too-limited category, considering their low caloric content, low cost, refreshingly tart flavor, and excellent storage qualities. In addition to sauce, which can be used with meats and with cheese dishes as well as with fowl, cranberries can be used in pancakes, breads, muffins, cookies, puddings, juice, and preserves (see recipes on pp. 288, 542, and 607). Cranberries, which grow wild in some of our northern states, are readily available in cultivated form in the fall. They are nearly always sold prepackaged in plastic bags. The bags used to hold a pound—about 4 cups—of berries, but now they contain only 12 ounces—or 3 cups—of cranberries for the same price, if not more. *Choose* bags with firm, plump, lustrous red berries and no sign of leakage. Uncooked, cranberries can be kept refrigerated for about a week. To assure yourself of a supply between Thanksgiving and the following October, buy extra bags in the fall and place them directly into the freezer without washing the berries; you can pour them out as needed and keep the rest frozen. There are only 44 calories in a cup of whole cranberries (before you add sugar), but aside from fiber, their nutrient content is low.

FIGS. Once Adam and Eve ate the apple, they felt obliged to cover themselves with fig leaves. Figs have been a human delicacy for at least 5,000 years, and, though native to Asia, they have been most prominent in the Middle Eastern and Mediterranean cultures. Fresh figs are not common in American markets but are definitely worth trying if you find them, usually during the summer and early fall, and if you can afford their gourmet price (about 79 cents each!). The most popular varieties are *Calimyrna* (or *Smyrna*), which are large and yellow-green; *Mission,* deep purple with small seeds; and *Kadota,* yellow-green and thick-skinned with very small seeds. *Choose* figs that are ripe (soft when gently squeezed) and plump. They should smell sweet, not sour. Refrigerate and use them as soon as possible, within a day or 2. Figs are very high in dietary fiber (a common home cure for constipation), and they are fairly high in potassium. There are 40 calories in one medium-sized fig (9 to a pound).

GRAPEFRUIT. Grapefruit has been a cultivated fruit for only about 150 years, but judging from the popularity it now enjoys, its future in the human diet is assured. Although it is grown in subtropical and tropical climates worldwide, the United States produces by far the largest crop, primarily in Florida, Texas, California, and Arizona. The flesh is usually white or pink, and sometimes red. Grapefruits are available year round for eating "on the half shell," sectioned in salads, or sugared and broiled for dessert. *Choose* thin-skinned fruits that feel heavy for their size (they will have more juice) and firm but springy when pressed. Minor skin blemishes can be ignored, but avoid those with obvious bruised or soft spots. Grapefruits do not ripen after harvest. Whole grapefruits will keep for two weeks in the refrigerator; cut grapefruits should be covered with plastic wrap and eaten within 2 days. Grapefruits are very rich in vitamin C and potassium. Pink grapefruits are also high in vitamin A.

GRAPES. As one of the oldest human foods, grapes have been cultivated for more than 6,000 years and were eaten in their wild form long before that. The ability of grapes to ferment into wine stimulated breeding programs that have resulted in hundreds of grape varieties, each suitable for different growing conditions and tastes. Although the small, green *Thompson Seedless* grapes are by far the most popular table variety, there are many others available, including the deliciously sweet new *red seedless* grapes, the foxy and very flavorful *Concord* grapes (available fresh only in the fall), *Emperor* grapes (thin-skinned and red), *Ribier* grapes (large, blue-black grapes with tough skins), and *Tokay* grapes (mild, red, oval, and thick-skinned). *Choose* plump, firm grapes that are firmly attached to their stems,

which should be supple and green. Check the fruit for full color and absence of discolorations. Green grapes are best if some yellow is mixed with the green, but there should be no evidence of browning or whitening at the stem end. Store unwashed grapes in the refrigerator in a plastic bag, and use them within a week. Grapes are high in fiber but not much else except fruit sugar. There are 70 calories in a cup of Concord grapes, and about 100 in a cup of Thompson Seedless.

KIWI FRUIT. A relative newcomer to the American market, this egg-shaped fruit with a brown fuzzy skin hails from New Zealand, where it was named for that country's native flightless bird. Its quick adoption as a specialty fruit (sliced, it looks beautiful in tarts and on fruit platters) led to commercial cultivation in California and wider availability, although, oddly, no reduction in price. The kiwi, the very same fruit as the Chinese gooseberry, has bright green flesh and a circle of edible black seeds under its thin dull skin. The flavor is tart and reminiscent of the musty taste of some tropical fruits. Kiwis can be eaten from the half shell or peeled and sliced (crosswise for the best appearance). They are available year round except, perhaps, in spring. *Choose* ripe fruits that yield to gentle pressure, or buy them firm and ripen them at home at room temperature in a perforated paper bag. Once ripe, store the fruit in the refrigerator for up to 3 weeks. Kiwis are high in vitamin C; a 3-ounce fruit has twice the recommended daily amount of vitamin C for an adult.

LEMONS AND LIMES. These citrus fruits are not eaten as fruits in their raw state. Rather, their juice (and sometimes their rinds) is mainly used as a flavoring and in drinks. The bottled alternatives to fresh lemon and lime juice leave much to be desired. Far better to prepare your own; both can be frozen for later use (see p.

265). Lemon is especially popular as a culinary aid, used in preparing everything from soup to entrées to desserts. Both lemons and limes are very high in vitamin C. The use of limes to prevent scurvy (vitamin-C deficiency disease) during long voyages led to the nickname "limeys" for British sailors. *Choose* firm, plump fruits that are heavy for their size and have a rich color and slightly glossy skin. Some brownish mottling on the skin of limes does not affect the fruit.

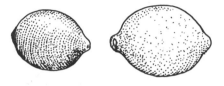

MANGOES. Native of the East Indies, mangoes are now grown throughout the tropics and in Florida and California. When they are good, they are very, very good, with slippery smooth yellow-orange flesh that is succulent and sweet; but when they are bad, they are horrid, with stringy flesh and a disagreeable flavor that has been likened to turpentine. To my taste, the most luscious mangoes come from Mexico. I first became acquainted with mangoes in the Central Desert of Baja California, where a crate of ripe Mexican mangoes, squirted with lime juice, sustained me through the scorching, parching heat. I have loved them ever since, slicing them into fruit salads and atop cold cereal and yogurt, or just eating the peeled fruit right off the pit. They can also be turned into an excellent chutney or a refreshing sorbet or drink (see the recipe on p. 288). Mangoes are now available in markets year round. They come in a wide range of sizes—from a few ounces to several pounds—and several shapes—round, oval, and more or less kidney-shaped. *Choose* firm, unblemished fruit that is on the large side (the pit takes up proportionately less space in big mangoes). The skin may be green or yellow, turning red and yellow as

the fruit ripens. A ripe fruit will yield to gentle pressure (but avoid one that is mushy) and will smell sweet and delicious, not fermented. Mangoes will ripen at room temperature, fastest in a perforated paper bag. Store ripe mangoes in a plastic bag in the refrigerator, and eat them within a day or 2. *Take care in peeling* the fruit—the skin contains a sap like that in poison ivy. Sensitive individuals (and you can suddenly become sensitive to this chemical) will get a blistering rash. After peeling mangoes (you may want to wear rubber gloves or hold the fruit in a paper towel while doing this), wash your hands and utensils well with soap and water. Never try to eat the fruit off the peel (I learned this the hard way after I got "poison ivy" in the corners of my mouth). Mangoes are very high in vitamins A and C, potassium, niacin, and fiber. A cup of mango slices has about 100 calories.

MELONS. In addition to the aforementioned cantaloupe, your market may offer any of several specialty melons that generally cost more but may taste even better than the best cantaloupe. The one you're most likely to find is the *honeydew* melon, off-white to yellowish-white on the outside, lime-green within, and so named for its honey-sweet flavor (if you get a good one). *Choose* a ripe melon, one with skin that has a dull appearance and feels velvety. Avoid dead-white or greenish-white melons and those with hard, smooth skins. The blossom end (bottom) should yield slightly to pressure, and you should be able to smell the melony aroma. If you shake it, you

should hear the seeds and juice slosh about. Larger melons are generally tastier. Other melons on the fresh market include *Persian,* with a yellow skin and finer netting than cantaloupe but more orange flesh and larger size; *crenshaw* (or *cranshaw*), with yellow-orange flesh and a mottled-green skin that turns to golden yellow as the melon ripens; *casaba,* which looks like the crenshaw but is more deeply furrowed and has no odor when ripe; and *Spanish melon,* a cross between the crenshaw and the casaba. See "cantaloupe" for buying, storing, and nutritional information. The honeydew and casaba have less vitamin A than the cantaloupe.

NECTARINES. Contrary to popular belief, the nectarine is not a cross between a peach and a plum, or a peach and anything else. It is an original ancient fruit, a smooth-skinned member of the peach family, and its name is believed to have come from the Greek word *nekter,* the drink of the gods, a testimony to its extraordinarily delicious flavor when ripe. Nectarines used to be available only during the summer months. After being in limited supply during the the 1970s, they appear to have made a comeback with the importation of delicious and inexpensive nectarines from Chile, which are available all winter here. *Choose* plump, full-color fruits (deep yellow or with a red blush) that are slightly soft along the seam. Avoid those that are hard and greenish since they may never ripen properly. The fruit should also have a fragrant aroma. A hard nectarine that was immature when picked will soften and become juicier (but not necessarily sweeter) when kept at room temperature in a perforated paper bag. Once ripe, store the fruit in the refrigerator in a plastic bag, and eat it within a few days (the flavor is best if eaten at room temperature). The cut flesh will darken upon exposure to air, so add it to fruit salads at the last minute or coat it with citrus juice. Nectarines are very high in vitamin A and potassium. One fruit about 2½ inches in diameter has 88 calories.

ORANGES. A native of the Far East, where it has been cultivated for at least 4,000 years, the orange did not become popular in this country until this century. Extensive cultivation in California and Florida as well as a transportation and processing network have combined to make oranges, either whole or as juice, daily fare in most American households. The orange is by far the nation's primary source of vitamin C. Of all the widely available fruits, oranges and their close relatives are probably the most durable and portable, though somewhat messier to eat than apples or bananas. Oranges can be bought for eating or for squeezing (juice oranges), or for making into marmalades and sauces (bitter oranges). Popular eating varieties include the *navel* (so named for the "belly button" at one end), *Temple, king,* and *Jaffa.* The *mandarin,* with segments that separate easily, is a small, very sweet relative of the orange. Also fine for eating out of hand are such relatives of the orange as the *Clementine* (a cross between an orange and a tangerine), *tangelo* (a cross between the tangerine or mandarin orange and the pomelo, a relative of grapefruit), and *tangerine* (a loose-skinned variety of mandarin orange). Among the popular juice oranges are *Valencia* (this thin-skinned orange can also be peeled and eaten out of hand), *Hamlin,* and *Parson Brown.* For making marmalade, the *Seville* orange is the one most often used, and for sauces, the *blood* orange (its pulp is reddish) is used. Fresh oranges both for eating and squeezing are now a year-round commodity in American markets, although the supply of good oranges dwindles in the summer months (however, many other luscious fruits are available then). *Choose* fruits that are firm and heavy for their size and free of soft spots and wrinkles. Brown streaks on the skin have no bearing on quality. Oranges do not ripen after harvest, and some green color on the skin does not necessarily mean the fruit is unripe. The skin of Florida oranges is commonly dyed to meet consumer "demand" (created largely by the industry itself) for uniformly orange-colored oranges. Although the government claims it is harmless, some scientists have doubts about the healthfulness of this dye. Unfortunately, the only way to know if an orange has been dyed is to check the shipping crate, which must be labeled "color added." If I am planning to use the rind in a recipe, I buy California oranges (for example, the Sunkist brand). Oranges can be kept at room temperature for several days but are best stored in a plastic bag in the refrigerator, where they will keep for weeks without significant nutrient loss. Oranges and their relatives are excellent sources of vitamin C (1 medium orange or its juice meets the daily requirement for an adult) and potassium, and are fairly high in vitamin A. Although the flavor and fiber content of freshly squeezed orange juice is unbeatable, juice made from frozen concentrate may actually contain more vitamin C because the concentrate is prepared from oranges that ripen on the tree, where vitamin-C content reaches its maximum, whereas oranges that are shipped out of state are picked before they reach peak maturity. A medium-sized orange has 65 calories; a cup of orange sections has 88.

PAPAYA. Here is another nutrient-rich, delectably flavored tropical fruit worth knowing. It goes by such pseudonyms as pawpaw, fruta bomba (in Cuba), and tree melon (the melonlike fruits, which are really berries, are produced just under the leafy canopy of fast-growing trees). Florida is the main producer of papayas in the continental United States. The fruits are elongated, something like an avocado, yellow to yellow-green in color, and range in size from a few ounces to several pounds. There are edible black seeds in the center (though most Americans discard them, the Mexicans use these high-protein seeds in salads and other dishes). When the fruit is sectioned crosswise, the seeds form the shape of a five-pointed star. Papayas can be eaten underripe as a cooked starchy vegetable or ripe as a sweet, fresh fruit. Although you may never have eaten papayas directly, chances are you've consumed their most popular ingredient, papain, an enzyme used to tenderize meat. (A related chemical, chymopapain, is used to dissolve herniated spinal disks.) Papayas are available all year but are at their peak in May and June. *Choose* those that are mostly yellow, yield slightly to gentle pressure, and have a pleasant aroma. Avoid fruits that are very soft or have rotten spots. Fruits that are at least partly yellow can be ripened at room temperature in a perforated paper bag. Store ripe fruit in the refrigerator, and use the fruit within a day or 2. *When peeling papaya, take care* not to touch the skin: it, like mango skin, can cause an allergic reaction. Papayas are very rich in vitamins A and C, and potassium. One cup of cubed fruit contains only 55 calories.

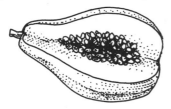

PEACHES. The peach originated in China, where it was known 2,000 years before the birth of Christ and was regarded as a symbol of immortality. The Chinese may have been on to something, judging from the reported effects of a peach on Madame Récamier, a French beauty of the nineteenth century. She was ill and refused all food, but her life was saved by a dish of peaches in syrup and cream, which restored her appetite and her will to live. Peaches today are among the most widely cultivated fruits. Popular varieties include "freestones" (the corrugated pits separate readily from the flesh), "clingstones" (with a firm hold on the pit), and "semifreestones" (in between freestones and clingstones). Fresh peaches are decidedly summer fruits. It is best to buy ripe or nearly ripe peaches if you want good flavor. *Choose* those with full color—yellow, yellow with a red blush, or mostly red—and a distinct peachy aroma. The fruit should be free of soft spots but yield slightly to

gentle pressure. If picked too green and hard, peaches will not ripen properly off the tree. You can soften the flesh of a too-firm peach by storing it at room temperature for a few days, but don't expect much improvement in flavor. Ripe peaches should be refrigerated in a plastic bag and consumed within a few days. They bruise easily, so handle them gently. Peaches are very rich in vitamin A and potassium, and contain a fair amount of niacin and some iron and vitamin C. One medium-sized fruit (4 per pound) has 38 calories; a cup of sliced fresh peaches has 65 calories.

PEARS. According to paleontological evidence from western Asia, pears may be one of the oldest of cultivated fruits, going back 35 to 40 centuries. They were certainly popular among the Greeks and Romans, and by now more than 5,000 varieties of pears have been developed. In this country, the most popular is the *Bartlett,* a very juicy, tasty pear with a yellow skin. It is also highly perishable and does not transport well when ripe. A similarly juicy variety is the *Comice,* with a red-blushed yellow skin and squat neck. More durable and, in my view, more satisfying to eat (they require chewing) are the *Bosc* (russet-colored with a long, slender neck), *Anjou* (yellow-green and squat neck), and *Seckel,* a tiny, firm pear with a slightly granular texture and surprisingly sweet, juicy flesh (the skin is green, often with a red blush). One variety or another is available in summer, fall, and winter (only March to July tends to be pearless). Unlike most fruits,

pears are best when ripened off the tree. *Choose* those that are firm, well shaped, and free of bruises, and be prepared to allow a few days to ripen them in a perforated paper bag at room temperature. They are ready to eat when the flesh at the stem end yields slightly to gentle pressure; color is not a reliable indicator. Pears contain a fair amount of potassium and fiber. There are about 100 calories in a Bartlett or an Anjou, 86 in a Bosc. A cup of sliced pears has 100 calories.

PINEAPPLE. A South American native, the pineapple was introduced to Europe by Columbus, who brought it to Spain from Guadeloupe. It got its curious name compliments of the Spanish, who dubbed it "piña" because it looked like a pine cone. By the end of the sixteenth century, this succulent, sweet fruit was being produced in Africa and Asia. Pineapples are grown on non-woody, slow-growing plants called bromeliads, and they must be ripened on the plant. (When a fruit ripens, starch is converted to sugar. In the case of pineapple, the starch is in the plant, not the fruit, so no sugar will enter the fruit unless it remains on the plant until ripe.) To prevent spoilage, ripe pineapples are flown to the continental United States from Hawaii, the Caribbean, Mexico, and Central America, making them costly as fruits go. A Hawaiian pineapple is likely to cost between $2.79 and $3.79, those from eastern countries about $1.79. Both types are available year round, with peak supply in spring. To my taste, the Hawaiian pineapples are worth paying for: they are far superior in flavor and are larger (about 4 pounds) and juicier than the ones from south of the border. Hawaiian pineapples are nearly always identified as such on a tag attached

to the green top. Given their cost, you want to be especially sure you're getting a good one. The longstanding belief that ripeness can be judged by pulling a leaf from the crown is incorrect. Neither is skin color a reliable sign: a fully ripe pineapple may be either green or gold or both. *Choose* a pineapple with fresh, deep-green leaves at the crown; a very slight separation of the eyes, which should not be shrunken; heaviness for its size (indicating juiciness); and a distinctly sweet, pineapply aroma. If it smells fermented or acidic, it will be, so don't buy it. Finally, the squeeze test: pressed with your fingertips, a ripe pineapple will yield slightly. If you select a larger fruit, you'll have relatively more flesh, since the waste in skinning a pineapple is the same no matter what its size. If the pineapple you get is not quite ripe, you can reduce its acidity by placing it in a perforated paper bag at room temperature for a few days. Store a ripe pineapple in the refrigerator and try to consume it within a few days, although a well-wrapped cut pineapple will keep in the refrigerator for about a week. Pineapple is a good source of potassium and has some vitamin C and iron. A cup of diced fresh pineapple has 81 calories.

PLUMS. There are many different sizes, shapes, and colors of plums, which are widely grown throughout the world, especially in eastern Europe, where plums are fermented and distilled to produce the potent brandy slivovitz. Among the more popular plums are *Italian prune,* small and oval with a dark purple-blue skin and meaty flesh that makes them a good cooking plum (which incidentally is not the kind that is dried into prunes); *Santa Rosa,* a Japanese variety with deep-red skin; *greengage,* or *Kelsey,* medium-sized with a green skin that gets slightly yellow when ripe; *El Dorado* and *President,* large with reddish-blue skins; *Friar,* a squat, mid-sized, dark-purple plum; *Empress,* also dark purple but shaped like a large egg; and *damson,* small, oval, and blue-black with a very tart flavor that is best suited for preserves and tarts to which sugar is added. Plums are available from May through October. *Choose* fruits with good color that are plump, slightly soft, and free of bruises and shriveled skin. Underripe fruits will soften at room

temperature and lose some of their acidity, but don't expect much improvement in flavor since plums have all the sugar they can get when they are picked. Store ripe plums in a plastic bag in the refrigerator, and use them within several days. Plums are rich in vitamin A, potassium, and fiber, and contain a fair amount of iron. One prune plum has 21 calories; a Santa Rosa, about 32 calories; and 1 cup of pitted plum halves has 89 calories.

RASPBERRIES. Raspberries, cultivated in England by the mid-sixteenth century, grow wild in Europe, eastern Asia, and North America. As a child, I and my family spent part of every July among the wild bushes to pick these luscious, fragile fruits, which were well worth their toll in scratches and mosquito bites. Today, due to problems with plant viruses, the need for hand care of the vines and hand-picking, along with the perishability of the fruits (they crush and mold quickly), there are few fresh raspberries available and those that are cost plenty. Even in the peak season, in July, ½ pint can cost $2 or more. If you can, get your raspberries from a farm or farm stand, where they're likely to be cheaper. As with all berries, raspberries must be picked ripe: pinkish-red or black in color (depending on the type), soft, and plump. Occasionally, pinkish-yellow raspberries, called *honeyberries,* reach the fresh market; these are, to my taste, the most succulent of the lot. You may also find *blackberries* for sale, a close relative of the raspberry. *Choose* fruits that are uncrushed, free of mold and stem caps, and in boxes that are not stained or leaking. Store them in the refrigerator in the box they come in, and use them within a day or 2. Do not wash the berries until just before use. Raspberries are rich in potassium and

niacin, and contain a fair amount of iron and vitamin C. A cup of red raspberries has 70 calories; a cup of black raspberries has 98 calories. Blackberries are a good source of potassium and contain some vitamin A, vitamin C, and iron. There are 98 calories in a cup.

RHUBARB. Rhubarb, a vegetable that resembles pinkish-red celery, is nearly always cooked with sugar and used as a fruit. The leaves of the rhubarb plant are highly toxic and should be removed and discarded right after purchase (if you find them still attached to the stalks). Rhubarb was originally cultivated for its roots, which have medicinal properties. Wise consumers, however, will concentrate on the stalks, which can be stewed with sugar or honey (making a superb dessert or topping for yogurt), baked in pies (strawberry-rhubarb pie is an all-time favorite of mine), chopped into cake batter, or made into jam (see recipes on pp. 591 and 621). Fresh rhubarb is usually available in the spring. It freezes well when stewed or chopped fresh. *Choose* firm, crisp stalks (the leaves, if still attached, should be fresh, not wilted), not too big but not too skinny either. Store the rhubarb in the refrigerator in a plastic bag, and use it within a week. Rhubarb is best noted for its laxative properties. It is also high in potassium and contains a fair amount of calcium and iron. A cup of diced raw rhubarb contains only 20 calories, an amount that is significantly increased when sweetener is added (add 18 calories for each teaspoon of sugar).

STRAWBERRIES. Strawberries are really false fruits; the true fruits are the tiny black "seeds" that dot the fleshy portion, which is actually a swollen stem. False or not, strawberries are something special, an essential ingredient in almost every fruit fancier's repertoire. *Wild strawberries* can be found throughout the temperate zones of the world. They are tiny, painstaking to pick, highly perishable, and highly prized for their extraordinary flavor. One Fourth of July weekend, my husband and I nearly got sunstroke because we stumbled upon a large patch of wild strawberries and, on hands, knees, and occasionally rear end, we spent hours in the blazing sun to pick 2 quarts of them. After eating as many as we dared, we turned the rest into jam, which we sparingly doled out only to our most special guests over the next 2 years. Cultivated strawberries are the result of a hybrid accidentally developed in the eighteenth century, a cross between two wild species from South America and North America. Although traditionally a fruit of late spring, in recent years strawberries have been available year round on the fresh market, thanks to crops from Mexico and Florida. The cost per pint in midwinter may be double that of spring berries, but what a wonderful treat to have fresh strawberries for New Year's Eve! *Choose* berries that are brightly colored, firm, and have hulls attached. Avoid boxes that are stained, are leaking, or show signs of mold. Peek through the holes at the bottom of the box to be sure unripe berries are not buried beneath a layer of ripe ones. Strawberries do not ripen after picking. Refrigerate the berries, and use them within a day or 2, washing and hulling them as you go. Strawberries are high in vitamin C but lose this vitamin rapidly after they are cut. They are also rich in potassium and contain a fair amount of iron. There are 55 calories in a cup of whole berries. A pint yields about 2 cups of sliced berries.

WATERMELON. Watermelons are the fruits of a plant in the cucumber family. They are believed to have originated in North Africa, although claims of provenance have been made for southern Italy and India. Today they come in at least three popular sizes: the very large, almost cylindrical *Charleston Gray* with smooth, mottled, light-green skin (the best shape for making watermelon "boats"); the smaller, spherical, and darker-green *Miyako* and *Crimson Sweet* melons, weighing 20 to 40 pounds; and the small, round, dark-green *Sugar Baby* melon that runs 6 to 10 pounds. Watermelons are popular as summertime thirst quenchers, which is easy to understand when you realize that 98 percent of a watermelon's weight is water. The fruit is also reputed to be a diuretic (my mother-in-law never eats it at night because she says it means a trip to the bathroom long before morning). Watermelons are a summer fruit, generally available from May through September. Buying a whole watermelon is chancy since you can't see the flesh beforehand. *Choose* one with a smooth surface, dullish sheen, and well-rounded ends that should yield slightly to pressure. The underside should be creamy-yellow in color. You might also try slapping the melon: if the sound is flat and dull, it may be underripe; and if it sounds hollow, it may be too ripe. If you're buying a piece, the flesh should be deep-red, firm, free of white streaks, and with dark seeds. Cut melon should be stored in the refrigerator covered with plastic wrap. Whole melons do best there, too, if they fit in; otherwise, keep them in the coolest part of the house or in a picnic cooler along with some ice. Use the melon within a few days. Watermelon is very rich in vitamin A and potassium, and contains some iron and vitamin C. An inch-thick slice that is 10 inches in diameter and weighs 7 ounces has 111 calories; a cup of diced melon has 42 calories.

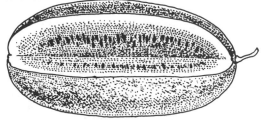

Dried Fruits: Use with Discretion

Dried fruits—among them apples, apricots, bananas, cherries, dates, figs, papaya, peaches, pears, pineapple, prunes, and raisins—are concentrated packages of nutrients, dietary fiber, sugar, and calories. When fruits are dried, most of their water is lost, greatly reducing their bulk. Thus, it is easy to eat a lot of them—and a lot of calories —before you feel full. Dates, for example, are about 60 percent sugar and supply 274 calories in 3½ ounces. Whereas a fresh apple has 58 calories in 3½ ounces, the same amount of dried apples has 275 calories. Dried fruits also cling tenaciously to teeth, providing decay-causing bacteria with a ready-made meal. It is best to brush soon after eating the fruits. Some people object to the additives used in processing dried fruits. The lighter-colored fruits, like golden raisins, apricots, apples, and pears, are often treated with sulfur dioxide to prevent discoloration, and some are treated with the preservative potassium sorbate to suppress the growth of molds and fungi. Imported dried fruits and some produced here are fumigated to destroy insects and their larvae.

Still, dried fruits are preferable to candy if you want a sweet snack; they are better than chocolate chips in cakes and cookies; and much healthier and tastier when added to dry cereal than are the commercial sugar coatings. They can also be cooked into a delicious fruit compote— no sugar necessary—and added to stuffings for poultry and meat.

Most dried fruits are high in iron, especially apricots, dates, figs, prunes, and raisins. Vitamin C is the only significant nutrient lost when fruits are dried, and most of the fruits involved were not good sources of this vitamin to begin with. Dried fruits are available year round, they are not subject to spoilage (however, store them in plastic bags to prevent them from getting dry and hard), and they keep for many months without refrigeration as long as no weevils live in your pantry. However, dates, which are moister than most dried fruits, do best stored in the refrigerator. You can also dry fruits at home if you have a food dehydrator.

A word of caution: Dried fruits can have a potent laxative effect, so don't eat too many unless you know your digestive tract can handle them.

CALORIES IN DRIED FRUIT

Fruit	Amount	Calories
Apple rings	1 cup (3 ounces)	234
Apricots	1 cup (28 large halves)	338
Dates	10 (3 ounces with pits)	219
Figs	7 medium (3½ ounces)	274
Lychees	46 (3½ ounces)	277
Peaches	1 cup (12 medium halves)	419
Pears	1 cup (10 halves)	480
Pineapple (candied)	3½ ounces	316
Prunes	10 large (3½ ounces)	215

III. Eat Your Way to Good Health and Weight Control

Introduction

If there is a nation more concerned about weight than ours and more unsuccessful at keeping it off, it must be buried under the mountain that could be made from all the discarded tried-and-false diet books and formulas. Millions of Americans go to desperate extremes to lose weight. Some live on high-protein liquid formulas, papayas and pineapples, or vinegar and seaweed for weeks. Others try vitamin-supplemented starvation or alternating days of feast and famine. One of the most popular diets of all time—the high-protein, low-carbohydrate scheme that has had dozens of reincarnations in the last hundred years—has dieters gorging on steaks, cheese, bacon, eggs, and other high-calorie, high-fat, high-cholesterol foods (as if a trim figure matters when you're six feet under). But as the number of diets and other weight-loss gimmicks multiplies, Americans continue to get fatter and repeatedly undermine their health in their futile battles against the bulge. The reasons for their failure to get off unwanted pounds and keep them off lie in the very methods most use to do it—*diets.*

What is a diet? Something you go on . . . to go off! And when you go off it, you return to the eating habits that had made you overweight in the first place. Slowly, your hard-won losses become unwanted gains, and you're ready to try the next desperation diet. The reason there are so many diet fads is that in the long run not one of them works. If any fad diet worked for the majority of people who tried it, there'd be no need for its dozens of successors. In truth, all that fad diets accomplish is to greatly enrich their inventors at the expense of a gullible public. More than 90 percent of people who go on them have regained the weight—and often then some—within a year (and often sooner).

Besides, low-calorie diets are self-defeating. Evolution has built a safety mechanism into the human body that helps to protect it from the ravages of starvation. When you eat significantly fewer calories than your body needs to sustain its current weight, a calorie-conservation system is triggered into action. In effect, your body lowers its thermostat so that fewer calories are used up in the normal course of the day. Your body's basal metabolic rate (BMR)—the rate at which calories are used when you are at rest—can drop by 10 percent to 45 percent. The more drastic your diet, the greater the drop in BMR is likely to be. Thus, if you were maintaining your weight on 2,000 calories a day and cut back to 1,000, the daily deficit may not be 1,000 calories but only 500. For some people, the calorie-conservation mechanism is so effective that after a few weeks they stop losing weight altogether, even though they are continuing to consume a very low-calorie diet. The discouragement that ensues is all too familiar to chronic dieters. This is not to mention the psychological stress associated with having to stick to a restricted-calorie diet and the fatigue that can accompany it, especially if the diet is very low in carbohydrates.

The problem is compounded if you then lapse from your diet and return to your former caloric intake. Now, with your BMR depressed, you can gain weight back faster than you lost it and maybe even more than you lost. Furthermore, you will gain back proportionately more body fat than you lost, and this will make it even harder for you to lose weight again when you decide to get back on the low-calorie bandwagon.

The secret to *permanent weight control* is not a diet but *an eating and exercise management plan* that you can go on and stay on for the rest of your life. It is not a lifetime of deprivation and self-denial, of eating awful-tasting and worse-looking foods, of alternately bingeing and starving, of measuring, weighing, and counting everything you put in your mouth, or of swallowing pills, potions, formulas, or fiber supplements. Nor is it a matter of sweating, massaging, or having your fat sucked out surgically or "dissolved" by magical enzymes. Rather, it is learning to eat three or more sensible meals a day, with wholesome snacks and occasional no-nos and plenty of satisfying complex carbohydrates, and making exercise as routine a part of your life as brushing your teeth.

Sure, calories count in weight control: if you eat more calories than your body uses up, the excess gets stored as fat. But for most overweight Americans, the problem is not so much the calories *in* as the calories *out*—or, rather, *not out!* Study after study has shown that most people with weight problems do not eat too much—they move too little. Cutting back on calories is not an alternative to exercise but rather an adjunct to it. Without exercise, recent studies show that nearly all attempts to lose weight and keep it off are doomed from the first spoonful of cottage cheese.

In fact, if you're already eating a reasonably good diet, you won't have to change your menu at all to shed those extra pounds. Exercise, as you will see in Chapter 14, can do it all, once and for all. And for those who may be consuming unneeded hidden calories, the chapters that follow it will show you how to clean up your caloric act without compromising the taste of food or having to eat boiled chicken and celery sticks while your friends are enjoying shrimp scampi. Whether you're dining at the local McDonald's or the Four Seasons, you can make choices that please your palate without fattening your frame or undermining your health.

11 ·

HOW TO EAT MORE AND WEIGH LESS (NOT FOR DIETERS ONLY)

Whether you are 50 pounds overweight or as trim as a fashion model, I hope you will read this chapter carefully. In it I have tried to show you how to trim unnecessary calories from your present diet and to outline a basic approach to meals and major nutrients that will help you to preserve your health and maintain a high energy level even if you have no extra pounds to shed. You will learn how to eat protein in reasonable amounts, with a greater emphasis on the healthier vegetable proteins and less on the fatty animal foods. You'll see how to de-fat your diet and reduce your dependence on salt without sacrificing flavor. And you'll learn how to cut your sugar consumption in half or more without having to give up all the sweet things in life. Together, these measures can help you shed unwanted pounds as well as improve your nutritional status and reduce your risk of developing heart disease, cancer, high blood pressure, stroke, diabetes, kidney disease, and a host of other ailments that currently plague millions of Americans. Not to mention the fact that you'll save a considerable amount of money on food, enough to buy some new clothes for your new figure or to treat yourself periodically to expensive but nutritious dining delights, like a fresh Hawaiian pineapple or strawberries out of season.

GETTING ENOUGH OF GOOD PROTEIN

With the average American already eating two to four times more protein than is really needed for good nutrition, nearly all of us could benefit from a cutback in protein consumption. Two ounces of a concentrated protein source is more than enough for most people at a single meal, but it is not unusual for an American adult to eat ½ pound of red meat, fish, or chicken for dinner. As I've said earlier, in my family that ½ pound of animal flesh feeds all four of us. But before you envision each of us sitting down to a tiny 2-ounce cube of meat on his or her plate (and from here on, I'll use the word *meat* to refer to *all flesh foods*), let me assure you that that's not how it is at all. We rarely serve meat as an intact chunk of food. Rather, we slice it, sliver it, cube it, chop it, or grind it, and combine it with lots of vegetables and starchy foods in a soup, stew, stir-fry, or casserole.

Some typical entrées for four would be stir-fried carrots and green beans with ½ pound of slivered pork served over a bed of rice; tomato sauce with ½ pound of lean ground beef (cooked first to remove the fat) served over pasta or rice; hearty soup made with lots of vegetables and potatoes, and ½ pound of cubed firm fish or baby shrimp or half the meat from a cooked chicken (all skin and fat removed, of course). (See, for example, recipes on pp. 334, 352, and 411.) In other words, the animal protein is treated more like a condiment and a complement to the protein in the starchy food rather than being the main focus of the meal. Often, in fact, the meal contains no animal flesh but rather uses milk, cheese, or eggs to enhance the protein value of a starch-based meal, or relies primarily on the protein in dried beans and peas without the need for any animal protein. Some favorites in this category include bean and vegetable soup with rice or pasta; pasta with vegetables and grated cheese; vegetable and cheese casserole; potatoes au gratin; pizza with vegetables and cheese; spaghetti pancakes; curried lentils and rice; meatless chili; vegetable lasagne; eggplant Parmesan; and a large "chef's" salad with kidney beans, green beans, sliced potatoes, and hard-boiled egg (see, for example, recipes on pp. 333, 394, and 402).

I'm not suggesting that you never again eat a steak or chops or fried chicken (we still do that from time to time) or that you revolutionize your diet overnight (it took our family years to evolve into our present dietary pattern). Too radical and abrupt a dietary shift will just provoke a counterrevolution because you'll miss the foods you're accustomed to eating. Instead, start by trying out the new approach for one or two, possibly three, meals a week, and as you become more familiar with this approach, gradually increase the proportion of carbohydrate-based meals and decrease those based on meat. Eventually, you're likely to find, as we did, that you think less and less about planning your meal around the meat and more and more about starting with the potatoes, rice, pasta, beans, and so forth, and adding in a little lean meat for flavor and the excellent nutrients it can provide when consumed in reasonable amounts.

Most of the menus and recipes in this book take this approach. Occasionally, when a meal contains a chunk of red meat, fish, or poultry, the amount of animal protein per serving is double our normal quantity—about 4 ounces instead of 2—but the fat content is still way below that of typical American meals. You will also find main-course recipes that include no animal protein but instead rely on combinations of plant proteins to provide complete protein as good as that in any animal food. Individually, plant foods contain incomplete proteins that are relatively deficient in one or more essential amino acids, the building blocks of protein. This means that unless two or more *complementary* plant proteins are combined in the same meal, the human body cannot make full use of all the protein in the plant food. It *doesn't* mean, however, that the body uses none of the protein in a plant food that is consumed alone, such as peanuts or oatmeal, just that all the available protein in that food cannot be assimilated by your body to manufacture new proteins for your tissues and cells. You may have seen complicated formulas for filling in the amino-acid deficiencies of plant foods,

---

Table 11   MEETING YOUR PROTEIN NEEDS

Protein needs are primarily determined by your age and your ideal body weight (that is, how much you *should* weigh). To calculate the number of grams of protein you should consume in a day, multiply your ideal weight by the appropriate number of grams listed below. Thus, if you are a 40-year-old woman who weighs (or who should weigh) 120 pounds, you need approximately 120 times 0.36, or 43 grams of protein a day.

Age (in years)	Grams of protein per pound	Age (in years)	Grams of protein per pound	Age (in years)	Grams of protein per pound
INFANTS		CHILDREN		ADULTS	
0–0.5	1.00	1–3	0.81	19 and over	0.36
0.5–1	0.90	4–6	0.68	Pregnant women	0.62
		7–10	0.55	Nursing women	0.53
		11–14	0.45		
		15–18	0.39		

Table 12   HOW MUCH PROTEIN IS IN YOUR FOODS?

Food	Serving size	Grams of protein	Food	Serving Size	Grams of protein
Barley	¼ cup raw	4	Noodles, egg	1 cup cooked	8
Bean curd (tofu)	4 ounces	10	Oatmeal	1 cup (in water)	5
Beans, kidney	½ cup cooked	7	Pancakes	3 4-inch cakes	6
Bean sprouts	½ cup	2	Peanut butter	2 tablespoons	8
Beef, lean cooked	2 ounces	16	Pizza	¼ 14-inch pie	16
Bran Flakes (40%)	1 cup	4	Pork, loin	2 ounces	14
Bread, whole-wheat	2 slices	5	Potato	7 ounces baked	4
Bulgur	½ cup cooked	3	Rice, brown	1 cup cooked	5
Cheese, Cheddar	1 ounce	7	Rice, white	1 cup cooked	4
Cheese, cottage	½ cup	15	Sesame seeds	2 tablespoons	3
Chicken, breast	¼ cup	11	Shrimp	2 ounces	14
Chicken, drumstick	1 small	12	Soybeans	½ cup cooked	10
Corn	½ cup	3	Spaghetti	1 cup	7
Eggs	2 medium	11	Spaghetti, high-protein	1 cup	13
Egg whites	2 medium	7	Squash, winter	1 cup baked	4
Flounder	3 ounces	26	Tuna, canned	3 ounces	24
Lentils	½ cup cooked	8	Turkey	2 ounces	18
Macaroni	1 cup cooked	7	Walnuts	6 large	4
Mackerel	3 ounces	19	Wheat flakes	1 cup	3
Milk, skim	1 cup	9	Yogurt, plain low-fat	1 cup	8
Muffin, corn	1 medium	3			

and chances are these seemingly elaborate schemes put you off. Who, after all, wants to have to think so hard to devise a nutritious meal and still worry that we may not have gotten all the protein we need? Well, you can relax: you don't need a computer to figure out how to balance plant protein, nor do you have to weigh and measure anything. There are just two simple approaches to obtaining complete protein from plant foods.

(1) Combine any legume (dried beans or peas, peanuts, or soy-based food) with any grain (for example, wheat, oats, corn, rice), nut, or seed. For example:

Lentils or black beans with rice
Peanut-butter sandwich
Bean taco or enchilada
Stir-fried tofu with rice
Stir-fried vegetables with rice and almonds
High-protein pasta (made with wheat and soy flours)
Pasta e fagioli (pasta and beans)
Felafel (chickpeas and sesame seeds)

(2) Combine any grain, legume, nut, or seed with small amounts of milk, cheese, yogurt, eggs, red meat, fish, or poultry. For example:

Oatmeal made with milk
Rice pudding
Pizza
Macaroni and cheese
Pancakes
Potatoes au gratin
Stir-fried pork and vegetables with rice
Spaghetti with clam sauce
Chicken soup with rice or pasta
Chef-style salad with chickpeas and cheese
Meatless chili topped with yogurt
Spanish rice

Many of these dishes, perhaps in slightly modified form, are doubtless already familiar to you. So including more of such foods in your diet and learning to rely upon them as main sources of protein need not be like adopting the exotic cuisine of a foreign country. Chances are, after a while you won't think of "pigging out" on animal protein because large amounts of flesh foods have lost their appeal. When served a large piece of meat, you may find you don't want to finish it. If you take the leftovers home, you can use them to make another meal (or two) and get double your money's worth while benefiting your health.

A WARNING ABOUT PROTEIN DIETS: If you have a weight problem (40 percent of Americans do and another 40 percent *think* they do), chances are you've either tried or been tempted by the plethora of high-protein, low-carbohydrate, and usually very low-calorie diets that periodically make a bundle for their inventors at the expense of gullible Americans, some of whom risk their health and their lives in a desperate attempt to shed unwanted pounds in a hurry. You *do* lose weight fast on these diets (it's hard not to if you're only eating 300 to 500 calories a day). But at what price? Aside from the monetary cost of the formulas or prepackaged meals and vitamin-mineral supplements you must buy, the combination of low calorie, low carbohydrate, and high protein throws your body's hormonal balance out of whack. Production of two essential hormones—thyroid hormone and norepinephrine—is significantly diminished. The result is likely to be such symptoms as feeling cold, dry skin and hair, constipation, abdominal bloating and nausea when you eat, fatigue, dizziness when you stand up, and generally feeling cruddy. What's more, when you go off such a diet, there is a risk, albeit small, of sudden death because of a rapid drop in blood levels of potassium and magnesium, which are needed to maintain a normal heart rhythm.

The rule of thumb for any weight-loss scheme should be: *Don't go on anything that you're not willing (or able) to stay on forever.* Since there's no way you could live indefinitely on any diet that distorts nutritional requirements and throws off basic body machinery, that's obviously not the kind of diet you should adopt to lose weight.

LESS DIETARY FAT MEANS LESS BODY FAT

Fat, as you've seen, is our most fattening nutrient. Ounce for ounce, fat contains two and a quarter times more calories than starch, sugar, or pure protein. Thus, even a seemingly small serving of fat can mean that a substantial proportion of the calories in your meal comes from fat. On average, Americans derive more than 40 percent of their daily calories from fat—three times the amount derived from protein and more than double that from added sugars. A typical adult eats the fat equivalent of *one stick of butter* daily. We would all be a lot healthier—and trimmer—if we cut that fat intake in half. Even if you replaced all the fat you would give up with an equivalent *amount* of starchy foods, you'd automatically reduce your caloric intake. Let's say that you now eat 2,000 calories a day and that 840 (42 percent) of those calories come from fat. That adds up to 93 grams of fat a day, since there are 9 calories in 1 gram of fat. If instead of 93 grams of fat you ate 93 grams of starch, you'd consume 372 starch calories, since there are only 4 calories in 1 gram of starch. That means a 468-calorie reduction in your daily caloric intake. All other things being equal, in a week's time you'd lose 1 pound of body fat just by making this ounce-for-ounce substitution of starch for fat. (Of course, you should not eliminate all fat from your diet. At least 1 tablespoon of vegetable fat—11 to 13 grams, providing 100 to 120 calories—is required each day for good nutrition.)

But, you say, you don't eat much fat. Chances are you're now consuming a lot more fat than you realize. Most of the fat we eat is *hidden* in our foods as part of the food naturally or as fat that is blended into the food when it is prepared. For example, 85 percent of the calories in a hot dog come from fat; 75 percent of the calories in hard cheese are fat calories; 62 percent of the calories in roast chicken (eaten with the skin) are fat calories; 55 percent of calories in tuna salad are fat; and even whole-milk yogurt is 49-percent fat calories. If you put a regular dressing on your salad, as many as 90 percent of the calories in the salad you eat would come from fat, turning an otherwise nutrient-dense food into a fat food of mostly empty calories. If you fry your potatoes, you add 219 fat calories to a cup of potatoes that naturally contains only 2 fat calories. If you drink whole milk instead of skim, you get 75 more fat calories per cup. If you fry chicken, you consume nearly twice the fat you would get if you ate it roasted and left the skin on your plate. If you add 1 tablespoon of butter or margarine to a serving of cooked pasta, you increase the calorie content by nearly 50 percent—from 210 to 310 calories. And if you eat tuna packed in oil, you get 339 fat calories in a 6½-ounce can, compared to just 13 fat calories from a can of tuna packed in water. Even if you drain off "all" the oil, the oil-packed tuna contains 103 more fat calories than the water-packed tuna does.

When you realize where all the fat is hidden in your diet and how much you really add to your food, you'll see that it's easy to reduce your consumption of expendable fat calories drastically. In fact, that may be the only change you need to make in your diet to start shedding unwanted pounds and improving your chances for a long and healthy life. Fat adds flavor to foods and increases their satiety value (how much the food satisfies your appetite), so you wouldn't want to eliminate all fat even if you could. The idea here is not to have foods taste bland and uninteresting or to deprive you of an occasional indulgence in a high-fat food. The goal is to raise your fat consciousness so that you can trim unnecessary fat calories where they count the least, leaving room in your diet for those that really matter to you. For example, by eating less high-fat cheese, you may have room for some ice cream now and then. Or by using a salad dressing that contains little or no oil, you could get away with adding a few slices of avocado, which is high in fat, to your salad. Or, if burgers are your passion, you can cut fat calories in half if you use lean ground beef instead of regular ground beef. Here are some tips to help you de-fat your daily menu.

LOW-FAT COOKING TECHNIQUES

- Use nonstick pots and pans for preparing foods that require some fat, such as pancakes, omelets, sautéed vegetables, and browned meats, and for reheating leftovers. You'll be able to prepare foods with much less fat and sometimes with none at all.
- Instead of adding a chunk of fat or spoonful of oil to the pan, use the end of the stick of butter or margarine or a pastry brush dipped in oil to smear on a light coating of fat. Or coat the pan with a nonstick vegetable oil spray, such as Pam or Mazola No Stick.
- For some foods, you may be able to skip the cooking fat altogether and use a nonfat liquid instead, such as chicken broth or tomato juice to prepare vegetables, or Worcestershire sauce to sauté mushrooms.
- Use a steamer rack to cook vegetables or prepare fish (put the seasoned fish on a heat-proof plate on the rack) and a steamer or microwave oven to reheat foods that would otherwise stick to the pan.
- Trim off all visible fat from meat *before* you cook it.
- Broil meats, poultry, and fish instead of frying them. You can also poach poultry or fish in broth or vegetable juice or water seasoned with lemon juice, vinegar, or dry wine, along with herbs and spices. Or try poaching fish in skim milk.
- Plan ahead when you cook foods like soups or stews that contain expendable fat. If possible, cook them far enough in advance to allow them to cool, and skim off the fat before you reheat and serve.

- After having prepared broth from meat bones or poultry, refrigerate the broth and skim off the fat that solidifies at the top before you use the liquid to make soup. Or pour the hot broth into a fat-straining cup (one with a spout that attaches at the bottom [see p. 237]); as soon as the fat rises to the top, you can pour off the fat-free broth even without cooling it. Use the same trick to make gravy from pan juices, or stir an ice cube into the juice to harden the fat.
- When you buy red meat, choose the leanest cuts. For beef, these are sirloin tip, eye of the round, round steak, chuck with round bone, flank steak, tenderloin, lean stew meat, and extra-lean ground beef. For pork, try pork loin or tenderloin, center-cut ham, and Canadian bacon. For lamb, the leanest cuts are the leg, lamb steak, and sirloin chop. All cuts of veal are lean except the breast.
- Avoid processed meats like bologna, salami, sausage (dried or fresh), and frankfurters. Far leaner choices in cold cuts would be sliced turkey breast, turkey "ham," smoked turkey or chicken breast, boiled ham, baked Virginia ham, and roast beef.
- Small chickens (broilers and fryers) are leaner than roasters, which in turn are leaner than large hens and capons. Turkey and Cornish game hens are also lean. Remove hunks of fat from inside the carcass before you cook the bird. For dishes made from chicken parts, skin the chicken *before* you cook it, since the skin is nearly all fat and accounts for half the fat in a bird. This includes fried and browned chicken parts, as well as chicken that is braised or prepared in a stew or casserole. When preparing soup, however, you can use the skin to flavor the broth, as long as you skim the fat off after cooking. When roasting a bird or broiling chicken, leave the skin on (it prevents the flesh from drying out) but *don't eat it!*
- Although most fish are low in fat, the least fatty are the white fish like cod, flounder, haddock, scrod, and halibut, along with squid and shellfish (shrimp, mussels, crab, oysters, clams, lobster). Much fattier are mackerel, salmon, and swordfish. Tuna, bluefish, and catfish are moderately fatty. When buying canned fish, such as tuna, salmon, sardines, or mackerel fillets, choose the water-packed type. When tuna is packed in water, you save 200 fat calories per serving. Note, however, that naturally fatty fish can help protect against heart disease (see p. 11), so if weight is not an overriding concern, you may want to include such fish in your regular diet.
- It may not sound like much of a savings to buy skim milk (0 percent fat) or 1-percent milk (1 percent fat) instead of whole milk (3.5 percent fat), but the caloric difference is significant: 160 calories per cup of whole milk, 102 calories per cup of 1-percent milk, and only 86 calories per cup of skim milk. In making a switch from whole to low-fat or skim milk, do it gradually, possibly by combining the two, each time using a little more of the low-fat and less of the whole. Once you're used to the low-fat milk, whole milk will taste more like cream to you.
- In recipes calling for evaporated milk, substitute evaporated skim milk. When the recipe says cream, use whole milk (if it doesn't have to be whipped) or chilled evaporated skim milk (if whipping is needed).
- Despite its deceiving name, buttermilk is actually low in fat (made from skim or 1-percent milk) and can be used in place of whole milk to make pancakes and baked goods (just add ½ teaspoon of baking soda to the dry ingredients for

every cup of buttermilk you use). Buttermilk also makes a fine basis for salad dressing.

- In most recipes and dishes calling for sour cream, you can substitute plain yogurt and save 349 calories per cup. This substitution works especially well in salad dressings, dips, and toppings for foods like baked potatoes or chili. You can also substitute yogurt for half the mayonnaise when you make potato salad or coleslaw. To keep yogurt from separating in foods that are to be cooked or stirred vigorously, first mix 1 tablespoon of cornstarch with 1 tablespoon of yogurt and stir the mixture into the rest of the yogurt, then add it to your recipe.

- You'll also get less fat if you buy low-fat yogurt instead of yogurt made from whole milk. But there may not be much of a calorie savings because low-fat brands often contain added nonfat milk solids, which, by the way, mean more protein, vitamins, and minerals for you.

- Consider sherbert or frozen yogurt when you want a frozen dessert. It contains very little fat compared to ice cream, which has 10 percent to 16 percent butterfat. In general, the more expensive the ice cream, the higher the fat content. Another good choice is ice milk, which has a third (soft-serve) to a half (hard) less calories than ice cream. Fruit ices and sorbets contain no fat at all.

- Use farmer cheese, low-fat cottage cheese, yogurt cheese (see p. 641), or part-skim ricotta in place of cream cheese as a spread or recipe ingredient. Eighty-five percent of the calories in cream cheese are fat calories, whereas only 12 percent of the calories in low-fat cottage cheese (1-percent butterfat) come from fat. Cottage cheese contains less fat than ricotta and about half the calories. Whipped cream cheese has about a third less fat (by volume) than regular cream cheese, and it spreads more easily so you may use less.

- Other cheeses that are lower in fat include feta, part-skim and regular mozzarella, Neufchâtel, and Camembert. There are also some prepackaged reduced-fat processed cheeses and "imitation" cheese spreads available. However, don't be fooled by imitation cheeses in which the butterfat has been removed and replaced by vegetable oil; unless the package says otherwise, chances are these are not lower in calories than regular cheese although they are likely to be less damaging to your blood vessels. In general, most hard cheeses and cheese spreads should be considered high-fat foods and eaten with discretion. Instead of cutting hard cheese with a knife or buying it already sliced, you're likely to use less if you grate it or slice it with a cheese knife that skims off thin slivers (see p. 237).

- If you use margarine as a table spread, choose the "diet" brands; they contain half the fat of standard margarines. The first ingredient in diet margarines is usually water rather than fat, which makes these products cheaper as well as lower in fat and calories. Whipped butter also contains less fat and fewer calories per serving than regular butter.

- For dressing up cooked vegetables, try a few drops of a flavorful vegetable oil, such as Oriental sesame oil, or a little grated cheese instead of a chunk of butter or margarine. Or skip the fat, and season with herbs and spices.

- Try a few of the many no-oil salad dressings now on the market, or make your own (see recipes on pp. 549–553), and you'll save 100 to 200 calories per serving.

- When it comes to calories, it matters little whether you use vegetable oil, margarine, vegetable shortening, butter, lard, or suet; per tablespoon, they each have about 100 to 120 calories. However, olive oil, polyunsaturated vegetable oil, and soft margarines are less likely than the other fats to do damage to your blood vessels.
- Treat nuts, seeds, peanut butter, and avocados as fats, and consume them with discretion. They each contain about 85 percent fat calories. In buying peanut butter, look for the "old-fashioned," "real," or fresh-ground varieties rather than heavily processed brands that contain hydrogenated oil, sugar, and salt. Or grind your own from fresh roasted peanuts. If you or your family is already used to the heavily processed kind, mix them together, and, with each new batch, gradually increase the proportion of the plain-peanut peanut butter.
- Make pies with a single crust and save 75 to 100 fat calories per serving (plus the calories from the flour). Crumb crusts (for example, graham cracker, cereal, gingersnap, etc.) can be made lower in fat than traditional flour-based crusts (see recipes on pp. 626–630).

CURBING YOUR SWEET TOOTH

For most people who like sweets (and most people do), there's no such thing as "too sweet." And for some, there's no such thing as too many sweets. You probably know at least one person who will admit to having made short work of a whole box of candy or cookies or nibbled away at a cake until it was gone. Maybe that person is you! I did it—many times, in fact—in my previous incarnation as a sugarholic. But I couldn't do it now. Over the last 10 years I've retrained my taste buds so that now very sweet things don't taste good to me and I'm satisfied with a small amount of them, if I eat any at all.

This is not to say I don't eat foods with added sugar—I certainly do, and I make them as well. You'll find lots of my favorite recipes for sweet snacks and desserts in this book. But the sweets I now enjoy the most are just minimally sweet. They contain a half to a third the amount of sugar that you'd find in a commercially prepared version. And I find some foods so sweet—among them, pecan pie, most candies, commercial jellies, yogurt with preserves, and soft drinks—that I have no trouble resisting them.

My sons, by the way, were well on their way to becoming sugarholics by the age of 2. The very first phrase they said was "More cookie." When I realized how much they loved sweets, I got rid of all the commercial stuff and started making my own, using far less sugar than in store-bought versions. By the time they were 6, their reaction to very sweet foods was "Yuk, Mommy, this is too sweet." To this day they will pass up treats that are very sweet, and they eat only small amounts of candy infrequently.

You can change your taste preferences, too, no matter how much you now love sweets. Sweet tolerance, like salt tolerance, is a matter of habit. You can reduce yours by getting into the habit of eating sweet foods that are not very sweet. After a while you won't be tempted by sweet, rich, high-calorie desserts and snacks. You'll be satisfied with more nutritious choices that, in addition, are lower in calories. As with all other dietary changes, this one is best made gradually. For a while stop buying very sweet snacks and desserts to give your taste buds a chance to become more sensitive to sweetness. Try tea biscuits, fresh-fruit tarts, and coffeecakes instead of chocolate-laden cookies, pies, and layer cakes dripping with sweet icing. Try some of your favorite recipes with a third less sugar than you ordinarily use. After a while, as your taste buds adapt, use even less sugar, gradually reducing the amount of sweetener to the limit the recipe can bear and still turn out with the proper texture and an appealing flavor. (Most recipes can take a 50 percent to 75 percent reduction in sugar and still turn out okay. Sugar is most critical in high-volume cakes, like angel food.)

Table 13   SWEET CALORIES

Sweetener	Calories per tablespoon	Sweetener	Calories per tablespoon
White granulated (table) sugar	46	Molasses (dark)	46
Honey	64	Molasses (blackstrap)	43
Corn syrup	57	Sorghum syrup	55
Dark-brown sugar (packed)	52	Fructose	46
Maple syrup	50	Powdered sugar	42
Molasses (light)	50		

Don't make the mistake of substituting honey or fructose for ordinary sugar. These are just as sweet and no more nourishing, although you can use fewer calories worth of fructose to achieve the same level of sweetening you'd get from ordinary sugar and fructose may delay the return of hunger pangs. You will, of course, save calories when you use less sweetener, but the idea here is not so much one of saving calories as one of learning to like foods better when they're not very sweet. That way, when you do encounter a very sweet treat somewhere, you'll not be tempted to eat much, if any, of it.

The same goes for artificial sweeteners. These simply perpetuate your craving for very sweet foods. And animal experiments indicate that they may also help to drive up your body's set point—the level of weight you stabilize at when you do nothing in particular to control it. The more like the "real thing" the artificial sweetener tastes, the more effective it would be at raising the set point. Thus, the new sweetener aspartame may work even better than saccharin at keeping people fat.

Incidentally, no artificial sweetener has ever been shown to help people lose weight and keep it off. In fact, some people with the worst weight problems are among the heaviest saccharin users, and many successful losers never used artificial sweeteners to help them shed their weight or keep it off.

Saccharin, by the way, has another serious strike against it: since 1952, numerous animal studies have indicated that it can promote the growth of cancer. Although this effect has not yet been noted in people, researchers really haven't looked very carefully into the human cancer-saccharin relationship.

Only bladder cancer has been studied so far. Very large numbers of people would have to be studied over a period of many years to see if *any* types of cancer are increased among heavy saccharin users. For a society that is ostensibly concerned about cancer-causing chemicals in the diet and the general environment, I find it disturbing that so many people are willing to consume large amounts of a highly suspicious cancer promoter like saccharin. When the U.S. Food and Drug Administration tried to ban saccharin on the basis of the animal studies, the protest from the public was so loud and strong that Congress stayed the hand of this watchdog agency and has repeatedly renewed the legislated moratorium on a saccharin ban in order to keep this potential carcinogen in our food supply.

Although aspartame (NutraSweet and Equal) is more like a natural body chemical than is saccharin, its safety, too, is suspect. For one thing, it can change the level of chemicals that send nerve messages in the brain, the long-term effects of which are not yet known. And some people seem unusually sensitive to aspartame's effects: the Food and Drug Administration has received hundreds of complaints from consumers who say they have reacted to aspartame with such effects as depression, headache, irritability, dizziness, and seizures.

You'd be much better off learning to like less of the calorie-containing sweeteners than simply maintaining your addiction to sweets by switching to a no-calorie or low-calorie artificial sweetener. Here are some additional tips to help you along:

- Eat fruit for desserts and between-meal snacks. Fresh, of course, is best. If you buy canned fruits, choose those packed in water or juice—or, at worst, in light syrup. Frozen fruits are often less sweet than fruits canned in syrup. But go easy on dried fruits; these contain concentrated sugars, albeit "natural" sugars, and are high in calories. Fresh fruit salad is excellent year round. I keep one going almost all the time, varying the ingredients according to seasonal availability. I use fruit salad as a topping for pancakes and French toast, as an accompaniment to yogurt or cottage cheese, or I eat it plain as an appetizer, snack, or dessert. Once you get the hang of it, you'll find that you can make a beautiful and delicious multifruit salad for 4 in about 10 minutes.
- Drink fruit juices, unsweetened, perhaps mixed half and half with club soda or seltzer, instead of soft drinks. A typical soft drink has 9 to 12 teaspoons of sugar in a 12-ounce serving. Orange juice, grapefruit juice, and pineapple juice have less sugar and more valuable nutrients. Six ounces of juice mixed with 6 ounces of club soda or seltzer has only about 3½ teaspoons of sugar. But be wary of fruit nectars; many are made with a lot of added sugar and taste very sweet. Check the label before you buy.
- Make your own sweet treats—muffins, cookies, quick breads, jellies and jams, pies, and tarts—and use half the sugar in a standard recipe (the recipes in this book already have their sugar content drastically reduced, so you needn't cut back any further). You can also try substituting naturally sweet juice for the liquid and sugar in some recipes.
- Buy plain yogurt, and sweeten it with fresh fruit rather than with the very sugary preserves that are used in fruit-flavored yogurts.

- Use fruit purées or "butters," like unsweetened apple butter, in place of jams and jellies. You can make your own naturally sweet purées by processing very ripe fruit in the blender or food processor.
- Buy unsweetened cereals, and add sliced fruit or raisins instead of sugar. Some of the sweetened cereals contain up to 4 teaspoons of sugar in a 1-ounce serving. That's much more than you'd add even if you sprinkled sugar into a bowl of unsweetened cereal. Raisins, of course, add sugar but they also add vitamins, minerals, and fiber.
- Reward your children with something other than sweets—preferably something other than food! Ask your friends and relatives not to bring candy and the like "for the kids." A ball, a kite, a small toy, or even some coins would be more appropriate and appreciated by both the youngsters and their parents.
- Don't buy sweets to "have around the house" in case company comes. Chances are, you'll have finished them off long before you see your next guest. If you really find yourself "dying for something sweet," rather than purchase a whole box, buy one cookie, one small bar of candy, one sweet roll, or one ice cream bar or cone. It may cost more per serving that way, but you'll save yourself a lot of calories and psychological discomfort by avoiding the temptation to eat the rest of a box of cookies or ½ gallon of ice cream.

SHAKING THE SALT HABIT

What do you think would happen to the taste of food if for one day all the foods you ate contained no added salt? I asked this question of a salt-loving friend, and his reply was almost instantaneous: "Everything would taste the same—like cardboard." I asked another friend who's been on a salt-free diet for two years the reverse of this question: "What would happen if one day everything you ate was generously salted?" *His* reply was equally swift: "Everything would taste the same—like salt."

Is there something inherently different in the physiology of these two men? I think not. Rather, the difference lies in what they are used to eating. One is so attuned to salt that he can no longer distinguish the natural flavors of foods; the other is so used to the natural flavors of foods that adding salt would effectively disguise them. Like sugar, your taste for salt is a habit, one that you can retrain if you want to. This is not to say you have to live salt-free (unless your doctor says you should), but reducing your dependence on salt can actually enhance your enjoyment of foods.

Since salt is a noncaloric nutrient, you may wonder what it is doing in a section on weight control. First, the high-salt diet most of us live on is closely tied to another problem associated with overweight: high blood pressure, or hypertension. By eating less salt, you may diminish your risk of developing this disease, whether or not you lose weight (though of the two, weight loss is probably more important to preventing hypertension). Second, since salt holds water in your body, it can cause discouraging weight swings and bloating. You may be losing fat on your weight-control program, but you'd never know it from the scale or how your clothes fit, which may tempt you to forget the whole thing and eat with abandon.

As with the aforementioned dietary changes, reducing salt is best done gradually. That way you'll never notice the difference, at least not until you get down to little or no salt and then taste something salty that you once liked! There are many foods that I now find intolerably salty, and most of them are foods I have no business eating anyway (or at least eating very, very occasionally): processed and cured meats (bacon, salami, frankfurters, sausage, pepperoni, etc.); salted pretzels, nuts, and potato chips; many cheeses and especially processed cheese spreads; smoked fish; anchovies; salted pickles and sauerkraut; most regular commercial soups and soup mixes; packaged stuffing mixes; most commercial salad dressings and spaghetti sauces; and even some breakfast cereals (including my one-time favorites, Wheaties and Cheerios). And I have by no means cut salt completely out of my diet; I have just reduced the amount I use to about a quarter of what I once used.

Only about one-third of the salt in the American diet is added during home cooking and at the table. The rest comes from processed foods. You can go a long way toward reducing your salt intake by avoiding commercially prepared foods that are obviously salty. Some, such as regular canned soups, contain the recommended intake of salt for the whole day in just one serving. If you do more "cooking from scratch," using the recipes in this book for starters, you will have far more control over how much salt (as well as fat and sugar) gets into your foods. And if you gradually reduce the amount of salt you use, first cutting down to three-fourths your usual amount and then, after some weeks, cutting to a half, then to a quarter (and perhaps finally to none at all), you'll never miss the salt because you will have given your taste buds a chance to recover from their salt intoxication and tune in to the taste of real food.

While you're decreasing your dependence on salt, you can be exploring safe and delicious herbs and spices, garlic, onions, peppers, vinegars, lemon, and lime which can actually add variety to your salt-reduced meals. Instead of having everything taste a little bit salty, some foods can be garlicky, others flavored with basil, still others tangy with lemon, curry, cumin, cayenne, you name it. The choices are almost endless when you consider the possible combinations of various seasonings with different foods. (See some suggested combinations on pp. 183–184.)

For those who prefer to use some processed foods, in recent years major food processors have introduced "no added salt" and "reduced salt" product lines. For example, Del Monte and Libby's, major packers of canned vegetables, have more than 2 dozen no-added-salt products on the market, and Hunt's has introduced a full line of no-salt tomato products: sauces, canned tomatoes, tomato paste, tomato juice, and ketchup. Chicken of the Sea has a canned tuna with 50 percent less salt, and Season markets low-sodium sardines that are actually better than the usual salty kind. You may find salt-free pickles, pickled vegetables, and hot peppers (B an' G brand is one) and a variety of bottled sauces and condiments that have no added salt. There are also some no-salt ready-to-eat cereals by Kellogg, in addition to my all-time favorite, Shredded

Wheat, which was never made with salt (or sugar, for that matter). If you have access to a health food store, you'll probably find a number of other salt-free breakfast cereals, such as puffed corn, rice, and millet, as well as a crunchy oat cereal and wheat flakes. And, of course, in your supermarket there are the old stand-by hot cereals like oatmeal, farina, Maltex, and so forth, which are packaged without salt, allowing you to add the amount of salt you want, including none at all. Be careful, though, because some of the instant hot cereals have salt already added. Be sure to check the label; if salt has been added, it must be included in the ingredients list.

The Food and Drug Administration has established guidelines for foods that make claims about sodium. These guidelines can help you select wholesome processed foods. In addition to the following requirements, which are scheduled to take effect July 1986, any food that has nutritional labeling or that makes a sodium claim must list how many milligrams of sodium there are in a serving. This is especially important for foods described as "unsalted" since they may contain other sources of sodium besides salt, such as baking soda. According to the guidelines, if a food label states *sodium-free,* it must contain less than 5 milligrams of sodium per serving; *very low sodium,* it can contain 35 milligrams or less per serving; *low sodium,* it can have 140 milligrams or less per serving; *reduced sodium,* its sodium content must be reduced by 75 percent or more below what would be in the product it replaces; *unsalted, no salt added, without added salt,* no salt can have been added in processing to a food that would normally be processed with salt.

Here are some further tips for desalting your diet:

- Try rinsing certain processed foods that are prepared with salt. Duke University researchers showed that rinsing canned green beans for 1 minute lowered their sodium content by 41 percent; rinsing canned tuna dropped its sodium content by 76 percent; and rinsing cottage cheese eliminated 56 percent of its sodium. Salt is sodium chloride, and the sodium lost through rinsing comes from added salt.

- Read labels. Sodium is in more than just salt. Some telltale signs of sodium-containing ingredients are brine, sea salt, kelp, MSG (monosodium glutamate), soy sauce, baking soda, baking powder, and various sodium-containing additives (such as sodium citrate and saccharin).

- Avoid or reduce the amount you use of salty seasonings, such as soy sauce, tamari, miso, hydrolyzed vegetable protein (e.g., Maggi Seasoning), barbecue sauce, garlic salt, onion salt, celery salt, seasoned salt, dry soup mixes, bouillon cubes, ketchup, hot bean sauce, brown bean sauce, and oyster sauce. Instead use salt-free mustard and ketchup, garlic and onion powder (or, preferably, fresh garlic and onion), herbs and spices, hot pepper sauce, fresh peppers (both sweet and hot), fresh ginger, lemon, lime, fruits and fruit juices, vinegar, wine, and aromatic bitters to season foods. Worcestershire sauce has far less sodium than soy. There is also available a reduced-sodium soy sauce manufactured by Kikkoman (but it is still high in sodium: 605 milligrams per tablespoon, compared to 930 milligrams in a tablespoon of regular soy sauce). Still,

Kikkoman soy sauce has considerably less sodium than the American version by Chun King, which has 1,479 milligrams of sodium per tablespoon.

- Try low-sodium baking powder if you do a lot of baking. I use it, and I can rarely tell the difference in the results, especially if I double the amount called for in the recipe. You can buy it in health food stores if your supermarket doesn't carry it.
- Buy unsalted snacks if you must have snacks. Nuts, crackers, potato chips, pretzels, and corn chips can now be obtained without added salt. You may think unsalted chips are not worth eating, to which I would add: chips are not worth eating with or without salt because they are so high in fat. A far more wholesome and very low-calorie snack is popcorn, prepared without added fat or salt.
- When dining out, ask that your food be prepared without salt whenever

Sodium-Free Seasoning Mixes You Can Make

The mixture devised by the American Heart Association is a family favorite. We use it in salad dressings, omelets, tomato sauce, and to season vegetables, poultry, fish, and red meat. Although we otherwise would not use garlic powder or onion powder (the flavor of the "real thing" is far superior), in this premixed combination of dry seasonings, they do not result in an overwhelmingly artificial flavor.

AHA HERB MIX
(All-Purpose)

  ½ teaspoon cayenne (red pepper)
  1 tablespoon garlic powder
  1 teaspoon of each of the following *ground**
    seasonings: basil, thyme, parsley, savory, mace,
    onion powder, black pepper, sage

*If you start with leaves, use 1½ teaspoons of basil, parsley, and sage, and 1¼ teaspoons of thyme and savory.

Combine all the seasonings in a blender jar. Blend the ingredients at medium-high speed until they are ground.

possible, and order gravies, sauces, and salad dressings on the side. Or use oil and vinegar or lemon juice and freshly ground pepper to dress your salad.

A WARNING ON SALT SUBSTITUTES: There are now many brands of salt substitutes and of seasonings made with salt substitutes. These contain potassium chloride instead of sodium chloride. You should not use them without a physician's knowledge and guidance, since an overdose of potassium can be dangerous. Furthermore, for some people, potassium chloride leaves a bitter aftertaste (usually for the same people who find saccharin to have an unpleasant aftertaste). If you do use salt substitutes, use them with discretion; if you have been a heavy salter, do not make a one-to-one substitution of potassium chloride for sodium chloride.

The following herb mixes were suggested by the Cumberland Packing Corp. If you don't care for one of the seasonings used, you can substitute one you prefer, such as dill for sage in the blend for fish.

BLEND FOR VEGETABLES AND MEAT

1 teaspoon thyme
1 teaspoon marjoram
¾ teaspoon rosemary
½ teaspoon sage

BLEND FOR VEGETABLES, MEAT, AND POULTRY

¾ teaspoon marjoram
½ teaspoon thyme
½ teaspoon orégano
½ teaspoon sage
½ teaspoon rosemary

BLEND FOR FISH

¾ teaspoon parsley flakes
½ teaspoon onion powder
½ teaspoon sage
¼ teaspoon marjoram
¼ teaspoon paprika

BLEND FOR MEAT, POTATOES, AND VEGETABLES

1 teaspoon dry mustard
½ teaspoon sage
½ teaspoon thyme
¼ teaspoon marjoram

The following salt-free seasoning suggestions were prepared for the Hunt's Plan, based on information from the American Spice Trade Association. Groups of seasonings between semicolons are meant to be used together. However, you may wish to try some individually listed seasonings in combination. For example, I might use orégano, basil, garlic, and chili in a meatloaf.

Fish in tomato sauce: dillweed; fennel; thyme; chervil

Fish soup: bay leaf and thyme; tarragon; Italian seasoning

Beef stew: caraway; pickling spices; marjoram; tarragon; bay leaf; chili powder

Meatloaf: orégano; basil; garlic; chili powder; nutmeg

Chicken in tomato sauce: orégano, basil, and bay leaf; thyme and rosemary; basil, nutmeg, and garlic

Barbecued chicken: orégano, basil, and garlic; dry mustard, clove, and allspice; ginger, garlic, and dry mustard; chili powder

Vegetable soup: Italian seasoning; paprika; thyme; rosemary; fennel

Rice and vegetables: thyme, onion, paprika, rosemary, and garlic

Spanish rice: Italian seasoning; cumin, orégano, and basil

Spaghetti: orégano, basil, and nutmeg; red pepper and tarragon; Italian seasoning; nutmeg

Cabbage: minced onion and nutmeg; caraway, vinegar, allspice, and clove

Green beans: dillweed; savory and onion

Mushrooms: orégano; basil and thyme

Potatoes: caraway; onion; thyme and parsley

Zucchini: orégano and garlic; tarragon and basil; dillweed

Eggplant: onion and garlic; coriander, thyme, basil, and marjoram

Carrots: dillweed; Italian seasoning

HOW MUCH SODIUM ARE YOU USING?

The following table, prepared by the Hunt's Plan, shows the sodium equivalent per serving if you use the indicated amount of salt in preparing a recipe. Total daily sodium intake for a healthy person should be between 1,100 and 3,300 milligrams a day, according to the Food and Nutrition Board of the National Academy of Sciences–National Research Council.

AMOUNT OF SALT IN RECIPE	AMOUNT OF SODIUM PER SERVING, IN MILLIGRAMS, FROM SALT (NUMBER OF SERVINGS PER RECIPE)				
	1	*2*	*4*	*6*	*8*
¼ teaspoon	530	265	135	90	70
½ teaspoon	1,065	530	265	180	135
1 teaspoon	2,130	1,065	530	355	265
1½ teaspoons	3,195	1,600	800	530	400
2 teaspoons	4,260	2,130	1,065	710	530
2½ teaspoons	5,325	2,665	1,330	890	665
1 tablespoon	6,390	3,195	1,600	1,065	800
2 tablespoons	12,780	6,390	3,195	2,130	1,600

Table 14   SODIUM IN CONDIMENTS AND SEASONINGS

Food item	Amount	Sodium content (mg.)
Baking powder	1 teaspoon	339
Baking soda	1 teaspoon	821
Chili powder	1 teaspoon	26
Garlic salt	1 teaspoon	1,850
Horseradish, prepared	1 tablespoon	198
Meat tenderizer	1 teaspoon	1,750
MSG (monosodium glutamate)	1 teaspoon	492
Mustard, prepared	1 teaspoon	65
Olives, green	4	323
Olives, ripe	3	96
Onion salt	1 teaspoon	1,620
Pickle, dill	1	928
Pickle, sweet	1	128
Relish, sweet	1 tablespoon	124
SAUCES		
A.1.	1 tablespoon	275
Barbecue	1 tablespoon	130
Chili	1 tablespoon	227
Ketchup	1 tablespoon	156
Soy	1 tablespoon	1,029
Tabasco	1 teaspoon	24
Tartar	1 tablespoon	182
Teriyaki	1 tablespoon	690
Worcestershire	1 tablespoon	206
SALAD DRESSINGS		
Bleu cheese	1 tablespoon	135
French	1 tablespoon	214
Italian	1 tablespoon	116
Mayonnaise	1 tablespoon	78
Russian	1 tablespoon	133
Thousand Island	1 tablespoon	109

SOURCE: *The Sodium Content of Your Food,* Home and Garden Bulletin No. 233 (Washington, D.C.: United States Department of Agriculture, 1980).

A READING LIST FOR LOW-SALT EATING

The following books contain lists of the sodium content of foods or recipes for cooking without added salt.

American Heart Association. *Cooking without Your Salt Shaker.* Dallas: American Heart Association, n.d. A 145-page spiral-bound cookbook and dining-out guide. For purchase, contact your local chapter of the Heart Association.

Baltzell, Karin B. and Terry M. Parsley. *Living without Salt.* Elgin, Ill.: Brethren Press, 1982.

Brenner, Eleanor P. *Gourmet Cooking without Salt.* New York: Doubleday, 1981.

Claiborne, Craig. *Craig Claiborne's Gourmet Diet.* New York: Ballantine Books, 1981; New York: Times Books, 1980.

James, Janet, and Lois Goulder. *The Dell Color-coded Low-Salt Living Guide.* New York: Dell, 1980. A handy listing that quickly alerts you to high-sodium products, including over-the-counter drugs. Some recipes included.

Jones, Jeanne. *Secrets of Salt-Free Cooking.* San Francisco: 101 Productions, 1979.

Kraus, Barbara. *The Barbara Kraus 1983 Sodium Guide to Brand Names and Basic Foods.* New York: Signet, 1983. An alphabetized listing of foods showing differences between brands.

Low Salt Secrets for Your Diet. Berkeley, Calif.: Longevity Publications, 1981. A list that includes special low-sodium products, fast foods, and processed foods by brand name.

Margie, Joyce Daly, and Dr. James C. Hunt. *Living with High Blood Pressure: The Hypertension Diet Cookbook.* Radnor, Pa.: Chilton, 1979.

Minear, Ralph E., M.D. *The Joy of Living Salt-Free.* New York: Macmillan, 1984.

Sodium Content of Your Food. FDA Consumer Communications, HFE-88, 5600 Fishers Lane, Rockville, Maryland. A free guide to the sodium content of 789 foods and food products and over-the-counter drugs.

12 ·
WHEN TO EAT WHAT

PARENT: Don't eat that doughnut! You'll spoil your dinner.
  YOU: But I'm hungry now. Besides, I've got basketball practice tonight.

PARENT: You can't leave the house without breakfast.
  YOU: But I'm not hungry in the morning. Besides, I'm late for school.

PARENT: If you want to be healthy, you've got to eat three meals a day.
  YOU: But I'll get fat if I eat so much. Besides, I never have time for lunch.

Do any of these exchanges sound familiar to you? Few of us grew up eating the way our parents thought we should, and few of us had parents who followed their own dietary advice! Although we all learn early in life that we should eat three meals a day, not skipping any and not eating unnourishing snacks in place of nutritious meals, it was the rare paragon of nutritional virtue who adhered religiously to this "rule." Besides, many of the dietary dicta we encountered made no sense at the time and didn't fit in with the demands of childhood.

As we got older, other factors influenced our eating habits: jobs that dragged us out of the house at the crack of dawn or that got us home too late or too exhausted to apply the need to fit into that dress for the party next week; long business lunches or dinners; the frantic morning rush to get the kids off to school. Coupled with the temptations of quick fixes—diet formulas, packaged instant meals, vending machines, coffee carts, fast-food restaurants, street vendors—it was all too easy to pay more attention to the demands of life than to when and how we fueled our bodies.

Millions of Americans have fallen into a pattern of too-late-for-breakfast, grab-something-for-lunch, eat-a-big-dinner, and nibble-nonstop-until-bedtime. They starve their bodies when they most need fuel and stuff them when they'll be doing nothing more strenuous than flipping the TV dial or the pages of a book. When you think about it, the pattern makes no biological sense. Why should an organism be given fuel just before it's going to sleep and no fuel when it needs peak energy? That would be like trying to drive your car from New York to Washington, D.C., on an empty tank of gas and then filling the tank once you got there.

THE MORE MEALS, THE BETTER

While there is nothing sacred about a three-meal-a-day eating pattern (that was established mainly to suit the demands of work), eating just one or two meals a day may actually be harmful. This lopsided eating pattern encourages the storage of calories as fat and is partly responsible for the fact that so many people are bigger than they want to or should be. It also raises blood cholesterol levels and thus may increase the risk of heart disease. And it can lead to wide fluctuations in blood sugar and insulin levels, with possible adverse effects on emotional well-being as well as physical health.

Numerous studies of both laboratory animals and people have shown that eating several small meals a day—even as many as six minimeals—is far better for body and mind than stuffing down one or two big ones. To rely once again on the likely pattern established in the course of human evolution, early humans were undoubtedly nibblers who spent most days walking through field and forest picking fruits, nuts, berries, and other edible plants whenever they were hungry. Big feasts, comparable to a three-or-more-course American dinner, were only sometime events, not daily fare. Thus, our metabolic systems evolved to handle relatively small amounts of food at one time. And, to prevent starvation when the food supply ran short, we also evolved with a system for storing extra calories whenever they were available.

Therein lies the problem for people who seem to gain weight easily. They are actually better suited to survival than those who can't seem to put on an ounce—better suited, that is, if they lived in a place where the food supply was uncertain: feast one day, famine the next. Fortunately, or unfortunately, our food supply in late twentieth-century America is hardly uncertain. At the worst, a major snowstorm or a strike may cut off a city's supply of fresh milk and bread for a day or so, but affected residents would hardly go hungry with larders well stocked with meats, cheese, eggs, cereals, pasta, rice, frozen and canned vegetables and fruits, cookies, crackers, TV dinners, mix-and-serve meals, canned and packaged soups, and what have you. Not to mention the Pizza Hut, Burger King, or Kentucky Fried Chicken on the next block in case you get tired of "making do."

Here are some findings that may prompt you to rethink your current eating pattern:

- In an early study by the late Dr. Clarence Cohn of the Michael Reese Hospital in Chicago, 1,500 young laboratory rats were divided into two groups, one fed at "meal times" twice a day and the other allowed to eat whenever they wanted. However, the total amounts of food and nutrients consumed were the same for both groups. After 41 days, both groups had gained the same amount of weight, but the meal eaters had put on almost twice as much body fat.
- In a later study at Michigan State University, test animals were allowed to eat only during a 2-hour period, at a time equivalent to the animal's evening. After a few weeks, they were compared to animals that had continuous access to food and nibbled throughout the day. The meal eaters had actually consumed about

15 percent less, but they gained as much weight as the nibblers. Furthermore, the stomachs and small intestines of the meal eaters became enlarged, presumably to handle the big load of food efficiently. With a small intestine 40 percent larger, the rate at which the meal-fed animals could absorb nutrients and calories was about 40 percent greater.

- In a series of studies among hundreds of men in Prague, Dr. Paul Fabry showed that 57.2 percent of men who ate three meals a day or fewer were overweight, compared with 28.2 percent of men who ate five or more meals a day. The infrequent eaters also had higher serum cholesterol levels and a poorer ability to process blood sugar. And among 1,400 men in their 60s, the incidence of heart disease was highest among those who ate three meals a day or fewer and lowest among men who ate five meals or more. In rat studies, Dr. Fabry also showed that the number of fat cells (where body fat is stored) increased markedly in animals that were fed infrequently.

- In one of the latest studies, conducted at the University of Minnesota, 2 women and 4 men were fed 2,000 calories a day in one meal. For half the experiment, the meal was consumed at breakfast, for the other half, at supper. When they ate their 2,000 calories in the morning, they all lost weight; when the same meal with the same number of calories was eaten at night, 4 of the 6 gained weight and the other 2 lost less than they had on breakfast only. The weight difference resulting from the two eating patterns amounted to an average of 2½ pounds a week.

- Finally, in a study at the National Institutes of Health, 3 obese women were placed on a hospital-supervised 400-calorie-a-day diet. All the calories were given as one meal either for breakfast at 8 A.M. or for dinner at 5 P.M. After 10 days, 2 of the patients had lost significantly more weight while on the breakfast regimen than while eating their diet meal for dinner. Furthermore, the studies showed that these women had used up more of their body fat on the early-in-the-day meal schedule.

To be sure, not all researchers believe that frequent small meals are better than one or two large ones widely spaced. Nor does everyone agree that eating a big breakfast and small dinner is healthier than eating little or no breakfast and a big dinner. But it is almost impossible to make a rational biological case for the eater who skips breakfast, skimps on lunch, and stuffs at dinner. Nor can a sound case be made for eating a few big meals as opposed to a lot of little ones. Anytime a lot of food enters the body, large amounts of insulin are released from the pancreas to help process the sudden load. One of insulin's jobs is to put fat into storage, so, all other things being equal, the stuffer is nearly always going to be fatter than the nibbler. And, with a stretched stomach and intestine, the stuffer is also going to be able to hold and absorb more food at one time than the nibbler, whose gastrointestinal tract sends out distress signals when he tries to overeat.

BREAKFAST: THE MOST IMPORTANT MEAL

You've already seen that skipping breakfast is no shortcut to slimdom. If anything, the reverse is true: eating breakfast will help you to lose unwanted pounds. But that's only one of the advantages of eating a good breakfast. Through the years, various studies have demonstrated several others. Eating breakfast may even be a matter of life and death. In a decade-long study conducted among 7,000 men and women, researchers from the University of California at Los Angeles found that those who ate breakfast almost every day lived longer. In the study, death rates were 40 percent higher among men who said they rarely or never ate breakfast and were 28 percent higher among female breakfast skippers. While skipping breakfast may not in and of itself be fatal, as a part of an overall pattern of self-neglect, it is a significant factor in a person's health profile. A study many years ago by Dr. Raymond Pearl at Johns Hopkins University of people who lived into their 80s and 90s revealed only one factor they had in common: most of them had always eaten a large breakfast.

Even more important, eating breakfast has immediate benefits to your sense of well-being and how well you do your job. Studies by the University of Iowa Medical College showed a connection between eating a nutritious breakfast and improved physical and mental performance. Benefits to breakfast eaters, when compared to breakfast skippers, included a faster reaction time, higher productivity during the late morning hours, and less muscle fatigue. Children who skipped breakfast were likely to be listless and to have trouble concentrating. And a study by the Human Nutrition Center at the University of Texas in Houston showed that, among children aged 9 to 11, skipping breakfast interfered with their ability to solve problems.

Given the low level of blood sugar after an all-night fast, the above findings are hardly surprising. I don't know if anyone has examined this matter scientifically, but I'm willing to bet that until they eat lunch or supper, breakfast skippers are also more irritable, more impatient, and quicker to fly off the handle than breakfast eaters. That's what happens to most people when they are hungry and their blood-sugar level is low. Breakfast skippers may not be consciously aware of their hunger, but it's there. And by suppressing or ignoring hunger, breakfast skippers are bypassing nature's message that their bodies need fuel, which is the opposite of what they *should* be doing if they are concerned about their weight and health.

Finally, breakfast skippers are likely to shortchange their bodies on essential nutrients. First, many nutrients in typical breakfast fare are not consumed in significant amounts during the rest of the day's meals. And second, nutrients, including protein and calcium, are better absorbed if they are consumed in small amounts throughout the day than if large amounts of them are dumped into the digestive tract all at once. Calcium, riboflavin, and vitamin C are among the nutrients likely to be in short supply among those who skip breakfast. According to Dr. Helen A. Guthrie, professor of nutrition at the Pennsylvania State University, adolescents who skip breakfast take in 40 percent less calcium and vitamin C and 10 percent less iron and thiamin than those who eat breakfast.

Currently, in one half of American families, one or more persons regularly skips breakfast. Half of the nation's school children leave the house with little or no breakfast. And a 1983 national household survey indicated that breakfast skippers had increased by one-third since 1978. Yet, nearly everyone eats dinner, stuffing in more than half the day's food allotment when they least need the calories or the energy boost. We'd have a lot healthier nation if these statistics were reversed, with most people eating breakfast and half skipping dinner!

Some people insist they are never hungry in the morning and couldn't think of eating soon after they get up. Chances are this is more a matter of habit than native biology. But even if it is inborn, this doesn't mean their bodies should have to wait until lunch (or later) to get much-needed fuel. It's okay to delay breakfast for 2 or even 3 hours after you get up, as long as you eat something nourishing when food no longer seems "repulsive" to you. If you go to work or school, pack a brown-bag breakfast (see some suggestions on p. 196) and eat it when you get there or during a midmorning break.

WHAT'S IN A GOOD BREAKFAST? Juice and coffee are not breakfast. Nor are coffee and a piece of toast, or a so-called "breakfast bar." And breakfast is certainly not the potato chips and pop that many teen-agers down on their way to school. Breakfast, first of all, should contain a fair amount of *protein*. This is the nutrient that stimulates alertness (if you have a high-protein breakfast, you may not even need the kick you now get from caffeine). Protein also helps to stave off midmorning hunger, which is common after a breakfast of a sweet roll and coffee. A 1-ounce serving of ordinary breakfast cereal with ½ glass of milk is not enough protein for an adult's breakfast (a whole glass of milk would be better along with enough cereal to provide at least 4 grams of protein). On the other hand, the amount of protein in a "hearty" American-style breakfast of 2 eggs, 3 ounces of ham, 1 cup of milk, and 2 slices of toast would meet the entire *day's* protein needs for a 120-pound woman.

Ideally, your breakfast should contain about a third of your day's protein needs. For the average adult, this means 15 to 20 grams of protein, the amount in any of the following: ¼ cup of cottage cheese, 3 ounces of fish, 4 tablespoons of peanut butter, 2 ounces of hard cheese, 2 cups of milk or yogurt (low-fat or skim), one-fourth of a 14-inch pizza, 2 ounces of chicken or turkey, a 10-ounce serving of bean soup, 1 cup of kidney beans, or 6 ounces of high-protein pasta. If some of these foods are not exactly what you now consider "breakfast food," I hope this chapter will encourage you to have some new thoughts on how to start your day.

Another important part of breakfast is *juice or fruit* that contains vitamin C: orange, grapefruit, tomato, strawberries, cantaloupe, apple, or cranberry juice (if vitamin C is added). Recommended quantities are ½ cup of juice, half a grapefruit, a whole orange, one-fourth of a medium melon, or ½ cup of berries. If your stomach can't handle a high-acid juice or fruit first thing in the morning, skip it then (perhaps replacing it with milk) and have it later in the day. *Carbohydrates,* so important for immediate energy needs, should also be in your breakfast menu. Ideally, they should be *complex* carbohydrates—starchy foods —rich in original nutrients, such as a whole-grain bread or cereal, or a bran or oatmeal muffin. Limit the fat you put on bread to 1 teaspoon; a teaspoon of jelly (or, better yet, unsweetened apple butter) is okay to add. A *beverage* after all this is optional, but breakfast would hardly be the same without it. Coffee, regular or decaffeinated, is clearly America's favorite breakfast drink. Other liquid possibilities include tea, skim or low-fat milk, buttermilk, water, or more fruit juice. The liquid may aid in digestion of the other foods you eat and will help to give you a feeling of satisfaction. If you drink milk, you'll also give your body a hefty start on fulfilling the day's calcium needs. (For specific breakfast suggestions, see the menus on pp. 652–655.)

HOW TO "DO" BREAKFAST. Given the time constraints in most American households in the morning, it's no wonder so many people skip breakfast. There's getting up (after the snooze alarm has issued its third and final warning); making the coffee and drinking it while trying to catch the news, weather, and traffic report; walking the dog and/or exercising; getting the kids up and off to school; showering; drying and setting the hair; putting on make-up; dressing; taking something out of the freezer for dinner; then racing off to catch the train or bus or to join the millions of commuters who drive to work. All accomplished in less time than you'd be likely to have to wait in the doctor's office. Who's got time for breakfast? And, with all that racing around, whose stomach is calm enough to enjoy it?

Squeezing breakfast into such a morning may be difficult but not impossible. Here's how.

START THE NIGHT BEFORE: Decide what breakfast will be, and get it going as far as possible. Set the table or set up a tray with the needed utensils, dishes, and glassware. The juice (if frozen) can be defrosted and mixed or a fresh-fruit salad prepared; bread can be dipped in egg batter for French toast; the dry and wet ingredients for pancakes can be prepared, to be combined in a minute in the morning; the makings of cooked cereal can be measured and waiting; sandwiches can be made, to be eaten cold or grilled; leftover spaghetti or rice can be used to prepare a spaghetti pancake or rice-pudding cereal (see recipes on pp. 355 and 509); pita pizzas can be made ready to pop into the toaster oven (see the recipe on p. 475); leftovers can be combined into a ready-to-heat stir-fry. You can even mix up a batch of muffins and bake them before bed, to be eaten with peanut butter or cheese the next morning. The possibilities abound, limited only by your imagination and what may be in your refrigerator or cupboard.

Of course, if you can't cope with anything more complicated than pour and eat, there's nothing wrong with a ready-to-eat breakfast cereal topped with bananas, peaches, berries, or raisins and moistened with low-fat milk. Just be sure you pick a nourishing cereal (see pp. 193–195) and consume it with more than ½ glass of milk (or eat some other high-protein food as part of your breakfast). Other "instant" breakfasts include yogurt or cottage cheese with

How to Choose a Breakfast Cereal

When people are asked what they had for breakfast, they may reply apologetically, "Oh, just some cereal." Cereal, it seems, has acquired a bad reputation, perhaps because of the nutritionally questionable products that now glut the cereal market and the categorization of cereal as "instant" packaged food. But while some cereals clearly deserve their ill repute, others—particularly the old-fashioned ready-to-eat and hot cooked cereals—can be the foundation of a fast, nutritious breakfast that is certainly healthier than bacon and eggs and vastly superior to doughnuts and coffee.

On a winter morning, a steaming bowl of oatmeal or whole-wheat hot cereal can warm you down to your toes at the same time that it provides stick-to-the-ribs satisfaction, dietary fiber, and essential nutrients. On a summer day, a crunchy bowl of a whole-grain ready-to-eat cereal moistened with ice-cold milk and topped with fresh fruit is a cool and nourishing way to start the day. Surveys have shown that people who eat cereal for breakfast typically consume less fat, less cholesterol, less sodium, and fewer calories than those who start the day with other common breakfast fare. Ready-to-eat breakfast cereal served with low-fat or skim milk is also an excellent between-meal snack for youngsters and forever-starving teen-agers—far more nourishing, less fattening, and less expensive than cookies, cake, candy, ice cream, and chips.

But faced with the blinding array of cereal products now on supermarket shelves, shoppers interested in good nutrition as well as good taste can easily become confused. Bargain hunters usually do best, for the cheaper cereals are often nutritionally superior. Shoppers who succumb to price-raising gimmicks—such as "all natural," "fortified with 100% of 10 essential vitamins," "no preservatives," "no added sugar," "high fiber"—may miss the fact that the cereal is also high in fat, calories, natural sources of sugar, and/or salt.

Nutrition-conscious shoppers have a clear advantage when it comes to buying cereals:

nearly all cereal products offer *Nutrition Information* on the package label. Along with the *ingredients* list, this information can help you resist advertising pressures and choose products that will fill your body with nutritious food, not just line the pockets of food processors.

As a general rule, the shorter the list of ingredients, the more nutritious the product. For example, Nabisco's Spoon Size Shredded Wheat contains, very simply, 100-percent whole wheat; Wheatena, 100-percent toasted wheat; Quaker Oats, rolled oats; Kellogg's Nutri-Grain Corn Cereal, whole corn kernels, malt flavoring, salt, and baking soda; and Post Grape-Nuts, wheat, malted barley, salt, and yeast (plus 8 vitamins). Far less nourishing is Kellogg's Sugar Smacks, which lists the following ingredients: sugar, wheat, corn syrup, honey, hydrogenated soybean oil, salt, caramel color, and sodium acetate (plus 9 vitamins and minerals, and lecithin). If you shop in a health food store, you may find ready-to-eat cereals that contain only one ingredient, the grain (for example, "whole yellow corn" or "whole puffed wheat")—no sugar, salt, fat, preservatives, or added nutrients. While these cereals are nutritious and usually inexpensive, they also have little taste by themselves and take some getting used to. I have found them more interesting when they are mixed with another cereal, such as Grape-Nuts, or when a small amount of granola is used as a garnish along with sliced banana or some other fruit.

"Nutrition Information" and its sidekick "Carbohydrate Information" reveal much about the nutritional composition of the cereal. Many people are confused by this labeling, which lists major nutrients in grams per serving and lists vitamins and minerals as percentages of the U.S. Recommended Daily Allowances (USRDA). You needn't become fluent in the metric system or have a college degree in chemistry to benefit from the information on the package label. Here are some specific things to look for.

Serving Size and Calories per Serving. You can be easily deceived by cereals that promise high nutrient value unless you first determine how much cereal the manufacturer means by a serving and how many calories that serving contains. The usual serving size is 1 ounce of cereal, which can vary from ¼ cup for granolas to ½ cup for whole-bran cereals to 2 cups for some puffed cereals. Now look at "Calories per Serving." This can range from about 70 (per 1-ounce serving) for whole-bran cereals to 150 for some sugary and fatty granolas. In other words, if you eat 1 ounce of Quaker 100% Natural Cereal (a granola) for breakfast, you'll get ¼ cup of cereal that contains 130 calories before you add the milk. Contributing heavily to the caloric load are 9 grams of sugars and 6 grams of fat. But if you eat 1 ounce of Quaker Puffed Wheat, you'll get 2 cups of cereal that supplies 108 calories with no added sugar and less than ½ gram of fat.

The Grain. Look for a whole grain as the first ingredient listed. It can be whole wheat, whole rye, whole corn, oats (rolled or flour, since oats are always "whole"), whole barley, or whole millet, or it can be the bran of wheat, oats, or corn.

Dietary Fiber. You may find a listing for dietary fiber under "Carbohydrate Information" or a statement about fiber content somewhere else on the ingredients panel. Cereals made from bran are high in dietary fiber, with Kellogg's All-Bran and Nabisco's 100% Bran the highest, at 9 grams per serving, followed by Bran Buds, with 8 grams. Raisin Bran and 40% Bran Flakes have 4 grams of dietary fiber per serving, Corn Bran has 5, and Nutri-Grain and Wheaties, 2. Granolas, incidentally, have less fiber than you might think—less than Wheaties or Grape-Nuts and, in some products, less than Cheerios and Puffed Wheat. Although the label doesn't say so, oatmeal and cereals made from oats are good sources of a type of fiber that helps to lower cholesterol levels and control blood sugar. The amounts of "crude fiber" listed on some cereal packages mean relatively little, since the true fiber content is likely to be considerably higher.

Protein. Among the commonly consumed grains, oats contain the most protein and corn and rice the least. Among hot cereals, buckwheat (sold as groats and known as kasha) has good-quality protein and a lovely nutty flavor. Granolas that contain nuts and/or seeds may have more protein than ordinary flake cereals, but they have other disadvantages, such as lots of calories from fats and sugars (see below). Kellogg's Special K is high in protein, as cereals go, with 6 grams per serving. Under "Nutrition Information," look for a cereal that provides 3 or more grams of protein per 1-ounce serving (before adding milk). And don't stint on the milk; if you eat your cereal with 1 cup of milk, you'll add 8 grams of high-quality protein. When preparing hot cereal, you can also enhance its protein value significantly by substituting low-fat or skim milk for all or part of the water.

Fat. Grains, the basis for most cereals, are naturally low in fat, so most cereals are low-fat foods. Thus, under "Nutrition Information," you're likely to find the amount of fat per serving is only 1 or 2 grams, maybe 3 at most. Granolas, on the other hand, are made with a lot of fat—5 or more grams per serving, or up to 25 percent of the total calories—and very often that fat is mostly highly saturated coconut or palm oil or partly saturated hydrogenated vegetable oil. The fat content of granolas is also increased by the nuts and seeds these cereals often contain. If you make your own granola (see the recipe on p. 508), you can use considerably less total fat and less saturated fat.

Sugars. Avoid products in which sugar (or honey, corn syrup, fructose, or molasses) is listed as the first ingredient. Some presweetened cereals—among them Sugar Smacks, Apple Jacks, Froot Loops, Cocoa Pebbles, Sugar Frosted Flakes, and Cap'n Crunch—contain between 40 percent and 60 percent sugar by weight. That can mean as much as 4 teaspoons of sugar in a 1-ounce bowl of cereal. Often, there is more than one source of sweetener, so even if sugar is not listed as the first ingredient, there may well be more sugar in a cereal than anything else.

If a product has only a few ingredients, sugar or some other sweetener may appear near the top of the ingredients list even though the cereal may not contain much sugar. Therefore, it helps to check the "Carbohydrate Information" usually listed at the bottom of the ingredients panel. This listing separates the sugars from the nutritionally more desirable starches. Look for products that contain no more than 3 or 4 grams of "sucrose and other sugars" per serving (1 teaspoon of sugar weighs about 4 grams). Note that bran cereals, which without sweeteners are indistinguishable from sawdust, are somewhat higher in sugar: Nabisco's 100% Bran, Kellogg's All-Bran, and Quaker Corn Bran each have 6 grams of sucrose and other sugars in 1 ounce of cereal. Cereals that contain raisins or dates also have higher sugar contents, but much of their sugar comes from the fruit, which is rich in essential nutrients and not just "empty calories." Thus, whereas Nabisco's Shredded Wheat has no sugar, Nabisco's Toasted (shredded) Wheat & Raisins has 5 grams of sucrose and other sugars per serving, but all the sugar comes from the raisins. If sweetening is desired, far better to use fruit—fresh or dried—than sugar. In preparing hot cereal, try adding raisins or dried currants and/or chopped apples to the pot (see the recipe for Hearty Oatmeal on p. 509).

Sodium. Many cereals contain surprisingly large amounts of sodium, most of it as salt. When milk is added, which naturally contains sodium, the total sodium per serving can exceed 400 milligrams, about a sixth of the day's total sodium allotment. In some cereals, like Wheaties and Cheerios, salt is the predominant flavor. If you have reduced your dependence on salt, these products will probably taste salty to you. A 1-ounce serving of Cheerios, Kix, Rice Krispies, Corn Flakes, Wheaties, and Total all exceed 300 milligrams of sodium. More reasonable amounts of sodium—less than 200 milligrams—are found in the Nutri-Grain cereals, All-Bran, Most, Product 19, Grape-Nuts, and many of the presweetened cereals, including the granolas. And the puffed cereals, Shredded Wheat, and the Quaker 100% Natural cereals have almost no sodium.

If you prepare them without salt, hot cereals like oatmeal, Wheatena, Maltex, and Cream of Wheat have less than 10 milligrams of sodium per serving, making them ideal for low-sodium diets. But adding ⅛ teaspoon of salt per serving means an additional 275 milligrams of sodium. If you choose "instant" hot cereals, be sure to read the label first, since many already contain added salt. For example, while Old Fashioned Quaker Oats and Quick Quaker Oats have only 1 milligram of sodium (when cooked without added salt), Instant Quaker Oatmeal has 252 milligrams of sodium per serving.

Vitamins and Minerals. Fortification of cereals with vitamins and minerals is not in itself bad. But it sometimes is used more to benefit sales than to improve the nutrition of consumers, and occasionally it is used to disguise the fundamental unwholesomeness of an overly refined, sugary cereal. Take a look at Total, a whole-wheat cereal that is fortified with 100 percent of the USRDA for 10 vitamins and minerals. Or Kellogg's Most, which earned its name by providing 100 percent of the USRDA for 11 vitamins and minerals, the same level of fortification in Kellogg's Product 19. That doesn't even include the milk! Unless one serving of dry cereal is all you plan to eat for the rest of the day, there's no reason for your cereal to provide 100 percent of any required nutrient, let alone 10 or 11 of them.

A more reasonable level of fortification would be to 10 percent to 25 percent of the daily requirement (before adding milk). It would also cost you considerably less. For example, for the approximately 2 cents' worth of vitamins that General Mills adds to Total, consumers pay 40 cents more for a 12-ounce box than they would for the otherwise comparable General Mills product Wheaties, fortified up to the 25-percent level. Keep in mind, too, that no level of fortification can negate a high sugar or fat content. Nor can it make up for all the nutrients lost when grain is refined. Thus, it is always better to start with a whole-grain cereal.

Preservatives. BHA and BHT are "added to the packaging material" of some cereals to prolong their shelf life. Questions have been raised about the safety of these preservatives (they are banned in Great Britain), yet some studies have indicated that they have cancer-inhibiting properties and that BHT also inhibits the growth of viruses. If these or other preservatives are used, the label must say so.

fruit and granola, or with applesauce, raisins, and cinnamon; peanut butter or cheese on bread; a thick shake of buttermilk or yogurt and fruit, mixed in the blender; reheated hearty soup; or cold leftovers. You don't have to resort to the food industry's sometimes bizarre notions of instant breakfasts, like fruit pies that are popped in the toaster, granola bars (which are really cookies), and artificially flavored powdered mixes that are added to milk or water.

GET UP EARLIER: Just 15 extra minutes is all you'll need to put together a decent breakfast. Your body will be far more grateful for the breakfast than for the extra minutes of shuteye that are usually disturbed anyway by the foreboding tones of your alarm clock or the tumult of others in the household who get up before you. And if you have children, try to sit down and eat breakfast with them. Children learn best by mimickry: if they see you eating a proper breakfast, they are more likely to grow up eating that way, too.

OR PACK A PORTABLE BREAKFAST: If you "can't eat a thing" before you leave the house in the morning, take something nourishing with you to eat when you get there. A sandwich; yogurt and fruit; a single-serving box of cereal and a container of milk; a bran muffin and a piece of fruit and cheese—almost anything is better than more coffee and a doughnut. Similarly, for children who are too agitated to eat before leaving for school, hand them a portable "breakfast box" (or bag) to eat on the way—a sandwich, pita pizza, cheese and fruit, whatever is nourishing but no more difficult to get down than chips and Coke. Actually, you, too, can eat a portable breakfast. I often eat en route when I have to leave early to get to the airport or to a meeting.

LUNCH, SUPPER, AND SNACKS

Now that you've mastered breakfast, let's see what to do about the rest of the day's meals if you want to be trim and healthy. Lunch is nearly as important as breakfast, since it picks up where breakfast left off to fuel the rest of your day's activities. Like breakfast, lunch should contain at least a third of your day's protein along with a generous amount of complex carbohydrates to keep your internal fires burning brightly and stave off those hunger pangs throughout the afternoon. In addition, some nutrient-rich vegetables and/or fruit should be on the lunch menu.

Lunch is a problem for many people because they're at the mercy of the nearest cafeteria, restaurant, lunch wagon, or take-out. It can be very hard to choose the right thing when you have no idea how the food was prepared, there are a dozen other hungry people behind you in line, and you have only 45 minutes or less for lunch. The temptation is strong to grab the first thing you see that sounds appealing or the special of the day, which at least you know is ready to serve. (See p. 209 for specific tips on eating out.) I solved the workday-lunch dilemma by becoming a brown-bagger of both hot and cold meals. I acquired a small hot plate that I plug in near my desk to heat my hot meals, which include an everything-but-the-kitchen-sink soup, stir-fried leftovers, a homemade chili, curried lentils and rice, or some stew or pasta concoction. Sometimes, of course, I have a sandwich or a salad platter with tuna, sardines, cottage cheese, chicken, or shrimp. With a piece of bread, a drink, and fruit for dessert, I have a nourishing, low-fat, satisfying meal that keeps me from sagging midafternoon.

If such a meal is more than you can down at once, save part of it for a snack. Or, if you have a long stretch (as I do) between lunch and supper, pack a wholesome snack when you make your lunch. My favorite snack items include a homemade muffin, fruit bread, or sandwich bread with a thin slice of cheese or smear of peanut butter, washed down with decaffeinated coffee or herb tea; fruit and yogurt; fruit juice and cheese; and skim milk and a homemade cookie. Having come equipped with my own snack, I don't have to confront the high-calorie, unnourishing selections on the coffee cart or stare at vending machines that offer a choice between fatty corn chips and sugary candy bars.

You don't have to deny your sweet tooth constantly, but it does help to plan its indulgences. If you know you crave something sweet after lunch or midafternoon, bring along a minimally sweet treat or one small cookie to satisfying the craving. That way you won't be tempted to go overboard by buying a whole package of cookies or a 300-calorie candy bar. Throughout the two years I was losing weight I allowed myself one sweet treat a day—two small cookies, a couple of tablespoons of ice cream, a sliver of cake or pie. That way I never felt deprived or developed cravings that couldn't be satisfied on less than a box of cookies or a whole quart of ice cream. An alternative approach that works for some people is to designate one day a week for a generous high-calorie treat —a piece of pie à la mode, an ice-cream sundae, a towering piece of layer cake —and refrain from sweet indulgences the rest of the time.

If you're really struggling to keep your calorie intake low and simply need something to munch on midafternoon to quiet your growling stomach on the way home or to keep you from being ravenous for supper, try popcorn (only 23 calories a cup without butter), unsweetened ready-to-eat cereal (preferably one high in fiber, like shredded wheat or puffed cereals), vegetable sticks, or fresh fruit. I find apples, oranges, tangerines, firm pears, and grapefruit especially satisfying because they take longer to eat than other fruits. And keep in mind that you can eat a whole pint of steamed vegetables (for example, carrot sticks, broccoli flowerets, green beans, asparagus, etc.) for half the calories and probably hundreds of times the nutrients in one big cookie.

Given the demands of modern days and the disparate directions in which family members go, supper has become the "big meal," the time when people can get together and relax enough to down a three-course dinner. And as if the dinner weren't filling enough, the permission people give themselves to eat and finally satisfy the latent hunger that gnawed at them all day prompts many to make evening a nibbling marathon. But if you're concerned about weight, health, and a sound night's sleep, the end of the day is precisely the wrong time to pack in so many calories. By morning, a good number of them have already been converted into body fat and put into storage.

Unless you dine early—say, at 5 P.M. or 6 P.M.—and remain physically active for the next four or five hours, you'd be much better off with a light evening meal, such as soup with bread and salad, a pasta and vegetable dish, a chef's salad, or a vegetable and meat stir-fry with some rice. An ordinary entrée of meat, poultry, or fish, with two vegetables is also okay—if the portions are small: 2 or 3 ounces of the animal protein and about ½ cup of each vegetable, plus bread and perhaps fruit for dessert. It's important to limit protein and to include a generous serving of a starchy food in your end-of-the-day meal if you're interested in a tranquil evening and a good night's sleep. Carbohydrate foods prompt the entry of tryptophan into the brain, which in turn produces serotonin, a natural sleep-inducing chemical. But this effect can be obliterated if you eat too much protein. (Even though protein foods contain a lot of tryptophan, other substances in protein block its entry into the brain.)

Before or with your evening meal, you might also enjoy a cocktail, wine, or beer, if you can afford the calories. On the average, people who drink one or two drinks a day live longer and suffer fewer heart attacks than teetotalers. But keep in mind that alcohol diminishes your resistance to temptation, and some people find that even one drink prompts them to throw caution to the winds and overeat.

SOUP AS A SLIMMING FOOD

While there is no such thing as a food that causes your body to burn calories (all foods do to some extent since energy is needed to metabolize them, but no food uses up more energy than it contributes), some foods can help you to limit how many calories you subsequently consume. Soup, as an interesting study showed, is one of them. Participants in a weight-loss program at the Institute for Behavioral Education in King of Prussia, Pennsylvania, lost more weight the more often they ate soup. Those who ate soup less than four times a week lost an average of 15 percent of their excess weight, but those who consumed soup four or more times a week lost an average of 20 percent of their excess weight.

The researchers, headed by Dr. Henry A. Jordan, showed that the larger the role soup played in the dieters' meals, the fewer total calories they consumed. Total caloric intake at lunch, for example, was four times higher when soup contributed less than a quarter of the calories than when it accounted for more than three-quarters of the calories consumed. And when soup was eaten at lunch, it even helped to reduce the number of calories consumed at other meals, lowering the total daily intake by 92 calories. The researchers showed that by eating soup as a part of their meals, the dieters consumed calories at a slower rate: a third more calories were consumed per minute in nonsoup lunches than in those in which soup was eaten. Another study conducted at Baylor College of Medicine in Houston showed that soup eaters were also more likely than nonsoup eaters to maintain their weight loss a year later.

In other words, by starting your meals with soup, which has a lower caloric density than most solid foods and which takes a relatively long while to consume, you're likely to eat less. Eating soup gives your brain time to register satiety before you've overconsumed calories. You will find an abundance of delicious soup recipes in Part V: soups as first courses and as main courses. Main-dish soup has become my favorite meal; I even eat it for breakfast on occasion and often serve it for company dinner, with a big salad and bread.

But soup is not the only dieter's food aid. The Pennsylvania researchers noted that by choosing one type of food over another, you are likely to slow your rate of calorie consumption: baked potato versus French fries; artichokes versus string beans; apples versus applesauce; whole fish versus fish fillets; whole oranges versus orange juice; and hard rolls versus white bread. To this list I would add green salad with a low-fat dressing versus potato salad or coleslaw with mayonnaise, and plain yogurt with fresh fruit versus fruit-flavored yogurt.

DON'T FORGET DRINKS

Liquid, an essential ingredient in any weight reduction plan and a necessary part of every wholesome menu, can easily become a caloric and nutritional downfall if the drinks are not wisely chosen. A drink doesn't have to be high in calories to be a potential caloric problem. For example, diet soft drinks that are artificially sweetened can perpetuate your sweet craving and make you more likely to succumb to the temptation of calorie-laden sweets. Many soft drinks are also fairly high in sodium, which holds water in your body and may mask your progress in losing fat.

Alcohol can be both a diet aid and a detriment. A small glass of wine with a meal can help to relieve a dieter's anxiety and curb hunger sensations. One study of 35 obese men and women showed that those who drank wine with dinner lost a higher percentage of their body weight than those who abstained from alcohol. But too much alcohol can also weaken will power and lead you into temptation. A wine spritzer gets my vote as the best alcoholic drink for weight watchers: combine 3 to 4 ounces of white wine with ice cubes and 4 or more ounces of seltzer, club soda, or mineral water, then sip slowly. You can start this drink during the cocktail hour and nurse it all the way through dinner without need for a refill.

Like alcohol, caffeine in coffee, tea, and other beverages is also a mixed blessing. On the one hand, this stimulant can raise your metabolic rate, increasing the amount of calories your body uses up. On the other, it can lower blood sugar and speed the return of hunger sensations. Try to limit your consumption of caffeinated drinks to the equivalent of 2 cups of coffee a day. Alternatives include decaffeinated coffee and tea and various low-calorie grain-based beverages like Postum, Pero, and Cafix. Herb teas are another no-calorie alternative, but a cautious approach to them is necessary. Some herb teas contain potent drugs, so be sure to drink a variety of teas rather than depending on only one kind, and a brew a fresh cup each time to avoid strong concentrations of any chemicals they may contain.

Tomato juice may have fewer calories than orange or apple juice, but unless you buy a low-sodium brand, the large amount of salt in tomato juice will hold water in your tissues. Nectars tend to be much sweeter and higher in calories than ordinary unsweetened fruit juices. Grapefruit juice, although more sour than orange juice, contains no less sugar (just more acid) and no fewer calories. You might try fruit juice mixed half and half with seltzer or club soda for a refreshing and nutritious treat.

Water, of course, is the ideal drink. Down at least one glass before meals and one with meals for the supreme no-calorie filler-upper and digestive aid. If you're too chilly for cold water, drink it hot, perhaps with a squirt or two of lemon juice (for no extra calories).

OTHER CALORIE-TRIMMING TIPS

There was a popular love song in the 1950s called "Little Things Mean a Lot." The message is true not only for love but also for those "love handles" that tend to gather around waistlines. Small caloric savings here and there may not seem significant individually, but they can add up to (or, more accurately, subtract) a significant number of calories over the course of a day. By adopting some of these painless ways to trim your total caloric intake, you may be able to have your cake and eat it, too.

- Serve yourself on a small plate so that smaller portions don't look so skimpy. By eating 3 ounces of steak instead of 6, you'll save more than 300 calories.
- Put your eating utensils down between bites, and use a teaspoon rather than a tablespoon to eat soups and cereal.
- If you like sweetened yogurt, buy plain yogurt and add a teaspoon or 2 of preserves rather than buying presweetened Swiss-style yogurt or the type with 2 tablespoons of overly sweet preserves at the bottom. Better yet, eat the yogurt with fresh fruit, such as a sliced banana or fruit salad.
- Think high fiber when you are eating cereal, bread, or baked snacks. A bran muffin is more filling (and more nourishing) than a doughnut.
- Put crunchy raw vegetables into your salads, such as broccoli, cauliflower, and carrot and zucchini slices. They take longer to eat, and the chewing they require is satisfying.
- Mix powdered dressing mixes with yogurt, buttermilk, cottage cheese, and/or tomato juice instead of oil or sour cream. When a recipe calls for mayonnaise, try using half mayo and half low-fat yogurt.
- Use marinated vegetables and a few dashes of vinegar instead of an oil-based dressing to season your salads. Other low-calorie seasonings for a variety of foods include mustard, lemon juice, and vinegars (there are dozens of flavors and types to choose from).
- Sauté vegetables in a small amount of bouillon or stock instead of oil. For quick access, freeze stock in ice-cube trays (a tablespoon or 2 for each cube), and, when frozen, remove the cubes from the tray and place them in a plastic bag for convenient frozen storage.
- Pie lovers can save about 150 calories per serving by substituting fruit cobbler

for pies with a fat-rich crust. For nonfruit open-face pies, graham-cracker crusts are lower in fat and calories than dough crusts.

- Eggplant is a sponge when it comes to oil. Instead of frying this vegetable in oil for dishes like eggplant Parmesan or ratatouille, steam or boil the cut-up vegetable.
- Substitute skim milk for whole milk, whole milk for cream, and yogurt for sour cream in most recipes.
- To thicken cream soups, purée some of the vegetables in the broth and use low-fat or skim milk instead of adding sour cream or heavy cream.
- Puréed vegetables also make excellent low-fat sauces for fish, poultry, pasta, or vegetables.
- Use vegetables as "fillers" in recipes, such as in meat loaf or croquettes. In most recipes that already include vegetables, you can safely double the allotted quantity.
- Sautéed diced vegetables make a delicious low-calorie topping for pasta, baked or boiled potatoes, or rice.
- Instead of fat, marinate or baste foods with lemon or lime juice, tomato juice, wine, broth, or bouillon.
- Stuff fish and poultry with vegetables instead of bread.
- Rather than syrup, use fruit or a thin smear of jam to sweeten pancakes and French toast.
- Buy unsweetened fruit juices and applesauce (or make your own).

"LITE" AND DIET FOODS

The array of diet and dietetic foods available today could confuse even the most discerning shopper. The market for diet foods and beverages is expected to reach $41.2 billion a year by 1990. In the last decade, food manufacturers that cater to weight-conscious consumers have come a long way from low-calorie jellies and puddings and thinly sliced breads laced with wood fiber. Today you can buy everything from soup to nuts at a lower caloric cost (though usually a higher monetary cost) than the same food in its usual form. In most markets, you can now find low-cal salad dressing, syrup, pancake and gravy mixes, pasta, mayonnaise, margarine, cheese, beer, wine, peanuts, and a variety of frozen ready-to-heat-and-eat dinners (Weight Watchers and Stouffer's Lean Cuisine, to name two national brands of diet meals). If you add these to the low-cal choices among ordinary foods, such as low-fat milk, yogurt, and cottage cheese, tuna packed in water, and fruit canned in its own juice, you can probably eat low-cal without having to do much more than boil water. Not that I recommend the factory-food route to weight control. But I do realize that having such foods available can be an important aid on those days when other demands leave no time to cook and you've run out of your homemade calorie-controlled "TV dinners."

You *can* save quite a few calories by choosing the diet versions of various commercially prepared foods. Thus, a lunch of thinly sliced bread, tuna packed in water, diet mayonnaise, and unsweetened fruit cocktail, along with a no-calorie beverage can have almost 600 fewer calories than the regular alternative. For dinner, diet lasagne, garden salad with low-calorie dressing, light wine, and ice milk for dessert add up to 400 fewer calories than the nondiet counterparts (with ice cream for dessert).

But you can also become mired in the confusion of names and labels given to various supposedly "diet" foods. Because not all names are subject to government regulation, the consumer can easily be fooled into paying a premium price for a presumed diet food that actually offers no significant caloric saving. Here are some official definitions and common labeling designations.

- To be labeled *low calorie,* the Food and Drug Administration requires that a food contain no more than 40 calories per serving and no more than 40 calories per 100 grams (3½ ounces). However, a food that is naturally low in calories, such as mushrooms or celery, cannot be labeled "low calorie." Any food that is labeled "low calorie" must also bear nutrition labeling, showing nutrient and calorie content per serving. And if the label suggests that calories have been cut, it has to back up that claim with a numerical comparison to the unmodified food.
- To be labeled *reduced calorie,* a food must be at least one-third lower in calorie content than the comparable food in which calories have not been reduced. At the same time, however, the reduced-calorie food cannot be nutritionally inferior to its unmodified counterpart. As with foods labeled "low calorie," reduced-calorie foods must bear nutrition labeling and show the caloric comparison with unmodified versions of the same foods.
- If there exists a government standard specifying the contents of a food product, reduced-calorie versions of this food must be labeled *imitation.* This does not mean it is a fake food made from combinations of chemicals that mimic the real thing. It simply means that a serving of the food contains less fat (and, therefore, fewer calories) than the government definition states.
- Foods labeled *sugar-free* are not necessarily low in calories. Instead of ordinary sugars, they may contain sweeteners like sorbitol and mannitol, which have the same calorie value sugar has but are absorbed very slowly and incompletely, making them suitable sweeteners for diabetics who cannot handle a large sugar load at one time. Be careful about consuming too much of these sugar alternatives; they often cause diarrhea and intestinal gas because they are not fully absorbed by the body.
- Some sugar-free foods are labeled *artificially sweetened,* flavored with such sweet chemicals as saccharin or aspartame (NutraSweet), which for all intents and purposes provide no calories. However, artificial sweeteners are most often used in foods that offer little or no redeeming nutritional value and are best left out of the diet entirely. And, with regard to saccharin at least, there are strong doubts about its long-term safety (see p. 177).
- There is no official definition of *light* foods, and the nonlabel-reading consumer can easily be hoodwinked. Light beers and wines are made by decreasing the carbohydrate and alcohol content of the finished product, but there is a wide range in caloric content among the various brands. While Miller's Lite beer has 96 calories in a 12-ounce can, Michelob Light has 134, only 10 calories less

than regular beer. And all "light beer" is not low-calorie light; light on the label has been used for many years to distinguish pale-colored beers from dark ones. As for wines, the calorie saving is really minimal. The light versions contain about 50 to 60 calories in 3½ ounces (one wineglass) compared to 65 to 80 calories in the same amount of regular wine. Fritos recently introduced a "lights" version of its corn chips: the supposedly light chips contain 150 calories per one-serving bag, compared to 160 calories in regular Fritos corn chips. Like beers, certain foods are called "light" for reasons other than calories: light tuna (as opposed to darker-colored fish), light cream (as opposed to heavy), light salt (made with potassium instead of sodium), light syrup (made with less sugar), light chocolate (as opposed to dark), and light whiskey (stored in uncharred containers), light batter (as opposed to heavy).

13 ·
DINING OUT

No longer reserved for special occasions, celebrations, and vacations, eating out has become a daily event in American life. For many it is a logistical necessity since they live too far from work to go home for lunch. For others, it is an occupational necessity enforced by travel obligations or the need to conduct business over lunch or dinner. For still others, such as students, those who live alone, and those who think they can't cook, eating out is a psychosocial necessity, the alternative to grabbing something from a vending machine or going hungry.

More than one-third of American meals are now eaten outside the home, and that's not counting the doughnut and coffee many breakfast skippers pick up on their way to work. Some people get nearly all their meals from commercial eateries, most of which are more interested in making money than in keeping diners slender and healthy. Even the so-called health-food and natural-food restaurants often serve foods that are too high in fat, cholesterol, calories, and salt to be truly healthful.

A Cornell University analysis of the national Food Consumption Survey of 1977 showed that people who eat out more than one meal a day have a lower intake of essential nutrients, especially of thiamin and vitamins A and C. It's hard enough to know what you're eating when you start with supermarket packages. But at least *they* have labels; menus rarely do. Still, there are many ways to uncover the caloric and health value of various menu selections. If you're willing to read between the lines and to speak up to those who serve you, you won't have to be a fat, unhealthy victim of dining-outitis. Nor will you have to sacrifice the pleasures of a good meal.

Dining out healthfully is getting easier. A growing number of restaurants, cognizant of consumer interest in diet and health, are introducing more nutritious offerings: more foods cooked without fat and with little or no salt, more fresh vegetables and fruit, more fish and poultry, fewer heavy sauces, and more whole-wheat breads. Several hotel chains, including Marriott, Fairmont, and Sheraton, and restaurant chains like the Hungry Tiger and Sizzler Family Steak House have signed agreements with the American Heart Association to provide heart-healthy or "prudent" menus. A growing number of top gourmet restaurants, including those at Four Seasons hotels, are offering low-cal, low-fat, low-cholesterol "haute cuisine" (the chic Four Seasons Restaurant in New York calls it "spa cuisine") along with their traditional eggs-butter-and-cream dishes. Several fast-food chains, including Burger King, have even introduced salad bars. Of course, the restaurant industry's own survey in 1983 showed that consumer desire for less fat, sugar, salt, and calories was lagging behind the number of restaurants offering such foods, but the trends were highly encouraging. It may not be long before many, if not most, restaurants adopt the approach used by the Copper Alley, a family-dining favorite in Mankato, Minnesota, where a community-wide save-your-heart program has raised the nutrition consciousness of thousands of residents. The restaurant's salad menu has been greatly expanded, vegetable casseroles have been added, and all the fish dishes are now poached, steamed, or broiled (fried only on request). Since the menu reformation, the Copper Alley's business has grown by more than 30 percent, with the heaviest orders for the healthy-heart specials.

Of course, there are times when you won't want to have to think about calories and health. It's okay now and then to throw caution to the winds and indulge in some high-calorie dining. Just get back to normal the next day, and be sure to get in some vigorous exercise; it will help your body shed some of those extra calories you consumed the night before.

DINNER IN A RESTAURANT

There's no reason why dinner out should be a dietary disaster, provided you approach the meal as an epicure—someone with a refined taste for food and wine—rather than as a glutton. High-quality but low-calorie dining starts with selecting the right restaurant. Forget those all-you-can-eat feasts (the food is rarely good, just plentiful), and think twice before you choose a traditional French restaurant wedded to the eggs-butter-and-cream style of cooking or a steakhouse famous for its 10-ounce cuts. It's usually easier to order calorie-controlled meals in a seafood or Japanese restaurant. Restaurants with good salad bars can also make it easier for the weight-watcher as long as the selections are not mainly premixed salads, cold cuts, cheese, marinated vegetables (they're usually marinated in an oily dressing), nuts, and seeds. However, if you have asthma or know you are sensitive to sulfites, ask first whether these preservatives are used in any of the salad-bar offerings.

If possible, first look over the menu, or, when you call to make a reservation, first ask if at least some of the selections are prepared with little or no fat. If foods are made to order, you'll have an easier time asking that your food be prepared without added fat and with the sauces or dressings on the side so that you can use a dab instead of a dollop. But wherever you end up eating, the following tips should help you dine with elegance, not excessiveness.

- Don't start out famished. If you're very hungry when you order, chances are you'll overorder. Don't skip lunch because you know you're having dinner out.

Before you leave home, take the edge off your appetite by eating some raw vegetables, a piece of fruit, or a cup or two of unbuttered popcorn.

- Go easy on the alcohol. If you would like a cocktail, consider ordering a tall drink (long on nonalcoholic liquid) such as a white-wine spritzer or Scotch and soda or light beer. Try to limit yourself to one drink: if you plan to have wine with dinner, skip the cocktail before; you can always order mineral water with lime if your companions are starting with a drink.

- Order à la carte. The "bargain" full-course dinner may have some hidden costs to the body that eats it. Unless you're able to share the dinner with someone, you're better off ordering exactly what you want and no more. One of my favorite restaurant tricks is to order soup and an appetizer or two appetizers and a salad instead of a full entrée. In an Italian restaurant, you can order an antipasto or salad and a "first course" pasta dish as your main course.

- Consider selecting foods that require work before you can eat them: mussels or shrimp in their shells, crab legs, whole fish (and don't let the waiter remove the bones), unboned chicken.

- Before you order, ask the waiter how the food is prepared. You might say you're on a low-fat diet and want to know which dishes are made or *can* be made with little or no fat. Since most calorific sauces are added at the end of cooking, you can usually ask that they be left off or served on the side. Don't assume from the name of the dish that you know how it is prepared. (I recently encountered a recipe for steamed fish that included *six* sticks of butter, one for each serving!) At a wonderful restaurant in Pittsburgh, I inquired about the poached sole with shrimp (by itself, very low in fat and calories) and discovered it was served with a hollandaise sauce. I asked for the sauce served on the side, but the fish was so delicious that I was never even tempted to taste the sauce.

- Don't be afraid to send a dish back if it is not prepared the way you ordered it. If the fish you asked to be broiled without fat arrives in a pool of butter, send it back. Remember, you are paying for this meal, and if you eat food you really don't want, you're paying double.

- Beware of calorie-laden salad dressings and salads containing such high-fat ingredients as bacon, cheese, avocado, and olives. Always order salad dressing on the side so you can add a few teaspoons rather than the several tablespoons customarily used by restaurants. Or create your own dressing by asking for vinegar or lemon juice and oil (easy on the oil) and freshly ground pepper.

- It's okay to eat a roll or a few slices of bread with your meal. It's not the bread that's fattening; it's the butter you smear on it. Skip the fat, or spread it *very thinly*. Really good bread should not require any enhancement, and bread that is not really good should not be eaten.

- Forget about clean-plate clubs. The food you leave over is not shipped to starving people abroad or even given to the hungry in your home town. It is not immoral not to finish a meal, but it is of questionable morality to treat yourself like a waste-disposal system. If you'd rather not see food go to waste, ask for the leftovers to be placed in a doggie bag. No restaurant is too fancy for a doggie bag; in fact, the fancier the restaurant, the fancier the doggie bag. Many restaurants openly acknowledge the true use for take-home leftovers and put them in a containers labeled "people bag." By taking home leftovers, you can get two meals for the price of one.

- If possible, inquire about portion sizes before you order. If they are large, ask that you be served half a portion (perhaps half can be put in a doggie bag before it arrives at the table), or, if that is not feasible, eat only half of what you're served.

- As soon as you've eaten all you want, ask the waiter to remove your plate. That way you won't be tempted to keep picking at the leftovers.
- "Don't eat mediocre food; it's an insult to your palate as well as to your waistline," advises Dr. Judith S. Stern, associate professor of nutrition at the University of California at Davis. Another trick of mine is to eat the food on the plate I like best first. By then I'm often full enough to skip the foods I don't like as well. (If you eat the other way around, chances are you'll never leave behind your favorite foods.)
- Buffets and smorgasbords do not have to be a dieter's downfall. They can be a great boon (you and you alone determine your selections and portion sizes) if you approach them rationally. Beware of two major hazards: overloading your plate by taking too much of the first dishes offered and then not wanting to miss any down the line; and going back for seconds or even thirds before the firsts have had a chance to tell your brain that you've had enough. Before you even pick up a plate, survey the entire buffet display. Decide which dishes you *really* want to try, and skip the rest. Take reasonable portions. Remember, if something is truly wonderful, you can always go back for more later. If one of your selections turns out to be mediocre, leave it on your plate. Start your meal with soup if it's offered, and be sure to take plenty of fresh vegetables and salad greens.
- Wait until you've finished the rest of your meal before you order dessert. When you're full, you'll be less tempted by some calorific no-no. In a buffet, the richest desserts are often the first to go, so by waiting until you've finished your meal, you may spare yourself the agony of self-denial. Most restaurants have some low-cal offerings, such as fruit (fresh or poached). Order your berries without cream. A scoop of ice cream or sherbet has far fewer calories than a slice of cake or pie. Offer to share a fattening no-no with a companion, or, if you have no takers, order half a portion (and tell the waiter you'll gladly pay for a whole one to avoid being led into temptation). One of my favorite solutions to dessert is to hold on to a dinner roll to eat with my coffee.

BREAKFAST ON THE ROAD

Assuming you are now convinced that the first meal of the day is your most important one, how do you then escape from the eggs and bacon, cheese omelets and home fries, Egg McMuffins, pancakes and sausage, croissants and jam, sweet rolls and butter, and other such fare that deposit fat on your hips and cholesterol in your arteries? As someone who travels often, I am well acquainted with the problems of getting a quick, decent breakfast away from home. Here are some strategies I've found to work well most of the time.

BRING ALONG THE BASICS. When I have to be out of town for more than a day and I'm uncertain that I can get the kind of breakfast foods I'm willing to eat on a daily basis, I bring along some staples from home or pick them up in a market when I reach my destination. My favorites are whole-grain ready-to-eat cereals, like Spoon-Size Shredded Wheat, Nutri-Grain, Grape-Nuts, All-Bran, and perhaps some granola for garnish; peanut butter, unsweetened apple butter, and pita bread; and fresh fruit. In a market near my hotel, I often buy some orange juice and a container of low-fat or skim milk and keep them chilled in the hotel ice bucket. I also travel with an immersion heater (I have a good one that doesn't burn out and that can be used in foreign countries), a cup, some tea bags, instant coffee, and powdered milk. A few plastic-coated paper bowls and some plastic utensils are the only other tools I need for my hotel picnic breakfast. Sometimes dinner the night before provides me with the leftovers for a more exotic breakfast, such as shrimp or crabmeat or a sandwich of leftovers on a restaurant roll. I may even make a doggie bag of an in-flight meal that seemed edible and nutritious but was served at a time I was not ready to eat (the airsickness bag, believe it or not, is a handy waterproof container). Wrapped in a plastic bag (I travel with a few that I know are water-tight), your restaurant or airplane doggie bag can be stored in the hotel ice bucket until you're ready to dine on the contents.

Not only does this approach allow me to determine the healthfulness of the food that starts my day, it also gives me the flexibility I need in the morning, enabling me to eat breakfast when I want to without having to get dressed first or wait until the coffee shop opens or deal with slow service and smoking patrons at nearby tables.

TAKE ADVANTAGE OF ROOM SERVICE. For years I thought room service was an immoral extravagance for lazy people, the kind who get up late and like to have breakfast in bed. Now, as a frequent traveler, I find it an invaluable service for early risers who like to exercise and perhaps work in the morning, and who want to be sure they get the breakfast they want when they want it. Room service, especially at breakfast, is well worth the extra dollar or two it may cost. I usually order it the night before to arrive after I have returned from my morning run and have showered. I have found that specific requests are nearly always honored: an omelet made with one egg yolk and two whites; whole-wheat toast, unbuttered; skim milk for my cereal and coffee; oatmeal cooked in skim milk; berries without cream; and so forth. And if my day's schedule looks like there's no time for lunch, along with my breakfast I sometimes order a sandwich that will keep in my briefcase until lunchtime.

STAY AWAY FROM SPECIALS. Breakfast menus often specify combination meals that will save you money but are no bargain for your body because they include foods you shouldn't eat. Unless you have extraordinary will power or you're dining with someone who's willing to eat the items you won't, it's better to spend a little extra and get exactly what you want by ordering à la carte.

COPING WITH THE COFFEE BREAK

If three or four hours have elapsed since your last meal and your next one is two hours off, a midmorning and/or midafternoon snack may be the ideal way to stave off the voracious hunger that prompts many people to eat too much too fast at the next meal. Unfortunately, the choices that confront most people at coffee-break time are hardly ideal: oversized cookies, cake, pie, Danish pastry, doughnuts, and the like. Of course, if you've had a decent breakfast or lunch, you'll be less tempted to select fat- and- sugar-rich no-nos at coffee break. But they may be hard to resist if you have no other choice.

Better to *plan* your snack ahead of time by bringing it with you or by finding a nearby source of more nutritious fare. Consider saving a part of your breakfast or lunch, such as a roll or fruit, to have at coffee-break time. You may even be able to convince the coffee wagon at your worksite to stock more acceptable alternatives. In response to employee requests at my office, for example, the coffee cart now carries yogurt, apples, oranges, fruit juice, and skim milk in addition to the traditional high-calorie snacks, soft drinks, coffee, and tea. If you want something doughy, try a bagel, a roll, whole-wheat toast, or a toasted English muffin. If your choices are limited to sweetened baked goods, look for a corn or bran muffin instead of a doughnut or a piece of cake. And ask for milk to lighten your coffee or tea rather than high-fat cream or nondairy creamer (it is usually made from corn syrup and coconut oil). I keep a small jar of powdered nonfat milk in my desk for this purpose.

LUNCH AWAY FROM HOME

As the meal most often eaten out, lunch is a difficult time for most weight- and health-conscious consumers. Time is often short, and the choices of eating establishments limited. Here are some personally tested techniques for making lunch a wholesome experience that doesn't add permanently to the waistline.

KEEP A RESTAURANT LIST. Take an hour or two one day to visit nearby restaurants and look at their menus. Many establishments post the menus outside. But if not, go in and ask the maître d' if you may look at the menu for future reference. Write down the names, addresses, phone numbers, and serving hours of restaurants offering foods that are made to order and are not drowning in fats and calories.

THE FAST-FOOD MINI-FEAST. Though hardly gourmet dining, fast-food emporiums may be desired for their convenience, speed, accessibility, and predictability. Unfortunately, too often they can also be counted on to dish up a meal that contains all the calories you should be eating in a day. For example, a ¼-pound burger-with-everything-on-it, French fries, and a small shake add up to about 1,200 calories. But you'd halve the caloric total without sacrificing any of the valuable nutrients if instead you had a plain burger, coleslaw, and low-fat milk.

If fast food is your speed, try to pick a restaurant that has a salad bar, and start your meal by filling up on bulky vegetables (be sure to go easy on the oily dressings, or bring along your own low-fat favorite). Order sandwiches without dressings, a plain burger, or pizza with vegetables rather than sausage. Hot dogs usually have considerably more fat and always have more salt than burgers. If the chicken or fish is fried, remove the fat-soaked skin or crust. Skip the French fries (a baked potato is fine, however, as long as you don't drown it in butter). Instead of a shake or soft drink, order milk, coffee, tea, or fruit juice for your beverage.

CAFETERIA STRATEGY. You may have already noticed that most cafeteria lines start with dessert and proceed on to the more wholesome part of the meal. This greatly increases the probability that you'll select a high-calorie dessert because you enter the line hungry and are easily tempted by the first thing you see. I have a standing rule about cafeterias: I start *not* by getting in line but by surveying all the possibilities first and then deciding upon my selections without the pressure of people behind me. As for dessert, don't make your selection (unless it's fresh fruit) until you've finished the rest of your meal. You may decide it's not worth it to go through the line again just for dessert. An alternative approach is to share a rich dessert with a companion.

BROWN-BAGGING IT. By far my favorite solution to the luncheon debate is to bring my own meal from home. Not only does this give me complete control of my nutrient and calorie intake, it's also economical and time-saving. National surveys indicate that brown-bagging is on the rise. Interestingly, 70 percent of the brown-baggers are adults, and those who bring their lunch from home tend to be better educated and better off financially.

Most of my lunches are combinations of leftovers that I reheat at my desk (see p. 196). This approach has a hidden caloric advantage: because I want to have something left for lunch, I'm less likely to eat it all the first time the dish is served. You can also take cold salads in plastic containers: fruit salad and cottage cheese; garden salad and chicken or fish; lentil salad with greens and bread; and so forth. If sandwiches are more to your liking, fine. Just avoid the fatty luncheon meats, and go easy on the mayonnaise and butter. Mustard and ketchup are lower-calorie sandwich spreads. Use whole-grain bread or roll or pita bread. Good fillings include chicken or turkey breast, boiled ham, water-packed tuna or sardines, poached or broiled fish, or lean roast beef. You can add a thin sliver or two of cheese for flavor (see p. 496 for other sandwich "recipes"). But don't overdo the protein filling. Instead, fill out the sandwich with vegetables: lettuce, tomato, cucumber slices, sprouts, etc. For your beverage, try a small can of juice, low-fat milk, club soda or mineral water, coffee, or tea. Fresh fruit is the ideal dessert, perhaps with one small cookie to satisfy that craving for a crunchy sweet with your coffee.

If your worksite has no refrigerator in which to store your lunch, you might invest in a minicooler (perhaps the type used to hold a six-pack of beer) or an insulated bag kept cool by a water-filled plastic jar that you freeze overnight. If it's not terribly hot, many sandwiches—peanut butter, sardines, tuna, ham, felafel, hummus—will keep outside the refrigerator for the five hours or so until lunch. When I take soup or other frozen leftovers for lunch, I remove them from the freezer when I get up in the morning; that keeps them cold until I'm ready to heat them for lunch.

EATING IN TRANSIT

The food usually served on airplanes and trains and at rest stops along interstate highways is famous for its awfulness. If you're concerned about calories and nutrients, there's little room in your diet for awful food that does nothing more than fill your belly. But just because you're soaring 37,000 feet above sea level doesn't mean you're stuck with pancake-wrapped sausages for breakfast or a salami and cheese sandwich for lunch or a heavily sauced casserole for dinner. By planning ahead, you can have far more delicious and nutritious fare.

ON THE PLANE. Airlines rarely advertise the fact that passengers can order special meals at no extra cost by calling the airline at least 24 hours before the flight. Most major carriers and many smaller ones can provide vegetarian, low-cholesterol, low-sodium, low-calorie, low-carbohydrate, diabetic, or kosher meals, as well as certain special entrées. Choices of special entrées may include cold seafood platter (my favorite—an almost fat-free platter of shrimp and crabmeat, lettuce, tomato, and sometimes a hard-boiled egg, served with cocktail sauce), hot fish dinner or seafood terrine, chef's salad, or fruit platter. The special trays are individually prepared, but that's no guarantee of high quality. You may wonder, for instance, why the regular meal was served with a whole-wheat roll and the vegetarian dinner you ordered came with white bread. If you placed your order when you made your reservation, it's a good idea to re-confirm it the day before departure. When you check in to get your boarding pass, tell the attendant that you ordered a special meal, and once on board tell the flight attendant as well. This will speed service and avoid confusion when the meal is served.

Whatever you order on an airplane, don't expect it to look or taste like a gourmet dinner. At best, airplane food—prepared way in advance of consumption in assembly-line fashion and reheated on board—will approach the fare of a mediocre restaurant. If you're not happy about eating such food, bring something from home. You can always get something to drink on board.

A WORD OF WARNING: On most flights, when you finally get off the ground, you'll be offered drinks and some nibbles, usually high caloric, salty nuts you'd be wise to pass up. Alcohol is not the best drink to have when you fly (it impairs the ability of your ears to adjust to pressure changes, it adds to the dehydration inherent in flying, and it enhances jet lag), so you can save calories and money by sticking to the free offerings. My favorites are orange juice and club soda, which I sometimes ask the flight attendant to mix. If you're an aficionado of herb tea and carry your own tea bags, you can request hot water (with or without lemon) and make your own low-calorie beverage. I often drink hot water with lemon, which to me tastes better than most herb teas.

IN THE CAR. Carry low-calorie snacks with you: unbuttered popcorn, dry cereal, raw vegetables, fresh fruit. If you're not driving, take along something to do to keep your mind off food: a book or magazines, knitting, needlepoint, crossword puzzles, paper-and-pencil car games, a tape recorder with music or a learning tape. If you're the driver, you can also listen to tapes or have someone read to you.

Unless you know your route will take you near restaurants that prepare the kind of foods you're willing and able to eat, your best bet is to take along a cooler stocked with more acceptable fare. A roadside picnic is always cheaper and faster and usually more fun than eating in a mass-market diner. The diner can be a source of hot drinks, but you can pass on the overcooked roast beef, gray vegetables, white bread, and watery mashed potatoes swimming in gravy. We've found that having our own food along also reduces the number of stops we have to make to satisfy the hunger of our fast-growing sons, who seem to be struck by the hungries as soon as the car pulls off the block.

Our favorite cooler foods include baked, barbecued, or broiled chicken; potato salad or coleslaw; steamed vegetables (sometimes with a low-fat dip or salad dressing); lettuce, tomatoes, and cucumbers; sliced turkey breast; boiled ham; Swiss cheese; peanut butter; apple butter; whole-grain bread; yogurt; fresh fruit; skim milk; fruit juice; and homemade muffins or cookies. If your trip is just a day long, you can also take a thermos of hot soup.

If a cooler or roadside picnic is not a viable option and you're stuck with eating in roadside diners, order as sensibly as you can, starting perhaps with soup and salad, and then a sandwich or simple entrée. Be sure to ask for dressings and gravy on the side.

On bus and short train trips, it's best to carry your own snacks and sandwiches.

VACATIONS AND BUSINESS TRIPS

Being away from home for an extended period of time too often means more of you comes home than left. But that needn't be the case. In fact, I often lose a few pounds on a business trip because my access to food is limited and I'm more aware of the importance of eating carefully. On vacations, don't maintain lofty goals of trying to lose weight. Be content to hold your own or even to gain a pound or two, then go back into your weight-loss mode when you get home. Here are some steps to keep you from gaining anything more than a good time from your trip.

- Choose a hotel that has health-club facilities or other physical activities, and take advantage of them. I always try to stay in hotels with pools (indoors during the cooler seasons). Many also have jogging tracks, tennis courts, and workout rooms with exercise bicycles and other equipment.
- Stick to your regular exercise program as much as possible. I was a source of great amusement to Kenyan natives as I jogged through their countryside, but I

also managed to hold my weight through a three-week tour and I got to see many sights my stay-a-bed traveling companions missed.

- Walk to appointments whenever possible. I buy street maps of the cities I visit, plot out my appointments, and figure out how many I can walk to.

- Avoid American-plan hotels, or, if there's a choice of plan, choose to pay your way for meals. That way you'll be less tempted to eat as much as possible to get your money's worth. If American plan is the only choice, order carefully and ask your waiter to serve you small portions.

- If you know you'll be confronting three big meals a day, eat a good breakfast (easy on the sweet rolls) and a skimpy lunch. Or, better yet, eat a good breakfast and a good lunch and a skimpy dinner. And get plenty of exercise between meals.

- At banquets, you can usually find out in advance what is going to be served. If it's *verboten* fare that you can easily forgo, order a plain fish or vegetable dish, chef's salad, or fruit platter. Be sure to ask for your salad dressing on the side. Desserts at most banquets are high-calorie no-nos that look much better than they taste. If you must, ask a tablemate for a taste and ask the waiter for fruit or hang onto a dinner roll for your dessert.

WHEN YOU'RE A GUEST IN SOMEONE'S HOME

When someone else has determined the menu, you're less in control of food choices than you would be in a restaurant. But that shouldn't be used as an excuse to throw caution to the winds and eat everything in sight, regardless of its caloric or nutritional value (unless you've decided in advance that's the kind of experience you want).

- As with restaurant dining, it's best not to arrive famished. Have a filling but low-calorie snack before you leave home.

- Chances are the meal will begin with cocktails, usually accompanied by hors d'oeuvres, which alone could add up to the number of calories you would normally allot to dinner. Ask for either a nonalcoholic drink, a tall drink with a small amount of alcohol and lots of water or club soda, a wine spritzer, or a light beer. If they're offered, fill up on fresh vegetables (but easy on the dip). Avoid fried appetizers and those made in flaky (i.e., buttery) pastry. Keep in mind that cheese is loaded with fat and calories. If some rich appetizer seems especially tempting, try one, but only one.

- When the meal is about to be served, quietly ask your host for small portions or, if you serve yourself buffet-style, take small portions, filling up your plate with the lowest-calorie offerings. Eat lots of salad, if it's not swimming in an oily dressing. Don't skip the soup, but if it's a cream soup, ask for only one ladleful. By dessert, you should be full enough to be able to say honestly that you're too full for more than a taste.

- Skip the after-dinner alcoholic offerings, or, if you must, ask for a tiny bit of cognac or brandy and savor it, inhaling more than you drink.

SLIMMER PICKINGS AT CELEBRATIONS

Parties and holiday celebrations are practically synonymous with food and drink —and far more of both than you'd ordinarily indulge in. In addition, cooks commonly put their very best culinary feet forward at such times, preparing all-too-tempting treats that are often once-a-year offerings. Does watching your weight mean you can't have pumpkin pie for Thanksgiving dinner or potato pancakes for Hanukkah, or egg nog at the Christmas party? Not at all. But if you want to indulge in such treats, some precautions are in order. The five weeks between Thanksgiving and New Year's are expansive times for many people—especially around the waist and hips! A whole autumn of weight-watching may be lost to huge holiday dinners, countless cocktail and office parties, and well-intentioned but calorific gifts. The resulting holiday "spread" no doubt contributes to the after–New Year's letdown that many people experience. Here are some ways to help you enjoy parties and celebrations without remorse.

- Concentrate on dressing well, in your most slenderizing attire. If you leave for the party in clothes that just fit and are figure-revealing, you'll be less likely to overeat because it will "show" immediately.
- Taste everything you want, but be satisfied with less than a full portion of the most fattening foods. The fourth bite of Nesselrode pie tastes no better than the first three.
- No matter how busy you are, don't neglect daily exercise. If anything, do more than usual if you know you'll be eating more than usual. Vigorous exercise is especially helpful the day after you've overindulged.
- Limit your alcohol intake to one drink a day or less. If you're planning to have wine with dinner, skip the cocktail, or vice versa. Alcohol provides only nutritionally empty calories and undermines discretion and determination to eat discriminately. Have a comfortable excuse ready for the host who pushes drinks: "Doctor's orders"; "I'm driving"; "I've already been to another party"; "My stomach isn't up to it"; "There's a long evening ahead."
- If you expect to eat more than usual at a party or dinner, eat somewhat less for breakfast and lunch. But don't skip the early meals of the day. And never go to a party famished.
- A cocktail party that serves substantial and nutritious hors d'oeuvres may mean you can skip dinner. Or, if you know a dinner is to follow, arrive fashionably late for the cocktail hour.
- Position yourself as far from the hors d'oeuvres as you can, and find interesting people to talk to. It's not polite to talk with food in your mouth, and stimulating conversation will keep your mind off eating. If a waiter walks around with sumptious offerings, after you've had one or two say "No thanks" and turn your back as the tray approaches.
- Avoid wasting calories on ordinary high-calorie filler food—chips and dips, pretzels, cheese, and cheese spreads—and be wary of such fattening snacks as pâté, quiche, rich canapés, fruitcake, butter cookies, fudge, and so on. If you can stop at one, have a taste and move on.

- If you're willing, ask the host if you can bring something to the party and prepare a low-calorie appetizer: a vegetable platter and low-calorie dip; marinated shrimp; broiled marinated chicken bits; tabbouli (bulgur and parsley salad); or baba ghanoush (eggplant spread) with toasted pita crusts (see recipes on pp. 290, 293, and 540). That way you'll be sure there's something at the party you like that will like you back.
- Don't make candies, cookies, cakes, or other rich or sweet foods that you find irresistible to "have around the house" at holiday time. Chances are you'll eat more of them than your guests will. If you receive a gift of some fattening treat, serve it immediately to your guests or give it to a charitable organization (many churches and Y's have holiday parties and would be grateful for donations), or, if you can't part with it, "hide" it in the freezer or in an inaccessible cupboard and take it out only when you can serve it to a lot of people who are likely to eat it up.
- If you're the host of a holiday meal, keep in mind that your reputation doesn't ride on how many courses you can manage to cook and serve. Most guests will be more grateful for a three-course dinner than a seven-course one. Consider preparing low-cal alternatives to traditional dishes: pumpkin pie with evaporated skim milk instead of heavy cream; turkey stuffed with rice or bulgur moistened with vegetables instead of with a heavy bread stuffing moistened with fat; vegetables "sautéed" in broth instead of fat; chowder made with milk instead of cream.
- Whether you are host or guest, remember that this holiday dinner is not your first such meal nor is it likely to be your last. You'll get another crack at the special foods next year. And they'll be all the more delicious if you treat them with the discretion that something special deserves.
- Think about how terrific you'll feel the next day if you refrained from stuffing yourself or drinking too much the night before. But if you should overindulge one day, don't punish yourself by repeating the performance the day after and the day after that. Just get back to normal the next day. Remember, it's hard to eat an extra pound's worth of calories in one feast. If your scale does show a gain of a pound or 2, in all likelihood it's just water that will be lost in the next 24 to 48 hours of more controlled eating.

14 ·

EXERCISE: A NEW
DIETARY REQUIREMENT

Our species evolved on the move. Recent research on the effects of exercise and the consequences of sedentary living has shown that physical activity is crucial to the proper processing of foods that we eat. In fact, most of the chronic and often life-threatening ailments that besiege Americans in epidemic proportions could be tempered by regular exercise. Among them are heart disease, diabetes, high blood pressure, arthritis, and osteoporosis. But let's face it: most people are not motivated to exercise by what it may do for them 20 years down the pike. What gets people like me out moving every day is what exercise does for me right now, especially how it allows me to enjoy eating without gaining. I, along with millions of Americans, have discovered that exercise is the key to permanent and painless weight control.

After hearing a description of my usual daily exercise schedule—a morning run or bike ride and an evening swim, sometimes with an hour of tennis in between—some people remark, "Wouldn't it be a lot easier to eat one less bagel a day and skip all that exercise?" My answer is, "Easier, yes, but not nearly as effective nor as much fun." Here's why exercise, not dieting, is the best route to a leaner, lighter you.

EXERCISE ADJUSTS THE CALORIC EQUATION

Most of us are familiar with the basic biological "rule" that if calories *in* exceed calories *out,* you get fat. A small daily error in caloric intake—say, 100 extra calories, the equivalent of one large apple—can add up to 10 extra pounds on your frame within a year. Yet without counting every calorie they consume and use, most people are able to maintain a relatively stable weight—albeit sometimes more weight than they want—year in and year out even though caloric intake and output can vary greatly from day to day. There seems to be a built-in mechanism for balancing the calories you consume with the calories your body uses. But, the available evidence indicates, *the mechanism only works properly when you are reasonably active.* Sedentary individuals tend to overestimate their caloric needs, eating more than their bodies require and slowly acquiring excess pounds.

A study of 150 obese adults conducted in 1939 revealed that two-thirds of them started getting fat during a time when their activity was restricted, such as by an injury or illness. Only 3 percent gained weight because they began eating more than usual. Two decades later, Dr. Jean Mayer, then a nutrition scientist at the Harvard School of Public Health and now president of Tufts University, demonstrated this phenomenon in laboratory rats. Sedentary caged rats are overweight when compared to normally active wild rats. But when the caged animals are put on a program of moderate daily exercise, they eat less and lose weight, becoming lean like their wild counterparts.

Modern Americans are like caged animals: more sedentary than evolution intended them to be. The typical American *sits* in a vehicle on the way to work, *sits* at work for 8 or more hours, *sits* in the same vehicle to get home, *sits* down to dinner, then *sits* in front of the TV until it is time to *lie* down and go to sleep. This is not how the human species evolved, and our metabolic systems do not function right at this level of inactivity. For too many people, the result of sedentary living is a perennial, losing battle against the bulge: bursts of self-denial interspersed with guilt when self-denial inevitably yields to self-indulgence.

According to one prevalent theory of weight control, your normal (that is, usual) body weight is like water—it constantly seeks its own level. The weight at which you stabilize when you make no special effort to gain or lose is called your body's *set point.* When your weight drops below that set point, chemical signals of starvation seem to trigger a corrective system into action to bring you back to "normal," even though normal by your definition means fat. This may be a major reason behind the failure of diets to produce long-lasting weight loss for most people. Only a few highly controlled individuals seem able to fight their set point indefinitely. But before you conclude that keeping weight off is hopeless if it means a constant battle against an unseen biochemical enemy, the set-point theory offers you an out. Through exercise, you can safely and permanently lower your set point (as long as you keep exercising) so that you will now stabilize at a lower weight.

EXERCISE RESETS THE BODY THERMOSTAT

Everybody knows that exercise uses calories, and that the harder and longer you exercise, the more calories your body will burn. But when people look at how hard they would have to work to get rid of the calories in just one piece of pie à la mode (running fast for an hour or sawing wood for 2), not to mention what it takes to lose a pound (walking for 16 hours or swimming hard for 7), many sit down in self-defeat. The effort required hardly seems to pay. But what most people don't realize is that exercise does far more than just burn calories while you're exercising. Vigorous exercise also revs up the body engine—raises its idling speed, as it were—so that *your body continues to use extra calories for up to 15 hours after you stop exercising.* If you exercise twice a day—once in the morning and once in the evening—you get the calorie-burning bonus all day long, even while you sleep. Even if your metabolism is normally on the slow side, exercise can boost it permanently by 20 percent to 30 percent.

But that's not all. According to recent studies directed by Dr. David Levitsky at Cornell University, exercise provides a further calorie-burning benefit, especially after you've overeaten. The research showed that exercise done within 2 to 3 hours of a meal uses up more calories than the same exercise done on an empty stomach. Exercise does this by producing extra body heat, as would happen if you raised the thermostat in your home. If you exercise within a few hours of eating, your body's furnace burns more calories than are needed just to do the activity and helps you get rid of extra calories you consumed at your previous meal. Even the day after overindulgence, exercise "wastes" calories by causing the body to produce more heat than it otherwise would. And you don't have to jog or swim laps or play squash to achieve this effect. Walking briskly for 20 to 45 minutes will do, the Cornell studies showed.

At the same time, through regular exercise, body fat is lost and replaced by lean muscle tissue. Pound for pound, muscle tissue uses more calories to sustain itself than fat tissue does. The more muscle tissue you have and the less body fat, the more calories you can consume without gaining weight—or the faster you can lose weight without drastically reducing the amount of calories you consume. Furthermore, muscle tissue takes up less room than the same weight of body fat, so that even if you don't lose an ounce, you'll look thinner if you have good muscle tone and less fat. Dr. Joan Ullyot, runner, author, and exercise physiologist, says she lost no weight since she started running in the early 1970s, "but I've lost 20 pounds of fat and put on 20 pounds of muscle —and I've gone down two dress sizes." When your clothes and mirror pronounce you trim and fit, it matters not a whit what the scale says.

EXERCISE BURNS BODY FAT

Dr. Donald Layman of the University of Illinois took a group of obese laboratory rats and reduced them down to the weight of normal rats by feeding them less. The animals lost weight all right, and some even dropped three-fourths of their original body weight. But their body composition changed not a bit. "They went from being big, fat rats to small, fat rats," the Illinois nutritionist said. "Their percentage of body fat remained the same." Only when exercise was included in the animals' weight-loss program did they reduce their percentage of body fat. The same thing happens to people who try to lose weight without exercise: the fat person remains hidden within, just waiting for a chance to emerge once again.

When you go on a low-calorie diet, what you lose at first is mainly water and protein. The water is lost when your body burns glycogen—a form of stored sugar—for energy. Since each pound of glycogen holds 3 to 4 pounds of water, water accounts for most of your initial weight loss. It is a temporary loss at best, since your body will eventually have to replace the lost glycogen, which serves as its emergency energy supply and assures your brain of the sugar it needs to operate properly. The rest of what you lose at the start of a low-calorie diet is protein from your muscles, just what you don't want to lose if your goal is to look better and feel better. The combination of lost glycogen and muscle protein may be what causes dieter's fatigue, which in turns prompts you to reduce your activity level—just the opposite of what you should do if you want to lose weight permanently.

Only after several weeks on a low-calorie diet does your body start using a significant amount of body fat for energy. Ounce for ounce, fat contains more than twice the calories in either glycogen or protein. Thus, losing fat on a low-calorie diet is a slow process. All other things being equal, a 500-calorie deficit in your daily diet will add up to a 1-pound loss of body fat in a week. Thus, the same low-calorie diet that enabled you to shed 5 pounds of water and muscle during the first week or two now produces only a 1-pound loss of fat during the next. Discouraged by the slowdown, you may then lapse from your diet and regain the weight.

Far better for your health and your future to lose primarily fat in the first place. The only way to do that is through exercise, which uses body fat as its main source of energy. You may not see that initial rapid (but false) weight loss, but what you lose will be what you *want* to lose—fat, not muscle or water. Your loss will be slow but steady, and, if you make exercise a regular part of your life, chances are your loss will be permanent, too. If it's any consolation, studies have shown that in most cases, the faster people lose weight, the more likely they are to regain it. Slow loss, then, is the secret to lasting success.

Several studies have demonstrated the effectiveness of exercise as a weight-loss tool. One study involved 25 women who were 20 to 40 pounds overweight. They were divided into three groups: the women in one group cut 500 calories from their daily diet without changing their level of physical activity; those in the second group cut down by 250 calories and added enough exercise to use 250 extra calories a day; and those in the third group made no dietary changes but added activity that burned 500 extra calories a day. After 16 weeks, all three groups had lost weight, but the two groups that included exercise had lost significantly more fat and less muscle tissue than the diet-only group. Another study, conducted at the University of California, Irvine, started with a group of obese adults who had tried dieting countless times and failed. The group was told to forget about dieting, eat normally, and instead start a program of daily brisk walking. Those who worked up to at least a 30-minute walk five times a week began to lose weight without a diet. And, for the 11 women who stuck it out for a year and a half, each lost an average of 22 pounds and continued to lose even though they did not diet. In another study at the University of Minnesota, obese young men lost an average of 13 pounds each in 16 weeks through a program of brisk walking without a diet. And at Stanford University, 32 initially sedentary overweight men began a running program with no attempt to diet. As their mileage increased, so did their food intake and so did the amount of weight they lost. In the end, *those who ate the most lost the most, but only because they also exercised the most.*

If you want to lose weight faster than you can with just exercise, simply combine exercise with a reduced-calorie diet. Researchers at the University of California, Davis, showed that exercise can counter the metabolism-lowering effect of a low-calorie diet in many people. It also seems to curb the adverse caloric effect of aging on body metabolism. Whereas ordinarily your metabolism would slow down as you get older (which is one reason people get fatter in middle age even though they don't eat more), if you continue to exercise regularly, you may keep your youthful metabolic rate by maintaining a muscular body instead of losing muscle and putting on pounds of fat.

OTHER BENEFITS OF EXERCISE

The weight-control benefits of exercise go far beyond its direct effect on how many calories your body uses. Vigorous exercise also suppresses your appetite. After a hard run or an hour of tennis, for example, you may find you don't get hungry for an hour or more. And although you may eat more when you exercise, chances are the extra calories will be significantly less than what you used up through exercise. A study by Dr. Peter Wood at Stanford University Medical School showed that very active people consume about 600 calories more than their sedentary counterparts but weigh on the average 20 percent less.

Furthermore, exercise is a natural relaxant and produces a lasting euphoric effect. This, in turn, reduces the chances that you'll eat to relieve such emotions as tension, anxiety, anger, frustration, boredom, and depression. The good feelings induced by vigorous exercise most likely result from a natural tranquilizing chemical, beta-endorphin, that is released in the brain in response to exercise. This chemical is the body's equivalent of morphine or Valium but lacks the expense and adverse side effects associated with drugs. The release of beta-endorphin may account for the addictive quality of exercise and the fact that many exercise enthusiasts report that they don't feel as good when they are not able to exercise.

Finally, there are the many health and other benefits of exercise beyond weight control.

- Exercise counters heart disease and stroke by lowering serum cholesterol levels and blood pressure and by improving the ability of the heart to pump more blood with less effort.
- By enhancing muscle tone in the legs, exercise can prevent and sometimes reverse the symptoms of varicose veins.
- By facilitating the use of blood sugar by muscle tissue, exercise helps to lower blood sugar. This effect, along with exercise-induced improvements in blood circulation and weight control, helps to counter diabetes.
- Exercise strengthens bones by preventing the loss of calcium that weakens bones as people age.

- Exercise—as long as it's not abusive—helps to keep joints mobile and ward off the crippling effects of arthritis.
- Exercise is an important weapon against depression, and a growing number of therapists now insist that their depressed patients include daily exercise in their treatment program.
- Exercise improves the quality of sleep, and many people find that once they start a regular exercise program, they need less sleep than they used to because the sleep they now get is more restful.
- People who exercise regularly report that it improves their work efficiency and organization, probably because it establishes a daily routine and helps to free them of distractions and inhibitions caused by emotional tension. Thus, they are able to get more done in less time and with less effort.
- Exercise can enhance your sex life, perhaps because you feel better about your body when it has good muscle tone. However, if you become an exercise addict or marathon runner, you may not have time for sex!

HOW TO GET EXERCISE INTO YOUR LIFE

The real problem with exercise for most people is not a failure to realize that it's good for them but an unwillingness to work it into their daily lives, the most common excuse being "I don't have time." My answer to such people is (if you'll pardon the pun) "That's a lame excuse." People have always managed to find time for the things they really want to do. Finding time for exercise, then, starts with a realization of its importance and a decision—a commitment—to make it a regular part of your life. Just as you brush your teeth every day, eat every day, and sleep every day, you can exercise every day. After a while, you may find, as I did, with regular moderate exercise you get more rest from less sleep and you work so much more efficiently that you actually have *more* time now that you've given up some time to exercise.

To maximize the weight-control benefits of exercise, do three ½-hour sessions a week of an aerobic activity that uses at least 600 calories an hour (see Table 15, p. 226), or do more of a less vigorous activity. During an aerobic activity, your body uses oxygen, which is needed when fat is burned to produce body energy. Most effective are continuous-movement activities like fast walking, jogging, cycling, swimming, skating, rope jumping, aerobic dancing, cross-country skiing, hiking, and rowing. (These are the kinds of activities that "condition" your heart, improving its ability to withstand physical stress.) To be most effective, the activity should be done continuously for 20 minutes or longer three or more times a week, and you should work hard enough to get your pulse rate into the "target zone." This zone, counted as beats per minute, can be calculated roughly by first substracting your age from the number 220 (the resulting number represents your theoretical maximum heart rate), then multiplying the result first by 70 percent (0.70) and then by 85 percent (0.85). The two numbers that result represent the range of heart beats per minute that you should try to maintain during your aerobic exercise session. For example, if you are 40 years old, your maximum heart rate would be 220 minus 40, or 180, and your target heart rate for aerobic exercise would range from 126 (which is 70 percent of 180) to 153 (which is 80 percent of 180).

You can also use a lot of calories aerobically during such activities as tennis, squash, handball, basketball, football, volleyball, and downhill skiing, even though these sports don't involve continuous motion for 30 consecutive minutes. However, *anaerobic* activities, like weight lifting and sprinting, that leave you breathless are not effective fat-burning exercises. Nor are they good for the heart (they increase blood pressure by causing muscles to clamp down on blood vessels), although they can certainly increase your muscle strength.

If your chosen activity uses fewer than 300 calories in ½ hour, then it should be done for a longer time. And, if you're really serious about reaping the health benefits of exercise, it's best to make it part of your daily life, not just a few times a week, perhaps alternating two or more kinds of activities to reduce the risk of injury, boredom, and exercise "burnout." That way you never have to face the decision *"Should* I exercise today?" Your only daily decision needs to be *"How* should I exercise today?" And if on occasion your daily exercise is disrupted by matters beyond your control, you won't find yourself slipping back to two or even one exercise session a week.

In addition to setting aside time for a period of concentrated exercise each day, you can also incorporate more activity into the routine of your daily life. Here are some possibilities:

- Walk all or part of the way to a destination instead always hopping into a car, taxi, bus, or train. If you must take transportation to work, park the car some distance away, or get off the bus or train one stop before, and walk the rest of the way. If, while you're walking briskly for 20 minutes, you carry a heavy briefcase, shopping bag, or backpack (one that weighs 6 pounds or more), you can get enough exercise to condition your heart, Israeli researchers have shown.
- Take the stairs instead of the elevator or escalator. If you're going up more than three flights, ride only part of the way. If you're going down eight flights or less, walk.
- Use a hand mower and an old-fashioned hedge clipper instead of tools powered by gas or electricity.
- Prepare food by hand instead of always relying on a blender or food processor.
- If you bake bread, use your own power to knead it rather than an electrified dough hook. I can't promise you it will taste better, but it will be a more satisfying achievement.
- Carry your golf clubs, or pull them along, instead of riding in a motorized cart.
- Saw wood by hand, rather than using an electric saw for the entire job.

The possibilities are limited only by your imagination and the particular demands of your life. If for everything you do you think exercise, you'll doubtless find many enjoyable ways to get your body to use the energy it has in excess at the same time that you save some of the energy that the world has in short supply.

HOW TO START AN EXERCISE PROGRAM

There are probably more people who have started an exercise program and dropped out than you could line up ten across along the entire course of the New York City Marathon. If you add in the people who have *thought* about getting into exercise but haven't yet done it, you could probably cover every available inch of space in all 365 square miles of the Big Apple. Yet, millions of Americans do manage to exercise regularly, and most of them would not dream of giving it up. How do they do it? It's a lot easier than you may think. If you adopt a rational approach to exercise, you're likely to find yourself eagerly anticipating your workout and resentful of anything that threatens to interfere. Here are some guidelines to help you get moving toward a slimmer, trimmer you—with pleasure, not pain.

Pick an activity (or activities) you enjoy. Exercise is not some kind of punishment for dietary transgressions. It is a positive force, to be enjoyed, not suffered through. If you try to make yourself do something you truly dislike, you'll have no trouble finding a dozen excuses to keep from doing it. Think back to what you enjoyed doing as a child. Was it biking, skating, swimming, dancing? Chances are you'll still find them fun. If you were an inactive child or one who always hated sports, try something simple and noncompetitive, like brisk walking, jogging, or bicycling. Think, too, about your native abilities. An uncoordinated person or someone who never could see the ball can find activities like rope jumping or a racket sport to be frustrating. If that's you, walking, jogging, or swimming might be more appropriate. Also consider whether you'd prefer to exercise alone (this has the advantage of not having to coordinate your schedule with anyone else's) or whether working out with a friend would be more fun and more likely to keep you at it. When you make a commitment to join someone else, you'll be less likely to skip your exercise session for trivial reasons.

Consider your time and schedule. If you have to leave for work at 7 A.M. and don't get home until after the sun sets, you may be reluctant to exercise outdoors in the dark. For you, exercising at home on a stationary bicycle or rowing machine, jumping rope, swimming in a pool, or taking an aerobic dance class might be more suitable. If you think you can only spare ½ hour a day from start to finish, don't get into a sport like tennis that can easily chop 1½ to 2 hours out of your day for 1 hour's worth of exercise. Intense exercises that require minimal preparation, like jogging or rope jumping or working out on an exercise machine, would be more suitable. If you do have the time, you can use as many calories walking briskly as you would jogging over the same distance. Just remember that, for the same caloric benefit, it takes about twice as much time to walk that distance as to jog it.

Think about the cost and convenience. If money is tight, buying expensive equipment or a club membership or paying high court fees may be out of the question. On the other hand, jumping rope, walking briskly, or jogging need not cost much more than the protective shoes you should have on your feet. You may have an old bicycle that can be fixed up for a few dollars, or you may be able to pick up a used bike inexpensively. Check out your local Y or community center for low-cost exercise programs, such as swimming or aerobic dancing. Make sure you can tolerate the transportation and arranging involved in your chosen activity. If, for example, you have to search for tennis partners, juggle a complicated schedule, and then drive several miles to the court, that can discourage regular participation.

Take your current health into account. If you have physical limitations, these should be considered when you choose an exercise. A person with asthma or foot problems, for example, may not be able to jog, but could do very well with a swimming program. If you have any chronic illness or muscle or joint problem, consult your physician first. Similarly, if you are over 35 and have been inactive, it's wise to check with your doctor before starting a program of vigorous exercise. If you are over 40, an exercise stress test may be advisable to determine what level of activity your cardiovascular system can withstand. If you are over 50, it may be best to start with a walking program to get your body into condition *before* you get into something more vigorous.

Select a time for exercise. And stick to it every day. If you want exercise to be a habit, you have to make it one, just as other daily activities are habits that you do pretty much at the same time each day without having to think about them. If you can never get up in the morning, then try exercising at lunchtime or before supper. If you're a morning person who peters out after 4 P.M., exercising soon after you get up in the morning may better suit your biological clock, although if you can get yourself to exercise in the afternoon, you may find that it renews your energy and you get more done in the evening.

Give yourself time to enjoy it. Don't expect to love your new activity the moment you start it. It can take a while—months sometimes—before you begin to feel really good about what you're doing. Make a commitment to stick with your activity for at least 3 months before deciding whether it's for you. And don't try to do too much too soon. Work up gradually to your full-length exercise program to avoid muscle soreness and injury. When I started swimming, I could do only 10 lengths of the pool at first, but by the end of a year, I was swimming 44. The same with jogging: I started with ½ mile and gradually worked up to my present level of 3- to 4-mile runs. If you've been sedentary for years and now want to get into jogging, start with a jog-walk program by alternating walking and jogging in each workout, emphasizing walking at first and gradually increasing the proportion of jogging.

HOW MANY CALORIES WILL YOU USE?

Every movement of your body uses calories, and the harder and longer you use your muscles, the more calories you will use up. You can use as many calories scrubbing floors as cycling around the park. Walking briskly for 3 miles uses the same number of calories as jogging that distance. Remember, too, that you're not likely to perform all activities for the same amount of time. You'd probably play tennis for at least 1 hour but jump rope for perhaps 15 minutes, swim for 30, and jog for 40. Even for the same activity done over the same period of time, different people use different amounts of calories. The number of calories your body will use to perform a particular activity depends on many factors, among them:

- How big you are to begin with. Heavier people use more calories than thinner ones to do the same activity. If you weigh 90 pounds, in 1 hour of vigorous tennis you will use about 350 calories. But if you weigh 190 pounds, in that same hour you will use twice that amount of calories.
- The temperature of the air or water. The colder it is, the more calories used because some are expended to maintain body temperature. Of course, if you dress warmly, you counteract some of this effect.
- How hard you work. Tennis players who "get everything" and hit the ball hard use more calories than those who never run after balls and just tap them back over the net. When you swim a fast crawl, you use more calories than when you do a leisurely backstroke. Lifting up your feet when you jog uses more calories than shuffling along. Riding a three-speed bike over hilly terrain requires more energy, and thus uses more calories, than riding a 10-speed bike at the same pace.

Table 15 provides a usual range of caloric expenditure for a variety of common activities. It is presented mainly to give you an idea of the relative demands of different activities, both routine and extracurricular. Use it as a guide to your daily caloric expenditure, not to calculate a precise equation of calories in and calories out. The starred items are potentially valuable as aerobic exercises for conditioning your heart as well as revving up your body metabolism to enhance weight loss. However, to be of conditioning benefit, you should perform these activities nearly continuously for periods of 20 minutes or longer. Thus, depending on how you play the game, singles tennis can be a conditioning exercise or not. So can scrubbing floors and mowing the lawn with a hand mower.

FOR FURTHER READING

Bailey, Covert. Fit or Fat? Boston: Houghton Mifflin, 1978.

Bennett, William, M.D., and Joel Gurin. The Dieter's Dilemma: Eating Less and Weighing More. New York: Basic Books, 1982.

Katahn, Martin, Ph.D. The 200 Calorie Solution. New York: W. W. Norton, 1982.

Katahn, Martin. Beyond Diet. New York: W. W. Norton, 1984.

Mirkin, Gabe, M.D. Getting Thin. Boston: Little, Brown, 1983.

Wood, Dr. Peter. California Diet and Exercise Program. Mountain View, Calif.: Anderson World Books, 1983.

Table 15   CALORIC COST OF VARIOUS ACTIVITIES *(for a 154-pound person)*

Calories used per hour (approximate)	Activities	Calories used per hour (approximate)	Activities
72–84	Sitting Conversing	360–420	Roller skating* Horseback riding (posting to trot)* Canoeing 4 mph Digging garden Disco dancing
120–150	Strolling 1 mph Standing Playing cards	420–480	Hand lawn-mowing* Walking 5 mph* Cycling 11 mph* Tennis (singles)* Badminton (competitive) Downhill skiing (light) Water skiing Cross-country skiing 2.5 mph* Folk (square) dancing* Splitting wood Snow shoveling
150–240	Level walking 2 mph Level cycling 5 mph Typing on manual typewriter Riding lawn mower Golfing, using power cart Canoeing 2.5 mph Horseback riding (walk)		
240–300	Cleaning windows Mopping floors Vacuuming Pushing light power mower Bowling Walking 3 mph* Cycling 6 mph Golfing, pulling cart Horseback riding (sitting to trot) Volleyball (6-man, noncompetitive) Badminton (social doubles)	480–600	Sawing hardwood* Digging ditches Jogging 5 mph* Cycling 12 mph* Downhill skiing (vigorous) Touch football Paddleball Horseback (gallop)* Basketball Mountain climbing* Ice hockey*
300–360	Scrubbing floors* Walking 3.5 mph* Cycling 8 mph* Table tennis (Ping-Pong) Badminton (singles) Volleyball Golfing, carrying clubs Calisthenics (many)* Ballet exercises* Dancing (foxtrot) Tennis (doubles) Raking leaves or hoeing	600–660	Running 5.5 mph* Cycling 13 mph* Handball (social)* Squash (social)* Fencing Basketball (vigorous)* Cross-country skiing (4 mph)*
360–420	Walking 4 mph* Cycling 10 mph* Ice skating*	More than 660	Running 6 to 10 mph* Cross-country skiing 5 or more mph* Handball (competitive)* Squash (competitive)*

Note: Continuous swimming is also an excellent aerobic exercise that can burn a significant number of calories. However, the caloric range is very wide, depending on such factors as the skill of the swimmer, percentage body fat, stroke used, temperature of the water, and presence of a current.
*This means that the activity can result in cardiovascular conditioning.

IV. Helpful Hints for Wholesome Cooking

Introduction: Cooking from Scratch Efficiently

If until now you've relied primarily on packaged mixes and meals, frozen dinners, take-out, and ready-made foods to feed yourself and your family, cooking from "scratch" as I do may seem intimidating. Where do you begin? How do you find the time? What tools do you use? How do you shop for, store, and cook foods to minimize waste and wasted energy? If you never learned the tricks of the cooking trade at your mother's or father's elbow, or if you learned but never practiced them, you may feel at a loss when a recipe says skim off the fat, skin the chicken, score the fish, mince the parsley, or crush the garlic.

Like most American women today who are under 50, I learned most of what I know about cooking by trial and error (for example, after straining stock through a colander and watching bits and pieces "contaminate" my supposedly clear broth, I quickly learned to use a fine strainer). I have also spent time studying recipes, watching friends cook, and reading books and magazines on cooking techniques and principles. Because I like to squeeze a great deal into my life, I try to be efficient in all my endeavors, including cooking. I have discovered that you can prepare nearly all your food from scratch with just minimal reliance on processed foods and without spending half the day or the entire weekend in the kitchen. Through the years, I have acquired a certain amount of wisdom in efficient food preparation which I am pleased to be able to share with you. If you need further guidance, consult one or more of the books I listed on page 273. And if, at the end of this chapter, you still feel as if you are all thumbs in the kitchen, you might think about treating yourself to a good basic cooking course, one that stresses technique.

For most people, cooking can be a satisfying and enjoyable activity. The rewards, after all, are self-evident: a good meal and a healthy body (and, as you get better at it, an appreciative audience). As I became more adept at cooking and acquired an appreciation for the fundamentals of food chemistry (how, for example, to keep the yeast from dying and the milk from curdling), cooking became an important source of pleasure in my life, something I do to relax and take a break from my usual endeavors, rather than a necessary trial or tribulation like doing the laundry or scouring the sink. If you have a family, why not get others into the act (one at a time, if you can)? A child of 2 or 3 can lend a hand. Although, at first, it may seem like more work than doing it yourself, in the end you'll be grateful for an efficient kitchen helper. Older children can help with the shopping, unloading of groceries, and cleaning up, as well as with the actual cooking. And, of course, participation of spouse or housemate goes without saying, especially when both adults work outside the home. But even if you have to "go it alone," you can learn to put on a feast for a dozen without pulling out your hair. Forget all the "I can'ts," and read on.

15 ·
HOW TO EQUIP
YOUR KITCHEN

In the best of all possible worlds, we'd all have a modernized "country kitchen" —big enough to prepare three meals a day for an extended family of ten plus two farm hands but equipped with all the modern conveniences in the housewares and kitchen-appliances sections of the Sears catalogue. Alas, for most of us, this ideal will forever remain just that—a dream. The typical kitchen in an urban or suburban home may be a 10×15-foot L-shaped room or an even smaller section set off from the dining area by a counter top. And for the millions who live in apartments, a kitchen is often more like a walk-in closet with a refrigerator, stove, and sink and enough cupboard space for half a dozen pots and pans and eating utensils for four.

The trick in cooking efficiently is to make the best use of the space you have available to store essential equipment and basic ingredients. Obviously, an apartment dweller will have to be content with less than might be used by a self-employed caterer. Thus, I have listed by degrees of relative importance the equipment I regard as worth having. You needn't acquire all the "must haves" at one time. Better to purchase good equipment gradually, as finances and space allow, than to get everything at once but of poor quality. You might also put the items you're missing on your holiday or birthday gift list and let friends and family know what they can get you that you'd really appreciate.

Note, too, that the ranking reflects my own cooking style. You may disagree with some of my ratings and regard a tool I deem expendable as an absolute essential, or vice versa. Your most important task is to be realistic: What can you afford, and where can you put it? If a gadget like a food processor must be relegated to the back of the top cupboard and you must stand on a stool and move other items to get it down, it's going to be little used. You'd be better off with just a blender or food mill and some small hand tools that can fit in a drawer or that can be hung on the wall.

Which brings me to my first and most important hint: Forget notions of "house beautiful," and find ways to keep your most-used tools and ingredients as handy as possible. (Exercise caution, however, if you have toddlers in the house. Until they reach the age of reason, it might be wise to keep possibly hazardous equipment and ingredients in locked cupboards.) Most of my oft-used items are hanging on the kitchen walls at arm's reach, or are standing on the counter in squat vases, or are lined up along open shelves, or, if behind cupboard doors, are logically placed by type and frequency of use and always put back in their designated places. The less searching you have to do for the spatula or baking powder, the less harassed a cook you'll be and the faster the food will get done. It's easy to make pancakes from scratch if the flour, baking powder, baking soda, sugar, salt, and so forth are handy, obvious, and pretty much all in one place. The same is true of salad dressings and marinades if your vinegars and oils and other liquid condiments are all in one easy-to-reach spot in properly labeled and easy-to-pour containers. To minimize the chances that I'll run out of an important ingredient in the middle of a recipe, I store most items (like cornstarch, sugar, flours, grains) in clear glass or plastic containers. When an item starts to run low, I add it to the shopping list before I run out. At the least, I can tell at a glance before starting a recipe that I'm going to need more rolled oats than I have on hand.

KEY TO EQUIPMENT RATINGS:
★★★★means it's *a must* for me.
★★★means *if you can* afford and house it, it's very useful.
★★means *it would be nice* to have, but it's not essential.
★means *other techniques will do,* but I have it and use it fairly often.

★★★★ Knives, at least three good ones:

- *Paring knife*—small (2- to 4-inch blade), thin, and sharp, for delicate cutting of fruits, vegetables, and herbs.
- *Chef's knife*—heavy and sharp, for most of your cutting, slicing, and chopping tasks.
- *Bread knife*—long scalloped or serrated blade, for slicing bread and tomatoes.

I prefer carbon-steel knives (seasoned with oil to reduce rusting) because they keep a better edge. But you'll need at least one stainless-steel knife for cutting foods like peaches, onions, and avocados that turn black when they come into contact with carbon steel. All knives should be washed and dried (and put back in their place) immediately after use, but for carbon steel, this is a must to prevent rusting.

★★★ Other Knives:

- *Utility knife*—with a 6- to an 8-inch blade, for cutting small vegetables, deboning chicken, and other tasks for which a chef's knife may be too clumsy and a paring knife too delicate.
- *Chinese cleaver*—once you become adept in its use, it can be a more efficient cutting tool than a chef's knife.
- *Grapefruit knife (or pineapple knife)*—the curved blade simplifies a number of cutting chores.
- *Small serrated knife*—for slicing tomatoes and other tender foods without

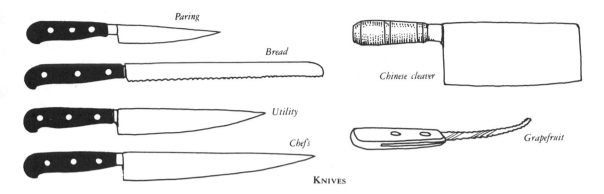

Paring

Bread

Chinese cleaver

Utility

Chef's

Grapefruit

KNIVES

crushing them (especially useful if you like to keep your bread knife dry at all times).

★★★★ **Knife Sharpener,** ideally a sharpening steel (either metal or ceramic) *and* a sharpening stone. No "modern" knife-sharpening gadget equals their ability to put a good edge on a knife without knicking the blade.

★★★★ **Potato Peeler,** a simple but sharp one. It is eminently useful for peeling all kinds of fruits and vegetables, including tomatoes.

★★★★ **Pots and Pans,** heavy ones (the best you can afford), preferably with nonstick (Silverstone type, not Teflon) coatings and tight-fitting covers, including the following:

- *Saucepans,* at least three—1-quart, 2-quart, and 3-quart.
- *Dutch oven or soup pot,* 5- or 6-quart size.
- *Skillets,* two or three—7- or 8-inch, 10-inch, and 12-inch.
- *Griddle,* 11 inches square.

★★★ **Other Pots,** if you have room, that are nearly essential include:

- *Cast-iron chicken fryer* (10 inches in diameter with deep straight sides) *with a cover.* The cover can double as a skillet.
- *8-quart pot* for cooking pasta and large quantities of soup.
- *Wok* (with cover and burner stand), about 12-inches in diameter, but only if you have a gas range (temperatures change too slowly in an electric wok). A steel wok (you must season it with oil) is best. Do not scour it (let a dark surface build up inside and out); wash or wipe it out immediately after use.
- *Pressure cooker,* especially useful for speedy cooking of dried beans and peas, stocks, beets, and other slow-cooking vegetables.
- *Roasting pan,* with a cover, for large birds and party-sized recipes.
- *Kettle,* at least a 2-quart size, for fast boiling and safe pouring of water (if you have no kettle, you can make do with a saucepan).

- *Double boiler,* for heating or melting ingredients that would otherwise scorch. In its place you can use a heat-proof glass bowl set in a pot of water.
- *Egg poacher,* either a separate pan or an inset for one of your skillets. Neater than poaching directly in water. Cholesterol-watchers can poach just the whites.
- *Coffee maker,* either an automatic electric or a fill-it-yourself drip type.

★★★★ **Steamer Rack or Pot,** for waterless cooking of vegetables and reheating of various foods that do best with moist heat. The steamer could also serve as a poacher for small fish. You can also get bamboo steamer racks that can be stacked in a wok. A double-decker steamer pot is the most-used cooking utensil in my house.

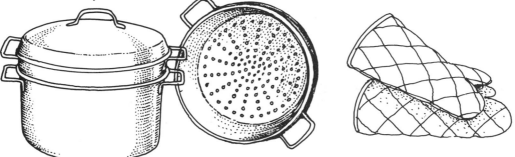

★★★★ **Baking Pans,** including the following:

- *Cookie sheet,* at least one big one, preferably two. Get the nonstick variety, if you are buying new ones.
- *13 × 9 × 2-inch pan,* at least one, in metal or oven-proof glass.
- *8 × 8 × 2-inch pan,* at least one, in metal or oven-proof glass.
- *Loaf pans* (about 9 × 5 × 3 inches), at least two, made of metal, pottery, or glass (note, however, that glass bakes faster; reduce the baking temperature by 25 degrees to compensate).
- *Muffin tin,* one or two, with 12 cups each.
- *Pie plate,* 9 inches in diameter, preferably of glass or ceramic.

★★★★ **Pot Holders,** at least two flat ones and two oven mitts that are well insulated. Handiest if they can hang by magnets or loops near the stove.

★★★★ **Aprons,** at least two (for when one is in the wash) with bibs, preferably with a pocket or loop to which a hand towel can be attached.

★★★★ **Towels,** two for the hands, two for the dishes, plus a handy rack or holder to keep them on.

★★★★ **Baker's Rack,** at least one square one, preferably a large one, for cooling breads, cakes, and pies. A rack permits air to circulate, reducing sogginess. In a pinch, use a cool oven rack or a toaster-oven rack in place of a baker's rack.

★★★★ **Casseroles,** at least two—1½ quarts and 3 quarts—preferably with covers.

★★★★ **Whisk,** at least one small one, the perfect tool for making smooth sauces.

★★★★ **Eggbeater or Small Electric Mixer,** needed for beating and whipping foods that should be aerated. For safe operation of an electric mixer, insert and remove the beaters only when the machine is unplugged.

★★★★ **Spatulas,** at least two—one elongated, the other with a nearly square base— for lifting and flipping foods during and after cooking. If your pans are treated with a nonstick coating, be sure your spatulas are nylon, not metal. If you have a wok, you will also need two convex-shaped spatulas for stir-frying.

★★★★ **Wooden Spoons,** preferably two but at least one heavy-duty one, for mixing bread dough, batters, beans, and soups.

★★★★ **Slotted Spoon,** of plastic or metal, for stirring thick soups and stews and for lifting out solids and leaving the liquid behind.

★★★★ **Ladle,** for serving soups and some sauces.

★★★★ **Juicer,** hand variety (it can be a simple type that sits atop a measuring cup), for preparing fresh lemon and lime juice (commercially prepared juices have an off-flavor).

★★★★ **Funnel,** at least one, preferably the type that has several screw-on adapters, among them a wide and narrow neck and a strainer.

★★★★ **Bowl Scrapers** (sometimes also called spatulas), preferably in malleable plastic, including at least one long, thin one.

★★★★ **Rolling Pin,** for making pie crusts, biscuits, and molded cookies. Also handy for crushing crackers (between sheets of wax paper).

★★★★ **Measuring Spoons,** at least two 4-spoon sets, each with sizes from ¼ teaspoon to 1 tablespoon. Use one for wet ingredients, the other for dry.

★★★★ **Measuring Cups,** at least a 1-cup and a 4-cup glass measure for liquids. Also desirable is one or two sets of nested cups in metal or plastic (usually four, ¼-cup to 1-cup size, but some have 6, from ⅛ cup to 2 cups); these are especially handy for measuring dry ingredients.

★★★★ **Mixing Bowls,** graduated sizes (about 1 quart to 5 quarts) that nest, preferably of heat-proof glass (e.g., Pyrex) or ceramic. Nested stainless-steel bowls up to 8 quarts in size are also useful.

★★★★ **Grater,** a small four-sided or six-sided hand grater, good for everything from apples to zucchini.

★★★★ **Strainers,** small wire-mesh type, at least two—a fine one that is 2½ or 3 inches in diameter, and a coarser 5-inch one. To keep the mesh clear, wash strainers immediately after use; use a toothbrush to clean clogged pores.

★★★★ **Colander,** big enough to hold 1 pound of cooked spaghetti, for draining pasta, washed greens, berries, and grapes.

★★★★ **Can Opener,** the hand-held or wall-mounted variety for removing lids. The most reliable one I've found is a manually operated Swing-Away that costs $3.98.

★★★★ **Bottle and Juice Can Opener,** the type often referred to as a "church key."

★★★★ **Corkscrew,** for opening wine bottles (not needed if you never drink wine or use only those wines that come in bottles with screw-off caps).

★★★★ **Tongs,** for lifting solid, unevenly shaped foods out of the cooking liquid or pan.

★★★★ **Long-handled Fork,** with two prongs and wooden handle. Useful for charring peppers over a flame and for removing heavy foods (e.g., roasted fowl) from cooking pans.

★★★★ **Pepper Mill,** at least one at the work counter, preferably another for the table, and perhaps a third for white peppercorns. The best are the French type that fill from the side so you don't have to readjust the grind each time.

★★★★ **Brushes,** one soft one for coating pastry, one heat-proof type for oiling pans (as when cooking crêpes and pancakes).

★★★★ **Cutting Board,** a wooden free-standing one at least 1-inch thick, useful even if your counter top is butcher block, essential if it is not. It can double as a bread board. To cut down on cleaning problems, some people use a separate board just for cutting garlic, onions, and other pungent ingredients. Keep your cutting board in A-1 condition by oiling it twice a year.

★★★★ **Kitchen Scissors,** with fine blades, for snipping herbs and string.

★★★★ **Melon Baller,** $1.29 variety with a different-sized baller on each end, useful not only for making decorative fruit salads but also for seeding cucumbers and squashes and hollowing out squashes, eggplants, and cherry tomatoes for stuffing.

★★★★ **Kitchen Timer,** at the least, one on your stove; preferably a digital type that can be set easily for minutes and seconds. I have a portable timer that can be set for up to 99 minutes and 99 seconds and that can be clipped onto my clothing. More expensive types can time three different things at once.

★★★★ **Spice Rack,** or similar handy holder or shelf, that permits easy access to alphabetically arranged herbs and spices.

★★★★ **Cheesecloth,** for squeezing out excess liquid or for fine straining, as in making clear broth or jelly. Old nylon stockings or gauze baby diapers work, too.

★★★★ **Disposables,** and, if possible, a wall rack to hold them. Include the following for myriad wrapping and food-preparation uses:

- *Plastic wrap* on a roll.
- *Aluminum foil,* the heavy-duty type is the most versatile.
- *Plastic bags,* both sandwich and food-size, with twist ties or "zip lock" closings.
- *Wax paper,* preferably double-sided, useful, among other things, for rolling dough, separating breaded foods before cooking, sealing pots with covers that don't close tightly.
- *Paper towels* with decent "wet strength."

★★★★ **Clean-Up Tools,** including the following:

- *Sponges,* at least two: one for dishes and/or counter tops, the other for the floor.
- *Plastic cloth or ball,* used for scouring away stuck food without scratching the nonstick finishes of utensils. Also useful for wiping out a wok.
- *Steel wool pads,* with or without soap, for scouring uncoated metal pots and pans.
- *Toothbrush,* an old one, for cleaning holes of strainers and graters and for cleaning or polishing nooks and crannies of pots.
- *Vegetable brush,* for scrubbing potatoes and other foods that grow underground. You can also use a plastic cloth or, if tough, bare hands.

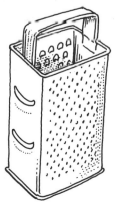

★★★★ **Storage Containers,** for convenient, bug-resistant storage of dry products as well as for refrigerating leftovers and freezing home-prepared foods. I find the following to be most useful:

- *Glass canning jars* (they come in sizes from ¼ liter to 2 or more liters) that close with rubber gaskets under glass lids, for storing grains, pasta, flours, cereals.
- *Plastic tubs* of various sizes, preferably translucent, for refrigerator and freezer storage. I save the containers that margarine, yogurt, and ricotta cheese come in. Also handy are waxed cardboard and plastic milk containers (1-quart and ½-gallon sizes, in particular) for freezing soups and purées.

★★★★ **Masking Tape and Waterproof Marking Pen,** for labeling what you store with contents and date. Affix the tape label to the container before you fill it with cold food; otherwise "sweating" prevents the tape from sticking.

★★★★ **Blender and/or Food Processor.** If you have room in your budget or your
or
★★★ kitchen for only one, I recommend the blender, unless you do a great deal of bulk cooking, in which case the food processor may be the better choice. In either case, get a good piece of equipment—for example, an Osterizer blender or a Cuisinart food processor.

★★★★ **Mortar with Pestle,** for grinding spices, herbs, and seeds. I prefer a ceramic
or
★★★ mortar to wooden one.

★★★★ **Garlic Press,** a good one (see illustration). I prefer mincing garlic with a knife.
or
★★★ But sometimes it needs crushing, and a press is more efficient to use than mortar and pestle and safer and neater than a knife handle.

★★★★ **Wooden Chopping/Salad Bowl,** large. Mine gets daily use for salad and
or
★★★ occasional use for chopping (as in liver or fish).

★★★★ **Rubber Gloves,** the thin variety, to keep hands free of irritating juices when
or
★★★ seeding and cutting hot fresh peppers. Paper toweling is not a good alternative.

★★★★ **Kitchen Twine,** for sewing or tying up stuffed birds or meat. Dental floss is
or
★★★ a more expensive, though more durable, substitute.

★★★ **Potato "Nails,"** aluminum spikes for speeding up the baking process. Get one for each diner.

★★★ **Salad Tongs or Servers,** for tossing and serving salad.

★★★ **Cheese Slicer,** Swedish-style (see illustration), for cutting slivers, rather than chunks, of hard cheese. This helps to "slenderize" portions of this fatty food.

★★★ **Jar Opener,** either a hand-held rubber disk, a vise-type twister, or the type that mounts beneath an overhanging cupboard (see illustration).

★★★ **Kitchen Scale,** preferably one that weighs in 1- or 2-ounce increments, up to 8 or 10 pounds.

★★★ **Dairy Thermometer,** especially useful if you bake with yeast or make your own yogurt or buttermilk.

★★★ **Fat-separating Measuring Cup,** two if possible—a 1½-cup (for pan juices and gravies) and a 4-cup size (for soups). The spout originates at the bottom of the cup so that the liquid can be poured off but the fat remains behind. These cups are expensive, considering they are made of plastic, but well worth it for the time and effort they save.

★★★ **Potato Ricer,** an old-fashioned hand tool that resembles a giant garlic press and makes smooth mashed potatoes in an instant. A potato masher (metal or cheap plastic) or strong fork is less efficient but will do. These tools are also handy for mashing foods like bananas.

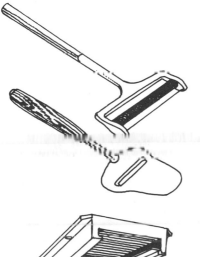

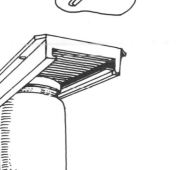

★★★ **Food Mill,** a hand-operated Foley-type sieve with a churn wheel and scraper attached. For simultaneously separating foods from seeds and puréeing them. Excellent for processing Concord grapes, uncored apples, or unseeded tomatoes, which cannot be done in a food processor or blender. Essential for puréeing fruits and vegetables if you do not have a food processor.

★★★ **Toaster,** for bread, especially if the bread has gotten a little stale.

★★★ **Salad Spinner,** for quick drying of greens without bruising them. A wire basket that doubles as a steamer rack would also do, if you have a yard in which to swing it around. Greens can also be dried with a dishcloth or paper towels.

★★★ **Mold,** 6-cup, with or without a center hole and without a bottom seam, for
or
★★ gelled dishes.

★★ **Grapefruit spoons,** one for each diner in the house. They eliminate the need for cutting grapefruit sections one by one and permit consumption of the fibrous section dividers. They are also useful for seeding cucumbers, and squashes.

★★ **Apple Slicer/Corer,** for simultaneously removing the core from apples and pears and cutting the fruit into even wedges. Children love to be served fruits cut into the shape of a flower with this device. It is very handy for making fast fruit salads, fruit slices for pie, and sautéed fruit for pancakes and crêpes. A sharp knife could also be used.

★★ **Apple Corer,** for removing just the core of fruits like apples and pears. Useful if you wish to cut fruit into rings or poach fruit whole.

★★ **Hand Chopper,** the type with a rounded single or double blade, if you have and would use a wooden chopping bowl. The blade must be kept sharp. The chopper is especially useful if you do not have a food processor for chopping meats and large amounts of vegetables.

★★ **Baster,** for safe basting of oven-cooked foods and for removing small amounts of liquid from pans.

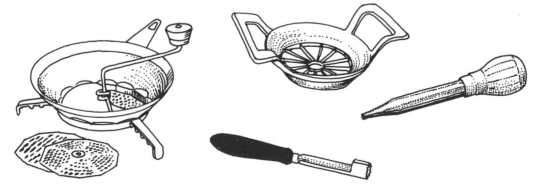

★★ **Microwave Oven,** especially useful for quick defrosting, heating of prepared foods and leftovers, keeping foods warm, and quick baking of potatoes and cooking of fresh vegetables. In vegetable cookery, the microwave preserves more nutrients than any other cooking technique. Many friends say having a microwave has helped them to cut down on nonnutritious snacks and fast foods, especially when they come home from work late, tired, and/or hungry. It is also useful when leaving behind a prepared meal for children to heat for themselves. Personally, for ordinary cooking I prefer the stove top and oven, although I can certainly appreciate the versatility offered by a microwave. It is not necessary to get a space-age computerized version unless you plan to do complicated food preparation in it.

★★ **Toaster Oven,** not necessary if you have a toaster and a microwave or broiler, but more energy-efficient than the oven for preparing one or two servings or reheating foods like pizza.

★★ **Pasta Rake,** or what I call a "spork"—a spoonlike paddle or scoop that has forklike projections at a 90-degree angle to the handle (see illustration). It is good for stirring spaghetti-type pasta while the pasta is cooking, and it is especially useful for serving the pasta.

★★ **Marble Slab,** at least 18 × 18 inches, for rolling out pastry and biscuit dough and for kneading bread (marble is easier to clean than a wooden board). I installed one as part of my counter top.

★★ **Ice-Cream Scoop,** for dishing up attractive portions of sherbet, sorbet, rice, and other grains, even if you never serve the high-fat real thing.

★★ **Boil-Control Disk,** in stainless steel or glass, for preventing boilovers when cooking foods like pasta or when heating milk.

★★ **Egg Slicer,** for fast, even slicing of hard-boiled eggs (slice them with the yolks, then remove the yellow if desired). A wire cheese slicer would also work, though it is harder to make even slices, but few knives are thin enough to do the job as well as an egg slicer. Another use for this gadget is in slicing small cooked new potatoes, beets, and mushrooms (place the mushroom cap side down).

★★ **Pounder,** for flattening and tenderizing meat and chicken cutlets. It works best if the food is placed between sheets of strong wax paper. It can also be used to crush ice cubes (place cubes inside a plastic bag, and place the plastic bag inside a heavy paper bag).

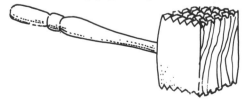

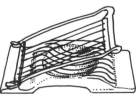

★★ **Convertible Slicer/Grater,** an inexpensive version of a mandolin (the hand-
or operated predecessor of a food processor), with replaceable inserts for different
★ functions. Mine cost about $6 and comes with me when I go camping or cook
in a summer cabin.

★★ **Butter-melting Pan,** either a very small cast-iron skillet or a warmer with sides
or that slant inward toward the top. A 1-quart saucepan also works.
★

★★ **Nut Grinder,** the $2.50 version, for fine chopping without having to wash a
or food processor and without having nuts scatter about the kitchen. The hopper
★ holds about ½ cup of nuts at a time. It is also useful for chopping hard-boiled
eggs.

★★ **Hot-Air Corn Popper,** for popcorn lovers who want to keep this nutritious
or snack lean. No fat is needed, nor does anyone have to shake the pot for 10
★ minutes.

★ **Flour Sifter,** handy if you bake a lot, to assure that dry ingredients are fluffy,
free of lumps, and well mixed. However, a mesh strainer or fork can be used
in its absence. Note that most white flour sold today is labeled "presifted."

★ **Pastry Blender,** the type with about four curved wire or metal blades that speed
the cutting in of shortening when making pie crusts and biscuits. Two knives
used crisscross fashion like swords also work.

★ **Nutmeg Grater,** essential if you buy whole nutmeg and don't have a fine side
on another grater. I find the taste of freshly grated nutmeg so superior to
packaged ground nutmeg that I no longer bother with the ready-made kind.

★ **Pastry Bag and Tips,** for decorating cakes and hors d'oeuvres with squeezable
mixtures.

★ **Extra Ice-Cube Trays,** preferably the twist-'em plastic type, for freezing small measured quantities of broth, lemon and lime juice, or pesto, and for preserving fresh herbs (place 1 tablespoon of minced herb in each compartment, add water, and freeze). Once the cubes have frozen, remove them from the trays and place them in labeled freezer containers.

★ **Top-of-Stove Potato Baker,** a useful energy saver for potato lovers, especially if you don't have a microwave. It can also be used for reheating foods that should not be steamed.

★ **Egg Separator,** for foolproof separation of yolks from whites. I have never used one. Cracking the egg against a sharp surface and gently transferring the yolk from one side of the shell to the other seems to work fine with just a little practice. The wise cook who needs clear whites breaks each egg separately over a small dish before transferring the white to the main bowl. Cold eggs are easier to separate than eggs at room temperature.

★ **Tea Strainer,** for brewing tea with loose leaves. Also useful for holding herbs when making soup stock.

WHERE TO BUY KITCHEN EQUIPMENT

Every kitchen tool listed in this chapter can be purchased by mail or phone from one or another of the following companies. All accept credit-card orders and will send a catalogue upon request.

Brookstone Homewares
5 Vose Farm Road
Peterborough, New Hampshire 03458
603 701 9511

The Chef's Catalog
3915 Commercial Avenue
Northbrook, Illinois 60062
312–480–9400

Colonial Garden Kitchens
270 West Merrick Road
Valley Stream, New York 11582
800–228–5000

Figi's Collection for Cooking
Marshfield, Wisconsin 54404
715–384–6101

S. E. Rykoff & Co.
P.O. Box 21467
Los Angeles, California 90021
800–421–9873

Sears "Especially for Cooks" Catalog
Sears, Roebuck and Co.
Chicago, Illinois 60607
or
Philadelphia, Pennsylvania 19132
(Check your phone book for a local number)

Williams-Sonoma
Mail Order Department
P.O. Box 7456
San Francisco, California 94120
415–652–9007

The Wooden Spoon
Route 6
Mahopac, New York 10541
800–431–2207

16 ·
HOW TO STOCK YOUR LARDER

My husband challenged me to come up with a list of "bare essential" cooking ingredients since my food cupboards look like the storerooms for a major metropolitan air-raid shelter. I do believe in being prepared: it gives me the freedom to make almost anything I want to at any time of the day or night, and it saves multiple emergency runs to the store for missing ingredients. However, you have to be reasonable, keeping on hand only "basics" that you are likely to use fairly often, that don't spoil with prolonged storage, and that fit in your available space. What follows is my ideal list, suited to the kind of cooking recommended in this book. If you know you dislike a particular seasoning or food item, forget about it. If I list something as a "must have" that you've never tasted before, buy it in a small quantity the first time or share a purchase with a friend. Other than saffron, no item listed exceeds the price of gold. And if you end up with something you'd rather not ever have again, give it away or throw it out.

KEY TO RATINGS:
**means *must have.*
*means *handy if you have the room.*

** Flours and Related Items:

- White flour, all-purpose unbleached
- Whole-wheat flour, stone-ground
- Rolled oats, regular or quick (not instant)
- Bread crumbs, unseasoned (you can make your own by grinding dried bread in a blender or food processor)

*Other Flours and Related Items:

- Unprocessed bran flakes
- Wheat germ
- Rye flour
- Whole-wheat pastry flour
- Corn meal, yellow, stone-ground

* Still Other Flours and Related Items:

- Soy flour
- Buckwheat flour
- Oat flour
- Graham-cracker crumbs

** Leavenings and Thickeners:

- Baking powder, double-acting or low-sodium single-acting (if the latter, double the amount given in the recipe)
- Baking soda
- Active dry or compressed yeast (assuming you bake bread)
- Cornstarch
- Unflavored gelatin

** Dry Seasonings:

- Allspice
- Basil leaves
- Bay leaves
- Caraway seeds
- Cardamom
- Cayenne pepper
- Celery seed
- Chili powder (hot and/or mild)
- Cinnamon, ground
- Cloves, whole and ground
- Coriander
- Cumin, ground
- Curry powder, hot and/or mild
- Dillweed (also, fresh dill, if available)
- Ginger, ground
- Mace
- Marjoram
- Mint leaves (unless you have fresh mint year round)
- Mustard powder
- Nutmeg, ground or whole (with grater)
- Orégano, ground and leaves
- Paprika
- Pepper, black peppercorns (with mill) and/or ground black pepper
- Pepper flakes, hot red
- Rosemary
- Sage
- Salt (keep this on hand for guests even if you don't cook with it)
- Salt-free seasoning mix, commercial or make your own (see p. 182)
- Sesame seeds, hulled
- Sugars, including white, dark brown, and confectioners' (if you bake)
- Tarragon
- Tartar, cream of (for whipping egg whites)

- Thyme, leaves preferred to ground
- Turmeric
- White pepper

* Other Dry Seasonings:

- Anise seed
- Broth mixes (chicken, beef, vegetable), low-salt type
- Chilies (whole dried red peppers)
- Cinnamon sticks
- Cocoa powder, unsweetened
- Cumin seed
- Dill seed
- Fennel seeds
- Five-spice powder
- Garlic powder (I use it only for making no-salt herb mix)
- Onion powder (I use it only for making no-salt herb mix)
- Parsley flakes (for no-salt herb mix and if you don't have ready access to fresh parsley)
- Poppy seeds
- Saffron (if you can afford it)
- Savory
- Vanilla bean
- White peppercorns (if you have a spare mill)

** Wet Seasonings:

- Almond extract
- Garlic, one or more heads
- Ginger, fresh (small piece) (see "Storage Tips," p. 247)
- Honey
- Horseradish (grated), in a small bottle
- Ketchup (regular or low-sodium)
- Mayonnaise (commercial if you don't make your own often)
- Molasses, light unsulphured
- Mustard, prepared, preferably Dijon
- Parmesan cheese, grated or for grating
- Pepper sauce, hot (Tabasco-type)
- Soy sauce, imported, reduced-sodium (store in the refrigerator)
- Vanilla extract
- Vinegars: white distilled, cider, white wine, red wine
- White wine, dry, for cooking
- Worcestershire sauce

* Other Wet Seasonings:

- Anchovy paste or flat anchovies (caution: salty)
- Brandy or cognac, small amount
- Capers (caution: salty)
- Chili oil (pepper-seasoned sesame oil, Oriental-type)

- Lemon rind, grated (store in the freezer)
- Liqueurs, various types (orange, etc.), in small amounts
- Orange rind, grated (store in the freezer)
- Peppers, fresh hot (e.g., chilies, jalapeño, serrano, cherry)
- Sesame tahini (Middle Eastern sesame paste)
- Sherry, dry
- Tamari soy
- Tomato paste, in tube or cans
- Vinegars, other kinds (e.g., balsamic, raspberry, herb)
- Wines, various types (like Madeira, Marsala, port)

** Oils:

- Corn, sunflower, or safflower, for cooking and salads
- Olive oil, good quality (in amounts you will use in a month)
- Peanut oil (buy in small quantities or refrigerate)
- Sesame oil, Oriental-type (a little goes a long way)
- Vegetable-oil cooking spray (for coating pans)

** Basic Ingredients to Have on Hand:

- Barley
- Beans and peas, cooked canned beans (especially kidney beans and chickpeas) and/or dried, various types (see pp. 104–106)
- Bread, whole-grain and other, if desired
- Bulgur (medium grain)
- Carrots
- Celery
- Coffee, regular and/or decaffeinated beans or ground beans or freeze-dried instant
- Evaporated skim milk, one or more cans
- Kasha (buckwheat groats), whole or coarse
- Lemons, or freshly squeezed and frozen juice
- Milk, nonfat powder (dried)
- Nuts, like walnuts, pecans, pine nuts
- Onions, yellow all-purpose
- Oranges or orange juice (small quantity for cooking)
- Pasta, dried, various sizes and shapes (see pp. 81–83)
- Potatoes, all-purpose
- Raisins, black seedless
- Rice, parboiled or converted white and/or long-grain brown
- Soft drinks, unflavored (seltzer, club soda, mineral water)
- Tea, herbal and/or regular leaf tea or tea bags
- Tomato sauce, a few small cans or homemade sauce frozen in small containers
- Tomatoes, canned peeled, regular or plum, in juice or purée, various can sizes (16, 28, and/or 35 ounces)
- Yogurt, plain low-fat

* Other Basic Ingredients:

- Bran cereal (not flakes), for baking
- Buttermilk, preferably fresh, but dried powder will do, or prepare a suitable substitute for cooking by mixing 2 tablespoons of vinegar into 8 ounces of milk
- Cheeses, hard, for grating (e.g., Cheddar, Monterey Jack, Swiss), stored in the freezer
- Corn grits (if you like them)
- Corn syrup (I rarely use it)
- Cottage cheese, low-fat type (can be "creamed")
- Couscous
- Currants
- Millet
- Peanut butter, preferably the natural kind without added fat, salt, or sugar
- Popping corn
- Shallots
- Sunflower seeds

STORAGE TIPS FOR BASIC INGREDIENTS

To reduce waste from spoilage and insect invasion, keep all the above ingredients in a cool place—a good trick since they are to be used in the kitchen and few of us have an extra refrigerator or freezer to house such items. At the least, try the following:

- Keep flours, grains, and bread crumbs in jars or canisters that close with a rubber seal or a tight screw-on top. I invested in a set of glass-top canning jars with rubber gaskets and metal catches. Put a bay leaf in each container to deter weevils. In the summer months, consider freezer storage for little-used items.
- Always keep opened wheat germ in the refrigerator to prevent rancidity.
- Bread keeps better in the refrigerator if not used in 3 or 4 days (unless it's a packaged type made with preservatives). For longer storage, wrap the bread very well in plastic and freeze it.
- Potatoes, onions, and shallots keep best when stored in a cool, dry, dark bin where air can circulate.
- Natural peanut butter keeps longer and is less likely to separate if stored in the refrigerator, but it is harder to spread when cold. If the jar is closed tightly and stored upside down, you'll have less trouble mixing in the oil if it should separate between uses.
- Paprika and cayenne pepper are particularly vulnerable to insect invasion. Buy them in small quantities, and consider storing them in the refrigerator.
- Keep herbs and spices in tightly closed containers (small glass jars are usually best) *away from the heat* of the stove and, if possible, away from light. If your spices are more than a year old, consider replacing them. Or use more than the recipe calls for to make up for lost pungency.
- Ketchup and mustard do not need refrigeration in most households, but mayonnaise always does.
- Olive and peanut oil are likely to turn rancid during prolonged storage. Buy

them in small quantities if they are used infrequently and/or keep them in the
refrigerator.

- Honey should not be refrigerated. If it crystallizes, place the jar in hot water to
  dissolve the crystals.
- Coffee beans keep longer than ground coffee. Store them all in the refrigerator
  or freezer, if possible.
- Raisins and other dried fruits can be stored in the freezer for many months.
- Unless used within a month or two, nuts are best stored in the freezer.
  Unshelled nuts have a longer shelf life (but are far less convenient to use in
  cooking).
- All canned foods can eventually deteriorate. Keep them in a cool, dry place,
  and discard without opening any cans that swell.
- If you find yourself with a half-used can of a basic ingredient (like tomato paste
  or broth), you can freeze it in the can (label it as to the amount remaining) or a
  in a smaller labeled container or in ice-cube trays (remove the cubes from the
  trays when the food has frozen).
- Start a collection of chicken scraps (bones, skin, wing tips, giblets except for
  liver, etc.) in a labeled bag in the freezer for making broth. Vegetable scraps
  can be similarly stored.
- Keep a jar in the refrigerator or freezer for vegetable cooking liquids to use in
  making broth.
- If freezer space is limited, you can boil down broth to a concentrate and
  reconstitute it with water when you defrost it. Broth can also be kept for weeks
  in the refrigerator if you reboil it every few days.
- Fresh herbs can be dried. Wash, dry, and hang them upside down in a dry,
  warm room. Crumble them when they have thoroughly dried.
- Many fresh herbs can be frozen. Wash and mince them (if the leaf is not
  already very small), place 1 or 2 tablespoons of herbs in each compartment of
  an ice-cube tray, add water to cover, and freeze the herbs. When they have
  frozen, remove them from the tray and store the herbs in a labeled container or
  a plastic bag.
- Fresh ginger should be kept uncovered in the refrigerator. For longer storage,
  peel and cut the root into small chunks, place them in a jar, and cover them
  with dry sherry. This will keep in the refrigerator for months, even years.
- Fresh herbs keep longer if stored with cut ends in water and tops lightly
  covered with a plastic bag. If you have the room, store celery and scallions the
  same way.
- Keep active dry yeast in the refrigerator (or freezer) in a closed plastic bag.
- To keep brown sugar soft, bag it in plastic and refrigerate it. If the sugar gets
  hard, grate it by hand or in the blender.
- You can freeze vine ripened tomatoes in season, instead of relying on canned
  ones all winter and spring. Wash the tomatoes, then cut them into quarters, and
  spread them on cookie sheets. Freeze them, then transfer them to plastic bags.
  When you are ready to use them, the peel will be easy to remove as the
  tomatoes begin to defrost.

17 ·
HOW TO SHOP
EFFICIENTLY

This is another topic that drew a dare from my husband, who's convinced he married a compulsive food shopper. I admit to being spoiled by living in a food-oriented city (New York), where dozens of well-stocked fruit and vegetable markets are open 24 hours a day, seven days a week, and where several supermarkets, mom-and-pop groceries, meat and fish markets, and bakeries are within walking or biking distance of my home (although none is open around the clock). Thus, I have the privilege of "forgetting" grocery items or changing my mind after I've done the main weekly shopping. I can also go from store to store to shop for the best prices and quality. I can pick up fresh fruits and vegetables daily on my way home from work (most of the markets are open late). And I have access year round to the most extraordinary selection of fresh foods, from basil and dill to melons and strawberries.

But I have also done a great deal of cooking in areas where food is not as conveniently located or varied in type. For example, I often cook in a rural home where I am at the mercy of one drive-to supermarket and in a country cabin where the nearest supermarket is 10 miles away and the nearby quick-pick-up store (a 20-minute bike ride) is erratically and sparingly stocked.

So the following tips are based on varied shopping/cooking experiences. They are designed with economy in mind—not just economy of budget, but also of time. Your time and your energy are worth money—more than money, in fact, since once squandered they cannot be bought back.

MAKING THE LIST

In few households these days do people have the opportunity to decide on a daily basis what they are going to eat. With all adults in a family working, and with youngsters scheduled tightly into various after-school activities and jobs, there is often no one around during the day to do grocery shopping and food preparation. In more and more homes, batch cooking on weekends is becoming routine: three main dishes may be prepared at one time on Saturday or Sunday to provide the family with six main meals during the week, with dinner out or a salad supper for the seventh day. There are now several cookbooks available to help people who cook in this fashion (see those mentioned on p. 650). If this pattern suits you, the following suggested action plan is a place to start. If you would rather shop and cook day to day, you can adapt this plan to suit those needs, too.

- For basics, keep a perennial shopping list going. Write down as soon as you think of it any item that has been used up or, preferably, that is running low. For example, when my flour supply drops below 2 pounds, I buy a new bag so I never run out. When the last roll of paper towels is put on the roller, paper towels go on the list.
- On Thursday or Friday evening, look through the menus and recipes in this book and others you may have and decide what you want to cook for the coming week, keeping in mind seasonal availability and best buys.
- Make a list of the ingredients you'll need for each selected recipe, including amounts. Also list the ingredients you'll need for vegetable side dishes, salads, bread, and fruit for desserts and snacks.
- Condense your list by combining like items in their needed quantities. For example, if one recipe calls for ½ cup of minced scallions (2 large or 4 small) and another calls for 4 scallions, sliced, you'll need at least one large bunch of scallions that week.
- Organize your shopping list by type of item: dairy products and eggs; meat, chicken, and fish; fruits and vegetables; canned goods; cereals, grains, pasta; and so forth. This simplifies filling the grocery cart once you are in the store surrounded by a confusing array of perhaps 18,000 different items.
- Write the list out clearly on a pad, and take it and a pen to the store with you so you can cross off the items as you put them in the cart. Not only will this help you know when it's time to get in the check-out line, but you'll also know at a glance what you were unable to find and may have to look for elsewhere (or that you must modify or replace a particular recipe).

TACKLING THE STORE

List in hand, it's time to develop a shopping battle plan so that you can choose wisely among the many similar offerings and end up with foods that will suit your health and tastes as well as your budget. This means shopping with ingredients as well as price and convenience in mind.

- Consider shopping when the stores are least crowded—first thing in the morning or in the evening (when you're probably too tired to do much else). However, you may find the shelves less than fully stocked at those times and have a harder time getting assistance from store clerks.
- If practical, plan to shop for fresh vegetables at least twice a week. Many vegetables lose quality and nutrients during prolonged refrigeration, and few people have large enough refrigerators to house a week's supply of fresh produce for an entire family. (See pp. 133–149 for selection tips.)
- Try to buy fruits and vegetables where you can pick them individually, rather than having to buy a prepackaged amount. Choose small, young vegetables

when possible, and as soon as you get home, remove leafy tops to reduce wilting. (Try cooking the tops of beets as a separate vegetable, and use celery tops in making stocks and soups.)

- Compare the ingredients lists on package labels. It won't take long before you realize that a brand of yogurt made from milk and milk solids and active cultures is superior to a brand that has added sugars, flavorings, colorings, and stabilizers. Check the amount of sugar in breakfast cereals by looking at the carbohydrate information supplied on most boxes. Unless you're buying a food specifically for its sweetness, sugar (or honey) should not be the first ingredient listed. Look for the kind of fat used (put back those products in which coconut or palm oil or unspecified vegetable oil is a prominent ingredient). Choose canned fruits that are packed in pure fruit juice, not syrup.

- Check for sodium information; very similar products can vary greatly in the amount of salt used in processing. Your best bet is no added salt. Then you can add seasonings to taste, most likely using far less than the manufacturer would have. (See pp. 179–185 for more information on sodium content of foods.)

- Avoid heavily processed "instant" foods and packaged mixes. Reading the ingredients listed on oil-free salad dressings may be all the stimulus you need to make your own (see recipes on pp. 549–553).

- If there's a choice between an "enriched" and a whole-grain product, choose the latter—it has nearly 2 dozen more nutrients.

- Don't be put off by the high cost of good-quality fruits and vegetables. Remember, you're saving a lot by buying very little meat and cheese, and few snack foods. (And you may be saving even more on future medical costs!) You can now afford to spend $3 on a 4-pound ripe pineapple flown in from Hawaii or $2 a pound for tender asparagus. And you deserve it.

- Avoid wilted vegetables and bruised fruits, even if they're a bargain. Chances are you'll end up discarding much of them, obliterating your savings.

- Check the expiration and "sell by" dates on perishable foods like dairy products, cereals, and breads. Always buy the item with the most distant date.

- Comparison-shop for price. Most markets now offer unit price information on the shelf. If not, or if you have a hard time finding the right labels, carry a tiny calculator with you and do the arithmetic yourself.

- Larger-sized packages are usually, but not always, cheaper. For example, in my market, you can buy two 12-ounce packages of cheese for less than a 24-ounce package of the identical cheese and two 6-ounce cans of frozen juice for less than one 12-ounce can.

- Watch out for deceptive packaging. Many products that once came in 1-pound packages (for example, raisins, kasha, and cranberries) now hold only 12 or 13 ounces in a container of the same apparent size.

- Store brands are usually comparable to or better in quality than nationally advertised ones, but may be much cheaper. For example, in my market, the store brand of pasta costs half of what the name brands do, and they have identical ingredients and few, if any, discernible differences in quality.

- When preparing your shopping list, check the market ads and newspaper for cents-off coupons and specials of the week. Stock up on nonperishable items when they're on sale.

- Try generic products. Some are as good as ordinary brands, but most of the generics I've tried have been distinctly inferior. Last winter my children used the generic raisin bran I bought to feed the birds.

- In some cities, "no frills" markets—where you unbox and package your own groceries—can mean a significant savings.
- Items sold in health food and natural food stores are usually, but not always, more expensive than the same foods in supermarkets. These stores may be your only access to certain wholesome foods like whole-grain flours and the more "exotic" grains, beans, nuts, and seeds. And on certain items, the health food store may be cheaper, especially for foods like rolled oats, bran, rice, and other grains, and nuts that the store repackages or sells in bulk.
- Check out local food co-ops. If handy, you're likely to get your best buys and quality from co-op shopping.
- Don't shop on an empty stomach. Studies have shown that hungry shoppers tend to be less discriminating and buy more "junk" foods than shoppers who have just eaten.

18 ·
HOW TO COOK
EFFICIENTLY

Aphorism of the day: The time and money you save in the kitchen is your own.

For too many cooks—myself included—developing techniques of food preparation has been like repeatedly rediscovering the wheel. After years of using some inefficient method (or wasting precious ingredients), a light bulb goes off and a better way to do the task comes to mind. Well, you no longer have to rely on sudden flashes of insight or the chance remark of a friend who tires of watching you do something the hard way. You can benefit from the years of accumulated wisdom among cooks throughout the world. Applying this wisdom to healthful cooking from scratch can shave hours a week off your kitchen time, save countless food dollars, and help to make the whole process of cooking a great adventure instead of an annoying chore.

REMOVING SKINS

CHICKEN is easier to skin when left whole than when cut up. With the legs pointing toward you, grab the far edge of the skin (i.e., the skin near the neck) and pull it off the bird as you would a pair of tights from a child. (Chances are you will not be able to skin the wings, so just leave them as is.) Save the skin along with the wing tips, hind end, and giblets (except for the liver) for making stock. Once skinned, the bird is easy to cut into serving pieces because the joints are visible.

CORN is easy to shuck (the process of removing the leafy coat), but the silks can adhere stubbornly to the cob. Run a damp paper or cloth towel over the cob from tip to stem end; the silks should come off easily.

FISH FILLETS can be skinned easily with a knife that has a long, thin, sharp blade. With one hand, hold one end of the fillet near you by the skin and with the other hand carefully work the knife away from you between the flesh and the skin.

GARLIC is easily peeled in one of two ways. (1) Lay a clove on a firm surface, and place the flat side of a knife blade against it. Punch the blade once with your fist; the skin should now be easy to remove. If you pound hard, it will simultaneously flatten the clove, which makes it easier to mince. (2) If you are peeling lots of garlic, you may prefer to place the cloves in boiling water for 30 to 60 seconds. Skins will then slip off easily.

ONIONS are best peeled from the growing tip downward. If you are going to slice or chop an onion, try to keep the peelings attached at the root end; they will help you hold on to the onion while cutting it. If you have lots of onions or shallots to peel (as in making stew with small white onions), place them in boiling water for 1 to 2 minutes to loosen the skins.

ORANGES can be peeled without traces of the white pith if plunged first into boiling water. Or place the oranges in a 350-degree oven for 5 minutes.

PEAS are easily shelled after 10 minutes in the steamer.

PEPPERS are easy to skin if they are placed in a preheated broiler for a few minutes, then immediately placed in a tightly closed plastic bag. When the peppers cool enough to handle, the skins should come off easily. If you are roasting the peppers, leave them in the broiler (about 2 inches from the heat) for about 20 minutes, turning them several times to char the skin on all sides. Then enclose them in a plastic bag to cool.

PINEAPPLE skin can be removed with minimum waste if you first cut the top and bottom off, leaving a flat base. Then one of two methods can be used to remove the outer shell. (1) Stand the pineapple on end, and, with a large, heavy knife, slice downward just beneath the skin, rotating the pineapple after each slice to completely remove skin and "eyes." The pineapple can then be quartered lengthwise and the tough core removed by slicing off the center piece of each quarter. (2) Quarter the unpeeled pineapple (after the top and bottom ends have been removed), and use a pineapple or grapefruit knife (with curved blade) to cut between the flesh and the skin. Forget about commercial peeler-corers unless you own a pineapple plantation; too much of the fruit ends up in the garbage.

POTATOES are best peeled after they are cooked whole, if you're concerned about preserving nutrients. They peel easily while hot. Impale them on a two-pronged fork, and slip the skins off with a paring knife.

TOMATO-peeling techniques are a matter of personal preference. If I am just doing a few tomatoes, and especially if they are to be served uncooked, I prefer to pierce the skin with a knife and then peel it off with a sharp potato peeler or slender paring knife (this works best if the tomatoes are fairly firm). For large quantities of tomatoes that will ultimately be cooked or canned, bring a large pot of water to a boil, add a few tomatoes at a time, and return the water to a boil, boiling the tomatoes for 10 to 20 seconds, depending on their firmness. Remove the tomatoes with a slotted spoon, and rinse them immediately under cold water. (Alternatively, drop the tomatoes into boiling water for 1 minute, then remove and place them in cold water for another minute.) Then peel the tomatoes from bottom to stem end with a small knife. In a third technique (best for small quantities), the tomato is impaled on a two-tined fork with a long wooden handle and rotated slowly over a gas flame until the skin begins to shrivel. When the tomato cools enough to handle, remove the peel with a knife.

CUTTING UP FOODS

The most important rule here is to use a *sharp* knife whose weight is appropriate to the size of the task. I prefer a chef's knife or Chinese cleaver for all slicing and chopping (see p. 230), using a small paring knife only for the delicate, gloved task of mincing hot peppers. However, many cooks use a utility knife (a small version of the chef's knife) for smaller fruits and vegetables. Whatever you use, sharpness is critical. The knife is much more likely to slip and cut you if it is dull, and the job will require more muscle power and turn out less neatly. When slicing and cutting, hold the knife with your thumb and index finger gripping the top of the blade; this gives you good leverage.

As for efficiency, it stands to reason that if you need large amounts of a particular cut food, the job will go a lot faster if you start with larger sizes of the food. There will be that much less to peel and fewer cuts to make.

WHEN SLICING ROUND FOODS, like potatoes, turnips, onions, etc., cut the food in half lengthwise and place the cut side down. Hold the object with thumb at the rear and remaining fingers curved on the top like a claw, fingertips pointing toward the rear. Slice straight down, pushing the object forward with your thumb and moving your top fingers back as you go.

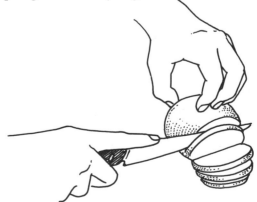

WHEN SLICING LONG FOODS like carrots and parsnips, to reduce slippage cut off a thin strip to create a flattened side. Place the cut side down, and slice crosswise, as you would a round food.

JULIENNE (MATCHSTICK) STRIPS are not difficult to cut if the food is first sliced lengthwise to create a flat surface. Placing the cut side down, slice the food lengthwise into ¼- or ⅛-inch strips (as desired), then lay some of those pieces down on their side and cut the same size strips in the same direction. For efficiency, you should be able to cut two or three layers at a time, but don't try to do too many or they'll slip from the pile.

CHOPPING OR DICING HARD FOODS like carrots, potatoes, and celery is fastest if you first cut julienne-like strips (although they can be thicker than julienne), and then align the strips and cut them crosswise into pieces.

CHOPPING, MINCING, OR DICING ONIONS is simplest if you take advantage of the fact that the onion rings already provide a natural cut in one direction. Peel the onion as described above, from growing tip toward the root end. Cut the onion in half in the same direction, and place the cut side down. Cut lengthwise strips across the onion, cutting almost to the root end, which will help to hold the strips together. Then cut crosswise slices, starting at the growing tip, as in slicing round foods (above). Make the size of your strips and slices smaller if you want to end up with minced onions, larger if you want them diced. To *mince a scallion,* cut the bulb in half lengthwise, lay it down flat on its cut sides, then cut several lengthwise strips. Bunch the strips together, and cut small crosswise slices. To reduce tears when cutting up members of the onion family, partially freeze the vegetables first.

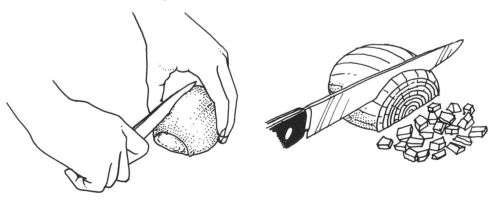

MINCING GARLIC AND FRESH GINGER. Garlic is easy to mince if the clove is either flattened first by pounding it with the flat side of a knife blade or by slicing it in half lengthwise. First, cut the clove into lengthwise strips, then crosswise slices. If smaller pieces are needed, chop the garlic by rocking your knife blade across the pieces (with the palm of your hand, hold the tip of the blade against the cutting surface and cut down repeatedly toward the heel of the blade, working the heel of the knife in a semicircle and pushing the pieces of garlic into a heap as you go). For fresh ginger, first cut a peeled chunk into crosswise slices, then cut the slices into narrow strips in both directions, as in chopping hard foods. If further mincing is needed, use the blade in a rocking motion, as with garlic.

CHOPPING OR MINCING FRESH PARSLEY is easiest if the herb is dry. Use a chef's knife or cleaver. Align the bunch with stems facing away from your knife hand, bunch the foliage together (holding with fingertips pointing toward the stems), and cut crosswise slices until you reach the stems (which should be discarded or saved for stock). Then hold the knife blade by both ends and chop, pushing the pieces repeatedly into a heap under the knife. Or rock the knife from tip to heel, lifting only from the handle and moving the heel in a semicircle.

SNIP HERBS like dill and chives with a sharp scissors to avoid crushing the delicate leaves. Otherwise, use a paring knife with a very sharp, thin blade.

HOT PEPPERS should never be seeded and cut unless you are wearing rubber gloves. Wash the knife, cutting surface, and your gloved hands while the gloves are still on you to minimize exposure to the irritating chemical that makes peppers "hot."

WHEN SLICING, CHOPPING, OR DICING APPLES AND PEARS, if you don't have a corer, quarter the (peeled, if desired) fruit lengthwise and cut off the corner containing the core. For slices, cut each quarter into two or more lengthwise wedges. For chopped or diced fruit, lay the quarters on one flat side, cut them into lengthwise slices, then lay the quarters on the other flat side, and repeat. Align the strips, and, holding them with fingertips pointing away from the knife, cut the strips crosswise into pieces. To keep cut apples from darkening (if you are preparing large amounts), toss them with 1 cup of cold water mixed with 1 tablespoon of lemon juice.

SLICING MUSHROOMS is a snap if you have an egg slicer. After trimming the stem end, place the mushroom in the slicer with the cap facing downward.

This also works for firm cooked new potatoes and small beets as well as eggs, all of which slice best when cold.

SLICE BREADS using a long serrated or scalloped knife when the breads are cool or partly frozen. Bread is compressed when sliced hot.

SLICING MEAT PAPER-THIN is easiest if the well-trimmed meat is partially frozen, then sliced across the grain with a chef's knife or cleaver.

BONING CHICKEN is easier if the pieces are first partially frozen.

SLICING OR CHOPPING DATES AND CRANBERRIES is simpler if the fruits are first placed in the freezer for 1 to 2 hours.

GRATING, GRINDING, AND SHREDDING

These are jobs now often relegated to a food processor. But unless you are doing large amounts or several such tasks, the job of cleaning the processor may be more trouble than it's worth. In those cases, a multisided grater may be your most efficient tool.

GRATING CHEESE is a job best done just before you are going to use it. Unless the cheese is very hard, like Parmesan or Romano, it will congeal into a mass if it sits around too long. To simplify the job of grating softer cheeses (like mozzarella or Monterey Jack), place the cheese in the freezer for 30 to 45 minutes beforehand.

GRATING RINDS OF LEMON, LIME, OR ORANGE must be done while the fruit is still whole (this will also help to release more juice when you later squeeze the skinned fruit). Remember, if a recipe calls for both juice and grated rind, grate the rind first. To simplify the job, first place the fruit in the freezer for 15 minutes, and then push it diagonally across the grater rather than straight up and down. Grate only the outer rind, not the white pith. Grated rind can be frozen for future use: spread grated rind in a pan lined with wax paper, and place it in the freezer. When the rind is frozen, transfer it to a labeled jar with a lid that closes tightly, and place the jar immediately in the freezer.

TO SIMPLIFY GRATER CLEANUP, smear the grater with some vegetable oil or spray it with vegetable-oil coating before grating cheese or citrus rinds.

SHREDDING CABBAGE is easy to do with a heavy chef's knife or cleaver. Cut the cabbage lengthwise into quarters, remove the hard core from each quarter, lay the quarters on a flat side, and slice the cabbage thinly either lengthwise or crosswise, as desired.

POTATOES can be grated into a bowl of ice water (perhaps with a teaspoon of lemon juice in it) to prevent darkening, which occurs almost immediately upon exposure to air. Drain the potatoes well, and pat them dry before use.

GRIND SPICES like pepper and nutmeg onto a small sheet of wax paper to simplify measuring them.

GRIND YOUR OWN EXOTIC FLOURS in the blender. This works with oats, millet, barley, rice, lentils, dried beans, and uncooked hot cereal.

GRIND NUTS quickly by crushing them with a rolling pin or wooden mallet.

CRUSH GRAHAM CRACKERS in a flat-bottomed bowl with the base of a heavy flat-bottomed glass or jar to reduce scatter and cleanup chores.

MAKE SEASONED BREAD CRUMBS in the blender by combining pieces of dried bread or unsweetened breakfast cereal with dried herbs and seasonings to taste and/or grated Parmesan.

SEEDING AND CORING

TOMATOES are easy to seed if you cut them in half *crosswise,* then scoop out the seedy pulp from each half with a fingertip. If you need to save the pulp and juice, seed the tomato into a fine strainer that has been placed over a bowl and press what you collect through the strainer into that bowl. This will leave just the seeds in the strainer.

CUCUMBERS, SQUASH, AND MELONS (like cantaloupe and honeydew) are easiest to seed when they are cut in half lengthwise and the seedy mass is scooped out with a melon baller or serrated grapefruit spoon.

CHERRY TOMATOES can be pulped for stuffing by slicing off a small cap at the stem end, then scooping out the pulp with the small side of a melon baller. Place the tomatoes cut side down on paper towels so that they can drain before filling.

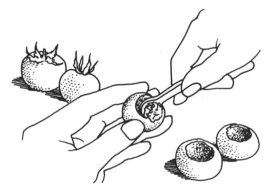

APPLES AND PEARS are easiest to core if they are first cut into quarters lengthwise. However, if you wish to cut the fruit into rings, you will need a vertical corer.

APPLESAUCE can be made without first coring the apples (do, however, remove the stem and blossom ends) if the cooked apples are to be puréed in a food mill (see p. 238).

SEEDING GRAPES when you want to preserve the skin (as in making Concord grape conserve or pie) is a laborious task that goes much faster if two or more people do it together. Holding a small cluster in one hand, pull off one grape at a time and squeeze the pulp into a saucepan. Save the skin in a bowl. When all the grapes have been peeled, cook the pulp over medium heat for about 5 minutes to loosen the seeds. Then place the pulp in a food mill or strainer set over a bowl to separate the pulp from the seeds. At the appropriate point in the recipe, add the reserved skins to the pulp and proceed.

FREEZING FOODS

Many households today are equipped with a free-standing freezer, and those that are not are likely to have a larger freezer compartment atop or alongside the refrigerator. For a food-conscious household in which working adults have little time and energy for daily food preparation, a freezer can be a wise investment, enabling you to store a variety of nuts and grains, breads and muffins, fresh foods in season (like blueberries) for future use, home-prepared basic ingredients (like broth and lemon juice) in ready-to-use amounts, foods prepared in advance for parties and gifts, and, most important of all, ready-to-heat-and-eat homemade meals. There are several important things to consider when freezing foods:

- Leave room at the top of the container for expansion. Liquids expand more than solids when frozen.
- To reduce the risk of breakage, it is best to freeze in plastic, rather than glass, containers.
- Wrap the food airtight to prevent dehydration. Tight-fitting lids on containers or a tight layer of plastic wrap around the food helps.
- With an indelible marking pen and a label that won't fall off (I put the label on the inside of a plastic bag), indicate on every package its contents (type and amount) and date frozen. When using frozen foods, use the oldest packages first.
- You can refreeze partially or completely thawed foods as long as they have *not* been kept at room temperature or subject to other sources of bacterial contamination or growth. The foods to be especially careful about are those containing cream, uncooked eggs, and shellfish; it is best not to refreeze these if they have thawed completely. But safety is only one consideration. Many foods lose quality if frozen more than once.
- Make sure the food *can,* in fact, be frozen without wrecking its texture or consistency.

The following is a list of foods that freeze well:

- Red meats and poultry, both raw and cooked.
- Raw shrimp and scallops. Other kinds of fish can also be frozen, but not without a loss in quality. You can, however, freeze the bones, heads, and tails of nonoily fish for making stock.
- Stocks and most soups, except those with a gelatin base or chunks of potato (unless you don't mind the fact that the potatoes will be mushy after defrosting). Soups "creamed" by the addition of yogurt, buttermilk, or sour cream are best frozen before this step. For convenient use of stocks in making sauces or in fat-free "sautéeing," freeze 2-tablespoon portions in ice-cube trays.
- Puréed cooked vegetables.
- Blanched vegetables and fruit (the heat in blanching destroys enzyme action that causes deterioration).
- Fruits mixed with sugar or ascorbic acid (which has the same effect as blanching).
- Hard cheeses, although some are crumbly after defrosting.
- Raw eggs, either whole or separated. Yolks do best when mixed with a little water and honey before freezing.
- All flours, uncooked cereals like rolled oats, and bread and cracker crumbs.
- Breads, muffins, cookies (except macaroons), pies (except custard and cream), and cakes, preferably before being iced.
- Nuts and dried fruits.
- Pancakes, crêpes, French toast, and waffles. Separate layers with sheets of wax paper.
- Pastry and bread dough.
- Leftover rice, for use in cooked dishes.
- Butter, margarine, and evaporated milk.
- Coffee (beans, ground, or instant).
- Chopped onions and chopped green peppers.
- Grated citrus rinds.
- Fruit juices, including lemon and lime juice (freeze 1 or 2 tablespoons of juice in individual compartments of ice-cube trays).
- Partially used containers of olives, pimientos, pickles, water chestnuts, and bamboo shoots.
- Blueberries, strawberries, and raspberries can be frozen, unwashed, spread on trays, then transferred to freezer containers for storage. Cranberries should be frozen in the bags they come in; you will be able to pour them out in needed quantities.
- Fresh ginger.
- Fresh mushrooms, sliced or whole, for use in cooked dishes only.
- Whole unpeeled bananas, to be eaten frozen. Sliced bananas, frozen separately on a tray, for pies or snacks. Mashed bananas, mixed with 1 teaspoon of lemon juice, for baking muffins or breads.
- Tomato sauce, pesto, ratatouille, and many other sauces.
- Dips like hummus and baba ghanoush that are not made with "liquid" dairy products.

- Casseroles and stews of all kinds. A good trick is to line the casserole dish with foil before putting in the food to be frozen. When the food is fully frozen, you can remove it, foil and all, and wrap it well in plastic. Then you will have the casserole dish free for other uses.

Foods that *do not* freeze well include:

- Cooked pasta (except for casseroles like lasagne) and bulgur.
- Gelatin dishes.
- Yogurt, sour cream, and cottage cheese.
- Melons, uncooked apples, pears, plums.
- Hard-boiled egg whites.
- Raw or cooked potatoes.
- Custards and creams.
- Mayonnaise.
- Raw tomatoes and most other raw unprocessed vegetables (freezing causes their cells to rupture, leaving them formless when defrosted).

DESALTING

Many foods and condiments are too salty for today's health- and taste-conscious consumer. Yet their basic flavoring or texture can add much to a dish. Here are some tips for desalting foods.

- You can significantly reduce the salt content of the following foods by soaking them for 15 minutes or longer in cold water, changing the water once or twice if the food is extremely salty: anchovies, capers, feta cheese, caviar, ham (chunks, steaks, or bones), sauerkraut or other pickled vegetables.
- If a cooking liquid or soup is too salty, add some sliced raw potatoes to it and cook the soup until the potatoes are just soft, then remove the potatoes.
- Dilute the soup with fresh water, and cook rice or small pasta in it.

DEFATTING

Most ordinary recipes call for much more fat than is needed to prepare the food or provide a good flavor. The trick in defatting foods is to know what you can do to cut fat corners without wrecking the recipe. Here are some tricks I've used successfully.

- Except when roasting or broiling, discard all chicken skin before cooking. To end up with moist, tasty chicken, marinate it first or cook it in a stew.
- Use a brush to oil pans, or spray the pans with vegetable-oil cooking spray.
- Pour soup stocks and pan juices into a fat-separating measuring cup (the kind where the spout comes out from the bottom [see the illustration on p. 237]), or refrigerate them to solidify the fat for easy removal. If you are in a hurry, skim ice cubes through the liquid to harden the fat.

- Trim all meats of visible fat before you cook them.
- Adapt the sauté to modern needs: use broth instead of fat to "sauté" vegetables like onions and mushrooms.
- In salad dressings, substitute jelled broth, puréed vegetables, or yogurt for some of the oil or mayonnaise.
- Refrigerate canned broth before opening; the fat can then be easily removed.
- In baking muffins and cakes, replace some of the fat with puréed fruit, like applesauce.
- Whip powdered skim milk into mashed potatoes, moistening the food with some of the cooking liquid or broth instead of with butter.
- Cook stews a day ahead; chill and remove the fat before reheating.
- Use a thin smear of mustard, sliced tomato, and/or lettuce instead of mayonnaise or butter to "moisten" sandwiches.
- Make your own nonfat yogurt and buttermilk. For yogurt, mix 1 packet (1⅓ cups) nonfat powdered milk into 3 cups of water. Heat the milk to 115–120 degrees Fahrenheit. Stir in 2 tablespoons of your favorite plain commercial yogurt with active cultures (or use some from your own previous batch), and set the milk in a warm place (such as the oven with the pilot light on) until it sets. For buttermilk, heat the milk to 90 degrees, and add ⅓ cup buttermilk with active cultures as a starter.

SUBSTITUTING INGREDIENTS: HOW TO CHANGE RECIPES

Even if you are among the most organized of cooks, you may sometimes find yourself missing an important ingredient in the middle of preparing a recipe. Or the recipe may call for an ingredient that you deem too high in fat (or saturated fat) or cholesterol to be suitable for your purposes. Or you may wish to substitute a liquid ingredient for a dry one, or vice versa. In these situations, it is often possible to make substitutions without doing much, if any, damage to the final result.

BACON. In place of this high-fat ingredient, use lean Canadian bacon or boiled or baked ham. You'll get a similar smoked flavor but much less fat and fewer calories.

BAKING MIX, COMMERCIAL. Make your own by combining in a large bowl 2 cups of all-purpose flour, 1 tablespoon of baking powder, 1 tablespoon of sugar, and 1 teaspoon of salt. Cut in ⅓ cup of solid vegetable shortening until the mixture resembles coarse grain. Store the mix in a tightly covered jar (refrigeration is not required).

BAKING POWDER. For 1 tablespoon baking powder, you can substitute 1½ teaspoons of cream of tartar mixed with 1 teaspoon of baking soda.

BREAD CRUMBS. Replace 1 cup of bread crumbs with ¾ cup of cracker or cereal crumbs.

BUTTERMILK. A reasonable cooking substitute can be made by combining 2 tablespoons of vinegar or lemon juice with 1 cup of skim or 1-percent milk, letting the mixture stand for 5 minutes. Or replace buttermilk with an equal amount of low-fat plain yogurt.

CAKE FLOUR. Substitute ⅞ cup of all-purpose flour for each 1 cup of cake flour.

CAYENNE PEPPER. Replace ⅛ teaspoon of cayenne with 4 drops of hot pepper sauce.

CHOCOLATE. Replace 1 ounce of unsweetened chocolate with ¼ cup of cocoa mixed with 2 teaspoons of shortening (oil, butter, margarine, or vegetable shortening will do).

CREAM CHEESE. Blend 1 cup low-fat cottage cheese with ¼ cup margarine to equal 1 cup cream cheese that is lower in saturated fat and cholesterol (but not lower in total fat).

EGGS. In most recipes calling for 1 or 2 eggs, 2 egg whites can be substituted for 1 yolk. If desired, add 1 to 3 teaspoons of vegetable oil for every yolk you omit. You might also try making mayonnaise with 2 whites instead of 1 yolk.

HERBS. When substituting dried herbs for fresh ones, use about one-third the amount called for in the recipe. However, in some recipes, such as pesto or tabbouli, fresh herbs are essential (all recipes in this book specify "fresh" when fresh is essential). One teaspoon of frozen chopped chives is approximately equal to 1 tablespoon of fresh chives. If your dried seasonings are more than a year old, they may have lost some verve; increase the amount needed by about 25 percent, or crumble the herbs in your hands or lightly crush them in a mortar with pestle to compensate.

LEMON JUICE. Replace 1 teaspoon of lemon juice with ½ teaspoon of vinegar.

MILK. In most recipes for cakes and muffins, fruit juice can be used in place of milk. Add ½ teaspoon of baking soda to the recipe if the juice is acid. If whole milk is needed, you can make it by adding 2 tablespoons of melted butter or margarine to 1 cup of skim milk; or mix ½ cup of evaporated (whole) milk with ½ cup of water.

MUSTARD. Use 2½ teaspoons of prepared mustard in place of 1 teaspoon of mustard powder.

SHORTENING. When substituting vegetable oil for vegetable shortening, butter, or margarine, use one-third less. Use 2 teaspoons of oil in place of 1 tablespoon of hard shortening.

SOUR CREAM. For a low-fat version to use in cooking, purée in a blender 1 cup of low-fat cottage cheese or part-skim ricotta with enough yogurt or buttermilk to achieve desired consistency, or combine the cheese with 2 tablespoons of skim milk and 1 tablespoon of lemon juice. Or whip ½ cup of *chilled* evaporated milk with 1 tablespoon of white vinegar to equal 1 cup sour cream.

SWEETENERS. Most regular dessert recipes (not those in this book or in most "diet" books, however) can stand a one-third or one-half reduction in the amount of sweetener recommended. If substituting honey for sugar, reduce the amount by 25 percent (e.g., use ¾ cup of honey in place of 1 cup of sugar) and reduce some other liquid ingredient as well (by ¼ cup for the example given). Baked goods made with honey are said to keep fresh longer than those made with sugar. To reverse the substitution, you can use 1¼ cups sugar plus ¼ cup water instead of 1 cup honey. You can make a reasonable facsimile of brown sugar by combining 1 cup of white sugar with ¼ cup of light molasses as a replacement for 1 cup of brown sugar.

THICKENERS. One tablespoon of cornstarch, arrowroot, or potato starch has the thickening power of 2 tablespoons of flour.

VINEGAR. Replace ½ teaspoon of vinegar with 1 teaspoon of lemon juice.

SEASONING

- Cold foods require more intense seasoning than hot foods.
- Pasta salads are usually best seasoned just before serving. If they are seasoned ahead, be prepared to add half again the amount of dressing just before serving.
- Do not add salt to dried peas and beans until they are cooked; it toughens them.
- Do not add salt to meat and chicken until they are well browned on both sides; it draws the liquid out of them.
- You will need less salt in soup if you add it at the end of cooking. This will season the broth rather than the other ingredients, and give the taste sensation of more salt.
- When increasing a recipe, do not increase the seasonings as drastically as the main ingredients. Make small changes, and taste.

THICKENING SOUPS AND DRESSINGS

A variety of wholesome tricks can be used to thicken soups, making it possible to use skim milk, say, instead of heavy cream in creamed soups (both hot and cold) or to help turn a soup with a thin broth into a heartier dish.

- Try adding bread crumbs, whole-grain or white, fresh or dried, to the soup.
- Add a few tablespoons of uncooked farina to the soup, and cook it, stirring, for about 5 minutes.
- Remove from the pot some of the broth along with about a third of the vegetables. Purée the mixture in a blender, and return the purée to the pot, leaving the remaining vegetables intact.
- Grate raw potato into the broth, and cook the broth for an additional 5 minutes.
- Purée leftover cooked vegetables, and add them to the soup pot.
- If you end up with a lot of thin broth, add tiny raw pasta to the pot and cook the soup for an additional 8 minutes. Or remove some of the broth, use it as the liquid to cook rice or bulgur, then add the cooked grain to the pot.
- If the soup can stand another ½ hour of cooking time, add lentils to the pot for extra protein as well as a thicker soup.
- Cornstarch will thicken a liquid without making it cloudy the way flour does. Mix 1 tablespoon of the starch with 2 tablespoons of cold water, and stir the mixture until it is smooth; add 2 tablespoons of the hot liquid, and stir the mixture again; then gradually add the whole mixture, stirring, to the liquid you

wish to thicken. Cook, stirring, for several minutes or until desired thickness is achieved.

- Other flours besides white flour can be used to thicken soups, among them rice, barley, and oat flour. For each 2 cups of hot liquid, mix 1 tablespoon of the flour first with 2 tablespoons cold water, then add some hot soup liquid, then add the mixture gradually to the pot. Cook the soup, stirring now and then, for 3 to 5 minutes so that the flour will not taste "raw."

For thicker salad dressings, sauces, or sandwich spreads, try the following:

- Use puréed low-fat cottage cheese or part-skim ricotta as the base or as part of the "liquid" ingredients.
- Whisk in 1 tablespoon or more of mashed potatoes.
- For a yogurt-based dressing, line a colander with several layers of cheesecloth or a thin (clean) kitchen towel, place the yogurt in the colander, and let the yogurt drain for an hour or longer before mixing it with the other ingredients.
- Add puréed cooked vegetables.
- If you are using an acidic ingredient in a flour-thickened sauce, you can expect the sauce to thin out somewhat. But contrary to what some cookbooks may tell you, it doesn't matter when you add the acid.

JUICING

There is an enormous difference in flavor between fresh lemon and lime juice and the bottled commercial juices. The fresh juice is vastly superior and worth going out of your way to use. However, some tricks can simplify your task.

- For more juice for your money, select citrus fruits with thin skins.
- You'll get more juice out of a lemon or lime if you roll it between your hands before cutting.
- When you need just a teaspoon or so of lemon or lime juice, you can avoid cutting open the fruit (which hastens its decay) and won't have to worry about pulp and seeds and cleaning several utensils if, after rolling the fruit between your hands to "loosen" up the juice, you use a fork to pierce a circle around the nipple end (opposite the stem end). Holding the pierced end downward, squeeze out the desired amount of juice through the holes, and refrigerate the fruit, unwrapped, until needed again.
- If a recipe calls for both juice and grated rind of a lemon, a lime, or an orange, be sure to grate the rind first before cutting into the fruit.
- Home-frozen juice is as good as fresh for virtually all cooking needs. When lemons or limes are inexpensive, buy a large quantity, squeeze them all (you might want to grate some of the rind first), and measure 1 or 2 tablespoons of the juice into the individual compartments of a plastic ice-cube tray. Freeze the juice, and, when solid, remove the cubes and place them in a labeled, tightly closed freezer container. The cubes melt quickly when you need them. For ¼ cup of juice, use 4 tablespoons worth of cubes.

- For most recipes, reconstituted frozen orange juice concentrate is an acceptable substitute for freshly squeezed orange juice.

GELLING AND UNMOLDING

Gelatin is an especially useful substance for the health-conscious cook. It can be used to thicken many low-fat versions of richer foods, such as pies and puddings and even salad dressings. It is especially handy for advance preparation of foods like molded salads, appetizers, and desserts. Although some people have a prejudice against gelatin-based foods (perhaps because "slimy" jelled desserts were repeatedly foisted upon them in childhood), I have discovered that it is a prejudice easily overcome when the food is interestingly prepared. Some cooks, too, have a prejudice against jelled dishes because they fear either that the gelatin won't set (or will set too firmly) or that the dish won't unmold neatly. But through trial and error and advice from experienced cooks, I have found that these concerns can quickly be put to rest. Here's what I've learned about successful use of gelatin.

AMOUNTS. One tablespoon of gelatin (one packet of commercial unflavored gelatin, such as Knox) will gel approximately 2 cups of liquid. If there are a lot of solids in the dish you are preparing (as in a salmon mousse), the recipe is likely to call for an additional packet (or tablespoon) of gelatin.

DISSOLVING. Gelatin cannot set unless it has first been dissolved. Start by sprinkling unflavored gelatin over cold water in a small saucepan. Let the mixture stand for 1 to 2 minutes to soften the granules. Then, stirring the mixture constantly, warm the gelatin over low heat until the granules are completely dissolved (you should not be able to see them), about 3 minutes. Remove the gelatin from the heat.

SUBSTITUTING LIQUIDS. You can "enrich" your dish or enhance its flavor by substituting a variety of juices for water: any canned fruit or vegetable juice; the liquid from canned fruits and vegetables; fresh orange, grapefruit, or tomato (but not fresh pineapple) juice. Milk or yogurt can also be used in place of some or all of the water (except for the water needed to dissolve the gelatin). You can make a quick protein-rich dessert with packaged flavored gelatin by replacing 1 cup of the water with 1 cup of plain low-fat yogurt.

SETTING. Certain fruits and fruit juices contain an enzyme that breaks down the gelatin protein and keeps it from setting. These should *not* be used in gelatin-based dishes: *fresh or frozen* pineapple, mangoes, papayas, and figs. However, canned or poached fresh versions of these foods are okay, since the heat destroys the enzyme in question. If a solid food is to be added to a gelatin mixture, let the mixture partially harden first or the food will sink to the bottom. If you are adding canned fruits or vegetables, be sure to drain them well first. Gelatin-based dishes should be chilled to set properly, although they will usually harden eventually at room temperature. To speed up the process of setting, prepare the gelatin mixture with an iced liquid, and chill the mold in the freezer before you add the gelatin mixture. If you are planning to add solids to the mixture, it can be partially frozen by placing it in the freezer, so long as you check on it often and stir it occasionally to prevent it from setting too firmly.

WHIPPING. Gelatin mixtures can be fluffed if the partially set, chilled mixture is beaten with an electric mixer or eggbeater. Return the whipped mixture to the refrigerator so that it may set firmly.

MOLDING. Thin metal molds—shallow ones or, if deep, those shaped like a tube—are most successful for making attractive and easily removed gelatin dishes. Flexible plastic molds also work. A glass or ceramic bowl can be used in a pinch, especially if you will be serving from the bowl rather than trying to unmold the food first. Some cooks prefer to use individual molds; these can be purchased in ½-cup and 1-cup sizes. Whatever you choose, you will have an easier time unmolding if, before you pour in your gelatin mixture, you rinse the mold in cold water and coat it thinly with vegetable-oil spray or salad oil.

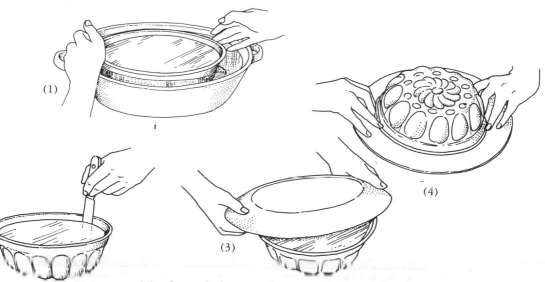

UNMOLDING. The first rule is not to leave unmolding to the last minute, especially if you're serving it to company. Before you try to unmold, make sure the gelatin is completely set. Fill a bowl larger than the diameter of the mold (you may have to use your sink for this) with *hot* but *not boiling* water. Set the mold in the water to a point just below the rim, and hold the mold there for 10 seconds—no longer—wiggling it slightly from side to side to loosen it. Remove the mold from the water, and run a knife around its edge if the gelatin is not already loosened. Set the serving platter upside down over the mold, and, holding the platter and mold together with both hands, invert them quickly. You may have to shake the mold a little or tap it gently with the handle of a knife to free the gelatin. If the food still remains stuck, turn the mold upright (keeping the platter in place), and repeat the water bath for 5 seconds or so. If the gelatin should get too soft and start to melt before you unmold it, set the mold in the freezer for 5 minutes and then try the unmolding process again, leaving the mold in the hot water for just 5 seconds this time.

ADVANCE PREPARATION

The secret of setting a "good table"—be it for family or friends—is organization, which means planning ahead. Even if you have but half an hour to get a meal on the table, you can make it a good one, prepared from scratch, if you get most of the ingredients ready ahead of time. While it is true that cutting up vegetables in advance sacrifices some nutrients, it is also true that you will still end up ahead nutritionally if you make your own instead of relying on prepackaged and take-out meals (talk about cutting up foods ahead of time!).

I first learned the tricks of getting ingredients ready to cook when I studied Chinese cooking with Norman Weinstein (The Hot Wok, in Brooklyn, New York). Norman would not let his students turn on the stove until everything was cut or mixed and lined up in the order they would be used. The technique took all the confusion out of Chinese cooking, which can have a dozen different major ingredients in one dish. The value of advance preparation was further driven home to me while testing the recipes for this book. Most of my tasting parties involved 10 or more different dishes. To have had to make them all within hours of the party would have required a team of cooks and at least two full kitchens. Having neither at my disposal, I learned to "make ahead" (and throughout the recipe section, where the opportunity for advance preparation is not already obvious, I indicate up to what point a dish can be prepared long before eating time).

Many dishes can be fully prepared in advance, to be reheated at serving time. Some—like most soups and stews—even improve when allowed to sit for a day or two. Others, including most casseroles and soups, can be frozen weeks in advance. And for still others, all the ingredients can be prepared, Chinese style, for quick, last-minute cooking. Here are some handy tips I use all the time.

- Always read the recipe *all the way through* before you start it—even before you decide to prepare it. I have yet to live down the results of failing to do this early in my marriage. We were having a dinner party one evening, and at 5 P.M. I got to the step in the recipe that said "Let stand overnight." Not entirely in jest, my husband suggested we call our guests and ask them to come tomorrow night instead.
- Make sure you have all the ingredients on hand in adequate amounts before you start to cook, so you won't have to make a last-minute dash to the market.
- If you are preparing several recipes that use some of the same ingredients, you'll save time and effort in preparation and cleanup if you add up the amounts of repeated ingredients from all the recipes and prepare all you need at one time. For example, if one recipe calls for ¼ cup of minced parsley and another specifies ½ cup, cut up ¾ cup to start with. Other often-repeated ingredients to be on the alert for include lemon juice, grated Parmesan,

chopped onions, chicken broth, bread crumbs, freshly ground black pepper, and minced scallions.

- All ingredients that require cutting, slicing, mincing, and so forth that will not be spoiled by prolonged exposure to air can be prepared hours—sometimes days—before cooking time. Those foods, like apples and pears, that darken after cutting can usually be kept fresh-looking by tossing the cut pieces with a little bit of lemon juice and water. Potatoes can be sliced, diced, or grated into cold water to prevent darkening and wilting, then thoroughly drained before use.
- Be sure to wrap all cut-up foods as airtight as possible, or enclose them in covered refrigerator dishes, and keep them chilled.
- Store cut-up odoriferous foods, like onions and garlic, in glass containers (plastic picks up odors) covered with plastic wrap. An alternative is always to use the same plastic containers for these ingredients.
- If you are setting up more than one recipe in advance, label your prepared ingredients in such a way that you can tell immediately which ingredient goes with which recipe. Or enclose all the individually wrapped ingredients for a particular recipe in one large bag. I find this trick especially helpful when I'm planning to make a soup, stew, or stir-fry. I simply whip out the bag for 10-vegetable soup, and I'm ready to go.
- Most sauces, liquid ingredients, and salad dressings can be mixed in advance— often days ahead—and refrigerated in labeled containers (old screw-top jars are useful here).
- Pancakes and muffins can be prepared quickly for a work-day breakfast if the night before you mix all the wet ingredients in one bowl (and refrigerate it) and the dry ingredients in another. In the morning, combine the two, and cook. Cake batter can also be set up this way; just be sure to bake the cake shortly after combining the wet and dry ingredients so that the leavening doesn't lose its punch.
- Most sandwiches can be made the night before and refrigerated. If the filling is moist, coat the bread with a thin layer of butter, margarine, or mustard. Or place limp pieces of lettuce between the filling and bread on both sides (crisp lettuce is best inserted just before eating the sandwich, since it will otherwise give off its moisture to the bread). If the filling is firm, such as cheese or sliced turkey, place it next to the bread and put the lettuce and mayonnaise in the middle.
- Although considered sacrilegious by purists, pasta *can* be cooked in advance, if that will simplify your last-minute preparations. There are just a few provisos: undercook it slightly, and rinse it immediately in cold water; then cover it with cold water (to prevent it from getting stuck in a congealed mass), and refrigerate it. Just before serving time, drain the pasta, and immerse it in boiling water for 1 to 2 minutes until it is heated through.
- Potatoes, both baked and mashed, can also be prepared ahead. If you do not have a microwave oven, which greatly simplifies the reheating procedure, moisten the baked potatoes and place them in a moderate oven for about 15 minutes. Mashed potatoes can be reheated in the top of a double boiler; grease the pan first, or coat the bottom of the pan with milk.
- Steamer pots and racks are excellent for reheating foods that you want to keep moist, such as cooked grains or stuffed pasta. If the pieces are large enough not

to fall through the holes of the rack, you can set the food directly on the rack (grease it first if the food is likely to stick). Or place the food in a shallow heat-proof bowl or platter, and set the dish on the steamer rack over an inch of water. Cover the pot, and steam the food over moderate heat until the food is heated through.

- Nearly all breads and sweet breads, muffins, and most cookies can be made in advance and frozen. You can also freeze the layers of a cake, to be frosted once they are defrosted. Just be sure to wrap all baked goods airtight. You can even slice bread before freezing it, if you wrap it well. At serving time, you can make a homemade bread taste freshly baked if you sprinkle it lightly with water, wrap it in foil, then heat it in a moderate oven for about 20 minutes.
- Freeze leftover soups, stews, casseroles, and so forth in individual serving containers for an instant meal or brown-bag lunch.
- You can get salad ingredients ready in advance if you enclose the rinsed and dried greens in plastic bags, separated from the other ingredients. However, mushrooms and avocados are best sliced at the last minute. At serving time, just toss it all in a bowl, dress and toss the salad, or serve the dressing on the side.

CLEANUP

All your time-saving cooking steps will be for naught if you are then faced with an hour-long job of cleaning up the kitchen. Here are some handy shortcuts:

- Wash utensils—and especially knives—(and dishes, if possible) as you go. Also wipe up counter tops and any spills on the stove or floor. When the utensil you need is dirty in the sink, you'll waste time and become distracted if you have to stop your recipe in the middle to wash the utensil. Also, utensils are likely to be harder to clean if they are allowed to dry with food residue on them.
- Add cold water immediately to pans, dishes, and utensils that were exposed to raw eggs, hot milk, and cooked cereal or other sticky starches.
- Reusable containers that held milk or juice should be rinsed as soon as they are emptied. If they get smelly, refresh them by soaking them in a mixture of water and 1 tablespoon of baking soda.
- Keep a toothbrush by the sink for cleaning graters, strainers, eggbeaters, and other utensils with hard-to-clean nooks and crannies that tend to collect food scraps.
- To reduce odors and stains on counter tops, coat the cutting surface with vegetable-oil spray before cutting up onions or garlic or handling berries.
- Any acidic substance can counteract fishy odors: lemon juice, vinegar, beer, wine. Use it in cooking fish and in cleaning up afterward.
- Simplify cleanup of vegetable scraps by peeling and trimming vegetables over a paper towel or sheet of newspaper.
- Always use glass or stainless-steel bowls and containers for preparing foods that leave odors behind, like onions, scallions, and garlic.
- To get rid of pungent odors on your cutting board, wash the board with a paste of baking soda or rub a wedge of lemon or lime over the area.
- For most recipes that use the food processor to prepare a succession of ingredients, you need not wash the machine between steps. But be sure to clean it thoroughly with soapy water after you're done.

- When washing a doughy counter, sprinkle salt on your cloth or sponge first to keep the dough from sticking to it.
- When barbecuing or broiling, the grate or tray will be easier to clean if you oil it or spray it with vegetable spray before cooking. Similarly, oil or spray the pan before scalding milk or cooking hot cereal.

STORAGE

- Make sure your refrigerator and freezer are at the proper temperature: 40 degrees Fahrenheit or less for the refrigerator; 0 degrees or less for the freezer.
- After opening, refrigerate wheat germ, pure maple syrup, vegetable shortening, salad dressing, jams and jellies, and shelled nuts.
- In warm weather (unless your kitchen is air-conditioned), consider storing whole-grain flours, crackers, and breads in the refrigerator or freezer, unless you can use them quickly. Refrigeration tends to dry out breads, so they are best kept in the freezer (you can slice them first), unless they will be eaten within 3 or 4 days.
- Honey keeps best in a warm, dark place. Do not refrigerate it.
- Uncooked bulgur, which is parboiled, does not require refrigeration even during the dog days of summer. Neither does white rice. And I personally have had no trouble leaving brown rice unrefrigerated.
- If you buy tofu (bean curd) in bulk or after you open a sealed packet, store it under cold water in the refrigerator and replace the water at least every other day to keep it fresh. Water chestnuts, bamboo shoots, or bean sprouts will also stay fresh longer if stored in a container other than its original one and under water that is replaced often.
- When you buy additional basic ingredients, such as canned broth or tomatoes, rotate the older containers to the front of your cupboard or refrigerator and be sure to use them first. Or date them with a marking pen or pencil when you buy them, and use the oldest ones first.
- Prevent contamination of food in containers: always use a clean utensil to scoop out mayonnaise, peanut butter, tomato paste, and so forth, and never eat directly from the main container (except for one taste with a clean utensil).
- To reduce contact with air (which may cause the food to deteriorate more quickly), store foods and leftovers in the smallest possible containers. This will also give you more room in the refrigerator.
- Always label and date stored leftovers. Throw out any food that looks or smells questionable or any leftover that has been in the refrigerator for more than a week (unless it is well preserved).

MISCELLANEOUS TIPS

Here are some more handy hints for efficient, healthful cooking.

- When you have to divide a chunk of food into numerous equal-size pieces, such as the ground-meat mixture for making meatballs or the dough for making rolls or refrigerator cookies, form the chunk into a square or rectangle or cylinder on a sheet of wax paper and cut it into the desired number of pieces. For example, if you have dough for a dozen rolls, shape it into a 12-inch-long cylinder and slice off 1-inch-wide circles.

- When rolling out pastry dough on or between sheets of wax paper, you can keep the paper from slipping if you first dampen the counter.
- Dried fruits and nuts will be less likely to sink to the bottom of a cake batter if they are sprinkled with flour before being added to the batter.
- If a recipe calls for both oil and honey or molasses, measure the oil first, then use the same cup for the sweetener, which will slide out easily.
- Save the ends and old pieces of bread for crumbs. Let them dry thoroughly in the open air, then reduce them to crumbs in a food processor or in batches in the blender. Or crush them by enclosing them in a heavy paper bag and pounding them with a mallet.
- You can use milk that's gone sour or cottage cheese or yogurt that's gotten old to make delicious pancakes and muffins. Just add ½ teaspoon of baking soda to the recipe to counteract the acidity.
- Old wine that's begun to sour can be used to make wine vinegar. Depending on whether the wine is white or red, add 2 tablespoons of red or white wine vinegar for each cup of wine. Let the mixture stand uncovered for 2 days at room temperature.
- To keep the bottom of a cake from sticking to the plate or doily, sprinkle the plate or doily first with confectioners' sugar.
- When a pan must be oiled and floured (especially a muffin pan), use a small fine strainer or sifter to sprinkle the flour (just lightly tap the side of the strainer). It reduces waste and mess, and gives the pan an even light coating.
- If the flour you buy is marked "presifted," there's no need to sift it again. But when measuring a cupful, use a scant cup.
- Eggs are easier to separate when they are cold. But egg whites are easier to whip when they are at room temperature.
- Beat egg whites in a *clean* glass, copper, or stainless-steel bowl, not in plastic or aluminum. Any residue of grease will inhibit foaming.
- If a recipe calls for both an egg white and a whole egg, separate the white first. In case you drop the yolk, you'll have another chance with the second egg.
- To cover a cake or pie with plastic wrap without harming the surface, stick several toothpicks in the top of the cake or pie and lay the plastic across them lightly.
- To open a vacuum-packed jar that's giving you trouble, press down on the lid as you try to turn it; this will help to release the vacuum. Other time-honored tricks include letting hot water run over the cover (the metal will expand more than the glass) or tapping the lid gently with the handle of a knife (this is risky, however, since the cap might bend, making the jar even harder to open).
- Store cut-up fruits in glass, ceramic, or plastic containers, not metal ones, to prevent discoloration.

FOR FURTHER READING

There are a number of very useful books of cooking hints that you may want to consult for additional tips. One in particular—*The Cook Book Decoder*—is especially useful for cooks who want to understand the "whys" behind many cookbook instructions and to gain an insight into the chemistry of food preparation. It is also fun to read, and you needn't have a degree in chemistry to understand it.

Arkin, Frieda. *The Cook's Companion.* New York: Doubleday, 1968.

————. *Kitchen Wisdom: A Compendium of Food and Cooking Lore.* New York: Holt, Rinehart and Winston, 1977. This paperback volume, done as a special edition for Consumers Union, is partly derived from *The Cook's Companion.*

————. *More Kitchen Wisdom.* New York: Consumers Union, 1982. This paperback volume is partly derived from *The Cook's Companion.*

Bloch, Barbara. *If It Doesn't Pan Out: How to Cope with Cooking Disasters.* New York: W. W. Norton, 1981.

Grosser, Arthur E. *The Cook Book Decoder, or Culinary Alchemy Explained.* New York and Toronto: Beaufort Books, 1981. Also available in paperback.

Hillman, Howard. *Kitchen Science: A Compendium of Essential Information for Every Cook.* Boston: Houghton Mifflin, 1981.

McGee, Harold. *On Food and Cooking: The Science and Lore of the Kitchen.* New York: Charles Scribner's Sons, 1984. This is a 600-page volume filled with everything you could ever want to know about foods and drinks, from history to cooking techniques.

Pierot, Suzanne Warner. *Suzanne's Cooking Secrets.* New York: W. W. Norton, 1981.

19 ·
YIELDS, EQUIVALENTS, AND MEASUREMENTS

One of the greatest frustrations involved in trying to prepare certain recipes is the inability to determine just how much of a particular ingredient you will need in order to end up with the amount specified. This is especially true for ingredients that are bought by the pound or bunch but are to be cut up and measured by the cup. Adding to this frustration is the fact that how small you cut your pieces, how tightly you pack them, or how moist they happen to be can influence the volume they take up. Even the weather can change the measurement for an ingredient that attracts moisture from the air.

The confusion is compounded by the fact that some recipes specify amounts in pounds of the whole food and others state measured quantities of the prepared food, as in "2 pounds potatoes, diced" or "2 cups diced potatoes." Such designations at least permit you to know precisely the right amount you should be cooking and are the kind of instructions I have tried to give throughout the recipe section (Part V) of this book. My biggest complaint, however, involves the nonspecific instruction, like "2 potatoes" or even "2 medium potatoes." What's medium to one person may be large or small to another, depending upon how well they like potatoes or the size potatoes they normally buy.

Since I have found wide variations in the estimated yields given in different cookbooks, in most cases I have started from scratch and devised my own. In this section, I have tried to give you a reasonable guide to yields and equivalents as I have measured them. Refer to it often, and, if in some cases you find you're consistently ending up with different amounts, change them in the book.

YIELDS AND EQUIVALENTS

BEANS AND PEAS, DRIED

Large beans (e.g., kidney)
1 pound = 2 cups uncooked
         = 5½ cups cooked
1 cup = 2 to 3 cups cooked

Small beans (e.g., navy)
1 pound = 2⅓ cups uncooked
         = 5½ cups cooked
1 cup = 2 to 3 cups cooked

Lentils
1 cup = 3 cups cooked

Split peas
1 pound = 2 cups uncooked
         = 5 cups cooked
1 cup = 2½ cups cooked

BREADS AND CRACKERS

Loaf
1 pound = 12 to 16 slices
1 slice fresh = ½ cup fresh crumbs
1 slice dried = ⅓ cup dry crumbs

Graham crackers
12 squares = 1 cup crumbs
1 packet = 1¼ cups crumbs

Saltine-type crackers
22 = 1 cup crumbs

CEREALS AND GRAINS

Barley
1 cup = 3½ cups cooked

Buckwheat groats (kasha)
1 cup = 2½ to 3 cups cooked

Bulgur (cracked wheat)
1 cup = 2½ to 3 cups cooked

Corn meal
1 cup = 4 cups cooked
1 pound = 3 to 3½ cups uncooked

Farina
½ cup = 2⅔ cups cooked

Millet
1 cup raw = 3½ cups cooked

Oats (regular or quick)
1 pound rolled oats = 5 cups uncooked
1 cup = 1¾ cups cooked

Pasta
1 pound macaroni = 5 cups uncooked
= 8 to 10 cups cooked
2 ounces spaghetti = 1 cup cooked
1 cup small pasta = 1¾ cups cooked
1 cup noodles = 1¾ cups cooked

Rice (long-grain), white or brown
1 pound = 2½ cups uncooked
1 cup raw = 3 cups cooked

Wheat berries
1 cup = 2⅔ cups cooked

Wild rice
1 cup raw = 4 cups cooked

CHEESES

Cottage cheese
1 pound (16 ounces) = 2 cups

Ricotta
15 ounces = 2 cups

Grating cheese (e.g., Parmesan, Romano)
3 ounces = 1 cup grated

Hard cheese (e.g., Cheddar, Swiss, mozzarella)
4 ounces = 1 to 1⅓ cups shredded

EGGS

Yolk
1 large = 1 tablespoon

White
1 large = 2 tablespoons

FATS AND OILS

Butter or margarine
1 stick = ½ cup or 8 tablespoons
or 4 ounces
1 pound = 2 cups
1 pound whipped = 3 cups

Diet margarine
1 cup = ½ cup butter or stick margarine (in cooking)

Vegetable oil
16 ounces = 2 cups

Vegetable shortening
1 pound = 2⅓ cups

FLOURS

Rye (medium)
1 pound = 4½ cups

White, all-purpose
1 pound = 3½ cups unsifted
= 4 cups sifted
1 cup = ½ cup barley flour
= 1⅛ cups cake flour
= 1 cup corn meal
= ½ cup potato flour
= ⅞ cup rice flour
= 1½ cups rye flour
= 1½ cups oat flour
= ¾ cup gluten flour

Whole wheat
1 pound = 3⅓ to 3¾ cups

FRUITS

Apples
1 pound = 3 medium
         = 3 cups slices or diced pieces

Apricots
1 pound fresh = about 10 medium
              = 3 cups cooked
1 pound dried = 3 cups dry
              = 4½ cups cooked

Bananas
1 pound = 3 to 4 medium
        = 2 cups slices
        = 1½ cups mashed

Berries (blueberries, strawberries, etc.)
1 pint = 2 cups

Cherries
1 pound = 2 cups pitted

Coconut
3½ ounces flaked = 1⅓ cups

Cranberries
12 ounces = 3 cups raw

Currants (dried)
1 pound = 3 cups

Dates
1 pound = 2½ cups pitted

Grapefruit
1 pound = 2 cups sections (approximately)

Grapes
1 pound seedless = 2½ cups

Lemon
1 whole = 2 to 3 tablespoons juice
        = 2 teaspoons grated rind
1 dozen = about 2½ cups juice

Lime
1 whole = 1½ to 2 tablespoon juice
        = 1 to 1½ teaspoons grated rind

Oranges
1 medium = about 6 tablespoons juice
         = about 2 tablespoons grated rind

Peaches
1 pound = 4 to 6 peaches
        = 2 cups slices

Pears
1 pound = 3 to 5 pears
        = 2 cups slices

Pineapple
2 pounds fresh = 3 cups cubes

Plums
1 pound fresh = 2 cups cooked

Prunes (dried)
1 pound raw = 2¼ cups pitted

Raisins
1 pound = 2¾ to 3 cups

Rhubarb
1 pound fresh = 3½ cups cut raw
              = 2 cups cooked

MILK

Fresh milk (whole, low-fat, or skim)
1 quart = 4 cups

Dry milk powder
1 to 1⅓ cups = 1 quart milk reconstituted
¼ to ⅓ cup milk powder = 1 cup milk,
                        reconstituted

Evaporated milk
1 13-ounce can = nearly 1⅓ cups

NUTS

Almonds
1 cup = 6 ounces whole
      = 5⅓ ounces blanched
1 pound unshelled = 1 to 1½ cups shelled
1 pound shelled = 3¼ cups

Peanuts
1 pound unshelled = 2 cups shelled
1 pound shelled = 4 cups

Pecans
1 pound unshelled = 2¼ cups shelled
1 pound shelled = 3½ cups

Walnuts
1 pound unshelled = 2 cups shelled
1 pound shelled = 3½ cups

NOTE: For most nuts, 1 cup whole (about ¼ pound) approximately equals 1 cup chopped.

SWEETENERS

Granulated (white) sugar
1 pound = 2 cups (approximately)

Brown sugar (packed)
1 pound = 2¼ cups
1 cup = 1 cup granulated sugar plus
        ¼ cup molasses

Corn syrup
1½ cups = 1 cup granulated sugar

Powdered (confectioners') sugar
1 pound = 4½ cups unsifted
1¾ cups packed = 1 cup granulated

Honey
1 pound = 1⅓ cups
      = 1⅔ cups sugar

VEGETABLES

Asparagus
1 pound spears = 3½ to 4 cups cooked

Avocados
1 pound = 2½ cups cubes

Beans, green or wax
1 pound = 2½ to 3 cups cooked

Beets
1 pound = 2 cups cooked, diced or sliced

Broccoli
1 pound head = 2 cups cooked flowerets

Brussels sprouts
1 pound = 3 cups cooked

Cabbage
1 pound = 6 cups shredded (packed)
      = 2 to 3 cups cooked

Carrots
1 pound = 3 cups sliced
      = 2½ cups shredded

Cauliflower
1 pound = 1½ to 2 cups cooked

Celery
1¼ pound bunch = 3 cups raw diced
             = 2 cups cooked
2 medium stalks = 3 to 4 ounces
             = ¾ to 1 cup sliced

Corn
4 medium ears = 1 cup kernels
10 ounces frozen kernels = 2 cups

Eggplant
1 pound = 15 ⅓-inch slices
      = 4½ cups raw diced
      = 1¾ cups cooked diced
      = 3 cups raw chopped

Garlic
1 large head = 10 to 15 cloves
1 small clove = ½ teaspoon minced
           = ⅛ teaspoon garlic powder
1 medium clove = ¾ teaspoon minced
1 large clove = 1 teaspoon minced
1 tablespoon minced = 3 large cloves

Mushrooms
1 pound fresh = 5 to 6 cups sliced
6 ounces canned = 1 pound fresh
3 ounces dried = 1 pound fresh

Okra
1 pound fresh = 2¼ cups cooked

Onions
1 pound = 3 large
1 large onion = 1 cup diced or chopped
1 medium onion = ½ to ⅔ cup chopped
1 small onion = ¼ to ⅓ cup chopped

Parsnips
1 pound = 4 medium
      = 2½ cups cooked and diced

Peas
1 pound in pods = 1 cup shelled and cooked
10 ounces frozen = 2 cups

Potatoes
1 pound all-purpose = 3 medium
             = 3 cups sliced or diced
             = about 2 cups mashed

Rutabaga and turnips
1 pound = 2⅔ cups cooked, diced
      = 2 cups mashed

Scallions
One bunch (6 bulbs) = ¾ cup minced or
                sliced

Spinach and similar greens
1 pound fresh = 4 to 8 cups raw leaves
                 = 1½ to 2 cups cooked
10 ounces frozen = 1¼ cups cooked
                 = 1 cup well drained

Squash, summer (e.g., zucchini)
1 pound = 3 cups raw slices
           = 1½ cups cooked
           = 2½ cups shredded

Squash, winter (e.g. Hubbard)
1 pound = 1 cup cooked mashed

Tomatoes
1 pound fresh = 2 large or 4 small
                = 2 cups diced
1 pound seeded and chopped = 1½ cups pulp
16-ounce can, drained = 1¼ cups
28-ounce can, drained = 2 cups
35-ounce can, drained = 2½ cups

MISCELLANEOUS

Chocolate, baker's
1 square = 1 ounce
          = 3 to 4 tablespoons grated

Chocolate chips
6 ounces = 1 cup

Cocoa
8 ounces = 2 cups

Coffee
1 pound = 40 cups brewed (approximately)

Gelatin
1 packet unflavored (¼ ounce) = 1 tablespoon

Herbs
1 tablespoon fresh = ½ to 1 teaspoon dried

Horseradish
1 tablespoon freshly grated = 2 tablespoons
                                     bottled

Meat
1 pound boneless = 2 cups ground

Tea
1 pound leaves = 125 cups brewed

Yeast
1 packet dry active = 1 scant tablespoon

BASIC MEASUREMENTS

VOLUME MEASURES

Pinch = about $\frac{1}{16}$ teaspoon
Dash = 6 drops or about $\frac{1}{8}$ teaspoon
3 teaspoons = 1 tablespoon
2 tablespoons = $\frac{1}{8}$ cup or 1 fluid ounce
4 tablespoons = $\frac{1}{4}$ cup or 2 ounces
$5\frac{1}{3}$ tablespoons = $\frac{1}{3}$ cup
8 tablespoons = $\frac{1}{2}$ cup or 4 ounces
$10\frac{2}{3}$ tablespoons = $\frac{2}{3}$ cup
12 tablespoons = $\frac{3}{4}$ cup or 6 ounces
16 tablespoons = 1 cup or $\frac{1}{2}$ pint or 8 ounces
1 pint = 2 cups or 16 ounces
2 pints = 4 cups or 1 quart or 32 ounces
1 liter = 1 quart plus 3 ounces
1 jigger = $1\frac{1}{2}$ ounces

WEIGHTS

2 ounces = $\frac{1}{8}$ pound
4 ounces = $\frac{1}{4}$ pound
8 ounces = $\frac{1}{2}$ pound
16 ounces = 1 pound

CAPACITIES

Rectangular cake pans
$8 \times 8 \times 2$ inches = 6 cups
$9 \times 9 \times 1\frac{1}{2}$ inches = 8 cups
$9 \times 9 \times 2$ inches = 10 cups

Round cake pans
$8 \times 1\frac{1}{2}$ inches = 4 cups
$9 \times 1\frac{1}{2}$ inches = 6 cups

Pie plates
$8 \times 1\frac{1}{4}$ inches = 3 level cups
$9 \times 1\frac{1}{2}$ inches = 4 level cups

Loaf pans
$8\frac{1}{2} \times 4\frac{1}{2} \times 2\frac{1}{2}$ inches = 6 cups
$9 \times 5 \times 3$ inches = 8 cups

V. Recipes I Have Known and Loved

Introduction

Developing and choosing the recipes to be included in this book was one of the greatest challenges I have faced as a health writer. My standards are high: food must be good for you, *and* it must taste good—not just okay, but really good. The most nutritious recipe is for naught if no one likes it. Healthful eating should be a pleasure, not a punishment, and it should leave the diner feeling satisfied, not deprived. Food also must look good, smell good, and be relatively easy to prepare—in many cases well in advance of serving time. With time-pressured, two-career families now the national norm, few people can or would want to spend hours in the kitchen each day to put food on the table.

To be sure, there have been many cookbooks written to cater to one or another of these demands. There are save-your-heart cookbooks, prevent-cancer cookbooks, live-longer cookbooks, cook-ahead cookbooks, salt- and/or sugar-free cookbooks, low-fat cookbooks, high-fiber cookbooks, natural-foods cookbooks, vegetarian cookbooks, vegetable cookbooks, and, of course, a seemingly endless stream of diet cookbooks. And some of these books are fine works for what they purport to do.

So why another one? Because to my mind none of the existing cookbooks adequately meets *all* the criteria I outlined above. Many are filled with nutritious recipes that require a lot of getting used to before you could say you "like" them—if, indeed, you ever would like them. Some books satisfy one need—for example, less sugar—but still use too much fat and salt. Some claim to use no sugar or salt, but instead the recipes are riddled with honey and soy sauce. Others emphasize replacing animal fats with vegetable fats but don't do enough to reduce *total* fat. And nearly all (except the vegetarian books) preserve the traditional American meal plan: a hunk of animal protein surrounded by a vegetable and a small dab of a starchy food. To me, this approach to eating is self-defeating and restricting. It dooms the health- and weight-watcher to small, unsatisfying portions of often tasteless meats. My approach is to use meat and other animal proteins as condiments—the complements to protein in starches and vegetables, which together represent the bulk of the meal. And in meals that contain no animal flesh, high-protein plant foods (i.e., dried peas and beans), dairy products, and eggs complement the starches and vegetables, which usually remain the most prominent ingredients.

I have been gathering recipes, both wholesome and "sinfully delicious," for twenty-two years, ever since I first had regular access to a stove and no one to cook for me. Many of the recipes included herein are old favorites that through the years I modified as my nutrition consciousness was raised, all the while preserving the essence of good eating—a pleasing flavor, texture, and appearance. Some recipes were contributed by friends who appreciate the fact that good health is important to the continuing ability to enjoy good food. But most of the recipes are newly developed or were discovered in the course of perusing hundreds of cookbooks and cooking magazines, as well as other periodicals that print food articles and recipes. I mixed and matched thousands of recipes until I came up with ones that met my criteria for healthful, enjoyable eating. If a recipe was closely derived from one that was published elsewhere, I have identified the source (when I knew it) and, in many cases, noted how I changed the original. This should help you to realize that you can use traditional sources for new recipes and make modifications to conform to a more wholesome diet without sacrificing food quality (see pp. 262–264).

I have personally tested all the recipes in this book, and most of them have been taste-tested by friends as well as family. People of all ages and tastes and from all parts of the country participated in my taste tests. Most recipes passed with flying colors. Those that did not were either modified and retested or scrapped. Many of the recipes were further tested by Lori Longbotham, a professional cook, as well as by friends.

A Special Plea: Write to Me

If in cooking any of the recipes you encounter difficulty or think of ways to improve them, I'd like to hear from you. I'd also love to receive your favorite health-promoting recipe(s) for testing and possible inclusion—with due credit, of course—in future editions of *Jane Brody's Good Food Book.* You can write to me c/o W. W. Norton & Company, Inc., 500 Fifth Avenue, New York, New York 10110.

You should know at the outset that I am not a professional cook. Although I briefly studied Chinese cooking, I have never taken a course in basic cooking principles and techniques. Nor did I learn much at my mother's elbow, although she was a good down-home cook, she died before I took an interest in food preparation. What I now know I have learned through reading and watching, but mostly through trial and error. To help you avoid the mistakes I made, I offer cooking tips to streamline your kitchen time and effort (see pp. 252–273 as well as the preparation tips that accompany most recipes). But I must confess that I enjoy cooking. I find it relaxing, creative, and emotionally satisfying to put a meal on the table that gives people pleasure. I also enjoy eating. It has always been—and I hope always will be—one of the great joys of my life. The recipes I have chosen and the preparation tips I offer will, I hope, make cooking and eating as pleasurable for you as it is for me.

There are several characteristics of the recipes that warrant some explanation.

FATS. In all of these recipes, I use as little fat as I deem possible to prepare the dish and to create something that tastes good. If your cookware has nonstick surfaces, you may find that in some cases you can get away with even less fat than is specified. If your cookware is not nonstick or well seasoned, however, you may need to increase the fat or cover the pan for a few minutes (so that the food steams a bit) to allow the food to cook without sticking or burning. You'll notice that in recipes that call for a hard fat, I suggest using either butter or margarine. This is a switch from my earlier view that margarine should always replace butter in a healthy diet. That was before I realized how little butter one needs to use to make a good-tasting recipe. When the amount is as low as that called for in the recipes in this book, it matters little from a health perspective whether you use butter or margarine. Although some scientists believe margarine contains substances that increase the risk of cancer and other diseases, the evidence for this is, in my view, skimpy and not sufficiently sound scientifically to warrant avoiding this fat. However, to me, margarine never tasted as good as butter, and it certainly doesn't cook as well as butter. I cook with the recently introduced butter-margarine blends (usually 60 percent vegetable oil, 40 percent butter), which taste and cook more like butter but are much lower in saturated fats and cholesterol than "the real thing." When just a coating of fat is needed, I often use one of the new butter-flavored vegetable-oil sprays (for example, Mazola No Stick and Pam). If you are on a strict low-cholesterol diet, by all means substitute margarine or even a polyunsaturated vegetable oil, which would be preferable to butter or a butter blend from a cholesterol perspective. But whatever fat you choose, the point is to keep the amount as low as possible.

SALT. This is not a no-salt cookbook, although for anyone already on a no-added-salt diet, the recipes are adequately seasoned to make salt superfluous. And for anyone interested in eliminating added salt, these recipes will help you take a giant step in that direction. Start with the amount of salt recommended (which is always considerably less than you'd find in a traditional recipe), and then gradually reduce how much you add each time you prepare the dish. In all but the few recipes in which salt is used to extract water from a vegetable prior to cooking, salt is listed as an optional ingredient. And when a recipe contains more salt than would be considered desirable on a low-salt diet, I note that fact in the introduction that precedes the ingredients list. Don't be fooled by sea salt; it's just as salty and no more nourishing than any other kind of salt. And keep in mind that many condiments that don't say "salt" are nonetheless loaded with it, including soy sauce, tamari, hydrolyzed vegetable protein, pickled vegetables, cured meats and fish, baking soda and baking powder, bouillon cubes, powdered seasoning mixes, and canned broths.

SWEETENERS. This is also not a no-sugar cookbook, although again, as with salt, the recipes contain far less sweetener than usual. Bear in mind that it doesn't matter to your body whether the sweetening comes from honey, brown sugar, raw sugar, or ordinary white table sugar. Sugar is sugar. The only real difference between the various sugars is the consistency and flavor. (Only dark molasses has a significant amount of nutrients, and only fructose seems to be handled by the body differently, which could make it preferable to white sugar for people with diabetes, for example.) By all means, use honey instead of white sugar if you like it better (just reduce the liquid in the recipe a bit to compensate), but don't kid yourself into thinking you're improving your nutrition by doing so. I do not, however, recommend the use of artificial sweeteners. These are all of questionable safety and of even more questionable benefit. In general, they perpetuate your sweet tooth, instead of teaching you to enjoy foods that are not so sweet. Some, like saccharin, stimulate your appetite, and so may be counter-productive if you're concerned about caloric intake. None has been demonstrated in proper scientific studies to help people lose weight or even to help those with diabetes control their disease.

ARTIFICIAL INGREDIENTS AND ERSATZ FOODS. With so many good-tasting and good-for-you real foods available, I see no point in substituting simulated ingredients, like fake cream, imitation meats, fat-modified cheeses, seasonings with potassium chloride in place of salt, artificial sweeteners, and so forth. Of course, if you must avoid all egg yolks, you can replace the eggs called for in most of my recipes with no-yolk egg substitutes. And if you are a semivegetarian who refrains from all red meat, you can use soy-based meat analogues instead (just be aware that most are very high in salt). And if you keep a kosher home, you can use nondairy creamer instead of milk in your coffee or tea (but bear in mind that most of these creamers are made from corn syrup and highly saturated vegetable fats—milk is decidedly better for you). But for the average person, I see no reason to replace the real thing with some laboratory-made ingredient.

"NO-NOS." I am not a fanatic about diet. I believe that the average person can continue to eat every food he or she loves, even those that are not particularly wholesome, as long as the unwholesome foods are eaten infrequently or in very small quantities. Thus, you will find some recipes that contain sausage or smoked meats, and even more that have cheeses. These ingredients are used primarily as flavoring agents and as complements to vegetable protein rather than as the main focus of the meal. You'll also find a number of sweet desserts, but in virtually all the sugar content is much reduced from what would be used in an ordinary recipe.

NUTRITION AND CALORIE INFORMATION. I purposely *did not* provide a nutrition analysis for my recipes. After reading thousands of recipes for which these analyses have been done, I realized that many were inaccurate and impossible to use in a meaningful way. All are based on old U.S. Department of Agriculture data, which are now being revised and extended. These analyses rarely take into account such factors as removal of skin or draining of fat prior to food consumption. And they cannot accommodate flexibility in recipes, such as the use of "4 to 5 cups of flour" or of "skim or low-fat milk." The analyses are also incomplete. Important health-related details are missing. For example, they do not show the ratio of saturated to unsaturated fats. Fiber content is either incomplete or totally inaccurate because there is no currently available accurate analysis of dietary fiber in all plant foods. Nor is there information on the sugar, as opposed to the starch, content of foods; instead, both are lumped together as "carbohydrates" as if starch and sugar were of equal value to your body. Furthermore, for some of the reasons outlined above and the fact that few people weigh and measure servings, the caloric values given in recipes with nutrition information are often highly misleading. Besides, you should not have to "count calories" per se to eat nutritiously and to achieve and maintain a normal body weight. Rather, you should know where high-calorie ingredients lurk and learn to avoid those foods or consume them in reduced amounts. For the most part, the recipes in this book limit the use of high-calorie ingredients, so if you eat normal-sized portions of the foods, you should not have to be concerned about their precise caloric contribution. In my view, people should be eating food, not numbers, and if they find that the amount of food they are eating is making them fat, they should eat less of it or increase their daily exercise.

Now, let's get to the heart of the matter: cooking and enjoying good, wholesome food.

DRINK TO YOUR HEALTH

Liquid refreshments can contribute to good nutrition. Party time need not mean straight alcohol, with or without a sugary mixer, or a high-calorie, cholesterol-rich drink like eggnog. Here are some fruit-based drinks my guests rave about.

MULLED CIDER *(Nonalcoholic)*

16 ½-cup servings

More and more people are steering clear of alcohol these days. This is a winter party drink that even the kids can enjoy.

    2 quarts apple cider or juice
    1 orange, sliced
    1 lemon, sliced
    4 sticks cinnamon
    6 whole cloves
    ¼ teaspoon nutmeg
    ¼ teaspoon powdered ginger

In a large saucepan combine all the ingredients, bring the mixture to a boil, reduce the heat to low, and simmer the cider for 30 to 40 minutes. Strain the cider, and serve hot.

CRANBERRY-WINE PUNCH   *about 30 servings*

Preparation tip: This punch can be served at any time of the year if you have the foresight and space to freeze a few bags of cranberries when they're in season. Or you can prepare the cranberry juice through step 2 and freeze it for later use. Note that the recipe calls for 1 *pound* of cranberries (the usual bag contains 12 ounces). If you use 12 ounces instead of a pound, reduce the sugar to 1½ cups.

    1 pound cranberries
    1 quart boiling water
    2 cups sugar
    1 bottle (fifth) dry red wine, chilled
    1 6-ounce can frozen orange-juice concentrate,
      defrosted
    ⅓ cup lemon juice
    Block of ice
    1 28-ounce bottle seltzer or club soda, chilled

1. In a medium saucepan, cook the cranberries in the boiling water until the berries pop. Strain the liquid through a fine sieve (a strainer lined with cheesecloth will catch the seeds), pressing on the pulp.
2. Return the juice to the saucepan, add the sugar, and stir the mixture over low heat until the sugar dissolves. Chill the cranberry juice.
3. At serving time, combine the cranberry juice with the wine, orange-juice concentrate, and lemon juice in a punch bowl. Add a block of ice and the seltzer, and stir the punch.

MANGO COCKTAIL *(Nonalcoholic)*   *8 servings*

Here's a refreshing treat for your "nondrinking" guests (or for you, if you want to keep your serving wits about you) that you can offer when others are drinking fruity cocktails like daiquiris. If you have any leftover, try blending it with buttermilk or yogurt for a summer's day breakfast or pick-me-up.

    2 cups ripe mango (fresh or canned), cut up
    2 cups orange juice
    ¼ cup sugar, or less if mango is canned
    ¼ cup fresh lemon or lime juice
    2 cups cold water

Combine all the ingredients in a blender, and blend the mixture at high speed for about 1 minute. Pour the liquid through a coarse strainer into a serving pitcher. Serve the cocktails over ice.

MANGO DAIQUIRI

4 ½-cup servings

The sweet but low-calorie mango (the best ones come from Mexico) makes an excellent daiquiri with a true tropical-fruit flavor.

  2 cups crushed ice
  1 large mango, peeled and cut from pit (about 1
    cup pulp)
  ½ cup light rum
  ⅓ cup fresh lime juice
  2 tablespoons sugar
  Lime slices for garnish (optional)

In a blender, combine the ice, mango pulp, rum, lime juice, and sugar. Blend the mixture for 2 minutes at medium speed. Serve the drinks immediately, garnished with lime slices, if desired.

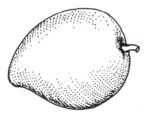

STRAWBERRY DAIQUIRI

4 servings

As delicious as it is beautiful, this simply prepared drink starts with frozen fruit, eliminating the need for crushed ice. If your freezer freezes very hard, remove the berries about 5 minutes beforehand or plan to mix the drink in a food processor.

  6 ounces light rum
  ⅓ cup fresh lime juice
  ¼ cup sugar
  4 cups frozen whole strawberries
  Lime slices for garnish (optional)

1. In a blender or food processor, combine the rum, lime juice, and sugar, and blend the mixture until the sugar has dissolved.
2. Add the strawberries, and blend the mixture at high speed until it is smooth. Serve the drinks garnished with lime slices, if desired.

HORS D'OEUVRES AND APPETIZERS

Traditionally, perhaps because they are eaten in relatively small quantities, hors d'oeuvres and appetizers are loaded with fat, calories, and salt: cheese and crackers, pâtés, miniquiches, pigs-in-blankets, and the like. What a way to start a meal! Or, if the party is strictly for cocktails, what a way to keep guests from overimbibing (the rich and salty nibbles only encourage excessive drinking). At dozens of gatherings, I've discovered that hors d'oeuvres need not undermine the principles of sound nutrition while upholding high culinary standards of good taste and attractive presentation. The following offerings have been favorites among partygoers across the country. Many make fine take-along dishes if you're an invited guest, and virtually all can be prepared in advance, with perhaps only last-minute heating in the oven required.

THE VEGETABLE PLATTER

Nothing has pleased my palate and my eye more nor has done more to improve the nutritional value of the American cocktail party than the advent of hors d'oeuvre vegetable platters, known in sophisticated culinary circles as crudités. Crunchy raw and tender-crisp cooked cold vegetables are a low-calorie, high-nutrient way to curb your hunger and calm your nerves at such affairs. Besides, they're delicious. Unfortunately, the dips usually served with such platters add too many nonnourishing fat calories. But this need not be the case. Or, if a high-fat ingredient is used, it can be a nutritious one, like a nut or seed butter. But first, the vegetable platter. Here are some possibilities to consider. Be sure to include a variety of colors and shapes to maximize the platter's appeal.

Asparagus, steamed tender-crisp
Beet slices, cooked
Belgian endive leaves
Broccoli, raw or blanched
Brussels sprouts (tiny), steamed or boiled tender-crisp

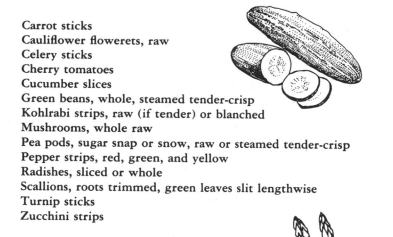

Carrot sticks
Cauliflower flowerets, raw
Celery sticks
Cherry tomatoes
Cucumber slices
Green beans, whole, steamed tender-crisp
Kohlrabi strips, raw (if tender) or blanched
Mushrooms, whole raw
Pea pods, sugar snap or snow, raw or steamed tender-crisp
Pepper strips, red, green, and yellow
Radishes, sliced or whole
Scallions, roots trimmed, green leaves slit lengthwise
Turnip sticks
Zucchini strips

TORTILLA CHIPS FOR DIPS

80 chips (from a package of 10 tortillas)

You need not rely on fatty fried and/or overly salted commercial tortilla chips. It's a snap to make your own low-fat, no-salt-added chips that enhance, not disguise, the flavor of a delicious dip. *Preparation tip:* Don't go too far from the stove while the chips are in the oven, lest they become overbaked.

  1 package flour or corn tortillas
  2 tablespoons oil

1. With a pastry brush, paint a very light coating of oil on one side of each tortilla. Stack the tortillas greased side up in an even pile. With a sharp, heavy knife (or serrated knife) cut the stack in half, then into quarters, then into eighths.
2. Separate the pieces, and arrange them greased side up on lightly oiled baking sheets. Toast the chips in a preheated 350° oven for about 10 minutes or until they are crisp and just beginning to brown lightly.

CHILIED BEAN DIP

1 ⅓ cups

This dip is very good, very easy, and very low in calories because it contains no added fat. *Preparation tip:* The hotness of the dip is readily adjusted by varying the amounts of hot peppers (or omitting them entirely) and chili powder. Hot or mild chili powder can be used. For a chunkier dip, mash the beans with a fork, leaving small pieces, and stir in the remaining ingredients.

 1 16-ounce can kidney or pinto beans, drained
   and rinsed
 2 or more tablespoons finely chopped canned or
   fresh green chilies or jalapeño peppers, to
   taste (optional)
 1 tablespoon vinegar
 1 teaspoon chili powder, or to taste
 ⅛ teaspoon cumin
 2 teaspoons minced onion
 2 teaspoons minced fresh parsley

1. Place in the jar of a blender the beans, peppers (if used), vinegar, chili powder, and cumin. Blend the ingredients until they are smooth. Transfer the mixture to a bowl.
2. Stir in the onion and parsley, and serve.

HUMMUS *(Chickpea-Tahini Spread)*

3 cups

If I had to choose between hummus and baba ghanoush (see p. 293) as my favorite food from the Mideast, it would be a standoff. Hummus is higher in calories but, when eaten on pita, provides complete protein. In Middle Eastern restaurants, I often make a meal of the two with a garden salad. My own hummus recipe is more complicated to prepare than the usual versions, but it is worth the extra effort. *Preparation tip:* Hummus can be made hours ahead. If tahini is unavailable, you can make it in a blender by combining 1 teaspoon of lemon juice, ½ teaspoon of oil, 2 tablespoons of water, and ¼ cup of finely ground (in a blender or mortar with pestle) sesame seeds.

 1 large onion, minced
 1 to 2 cloves minced garlic, to taste
 1 tablespoon vegetable oil
 2 cups cooked chickpeas (garbanzos), drained
   and rinsed if canned
 ½ cup fresh lemon juice
 1 tablespoon reduced-sodium soy sauce

Salt, if desired, to taste
¼ cup tahini (sesame paste)
½ cup sesame seeds, toasted (see p. 296) and
   ground

1. Sauté the onion and garlic in the oil until the vegetables are soft. Set the mixture aside.
2. In a blender or food processor, purée the chickpeas with the onion and garlic, lemon juice, soy sauce, salt, tahini, and sesame seeds. Serve the hummus with pita, fresh or toasted, and/or as a dip for fresh vegetables.

BABA GHANOUSH *(Eggplant-Tahini Spread)* — *about 2½ cups*

This eggplant appetizer is too wonderful to miss unless you are on a very strict low-fat diet. *Preparation tip:* This can be made hours ahead. See the preparation tip for hummus on page 292 for directions on making your own tahini if this ingredient is not available.

2 pounds eggplant (2 medium or 1 large),
   whole and unpeeled
¼ cup tahini (sesame paste)
¼ cup fresh lemon juice
1 large clove garlic, crushed
¼ cup finely minced onion
Salt, if desired, to taste
Freshly ground black pepper, to taste
1 tablespoon oil, preferably olive (optional)
2 tablespoons minced fresh parsley

1. Prick the eggplant in several places with a fork, place it on a baking sheet, and broil it in a preheated broiler for about 20 minutes, turning the vegetable several times so that the skin chars on all sides. Let the eggplant cool.
2. When the eggplant is cool enough to handle, cut it in half, scrape out the flesh into a bowl, discard the skin, and mash the eggplant with the tahini, lemon juice, garlic, onion, salt, and pepper. Cover the mixture, and refrigerate it.
3. Before serving, sprinkle the spread with oil, if desired, and minced parsley, and serve it with pita, fresh or toasted, or as a dip for fresh vegetables.

SARDINE SPREAD

about 2 cups

A simple-to-prepare, high-calcium spread that is low in fat and as good as a sandwich spread as it is on no-salt crackers or vegetables for an hors d'oeuvre. *Preparation tip:* Those on strict low-sodium diets should be sure to use low-sodium sardines, no-salt mustard, and low-sodium or imported Swiss cheese.

> 2 3¾-ounce cans sardines, preferably
>   low-sodium and water-packed, drained
> 1 cup finely shredded Monterey Jack or Swiss
>   cheese (about 3 ounces)
> ½ cup sliced scallions, with some tops
> 2 tablespoons Dijon mustard
> 2 teaspoons grated lemon rind
> 2 tablespoons lemon juice
> 1 to 2 tablespoons minced parsley for garnish

1. Mash the sardines—skin, bones, and all—in a bowl with a fork.
2. Mix in the cheese, scallions, mustard, lemon rind, and lemon juice. Garnish the spread with parsley, and serve it with crackers, bread, or vegetables such as celery stalks or wedges of green or red sweet pepper.

GUACAMOLE (*Avocado Spread*)

about 1¼ cups

Because avocadoes are rich in fat (the fat is an unsaturated vegetable oil), no other fat needs to be added to create a luscious dip or appetizer. *Preparation tip:* If you wish to prepare this in advance, bear in mind that avocado darkens upon exposure to air. The lemon juice retards this process, as does leaving the pit in the mixture until serving time.

> 1 large ripe avocado
> 1½ tablespoons fresh lemon or lime juice
> ¼ cup minced onion
> 1 tablespoon finely diced green chilies
> 1 small tomato, seeded and finely chopped
> 1 clove garlic, finely minced
> ¼ teaspoon salt, if desired

1. Skin the avocado, and remove the flesh from the pit. Place the flesh in a medium bowl, add the lemon or lime juice, and mash the avocado with a fork.
2. Stir in the onion, chilies, tomato, garlic, and salt. Chill the guacamole before serving, if prepared ahead, but serve it at room temperature.

INDIAN PEANUT DIP

1 cup

This dip, devised for a peanut promotion campaign, got raves from my tasters. It is a firm dip best suited for crisp vegetables.

½ cup smooth peanut butter (preferably natural)
¼ cup minced onion
¼ cup fresh lemon juice
1 tablespoon soy sauce (preferably reduced-sodium)
2 teaspoons minced garlic (2 large cloves)
1 teaspoon ground coriander
¼ cup minced fresh parsley

In a blender or food processor, combine all the ingredients and blend them for about 1 minute or until they are well mixed. Serve the dip at room temperature.

SALSA DIP

about 1¾ cups

Salsa, the Spanish word for "salad," can be used as a dip for some vegetables and for homemade tortilla chips (see p. 291) if the ingredients are finely chopped. This version is loaded with flavor and nutrients but very low in fat and calories (about 7½ per tablespoon) and practically free of sodium.

2 medium tomatoes, finely chopped
½ cup chopped scallions
2 tablespoons very finely chopped hot pepper (either canned or fresh green chilies or jalapeño pepper)
1 tablespoon red wine vinegar
1 tablespoon oil

Combine all the ingredients in a small bowl, and chill the dip for 30 minutes or longer before serving.

CURRIED YOGURT DIP

1 cup

By combining yogurt with sour cream, this simple dip retains the creamy consistency but not the fat content of sour cream–based dips.

⅔ cup plain low-fat yogurt
⅓ cup sour cream
1 tablespoon curry powder, or to taste
1 teaspoon lemon juice
½ teaspoon salt, if desired
⅛ teaspoon white or black pepper, or to taste

In a bowl, combine all the ingredients, stirring them well. Chill the dip, covered, for 1 hour or longer before serving.

BROCCOLI CHINOISE

about 4 cups

This dish could be used as an hors d'oeuvre or salad. It received top billing at one of my tasting parties. *Preparation tip:* Do not use the health-food variety of sesame oil; its flavor is quite different from that of Oriental sesame oil.

1 large bunch broccoli (about 3 stalks)
1 tablespoon sesame seeds

DRESSING
2 tablespoons Oriental sesame oil
¼ cup rice vinegar or white wine vinegar
1 tablespoon imported soy sauce (preferably reduced-sodium)
½ teaspoon sugar
Freshly ground black pepper to taste
Red pepper flakes to taste

1. Cut the flowerets off the broccoli stalks, cut the stems on a slant into slices about ⅜ inch thick, and cut the flowerets into bite-sized pieces. Place the broccoli on a steamer rack, and steam the vegetable until it is tender-crisp, about 5 to 7 minutes. Cool the broccoli immediately under cold running water.
2. In a heavy skillet over medium heat, toast the sesame seeds until they are golden, shaking pan to avoid burning the seeds. Remove the seeds from the pan, and, when they are cool, sprinkle them over the broccoli.
3. Combine the dressing ingredients, and pour the dressing over the broccoli, tossing to mix the salad well.

SCALLOP CEVICHE

6 first-course servings

Ceviche is an appetizer of fish "cured" in lime juice. Few would guess that in most ceviches the fish is not cooked (at least, not by heat): the lime juice gives the fish a milky-white cooked appearance and breaks up the fibers so that the fish "feels" cooked when you chew it. This is a tasty and colorful appetizer. See also the Squid Salad on page 408, which can be served as a first course as well as a salad meal. *Preparation tip:* You can also use an unroasted pepper or a roasted pepper that comes in a jar. Serve the ceviche on a crisp lettuce leaf with a slice of lime.

   1 pound bay scallops
 ⅓ cup fresh lime juice
   1 large red or green sweet pepper, roasted,
     peeled, seeded, and diced
 ½ cup red sweet onion, coarsely chopped
   1 tablespoon finely chopped green chilies, fresh
     or canned, seeded
 ¼ cup finely minced fresh parsley
   1 tablespoon olive oil
 ¼ teaspoon salt, or to taste, if desired
 ⅛ teaspoon freshly ground pepper, or more,
     to taste
   2 teaspoons tequila (optional)

1. In a medium bowl, combine the scallops and lime juice. Cover the bowl, and refrigerate the scallops for 4 hours or longer.
2. Remove the scallops from the refrigerator, pour off the marinade, and discard it. Add the sweet pepper, onion, chilies, and parsley to the scallops.
3. In a small bowl, combine the oil, salt, pepper, and tequila. Pour this over the scallop mixture, and combine the two. Chill the ceviche before serving.

CHICKEN TIDBITS

about 40 pieces

This was declared a winner by every one of twenty-five tasters. The cook loved it, too, because it was so easy to prepare and looked so good when served. The sodium content is moderate if reduced-sodium soy sauce is used. *Preparation tip:* Prepare this dish several hours ahead (even the day before), and refrigerate it, covered with plastic wrap, until serving time.

    2 large whole chicken breasts, skinned and
      boned
    ¼ cup imported soy sauce (preferably
      reduced-sodium)
    2 tablespoons rice vinegar
    2 teaspoons sugar
    6 scallions with tops, chopped
    1 6½-ounce jar roasted red peppers, drained and
      coarsely chopped

1. Trim all the fat from the chicken. If necessary, flatten the breasts with a mallet or by slicing them so that they are about ½ inch thick.
2. In a medium bowl, combine the soy sauce, vinegar, and sugar, and add the chicken. Marinate the chicken for 1 hour or longer in the refrigerator.
3. Remove the chicken from the marinade, and place it on a heat-proof platter. Set the platter in a pan on a flat steamer rack over about 1 inch of boiling water.
3. Cover the chicken with the scallions and peppers.
4. Cover the pan, and steam the chicken for about 5 minutes, or until the chicken is firm. When the chicken is cool, cover it with plastic wrap and chill it until serving time, for at least 2 hours. Before serving, cut it into bite-sized pieces without disturbing the vegetable topping.

STUFFED CUCUMBERS

6 servings

This recipe is compliments of a Minneapolis friend, Karen Knudsen. It is a refreshing hors d'oeuvre on a hot summer day.

    4 cucumbers, chilled and peeled
    ½ cup crumbled feta cheese
    1 tablespoon mayonnaise
    2 drops Worcestershire sauce
    1 tablespoon minced parsley

1. Cut the cucumbers in half lengthwise, and with a teaspoon scrape out the centers containing the seeds.
2. In a small bowl, blend the feta, mayonnaise, and Worcestershire sauce into a smooth mixture.
3. Fill the centers of cucumbers with the cheese mixture. Sprinkle the cucumbers with parsley, and chill them. Before serving, slice the cucumbers crosswise into bite-sized pieces.

HONEYDEW-SHRIMP APPETIZER

4 servings

Reading the ingredients of this recipe may cause you to wonder: Has she lost her head? But it's delicious and refreshing. It is also simple to prepare and elegant to serve.

1 small honeydew melon
16 medium shrimp, boiled, shelled, and cooled
1½ tablespoons fresh lemon juice

DRESSING
½ cup part-skim ricotta or low-fat cottage cheese
6 tablespoons buttermilk (approximately)
Salt, if desired, to taste
Freshly ground black pepper to taste
1 teaspoon lemon juice or vinegar
2½ tablespoons snipped fresh dill

1. Make melon balls, or cut the melon into small cubes. Combine the melon with the shrimp and 1½ tablespoons lemon juice.
2. In a blender, whip the cheese with a few tablespoons of the buttermilk, gradually adding more buttermilk until the mixture achieves the consistency of heavy cream. Transfer the mixture to a small bowl, and add the salt and pepper, 1 teaspoon of lemon juice or vinegar, and the dill.
3. Pour the dressing over the melon and shrimp. Toss the ingredients, and chill the mixture for 1 hour before serving. To serve, arrange the honeydew-shrimp mixture on a crisp lettuce leaf (red leaf lettuce is especially attractive).

COCKTAIL KNISHES

about 80 hors d'oeuvres

A beloved relic from my Russian-Jewish childhood, knishes will always be dear to my heart and taste buds, and I will always be willing to put up with the bother of making them. They can be made large as a side dish or small as an hors d'oeuvre. I offer two fillings—potato and kasha or bulgur—but you might like to experiment with some of your own. *Preparation tip:* These can be made in large quantities in advance through step 6 and frozen until baking time.

POTATO FILLING
1½ cups cooked mashed potatoes
   (can use leftovers)
½ cup finely chopped onion,
   sautéed in 1 teaspoon oil
2 tablespoons matzo meal or
   bread crumbs
2 tablespoons melted butter or
   margarine or vegetable oil
1 egg, beaten
¼ teaspoon salt, if desired
⅛ teaspoon freshly ground black
   pepper

KASHA OR BULGUR FILLING
½ cup finely chopped onion,
   sautéed in 1 teaspoon oil
½ cup medium-granulation kasha
   or medium-grain bulgur,
   uncooked
1 cup boiling water or broth
¼ teaspoon salt, if desired
⅛ teaspoon freshly ground black
   pepper
1 egg, beaten

DOUGH
3 cups all-purpose flour, plus additional flour for
   kneading
1 teaspoon baking powder
½ teaspoon salt, if desired
1 cup water
1 egg
1 tablespoon vegetable oil

1. Prepare the potato filling by combining the mashed potatoes, sautéed onion, matzo meal or bread crumbs, melted butter or margarine or oil, beaten egg, salt, and pepper. Set the filling aside.
2. Prepare the kasha or bulgur filling by adding to the sautéed onion the uncooked kasha or bulgur, boiling water or broth, salt, and pepper in a medium saucepan. Cover the pan, and cook the kasha or bulgur for 10 to 15 minutes or until the liquid is absorbed. Stir in the egg. Set the filling aside.
3. Prepare the dough by combining the flour, baking powder, and salt in a medium bowl. In a separate bowl, combine the water, egg, and oil, and add this mixture to the flour mixture, stirring, the ingredients until they are well combined. Turn the dough out onto a floured surface, and knead the dough

until it is smooth and elastic, about 5 minutes, adding only enough flour to keep the dough from sticking to the surface. Cover the dough with an inverted bowl and let it rest for 5 minutes. Cut the dough in half, and on a lightly floured surface roll each half into a rectangle about 20 × 10 inches. Slice the rectangle in half lengthwise. You will end up with four strips, each 20 × 5 inches.

4. Using half the potato filling, align the mixture in a strip along the 20-inch side of the dough. Roll the dough up toward the other 20-inch side. With a very sharp knife, slice the roll into 1-inch pieces. Repeat with the remaining potato mixture on another dough strip.
5. Using the same technique as described in step 4, fill the remaining two strips of dough with the kasha or bulgur filling.
6. Place the pieces about ½ inch apart, seam side down, on greased cookie sheets.
7. Bake the knishes in a preheated 375° oven for 25 to 30 minutes or until the crust is lightly browned.

OYSTER-STUFFED SHELLS *about 48 hors d'oeuvres*

This simple, low-calorie, tasty recipe comes compliments of the Pasta Information Bureau, an industry organization. Each hors d'oeuvre has only about 15 calories. *Preparation tip:* Be sure to start with unbroken shells, and cook them gently. (You'll have your best luck with shells that are packaged in a box rather than a bag.) I prefer to make a whole pound of pasta, using only the best shells for this dish and saving the partly broken ones for another use.

1 pound large pasta shells, cooked *al dente* (add
   1 tablespoon oil to the cooking water)
2 teaspoons chopped fresh dill
2 teaspoons fresh lemon juice
1 teaspoon mild Dijon mustard
2 cans small smoked oysters, drained and patted
   dry
Fresh dill for garnish (optional)

1. Drain the cooked shells, rinse them with cold water, and drain them again. Separate the whole shells from the rest, and place the whole shells on a platter to keep them from sticking together.
2. In a small bowl combine the dill, lemon juice, and mustard, and add the oysters. Toss the ingredients together gently to coat the oysters well.
3. Place 1 oyster in each shell, and arrange the filled shells on a serving platter. Garnish the dish with additional dill, if desired. Serve the shells at room temperature.

SHRIMP-STUFFED SHELLS   *about 3 dozen hors d'oeuvres*

These are excellent cocktail snacks—tasty "finger food" at only about 10 calories each. *Preparation tip:* I make them with garlic chives because I have an abundance of them in my yard, but ordinary fresh chives will do (you can always add to the recipe a small clove of crushed garlic, if you like). Stuffed shells may *look* fussy, but they are very simple to make; it takes only about 10 minutes to stuff more than 3 dozen shells. The job is easiest if you use a tiny spoon, such as one used for serving mustard.

  ½ **pound raw shrimp (frozen shrimp are**
     acceptable)
  ⅓ **cup plain low-fat yogurt**
  2 **teaspoons minced fresh chives or garlic chives**
  ½ **teaspoon salt, if desired**
Cayenne to taste
  4 **ounces large macaroni shells, cooked** *al dente*
Chopped parsley and red sweet pepper, slivered,
    for garnish (optional)

1. Cook the shrimp in a small amount of boiling water for 1 minute or until they turn pink and firm. Drain them, rinse them, and drain them again. (Remove the shells and devein the shrimp, if you use raw shrimp.) Chop the shrimp fine.
2. In a small bowl combine the chopped shrimp with the yogurt, chives, salt, and cayenne. Cover the mixture, and chill it for about 1 hour.
3. Using a small spoon, fill each shell with a small amount of the shrimp mixture. Arrange the shells on a platter. Garnish the platter, if desired, with the parsley and the pepper.

COLD SESAME NOODLES   *10 to 12 appetizer servings*

No doubt you think this recipe belongs among the pasta main dishes or side dishes. To my thinking, however, these tasty noodles should be limited to a small first course or buffet sampling, since they are high in fat and salt. I hadn't planned on including this recipe in the book, but popular demand from friends who have had the noodles at my parties changed my mind. I have adapted the traditional recipe to reduce the fat and salt, but there's a limit as to how far one can go and still have sesame noodles that taste like sesame noodles should. So, dine with discretion and enjoy. *Preparation tip:* Five-spice powder is sold in Oriental markets. If you cannot get it, omit it or grind together a pinch each of anise, cinnamon, cloves, fennel seeds, and Szechuan peppercorns. Chili oil is Oriental sesame oil cooked with hot red chili peppers (see p. 352).

1 pound thin noodles (vermicilli, fine linguine,
    spaghetti, or Chinese egg noodles)
1 tablespoon oil
8 to 10 cloves garlic, finely minced
2-inch piece fresh ginger, finely minced
5 tablespoons water
6 tablespoons sesame-seed paste (Oriental-type)
3 tablespoons thin soy sauce or reduced-sodium
    soy sauce
3 tablespoons brewed tea
2 tablespoons sesame oil (dark Oriental-type)
1 tablespoon sherry
1 tablespoon vinegar (black Chinese or wine)
1 tablespoon sugar
¼ teaspoon five-spice powder (available in
    Oriental markets)
Chili oil to taste
6 scallions, minced

1. Cook the noodles *al dente* in lots of boiling water to which 1 tablespoon oil has been added. Drain the noodles, rinse them under cold water, and drain them again. Transfer the noodles to a large serving platter or bowl.
2. In a mortar or small bowl, pulverize the garlic, ginger, and water with a pestle or the end of a knife handle.
3. In a medium bowl, mix well the sesame-seed paste, soy sauce, tea, sesame oil, sherry, vinegar, sugar, five-spice powder, and chili oil. Then add to it the garlic-ginger mixture and the minced scallions. Mix the sauce again.
4. To serve, combine the noodles and sauce and toss the two to mix well.

PITA MEAT PIES

64 hors d'oeuvres

To say these were a hit would be an understatement; they were devoured by old and young alike. I thank *Gourmet* magazine for the idea. *Preparation tip:* You can make the meat mixture in advance, but I would not recommend spreading it on the pitas until baking time lest the bread get soggy. The breads may seem soft when they emerge from the oven, but they crisp up after a few minutes. If desired, you could toast the breads under the broiler for a few minutes (taking care not to burn them) before spreading them with the meat mixture. These are especially good served with the Sesame-Parsley Sauce on page 645.

    ½ cup bulgur
    1 cup boiling water
    1 pound extra-lean ground beef
    1 cup peeled, seeded, finely chopped, drained
       tomatoes
    ½ cup finely minced onion
    ½ cup minced fresh parsley
    ⅓ cup minced green pepper
    3 tablespoons tomato paste
    3 tablespoons lemon juice
    3 small cloves garlic, minced
    4 teaspoons minced fresh mint *or* 1 teaspoon
       dried and crumbled mint
    ⅛ teaspoon cayenne, or to taste
    Salt, if desired, to taste
    Freshly ground black pepper to taste
    4 6-inch whole-wheat pitas, halved horizontally,
       or 8 whole breads

1. Soak the bulgur in boiling water for 30 minutes. Drain the bulgur, squeezing out the extra liquid.
2. In a medium bowl, blend thoroughly the bulgur, beef, tomatoes, onion, parsley, green pepper, tomato paste, lemon juice, garlic, mint, cayenne, salt, and black pepper.
3. Preheat the oven to 450°.
4. Place the pitas, cut sides up, on ungreased baking sheets. Divide the meat mixture among them, spreading it evenly. Bake the pitas for about 10 minutes or until the edges of the breads begin to brown.
5. Using a broad spatula, transfer the breads to a cutting board, and cut each pita into 8 wedges.

RATATOUILLE PITA PIZZA

24 wedges

Pizzas made on pitas are a household staple. We eat them for breakfast, lunch, and supper. So why not as an appetizer? The types are limited only by your imagination and what you might have in the house. In cleaning out my freezer, I discovered some containers of ratatouille I had made more than a year earlier. Here was the start of another pita pizza—this time served as an hors d'oeuvre. *Preparation tip:* The pizzas can be set up in advance on a cookie sheet and baked at party time.

4 ounces tomato sauce (optional)
6 sandwich-sized whole-wheat pitas
3 cups ratatouille (see the recipe on p. 520)
3 ounces part-skim mozzarella, shredded
3 tablespoons grated Parmesan or Romano

1. If your ratatouille is not especially moist or tomatoey, spread about 1 tablespoon of tomato sauce on one side of each pita.
2. Spread ½ cup of ratatouille on top of each pita.
3. Sprinkle the mozzarella and Parmesan or Romano over the ratatouille.
4. Bake the pita pizzas in a preheated 450° oven for about 10 minutes or until the filling is hot and the cheese fully melted. To serve, cut each pita into 4 wedges.

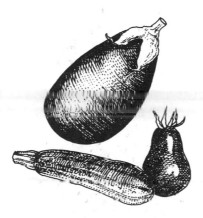

SPINACH AND CHEESE SQUARES   *about 54 squares*

No one would guess that these nibbles are nutritious—they taste too good. And they are easy to prepare. This is not a low-cholesterol recipe, but since only a small amount is likely to be consumed at any one time, it can be eaten by most people, even those on special diets. *Preparation tip:* The squares can be made ahead, refrigerated or frozen, and reheated at party time. In place of frozen spinach, you could use 12 ounces of fresh spinach, thoroughly washed, chopped, parboiled, and drained well.

  2 large eggs
  6 tablespoons whole-wheat flour
10 ounces frozen chopped spinach, defrosted and
    drained well (squeeze out extra liquid)
16 ounces (2 cups) low-fat cottage cheese
  6 ounces Cheddar, grated (2 cups)
¼ to ½ teaspoon freshly ground black pepper, to
    taste
⅛ teaspoon cayenne or to taste
Pinch nutmeg (optional)
  3 tablespoons wheat germ

1. In a large bowl, beat the eggs with the flour until the mixture is smooth.
2. Add the spinach, cottage cheese, Cheddar, pepper, cayenne, and nutmeg, and mix the ingredients well. Pour the mixture into a well-greased 13 × 9 × 2-inch baking pan.
3. Sprinkle the top with wheat germ, and bake the mixture in a preheated 350° oven for about 45 minutes. Let the spinach and cheese mixture stand for about 10 minutes, and then cut it into 1½-inch squares for serving.

BULGUR-STUFFED CHERRY TOMATOES

*about 3 dozen hors
d'oeuvres*

This was a hit at a large tasting party. Besides having a great flavor and combination of textures, it looks gorgeous. *Preparation tip:* The bulgur and tomatoes can be prepared separately well in advance (even the day before) and refrigerated. The tomatoes should be stuffed shortly before serving time. For the sake of efficiency, prepare the tomatoes and remaining ingredients while the bulgur soaks. If possible, select tomatoes that are at least 1 inch in diameter but not too large to be bite-sized hors d'oeuvres. The tomatoes are easy to pulp with the small end of a melon baller. The bulgur can also be stuffed into plum tomatoes, which have been halved lengthwise, pulp removed, and served as a first course.

¾ cup fine- or medium-grain bulgur, soaked in
   1½ cups boiling water for 45 minutes
2 pints cherry tomatoes
Salt, if desired
1 cup finely minced fresh parsley
½ cup finely chopped scallions
2 tablespoons minced fresh mint leaves, or
   more, to taste
¼ cup fresh lemon juice
2 tablespoons oil, preferably olive
¼ teaspoon freshly ground black pepper
⅛ teaspoon ground or crumbled orégano
⅛ teaspoon ground cumin
Sprigs of parsley for garnish (optional)

1. Pour the soaked bulgur into a cheesecloth or linen-type dishtowel, and squeeze it dry. Place the bulgur in a medium bowl, and set it aside.
2. Slice the tops off the tomatoes, and reserve them for decorating the platter, especially if they still have a cluster of leaves on them. Remove the pulp from the body of the tomatoes (use a melon baller, if available), and reserve it. Sprinkle the inside of the tomatoes with a little salt, if desired, and place the tomatoes cut side down on a platter lined with paper towels. Set the tomatoes aside to drain for about 30 minutes.
3. Separate the reserved tomato pulp from the seeds and juice, and chop the pulp, discarding the rest. Add the pulp to the soaked and dried bulgur along with the parsley, scallions, mint, lemon juice, oil, pepper, orégano, cumin, and additional salt, if desired.
4. Using a small spoon or a melon baller, stuff the drained tomatoes with the bulgur mixture. Decorate the platter with the reserved tomato tops and sprigs of parsley, if desired.

SOUPS

Soup Stocks

A rich, tasty stock or broth is the essence of a good soup. In addition, soup stocks in varying amounts (from a tablespoon to several cups) are often important ingredients in other recipes, including stir-fries, stews, fat-free "sautés," and salad dressings. Some commercial soup stocks (sold as broth or bouillon) are delicious, but nearly all are extremely salty. Although there are now no-salt-added broths available in some markets, they are very hard to find. Commercial broths also contain fat, although this can be removed before use if you chill it. Still, the best way to control salt and fat content—and to get that homemade flavor—is to make your own soup stocks. They are simple to prepare and can help you use up limp vegetables and leftovers that might otherwise go to waste. The following recipes, then, should not be considered ironclad. Many other ingredients and seasonings can be used. Your imagination is the limit.

Since stocks freeze very well (just be sure to leave room at the top of the container for expansion), they can be prepared whenever you happen to have the ingredients at hand. Or they can be made in large batches and frozen in meal-sized containers for future use. They can also be reduced—boiled down—for frozen storage and reconstituted with water when defrosted.

BEEF STOCK

about 8 cups

Beef bones used to be available for the asking from the butcher. But nowadays you may have to pay for them. This very rich stock is based on a recipe from Bert Greene's *Greene on Greens. Preparation tip:* Greene recommends roasting the bones first to give the stock a rich color; the lengthy simmering guarantees a rich flavor. However, you can make an acceptable beef stock just by dumping the bones in the water with all the remaining ingredients, but the pot should be allowed to simmer for at least 4 hours.

  4 pounds raw meaty beef and/or veal bones
  1 to 3 large onions, chopped
  2 to 4 carrots, coarsely chopped
  2 to 4 ribs celery with leaves, chopped
  2 cloves garlic
  4 to 6 parsley sprigs
  1 bay leaf
  4 whole cloves
10 peppercorns
Salt, if desired, to taste
3½ quarts (14 cups) cold water, divided
  2 tablespoons red wine vinegar (optional)

1. Roast the bones in a large pan in a hot oven (about 450°) for 30 minutes, turning them once.
2. Meanwhile, in a large, heavy stock pot, combine the onions, carrots, celery, garlic, parsley, bay leaf, cloves, peppercorns, salt, and all but 2 cups of the water. Bring the liquid to a boil, reduce the heat, and add the roasted bones.
3. Pour off the fat from the roasting pan, and add the remaining 2 cups of water to the pan, scraping the bottom and sides of the pan with a wooden spoon. Pour this liquid into the stock pot, and return the liquid to a boil. Reduce the heat, and let the stock simmer, partially covered, for 3 hours. Skim off froth as needed.
4. Stir in the vinegar, and continue simmering the stock, partially covered, for another 2 hours.
5. Pour the broth through a fine strainer or sieve.

CHICKEN STOCK

For easy identification, I keep a colored plastic bag in my freezer into which I put any and all chicken scraps: skin, fat, wing tips, giblets (except liver), bones, sinew, tail bone, and, if I'm lucky enough to get some, feet. Sometimes they are all I need to make a stock; other times I buy some chicken backs (at 9 cents a pound!) to add flesh to the pot. *Preparation tip:* The chicken scraps can be dumped frozen into the pot along with the remaining ingredients. Most cookbooks suggest enclosing the herbs in a cheesecloth bag (a tea strainer will also do), but since you are going to strain the broth in the end anyway, I don't see the need for this. Once the stock is prepared, I freeze it in several types of containers: ice-cube trays (for 1- and 2-tablespoon cubes), 1- and 2-cup plastic tubs, and 1-quart containers. I try to use containers that are wider at the top so I don't have to worry about defrosting the liquid before use.

2 pounds chicken scraps, including some bones
Cold water to cover (at least 2 quarts)
1 large onion, peeled and stuck with 3 or 4
  cloves
1 large clove garlic, peeled
1 or 2 ribs celery, halved crosswise, with leaves
  if available
1 or 2 carrots, cut into chunks
1 bay leaf
2 or more parsley sprigs *or* 1 tablespoon dried
  parsley flakes
1 teaspoon tarragon
½ teaspoon thyme
½ teaspoon dillweed
Salt, if desired, to taste
12 peppercorns *or* ¼ to ½ teaspoon freshly
  ground black pepper

1. Place all the ingredients in a large pot with a cover. Bring the liquid to a boil, reduce the heat, partially cover the pot, and simmer the stock for at least 1 hour. The longer the stock cooks, the richer it will become. But don't cook it until the broth evaporates.
2. Pour the stock through a fine strainer, sieve, or cheesecloth into a fat-separating measuring cup (see p. 237), bowl, or other suitable container. Press on the solids to extract as much liquid as possible.
3. If using the fat skimmer, decant the fat-free broth into containers for storage. Otherwise, refrigerate the broth until the fat hardens enough for easy removal. (Depending on the amount of gelatinous protein in the chicken scraps, the broth may gel at refrigerator temperatures.)

FISH STOCK

about 6 cups

You'll need the bones of a nonoily fish (any white fish) for this broth. The fish monger is usually more than willing to give them away. Or you can use the carcass of a white fish that you have filleted. Fish stock happens to be my favorite soup base because the flavor is so rich.

    2 pounds bones and trimmings (including heads
      but not viscera or gills) of any white fish
    1 cup sliced onion
    1 cup sliced celery
    1 bay leaf
    6 sprigs parsley
    ½ teaspoon thyme
    2 tablespoons lemon juice
    3 whole cloves
    ½ teaspoon salt, if desired
   10 peppercorns *or* ¼ teaspoon freshly ground
      black pepper
    6 cups cold water
    1 cup dry white wine

1. In a heavy saucepan, combine the bones, onion, celery, bay leaf, parsley, thyme, lemon juice, cloves, salt, and pepper. Cover the pan tightly, and let the ingredients steam in their own moisture over moderately low heat for 5 minutes.
2. Add the water and wine. Bring the stock to a boil, reduce the heat, skim off any froth, and simmer the stock for 20 minutes.
3. Pour the broth through a fine strainer, sieve, or cheesecloth, pressing all the liquid from the solids.

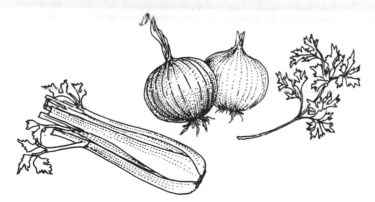

VEGETABLE STOCK

about 4 to 6 cups

Here's where you can clean out the refrigerator without wasting anything (as long as it's not rotten!). All kinds of raw and leftover cooked vegetables and vegetable peelings can go into a stock, as well as the liquid used for cooking vegetables. But if you want to follow a "standard" recipe, here's one.

    1 tablespoon butter or margarine
    ½ cup chopped onion
    ½ cup diced carrots
    ½ cup diced turnip
    ½ cup diced parsnip
    1 cup diced celery, plus some inner leaves
    1 cup shredded salad greens (optional)
    Vegetable scraps as available, such as tomato
        skins, potato peelings, mushroom bits (optional)
    3 sprigs parsley
    2 whole cloves
    1 bay leaf
    ½ teaspoon thyme
    ½ teaspoon salt, if desired, or to taste
    ⅛ teaspoon white pepper, or to taste
    Dash cayenne, or to taste
    Water and/or vegetable cooking liquid, to cover

1. In a large, heavy saucepan, melt the butter or margarine over moderate heat and cook the onions until they brown.
2. Add all the remaining ingredients to the pan, bring the stock to a boil, reduce the heat, and simmer the stock, partially covering the pan, for 30 minutes to 1½ hours (the longer, the better).
3. Strain the broth through a fine sieve, pressing the solids to extract the liquid.

First-Course Soups

Soup is a great way to start a meal—any meal. There's no limit to the variety. You can make a soup out of almost anything—even fruit. And when times are hard, people have been known to use virtually any edible in the soup kettle. Soups also are a boon to weight-watchers: they both speed the loss of unwanted pounds and help to assure that the pounds stay off (see p. 198). The best-tasting soups start with a base of broth or stock, usually chicken, beef, or vegetable, and sometimes fish. Usually I make my own. But if I use already-prepared broth from a can or, rarely, bouillon cubes or dehydrated granules dissolved in boiling water, I make adjustments for their high salt content: I use part broth and part water and/or I omit any additional salt.

The soups on the following pages merely scratch the surface of possibilities.

They have been selected because they are easy to prepare, nourishing, and, I and my family think, delicious. They are also low in fat. Virtually all of them can be frozen for later use with no discernible loss of flavor or texture. In general, first-course soups do not contain enough protein to be used as a main dish. However, those containing dried beans or peas, peanut butter, milk, or cheese make a reasonable protein contribution to a meal.

BLACK BEAN SOUP WITH CUMIN   *4 to 6 servings*

The cumin gives this black bean soup a distinctive and, my tasters said, appealing flavor. *Preparation tip:* For peak flavor, I use whole toasted cumin seed crushed in a mortar with a pestle. You may also use ground cumin. This soup freezes well (before the garnish is added). As with the Puréed Peanut Butter and Vegetable Soup (see the recipe on p. 319), this could also be used as the main dish of a light meal, perhaps topped with a generous dollop of plain low-fat yogurt.

1 cup black beans, soaked (see methods below)
7 cups broth (chicken, beef, or vegetable)
1 tablespoon vegetable oil
1 large onion, minced (1 cup)
1 large clove garlic, minced (1 teaspoon)
¼ cup diced celery
½ cup finely diced carrots
¾ teaspoon crushed cumin seed, or to taste
¼ teaspoon freshly ground black pepper
¼ teaspoon salt, if desired
1 chopped hard-boiled egg or egg white and
   chopped scallions for garnish

1. To soak the beans, place the washed beans in a bowl, cover them with cold water, and let them soak overnight or for at least 8 hours. *Or* place the washed beans in a saucepan, add 4 cups water, bring the beans to a boil, boil them for 2 minutes, turn off the heat, and let the beans stand for 1 hour.
2. Drain the soaked beans, add the broth, bring the beans to a boil, reduce the heat to low, and simmer the beans, partially covering the pan, for 2 to 3 hours or until the beans are thoroughly cooked.
3. In a heavy skillet, heat the oil, add the onion and garlic, and cook them, stirring, over a low heat, until they are transparent. Add the celery and carrots and cook the mixture, stirring, for a few minutes longer. Add the vegetables to the beans.
4. Season soup with cumin, pepper, and salt, if desired, and simmer the soup for another 30 minutes.
5. Purée the soup in a blender, food processor, or food mill. Serve the soup hot, garnished with chopped egg and minced scallions.

CURRIED CREAM OF BROCCOLI SOUP   *6 servings*

You needn't worry about the calories in creamed soups when the "cream" is actually milk (whole or low-fat). *Preparation tip:* This soup has enough flavor to permit omission of all added salt. It can be frozen before or after puréeing but preferably before the addition of the milk.

      1 tablespoon butter or margarine
      1 large onion, chopped (1 cup)
      2 cloves garlic, chopped (2 teaspoons)
      ¾ teaspoon curry powder, or more, to taste
 Freshly ground black pepper, if desired, to taste
 1⅔ cups chicken broth (canned or homemade)
      1 cup water
      1 bunch broccoli (about 1 pound), cut into
         flowerets, stems cut into ½-inch slices
      1 large potato, peeled and cut into ½-inch cubes
      1 cup milk (skim or low-fat)

1. In a large saucepan, melt the butter or margarine, and sauté the onion and garlic for a few minutes.
2. Add the curry, pepper, broth, and water to the pan, and bring the soup to a boil.
3. Add the broccoli and potato. When the mixture returns to a boil, reduce the heat, cover the pan, and simmer the soup for about 20 minutes or until the vegetables are tender.
4. Purée the soup in batches in a blender or food processor. Return the purée to the pan, stir in the milk, and cook the soup over low heat until it is hot (but do not boil it).

THREE "C" SOUP

(Cabbage, Carrots, and Caraway)

8 servings
(about 10 cups)

This soup is very flavorful even when it is made with only 1 teaspoon of salt (265 milligrams of sodium per serving). It is loaded with nutrients (including those in cancer-preventing cabbage and carrots) and is low in calories—about 100 per serving. My version is an adaptation of a recipe developed by the Division of Nutritional Sciences at Cornell University.

2 cups diced peeled potatoes
5 cups water
1 tablespoon vegetable oil
1 large onion, chopped (1 cup)
1½ teaspoons caraway seeds
1 teaspoon salt, if desired
¼ teaspoon AHA herb mix (see p. 182) or other
   no-salt seasoning (optional)
2 cups sliced carrots
½ cup diced celery (1 large stalk)
4 cups chopped cabbage (about 1 pound)
1 large beet, cooked (save the water),
   or 1 8-ounce can of beets, chopped
⅛ teaspoon freshly ground black pepper
½ teaspoon dillweed *or* 1 tablespoon fresh
   snipped dill
1 cup tomato purée

1. In a medium saucepan, cook the potatoes in the water until the potatoes are tender, about 10 to 15 minutes. Drain them, and *save the cooking water.*
2. In a large saucepan or Dutch oven, heat the oil, and sauté the onion until it is translucent.
3. Add the caraway seeds, salt, herb mix, carrots, celery, cabbage, and the water from the cooked potatoes. Bring the soup to a boil, reduce the heat, cover the pan, and cook the soup until the vegetables are tender, about 20 minutes.
4. Add the potatoes, beets, beet cooking liquid, pepper, dill, and tomato purée. Cover and simmer the soup for another 30 minutes.

PURÉE OF CARROT SOUP   *6 servings*

Lovely to look at, even lovelier to consume, this carrot soup has a richness all its own, without need of butter or cream.

    2 teaspoons vegetable oil
    1 pound carrots, sliced thin (about 3 cups)
    1 large onion, chopped (1 cup)
    ⅔ cup chopped celery
    1½ cups diced peeled potato
    1 clove garlic, minced (1 teaspoon)
    ½ teaspoon sugar
    4 whole cloves
Freshly ground black pepper to taste
    4 cups chicken broth

1. In a large saucepan, heat the oil, and add the carrots, onion, celery, potato, garlic, and sugar. Cover the pan, and cook the vegetables over low heat for about 10 minutes, stirring them occasionally.
2. Add the cloves, pepper, and broth, and bring the soup to a boil. Reduce the heat, and cook the soup, partially covering the pan, for about 20 minutes or until the vegetables are soft. *Remove and discard the cloves.*
3. Purée the soup in batches in a blender or food processor.

CREAM OF CAULIFLOWER SOUP   *4 to 6 servings*

Cauliflower has a subtle flavor that some find delightful. Here is a simple way to turn it into a tasty soup. *Preparation tip:* If desired, add a little curry in step 1. This soup can be served hot or chilled.

    1 large onion, chopped (1 cup)
    1 tablespoon butter or margarine
    4 cups broth (chicken or vegetable)
    1½-pound head of cauliflower, cut into flowerets
        (about 1 pound flowerets)
    1 carrot, peeled and diced
    1 cup low-fat milk (approximately)
Salt, if desired, to taste
    ¼ teaspoon nutmeg, preferably freshly grated
    ⅛ to ¼ teaspoon cayenne, if desired
Freshly ground black pepper to taste
Possible garnishes: sliced scallion tops, snipped
        chives or dill, hot paprika

1. In a medium saucepan or Dutch oven, sauté the onion in the butter or margarine for 3 minutes (if using curry, add 1 teaspoon or so at this point) or until it is soft but not browned.
2. Add the broth, cauliflower, and carrot. Bring the soup to a boil, reduce the heat, cover the pan, and simmer the soup for about 15 minutes or until the vegetables are soft. Remove the soup from the heat, and cool it down until it is warm.
3. Transfer the soup to a blender or food processor, add the milk, and purée the soup until it is smooth. (You may have to do this step in batches.)
4. Transfer the purée to a serving bowl or tureen, if it is to be eaten chilled, or pour it back into the pot for gentle reheating. If the soup is too thick, thin it with a little more milk. Add the seasonings. If the soup is to be eaten cold, chill it for at least 1 hour. Serve the soup garnished as desired.

GARLIC PIPERADE SOUP
4 servings

Here is a healthful treat from Marian Morash's *The Victory Garden Cookbook*. This soup has a mellow flavor despite the 20 cloves of garlic. *Preparation tip:* The thickness of the soup can be adjusted by adding more or less bread cubes. If the soup gets too thick, thin it with additional broth or water.

   20 garlic cloves
    2 cups sliced onions
    1 cup sliced green peppers
1½ tablespoons oil, preferably olive
    3 cups peeled, seeded, sliced ripe tomatoes (can use canned)
    2 cups beef broth
    3 to 4 slices crustless dark bread, cubed
Freshly ground black pepper to taste
Grated Parmesan for garnish (optional)

1. Blanch the garlic cloves in boiling water for 30 seconds, rinse them under cold water, drain them, and peel them. Slice the garlic thinly.
2. In a large saucepan, sauté the onions and peppers in the oil until they are soft and golden, about 8 to 10 minutes. Add the garlic and the tomatoes. Reduce the heat, cover the pan, and tightly simmer the vegetables for 30 minutes.
3. Pour in the broth, and heat the soup just to a boil. Add the bread cubes to thicken the soup to the desired consistency. Add pepper, and serve the soup with grated cheese, if desired.

HOT AND SOUR CHINESE SOUP   *2 to 4 servings*

This could be a main-course soup since it derives protein from the pork, bean curd, and egg and offers plenty to chew on. However, it is usually served as a first course, followed perhaps by a stir-fried dish with rice or noodles.

    3 cups chicken broth
    1 tablespoon reduced-sodium soy sauce
    4 dried Chinese mushrooms, soaked for 15
       minutes in boiling water, stems removed and
       caps cut into fine strips
    ½ cup bamboo shoots cut into 2-inch strips ¼
       inch wide
    ¼ pound raw lean pork, cut into narrow strips
    1 cake soybean curd (tofu), about 3 × 2 × 1
       inches, cut into 2-inch strips ¼ inch wide
    ¼ teaspoon white pepper
    2 tablespoons lemon juice
    2 tablespoons cornstarch mixed with 3
       tablespoons cold water
    1 egg, lightly beaten
    2 teaspoons Oriental sesame oil (*or* ¼ teaspoon
       hot chili oil or more to taste)
Finely chopped scallions for garnish

1. In a large saucepan, combine the broth, soy sauce, mushrooms, bamboo shoots, and pork. Bring the soup to a boil, reduce the heat, and simmer the soup for about 3 minutes.
2. Add the bean curd, pepper, and lemon juice. Bring the soup to a boil, and add the cornstarch mixture (stir the mixture again just before adding). Cook the soup, stirring, until it thickens slightly, and then pour in the egg very slowly, stirring the soup constantly.
3. Remove the soup from the heat, stir in the sesame oil *or* sprinkle with chili oil, and garnish with scallions.

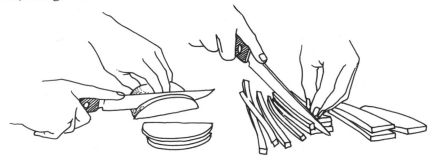

PURÉED PEANUT BUTTER AND VEGETABLE SOUP

4 to 6 servings

The unusual flavor of peanuts in soup has proved to be a winner among my tasters. Although this is a high-protein, high-nutrient soup, its richness suggests that it be served in small doses as a first course. Of course, it could be a fine light-meal main dish as well. *Preparation tip:* This soup can be prepared ahead and frozen, but purée it again before reheating.

    1 large onion, diced (1 cup)
    1 large clove garlic, minced (1 teaspoon)
    1 tablespoon vegetable oil (peanut, if available)
    1 stalk celery, diced
    2 carrots, diced
    2 cups peeled and diced potatoes
    2 leeks (white part only), washed well and diced
        (optional)
    4 cups chicken or vegetable broth
    ¼ teaspoon cayenne
    ¼ teaspoon freshly ground black pepper
    ¼ teaspoon salt, if desired, to taste
    ½ cup smooth peanut butter
Minced parsley and chopped scallions for garnish
        (optional)

1. In a large saucepan, sauté the onion and garlic in the oil, stirring, until the onions are transparent.
2. Add the celery, carrots, potatoes, leeks, and broth. Bring the soup to a boil, reduce the heat, cover the pan, and simmer the soup until the vegetables are tender, about 15 minutes.
3. Stir in the cayenne, black pepper, salt, and peanut butter. Transfer the soup to a blender and purée it.
4. Serve the soup hot, garnished, if desired, with parsley and scallions.

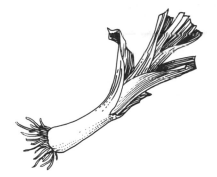

ALPINE POTATO-VEGETABLE SOUP   *6 servings*

This is a fall and winter favorite in our house, sufficiently peppery to get the blood circulating but not so seasoned that the taste of the individual vegetables is disguised. *Preparation tip:* I do not suggest freezing this, since the vegetables lose some of their texture.

    1 clove garlic, minced
    1 large onion, chopped (1 cup)
    1 tablespoon butter or margarine
    5 cups chicken broth (homemade, canned, or
        made from bouillon cubes)
    3 medium russet potatoes, peeled and cubed
    2 medium carrots, sliced
    2 medium celery stalks, sliced (reserve and slice
        the tops separately)
    1 zucchini, sliced
    1 tablespoon snipped fresh dill *or* 1 teaspoon
        dried dillweed
    2 or 3 sprigs fresh parsley, minced
    1 teaspoon salt, if desired (omit if using canned
        broth or bouillon cubes)
    ½ teaspoon freshly ground black pepper
    Thickener (optional): 1 tablespoon cornstarch
        dissolved in 3 tablespoons cold water

1. In a large saucepan, sauté the garlic and the onion in the butter or margarine until the onion is translucent.
2. Add the broth, potatoes, carrots, celery (without the tops), and zucchini to the pan.
3. Bring the soup to a boil, and simmer it for 15 to 20 minutes or until the potatoes are just tender.
4. Add the dill, parsley, salt, pepper, reserved sliced celery tops, and, if desired, the thickener, and simmer the soup until it is slightly thickened. Serve it immediately, with croutons, if desired.

POTATO AND TURNIP SOUP

6 servings

A simple, satisfying, low-fat soup. *Preparation tip:* It can be made ahead through step 2 and frozen. If you use salted chicken broth, no further salt should be needed. Although the addition of evaporated skim milk is optional, it does give the soup a richer consistency and flavor without many extra calories.

1 small onion, sliced thin (¼ cup)
2 small white turnips (about ⅓ pound), peeled
  and thinly sliced
1 pound potatoes (about 3 medium), peeled and
  thinly sliced
3 cups chicken broth (homemade, *or* 13½-ounce
  can of broth plus water to make 3 cups)
1 cup skim milk
Salt, if desired, to taste
Freshly ground black pepper to taste
2 to 4 tablespoons evaporated skim milk
  (optional)

1. In a large saucepan, combine the onion, turnips, potatoes, and broth. Bring the soup to a boil, reduce the heat, partially cover the pan, and simmer the soup until the vegetables are tender, about 10 minutes.
2. Transfer the vegetables and cooking liquid to a blender or food processor (in batches, if necessary), and purée them (*or* mash the vegetables and force them through a sieve).
3. Just before serving, return the purée to a saucepan and heat the purée over a moderately low flame. Add the skim milk, salt, and pepper, and heat the soup to just below boiling. Stir in the evaporated milk, and serve.

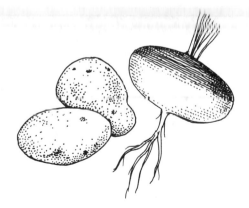

POTATO-LEEK CHOWDER

4 servings

A tasty and easy-to-prepare soup that could be a main dish for lunch. *Preparation tip:* If desired, the soup can be puréed in a blender before the milk is added.

  2 large leeks (white parts only)
  1 pound potatoes (about 3 medium), peeled and
    diced
  1 tablespoon butter or margarine
  2 cups chicken broth (homemade or canned)
Freshly ground pepper to taste
Salt, if desired (omit if using canned broth)
  1 cup skim milk
  2 tablespoons minced fresh parsley *or* 2
    teaspoons dried parsley flakes
½ cup grated Cheddar (2 ounces)

1. Separate and wash the leeks. Slice them into ½-inch pieces.
2. In a nonstick large saucepan, sauté the potatoes and leeks in the butter or margarine for several minutes, stirring the vegetables to prevent browning.
3. Add the broth, pepper, and salt. Bring the chowder to a boil, reduce the heat, cover the pan, and simmer the chowder for 20 to 30 minutes or until the vegetables are tender.
4. Add the milk gradually, and heat the chowder gently but do not boil.
5. Stir in the parsley. Serve the chowder with a generous sprinkle of grated cheese.

PUMPKIN SOUP

6 to 8 servings

This has been a long-standing family favorite sent to me by my mother-in-law, Anna Engquist. On sinful days, I serve it topped with a dollop of lightly salted whipped cream. But it is delicious as is or enhanced by plain croutons. *Preparation tip:* The soup base can be frozen after step 2.

  6 cups chicken broth *or* 2 cans consommé and
    2½ cups water
  2 pounds pumpkin, peeled and cut into 1-inch
    cubes
  2 medium onions, chopped (about 1¼ cups)
Salt, if desired, to taste
¼ teaspoon freshly ground black pepper

1 tablespoon flour
¼ cup cold water
1 cup milk (whole or 2-percent)

1. In a large saucepan, heat the broth and add the pumpkin, onions, salt, and pepper. Cook the soup until the pumpkin is soft, about 20 minutes.
2. Purée the soup in batches in a blender or food processor, or force the soup through a sieve.
3. Return the soup to the pan. Put the flour in a cup, and add the water, stirring the mixture until it is smooth. Add the flour mixture to the soup and heat, stirring, until the soup comes to a boil.
4. Add the milk, and correct the seasonings before serving.

ROOT SOUP *(Turnips, Parsnips, and Carrots)*   *6 servings*

This soup is just this side of heaven if you happen to be a fan of root vegetables. The seasonings can be adjusted to taste.

4 small white turnips, peeled
2 parsnips, scraped
2 carrots, scraped
2 onions
½ cup chopped parsley
½ cup barley
4 cups chicken broth *or* 4 cups water and 2
    bouillon cubes
1 tablespoon dried basil
2 dashes Tabasco or cayenne, to taste
¼ teaspoon curry powder (optional)
Salt, if desired, to taste
Freshly ground black pepper to taste
2 to 3 tablespoons snipped fresh dill *or* 1
    teaspoon dried dillweed

1. Grate the turnips, parsnips, carrots, and onions by hand or in a food processor.
2. Put the grated vegetables in a large saucepan. Add the parsley, barley, broth, and basil, and bring the soup to a boil. Reduce the heat, cover the pan, and simmer the soup for 1 to 2 hours. Check the soup periodically, and add water if needed.
3. Stir in the Tabasco or cayenne, curry, salt, and pepper. Sprinkle the soup with dill before serving.

PURÉED SPLIT PEA SOUP

about 8 servings

Dill gives this pea soup a wonderful flavor. All my tasters gave it top billing.
Preparation tip: Because the tamari and pork have salt, I use a salt-free broth in
preparing it. This soup freezes well.

   2 cups dried green split peas
   6 cups water
   1 tablespoon olive oil
   1 large onion, chopped (1 cup)
   2 cloves garlic, minced
   1 cup chopped carrots
   1 cup chopped celery (2 medium stalks)
   4 cups chicken broth (homemade or canned, but
      preferably without salt)
   2 teaspoons tamari *or* reduced-sodium soy sauce
   ¼ teaspoon freshly ground black pepper
   ½ cup snipped fresh dill
   1 slice (2 ounces) smoked pork or ham
      (optional)
   1 cup broth or skim milk, approximately

1. Place the peas and the water in a large, heavy saucepan, bring the water to
   a boil, boil the peas for 2 minutes, turn off the heat, and let the peas stand
   for 1 hour.
2. Heat the oil in a skillet (preferably nonstick), add the onion, garlic, carrots,
   and celery, and cook the vegetables, stirring them, for about 5 minutes.
   Add the vegetables to the soaked peas.
3. Add the broth, tamari, pepper, dill, and pork to the pan. Bring the soup
   to a boil, reduce the heat to low, and simmer the soup, partially covering
   the pan, for about 1½ hours (check now and again to be sure the soup is
   not scorching, and add water if needed).
4. In a blender or food processor, purée the soup with the meat, thinning the
   soup to the desired consistency with broth or milk. Heat the soup before
   serving.

CREAM OF SQUASH SOUP

4 to 6 servings

This is a simple and delicious soup for a first course or an accompaniment to
a sandwich. It is especially rich in beta-carotene (the chemical parent to vitamin
A), a cancer-fighting nutrient. *Preparation tip:* This soup freezes well.

1 tablespoon butter or margarine
½ cup chopped onion
2 cloves garlic, minced
¼ teaspoon freshly ground pepper or more, to
    taste
2½ cups chicken broth (if not salted, add ½
    teaspoon salt, if desired)
3 pounds winter squash (e.g., Hubbard or
    butternut), peeled, seeded, and diced
1½ to 2 cups skim milk
Dash nutmeg, or to taste

1. In a large, heavy saucepan, melt the butter or margarine, and sauté the onion and garlic until they are transparent.
2. Add the pepper, broth, and salt (if desired), and bring the liquid to a boil.
3. Add the squash, reduce the heat, cover the pan, and simmer the soup for about 8 minutes or until the squash is tender.
4. Remove the soup from the heat, and stir in the milk and nutmeg.
5. Purée the soup in a blender or food processor, and return it to the pan. Heat it before serving, but do not boil.

COLD CABBAGE SOUP

6 servings

Delicious and easy to prepare, this soup makes a wonderful warm-weather lunch accompanied by a dark, heavy bread and a slice of cheese or turkey.

2 cups broth (chicken, vegetable, or beef)
1 cup finely shredded green cabbage
1 tablespoon minced fresh dill or 1 teaspoon
    dried dillweed
1 tablespoon prepared mustard
1 teaspoon sugar
½ medium cucumber (peel if waxed), cored to
    remove seeds and finely diced
2 cups buttermilk
2 tablespoons minced fresh parsley for garnish
    (optional)

1. In a medium saucepan, heat the broth, add the cabbage, and simmer the soup for 5 minutes.
2. Remove the pan from the heat, and stir in the dill, mustard, and sugar. Then add the cucumber and buttermilk. Chill the soup thoroughly before serving. Serve the soup ice cold, garnished with parsley, if desired.

COLD CUCUMBER AND YOGURT SOUP

6 servings

Talk about winners—this soup was a unanimous favorite among very discerning tasters. It requires no cooking and is so easy to prepare that a child could make it. It is a very refreshing dish on a hot day or when you are eating "hot" foods. *Preparation tip:* Four teaspoons of chopped fresh mint can be used in place of or in addition to the dill. Do not add salt to the finished soup until you've tasted it, since the cucumbers are salted to drain some of the water out of them. For those on strict low-sodium diets, the soup can be made without draining the cucumbers and with no added salt (in other words, skip step 1).

2 medium cucumbers (1 pound), peeled, seeded, and finely diced
½ teaspoon salt
2 cloves garlic, finely minced
1 tablespoon olive oil (optional)
1 tablespoon snipped fresh dill *or* 1 teaspoon dried dillweed
4 cups (1 quart) plain low-fat yogurt
Freshly ground black pepper to taste
1 tablespoon finely chopped fresh mint *or* 1 teaspoon dried and crumbled mint (optional)

1. Place the diced cucumbers in a colander over a bowl or the sink and sprinkle them with the salt, tossing to coat. Let the cucumbers stand for 15 to 30 minutes.
2. In a large serving bowl or tureen, combine the drained cucumbers, garlic, oil (if desired), dill, and yogurt. Mix the ingredients well.
3. Chill for at least 1 hour. Before serving, check the seasonings and add more salt, if desired, and pepper. Add mint, if desired. If the soup is too thick, dilute it with a little ice water.

GAZPACHO GRANDE
about 6 servings

It's hard to think of anything more delightful to eat—or to prepare—for a late-summer meal than gazpacho—a no-cook Spanish soup of garden-fresh vegetables and just the right amount of zing to make them interesting. I keep the calorie count low by using much less oil than is traditionally put in gazpacho. The vegetables are divided: half are puréed to give the soup body; half are chopped and added for texture. The result is wonderful. *Preparation tip:* This recipe uses canned tomato juice, so be gentle on the salt unless you buy or make juice with no added salt.

 1 large cucumber, peeled, halved lengthwise,
   and cored to remove seeds, divided
 2 large tomatoes, peeled, cored, and seeded,
   divided
 1 green pepper, halved and seeded, divided
 1 medium onion, peeled and halved, divided
 1 pimiento
 3 cups tomato juice, divided
 ⅓ cup red wine vinegar
 1 tablespoon olive or vegetable oil
 ¼ teaspoon hot pepper sauce (Tabasco)
 ¼ teaspoon salt, if desired
 ⅛ teaspoon freshly ground black pepper or
   more, to taste
 3 to 4 cloves garlic, finely minced or crushed
Croutons for garnish (optional)

1. In a blender, combine half the cucumber, 1 tomato, half the green pepper, half the onion, the whole pimiento, and 1 cup of the tomato juice. Purée the ingredients at high speed.
2. Chop the remaining cucumber, tomato, green pepper, and onion. Place the vegetables in a bowl, cover it, and refrigerate it until serving time.
3. Pour the purée into a large serving bowl or tureen, and add the remaining 2 cups tomato juice, the vinegar, oil, pepper sauce, salt, pepper, and garlic. Refrigerate the gazpacho, covered, for at least 2 hours.
4. Just before serving the soup, add the reserved chopped vegetables to the purée mixture. Check the seasonings. Serve the gazpacho with croutons, if desired.

TWO-MELON SOUP   *6 servings*

Gourmet magazine is the source of this simple yet elegant and delicious summer soup. It's so easy to prepare, you needn't wait for company. For a refreshing breakfast or lunch, serve the soup with a generous dollop of plain low-fat yogurt. *Preparation tip:* Start with equal weights of cantaloupe and honeydew. Note that the purées need to be chilled for at least 3 hours. You can prepare them a day or two ahead and store them in separate containers in the refrigerator until serving time. Just be sure to stir them well before pouring.

    1 ripe cantaloupe, seeded and flesh diced
    2 tablespoons fresh lemon juice
    1 small honeydew (or ½ large), seeded and flesh
      diced
    2 tablespoons fresh lime juice
1½ teaspoons minced fresh mint, or to taste
Mint sprigs for garnish (optional)

1. In a blender, purée the cantaloupe with the lemon juice until the mixture is smooth. Transfer the purée to a suitable container, and refrigerate it, covered, for at least 3 hours.
2. Rinse out the blender, and purée the honeydew with the lime juice and mint until the mixture is smooth. Transfer the purée to a suitable container, and refrigerate it, covered, for at least 3 hours.
3. At serving time, transfer the purées to separate measuring cups or to pitchers with pouring spouts. With one cup in each hand, simultaneously pour equal amounts of the purées into individual serving bowls. The purées will stay separated, with the cantaloupe on one side and the honeydew on the other, even when carried to the table and while being eaten. If desired, garnish each dish with a sprig of mint.

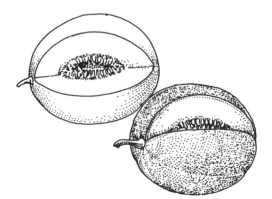

VICHYSSOISE *(Potato and Leek)*   *about 6 servings*

This classic cold French potato-and-leek soup is too often needlessly rich in fat. The potatoes, especially if you use new potatoes, give it enough body to justify the use of very little butter and the substitution of low-fat milk for cream.

  1 cup thinly sliced leeks (white part only),
     washed well
  1 tablespoon butter or margarine
  4 cups peeled and thinly sliced new potatoes
     (about 1½ pounds)
  3 cups chicken broth (dilute with water if
     canned salted broth is used)
Dash nutmeg
2½ cups low-fat milk
Salt, if desired, to taste
Pinch white pepper, or to taste
  2 tablespoons snipped chives for garnish
     (optional)

1. In a medium saucepan, sauté the leeks in the butter or margarine until they are tender but not brown.
2. Add the potatoes, broth, and nutmeg. Bring the soup to a boil, reduce the heat, and simmer the soup, partially covering the pan, for 30 minutes.
3. Purée the soup in a blender or a food mill. Pour the soup into a large serving bowl or tureen. Add the milk, salt, and pepper. Cover the soup, and chill it. Serve the vichyssoise garnished with chives.

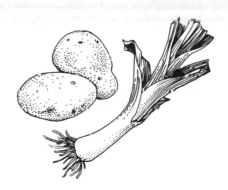

COLD WATERCRESS-TOMATO SOUP   *4 servings*

Watercress is one of my favorite vegetables. In addition to its snappy flavor, it has an ample supply of nutrients. This soup, devised by Jinx and Jefferson Morgan and originally published in *Bon Appétit* magazine, has a lovely color, compliments of the tomato, and gains body from the potato, obviating the need for cream. *Preparation tip:* It can be prepared a day ahead.

   1 tablespoon butter or margarine
   1 leek (about ½ inch in diameter), white part
     only, sliced and washed well
 ¼ cup chopped onion
   1 large clove garlic, minced (1 teaspoon)
1½ cups chicken broth
   1 medium-large potato, peeled and cubed (about
     1 cup)
   2 cups peeled, seeded, and chopped tomatoes
   1 bunch watercress (reserve a few sprigs for
     garnish), stems removed (about 1 cup packed
     leaves)
   1 tablespoon minced fresh parsley
Pinch sugar
 ½ cup low-fat milk
Salt, if desired, to taste
Freshly ground black pepper to taste

1. In a medium saucepan, melt the butter or margarine, and add the leek, onion, and garlic. Cover the pan, and cook the vegetables over low heat for about 10 minutes, stirring a few times.
2. Add the broth, potato, and tomatoes, and bring the soup to a boil. Reduce the heat, and simmer the soup for about 10 minutes. Add the watercress leaves, parsley, and sugar, and simmer the soup for another 10 minutes. Cool the soup to room temperature.
3. Purée the soup in a blender until it is smooth. Stir in the milk, salt, and pepper. Chill the soup before serving, and garnish it with watercress sprigs.

BUTTERMILK-ZUCCHINI SOUP   *about 6 servings*

This curry-flavored cold soup is a good way to make a dent in the late-summer mother lode of zucchini. If desired, it can be colorfully garnished with thin slices of carrots, zucchini, and radishes or minced parsley.

    2 tablespoons butter or margarine
    2 pounds zucchini, ends trimmed but not
       peeled, chopped
    1 cup thinly sliced scallions
    1 tablespoon ground cumin
    1 tablespoon curry powder
    2 cups chicken broth
    3 cups buttermilk
    Salt, if desired, to taste
    Freshly ground black pepper, to taste
    Thinly sliced vegetables for garnish (optional)

1. Melt the butter or margarine in a large, heavy saucepan. Add the zucchini and scallions, cover the pan tightly, and cook the vegetables over moderate heat for about 10 minutes or until the zucchini is soft.
2. Stir in the cumin and curry, and cook the mixture, stirring, for about 2 minutes.
3. Add the broth, and purée the mixture in a blender or food processor.
4. Transfer the purée to a large serving bowl or tureen. Stir in the buttermilk, and add salt and pepper. Chill the soup for 4 hours or longer. If desired, serve the soup garnished with thinly sliced vegetables.

ENTRÉES

Main-Dish Soups

The following soups are substantial enough to serve as a main course for lunch or supper. Soups like these constitute a large proportion of our main meals, especially during the colder months of the year. I have even used some as entrées at dinner parties. Most such soups have the undeniable virtue of allowing advance preparation, requiring only reheating at serving time. Those that do not contain milk can even be frozen for later use. And those that do contain milk can be prepared up to the point of adding milk and the soup base can be frozen, with the milk (and cheese) added after defrosting.

All these soups contain substantial amounts of complete protein, even though the amount of animal protein is limited, and all provide stick-to-the-ribs, nutritious goodness. Because they also include a lot of vegetables, they are essentially one-pot dishes. Served with a salad, bread, and perhaps fruit for dessert, they are filling but calorie-controlled meals-in-a-bowl. You may recall the studies that showed that people who eat soup often tend to consume fewer calories and lose weight faster than infrequent soup eaters (see p. 198).

BEAN AND TORTILLA SOUP   *4 servings*

Here I wave my avoidance of fried ingredients to bring you this unusual soup. It represents an unorthodox version of how Mexicans traditionally obtain complete protein: by mixing beans and corn. *Preparation tip:* If you prefer your foods relatively unspicy, use 1 teaspoon mild chili powder and omit the hot chili powder and crushed red pepper. A few dashes of Tabasco can also substitute for the hot chili powder. I would recommend using a nonstick pan to prepare the tortilla strips and to sauté the vegetables; otherwise you may have to use twice the amount of oil.

    2 cloves garlic, crushed with knife handle
    2 tablespoons plus 1 teaspoon oil, divided
    4 6-inch corn tortillas, cut into strips about
        ¼ × 1 inch
    1 medium onion, thinly sliced
    ½ cup diced celery
    ½ cup diced carrots
2½ cups water
    1 8-ounce can tomato sauce *or* 1 cup homemade
        sauce
    1 bay leaf
    ¾ teaspoon mild chili powder
    ¼ teaspoon hot chili powder
    1 16-ounce can red kidney beans, drained and
        rinsed, *or* 2 cups home-cooked beans
    1 teaspoon lime juice (optional)
Hot red pepper flakes to taste (optional)

1. In a heavy (preferably nonstick) frying pan or broad-bottomed saucepan, sauté the garlic in the 2 tablespoons of oil over medium heat until the garlic is lightly browned. Remove the garlic, and discard it.
2. Fry the tortilla strips in the flavored oil, turning them often to brown lightly. When they are crisp, remove them and place them on a paper towel.
3. In a heavy nonstick saucepan, heat 1 teaspoon of oil over a medium heat. Add the onion, celery, and carrots, and sauté the vegetables, stirring them often, until the onion starts to brown. Be careful not to burn the vegetables.
4. Add the water, tomato sauce, bay leaf, and chili powders. Simmer the soup, uncovered, for 15 minutes or until it begins to thicken.
5. Stir in the beans and lime juice, if desired, and simmer the soup until it is heated through.
6. Discard the bay leaf. To serve, divide the tortilla strips among four soup bowls, and ladle the soup over the strips. Sprinkle each portion with red pepper flakes, if desired.

"SEA" SOUP *(Shrimp and Navy Beans)*

The combination of shrimp and navy beans gives this seaworthy soup its name. It is good any season since it can be served hot or cold. *Preparation tip:* Don't forget to allot time to soak the beans before they are cooked. Be sure to do step 3 while the beans are coming to a boil in step 2.

    1 pound navy beans or other small white dried
      beans, such as pea beans
    7 cups water
3½ cups chicken broth (homemade or canned)
Salt, if desired, to taste
1½ teaspoons curry powder
  ½ teaspoon white pepper
    2 tablespoons butter or margarine
1½ cups chopped onion (1½ large)
1½ cups diced carrots (2 large)
1½ cups diced celery (3 large stalks)
  ¼ cup minced fresh parsley
    1 pound small fresh shrimp, peeled and
      deveined, *or* 12 ounces frozen shelled shrimp
    3 scallions, cut into 1-inch lengths

1. Soak the beans either overnight in four times their volume of water, or use the quick-soak method (bring the beans and water to a boil, let them boil for 2 minutes, remove the beans from the heat, and let the beans stand for 1 hour). Drain the beans.
2. In a heavy Dutch oven or 5-quart pot, combine the soaked beans with the 7 cups water, broth, salt, curry, and pepper. Bring the soup to a boil.
3. Meanwhile, in a large skillet, melt the butter or margarine, and add the onion, carrots, celery, and parsley and cook them for 5 minutes, stirring them often. With a slotted spoon, remove the vegetable mixture from the skillet and add it to the beans. *Do not wash the skillet.*
4. When the bean-and-vegetable mixture boils, reduce the heat to low, cover the pot, and simmer the soup for about 1 hour 15 minutes or until the beans are very tender. Remove the soup from the heat.
5. Purée the soup in batches in a blender or food processor, transferring the purée to a large bowl or tureen as you go.
6. Reheat the butter left in the unwashed skillet, add the shrimp and scallions, and stir-fry them for 3 to 4 minutes or until the shrimp have turned pinkish-white. Add them to the purée. Serve the soup hot, or chill the soup and serve it cold.

BROCCOLI AND CRAB BISQUE
6 servings

With crab meat in my neighborhood costing well in excess of $10 a pound, I make this soup with "sea legs"—a Japanese imitation of king crab legs made from fish that is reconstituted and rolled. Its red outer coating contrasts beautifully with the bright-green broccoli, resulting in a visually appealing as well as delicious soup.

1½ cups chopped onion
 2 teaspoons butter, margarine, or oil
 5 cups broth (fish, chicken, or vegetable)
 1 large head broccoli, stems sliced crosswise and
 flowerets reserved
 4 medium potatoes, peeled and diced, divided
1½ cups diced carrots, divided
 ¾ cup chopped celery
 ½ teaspoon freshly ground black pepper, or to
 taste
 1 teaspoon lemon juice
 ¼ teaspoon thyme leaves, crushed
 1 bay leaf
 ¾ teaspoon salt (or less if broth was salted), if
 desired
Dash cayenne, or to taste
 2 cups skim milk
 1 pound crab meat or sea legs, sliced into
 ½-inch pieces

1. In a large saucepan, sauté the onion in the butter, margarine, or oil until it is soft.
2. Add the broth, *broccoli stems,* half the potatoes, half the carrots, celery, pepper, lemon juice, thyme, bay leaf, salt, and cayenne. Bring the soup to a boil, reduce the heat, and simmer the soup for about 15 minutes or until the vegetables are tender.
3. Remove the bay leaf, and purée the vegetables and broth in a blender. Return the purée to the pot.
4. Add the remaining potatoes and carrots, and cook the soup over a low heat for about 10 minutes.
5. When the potatoes and carrots are nearly soft, add the *broccoli flowerets* to the pot, and cook the soup for another 5 to 10 minutes or until the broccoli is tender-crisp.
6. Add the milk and the crab meat or sea legs, and heat the bisque but do not boil it. Serve the bisque with croutons, if desired.

VEGETABLE-BEAN SOUP WITH PISTOU

10 to 12 servings

Even kids who dislike vegetables seemed to go for this soup, which has a garden full of them. It is the French equivalent of minestrone soup. The recipe makes a two-day supply, and chances are you'll be glad of it. *Preparation tip:* This soup can be made with a wide range of ingredients to suit individual tastes. The only requirement is that vegetables be added according to their respective cooking times so that none turns to mush. Pistou, the nutless French version of Italian pesto (see p. 642), adds richness to the soup, so it is best not to start out using too much of it. More can be added at serving time. I have found that the flavor improves as the soup sits and thus would recommend preparing it a day or two in advance of serving it. Heat the soup gently, stirring it often, just before serving.

SOUP

- 1 tablespoon butter or margarine
- 1 tablespoon oil
- 1 medium onion, chopped (½ to ⅔ cup)
- 2 large leeks, washed well and chopped (1 cup)
- 2 large carrots, chopped (1½ cups)
- 1 large potato, peeled and diced
- 8 cups boiling water
- 1 teaspoon salt, if desired, to taste
- ¼ pound fresh spinach or Swiss chard, coarsely chopped
- ½ pound green beans, cut into 1-inch pieces
- ½ pound tomatoes, peeled, cored, and coarsely chopped
- ½ pound zucchini, halved lengthwise, then sliced ¼ inch thick
- 2 cups cooked small dried beans, such as navy, pea, small white, or Great Northern (rinse if canned)
- ½ cup small soup macaroni

Freshly ground black pepper to taste

PISTOU

- 3 cloves garlic, mashed
- ½ to 1 cup finely chopped basil leaves
- ¼ cup olive oil
- ⅓ cup grated Parmesan

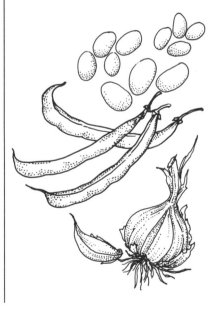

1. In a large stock pot or 5- or 6-quart Dutch oven, heat the butter or margarine and oil and add the onion, leeks, and carrots. Sauté the vegetables for 5 minutes, and then add the potato, boiling water, and salt. Bring the soup

to a boil, reduce the heat, and simmer the soup, uncovered, for about 30 minutes.

2. Meanwhile, prepare the pistou. In a blender or food processor, process the garlic and basil, gradually adding the oil. Transfer the mixture to a bowl, and stir in the Parmesan. Set the pistou aside.

3. To the soup pot, add the spinach or Swiss chard, green beans, tomatoes, zucchini, cooked beans, and macaroni. Bring the soup to a boil, reduce the heat, and simmer the soup until the pasta is cooked (about 8 to 10 minutes).

4. Stir in half the pistou, saving the rest for table use or some other purpose. Season the soup with pepper and additional salt, if desired.

PEANUT BUTTER–VEGETABLE CHICKEN SOUP

about 8 servings

To say this hearty, protein-packed soup is wonderful is almost an insult. It was devised by *Environmental Nutrition,* a newsletter for consumers and health professionals concerned about food quality and health.

    8 cups chicken broth (if broth is salty, use only
        4 cups broth, the rest water)
    2 cups diced cooked chicken
    1 cup peeled and diced potatoes
    1 cup diced carrots
    1 cup diced zucchini (do not peel)
    1 cup broccoli or cauliflower flowerets
    1 cup tomatoes (fresh or canned), chopped
    ½ cup chopped celery
    ½ cup chopped onion
    ½ cup chopped green pepper
    2 cloves garlic, minced (2 teaspoons)
    1 cup peanut butter, preferably natural smooth
    1 tablespoon minced fresh parsley *or* 1 teaspoon
        dried parsley flakes
    ½ to 1 teaspoon freshly ground black pepper, to
        taste
Salt, if desired, to taste

1. In a large stock pot, combine the broth, chicken, potatoes, and carrots. Bring the soup to a boil, and cook it over medium heat until the vegetables are nearly tender, about 10 minutes.

2. Add the zucchini, broccoli or cauliflower, tomatoes, celery, onion, green pepper, and garlic. Simmer the soup for about 8 minutes.

3. Add the peanut butter, parsley, pepper, and salt, stirring the soup until the peanut butter is fully blended. Simmer the soup for 3 minutes longer.

CHICKEN "BARLEYCORN" SOUP

8 servings
(about 12 cups)

Despite its peasant ingredients, this is a soup fit for royalty. *Preparation tip:* Although the preparation time is long, the soup is not hard to make, and it can be prepared ahead and frozen. The first two steps—preparation of the stock—should be done in advance, perhaps even the night before, to permit removal of the fat. If you prefer to use less than a whole chicken in the soup, you can save half the chicken pieces for another use.

      1 3-pound broiler-fryer chicken with giblets
      6 cups water
      4 cups chicken stock or canned broth
      1 onion stuck with 4 cloves
      3 carrots, divided
      3 stalks of celery, divided
      6 sprigs parsley
      1 bay leaf
 1½ teaspoons dried basil, divided
      1 teaspoon thyme leaves, divided
      ½ cup barley, washed and drained
      4 cups corn kernels (2 10-ounce packages frozen
         kernels, thawed), divided
      ½ cup thinly sliced scallions
      2 tablespoons finely chopped parsley *or* 1
         teaspoon dried parsley flakes
      ½ teaspoon ground cumin
      ¼ teaspoon hot pepper sauce (Tabasco), or to
         taste
Salt, if desired to taste
Freshly ground black pepper to taste

1. In a large pot, combine the chicken and giblets (except the liver), water, stock, onion, 1 carrot, 1 celery stalk, parsley, bay leaf, 1 teaspoon of basil, and ½ teaspoon of thyme. Bring the stock to a boil, reduce the heat, and simmer the stock, covering the pot, for about 45 minutes.
2. Remove the chicken from the stock, and let the chicken cool. Strain the stock into a large bowl, and chill it overnight to facilitate the removal of the fat, or pour the stock into a fat-separating cup (see p. 237) for immediate use.
3. When the chicken is cool enough to handle, remove and discard the skin and bones, and cut the chicken into ½-inch pieces. Set the chicken aside.
4. After the stock has been skimmed of fat, return it to the pot, bring it to a boil, and add the barley and the remaining ½ teaspoon each of basil and thyme. Simmer the soup, covered, for 45 minutes.

5. Meanwhile, purée in a blender or food processor 2 cups of the corn in 1 cup of stock. Dice the remaining 2 carrots and 2 stalks of celery.
6. When the barley is cooked, add the corn purée to the pot along with the remaining corn kernels, diced celery, and diced carrots. Simmer the soup, covered, for about 10 minutes, stirring it occasionally.
7. Add the chicken pieces, scallions, parsley, cumin, and pepper sauce to the pot, and simmer the soup, stirring, for another 5 minutes. Season the soup with salt, if desired, and black pepper.

CHICKPEA AND PASTA SOUP

*4 servings
(about 6 cups)*

This is a simple-to-make, tasty, hearty soup that derives balanced protein from vegetables by combining chickpeas (a legume) with pasta (a grain).

1 tablespoon unsalted butter or margarine
1 medium onion, minced
½ teaspoon dried thyme
1 16-ounce can tomatoes, including juice, chopped
2 garlic cloves, minced (about 2 teaspoons)
2 cups beef broth (canned or cubes or homemade), or more
2 cups cooked chickpeas (garbanzo beans), drained and rinsed if canned
½ cup small pasta (shells, elbows, etc.), cooked *al dente*
Freshly ground black pepper to taste
¼ cup grated Parmesan

1. In a large saucepan, melt the butter or margarine, and cook the onion with the thyme, stirring, for 5 minutes.
2. Add the tomatoes, their juice, and the garlic, and simmer the mixture, stirring occasionally, for 15 minutes.
3. Add the broth and chickpeas, and simmer the soup, stirring occasionally, for another 15 minutes.
4. Add the pasta and pepper, and cook the soup until the pasta is warm. Thin the soup with additional stock or water, if necessary. Serve the soup with a tablespoon of Parmesan sprinkled in each bowl.

GYPSY SOUP *(Sweet Potato and Chickpeas)*   *4 large servings*

Mollie Katzen, author of *The Moosewood Cookbook,* says this chickpea and vegetable soup is of Spanish and Dickensonian origins. Whatever its roots, it can grow into whatever you wish to make of it since the vegetables can be varied according to taste and availability. *Preparation tip:* Katzen suggests combining any orange vegetable with green, such as green peas or beans in place of the peppers, or carrots instead of the winter squash or sweet potato. You can use canned chickpeas or cook your own, allowing an hour for a quick soak (see p. 103) and 1½ hours cooking time. If you use canned salted broth, do not add more salt until you taste the completed soup.

> 2 tablespoons olive oil
> 2 large onions, chopped (2 cups)
> 2 large cloves garlic, crushed
> ½ cup chopped celery (1 large stalk)
> 2 cups peeled, chopped sweet potatoes or
>   winter squash
> 3 cups broth or water
> 1 bay leaf
> 2 teaspoons paprika
> 1 teaspoon turmeric
> 1 teaspoon dried basil
> Salt, if desired, to taste
> Dash cinnamon
> Dash cayenne
> 1 cup chopped fresh tomatoes
> ¾ cup chopped green pepper (1 large)
> 1½ cups cooked chickpeas
> 1 tablespoon tamari *or* reduced-sodium soy
>   sauce

1. In a large saucepan or stock pot, heat the oil, and sauté the onions, garlic, celery, and sweet potatoes or winter squash for about 5 minutes.
2. Add the broth or water, bay leaf, paprika, turmeric, basil, salt, cinnamon, and cayenne. Bring the soup to a boil, reduce the heat, cover the pot, and simmer the soup for 15 minutes.
3. Add the tomatoes, pepper, and chickpeas, and simmer the soup for about 10 minutes longer. Stir in the tamari, and serve the soup.

FINE FISH CHOWDER

6 to 8 servings

A hearty soup that is both easy to make and delicious to eat.

   1 tablespoon butter or margarine
   2 cups peeled, cubed potatoes (2 medium)
   2 cups sliced carrots (3 medium)
   2 cups sliced onion (2 large)
Salt, if desired, to taste
   2 whole cloves
   1 teaspoon dried dillweed *or* 1 tablespoon fresh
     snipped dill
   1 bay leaf
   2 tablespoons flour
   2 cups boiling water
   1 pound thick fish fillets (halibut, cod, pollack,
     etc.), cut into 1-inch pieces
½ cup dry white wine
   1 cup milk (skim or low-fat)
Freshly ground black pepper to taste
   2 tablespoons minced parsley

1. In a large saucepan or Dutch oven (6-quart capacity), melt the butter or margarine, and add the potatoes, carrots, onion, salt, cloves, dill, and bay leaf. Sauté, stirring, for about 5 minutes. Add the flour, and cook for another 30 seconds.
2. Add the boiling water, and cover the pot tightly. Simmer the chowder over very low heat for about 15 minutes or until the vegetables are tender.
3. Add the fish and wine. Cover the pot, and simmer the chowder for another 10 minutes or until the fish flakes easily with a fork. Discard the bay leaf.
4. Add the milk to the soup, and cook the soup, stirring, until it is hot.
5. Season the chowder with pepper, and serve it sprinkled with parsley.

ITALIAN FISH SOUP

5 to 6 servings

Since it has no starchy ingredient, this is a lighter soup than the Fine Fish Chowder (p. 341), and it is best served with a crusty bread such as a whole-wheat French-style loaf. With salad and dessert, it would make an elegant company meal. *Preparation tip:* To prepare it, you'll need a fish stock already made (see p. 311). After that, the recipe is straightforward.

   2 carrots, finely diced (1½ cups)
   1 medium onion, finely diced (⅔ cup)
   1 leek, washed well and diced
1½ tablespoons olive oil
   2 large cloves garlic, minced (2 teaspoons)
   ¾ teaspoon thyme
   4 large tomatoes, peeled, seeded, and coarsely
       chopped
   ⅓ cup dry white wine
1½ pounds assorted firm fish fillets (e.g.,
       monkfish, halibut, red snapper), cut into
       1-inch pieces
   ½ pound bay scallops
   4 cups fish stock, heated
   2 tablespoons minced fresh parsley
Salt, if desired, to taste
Freshly ground black pepper to taste

1. In a large, heavy saucepan, cook the carrots, onion, and leek in the oil, stirring, until the onion is translucent, about 5 minutes. Stir in the garlic, and cook the vegetables for another minute.
2. Add the thyme, tomatoes, and wine, and simmer the mixture for 5 minutes.
3. Add the fish, and simmer the mixture for another 5 minutes.
4. Add the scallops and hot stock, bring the soup to a boil, and simmer it for 5 minutes.
5. Stir in the parsley, salt, and pepper. Serve the soup.

MY FAVORITE LENTIL SOUP

8 servings

This soup is so delicious that I usually double the recipe and freeze several lunch servings. It is very good even without the grated cheese, but the cheese completes the protein in the lentils, making this a main-dish soup. *Preparation tip:* In place of homemade broth, you can use 3 bouillon cubes with 7 cups of water or 3½ cups of canned broth and 3½ cups of water. But if you do, do not add salt.

   2 tablespoons olive or vegetable oil
   2 large or 3 medium onions, chopped (2 cups)
   3 carrots, coarsely grated
   ¾ teaspoon marjoram, crumbled
   ¾ teaspoon thyme leaves, crumbled
   1 28-ounce can tomatoes with their juice,
     coarsely chopped
   7 cups broth (beef, chicken, or vegetable)
1½ cups dried lentils, rinsed and picked over
   ½ teaspoon salt, if desired
   ¼ to ½ teaspoon freshly ground black pepper, to
     taste
   6 ounces dry white wine
   ⅓ cup chopped fresh parsley *or* 2 tablespoons
     dried parsley flakes
   4 ounces Cheddar, grated

1. Heat the oil in a large saucepan, and sauté the onions, carrots, marjoram, and thyme, stirring the vegetables, for about 5 minutes.
2. Add the tomatoes, broth, and lentils. Bring the soup to a boil, reduce the heat, cover the pan, and simmer the soup for about 1 hour or until the lentils are tender.
3. Add the salt, pepper, wine, and parsley, and simmer the soup for a few minutes. Serve with cheese sprinkled on each portion.

LENTIL AND BROWN RICE SOUP   *8 to 10 servings*

No changes were necessary in this nourishing and delicious soup devised by *Gourmet* magazine. With the protein of the rice complementing that of the lentils, you have the protein quality of beef without the cost or the fat. It is the easiest soup meal I've ever made: all that gets dirty is a knife and a measuring spoon. *Preparation tip:* If this soup is made ahead to be frozen, stop after step 1 and add the parsley and seasonings after reheating.

       5 cups chicken broth, or more
       3 cups water, or more
    1½ cups lentils, picked over and rinsed
       1 cup long-grain brown rice
       1 35-ounce can tomatoes, drained (save the
          juice) and chopped
       3 carrots, halved lengthwise and cut crosswise
          into ¼-inch pieces
       1 large onion, chopped (1 cup)
       1 large stalk celery, chopped (½ cup)
       3 large cloves garlic, minced (1 tablespoon)
      ½ teaspoon crumbled dried basil
      ½ teaspoon crumbled orégano
      ½ teaspoon crumbled thyme
       1 bay leaf
      ½ cup minced fresh parsley
       2 tablespoons cider vinegar, or to taste
    Salt, if desired, to taste
    Freshly ground black pepper to taste

1. In a large, heavy saucepan or Dutch oven, combine the broth, water, lentils, rice, tomatoes, reserved tomato juice, carrots, onion, celery, garlic, basil, orégano, thyme, and bay leaf. Bring the soup to a boil, reduce the heat, cover the pan, and simmer the soup, stirring it occasionally, for 45 to 55 minutes or until the lentils and rice are both tender. Remove and discard the bay leaf.
2. Stir in the parsley, vinegar, salt, and pepper. If necessary, thin the soup with additional hot broth or water.

PORK AND POTATO CHOWDER

4 servings

When you want to whip up a quick winter lunch or supper, this soup may be your answer.

- ¼ pound lean smoked pork or Canadian bacon, finely diced
- 1 teaspoon butter or olive oil
- 1 large onion, chopped (1 cup)
- 4 cups diced all-purpose potatoes (about 4 medium)
- 2 tablespoons chopped fresh parsley *or* 1 teaspoon dried parsley flakes
- 2 cups boiling water
- 1 cup corn kernels
- 2 cups low-fat milk
- Freshly ground black pepper to taste
- Dash hot pepper sauce (Tabasco), or to taste
- Salt, if desired

1. In a nonstick skillet, briefly cook the pork or bacon, stirring to prevent scorching.
2. Add the butter or oil, and sauté the onion until it is golden.
3. Combine the pork, onion, potatoes, and parsley in a large saucepan. Add the water, bring the chowder to a boil, reduce the heat, cover the pan, and simmer the chowder for about 20 minutes.
4. Add the corn kernels and milk, heat but do not boil the chowder, and simmer it for about 5 minutes. Add the pepper, hot pepper sauce, and salt, if desired.

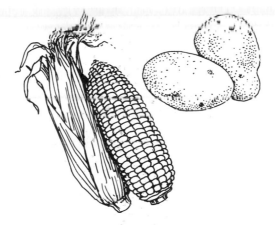

DUTCH SPLIT PEA SOUP

6 servings

A long-simmering soup with a delicate smoky flavor. *Preparation tip:* The flavor of this soup improves with age. The soup can be frozen. If needed, add more broth when reheating it.

　1 pound dried green split peas
　6 cups water
　4 cups (approximately) broth (chicken or beef)
¼ pound smoked pork or ham, diced
¾ cup chopped celery, with some leaves
　2 leeks (white part only), thinly sliced and
　　washed well
　1 large onion, chopped (1 cup)
2½ cups diced potatoes (about ¾ pound)
1½ cups diced carrots (2 large)
½ teaspoon salt, if desired
¼ teaspoon freshly ground black pepper
Dash hot pepper sauce (Tabasco), or to taste

1. In a large saucepan, combine the peas and water. Bring the water to a boil, and cook the peas for 2 minutes. Remove the peas from the heat, cover the pan, and let it stand for 1 hour.
2. Add the broth, pork or ham, celery, leeks, and onion. Bring the soup to a boil, reduce the heat, cover the pan, and simmer the soup for 1½ hours.
3. Add the potatoes and carrots, and cook the soup for another 15 to 30 minutes (the peas should disintegrate). If the soup gets too thick, thin it with additional broth.
4. Season the soup with salt, pepper, and hot pepper sauce.

TURKEY CHOWDER

6 to 8 servings

This gut-warming winter soup can also be made with smoked turkey (for a more distinctive flavor) or cooked chicken. *Preparation tip:* If canned broth or bouillon cubes are used, omit the salt, perhaps adding it to taste after the soup is finished. This soup is especially good when served with seasoned croutons or a hearty dark bread.

1½ tablespoons butter or margarine
  1 large onion, thinly sliced (about 1 cup)
  ¼ cup chopped green pepper
1½ cups broth (chicken or turkey)
  2 cups diced carrots (3 medium)
  3 cups peeled, diced potatoes (3 medium)
  1 cup thinly sliced celery (2 medium stalks)
  ½ teaspoon salt, if desired
  3 cups cooked, diced turkey
  1 17-ounce can cream-style corn
  2 tablespoons chopped pimiento or roasted red
    pepper
  ½ teaspoon dried thyme leaves
  ½ teaspoon AHA herb mix (see p. 182) or other
    no-salt seasoning
Freshly ground black pepper to taste
  3 cups low-fat milk
  ¼ cup finely chopped fresh parsley *or* 1
    tablespoon dried parsley flakes

1. In a large saucepan, melt the butter or margarine, and sauté the onion and pepper until they are tender.
2. Add the broth and carrots. Heat the chowder to boiling, reduce the heat, cover the pan, and simmer the chowder for 5 minutes. Add the potatoes, celery, and salt. Simmer the chowder, covered, for another 10 minutes or until the potatoes and carrots are tender.
3. Stir in the turkey, corn, pimiento, thyme, herb mix, pepper, and milk. Heat the chowder thoroughly, but do not let it come to a boil.
4. Just before serving, sprinkle the chowder with chopped parsley.

TURKEY CARCASS SOUP

4 servings
(about 6 cups)

This is the ideal soup for a waste-not, want-not cook. Even the bones contribute nutrients and flavor to this recipe. It requires starting with the remains of a roast turkey, preferably a skeleton that has not been picked completely clean of all meat. It is my favorite soup meal; my husband is convinced that I roast turkeys now and again just to get the carcass! If you have no reason to roast a turkey, perhaps a friend or relative will donate a carcass to you. (Just don't let the donor taste the soup you make, or you may never get another skeleton.) *Preparation tip:* The stock can be frozen or used right away to make this or some other soup.

STOCK   *8 to 10 cups stock*
  1 turkey carcass, broken into pieces
Any defatted pan juices or gravy that may be
    left over
12 cups water, or enough to cover the carcass
    completely
  2 medium onions, coarsely chopped
  2 ribs of celery, diced, with leaves, if available
  ½ cup diced carrots
  ½ cup diced well-washed leek (optional)
  ½ cup diced turnip
  1 clove garlic, minced
  1 teaspoon salt, if desired
Bouquet garni, made by tying in cheesecloth
    6 sprigs fresh parsley (*or* 2 teaspoons dried
    parsley flakes), ½ teaspoon thyme leaves, and
    1 bay leaf

1. Combine all the ingredients in a large pot, bring the stock to a boil, and simmer it, partially covering the pot, for 2 to 3 hours. (This stock tastes better the longer it simmers, as long as you don't cook away the liquid.)
2. Strain the stock, and skim off the fat.
3. If desired, remove all the bones, reserving any piece of turkey meat. Discard the bouquet garni and bay leaf. In a blender, food processor, or a hand sieve, purée the remaining vegetables in a cup of the stock and save the mixture for another soup or for flavoring a stew or sauce.

SOUP
  2 tablespoons minced onion
  1 clove garlic, minced
  1 tablespoon butter, margarine, or oil
 1 cup diced carrots
  ½ cup diced celery

½ cup finely chopped mushrooms
1½ tablespoons flour
  6 to 7 cups turkey stock (see the recipe, above)
  1 teaspoon marjoram
AHA herb mix (see p. 182) *or* salt and pepper, to
    taste
  1 cup cooked barley or rice, *or* ⅓ cup raw
    barley or rice
  1 cup diced turkey meat
Dash hot pepper sauce (Tabasco), or to taste
    (optional)
  2 tablespoons chopped parsley

1. In a large saucepan, sauté the onion and garlic in butter, margarine, or oil until they are soft.
2. Add the carrots, celery, and mushrooms, and cook the vegetables, stirring them, 3 to 5 minutes longer.
3. Add the flour, and cook the mixture, stirring it, for another minute.
4. Add the stock, marjoram, herb mix, and barley. Bring the soup to a boil, reduce the heat, partially cover the pan, and simmer the soup for about 1 hour.
5. Add the turkey meat and hot pepper sauce, adjust the seasonings, and heat the soup to boiling.
6. Sprinkle the soup with parsley just before serving.

MEXICAN ZUCCHINI SOUP

4 main or 6 first-course
servings

Betty Crocker's Mexican Cookbook provided the inspiration for this simple-to-prepare yet scrumptious soup that is a perfect main course for a light lunch or supper any season of the year. Even though they were forewarned that there were 10 more dishes to sample, my tasters gobbled up the potful, returning for seconds and thirds. *Preparation tip:* In winter, use frozen or canned corn kernels, but in summer, try making it with fresh corn cut from the cob.

    1 small onion, chopped (⅓ cup)
1½ teaspoons butter or margarine
    2 cups broth (chicken or vegetable)
    2 cups unpeeled, diced zucchini (10 ounces, or 2 small)
1½ cups corn kernels (about 8 ounces)
    2 tablespoons finely chopped green chilies or jalapeño peppers (fresh or canned)
    ½ teaspoon salt, if desired, or to taste
    ⅛ teaspoon freshly ground black pepper
    1 cup low-fat or skim milk
    2 ounces Monterey Jack cheese, cut into ¼-inch cubes
Minced fresh parsley and ground nutmeg for garnish

1. In a large saucepan, sauté the onion in the butter or margarine until it is tender, about 3 minutes.
2. Stir in the broth, zucchini, corn, chilies, salt, and pepper. Bring the soup to a boil, reduce the heat, cover the pan, and cook the soup until the zucchini is tender, about 5 minutes.
3. Stir in the milk, and heat the soup until it is hot but not boiling. Remove the soup from the heat, and stir in the cheese. Garnish the soup with parsley and nutmeg.

Pasta Main Dishes and Sauces

The tasty entrées that can be prepared from pasta are limited only by your imagination. A 5-ounce serving of ordinary pasta (cooked) contributes nearly half the protein recommended for a main course. If you then add a protein-rich ingredient like shellfish, dried beans, egg, or cheese, along with vegetables, you've got a full meal. Alternatively, you can use high-protein pasta (made with soy flour as well as wheat flour), and add a bit of protein or eat a larger serving to bring the protein total up to 16 to 20 grams. Many pasta main dishes can be fully prepared or set up for final cooking well in advance; others cook quickly (you can prepare the remaining ingredients while the water boils and the pasta cooks). Either way, they are handy weekday meals for working cooks.

The low-fat yet appetite-satisfying value of pasta can—and often is—subverted by the use of high-calorie sauces rich in fatty cheeses, butter, cream, or oil. Fettucine Alfredo is not the way to go if you're interested in eating health-enhancing, calorie-controlled meals. From personal experience, I can assure you that you can easily prepare delicious pasta meals with low-fat ingredients. Some of the them, in fact, would even fool gourmets into thinking that the dishes were richer than they really are. Try some of the following, and see if you don't agree.

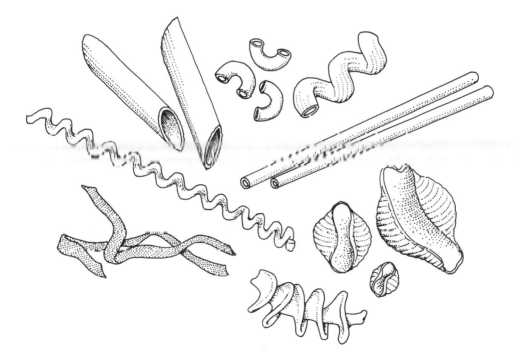

BUCKWHEAT NOODLE STIR-FRY   *4 servings*

Buckwheat noodles have a wonderful flavor and texture, providing quite a different pasta experience than traditional Italian spaghetti. They are not cheap (a 12-ounce package may cost $2 or more) but well worth the higher cost in terms of taste and nutrient value. They are usually available at Oriental markets or natural food stores. Hot pepper oil is also available in Oriental markets; or you can make your own by slowly cooking several dried chili peppers in sesame oil; when they blacken, remove and discard them.

    12 ounces soba (Japanese buckwheat noodles)
     2 tablespoons Worcestershire sauce
     1 tablespoon soy sauce (preferably
        reduced-sodium)
     1 tablespoon sherry
     2 tablespoons vegetable oil, divided
     3 scallions, thinly sliced
     3 cloves garlic, minced (1 tablespoon)
     1 red sweet pepper, cut in thin strips
     5 cups shredded cabbage
     1 cup cooked chicken, beef, or pork, cut in
        shreds
    ½ cup broth (any type)
     1 teaspoon hot pepper oil, or to taste

1. In a large kettle of boiling water (add salt, if desired), cook the noodles for 3 minutes or until they are *al dente,* and drain them.
2. In a small bowl, combine the Worcestershire sauce, soy sauce, and sherry, and set the mixture aside.
3. In a wok or large skillet, heat 1 tablespoon of the oil and stir-fry the scallions, garlic, and red pepper for about 1 minute. Add the cabbage, and stir-fry the vegetables for another minute. Add the chicken or meat, and stir-fry the mixture a minute longer. Transfer the mixture to a bowl.
4. Heat the remaining tablespoon of oil in the wok or skillet over high heat, and add the noodles, letting them brown for about 2 minutes. Reduce the heat, and add the broth, stirring to combine well.
5. Add the vegetable mixture and Worcestershire-sauce mixture to the noodles, and toss the ingredients well. Heat the stir-fry for about 1 minute, sprinkling it with hot pepper oil just before serving.

EGGPLANT AND ZITI PARMESAN   *4 servings*

Preparation tip: Note that the eggplant needs to drain for half an hour. Since the eggplant is salted to remove the bitter juices, and the grated cheese contains salt, no added salt is needed. If you do not have homemade tomato sauce handy, consider using a commercial variety with no salt added. You can prepare this dish in advance through step 6.

1¼ pounds eggplant, peeled and cut into ¼-inch
    slices crosswise
Salt
  8 ounces ziti
  1 tablespoon oil
  1 large clove garlic, crushed
Freshly ground black pepper to taste
1⅓ cups part-skim ricotta or low-fat cottage
    cheese
  1 cup grated Parmesan, divided
  ¼ cup minced fresh parsley *or* 1 tablespoon
    dried parsley flakes
  ½ teaspoon dried basil
  ½ teaspoon orégano
  ¼ teaspoon hot red pepper flakes (optional)
  2 cups tomato sauce

1. Sprinkle the eggplant with salt. Place the eggplant in a colander, and let it drain for 30 minutes. Rinse the eggplant, and pat it dry.
2. Cook the ziti *al dente* according to package directions. Drain and rinse the pasta, and set it aside.
3. Combine the oil and garlic, and smear it on the eggplant slices. Then sprinkle the slices generously with pepper.
4. Broil the eggplant slices about 4 inches from the heat, turning them once, for a total of about 5 minutes. (You may have to do this in two batches).
5. In a large bowl, combine the ricotta or cottage cheese, all but 2 tablespoons of the Parmesan, the parsley, basil, orégano, and pepper flakes. Toss the cheese mixture with the ziti.
6. On the bottom of a 2½- to 3-quart casserole, spread a thin layer of tomato sauce, add half the ziti mixture, then half the eggplant slices, then half the remaining tomato sauce. Repeat the ziti, eggplant, and sauce layers. Top with the reserved 2 tablespoons of Parmesan.
7. Cover the casserole, and bake it in a preheated 400° oven for 30 minutes. Remove the cover, and bake the casserole for another 15 minutes or until the top is lightly browned.

QUICK LASAGNE WITH BEAN SAUCE

8 servings

Nikki and David Goldbeck, authors of the extensive vegetarian cookbook *American Wholefoods Cuisine,* introduced me to instant lasagne, made with uncooked noodles, and to a new taste sensation in lasagne—beans. The dish was unanimously loved by more than a dozen tasters. *Preparation tip:* If you precook the noodles, bake the casserole uncovered for 25 minutes. An alternative to the bean sauce is 4 cups of already prepared tomato sauce to which beans, mushrooms, eggplant, or zucchini are added. For a cheesier lasagne, you can add more ricotta or mix it with some cottage cheese or mashed tofu (bean curd). The dish can be prepared for baking through step 2 and stored in the refrigerator or freezer. Cooked lasagne can be frozen and reheated without defrosting, if it is covered tightly.

BEAN SAUCE
- 1 tablespoon oil
- 2 teaspoons minced garlic
- 1 small onion, finely chopped
- 2 cups cooked beans (red or brown, canned or home-cooked), drained and coarsely chopped
- 4 cups tomato purée *or* 2 cups tomato sauce and 2 cups purée
- 1 teaspoon orégano
- 1 teaspoon dried basil
- Freshly ground black pepper to taste

REMAINING INGREDIENTS
- ¾ pound (approximately) uncooked lasagne noodles, white or whole-wheat
- 2 cups part-skim ricotta
- 8 ounces part-skim mozzarella, thinly sliced
- ¼ cup grated Parmesan

1. Prepare the sauce by heating the oil in a medium saucepan and sautéeing the garlic and onions for a minute. Add the chopped beans, and cook the mixture, stirring it, for several minutes longer. Add the tomato purée (or sauce and purée), orégano, basil, and pepper. Bring the sauce to a boil, and simmer it for 5 minutes.
2. To assemble the lasagne, spread a thin layer of the bean sauce on the bottom of a 9 × 13-inch baking pan or shallow casserole. Arrange a layer of noodles along the bottom of the pan to cover the sauce in such a way that they touch but do not overlap. You should use about a third of the noodles. Cover the noodle layer with half the ricotta, half the mozzarella, and one-third of the remaining sauce. Repeat with a layer of noodles, ricotta, mozzarella, and sauce. Finish off with layers of the remaining noodles and sauce. Then sprinkle the Parmesan on top.

3. Cover the pan tightly with foil. Bake the lasagne in a preheated 350° oven for about 1 hour or until the pasta is cooked. If there is too much liquid remaining in the pan, remove the foil and bake the lasagne for another 10 to 15 minutes.

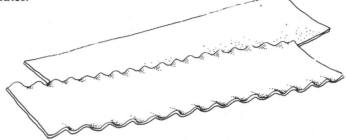

SPAGHETTI PANCAKE

4 servings

Although it's hard in our house to make enough spaghetti to have leftovers for the next day, every now and then one of my sons will exercise restraint because he wants to have a spaghetti pancake for breakfast. This simple dish is also good for lunch or supper. *Preparation tip:* This is easiest to prepare in a nonstick skillet. If you don't have one, grease a regular skillet with a generous coating of vgetable-oil spray. You can add herbs or minced hot peppers to taste.

4 cups cooked spaghetti (about ½ pound dry)
1 egg white plus 1 whole egg, lightly beaten
2 tablespoons milk
¼ to ⅓ cup grated Parmesan
¼ teaspoon dried orégano (optional)
Salt, if desired, to taste
Freshly ground black pepper to taste
Dash cayenne
2 teaspoons butter or margarine

1. In a medium bowl, combine the spaghetti, beaten egg white and egg, milk, cheese, orégano, salt, black pepper, and cayenne.
2. In a 10 inch skillet (preferably nonstick), heat the butter or margarine. Add the spaghetti mixture, spreading it evenly to form a tight cake. Cook the pancake over medium-low heat until its bottom is golden brown, about 10 minutes.
3. Using the edge of the spatula, divide the pancake into 4 sectors, and turn it one section at a time. (If you feel insecure about flipping the pancake, you could also place the entire pan under the broiler—providing its handle is oven-proof—to bake the top, although this method tends to dry it too much.) Brown the pancake on the other side, 3 to 5 minutes.

VEGETABLE LASAGNE   *8 servings*

To my family and guests, this dish ranks higher on the scale of culinary treats than regular lasagne. And to think it's good for you—low in fat and high in fiber, vitamins, and minerals. I thank Susan Oakley for introducing me to the particular combination of ingredients. *Preparation tip:* Lasagne, like eggplant Parmesan, is a multistep dish to prepare, which discourages some cooks. But it is excellent company or party food because it can be made weeks ahead and frozen unbaked. To me, it is especially wonderful after a day of outdoor winter activity: if defrosted, it bakes in less than half an hour while you're putting things away and preparing a salad. If you're making it for your family, I'd recommend preparing two pans: one to eat right away and another to freeze for later use.

1½ cups chopped onion (1½ large)
  2 large cloves garlic, finely minced (2 teaspoons)
  6 ounces mushrooms, coarsely chopped
  3 tablespoons sherry
  1 tablespoon butter or margarine
  2 large stalks broccoli (stems and flowerets), chopped (about 4 cups)
  ½ pound spinach, washed well and chopped (about 2 cups, packed)
  ½ teaspoon AHA herb mix (see p. 182) or low-salt alternative
 16 ounces (2 cups) low-fat cottage cheese
  4 ounces part-skim mozzarella, shredded (about 1 cup)
  3 tablespoons grated Parmesan
  ¼ cup chopped fresh parsley *or* 1 tablespoon dried parsley flakes
  2 eggs
  ¼ teaspoon freshly ground black pepper
  ¼ teaspoon salt, if desired
  3 cups tomato sauce (homemade or canned)
  8 ounces lasagne noodles, cooked *al dente* and spread on foil or wax paper

1. In a large skillet, sauté the onion, garlic, and mushrooms in sherry and butter until the vegetables are soft.
2. Add the chopped broccoli, spinach, and herb mix. Stir to combine the ingredients, reduce the heat, cover the skillet, and simmer the mixture for about 5 minutes or until the broccoli is tender-crisp.
3. In a medium bowl, combine the cottage cheese, mozzarella, Parmesan, parsley, eggs, pepper, and salt.
4. In a baking pan approximately 13 × 9 × 2 inches, spread ½ cup of tomato

sauce on bottom. Layer the lasagne ingredients as follows: Arrange three strips of lasagne noodles on the bottom. Spread half of the cheese mixture on noodles, then half of the vegetable mixture, and 1 cup of the tomato sauce. Repeat, starting from the noodles. End with a layer of noodles topped with the remaining ½ cup of tomato sauce. Sprinkle the top of the lasagne with additional Parmesan, if desired.

5. Bake the lasagne at 375° for 25 minutes. Let it stand for about 10 minute before serving it.

CHICKPEA SAUCE AND SPAGHETTI   *6 servings*

The unusual flavor of this sauce comes from rosemary. It provides a welcome change from the "traditional" Italian seasonings used in pasta dishes. Since canned chickpeas and Parmesan contain ample salt, the sauce doesn't need any extra. *Preparation tip:* The sauce can be prepared while the pasta cooks, or it can be made ahead and reheated when you are ready to cook the pasta.

```
 2 15-ounce cans chickpeas, divided (do not
   drain)
 2 tablespoons vegetable oil, preferably olive
 4 large cloves garlic, minced (4 teaspoons)
1½ cups thinly sliced onions (1½ large)
 1 16-ounce can tomatoes, drained and cut up,
   with liquid reserved
 1 teaspoon rosemary, crushed
¼ cup minced fresh parsley
Freshly ground black pepper to taste
 1 pound spaghetti, cooked and drained
¼ cup grated Parmesan
```

1. In a blender or food processor or sieve, purée *1 can* of chickpeas with its liquid.
2. In a large saucepan, heat the oil and sauté the garlic and onions until the garlic begins to brown.
3. Add the tomatoes and their liquid, rosemary, chickpea purée, and the remaining can of chickpeas with its liquid to the saucepan. Stirring it often, heat the mixture for about 15 minutes or until it has thickened. Add the parsley and pepper.
4. Toss the hot cooked spaghetti with the sauce, and sprinkle it with Parmesan before serving.

FETTUCINE WITH MUSSEL SAUCE   *6 servings*

This is a delicious sauce so low in calories that you hardly need to count them at all! The dish can be a first course or main course. *Preparation tip:* If you have access to cultured mussels, the cleaning job will be that much faster since the mussels will not need to be soaked. This sauce also goes well with a pasta broader than fettucine or an open macaroni like medium shells. You can prepare both the tomato mixture and the steamed mussels ahead of time and, at serving time, combine and cook them together for 10 minutes while the pasta cooks. Purists say that grated cheese should not be used with a seafood sauce, but I like just a light sprinkling on this one.

    4 pounds mussels, beards removed, scrubbed,
       and, if necessary, soaked in cold water,
       drained, and rinsed
    1 cup boiling water
    1 tablespoon olive oil
    1 tablespoon minced garlic (3 large cloves)
    ¼ cup minced shallots (2 large) *or* 2 tablespoons
       minced onion
    1 35-ounce can plum tomatoes, undrained
    ½ teaspoon marjoram, crumbled
    ¼ teapoon salt, if desired
    ¼ teaspoon sugar
    ⅛ to ¼ teaspoon freshly ground black pepper, to
       taste
    1 pound fettucine or similar pasta, cooked *al
       dente*
    Grated Parmesan (optional)

1. Place the cleaned mussels in a large pot, add the boiling water, cover the pot and steam the mussels until they open. Set them aside to cool, discarding any mussels that haven't opened.
2. In a large, deep skillet or large saucepan, heat the oil briefly, and sauté the garlic and shallots or onions, stirring them, until they are soft, about 1 or 2 minutes. Add the tomatoes and their liquid, breaking up the tomatoes with a spatula or wooden spoon, and stir in the marjoram, salt, sugar, and pepper. Heat the sauce to the boiling point, and simmer it, uncovered, for 20 to 30 minutes or until much of the tomato liquid has been reduced.
3. Meanwhile, remove the mussels from their cooking liquid, and set them aside. Strain the liquid through a very fine sieve or cheesecloth, and reserve it. Remove the mussels from their shells, saving 12 small ones in their shells for garnish.

4. When the tomato mixture has cooked down to the desired consistency, stir in the shelled mussels and 1½ cups of the reserved strained mussel liquid (or more, if you like a thinner sauce). (Any leftover liquid can be stored in the refrigerator or freezer to make soups or to poach fish or shellfish.) Simmer the sauce, uncovered, for 10 minutes, stirring often.
5. Place the cooked pasta on individual dishes (preferably with raised rims) or in shallow bowls. Spoon some sauce on top of the pasta, and garnish each serving with 1 or 2 of the mussels that were left in their shells. Serve with grated Parmesan, if desired.

"SZECHUAN" NOODLES WITH PEANUT SAUCE

4 servings

You may have had traditional Szechuan noodles with Oriental sesame paste (see p. 302). Here is an equally tasty version that you can make with ordinary supermarket ingredients. And only the pasta needs cooking! Although you may think of this as a side dish, it actually provides adequate protein and calories to serve as a main course, complemented with a green vegetable or salad. The dish is good both hot and at room temperature. *Preparation tip:* The sauce can be fully prepared while the pasta cooks, and you're ready to eat in about 20 minutes.

PASTA
12 ounces spaghetti, linguine, or similar pasta

SAUCE
⅓ cup hot water
⅓ cup smooth peanut butter (preferably all-natural)
2 teaspoons reduced-sodium soy sauce
2 teaspoons vinegar (I use white wine or rice vinegar)
2 scallions, finely chopped, divided
2 cloves garlic, very finely minced
1 teaspoon sugar
¼ teaspoon hot red pepper flakes, or more, to taste

1. Cook the pasta in boiling water until it is *al dente*. Drain the pasta, set it aside, and keep it warm.
2. Meanwhile, in a medium bowl, blend the water and peanut butter. Stir in the soy sauce, vinegar, all but 1 tablespoon of the scallions, garlic, sugar, and hot pepper flakes.
3. Combine the sauce with the hot spaghetti in a heated serving bowl. Garnish the dish with the 1 tablespoon of reserved scallions.

PERFECT PASTA PRIMAVERA   *4 generous servings*

This dish is the standard-bearer for my nutrition principles: based on complex carbohydrates (pasta), loaded with high-fiber and nutrient-rich vegetables, adequate in protein (from the pasta and cheese), and very low in fat, yet as tasty and attractive as anyone could want. *Preparation tip:* The specific vegetable ingredients can be varied, according to what you have available. I originally prepared this with the idea of clearing out bits and pieces from the refrigerator. Hence the particular vegetables listed should be used as a guide, not a rule. Whatever you use, keep in mind that the vegetables should be crunchy. If you have the vegetables cut and sauce ingredients ready, you can prepare them while the pasta cooks.

MAIN INGREDIENTS
- 1 cup broccoli flowerets, steamed for 5 minutes
- 1 cup 1-inch asparagus pieces, steamed for 5 minutes
- 1 cup sugar snap or snow peas, blanched for 1 minute
- 1 small zucchini or yellow summer squash, unpeeled, sliced in half lengthwise, then cut into 1-inch chunks and blanched for 1 minute
- 1 cup corn kernels (canned or, if fresh or frozen, blanched)
- 1 tablespoon finely minced garlic (3 large cloves)
- 1 tablespoon olive oil
- 1 large *or* 2 small tomatoes, diced
- ½ cup mushrooms, sliced
- ½ cup shredded carrot
- ¼ cup finely minced parsley
- ½ teaspoon freshly ground black pepper

- 12 ounces high-protein spaghetti or linguine

SAUCE
- 2 teaspoons butter or margarine
- 1 tablespoon flour
- 1 cup skim or 1-percent milk
- ½ cup chicken stock
- ½ cup grated Parmesan
- ¼ cup finely minced fresh basil *or* 1 teaspoon dried basil

1. Steam or blanch the various vegetables (broccoli, asparagus, peas, zucchini or squash, and corn) as indicated, combine them, and keep them warm.
2. In a skillet, sauté the garlic in the oil for 1 minute, but do not brown the garlic. Add the tomatoes, mushrooms, carrot, parsley, and pepper, and cook the mixture for 4 minutes. Add this to the reserved vegetables, tossing the ingredients gently to combine them well.

3. To prepare the sauce, in a small, heavy saucepan, melt the butter or margarine, and add the flour, whisking the roux over medium-low heat for 1 minute. Gradually add the milk and stock, stirring constantly until the sauce thickens slightly. Stir in the Parmesan and basil, and heat the sauce over medium-low flame, stirring it until the cheese is melted. Pour the sauce over the vegetable mixture, and toss the two gently to coat.

4. Cook the spaghetti or linguine *al dente,* drain it, and keep it warm.

5. Place the cooked pasta in a large heated serving bowl or platter. Spread the vegetable-and-sauce mixture over the pasta, toss the pasta gently once or twice, and serve it.

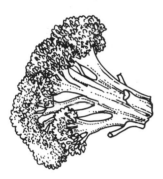

SPINACH-CHEESE NOODLES

4 servings

One of my favorite quickie meals dating back to childhood is egg noodles and cottage cheese. I make it for breakfast or lunch whenever there are some leftover noodles, white or green (I reheat the noodles by pouring boiling water over them, then drain them and add the cheese). Here is a more sophisticated cotatge-cheese-and-noodle dish that adds spinach and seasonings and heats the cottage cheese. If you use ricotta, bear in mind that it is fattier and therefore, more caloric. *Preparation tip:* If you have the ingredients ready, the sauce can be prepared while the noodles cook.

    8 ounces medium or wide egg noodles (you can
      use spinach noodles)
    1 tablespoon oil
    1 large clove garlic, minced (1 teaspoon)
    1 10-ounce package frozen chopped spinach,
      thawed and drained *or* 1 pound well-washed
      fresh spinach, stems removed, leaves blanched
      and chopped
    2 teaspoons fresh minced basil *or* ½ teaspoon
      dried basil
    ¼ cup minced fresh parsley *or* 1 tablespoon
      dried parsley flakes
    1 cup low-fat cottage cheese or part-skim ricotta
    ¼ teaspoon salt, if desired, to taste
    Freshly ground black pepper to taste
    2 tablespoons grated Parmesan
    1 pimiento, coarsely chopped, for garnish
      (optional)

1. Cook the noodles *al dente.* Drain them, and keep them warm in a large heated serving bowl.
2. Meanwhile, heat the oil in a skillet (about 10 inches, preferably nonstick), and sauté the garlic and spinach, stirring the vegetables, for 5 minutes.
3. Add the basil, parsley, cottage cheese or ricotta, salt, and pepper. Cook the mixture over low heat, stirring it until it is blended and heated through, about 2 minutes.
4. Add the spinach-and-cheese mixture to the noodles, and toss the two to combine. Sprinkle the noodles with Parmesan, and garnish with pimiento, if desired.

TURKEY TETRAZZINI

6 servings

It may have an Italian name, but this casserole of spaghetti, turkey, cheese, and milk is unquestionably American. It is good enough for a buffet as well as a family meal. *Preparation tip:* This is a great way to use up leftover turkey. Chicken can be used as well. You may also add leftover cooked vegetables such as broccoli, peas, or green beans in step 3. The dish can be prepared ahead through step 3 and baked just before mealtime.

½ pound mushrooms, sliced (about 3 cups)
1 tablespoon butter or margarine
2 tablespoons flour
½ teaspoon salt, if desired
½ teaspoon freshly ground black pepper
2 cups skim or low-fat milk
1 teaspoon Worcestershire sauce
½ cup shredded Swiss cheese or Cheddar (2 ounces)
1 green pepper, seeded and diced
⅓ cup sliced scallions
2 pimientos, finely chopped
2 cups cooked turkey (about ½ pound), cut into small cubes
½ pound spaghetti, cooked *al dente* and drained
¼ cup grated Parmesan

1. In a large, heavy saucepan over medium heat, sauté the mushrooms in the butter or margarine, stirring them often, until they are just tender.
2. Stir in the flour, salt, and pepper. Gradually add the milk, stirring constantly. Add the Worcestershire sauce, and simmer the sauce, stirring it, until it has thickened somewhat.
3. Add the Swiss cheese or Cheddar, green pepper, scallions, and pimientos to the sauce, and mix the ingredients well. Stir in the turkey and spaghetti, combining the mixture well. Pour the mixture into a greased 2-quart shallow casserole or baking dish. Sprinkle the top of the casserole with the Parmesan.
4. Bake the casserole, uncovered, in a preheated 350° oven for about 20 minutes or until it is heated through.

BEEF AND TOMATO SAUCE

4 to 6 servings
(for 1 pound of pasta)

This is probably the most frequently prepared pasta sauce in our household because it is quick, easy, and familiar enough to appeal to diners of all ages. As well as any recipe can, it represents the essence of my approach to cooking with meat: with a complex carbohydrate (pasta) as the centerpiece, a small but adequate amount of low-fat beef is combined with a vegetable sauce to make a complete meal, if you add a salad. The leaner the meat you start with and/or the more fat you drain off, the lower the fat and calorie count of the sauce will be and the more pasta you'll be able to eat without overloading on calories. Extra-lean ground beef may cost considerably more than regular kind, but, remember, you'll be throwing away a lot less of it, so you get more protein and less waste for your food dollar. *Preparation tip:* The optional ingredients are just that: make this sauce to suit your family's tastes. If the kids hate mushrooms or "pieces" of any kind, leave them out or purée them before adding the tomatoes.

½ pound extra-lean ground beef
2 teaspoon olive or vegetable oil
1 medium onion, minced (½ cup)
2 cloves garlic, finely minced (2 teaspoons)
½ cup finely diced celery (optional)
½ cup finely diced green or red sweet pepper
    (optional)
1 cup finely sliced small mushrooms (optional)
1 28-ounce can plum tomatoes with juice or
    purée
1 6-ounce can tomato paste
1 teaspoon sugar
1 teaspoon dried basil, crumbled
½ to 1 teaspoon orégano, crumbled, to taste
¼ teaspoon cardamom
¼ teaspoon salt, if desired
¼ teaspoon freshly ground black peper
Several dashes cayenne, to taste

1. In a large, deep skillet or broad-based saucepan (preferably nonstick), lightly brown the beef, crumbling it with a spatula into very small bits. Remove the beef with a slotted utensil to a plate lined with a paper towel. Pour off any fat in the pan, and wipe the pan out.
2. Heat the oil briefly in the pan, add the onion and garlic, and sauté them, stirring often, until they are translucent, about 2 minutes. (Do not let them brown.) Add the celery, sweet pepper, and mushrooms, if desired, and sauté the vegetables, stirring them, for another minute.

3. Add the tomatoes with their liquid, breaking them up with the spatula into small chunks. Add the tomato paste, sugar, basil, orégano, cardamom, salt, black pepper, cayenne, and reserved cooked beef. Bring the sauce to a boil over medium-heat heat, reduce the heat to low, and let the sauce simmer, uncovered, stirring it occasionally, for about 30 minutes or until it reaches the desired thickness.

WHITE CLAM SAUCE

4 servings

In a hurry? You can start with canned whole clams, even minced ones, rather than fresh. This sauce is excellent with green noodles or a flat pasta like fettucine.

2 dozen littleneck clams *or* 1 10-ounce can
  whole clams or minced clams
¼ cup water
1 clove garlic, minced
2 tablespoons olive oil
Salt, if desired, to taste (omit if using canned
  clams)
Freshly ground black pepper to taste
¼ cup minced fresh parsley
Grated Parmesan (optional)

1. In a pot with a cover, steam the clams in the water. As soon as the clams open, remove them from their shells, and chop them. Save the liquid in the pot and any that drips from the shells. Strain the juice. (If you used canned clams, chop them, and save the juice.)
2. In a heavy saucepan, sauté the garlic in the oil for 1 minute, but do not let the garlic brown.
3. Add the chopped clams and enough of the reserved clam juice to the sauce so that the desired consistency is reached. Add the salt and pepper. Stir in the parsley.
4. Serve the sauce over pasta, sprinkled with Parmesan, if desired.

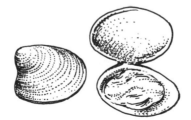

RED CLAM SAUCE

4 servings

For those who prefer tomato sauce on pasta, here's a simple variation on the theme that turns pasta with tomato sauce into a complete main dish. Since tomato sauce should simmer for a while, this sauce takes longer to prepare than white clam sauce.

  2 dozen littleneck clams *or* 1 10-ounce can
     clams, whole or minced
¼ cup water
  1 clove garlic, minced
  2 tablespoons olive oil
  2 tablespoons minced fresh parsley
  2 cups tomatoes (1 16-ounce can with liquid *or,*
     if fresh, peeled and cored), chopped
  2 tablespoons tomato paste
¼ teaspoon orégano, crumbled
Salt, if desired, to taste (omit if using canned
     clams)
Freshly ground black pepper to taste

1. In a covered pot, steam the clams in the water until they open. Remove them from their shells, saving the juice, and chop them. Strain the juice. (If you used canned clams, chop them, and save the juice.)
2. In a heavy saucepan, sauté the garlic in the oil for 1 minute, but do not let the garlic brown.
3. Add the parsley, tomatoes and their juice, tomato paste, and ½ cup of the clam juice. Simmer the sauce, uncovered, for about 40 minutes or until the sauce is thickened.
4. Add the clams, orégano, salt, and pepper, and simmer the sauce 2 minutes longer.

SHRIMP SAUCE

4 servings

I'm a great fan of shrimp because it is so low in calories, high in protein, and easy to prepare. Although for special events I use fresh, raw shrimp, for most other purposes I find that good-quality frozen shrimp serve the purpose. I buy 1½-pound bags of medium-sized peeled frozen shrimp from a fish market and keep them on hand in the freezer. *Preparation tip:* The recipe makes enough sauce for about 12 ounces of pasta, and the dish can be served either hot or at room temperature. If your ingredients are ready to go, you can start preparing this sauce while your pasta cooks.

½ pound raw medium-sized shrimp (if frozen,
   defrost)
1 tablespoon olive or salad oil
1 medium onion, chopped (½ cup)
2 cloves garlic, crushed
1 16-ounce can tomatoes, with juice, *or* 3
   medium-sized fresh tomatoes, peeled and
   coarsely chopped
⅛ teaspoon freshly ground black pepper
Few dashes cayenne
1 teaspoon dried basil
¼ teaspoon salt, if desired
¼ cup minced fresh parsley
½ cup pitted black olives, halved lengthwise, for
   garnish
Grated Parmesan (optional)

1. Cut the shrimp in half lengthwise.
2. Heat the oil in a medium skillet, add the onion, garlic, and shrimp, and sauté the ingredients, stirring, until the shrimp turn pink, about 3 minutes. Remove the shrimp, and set them aside.
3. Add the tomatoes and juice, black pepper, cayenne, basil, and salt to the skillet. Bring the mixture to a boil, reduce the heat, and simmer it, uncovered, for 5 minutes. Add the shrimp and parsley to the tomato mixture, and serve the sauce over spaghetti or other pasta garnished with olives and sprinkled with Parmesan, if desired.

SQUID-TOMATO SAUCE

4 to 6 servings
(for 1 pound of pasta)

Here's one I'd serve to company anytime. But I wouldn't reveal the name of the main ingredient until after everyone tasted it: one bite should cure all of any squeamishness about squid, a nutritious gem from the sea. *Preparation tip:* Clam juice is salty, so if you use it, omit any additional salt. This sauce works best with pasta that has a cuplike shape (e.g., shells or cavatelli) or a center hole (e.g., penne or ziti) that would catch the pieces. (See the note, below, for instructions on how to clean squid.)

 1 pound squid, cleaned and cut into ¼-inch
   pieces (see *Note*)
 2 tablespoons lemon juice
 ½ teaspoon salt, if desired
 2 large onions, sliced
 1½ tablespoons olive oil
 ⅔ cup peeled, seeded, chopped tomato, fresh or
   canned
 3 cloves garlic, crushed or finely minced
 ¼ teaspoon thyme
 ¼ teaspoon marjoram
 ⅓ cup dry red wine
 1 tablespoon tomato paste
 1 cup fish stock or bottled clam juice
 1 tablespoon flour
 1 tablespoon cold water
Freshly ground black pepper to taste

1. In a glass or ceramic bowl, combine the squid, lemon juice, and salt. Set this aside.
2. In a heavy saucepan, sauté the onions in the oil, stirring them, for 10 minutes or until the onions turn golden.
3. Add the squid, and cook the mixture, stirring it, for another 5 minutes.
4. Add the tomato, garlic, thyme, marjoram, wine, tomato paste, and stock or clam juice, and mix the ingredients well. Cover the sauce, and simmer it, stirring it occasionally, for 15 minutes (or for as long as 1 hour).
5. In a cup, combine the flour and water, and add them to the squid mixture. Cook the sauce, uncovered, for another 15 minutes, stirring it occasionally. Add the pepper, and serve it over cooked pasta.

NOTE: To clean squid, cut off the tentacles just in front of the eyes (temporarily leaving the eyes on the body portion) and squeeze the tentacles just below the cut to remove the hard white "beak" inside. Discard the beak, and cut the tentacles into pieces of desired size. Now cut the rest of the head from the body, just the other side of the eyes, and pull out innards, including the hard, translucent, sword-shaped "spine." Discard these and, holding the body under cold running water, slip off the outer speckled skin. Cut the body into pieces.

TUNA AND TOMATO SAUCE

4 servings
(for 1 pound of pasta)

Here is a sauce for tuna lovers that will turn any pasta into a main dish. I like it best with a macaroni that holds the sauce, such as rotini (corkscrew pasta). *Preparation tip:* The anchovy paste is salty, so no further salt is needed. You can prepare a reasonable facsimile of anchovy paste by mashing canned anchovies. I use reduced-salt tuna. If you have only regular tuna, you might consider using less anchovy paste.

- 1 tablespoon oil, preferably olive
- 2 teaspoons finely minced garlic (2 large cloves)
- ¾ teaspoon anchovy paste
- ¼ to ½ teaspoon hot red pepper flakes, or to taste
- 2 cups canned tomatoes, puréed in a blender with half their juice *or* 2 cups tomato purée
- ¼ teaspoon freshly ground black pepper
- 1 7-ounce can tuna packed in water, drained and flaked
- ¼ cup minced fresh parsley, divided

1. In a medium saucepan, heat the oil briefly, add the garlic, and cook it for 30 seconds. Remove the pan from the heat, and stir in the anchovy paste and pepper flakes.
2. Add the puréed tomatoes and black pepper, heat the sauce to the boiling point, reduce the heat, and simmer the sauce for about 20 minutes.
3. Add the flaked tuna and half the parsley, and simmer the sauce for another 10 minutes. To serve, toss the sauce with hot pasta, and sprinkle on the remaining parsley.

Greatness from Grains

Although nearly everyone has had lifelong culinary experience with grains in certain common forms—wheat as hot cereal, oats as oatmeal, rice as a side dish or pudding—few Americans have cooked these grains in their whole or natural forms (wheat berries, oat groats, brown rice). Nor have many eaten the less common grains and grain forms found in cuisines throughout the world such as millet, buckwheat groats, couscous, and wild rice. There are various recipes in this book using such grains to prepare main dishes, salads, side dishes, appetizers, and so forth (see the index under the respective grain). Here are some hot dishes in which the grain holds center court as an entrée.

BULGUR FRIED "RICE"   *4 servings*

Nearly everyone is familiar with Chinese-style fried rice. Here is a version in which bulgur (cracked wheat) is used in place of the less tasty and somewhat less nourishing white grains of rice. This dish is *not* low in sodium, but much lower than comparable Chinese recipes. *Preparation tip:* If you happen to have 3 cups of leftover cooked bulgur, you can use it in this dish.

   2 cups boiling water
   1 cup coarse bulgur
   4 teaspoons peanut or salad oil, divided
   1 egg white and 1 whole egg, slightly beaten
       with salt, if desired, and pepper to taste
   1 teaspoon minced fresh ginger (optional)
   ½ cup thinly sliced scallions, including about 2
       inches of green top from each scallion
   1 cup diced cooked chicken, pork, ham, or beef
   ½ cup sliced water chestnuts
   ½ cup sliced mushrooms
   2 tablespoons reduced-sodium soy sauce
   ½ teaspoon sugar
   Freshly ground black pepper to taste

1. In a bowl, combine the boiling water and bulgur. Let the bulgur soak for about 10 minutes, and drain off any water that was not absorbed. Or you can cook the bulgur in water for about 5 minutes and drain off any remaining water.
2. In a large nonstick skillet or a wok, heat 2 teaspoons of the oil. Add the egg white and whole egg, and cook them until they are just set. Transfer them to a plate, and when they are cool, cut them into shreds.
3. Heat the remaining 2 teaspoons of oil in the skillet, and add the ginger and scallions. Cook them, stirring, for about 1 minute.

4. Add the chicken or meat, water chestnuts, mushrooms, and bulgur, and sauté the mixture, stirring it, over high heat until it is hot.
5. Combine the soy sauce, sugar, and pepper, and add the sauce and the shredded eggs to the bulgur mixture, tossing the ingredients to combine well.

KASHA VARNISHKAS
4 servings

Every December, the arrival of the Jewish holiday Hanukkah provides me with a perfect excuse to prepare one of my childhood favorites: kasha varnishkas. This is a mixture of thick, shaped egg noodles (I nearly always use egg bows) and a grainlike food called buckwheat groats. I offered a recipe for this dish in *Jane Brody's Nutrition Book,* anglicizing its name to "Buckwheat and Bows." One devoted but very literal reader called me on the translation: "Call a spade a spade," he said. So I will. Kasha varnishkas it is! No need to wait for December to enjoy this traditional dish; it's good any time of the year. But I must admit that it's especially inviting on cold winter days, eaten for supper, lunch, or even breakfast. The egg complements the protein in the grain, turning this into a main dish.

2 teaspoons butter, margarine, or oil
1 medium onion, chopped fine (½ to ⅔ cup)
1 egg, slightly beaten
1 cup buckwheat groats (kasha), coarse granulation or whole
2 cups boiling broth, bouillon, or water
Salt, if desired, to taste (omit if using salty broth)
Freshly ground black pepper to taste (be generous)
¼ to ½ pound (as desired) egg bow macaroni (large size, not soup size), cooked, drained, and kept warm

1. In a skillet that has a cover, melt the butter or margarine or heat the oil, and sauté the onion until it is translucent.
2. In a small bowl, mix the egg with the buckwheat groats, and add this to the skillet. Cook the groats, stirring them, until the grains are dry and separated.
3. Add the broth or bouillon or water, salt, and pepper, cover the skillet, and simmer the kasha for 10 to 15 minutes or until all the liquid is absorbed.
4. Stir in the macaroni, and serve.

TEX-MEX KASHA

My friend and colleague Marian Burros, author of *Keep It Simple* and *You've Got It Made,* devised this dish, which is tasty without added salt. It would make a fine lunch or light supper. *Preparation tip:* This recipe can be prepared through step 2 and frozen. If so, sprinkle with cheese after reheating.

   1 tablespoon vegetable oil
   1 large onion, chopped (1 cup)
   1 stalk celery, chopped (½ cup)
   1 large green pepper, chopped (¾ cup)
   1 clove garlic, minced
   1 teaspoon orégano
   ½ teaspoon cumin
   1 teaspoon mild chili powder
   ¾ cup buckwheat groats (kasha), preferably
      whole
   1 35-ounce can tomatoes, coarsely chopped,
      liquid reserved
Freshly ground black pepper to taste
   1 cup coarsely grated Monterey Jack (3 ounces)

1. In a large skillet with a tight-fitting cover, heat the oil. Add the onion, celery, green pepper, and garlic, and sauté the vegetables until the onion is soft, about 5 minutes.
2. Stir in the orégano, cumin, chili powder, buckwheat groats, and tomatoes with their liquid. Season the mixture with black pepper. Bring it to a boil, reduce the heat, cover the skillet, and simmer the kasha for 10 to 15 minutes or until the liquid has been absorbed and the kasha is cooked.
3. Sprinkle the kasha with cheese, cover the skillet, and let the kasha stand for another minute or so to melt the cheese.

MILLET WITH CHICKPEA AND
VEGETABLE STEW

4 generous servings

Here's an offering from Mollie Katzen's *The Enchanted Broccoli Forest* (a wonderful vegetarian cookbook) that provides complete protein by combining chickpeas and nuts with millet. It is one of the tastiest ways to eat millet. I have modified the recipe to reduce the fat and salt. *Preparation tip:* Note that the recipe calls for *cooked* chickpeas (see p. 103 or use canned ones) and *cooked* millet.

2 teaspoons olive oil
2 teaspoon butter or margarine
2 medium onions, chopped (1⅓ cups)
¼ teaspoon salt, if desired, or to taste
1 pound fresh mushrooms, chopped
3 tablespoons fresh lemon juice
1 pound fresh broccoli, chopped
2 cups cooked, drained chickpeas (garbanzos)
½ cup (packed) currants
½ teaspoon paprika
Freshly ground black pepper to taste
Several dashes cayenne to taste
⅔ cup chopped, roasted cashews
4 cups cooked millet (see p. 71)

1. In a large, heavy skillet, heat the oil and the butter or margarine, and sauté the onions with salt for about 2 or 3 minutes, or until the onions soften.
2. Add the mushrooms, lemon juice, and broccoli. Cover the skillet, and cook the mixture over a medium-low heat for 4 or 5 minutes or until the broccoli is bright green and just tender.
3. Add the chickpeas, currants, paprika, black pepper, and cayenne, and simmer the stew, covered, for another 1 to 2 minutes to heat it through. Stir in the cashews, and serve the stew atop cooked millet.

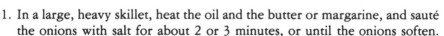

BROWN RICE CURRY WITH VEGETABLES AND SHRIMP

6 servings

A simple and tasty dish, the ingredients of which can be varied according to taste. *Preparation tip:* You can, for example, substitute small chunks of chicken or beef for shrimp; just add them sooner to the vegetable stew to give them time to cook through. Or you can leave out the "meat" altogether and make just a vegetable curry, perhaps adding cooked chickpeas, beans, or tofu for a protein boost. You can also vary the vegetables, adding them according to how long they take to cook. Broccoli or cauliflower, for example, could be used as a substitute for the zucchini. The vegetables and shrimp can be prepared while the rice is cooking (brown rice takes about 35 to 40 minutes to cook). The dish is delicious hot or cold.

    2 teaspoons oil
    1 large onion, sliced
    2 large cloves garlic, minced (2 teaspoons)
    1 *tablespoon* curry powder, or to taste
    ¼ teaspoon cinnamon
    ½ teaspoon salt, if desired
 1¼ cups water
    2 large carrots, sliced ¼-inch thick
    2 large potatoes, peeled and cut into ½-inch
      cubes
    1 large zucchini (about ¾ pound), quartered
      lengthwise then sliced crosswise ½-inch thick
    1 16-ounce can tomatoes, with their juice, cut
      into chunks
    ¼ cup raisins
    ½ pound shrimp (frozen or fresh, shelled, and
      deveined)
    4 cups hot cooked brown rice (1⅓ cups raw)
      (see p. 58)
    1 large banana, coarsely chopped (optional)

1. In a large saucepan or deep skillet (preferably nonstick), heat the oil briefly, and sauté the onion and garlic until they are soft.
2. Stir in the curry powder, cinnamon, salt, and water. Bring the mixture to a boil, and add the carrots and potatoes. Cover the pan, and simmer the mixture for 10 minutes.
3. Add the zucchini, tomatoes with their juice, raisins, and shrimp, cover the pan, and simmer the mixture 10 minutes longer.
4. Place the cooked rice in a serving dish, and pour the vegetable-and-shrimp mixture over it. Sprinkle the curry with chopped banana, if desired.

RICE, CORN, AND CHEESE CASSEROLE   *6 servings*

There could hardly be a simpler main dish to prepare, especially if you have on hand some leftover cooked rice. *Preparation tip:* For added interest, you could add chopped pimiento and minced green chilies or jalapeño peppers (canned or fresh) to give the dish more color or kick. The casserole can be prepared a day or two in advance for baking.

       3 cups cooked brown or white rice (1 cup raw)
           (see p. 58)
       2 cups corn kernels (1 10-ounce package frozen
           kernels, thawed, *or* 1 15-ounce can, drained)
       1 small onion, finely chopped (⅓ cup)
       2 cups grated sharp Cheddar (about 6 ounces)
    1½ cups skim or low-fat milk
       ½ teaspoon salt, if desired
       ½ teaspoon chili powder, or more, to taste
       ¼ teaspoon freshly ground black pepper
    Paprika

1. In a large mixing bowl, combine all the ingredients except the paprika, and mix them well.
2. Pour the ingredients into a greased 2-quart casserole. Sprinkle with paprika, and bake the casserole in a 350° oven for 40 to 45 minutes.

COMPANY RICE WITH BEANS   *4 servings*

This dish is named for the first time I made it. Unexpected guests dropped in late one summer afternoon, and these were the ingredients I had on hand to whip together a quick, tasty, and nutritious supper. The recipe is so simple I could even talk to my guests while I cooked. I served the dish with garden-fresh steamed green beans, a salad, and a refreshing fruit salad for dessert. *Preparation tip:* The bean-and-vegetable sauce can be prepared while the rice is cooking. Or you can start with 3 cups of cooked rice.

1 cup rice, brown or white
2 cups water
1 tablespoon oil
1 medium onion, coarsely chopped (⅔ cup)
2 cloves garlic, crushed or finely minced
2 medium tomatoes, finely diced
1 medium zucchini (about ½ pound), coarsely
    chopped
½ teaspoon orégano
1 16-ounce can beans (kidney, pink, black, or
    garbanzo), drained
Salt, if desired, to taste
Freshly ground black pepper to taste
1 cup shredded cheese (e.g., Cheddar)

1. In a medium saucepan, combine the rice and water, bring the mixture to a boil, reduce the heat, cover the pan, and simmer the mixture for 20 minutes (35 minutes for brown rice). Keep the pan covered until the vegetable mixture is done.
2. Meanwhile, heat the oil in a large skillet, add the onion and garlic, sauté them until they are soft.
3. Add the tomatoes, zucchini, and orégano. Cover the skillet, and simmer the mixture for about 5 minutes or until the vegetables are tender-crisp.
4. Add the beans, and simmer the mixture, stirring it occasionally, until it is heated through. Season with salt if desired, and pepper.
5. To serve, spoon the vegetable-bean mixture over the hot rice, and sprinkle the cheese on top.

PILAF WITH A PURPOSE

4 servings

Alice Antreassian, author of *Armenian Cooking Today,* suggested this combination of ingredients, which make up a main-course grain-based dish that is delicious and surprising. The mixing of bulgur, pasta, chickpeas, and nuts results in complete protein. The onion is my addition.

1½ teaspoons olive oil
 1 teaspoon butter or margarine
 ½ cup broken very thin pasta (capellini or
    capellini d'angeli)
 1 medium onion, chopped (⅔ cup)
 1 cup bulgur
 2 cups chicken broth
 ¼ teaspoon salt, if desired (omit if broth is salty)
Freshly ground black pepper to taste
 ⅓ cup chopped fresh basil *or* 1 tablespoon dried
    basil
 ¼ cup chopped walnuts
 ¾ cup cooked chickpeas, drained (about ½ can)

1. Heat the oil and the butter or margarine in a deep saucepan with a tight-fitting cover. Add the pasta, and cook it over medium heat, stirring constantly, until the pasta is golden brown. Add the onion and the bulgur, and cook the mixture, stirring it, another 1 to 2 minutes.
2. Add all the remaining ingredients, bring the pilaf to a boil, reduce the heat to very low, cover the pan, and simmer the pilaf for 20 minutes.

Maine-ly Potatoes

Actually, I get my potatoes from lots of places besides Maine—Long Island and Idaho among them. But in naming this section, I wanted to make a point. Most Americans think of potatoes only as a side dish—fries with burgers, a scoop of mashed potatoes with meat and gravy, home fries with scrambled eggs, potato nuggets atop a hamburger hot dish. In the following recipes, potatoes take center stage, providing a substantial portion of the protein, vitamins, and minerals (see p. 31) as well as the substance and calories. Keep in mind that before the potato blight struck Ireland, the Irish did quite well surviving mainly on potatoes. The recipes offered here aim to please without overwhelming this nutritious starchy food with fat and salt. I usually recommend boiling or steaming potatoes in their skin since this preserves more of the nutrients. Either way, save the water for baking breads or making soup stock; the starch that leaches out is an excellent dough conditioner and thickener.

MEAL-IN-A-BOWL POTATO SALAD   *4 servings*

This salad is both tasty and attractive without a fatty dressing. It makes an excellent picnic food as well as an appealing summer lunch or supper. *Preparation tip:* The flavor seems to improve as it stands, so I would suggest adding the dressing an hour or so beforehand, even though the salad may get a little watery as a result (you can always pour off the excess liquid). Those concerned about cholesterol should discard the yolks after the eggs are hard-boiled.

1½ pounds small red new potatoes, *unpeeled*	**DRESSING**
	1¼ cups plain low-fat yogurt
1 green pepper, seeded and sliced crosswise into rings	3 tablespoons snipped fresh dill
	1 tablespoon fresh lemon juice
4 hard-boiled eggs	1 tablespoon olive oil
½ small red onion, thinly sliced and separated into rings	1½ teaspoons Dijon mustard
	½ teaspoons sugar
½ cup pitted ripe black olives, sliced in half crosswise	¼ teaspoon salt, if desired, or to taste
¼ cup minced fresh parsley	¼ to ½ teaspoon freshly ground black pepper, to taste

1. Steam the unpeeled potatoes until they are just tender when pierced with a fork, but not mushy. If they are very small, leave them whole, or, when cool enough to handle, cut them in half or quarters with a very sharp knife, taking care not to pull off the skin. Place them in a large bowl or on a serving platter surrounded by the green pepper rings.
2. Slice the eggs crosswise, but remove and discard two of the yolks. Arrange the slices over the potatoes.
3. Add the onion rings and olives, and sprinkle the salad with the parsley.
4. In a small bowl, combine the dressing ingredients. Pour the dressing over the salad. Either serve the salad as is, or toss it gently. The salad may be served at room temperature or chilled.

COLCANNON *(Potato and Cabbage Casserole)*   *4 main-dish servings*

Colcannon, a combination of mashed potatoes and a member of the cabbage family (cabbage or kale), is a favorite food in Ireland and Scotland. According to Marian Morash, author of *The Victory Garden Cookbook* (a "must have" for all vegetable lovers), colcannon is traditionally eaten at Halloween, with symbols of fortune buried in it (a golden ring predicting marriage within a year, a sixpence for forthcoming wealth, a thimble for spinsterhood, and a button for bachelorhood). With or without the symbols, it will be your good fortune to try this simple version. The milk and cheese, which is not traditional, turn this into a main dish. *Preparation tip:* The cheese can either be mixed into the dish, as indicated, or placed on top. Taste the colcannon before adding salt since the cheese may provide enough. The dish can be prepared in advance through step 5, refrigerated, and heated at serving time.

> 1 pound all-purpose potatoes, washed but not
>   peeled
> 1 pound green cabbage, shredded (4 cups)
> 1 large onion, chopped (1 cup)
> ¼ cup skim or low-fat milk
> 1 tablespoon butter or margarine
> 3 ounces sharp Cheddar (or other hard cheese),
>   coarsely grated, divided
> Freshly ground black pepper to taste
> Salt, if desired, to taste

1. Boil the potatoes in lightly salted water until they are very tender but not mushy. Drain them, reserving the cooking liquid, and set them aside to cool somewhat.
2. Using the potato water (you may have to add more water), boil the cabbage and onion for about 5 minutes. Drain the vegetables set them aside.
3. When the potatoes are cool enough to handle, peel off the skin, place the potatoes in a bowl, add the milk and the butter or margarine, and mash them until they are smooth.
4. Add the reserved boiled cabbage and onion to the potato mixture.
5. Mix two-thirds of the cheese with the potato mixture. Season the colcannon with pepper and salt, if desired, and transfer it to a greased casserole or shallow baking dish. Sprinkle the remaining cheese on top.
6. Before serving the colcannon, heat it through in a moderately hot oven (the temperature is not critical—it can be between 350° and 425°, depending on what else you are using the oven for). Let the cheese on top brown slightly.

POTATO-BEAN PATTIES

4 servings

Even children who would otherwise never touch a bean devoured these soft croquettes which have a crisp outer shell. They are excellent as a lunch or supper entrée, accompanied by a green vegetable and salad. If you have precooked the beans, the patties can be prepared quickly. *Preparation tip:* Adzuki (or aduki) beans are very small and kidney-red; they are widely available in natural food stores. The closest substitute would be small red beans. For added nutrients and flavor, use the potato water for part of the liquid to cook the beans. The "batter" or patties can be fully prepared even a day ahead and refrigerated. Because the patties are soft, it is important to fry them with enough space between them so that they can be turned easily. They are easiest to handle on a pancake griddle (preferably one with a nonstick surface) rather than in a frying pan.

    1 pound unpeeled potatoes, scrubbed and boiled
        in lightly salted water until tender
    1 egg white
    3 tablespoons milk
    1 teaspoon butter or margarine
    Freshly ground black pepper to taste
    2 tablespoons minced fresh parsley
    ½ cup dried adzuki beans, soaked and cooked
        until tender but not mushy (see p. 103)
    ½ cup grated Parmesan
    Vegetable oil for frying (2 to 3 tablespoons)

1. When the potatoes are cool enough to handle, peel and mash them with egg white, milk, butter or margarine, and pepper.
2. Stir in the parsley, and fold in the cooked beans.
3. Form the mixture into 16 patties (about 2½ inches in diameter), coating each one on both sides with the grated cheese. Place them on a flat surface on a sheet of wax paper, but do not let them touch.
4. In batches on an oiled griddle or in a skillet, fry the patties until they are browned on both sides, taking care when turning them not to mush them. Keep the cooked patties warm in the oven until serving time.

POTATO-SALMON CROQUETTES   *6 servings*

For a quick, nutritious, and tasty meal any time of day, try these simple patties.

1½ pounds *cooked* all-purpose potatoes, peeled
    and finely diced (about 4 cups)
  1 7½-ounce can salmon, drained, skin discarded,
    bones crushed and saved, flaked
  ⅓ cup finely chopped green pepper
  2 tablespoons minced onion
  1 egg *or* 1 egg white, lightly beaten
Freshly ground black pepper to taste
Vegetable oil for frying

1. Combine the potatoes, salmon and crushed bones, green pepper, onion, egg or egg white, and pepper. Shape the mixture into 12 patties.
2. Fry the croquettes in a lightly oiled skillet or on a griddle, preferably nonstick, until they are browned on both sides.

VEGETARIAN SHEPHERD'S PIE   *6 servings*

This is an ideal dish for vegetable lovers. But for children who don't share this passion, it's—as one put it—"a good way to spoil mashed potatoes." One punning young taster suggested that the vegetables be fed to the sheep! *Nutrition Action,* the newletter of the Center for Science in the Public Interest, recommends this dish as a way of clearing the refrigerator of miscellaneous vegetables. *Preparation tip:* Anything goes as the underlayer for the mashed potatoes: green peas or beans, lima beans, diced turnips, sliced celery, etc. For extra protein you could add some cooked chickpeas or kidney beans. Therefore, do not be wedded to the ingredients listed, although they work well. The casserole can be prepared in advance for baking through step 4.

TOPPING

2 pounds all-purpose potatoes, scrubbed, *unpeeled,* and quartered
1 tablespoon butter or margarine
¼ cup skim or low-fat milk
1 teaspoon tamari or reduced-sodium soy sauce
1 garlic clove, crushed
½ cup grated cheese (any kind you like), divided
Several dashes cayenne, to taste
Paprika for garnish

FILLING

1 teaspoon oil
1 large onion, chopped (1 cup)
5 large fresh tomatoes *or* 1 35-ounce can of tomatoes with their juice, coarsely chopped
1 pound carrots, sliced
1 green pepper, seeded and diced
1½ cups shredded green cabbage
1 head of cauliflower or broccoli, cut into bite-sized chunks
1 bay leaf
1 *tablespoon* dried basil
2 cups chopped greens (spinach, kale, or Swiss chard)
1 teaspoon tamari or reduced-sodium soy sauce
1 clove garlic, minced

1. Cook the potatoes in lightly salted water to cover until they are soft. Drain the potatoes (save water for soup or bread) and, when they are cool enough to handle, remove and discard their skins, add the butter or margarine and the milk, and mash the potatoes until they are smooth. Mix in the tamari or soy sauce, the garlic, and two-thirds of the cheese. Set the mixture aside.
2. Prepare the filling in a large skillet or Dutch oven. Heat the oil, and sauté the onion until it is soft. Add the tomatoes, carrots, green pepper, cabbage, cauliflower or broccoli, bay leaf, and basil. Bring the mixture to a boil, reduce the heat, and simmer the mixture for 20 minutes.
3. Add the greens, tamari or soy sauce, and garlic, and simmer the mixture 5 minutes longer. Discard the bay leaf.

4. Transfer the vegetables to a large casserole (3- or 4-quart size). Spread the mashed-potato topping over the vegetables. Sprinkle on the remaining cheese plus the cayenne and paprika.

5. Bake the pie in a preheated 350° oven for 15 to 20 minutes or until it is heated through and the topping is lightly browned.

POLISH POTATO CASSEROLE　　*4 to 6 servings*

Of three potato-kielbasa casseroles I've made, this one is the easiest to prepare. *Preparation tip:* To keep the potatoes from darkening, slice them into a bowl of cold water, or wait to slice them until after the sauce is ready (step 1). If desired, cook the sausage in a skillet to remove some of the fat before assembling the casserole.

  1 tablespoon butter or margarine
  2 tablespoons all-purpose flour
  2 cups skim or low-fat milk
  ¼ to ½ teaspoon salt, if desired, to taste
  ¼ teaspoon freshly ground black pepper
  4 large potatoes (about 2 pounds), peeled and
    sliced thin
  1 large onion, sliced thin
  ½ pound green cabbage, shredded (2 cups), or
    more, if desired
  ½ pound kielbasa (Polish garlic sausage), sliced
    thin

1. In a medium saucepan, melt the butter or margarine, and stir in the flour. Cook the roux, stirring, for 1 minute, and then gradually add the milk, stirring constantly to eliminate lumps. Cook the mixture over moderately low heat, stirring it, until the sauce begins to thicken to the consistency of buttermilk. Stir in the salt, if desired, and pepper. Set the sauce aside.

2. Grease a 2½- to 3-quart casserole. Spread one-third of the potato slices on the bottom. Distribute half the onion slices followed by half the cabbage and half the kielbasa in layers over the potatoes. Add one-third of the sauce. Repeat with another third of the potato slices, the rest of the onion, cabbage, and sausage, and another third of the sauce. Top with the remaining potato slices and the remaining sauce.

3. Cover the casserole, and bake it in a 350° oven for 1 hour 15 minutes or until the potatoes are tender. If desired (and if there is enough liquid in the casserole), remove the cover for the last 15 minutes of baking time.

SCALLOPED POTATO SPECIAL   *6 servings*

Instead of cream sauce, these scalloped potatoes are baked with an onion-tomato sauce and a modest amount of cheese, which complements the protein in the potatoes and turns the dish into a main course. *Preparation tip:* The length of time the casserole should be covered is determined by the amount of moisture in the potatotes: the drier they are, the longer the cover should be kept on.

    2 teaspoons olive oil
    1 teaspoon butter or margarine
    3 cups thinly sliced onions (about 4 medium)
    4 cloves garlic, crushed or finely minced
    1 35-ounce can tomatoes, drained well and
        diced, *or* 2 pounds fresh tomatoes, peeled,
        seeded, drained, and diced
    ½ teaspoon salt, if desired, divided
Freshly ground black pepper to taste
    2 tablespoons minced fresh parsley *or* 2
        teaspoons dried parsley flakes
    ½ teaspoon dried basil
    ¼ teaspoon orégano
2½ pounds raw potatoes
    1 cup shredded Swiss cheese (4 ounces), divided
    2 tablespoons grated Parmesan, divided

1. Heat the oil and the butter or margarine in a medium skillet. Add the onions and garlic, and sauté them, stirring, for 1 minute. Cover the skillet, and cook the vegetables over moderately low heat for a few minutes longer or until the onions are soft but not brown (do not let the garlic burn).
2. Remove the skillet from the heat, and add the tomatoes, ¼ teaspoon of the salt, pepper, parsley, basil, and orégano. Mix the ingredients gently to combine them well.
3. Preheat the oven to 325°.
4. Peel and slice the potatoes very thin.
5. To assemble the casserole, place *one-third* of the onion-tomato mixture in the bottom of a greased 3-quart casserole. Spread *one-half* of the potatoes on top. Sprinkle them with half the remaining salt (⅛ teaspoon), if desired, and some pepper. Sprinkle *one-half* of the Swiss cheese and *1* tablespoon of the Parmesan on the potatoes. Repeat the layers: another third of the onion-tomato mixture, the rest of the potatoes, salt and pepper, and the remaining Swiss cheese and Parmesan. Top the casserole with the remaining onion-tomato mixture.

6. Bake the casserole, covered, in the preheated over for 1 hour 15 minutes. Uncover the casserole, and bake it 45 minutes longer or until the potatoes are tender but not mushy.

STUFFED BAKED POTATOES   *4 servings*

The fast-food chain, Wendy's, has gotten millions of Americans interested in the baked potato, topped by any number of "sauces," most of which are too high in fat and/or salt to suit me. However, this recipe, derived from one in *Stuffed Spuds* by Jeanne Jones, turns the baked potato into a complete and nutritious meal. *Preparation tip:* You can set this up well in advance through step 2, to be heated through at mealtime (simple enough for the kids to do for themselves, as soon as they're old enough to turn on the oven). Chances are you'll have more stuffing than you can fit into the potatoes. Put the leftover stuffing in an ovenproof custard cup, and bake it along with the stuffed potatoes. The stuffed potatoes can also be heated in a microwave oven.

  4 large baked potatoes (about 7 ounces each)
  ½ cup low-fat or skim milk, warmed
  1 cup part-skim ricotta
  2 small cloves garlic, crushed
  ¼ teaspoon salt, if desired
  ⅛ teaspoon freshly ground black pepper
  2 cups chopped cooked broccoli (stems or flowerets) or spinach
  ¼ cup grated Parmesan, divided

1. Take thin slices off the potatoes lengthwise. With a melon baller or small sharp spoon, carefully scoop out the flesh without tearing the skin. Reserve the skins (but not the slices).
2. In a medium bowl, mash the potato flesh with the warm milk. Combine it well with the ricotta, garlic, salt, pepper, broccoli or spinach, and 2 tablespoons of the Parmesan. Stuff the potato mixture into the reserved potato skins, piling it high. Sprinkle the stuffed potatoes with the remaining cheese.
3. Place the potatoes in a pan, and bake them in a preheated 350° oven for 20 minutes (longer if the potatoes were cold to start with).

Vegetarian Main Dishes

There once was a time when a meal without meat was considered un-American (unless it was macaroni and cheese), and that time was not so long ago! Vegetarians were looked upon as freaks who were asking for ill health because they refused to eat the flesh of animals. Now we know that a well-designed vegetarian diet can be healthier than a meat-based diet and that most vegetarians have a lower risk of developing heart disease, cancer, high blood pressure, and obesity than do meat-eating Americans. Many of us have also discovered that vegetarian dishes need not taste or look like animal feed. In fact, some of my family's favorite main dishes are meatless, and I don't hesitate to serve them to company.

The trick, however, is not to omit the meat and instead load the dish with fatty cheese and cream. Many of the dishes in this section use cheese as a protein source, but the amount is limited usually to an ounce or less per serving. In addition to the recipes in this section, you will find numerous other meatless main dishes in the sections on pasta, grains, eggs, soups, and salads.

CHILI WITHOUT CARNE   *4 servings*

If you try this recipe, you'll quickly realize that it's not the meat that makes chili wonderful—it's the seasonings and the beans. When served with rice (or any other grain) or bread, the protein in the beans is completed, making meat unnecessary for good nutrition. For introducing me to the ultimate in fine chili seasonings, I thank Marian Burros, noted food writer and author of many fine cookbooks, including *Keep It Simple* and *You've Got It Made.* The following is a minor modification of her recipe for meatless chili. *Preparation tip:* Don't be put off by the long list of ingredients—they're mostly seasonings. The entire recipe takes but 15 minutes to throw together. Besides, chili flavors improve with age, so this is a fine dish to make in advance for reheating at serving time. If you miss the meat, try adding coarse-grain bulgur (soak ⅓ cup of bulgur in ⅔ cup of boiling water for 15 minutes, then add it in step 2 along with the beans).

1 tablespoon olive or vegetable oil
2 medium onions, chopped (1 heaping cup)
3 large cloves garlic, minced (1 tablespoon)
1 green pepper, chopped
1 fresh jalapeño pepper, finely chopped (wear rubber gloves), *or* 2 tablespoons chopped canned hot peppers (jalapeño or green chilies)
1 28-ounce can tomatoes in purée *or* drained tomatoes, chopped, plus a 15-ounce can of purée
½ teaspoon ground coriander
¼ teaspoon whole cloves *or* generous pinch ground cloves
¼ teaspoon allspice berries *or* generous pinch ground allspice
2 teaspoons orégano
2 tablespoons brown sugar
2 tablespoons mild chili powder
2 tablespoons ground cumin
2 cups cooked kidney or pinto beans
1 cup raw rice, brown or white
2 cups boiling water

1. In a Dutch oven or large, heavy saucepan, heat the oil, and sauté the onions, garlic, green pepper, and jalapeño pepper until they are softened.
2. Add the tomatoes (and purée), coriander, cloves, allspice, orégano, brown sugar, chili, cumin, and beans. Bring the chili to a boil, reduce the heat, cover the pan, and simmer the chili for 30 minutes.
3. While the chili is cooking, in a medium saucepan add the rice to the boiling water, reduce the heat, cover the pan tightly, and simmer the rice for 15 to 35 minutes, according to package directions (depending upon the type of rice you use). Serve the chili over the rice.

VEGETABLE CHILI

4 generous servings

Here's an "anything goes" recipe, as long as you use fresh vegetables that don't get mushy. The ones listed here remain crunchy, and the result is a flavor-filled, satisfying meal, completed by a piece of whole-grain bread. Or you can serve the chili with rice or any other grain. *Preparation tip:* You can make this into a quick-cook dish by cutting up the vegetables in advance and storing them in separate plastic bags or containers in the refrigerator until cooking time. Or you can make the entire dish in advance, to be reheated at serving time; the flavors improve with age. The fully cooked dish also can be frozen.

    1 tablespoon oil
    1 teaspoon butter or margarine
    1 tablespoon minced garlic (3 large cloves)
    1 tablespoon chili powder, or more, to taste
    ½ teaspoon dry mustard
    ½ teaspoon ground cumin
    ¼ teaspoon celery seeds
    ¼ teaspoon freshly ground black pepper
    ¾ pound green beans *or* half green beans and
        half wax beans, cut into 1-inch pieces
    1½ cups carrot slices, cut ¼-inch thick (2 large
        carrots)
    1 cup sliced celery, cut on the diagonal into
        ½-inch lengths (1 medium-large stalk)
    1 16-ounce can tomatoes with juice reserved
    1 cup diced onions (1 large)
    2 cups strips of red and/or green peppers, about
        ¼ × 1½ inches (2 large peppers)
    1⅔ cups cooked kidney beans (1 16-ounce can
        with liquid)
    Plain low-fat yogurt *or* cucumber-yogurt sauce
        (see p. 641) for garnish (optional)

1. In a large, deep skillet or shallow saucepan or Dutch oven, heat the oil and butter or margarine, and add the garlic, chili powder, mustard, cumin, celery seeds, and black pepper. Sauté the mixture over a low flame, stirring it, for 1 to 2 minutes.
2. Add the green beans, carrots, celery, and ½ cup of the juice from the canned tomatoes. Stir the mixture well, cover the pan, and cook the mixture for about 10 minutes.
3. Add the onions and the red and/or green peppers, and cook the mixture, covered, for another 10 minutes.
4. Add the tomatoes, their remaining juice, and the kidney beans with their juice, and cook the chili 10 minutes longer. Serve the chili hot with a dollop of yogurt or cucumber-yogurt sauce on top, if desired.

MEATLESS TAMALE PIE   *6 servings*

Although tamale pie is traditionally made with beef, this one, based on a recipe from *Sharon Cadwallader's Complete Cookbook,* is made with beans and, to my taste, is just as delicious, not to mention less expensive. *Preparation tip:* Since green olives are salty, I prepare the beans without any salt and do not otherwise add salt to the filling. If you are on a strict low-sodium diet, leave out the olives as well. You could probably also skip the salt in the crust, since both the cheese and the chilies contain salt. The filling can be prepared in advance, with the batter added when you are ready to bake it.

FILLING

- 1 small onion, chopped (⅓ cup)
- 2 cloves garlic, minced
- 1 cup finely chopped green pepper (2 medium)
- 1 tablespoon oil
- 2 tablespoons tomato paste
- 1 heaping teaspoon chili powder
- ½ cup water
- 3 cups cooked, mashed beans (kidney, pinto, or pink)
- ¼ cup sliced green olives (with or without pimiento)
- 3 tablespoons minced fresh parsley
- Freshly ground black pepper to taste

CRUST

- 1 cup yellow corn meal, preferably stone-ground
- 1 tablespoon flour
- ¼ teaspoon salt, if desired
- 1½ teaspoons baking powder
- 1 egg, lightly beaten
- ½ cup skim or low-fat milk
- 2 tablespoons oil
- 2 tablespoons chopped green chilies, or more, to taste

TOPPING

- ½ cup grated sharp Cheddar

1. Sauté the onions, garlic, and green pepper in the oil in a large, nonstick skillet until the vegetables are softened (you may cover the skillet for a few minutes).
2. Stir in the tomato paste and chili powder, then add the water, beans, olives, parsley, and pepper. Simmer the mixture, stirring it, until it is heated through.
3. Grease an 8-inch baking dish or shallow casserole, and spread the bean mixture in it evenly.
4. In a medium bowl, combine the corn meal, flour, salt, and baking powder. Add the egg, milk, oil, and green chilies, and stir the mixture just to combine the ingredients.
5. Spread the batter over the bean mixture, top with the cheese, and bake the pie, uncovered, at 400° for 20 minutes or until the dough rises and is golden brown.

EGGPLANT-STUFFED "RAVIOLI"   *6 to 8 servings*

My children, who wouldn't normally let eggplant cross their lips, enjoyed this dish, which is based on a recipe from *Gourmet* magazine, even after I told them what was inside the won ton skins! My husband and I liked them as is, but for the boys I served them topped with a little tomato sauce. Like Intercontinental "Ravioli" (see p. 392), it would be a great party dish since the ravioli taste good at room temperature. *Preparation tip:* Won ton wrappers are available in Oriental markets and in the produce section of many supermarkets. They can be frozen (defrost them before using them). The unfilled won ton wrappers should be kept covered with plastic wrap or a damp cloth to prevent them from drying out while you are filling them. This is a large recipe, but leftovers will keep for about 5 days in the refrigerator.

       2 tablespoons olive or salad oil
       1 medium eggplant (about 1 pound), peeled and
         finely chopped (3 cups)
     ¼ cup very finely chopped onion
     ¼ cup very finely chopped green pepper
     ¾ teaspoon minced garlic (1 medium clove)
     ½ teaspoon orégano
       1 tablespoon fresh chopped basil *or* ½ teaspoon
         dried crumbled basil
   1½ cups water
     ⅔ cup part-skim ricotta
       1 cup grated Parmesan, divided
     ⅓ cup minced fresh parsley, divided
     ¼ teaspoon salt, if desired
   Freshly ground black pepper to taste
     48 won ton wrappers (approximately)

1. In a large skillet, heat the oil, and cook the eggplant, onion, green pepper, garlic, orégano, and basil over moderate heat for about 1 minute.
2. Add the water, and cook the mixture 10 minutes longer or until the liquid has evaporated. Place the mixture in a large bowl, and let it cool slightly.
3. Add the ricotta, ¼ cup of the Parmesan, 3 tablespoons of the parsley, salt, and pepper. Stir the mixture to combine the ingredients thoroughly.
4. To stuff the ravioli, place the won ton skins, one by one, on a work surface with a corner facing you. Put about 2 teaspoons of filling in the center of the skin (do not overfill). Using your fingertip and warm water, wet the rim of the won ton skin on all four sides. Fold the skin diagonally to form a triangle, pinching the edges together to seal them. Repeat with the remaining skins and stuffing.
5. Bring a large pot of water (salted, if desired) to a boil, reduce the heat to

a simmer, and add the stuffed won tons in batches of 8, cooking each batch for about 8 minutes. Carefully remove the cooked won tons with a slotted spoon, letting the water drain off before placing them on a warm platter. If necessary, cover them lightly with a damp cloth, and keep them warm in the oven while the rest cook. To serve, sprinkle the "ravioli" with the remaining Parmesan and parsley.

INTERCONTINENTAL "RAVIOLI"

4 main or 8 first-course servings

A Californian, Roxanne Chan, offered this recipe to the readers of *Bon Appétit* magazine. It is not only lovely to look at and delicious to eat, but it is easier to prepare than one would guess. It is excellent as a buffet offering, a first course at a company dinner, or a special treat for a family lunch or supper. *Preparation tip:* Dishes like this are easier to throw together if you have some homemade pesto (see p. 642) in the freezer (I freeze it in 2-tablespoon portions in ice-cube trays). Pesto can also be purchased in small jars in specialty food stores. Won ton wrappers and daikon are sold in Oriental markets and many supermarkets. The wrappers can be stored in the freezer for long periods of time if well wrapped. When working with them, keep all but the one you are filling covered with a plastic wrap or a damp cloth to prevent them from drying out. You will need a steamer rack to cook the filled "ravioli."

RAVIOLI
  8 ounces part-skim ricotta
  ¼ cup pesto
  24 won ton wrappers

REMAINING INGREDIENTS
  1 large daikon (Japanese white radish), peeled and grated
  ½ cup pine nuts, toasted
  Chopped basil leaves for garnish (optional)

DRESSING
  2 tablespoons olive oil
  2 tablespoons white wine or rice vinegar
  2 or more tablespoons chopped pimiento
  1 garlic clove, minced
  Salt, if desired, to taste
  Freshly ground black pepper to taste

1. In a medium bowl, combine the ricotta and pesto. To fill won ton wrappers one at a time, place a heaping teaspoon of the cheese mixture in the middle of the wrapper, wet the edges of the wrapper with water (a fingertip works well), fold the wrapper diagonally into a triangle, and seal the edges by pressing them together firmly to enclose the filling.
2. Bring 1½ inches of water to boil in a wok or steamer. Lightly oil the steamer rack, and set it over the water, making sure the rack does not touch the water. Arrange on the rack as many of the ravioli as fit comfortably without touching, cover the pot, and steam the ravioli for 5 minutes. Remove the ravioli, and set them aside. Repeat this procedure with the remaining ravioli, placing the cooked ravioli in a single layer if possible. Cover the ravioli with plastic wrap, and cool the ravioli completely.
3. In a small bowl combine all the dressing ingredients. Set the dressing aside.
4. Spread the grated daikon on a large serving platter. Pour half the dressing over it. Arrange the ravioli on top. Pour the remaining dressing over them. Before serving, sprinkle the ravioli with pine nuts and basil.

EGGPLANT-CHEESE PIE WITH ZUCCHINI CRUST

6 main-dish servings

A Minnesota friend, Laura Johnson, first served me this delicious dish. I reduced the fat and calories but, I think, preserved the flavor and essential nutrients. *Preparation tip:* The pie can be prepared in advance for baking. Or it can be baked through and reheated at serving time.

1½ tablespoons butter or margarine
  1 medium onion, chopped (about ½ cup)
  2 cloves garlic, minced
  1 pound eggplant, unpeeled, cut into ½-inch
    cubes (about 4½ cups)
 ½ teaspoon salt, if desired, or to taste
 ¾ teaspoon orégano
 ¾ teaspoon dried basil
Dash or 2 cayenne
  1 small zucchini, *unpeeled,* sliced
 ⅔ cup (1 small can) evaporated skim milk
  1 egg (omit yolk if you prefer)
  8 ounces part-skim mozzarella, grated (about 2
    cups)

1. In a large skillet, melt the butter or margarine, and sauté the onion, garlic, and eggplant for 2 minutes. Cover the skillet, and continue cooking the vegetables for about 5 minutes or until the eggplant is soft, stirring the mixture a few times.
2. Add the salt, orégano, basil, and cayenne, and stir the mixture well.
3. Line the bottom and sides of a greased 10-inch pie plate with the zucchini slices. Carefully spoon the eggplant mixture over them.
4. In a bowl, combine the evaporated milk, eggs, and cheese. Pour this mixture over the vegetables.
5. Bake the pie in a preheated 375° oven for 30 minutes.

SIMPLE TOFU STIR-FRY

4 servings

Here's a quick and easy way to prepare protein-rich but low-fat tofu (soybean curd). This could easily serve as an after-work supper or weekend lunch. Firm-style tofu is sold in sealed and dated plastic containers in the refrigerated section of most health and natural food stores and in the produce section of many supermarkets. Ask if you don't see it. *Preparation tip:* Start 1 cup of rice cooking before you begin to prepare your stir-fry. They both should be ready at about the same time—in 20 minutes or so, depending on the type of rice you use.

SAUCE
¼ cup broth (chicken, vegetable, or beef), or more if you like a lot of sauce
1 tablespoon reduced-sodium soy sauce
1 tablespoon mild vinegar (rice wine or white wine)
¼ teaspoon sugar

STIR-FRY
2 teaspoons vegetable oil
1 teaspoon Oriental sesame oil
1 tablespoon minced garlic
½ teaspoon hot red pepper flakes, or to taste
½ to 1 cup thinly sliced scallions with some green tops, to taste
¼ pound mushrooms, sliced (1¼ cups)
1 pound firm-style tofu, cut into thin slices (about 1 × ½ × ½ inch) or julienne strips
1 bunch watercress (coarse stems discarded) *or* ½ pound spinach, torn into bite-sized pieces
2 tablespoons lightly toasted sesame seeds (see p. 296)

1. In a small bowl, combine the broth, soy sauce, vinegar, and sugar. Set the sauce aside.
2. In a large skillet (preferably nonstick) or wok, heat the vegetable oil and sesame oil for about 30 seconds. Add the garlic, pepper flakes, and scallions, and stir-fry these ingredients for about 30 seconds. Add the mushrooms, and stir-fry the mixture for 1 to 2 minutes or until the mushrooms wilt and begin to release their liquid.
3. Add the tofu and the reserved sauce, tossing the ingredients gently to combine them. Top the stir-fry with watercress (or spinach), reduce the heat to medium, and cover the pan, cooking the stir-fry until the tofu is heated through and the cress is wilted. Sprinkle the stir-fry with toasted sesame seeds, and serve it with cooked rice.

TORTILLA CASSEROLE

8 servings

I've seen many recipes for Mexican-type casseroles that call for crumbled tortilla chips, the kind that are fried and salted. Here's one that uses the tortillas as is and thus is lower in fat and sodium. The tofu provides low-fat protein and texture without distorting the Mexican flavor. *Preparation tip: Nutrition Action,* the newsletter of the Center for Science in the Public Interest, designed this protein-rich dish to meet the needs of working families. It can be assembled in four 2-serving pie tins, frozen, and even baked frozen. Or you can prepare it in two large shallow baking pans. For 4 servings, prepare half the recipe.

    1 tablespoon vegetable oil
    2 medium-large onions, chopped (1⅓ cups)
    4 large cloves garlic, minced (4 teaspoons)
    1 28-ounce can tomatoes, coarsely chopped,
        with their juice
    2 tablespoons chili powder (mild or hot or both)
 1½ teaspoons orégano
    ½ teaspoon caraway seeds (optional)
    ½ teaspoon ground cumin
    ⅛ teaspoon cayenne, *or* ¼ teaspoon black pepper
    4 cups cooked small red beans or pinto beans
        (rinsed and drained, if canned), partially mashed
    1 4-ounce can green chilies, finely chopped
    1 pound firm-style tofu (soybean curd), crumbled
   12 corn tortillas, toasted on an oven rack for 10
        minutes at 350° until crisp
 1⅓ cups coarsely shredded Monterey Jack or mild
        Cheddar (about 5 ounces)

1. In a deep cast-iron skillet or medium saucepan, heat the oil, and cook the onions and garlic for about 5 minutes, stirring them often.
2. Add the tomatoes and their juice, chili powder, orégano, caraway, cumin, and cayenne or black pepper. Bring the mixture to a boil, reduce the heat, and simmer the mixture for 15 minutes, stirring it often. Remove the pan from the heat.
3. Add the beans, chilies, and tofu, and stir the ingredients well.
4. To assemble the casserole, spread a thin layer of the bean sauce on the bottom of each of four 8-inch cake or pie pans. Spread a layer of 1½ broken tortillas in each pan. Using half the remaining sauce, divide it among the four pans. Top this with another layer of broken tortillas (1½ tortillas to each pan) and the remaining sauce. Sprinkle ⅓ cup of the grated cheese on top of each pan.
5. Cover the pans with foil, and bake them in a 375° oven for about 20 minutes. If they are frozen, bake them for 30 to 40 minutes.

VEGETABLE CURRY

8 servings

My tasters and I adored this one. From a huge pot there was but one portion left, which I ate with plain yogurt for breakfast the next morning. Now I automatically make extra in hopes of having some leftovers for lunch. *Preparation tip:* Like Vegetable Chili (see p. 388), this dish can be host to a wide variety of vegetables, from aubergine (the French name for eggplant) to zucchini. The trick is to add them according to their cooking time so that they all retain a distinctive texture. Other possibilities than the ones listed include green peas, green or wax beans, sweet red peppers, and coarsely chopped cabbage. If you are on a strict low-sodium diet, don't sprinkle the eggplant with salt in step 1.

1 pound eggplant, peeled and cut into 1-inch cubes (about 4 cups)
½ teaspoon salt
1 tablespoon plus 2 teaspoons oil, divided
2 tablespoons curry powder (mild, hot, or both), or to taste
1 teaspoon ground cumin
2 large cloves garlic, finely minced (2 teaspoons)
Freshly ground black pepper to taste
Salt, if desired, to taste
½ cup broth (chicken or vegetable)
2 medium carrots, thinly sliced
2 cups diced potatoes (2 medium)
1 green pepper, thinly sliced
2 large onions, thinly sliced (2 cups)
2 cups bite-sized cauliflower flowerets (about ½ large head)
1 medium zucchini, sliced
2 cups peeled, seeded, and chopped tomatoes (save liquid)
¼ cup tomato liquid *or* more broth
1 16-ounce can chickpeas (garbanzos), drained
¼ cup raisins
Plain low-fat yogurt or cucumber-yogurt sauce (see p. 641) for garnish (optional)

1. Place the eggplant in a colander, and sprinkle it with the salt, tossing it to coat all pieces. Set the eggplant aside to drain for 30 minutes, then pat it dry.
2. Heat 1 tablespoon of oil in a large nonstick skillet or Dutch oven. Add the eggplant, and cook it, stirring it often, for about 5 minutes. Remove the eggplant from the pan, and set it aside.

3. Heat the 2 teaspoons oil in the skillet or Dutch oven, and add the curry, cumin, garlic, pepper, and salt, if desired. Stir in the broth, and cook the mixture for 2 minutes.

4. Add the carrots, potatoes, green pepper, onions, and cauliflower. Cover the pan, and simmer the curry for 5 to 7 minutes or until the vegetables are tender-crisp. Return the eggplant to the pan, and add the zucchini, tomatoes, tomato liquid or broth, chickpeas, and raisins. Cover the pan, and simmer the curry for 10 minutes.

5. Serve the curry with a dollop of yogurt or yogurt-cucumber sauce, if desired.

VEGETABLE-CHEESE PIE

6 main-dish servings

Here is a delicious one-crust pie that's a complete meal suitable for breakfast, brunch, lunch, or supper. Serve with a green salad and fruit for dessert, and you'll really pack in the nutrients while satisfying the taste buds. *Preparation tip:* The pie can be prepared in advance for baking at serving time. Swiss cheese can be used in place of Jarlsberg. If you have a large steamer basket, you can prepare the vegetables efficiently at one time by starting the carrots first, then adding the parsnips 4 minutes later, and the zucchini 1 minute after that.

   3 tablespoons cornstarch
   ¼ teaspoon salt, if desired
   ⅛ teaspoon freshly ground black pepper, or
     more, to taste
2½ cups skim or low-fat milk
   1 tablespoon butter or margarine
   ½ pound mushrooms, sliced (about 2½ cups)
   1 bunch scallions, sliced (about ¾ cup)
1½ cups shredded Jarlsberg (about 6 ounces)
   2 cups sliced carrots, steamed for 7 minutes
   2 cups sliced parsnips, steamed for 3 minutes
   3 cups sliced zucchini, steamed for 2 minutes
Single crust for 9-inch pie (see p. 632)

1. In a medium bowl, combine the cornstarch, salt, and pepper, and whisk in the milk until there are no lumps. Set the mixture aside.
2. In a medium saucepan, melt the butter or margarine, and sauté the mushrooms and scallions, stirring them often, for about 3 minutes.
3. Stir the reserved cornstarch mixture, and add it to the mushroom-scallion mixture. Stirring constantly, bring the mixture to a boil over medium heat, and boil it for 1 minute. Remove it from the heat, and stir in the cheese.
4. Add the carrots, parsnips, and zucchini to the cheese sauce, and combine everything well. Transfer the mixture to a 9-inch deep-dish pie plate.
5. Place the pie crust on top of the vegetable-cheese mixture, flute the edges of the crust to form a decorative rim, and cut slits in the top of the crust to let the steam escape.
6. Bake the pie in a preheated 375° oven for 35 to 40 minutes or until the crust is lightly browned.

MARLYS'S ZUCCHINI AND CHEESE CASSEROLE

6 servings

I got more requests for this simple recipe from my tasters than for any other squash-based dish, and I thank my Scandia, Minnesota, friend Marlys Ostrand for sharing it with me. *Preparation tip:* You can prepare the casserole ahead through step 2, or complete the entire dish in advance and reheat it at serving time.

   3 pounds zucchini, unpeeled, cut into 1-inch
      chunks (discard the seedy core if using very
      large zucchinis)
   1 cup low-fat cottage cheese
   1 cup shredded Monterey Jack (3 to 4 ounces)
   2 eggs *or* 2 egg whites and 1 egg, beaten
   1 teaspoon dill seeds
  ¼ teaspoon salt, if desired, or to taste
  ½ cup dried bread crumbs
   1 tablespoon butter or margarine, cut up

1. Simmer the zucchini chunks in salted water to cover for 5 minutes. Drain the zucchini very well.
2. In a large casserole dish, combine the zucchini with the cottage cheese, Monterey Jack, eggs, dill seeds, and salt.
3. Bake the casserole, uncovered, in a preheated 350° oven for 15 minutes.
4. Sprinkle the bread crumbs on top of the zucchini mixture, and dot it with the butter or margarine. Bake the casserole for another 15 minutes.

ZUCCHINI LASAGNE

6 servings

I have no objections to pasta. But this recipe, which uses strips of fried zucchini in place of pasta, is an interesting variation on the theme. *Preparation tip:* Like pasta-based lasagne, this dish can be prepared ahead and frozen before baking. If you are concerned about sodium, use no-salt-added ricotta and homemade spaghetti sauce.

  2 large zucchinis
 ¼ cup white or whole-wheat pastry flour
 Salt, if desired, to taste
 Freshly ground black pepper to taste
 Oil for frying (use as little as possible)
  1 15-ounce container part-skim ricotta
  1 egg white plus 1 whole egg
  1 teaspoon orégano
 ¼ cup grated Parmesan, divided
  2 cups spaghetti sauce, homemade or from a jar,
    divided
 ½ pound part-skim mozzarella, shredded, divided

1. Slice the zucchinis lengthwise into ¼-inch slices. Mix the flour with the salt and pepper (or alternate no-salt seasoning), and dip both sides of the zucchini slices into the mixture.
2. In a large, nonstick skillet, heat the oil, and fry the zucchini slices, half at a time, over medium heat until they are golden, turning them once. Remove the zucchini to a platter covered with a paper towel.
3. In a medium bowl, combine the ricotta, egg white and whole egg, orégano, and 3 tablespoons of the Parmesan.
4. In the bottom of a baking pan approximately 12 × 8 × 2 inches, spread 1 cup of the spaghetti sauce, top with half the zucchini slices, then half the ricotta mixture, and half the mozzarella. Repeat the layers. Sprinkle the lasagne with the remaining Parmesan.
5. Bake the lasagne in a preheated 350° oven for 45 minutes or until the lasagne is bubbly. Let the lasagne stand for about 10 minutes before serving.

WINTER SQUASH STUFFED WITH APPLES AND CHEESE

4 servings

Mollie Katzen's *The Moosewoood Cookbook* is the original source of this simple stuffed squash, which my tasters said should have broad appeal to eaters of all ages. *Preparation tip:* Prepare the stuffing while the squash bakes. You can add ½ cup of chopped nuts for a crunchier stuffing. If you should end up with more stuffing than the squashes can accommodate, bake the extra in a small casserole, and eat it plain, perhaps with toasted whole-grain bread.

2 medium-sized acorn squashes *or* 2 small butternut squashes, about 1¼ pounds each
1 tablespoon butter or margarine
3 cups peeled chopped apples, preferably tart cooking apples
½ cup chopped onion
2 cups low-fat cottage cheese
¾ cup grated cheese (e.g., Cheddar, Gouda, or Swiss)
¼ cup lemon juice
2 tablespoons currants or raisins
¼ teaspoon cinnamon plus a few sprinkles for garnish

1. Cut the squashes in half lengthwise (through the stem to the flower end), scoop out and discard the seeds and strings, and place the squashes cut side down on an oiled baking pan. Bake the squashes in a 350° oven for about 30 minutes or until they are tender.
2. In a small skillet, melt the butter or margarine, and sauté the apples and onion for about 5 minutes or until the onion is translucent.
3. In a large bowl, combine the apple-onion mixture with the cottage cheese, grated cheese, lemon juice, currants or raisins, and ¼ teaspoon cinnamon. Fill the cavities of the baked squashes with the stuffing. Sprinkle them with additional cinnamon. Place the stuffed squashes on a baking sheet or in a shallow pan, and cover them with foil.
4. Bake the squashes in a 350° for about 20 minutes or until they are heated through.

Main-Dish Salads

By adding one or more high-protein ingredients, you can turn a salad into a satisfying and nutritious main course. Most Americans are familiar with the so-called chef's salad, in which the protein usually comes from fatty meats and cheese. However, in most of the salad entrées offered here, the protein source is a low-fat food like turkey, chicken, shellfish, or beans. The dressings, too, are low in fat, so you end up with a lot of nutrient-packed food in your stomach at a relatively low caloric cost.

VEGETABLE-BEAN SALAD
WITH RICE OR PASTA
4 main-dish servings

This is a vegetarian salad with complete protein, thanks to the combination of rice (or pasta) and beans. *Preparation tip:* The salad can be prepared several hours to one day in advance.

SALAD
- 1 cup raw long-grain rice, white or brown, cooked without butter, *or* 3 cups cooked orzo
- 1 15-ounce can kidney beans, drained and rinsed
- 1 large stalk broccoli, flowerets cut, stems sliced, and steamed for 5 minutes or blanched for 2 minutes
- ½ pound snow peas or sugar snap peas
- ½ pound mushrooms, sliced thin (about 2½ cups)
- 1 green or red sweet pepper (or both), cut in strips about ¼ inch wide
- 4 to 6 scallions, sliced thin

DRESSING
- ¼ cup olive oil
- 2 tablespoons lemon juice
- 3 tablespoons vinegar
- 2 large cloves garlic, crushed
- 1 teaspoon dry mustard
- ¾ teaspoon tarragon, crumbled
- ½ teaspoon salt, if desired
- ½ teaspoon freshly ground black pepper, or to taste

GARNISH
- Greens for serving
- 1 pint cherry tomatoes, halved (optional)

1. In a large bowl, combine all the salad ingredients.
2. In a jar, combine all the dressing ingredients. Cover the jar, shake it well, and pour the dressing over the rice and vegetable mixture. Toss the salad to mix it thoroughly. Refrigerate the salad until serving time.
3. On a large platter, serve the salad on bed of greens surrounded by a necklace of cherry tomato halves, if desired.

ORIENTAL CHICKEN AND RICE SALAD

4 generous servings

This salad tastes as good as it looks, and the sodium content per serving is moderate. *Preparation tip:* Marinating the chicken is optional but improves the flavor. An alternative is to use chicken that was marinated in an Oriental dressing before it was cooked.

DRESSING

- 2 tablespoons reduced-sodium soy sauce
- 2 tablespoons rice vinegar or white wine vinegar
- 1 tablespoon Oriental sesame oil
- 1 tablespoon salad oil
- 1 tablespoon minced fresh ginger
- 2 cloves garlic, minced
- ½ teaspoon sugar
- ¼ teaspoon freshly ground black pepper
- ¼ teaspoon dry mustard

SALAD

- 2 cups cooked slivered chicken breasts
- 3 cups cooked rice (white or brown)
- 1 cup sliced celery
- 1 cup bean sprouts
- ½ cup sliced scallions
- 5 radishes, thinly sliced
- ¼ pound snow peas, blanched for 1 minute and cut diagonally into slivers
- 2 tablespoons toasted sesame seeds (see p. 412)
- 1 cup loosely packed watercress (optional)

1. In a medium bowl, combine all the dressing ingredients. Add the slivered cooked chicken, and let it stand for 30 minutes or longer.
2. Combine the chicken and dressing with the rice, celery, sprouts, scallions, radishes, snow peas, and sesame seeds. Toss the salad. Add the watercress just before serving, and toss the salad again.

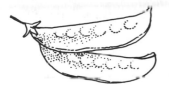

TRICOLOR CHICKPEA SALAD   *3 to 4 servings*

It took considerable restraint to keep from gobbling up this salad right after I made it. It is equally delicious warm or at room temperature. It looks lovely served on a bed of curly lettuce and surrounded by sliced or cherry tomatoes. *Preparation tip:* Do step 2 while the vegetables cook in step 1.

    1 large carrot, sliced into ¼-inch pieces
    1 medium potato, peeled and cut into ½-inch
       cubes
    ½ cup peas, fresh or frozen
    1 16-ounce can chickpeas, drained and rinsed
    2 teaspoons olive oil
    1 large onion, cut into ¼-inch slices
    4 cloves garlic, minced (about 4 teaspoons)
    2 ounces Swiss or other firm cheese, cut into
       ⅓-inch cubes
    2 tablespoons red wine vinegar
    2 tablespoons fresh snipped dill *or* 2 teaspoons
       dried dillweed
Freshly ground black pepper to taste (be
       generous)
Dash salt, if desired

1. In a saucepan, place the carrot in water to cover plus 1 inch. Bring the water to a boil, reduce the heat to moderately low, and cook the carrot for 5 minutes. Add the potato and peas (if fresh), and cook for another 10 minutes. If you are using frozen peas, add them during the last 2 minutes of cooking time. Remove the pan from the heat, and add the chickpeas, tossing to warm them.
2. Meanwhile, heat the oil in a small skillet, and sauté the onion and garlic until they are just tender—do not let them brown.
3. Drain the chickpea mixture, and transfer it to a serving bowl. Add the onion-garlic mixture and the cheese.
4. Add the vinegar, dill, pepper, and salt. Toss the ingredients gently to combine them well. Serve the salad warm or at room temperature.

LENTIL AND BULGUR SALAD

A vegetarian main-dish salad that derives complete protein from the combination of lentils and bulgur, with the added nutrients of vitamin-rich parsley. With a cold puréed soup and bread, this makes an excellent hot-weather meal.

SALAD
- 1 cup lentils
- 4 cups homemade broth *or* 4 cups water with 1 bouillon cube
- 1 cup bulgur
- 2 cups boiling water
- ½ cup finely chopped sweet onion (e.g., Spanish or red)
- 1 cup minced fresh parsley

- ½ cup thinly sliced scallions

DRESSING
- 2 cloves garlic, minced (2 teaspoons)
- 1 tablespoon Dijon mustard
- ¼ cup chicken broth
- 1 tablespoon olive oil
- 2 tablespoons aceto balsamico vinegar or red wine vinegar
- 1 tablespoon cider vinegar
- ⅛ teaspoon hot pepper sauce (Tabasco)
- ½ teaspoon Worcestershire sauce
- 1 teaspoon orégano
- ½ teaspoon dried basil
- ¼ teaspoon ground cumin
- ¼ teaspoon salt, if desired, or to taste
- Freshly ground black pepper to taste

1. In a medium saucepan, cook the lentils in the broth or water for 30 minutes. Let the lentils stand 10 minutes longer, then drain them.
2. Meanwhile, put the bulgur in a heat-proof bowl, pour boiling water over it, let it stand 10 minutes or so, and then drain it.
3. Combine the lentils and bulgur in a large bowl. Add the onion and parsley.
4. In a jar or small bowl, combine all the dressing ingredients. Pour the dressing over the lentil mixture, and toss the salad.
5. Add the scallions at serving time, and toss the salad again.

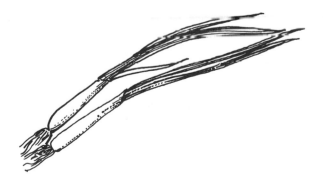

SARDINE SALAD WITH BROCCOLI

2 main-dish servings

For sardine lovers, here's a snappy salad meal that's loaded with calcium and vitamin A. It is not, however, a dish for those on very low-sodium diets. *Preparation tip:* Allow at least 30 minutes for the salad to marinate. See page 296 for instructions on toasting sesame seeds.

DRESSING
- 2 tablespoons reduced-sodium soy sauce
- 1 tablespoon olive or salad oil
- 1 tablespoon sugar
- ¼ teaspoon hot red pepper flakes, or to taste
- 1 clove garlic, crushed

SALAD
- 1 bunch broccoli flowerets, steamed tender-crisp and cooled
- 2 cans low-sodium sardines (with bones) packed in water, drained and broken into pieces
- 1 tablespoon toasted sesame seeds for garnish (optional)

1. In a small bowl, combine all the dressing ingredients.
2. In a medium bowl, combine the broccoli and sardines. Pour the dressing over them, and toss the salad gently. Chill the salad for 30 minutes or longer. Toss the salad once more just before serving. Sprinkle the salad with toasted sesame seeds, if desired.

TOMATO-SEAFOOD ASPIC

8 servings

This is a beautiful first-course or buffet dish or main-course luncheon salad. A number of my guests who insisted they "don't like aspics" said this one was the exception. *Preparation tip:* You can vary the seafood: small scallops are my favorite, but small shrimp or crab meat (if you can afford it) are also excellent.

- ½ cup cold water
- 3 envelopes unflavored gelatin
- 3 cups tomato juice
- 6 tablespoons sugar
- 3 tablespoons fresh chopped dill *or* 2 teaspoons dried dillweed
- ½ cup fresh lemon juice (the juice of about 3 lemons)
- 1 pound bay scallops, poached for 3 to 5 minutes
- Optional garnishes: watercress or parsley, sliced hard-boiled eggs

1. Place the cold water in a large bowl, sprinkle in the gelatin, and let the mixture stand for 5 minutes to soften.
2. In a small saucepan, boil the tomato juice, and add it to the gelatin mixture, stirring to dissolve the gelatin.
3. Stir in the sugar, dill, and lemon juice, and allow the mixture to cool.
4. Pour about one-third of the tomato-juice mixture into a large, lightly greased mold or serving bowl. Chill the aspic until it starts to set.
5. Arrange half the scallops on the hardening mixture, add another one-third of the tomato mixture, and chill the aspic until this layer sets. Repeat with the rest of the seafood and tomato mixture. Chill the aspic until it is very firm.
6. At serving time, unmold the aspic by holding the mold in a pan of very warm water for 10 to 20 seconds. Place a serving platter over the mold, and quickly turn the mold over. Serve the aspic garnished with watercress or parsley and sliced hard-boiled eggs, if desired.

CURRIED SHRIMP SALAD   *2 main-dish servings*

Not a scrap was left of this tasty, low-fat, low-salt salad, which would make a fine lunch or first course for a company dinner. *Preparation tip:* Crab meat or sea legs can be used in place of shrimp.

DRESSING
1 teaspoon oil
1 teaspoon curry powder
½ teaspoon finely minced fresh ginger
⅓ cup plain low-fat yogurt

SALAD
1 cup chopped cooked shrimp
½ cup raisins
¼ cup coarsely chopped toasted cashews
Salt, if desired, to taste
Freshly ground black pepper to taste
¼ cup finely chopped scallions, divided

1. In a small skillet, heat the oil, add the curry powder, and cook the mixture for about 30 seconds to eliminate the "raw" taste of the curry. Then in a medium bowl, mix the curry powder and oil with the ginger and the yogurt.
2. Add the shrimp, raisins, cashews, salt, pepper, and 2 tablespoons of the scallions. Toss the ingredients to combine them thoroughly. Before serving, bring the salad to room temperature, and garnish it with the remaining 2 tablespoons of scallions.

SQUID SALAD

4 to 6 servings

I love the looks of squid in a salad. The white curls of the cut body sacs and the wriggly tentacles contrast beautifully with the vegetables. *Preparation tip:* See page 368 for instructions on how to clean squid. Pay attention to the short cooking time: squid must be cooked either very briefly or very long to avoid chewiness. If you cannot get fresh or canned hot peppers, substitute ¼ teaspoon or more of hot red pepper flakes. If fresh limes are not available, substitute 2 tablespoons of lemon juice and 1 tablespoon of wine vinegar.

SALAD

2 pounds squid, cleaned, bodies cut into ½-inch rings and tentacles cut into bite-sized pieces (you should end up with about 3 cups)

¼ cup dry white wine

2 cups boiling water (approximately)

Salt, if desired, to taste

1 pint cherry tomatoes, halved

DRESSING

1 large red onion, chopped (1 cup)

2 tablespoons minced fresh parsley

1 tablespoon finely minced jalapeño pepper (use rubber gloves)

1 tablespoon finely minced garlic (3 large cloves)

¼ cup fresh lime juice

2 tablespoons olive oil

Freshly ground black pepper to taste

1. Place the squid in a medium saucepan, and add the wine, boiling water to cover, and salt to taste. Bring the ingredients to a boil, reduce the heat, and simmer the squid for 1 minute. Drain the squid, and let them cool. Transfer the cooled squid to a medium bowl.
2. In a small bowl, combine all the dressing ingredients, and add the dressing to the cooled squid. Toss the ingredients well, and refrigerate the salad, covered, until serving time.
3. Before serving, toss in the tomatoes, and bring the salad to room temperature.

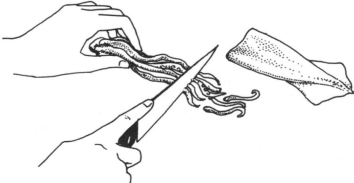

TURKEY AND RICE SALAD

6 main-course servings

Here is a beautiful as well as delicious and wholesome salad, ideal for company. *Preparation tip:* You can also use 1½ cups of packaged wild-rice-and-white-rice combination, cooked according to package directions (but omitting the butter). The rice should be prepared ahead to allow adequate time for it to chill. All the remaining salad ingredients and the dressing can also be prepared ahead of time, up to 12 hours before serving. It is important, though, to add the dressing just before serving; it loses its punch when it stands too long. Leftover cooked turkey or chicken is fine, but if you should be lucky enough to have access to smoked turkey or chicken, they're even better. The vegetables can be varied according to taste. For example, halved cherry tomatoes might be added to the salad or substituted for the red pepper. Steamed sliced carrots, broccoli flowerets, or tiny Brussels sprouts would be welcomed additions.

SALAD
- ¾ cup wild rice
- 2 cups chicken broth (homemade, canned, or made from cubes)
- 1 cup water
- ¾ cup long-grain white rice
- 2 cups cooked turkey, diced into bite-sized pieces
- 3 scallions, with tops, sliced
- ¼ pound mushrooms, quartered
- 1 large red sweet pepper, diced
- 1 cup (packed) spinach leaves, sliced into strips
- 2 tablespoons minced fresh parsley (optional)

DRESSING
- ⅓ cup dry white wine
- 2 tablespoons olive or salad oil
- 2 teaspoons sugar
- ½ teaspoon dry mustard
- ¼ teaspoon salt, if desired, or to taste
- ¼ teaspoon freshly ground black pepper, or to taste

GARNISH
- 1 small can mandarin oranges, drained (optional)

1. In a medium saucepan, combine the wild rice, broth, and water. Bring the liquid to a boil, reduce the heat, cover the pan, and simmer the rice for 15 minutes.
2. Add the long-grain white rice to the wild rice, cover the pan, and continue cooking the rice for another 20 to 25 minutes or until all the liquid is absorbed. Chill the rice.
3. Combine *all* the salad ingredients—rice, turkey, and vegetables.
4. In a small bowl or jar, combine all the dressing ingredients, and mix them well. Just before serving, add the dressing to the salad, and toss the ingredients to combine them. Garnish the salad with mandarin oranges, if desired.

TURKEY WALDORF SALAD

4 servings

Impress those who drop in on Thanksgiving weekend or your family any time you have cooked turkey on hand. Smoked turkey is especially good in this salad, although higher in salt.

SALAD
- 2 cups cooked, diced turkey (about 10 ounces)
- 1½ cups fresh bean sprouts
- 1 apple, unpeeled, diced
- 1 stalk celery, diced
- ¼ cup dried currants (raisins may be substituted)
- 3 tablespoons chopped walnuts (optional)

DRESSING
- 3 tablespoons plain low-fat yogurt
- 2 tablespoons mayonnaise
- 2 tablespoons orange juice
- 1 teaspoon grated orange rind

1. In a medium bowl, combine all the salad ingredients.
2. In a small bowl, combine all the dressing ingredients. Pour the dressing over the turkey mixture, and toss the salad.

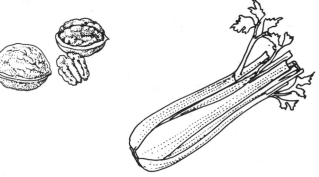

Pasta Main-Dish Salads

A combination of the pasta revolution and the rising health consciousness that says salads are good for you led, perhaps inevitably, to a panoply of pasta salads. Just about everywhere you dine these days—be it at sit-down restaurants, deli counters, buffets, parties, picnics—there's one or more pasta salads to turn your head. Unfortunately, most of those that taste good are not all that good for you because the sauces are loaded with salt and fat. It's hard to make a tasty pasta salad that isn't so adorned, especially since the seasonings seem to "disappear" as the salad sits awhile. I've prepared many healthful pasta salads I didn't think were worth the effort and a few that I and my tasters really liked. These I pass along to you.

BEEF-AND-VEGETABLE FETTUCINE SALAD

6 main-course servings

Preparation tip: This very colorful and tasty salad can also be made with cooked chicken, pork, or seafood. Or you can leave the animal protein out altogether and use high-protein fettucine to provide main-course protein. Fresh parsley and basil are important to the tastiness of the dressing, but you could substitute dried basil if need be. You can prepare this dish as much as a day ahead.

SALAD

- 2 medium zucchinis (about 1 pound), cut into ¼-inch strips
- 2 red sweet peppers, seeded and cut into slivers
- 1 pound cauliflower flowerets, steamed tender-crisp
- ¼ pound snow peas, strings removed and blanched or steamed tender-crisp
- 2 large carrots, coarsely shredded
- 1 medium red onion, quartered and sliced thin crosswise
- ¾ pound cooked beef, slivered
- ½ pound spinach fettucine, broken into 4-inch strips and cooked *al dente*

DRESSING

- ¼ cup minced fresh parsley
- ¼ cup fresh basil leaves, minced, *or* 1 tablespoon dried basil
- 1 very large clove garlic, crushed
- ¼ cup olive or vegetable oil
- ¼ cup chicken broth
- ¼ cup red wine vinegar
- 4 teaspoons Dijon mustard
- 2 teaspoons sugar
- ½ teaspoon salt, if desired, or to taste
- Freshly ground black pepper to taste

1. In a large bowl, combine all the salad ingredients.
2. In a small bowl, combine all the dressing ingredients. Pour the dressing over the pasta mixture, and toss the ingredients to combine them well. Chill the salad 1 hour or longer before serving.

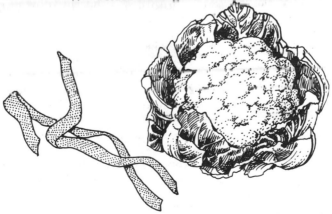

CHINESE SPAGHETTI SALAD

(with Chicken)   *8 main-dish servings*

This is a beautiful dish with a delightful textural contrast of soft noodles against crunchy vegetables. The addition of cooked chicken makes it a main dish with adequate protein. It could also be served as a side dish without the "meat." Alas, it is not a low-sodium dish. *Preparation tip:* You can prepare this in smaller quantities with leftover spaghetti or other similar pasta—just reheat it by pouring boiling water over it, then drain and mix the warm pasta with the pasta dressing. Any cooked "meat" can be used in place of chicken—turkey, beef, pork, or ham. If you are starting from scratch, simply poach the whole chicken breasts in water for about 30 minutes; then skin, bone, and cut them into slivers. Toast sesame seeds by placing them in a dry skillet over moderately low heat and stirring or shaking the skillet periodically until the seeds are lightly browned. Chili oil (Oriental sesame oil flavored with hot red chili peppers) should be used with care since it is very hot. You can substitute some hot red pepper flakes in the dressing, or you can make your own chili oil by cooking 1 or 2 dried chili peppers in sesame oil over moderately low heat until the peppers are charred (then discard them), or you can leave out the hot seasoning altogether and have a more delicate-tasting salad, perhaps serving the chili oil on the side for diners to add to individual portions.

DRESSING FOR PASTA
- 1 tablespoon Oriental sesame oil
- 2 teaspoons salad oil *or* another 2 teaspoons sesame oil
- 4 teaspoons reduced-sodium soy sauce

- 1 pound spaghetti, cooked and warm

DRESSING FOR SALAD
- ¼ cup broth (low salt)
- 3 tablespoons reduced-sodium soy sauce
- 2 tablespoons red wine vinegar
- 1 tablespoon Oriental sesame oil
- 1 teaspoon dry mustard
- ⅛ teaspoon cayenne, or to taste
- Chili oil to taste

SALAD
- 2 cups slivered cooked chicken breast (2 small whole breasts)
- ½ pound snow peas, ends trimmed and cut diagonally into 1-inch pieces, blanched for 1 minute, then quickly drained and cooled under cold water
- 2 cucumbers, peeled, seeded, cut into strips ¼ × 1½ inches
- 2 sweet red peppers, cut into strips ¼ × 1½ inches
- ¾ cup sliced scallions (cut diagonally), including some green tops (1 bunch)
- 3 tablespoons chopped fresh parsley
- 2 tablespoons toasted sesame seeds

1. In a large bowl, combine all the dressing ingredients for *pasta,* and toss them with the warm pasta. Set the pasta aside. (This can be done as much as a day ahead, but the pasta should be brought to room temperature before completing the salad.)
2. In a small bowl or jar, combine all the dressing ingredients for *salad.* Set the dressing aside.
3. At serving time, toss the pasta with the dressing for salad. Add all the salad ingredients. Toss the salad again.

PESTO PASTA WITH SCALLOPS   *4 to 6 Servings*

The scallops in this dish are used to provide added interest and balanced protein —they are not meant to be the focal point of the meal. *Preparation tip:* Pesto is not low in calories because a fair amount of olive oil is used to hold it together. However, you can get away with substituting a few tablespoons of broth for some of the oil. (In this recipe, the scallop cooking liquid does the trick.) You cannot, however, get away without using fresh basil. This dish can be prepared a day ahead.

PESTO
  1 cup packed fresh basil leaves, washed, dried, and slivered
  2 large cloves garlic, crushed
  ½ teaspoon salt, if desired
  1 or 2 tablespoons pine nuts or chopped walnuts
  ¼ cup olive oil
  ¼ cup grated Parmesan

REMAINING INGREDIENTS
  ½ cup dry white wine
  2 tablespoons lemon juice
  Additional salt, if desired, to taste
  Freshly ground black pepper to taste
  1 pound bay scallops
  12 ounces capellini (very thin spaghetti)

1. In a blender or food processor, combine the basil, garlic, ½ teaspoon of salt, and nuts. With the motor running, gradually add the oil, blending the mixture to a smooth paste. Add the Parmesan, and process the mixture a few seconds longer to combine the ingredients thoroughly. Transfer the pesto to a large bowl.
2. In a small saucepan, bring the wine, lemon juice, salt, and pepper to a boil, and add the scallops. Cook the scallops for 2 to 3 minutes. Drain them, reserving the cooking liquid.
3. In a large pot of boiling, salted water, cook the capellini *al dente* (about 2 to 3 minutes). Drain the pasta, and add it to the bowl with the pesto, tossing the pasta to coat it with the sauce. Gradually add the reserved scallop cooking liquid, tossing the ingredients to mix them well. Add the scallops, mix the ingredients again, and refrigerate the mixture until serving time (an hour or longer).

PASTA AND PEANUT SALAD   *6 main-course servings*

This attractive salad, derived from a *Gourmet* magazine recipe, combines peanuts and pasta for main-dish protein. Or it can be served as a side dish (in which case it will serve 12). The hot pepper flakes give it a kick that is especially welcomed on a steamy summer day. *Preparation tip:* For maximum aesthetic value, slice the vegetables diagonally (especially if you use penne as your pasta). The pasta and vegetables can be prepared ahead, as can the sauce, to be combined shortly before serving.

SALAD
- 1 pound tubular pasta (penne, small ziti, elbow macaroni, etc.)
- Salt, if desired
- 1 tablespoon oil
- ½ pound green beans, blanched and cut into ½-inch pieces
- 2 large carrots, halved lengthwise and sliced thin crosswise
- 2 large cucumbers, quartered lengthwise, seeded (cored), and sliced thin crosswise
- 8 scallions, with green tops, sliced into ¼-inch pieces

- ⅓ cup roasted peanuts, coarsely chopped

DRESSING
- ½ cup smooth peanut butter (natural kind)
- 2 tablespoons reduced-sodium soy sauce
- 2 tablespoons fresh lemon juice
- 1 tablespoon hot water
- 1 teaspoon hot red pepper flakes, or to taste
- ¼ teaspoon ground cumin
- ⅛ teaspoon turmeric

1. Cook the pasta until just tender in plenty of boiling water to which salt, if desired, and 1 tablespoon of oil have been added. Drain the pasta, rinse it with cold water, and drain it again. Place the pasta in a large bowl.
2. Add the blanched beans, carrots, cucumbers, and scallions, and toss the ingredients to combine them.
3. In a small bowl or in a blender, combine all the dressing ingredients.
4. To serve, add the dressing to the pasta-vegetable mixture, and toss the salad well. Sprinkle the salad with the chopped peanuts.

SCANDINAVIAN SALMON SALAD

6 servings

Fresh snipped dill makes this an exemplary pasta salad. You can make it with any shell-shaped pasta; I prefer cavatelli to give the salad added interest. For an even lower-fat dish, you might try the dressing with just yogurt rather than the yogurt–sour cream mixture. Since the ingredients are rather colorless, consider garnishing the salad with parsley and/or sliced radishes.

DRESSING
- ½ cup sour cream
- ½ cup plain low-fat yogurt
- ¼ cup low-fat milk
- ¼ cup snipped fresh dill
- 1 tablespoon fresh lemon juice
- 1 teaspoon Dijon mustard
- ¼ teaspoon salt, if desired
- ⅛ teaspoon freshly ground black pepper

SALAD
- 1 15-ounce can salmon, drained, skin discarded, and flaked
- ¼ cup finely chopped scallions
- 12 ounces medium-sized macaroni shells, cooked *al dente* in water to which 1 tablespoon oil has been added

- 4 hard-boiled eggs, sliced or quartered (optional)

1. In a small bowl, combine all the dressing ingredients.
2. In a large bowl, combine the salmon, scallions, and cooked shells. Add the dressing, and toss the ingredients gently to combine them. Cover the salad, and chill it for at least 2 hours before serving it. Before serving, garnish the salad with eggs, if desired.

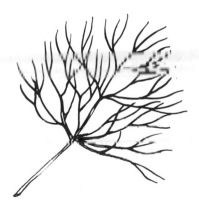

SESAME SPAGHETTI SALAD

4 to 6 main-course
servings

This salad captures some of the delectable sesame flavor of cold sesame noodles but without all the fat and heaviness (although it is not low in sodium). It is an excellent spring and summer dish since it is both light and zippy. In colder weather, it can be served hot. If you use high-protein spaghetti, the dish provides main-course protein without any meat or fish. *Preparation tip:* The trick with this dish, as with all Oriental stir-fries, is to have all your ingredients ready and lined up before you start to cook.

  2 tablespoons Oriental sesame oil (do not use
    health-food type)
  1 tablespoon vegetable oil
  2 large cloves garlic, finely minced (2 teaspoons)
  1 *tablespoon* minced fresh ginger
  1 cup minced scallions with some tops
  6 cups diced bok choy (Chinese cabbage)
  3 cups (about 1½ pounds) broccoli flowerets,
    steamed tender-crisp
  ¼ pound snow peas, trimmed and steamed
    tender-crisp
  1 large red sweet pepper, cut into thin strips
  2 large tomatoes, peeled, seeded, and diced
    (optional)
  1 tablespoon honey
 12 ounces spaghetti or linguine, cooked *al dente*
  2 tablespoons soy sauce (I use Oriental thin soy
    sauce)
  ¼ cup toasted sesame seeds (see p. 412)
  1 teaspoon Oriental chili oil, or to taste (see p.
    412)

1. Heat the sesame and vegetable oils in a wok over high heat for about 1 minute. Add the garlic, ginger, and scallions, and stir-fry the ingredients for about 30 seconds—do not let them burn.
2. Add the bok choy, broccoli, snow peas, and red pepper, and stir-fry the vegetables for about 2 minutes to heat the ingredients.
3. Add the tomatoes and honey, and stir-fry for another minute.
4. Add the cooked spaghetti or linguine, and sprinkle over the mixture the soy sauce, toasted sesame seeds, and chili oil, mixing well to combine all the ingredients and flavors.
5. Serve the salad immediately, or cool it to room temperature.

SHRIMP AND SHELLS

4 to 8 servings

This pasta salad can be served as a luncheon main dish or a dinner appetizer. The dressing can be varied according to taste.

SALAD
- ½ pound small pasta shells, tricolor if available
- ½ pound baby shrimp (can use frozen shrimp)
- 1 10-ounce package frozen peas
- 1 cup diced sweet red pepper
- ½ cup diced celery
- ¼ cup coarsely chopped red onion
- ¼ cup chopped fresh parsley (omit if not available; do not substitute dried parsley flakes)

DRESSING
- ½ cup plain low-fat yogurt
- 2 tablespoons mayonnaise
- 2 tablespoons snipped fresh dill *or* 2 teaspoons dried dillweed (optional)
- 1 tablespoon drained bottled horseradish
- 1 tablespoon lemon juice
- 1 teaspoon Dijon mustard
- White pepper to taste
- Salt, if desired, to taste

1. Cook the pasta *al dente* in boiling salted water (follow the package directions). Rinse the pasta under cold water, drain it, and let it cool.
2. Steam or poach the shrimp until they are pink and firm, 3 to 5 minutes. Refresh them under cold water, and let them cool.
3. Cook the peas in ½ cup of boiling water, or steam them for about 2 minutes (they should be firm). Refresh them under cold water, and let them cool.
4. Combine all the salad ingredients in a large bowl, and refrigerate them.
5. In a small bowl, combine all the dressing ingredients, and refrigerate the dressing. Dress the salad just before serving it.

Poultry Main Dishes

When it comes to entrées based on animal protein, I offer you more dishes made from chicken and other fowl than any other creature, for several reasons. Chicken is inexpensive, widely available, versatile, and appeals to a wide range of tastes. If properly prepared and eaten *without the skin,* it and related fowl (turkey and Cornish hens, but not ducks or geese) are also very low in fat. All in all, for health- and budget-conscious diners, they are truly "fowl-feathered friends." When poultry is prepared in the company of complex carbohydrates and/or lots of vegetables, individual portions can often be smaller than the traditional quarter or half a chicken. Leftovers are usually also wonderful, hot or cold, and can serve as a quick breakfast, lunch, or supper the next day. You'll find additional poultry-based entrées in the sections on main-dish soups and salads as well as in the sections on pancakes and sandwiches.

CHILIED CHICKEN FRICASSEE   *6 servings*

This low-fat, low-salt but still tasty dish is a complete meal when served with rice, noodles, or potatoes. *Preparation tip:* It can be prepared ahead and frozen. It can also be made with turkey breasts.

¼ cup yellow corn meal
½ teaspoon salt, if desired
¼ teaspoon AHA herb mix (see p. 182) or other
    no-salt seasoning
¼ teaspoon freshly ground black pepper
1¼ pounds boneless chicken breast, skin removed
    and flesh cut into 1½-inch cubes
4 teaspoons vegetable oil, divided
1 large onion, coarsely chopped (1 cup)
1 large green pepper, diced (¾ cup)
1 teaspoon minced garlic
2 to 3 teaspoons chili powder, or to taste
½ teaspoon ground cumin
1 cup chicken broth (I use no-salt broth)
1 28-ounce can tomatoes (without salt, if
    available), with juice, coarsely chopped
1 cup cooked corn kernels
1 cup green peas (frozen or, if fresh, boiled for
    3 minutes)
1 cup cooked pink beans (optional)

1. Combine the corn meal, salt, herb mix, and pepper in a shallow bowl or paper bag. Add the chicken pieces in batches, tossing them to coat them thoroughly with the corn-meal mixture.
2. Heat 3 teaspoons of the oil in a 4- to 5-quart Dutch oven or comparable heavy pot, preferably with a nonstick surface. Lightly brown the chicken chunks on all sides, remove them from the pot, place them in a bowl, and set the bowl aside.
3. Add the remaining teaspoon of oil to the pot, reduce the heat to moderately low, and add the onion, green pepper, garlic, chili powder, and cumin. Cook the mixture for about 5 minutes, stirring it often, until the onions are translucent.
4. Add the broth and the tomatoes with their juice to the pot, and bring the mixture to a boil. Reduce the heat to low, cover the pot, and simmer the mixture for 20 minutes.
5. Add the reserved chicken, cover the pot, and simmer the fricassee for another 25 minutes.
6. Add the corn, peas, and beans, if desired, and simmer the fricassee 5 minutes longer.

CHICKEN ENCHILADAS

4 servings

Enchiladas are really Mexican crêpes made of corn tortillas for the pancake and stuffed with various fillings: chicken, beef, mashed beans, cheese. Here's a version you can make from a leftover chicken breast and can count on everyone to enjoy. It saves on calories because the tortillas are softened in heated sauce instead of oil. *Preparation tip:* You can buy enchilada sauce mild or hot, according to your taste, or mix the sauces half and half. If you start with raw chicken breast on the bone, buy one that weighs about 1 pound, which will yield ½ pound of meat.

½ pound boneless chicken breast, cooked,
   skinned, and shredded
1 medium onion, chopped (½ cup)
4 ounces Monterey Jack, shredded (about 1
   cup), divided
1 10-ounce can enchilada sauce
½ cup water
8 6-inch corn tortillas

1. In a medium bowl, combine the chicken, onion, and half the shredded cheese. Set the mixture aside.
2. In a skillet, combine the enchilada sauce and water, and heat the sauce to boiling. Place a tortilla into the sauce. When the tortilla is limp, remove it to a platter, letting the excess sauce drain back into the skillet. Spoon a generous ¼ cup of chicken-cheese filling across the diameter of the tortilla. Roll up the tortilla, and set it seam side down in a baking pan or shallow casserole. Repeat this procedure with the remaining tortillas, one by one, arranging them in a pan in a single layer.
3. Pour the remaining sauce over the rolled tortillas, sprinkling the remaining cheese over them, cover the pan or casserole with foil, and bake the enchiladas in a preheated 350° oven for 15 minutes. Remove the foil, and bake the enchiladas for another 5 minutes or until they are heated through and lightly browned.

CHICKEN AND BARLEY BAKE   *6 servings*

Barley is one of the most satisfying grains to eat, yet it rarely finds its way to American tables other than in soup. A baked turkey and barley recipe in *Gourmet* magazine inspired me to put together this tasty casserole that is elegant enough for company. *Preparation tip:* If you should use turkey instead of chicken, bone it and cut the meat into 3-inch pieces. For quick service, the dish can be prepared ahead through step 5.

  1 tablespoon butter or margarine, divided
  1 tablespoon vegetable oil, divided
  1 large onion, minced (1 cup)
  2 large cloves garlic, minced (2 teaspoons)
½ cup minced celery (1 large stalk)
  2 sweet peppers (2 green or 2 red or 1 of each),
     minced
½ cup dry white wine
  1 28-ounce can tomatoes, drained and chopped
  1 cup barley, rinsed
  3 cups chicken broth (homemade or canned)
Salt, if desired, to taste
Freshly ground black pepper to taste
  6 chicken legs and thighs, skinned and
     separated
¼ cup milk (optional)
  3 scallions, minced, for garnish
  2 tablespoons snipped fresh dill for garnish
     (omit if fresh dill is not available)

1. Heat 1 *teaspoon* of the butter and 1 *teaspoon* of the oil in a large, heavy saucepan (3-quart size). Add the onion, garlic, celery, and peppers, and cook the vegetables, stirring them now and then, over moderate heat for about 5 minutes.
2. Add the wine, bring the mixture to a boil, and continue boiling and stirring until nearly all the liquid has evaporated.
3. Add the tomatoes, barley, and broth. Bring the mixture to a boil, reduce the heat, cover the pan, and cook the mixture, stirring it a few times, for 25 minutes. There should still be plenty of liquid in the pot. Stir in the salt (omit if broth is salty) and pepper, and transfer the mixture to a 3- or 4-quart casserole that has a cover.
4. While the barley is cooking, brown the chicken on both sides in a large skillet in the remaining 2 teaspoons of butter or margarine and 2 teaspoons of oil. Season the chicken with salt, if desired, and pepper, *or* sprinkle the chicken with a no-salt herb mix (see p. 182).
5. Transfer the chicken pieces to the casserole, imbedding them into the barley

mixture. Cover, and bake the casserole in a preheated 350° oven for 30 minutes.

6. Sprinkle the milk over the casserole, and bake the casserole, uncovered, for another 15 minutes or until the chicken is very tender. If the casserole seems to be drying out, cover it during this last step.

7. Serve the casserole garnished with scallions and dill.

OVEN-"FRIED" CHICKEN LEGS   *6 or more servings*

This is probably the most frequently prepared chicken dish in our house because it is (a) delicious, (b) simple, (c) gives the flavor of fried without the fat, (d) as good cold as it is hot any time of the day (I have even had it for breakfast). This is easy enough for the kids to prepare themselves without having to rely on salty, expensive "shake and bake" mixes.

6 chicken legs and thighs, skinned and trimmed
　of fat
Milk (skim or low-fat) for soaking the chicken
½ cup plain dry bread crumbs or cereal crumbs
⅓ cup grated Parmesan
1 tablespoon dried parsley flakes, crumbled
¼ teaspoon freshly ground black pepper, or to
　taste
Vegetable oil spray for the chicken, if desired

1. Place the chicken pieces in a shallow bowl or pan, and cover them with the milk. Let the chicken soak for 15 minutes or longer (refrigerate, if necessary, to keep the ingredients cold).

2. In a shallow bowl or pie plate, combine the bread crumbs or cereal crumbs, cheese, parsley flakes, and pepper.

3. One by one, dip the soaked chicken pieces in the breading mixture, coating the chicken on all sides. Set the coated chicken pieces on a greased baking sheet, preferably one with a nonstick surface. Lightly spray the chicken pieces with vegetable-oil spray, if desired.

4. Bake the chicken in a preheated 375° oven for about 45 minutes.

GREEK CHICKEN WITH CHEESE   *6 servings*

This is an especially delicious way to prepare chicken, an excellent, attractive meal for company as well as family. I made it for the first time when entertaining a Greek friend, who insisted that I give his wife the recipe. My recipe was inspired by Lydie Marshall's Chicken with Feta Cheese, as published in *The Pleasures of Cooking.* Marshall, a well-known cooking teacher and author of *Cooking with Lydie Marshall,* originally obtained it from a friend in Greece. My version is lower in fat and salt, and the cooking procedure is simplified. Feta, a cheese made from sheep's milk, is lower in fat than most cow's milk cheeses, and much of the salt can be soaked out of it. This dish is wonderful with spinach egg noodles, but ordinary noodles or macaroni or even rice would also be a good accompaniment.

½ pound feta cheese, sliced
6 chicken legs with thighs
1 tablespoon plus 1 teaspoon olive oil, divided
4 medium onions, thinly sliced
2 large cloves garlic, minced (2 teaspoons)
1 17-ounce can of plum tomatoes, with liquid,
   coarsely chopped
½ teaspoon orégano
¼ teaspoon salt, if desired
Freshly ground black pepper to taste

1. Place the feta in a bowl with cold water to cover, and set it aside.
2. Remove and discard the chicken skin, and trim away the pieces of fat.
3. Heat 1 tablespoon of oil in a 10-inch heavy skillet with a cover. Brown the chicken pieces over moderate heat, turning them several times. Transfer the chicken to a platter.
4. Add the teaspoon of oil to the pan along with the sliced onions. Cook the onions over moderately low heat, stirring them, for about 10 minutes. Add the garlic, and cook the vegetables for another 5 minutes or until the onions start to brown.
5. Add the chopped tomatoes and their liquid and the orégano, stirring the mixture to combine the ingredients.
6. Place the chicken pieces on the sauce, and sprinkle the ingredients with salt (if desired) and a generous amount of pepper. Cover the pan, bring the ingredients to a boil, reduce the heat to medium-low, and simmer the chicken for 30 minutes.
7. Remove the feta from the water, and arrange the slices on top of the chicken. Cover the skillet, and cook the chicken for another 15 minutes or until the cheese is melted.

CHICKEN CACCIATORE
WITH NOODLES

4 servings

I have a particular fondness for chicken cacciatore because it was the first main course I prepared totally on my own—and I did it on a camp stove! While I have no recollection of the quality of the results, I can assure you that the following simple version is quite tasty.

    1 small broiler-fryer, skinned and cut into
        serving pieces
AHA herb mix (see p. 182) *or* other no-salt
    seasoning
Salt, if desired, to taste
Freshly ground black pepper to taste
1½ tablespoons oil, divided
    1 medium onion, sliced
    1 large clove garlic, minced (1 teaspoon)
    1 16-ounce can *stewed* tomatoes, with their juice
    1 16-ounce can tomatoes, with their juice
    ½ cup white wine
    12 ounces wide egg noodles

1. Sprinkle the chicken pieces with herb mix, salt, and pepper.
2. Heat 1 tablespoon of the oil in a large skillet with a cover, and brown the chicken well on both sides. Remove the chicken from the skillet, and set the chicken aside.
3. Add the remaining oil to the skillet, and sauté the onion and garlic for about 3 minutes.
4. Add the stewed tomatoes with their juice, tomatoes with their juice, and wine, and bring the mixture to a boil.
5. Add the browned chicken pieces, reduce the heat, cover the skillet, and simmer the chicken for about 25 minutes or until the chicken is cooked through.
6. Meanwhile, cook the noodles according to package directions. Transfer the noodles to a serving platter, and spoon the chicken and sauce over them.

CHICKEN WITH CARROTS AND CABBAGE

6 to 8 servings

Here is a chicken dish that features two cancer-fighting foods: carrots and cabbage. It goes well with boiled or mashed potatoes or with noodles. *Preparation tip:* If desired, cup-up potatoes can be added to the carrots in step 1 during the last 15 minutes of cooking.

    3 cups chicken broth
    2 pounds carrots, scraped and cut into 2-inch
      lengths (cut thick pieces lengthwise)
    2 teaspoons sugar
    Freshly ground black pepper to taste, divided
    Salt, if desired, to taste
    2 pounds green cabbage, cored and cut into
      ½-inch slices
    1 chicken (about 3 to 4 pounds), skinned and
      cut into serving pieces
    AHA herb mix (see p. 182) or other no-salt
      seasoning
    1 tablespoon butter or margarine
    2 teaspoons vegetable oil
    3 large onions, sliced thin
    3 cloves garlic, minced (1 tablespoon)

1. In a medium saucepan, bring the broth to a boil, and add the carrots, sugar, pepper, and salt, if desired. Reduce the heat, cover the pan, and cook the carrots for about 30 minutes.
2. While the carrots are cooking, cook the cabbage in boiling water (lightly salted, if desired) for 5 minutes. Drain the cabbage.
3. Sprinkle the chicken pieces on both sides with the herb mix and black pepper.
4. In a large, deep skillet, heat the butter or margarine and the oil, and brown the chicken on both sides. Transfer the chicken to a bowl.
5. Add the onions and garlic to the skillet, and cook the vegetables, stirring them, for about 5 minutes. Add the parboiled cabbage, and cook the vegetables for another 3 minutes. Season the vegetables with pepper.
6. Return the chicken to the skillet with any juices that may have collected in the bowl. Cover the skillet, and simmer the chicken for 35 minutes.
7. Add the carrots and their cooking liquid to the skillet. Boil the liquid in the uncovered skillet for several minutes to reduce it.

STOVE-TOP BARBECUED CHICKEN   *6 servings*

On a cold winter day, you can entertain visions of a warm-weather barbecue without ever leaving the cosiness of your kitchen. This is a simple dish that can be enjoyed by all. Serve it with your favorite cooked grain (brown rice, for example) or with egg noodles.

 1 teaspoon oil
 1 medium onion, chopped (½ cup)
 ½ cup ketchup
 ½ cup water
 2 tablespoons vinegar
 2 tablespoons brown sugar
1½ teaspoons Worcestershire sauce
 ½ teaspoon chili powder
 ¼ teaspoon crushed celery seeds *or* ½ teaspoon
   crumbled celery flakes
 1 3-pound broiler-fryer, skinned and cut into
   serving pieces

1. Heat the oil in a large nonstick skillet. Add the onion, and cook it, stirring it, until it is softened.
2. Stir in the ketchup, water, vinegar, brown sugar, Worcestershire sauce, chili powder, and celery seeds or flakes. Bring the sauce to a boil.
3. Add the chicken to the skillet, placing what used to be the skin side down, and spoon the sauce over the pieces. Cover the skillet, and simmer the chicken for 30 minutes. Uncover the skillet, turn the chicken pieces over ("skin" side up), and cook the chicken for another 15 minutes or until it is tender.

GRANNY SMITH CHICKEN

(with Apples)   *4 servings*

Here is an easy way to prepare chicken that should suit family and company alike. *Preparation tip:* If you wish to prepare it ahead, refrigerate or freeze the dish after step 4. When you want to complete it, reheat the casserole before adding the hot milk.

> 1 small broiler-fryer (about 2½ pounds), skinned
>   and cut into serving pieces
> Freshly ground black pepper to taste
> Salt, if desired, to taste
> 1 tablespoon butter or margarine
> 1 medium onion, thinly sliced
> 1 large clove garlic, minced (1 teaspoon)
> ½ cup dry sherry or rice wine
> 1 tablespoon minced fresh parsley *or* 1 teaspoon
>   dried parsley flakes, crumbled
> ½ teaspoon thyme leaves
> 3 medium or 2 large Granny Smith apples,
>   peeled, cored, and cut into wedges
> ½ cup skim or low-fat milk
> ½ cup shredded Swiss cheese or Jarlsberg
>   (2 ounces)

1. Season the chicken with pepper and salt. Melt the butter or margarine in a large skillet that has a cover, and brown the chicken pieces well on both sides.
2. Add the onion and garlic to the skillet, and sauté the vegetables for about 3 minutes.
3. Add the sherry or rice wine, parsley, and thyme, cover the skillet, and simmer the chicken for 20 minutes.
4. Add the apples, and simmer the chicken, covered, for another 10 minutes, by which time the chicken should be tender. Transfer the chicken mixture to an oven-proof casserole.
5. In the skillet or in a small saucepan, heat the milk just to the boiling point, and pour it over the chicken. Sprinkle the casserole with the shredded cheese, and place it under a preheated broiler until the cheese is bubbly.

CHICKEN AND EGGPLANT

4 to 6 servings

Here's a tasty chicken dish with a sauce that resembles ratatouille. Unlike traditional ways of preparing eggplant, this recipe is very low in fat and spicy enough to be made without added salt. *Preparation tip:* If fresh tomatoes are not available, you can substitute 2 canned tomatoes.

    1 broiler-fryer (about 3 pounds), skinned and
      cut into serving pieces
Freshly ground black pepper to taste
    1 tablespoon vegetable oil
    1 large onion, halved vertically then sliced thin
      crosswise (about 1 cup)
    3 large cloves garlic, minced (1 tablespoon)
1½ pounds eggplant, unpeeled, cut into 1-inch
      cubes (about 5 cups)
    ½ pound tomatoes, cored and cut into 1-inch
      cubes
    ¼ cup red wine vinegar
    ½ cup dry white wine
    ½ cup chicken broth
    1 bay leaf
    ¼ teaspoon thyme leaves
    ¼ teaspoon hot red pepper flakes

1. Season the chicken with pepper.
2. In a large skillet with a cover, heat the oil, and brown the chicken for about 5 minutes on each side. Remove the chicken from the skillet, and place it in a bowl or on a platter.
3. Add the onion, garlic, and eggplant to the skillet, and cook the vegetables, stirring them, for about 1 minute. Then stir in the tomatoes.
4. Add the vinegar, wine, and broth. Bring the mixture to a boil, and stir in the bay leaf, thyme, and pepper flakes.
5. Return the chicken pieces to the skillet, and spoon the sauce over them. Cover the skillet, and simmer the chicken pieces, basting them occasionally with the sauce, for about 20 minutes or until the chicken is tender. Remove and discard the bay leaf before serving the chicken.

QUICK CURRIED CHICKEN

4 to 6 servings

This generously sauced curry can be made from start to finish in about 45 minutes. *Preparation tip:* If you prepare it in advance, stop after step 6. Store the chicken and purée separately, and reheat the purée before adding the milk and returning the chicken to the pan. If immediate service is planned, start cooking the rice or noodles after step 4.

    1 broiler-fryer (about 3 pounds), skinned and
        cut into serving pieces
Freshly ground black pepper to taste
AHA herb mix (see p. 182) or other no-salt
        seasoning
    1 tablespoon butter, margarine, or vegetable oil
    1 medium-large onion, finely chopped (¾ cup)
    ½ cup finely chopped celery (1 large stalk)
    1 teaspoon minced garlic (1 large clove)
    2 tablespoons curry powder, or to taste
    1 bay leaf
    1 large apple, diced (1 cup)
    1 medium banana, diced
    2 teaspoons tomato paste
1½ cups chicken broth
    ½ cup skim milk

1. Season the chicken with the pepper and the herb mix.
2. In a heavy skillet with a cover, heat the butter, margarine, or oil, and brown the chicken lightly on both sides.
3. Add the onion, celery, and garlic to the skillet, and cook them for a few minutes.
4. Sprinkle the contents of the skillet with the curry powder, then add the bay leaf, apple, and banana. Cook the chicken for 5 minutes.
5. Stir in the tomato paste and broth. Bring the sauce to a boil, reduce the heat, cover the skillet, and cook the chicken for 15 minutes or until it is tender. Remove the chicken from the skillet, and set it aside to keep it warm. Remove the bay leaf, and discard it.
6. In a blender or food processor, purée the remaining contents of skillet.
7. Return the purée to the skillet, stir in the milk, and add the chicken. Bring the sauce just to a boil. Serve over rice or noodles.

"CULTURED" CHICKEN

(with Buttermilk and Yogurt)   *4 to 6 servings*

This dish gets its name from two tangy low-fat cultured milk products: butter-milk and yogurt. It goes well with steamed or boiled potatoes. *Preparation tip:* You'll save time if you do step 3 while the chicken browns. To prepare this dish in advance, stop after step 4 before adding yogurt.

1 broiler-fryer (about 3 pounds), skinned and
  cut into serving pieces
1 tablespoon vegetable oil
½ cup sliced scallions (with some green tops),
  divided
1 35-ounce can tomatoes, drained (2½ cups)
¾ cup buttermilk
1 tablespoon snipped fresh dill *or* 1 teaspoon
  dried dillweed
½ teaspoon sugar
½ teaspoon salt, if desired
⅛ to ¼ teaspoon freshly ground black pepper, to
  taste
Dash hot pepper sauce (Tabasco), or to taste
½ cup plain low-fat yogurt
¼ cup grated Parmesan
¼ cup minced fresh parsley (omit rather than
  substitute dried parsley flakes)

1. Lightly brown the chicken pieces in the oil in a large skillet that has a cover.
2. Add ¼ cup of the scallions to the skillet, and cook the chicken and scallions for about 2 minutes. Turn off the heat.
3. In a blender or food processor, combine the tomatoes, buttermilk, dill, sugar, salt, pepper, and pepper sauce. Purée the mixture until it is smooth.
4. Pour the sauce over the chicken, bring the contents of the skillet to a boil, reduce the heat, cover the pan, and simmer the chicken for about 20 minutes or until it is tender.
5. Stir in the yogurt and the Parmesan and heat the chicken until the sauce is very hot but not boiling. Serve the chicken garnished with the remaining ¼ cup scallions, and the parsley.

ORIENTAL STEWED CHICKEN   *6 servings*

This simple chicken entrée is, alas, not a low-sodium dish, although using reduced-sodium soy sauce helps some. *Preparation tip:* Note that the chicken marinates for 1 hour. The dish can be prepared ahead and reheated at serving time while the rice or noodles are cooking.

> 2 tablespoons soy sauce (preferably reduced-sodium)
> ½ teaspoon chili powder, or to taste
> 2 large cloves garlic, minced (2 teaspoons)
> 1 broiler-fryer (about 3½ pounds), skinned and cut into serving pieces
> 3 scallions, cut in 1-inch sections, with green tops
> ½ cup chicken broth (if broth is salty, use ¼ cup broth and ¼ cup water)

1. In a large saucepan or Dutch oven, combine the soy sauce, chili powder, and garlic. Add the chicken and scallions, and stir to coat the chicken well. Marinate the chicken for 1 hour, turning the chicken pieces several times.
2. Add the broth, and bring the ingredients to a boil. Reduce the heat to low, cover the pan, and simmer the chicken for 1 hour or until it is tender. Serve the chicken with rice or noodles.

ARROZ CON POLLO   *6 servings*

Here is a wholesome variation on the theme of Spanish rice with chicken. I served it at a dinner attended by four generations—from age 2 to 80—and was delighted to find everyone reaching for more. It is not only delicious, it's also an attractive dish and well suited to a buffet dinner. The "heat" of the chili pepper is hardly noticeable in the finished product, but it definitely adds interest to the flavor of the entire meal. *Preparation tip:* Note that the chicken should marinate for 30 minutes. I use salt-free homemade broth in preparing it; if your broth is commercially salted bouillon, you might want to dilute it with an equal amount of water before adding it to the rice. The dish can be prepared hours —even a day—in advance through step 4 and reheated in the oven before finishing it off with the last addition of ingredients (step 5 can also be done in the oven). If saffron (at $3 for .002 ounce) is too rich for your blood, you can leave it out and use an extra ¼ teaspoon of turmeric.

> 1 large broiler-fryer (3 to 3½ pounds), skinned, trimmed of fat, and cut into small pieces
> ¼ teaspoon turmeric

⅛ teaspoon saffron threads, crushed
 2 tablespoons warm water
 1 tablespoon lemon juice
¼ teaspoon salt, if desired
 2 tablespoons vegetable oil, divided
1½ cups long-grain brown rice
 1 large clove garlic, finely minced (1 teaspoon)
 1 large onion, coarsely chopped (1 cup)
2½ to 3½ cups chicken broth
½ teaspoon orégano
¼ teaspoon freshly ground black pepper
¼ teaspoon paprika
 1 28-ounce can tomatoes with their juice
 1 dried chili pepper, crushed, *or* hot red pepper
   flakes, to taste (optional)
 2 tablespoons minced fresh parsley *or* 2
   teaspoons dried parsley flakes
 1 10-ounce package frozen peas
½ cup sliced black olives
¼ cup chopped pimiento

1. Place the chicken pieces in a bowl. In a cup, prepare a marinade by combining the turmeric and saffron with the warm water, stirring to dissolve the saffron. Add the lemon juice, salt, and 1 tablespoon of oil. Pour the marinade over the chicken, tossing the pieces to wet them. Refrigerate the chicken for 30 minutes or longer.

2. Heat the remaining tablespoon of oil in a nonstick skillet (if you have only a small pan that is nonstick, use it, doing this step in batches and using part of the oil for each batch). Remove the chicken from the marinade, reserving the marinade. Brown the chicken pieces in the oil, and remove them from the pan.

3. Add the rice to the pan, and "fry" it for about 3 to 5 minutes, stirring it constantly to coat it with oil and toast the grains. Stir in the garlic and onion, and fry them for 1 to 2 minutes, still stirring. Transfer the rice-vegetable mixture to a Dutch oven, and then add 2½ cups broth, the orégano, pepper, and paprika. Stir the ingredients to combine them, bring the mixture to a boil, reduce the heat to low, cover the pot tightly, and cook the rice for 30 minutes.

4. Stir in the reserved marinade (if any), tomatoes and their juice, chili pepper, and parsley, arrange the chicken pieces on top of the rice, cover the pot, and cook the chicken-rice mixture over low heat for 30 minutes or until the chicken is nearly done. Check once or twice, and add more broth if needed.

5. Sprinkle the peas, olives, and pimiento over the top of the chicken, add more broth or water, if necessary, cover the pot, and cook the mixture for another 10 to 15 minutes or until the chicken is tender, the rice fairly dry, and the peas hot.

COUSCOUS WITH CHICKEN   *6 servings*

Couscous, a grain made from hard durum wheat (semolina, the type used to make fine pasta), is basic to the Moroccan diet. The traditional lengthy recipe has been simplified for American fast-food habits with little or no sacrifice in flavor. Don't be intimidated by the long list of ingredients; many of them are just seasonings. *Preparation tip:* Couscous can often be found in specialty food stores, Arabian markets, or the specialty foods section of supermarkets. If it is unavailable, you can substitute bulgur or rice. For efficiency and a meal that needs no reheating, start preparing the couscous as you near the end of step 4 (it cooks in less than 5 minutes).

1 large onion, sliced thin crosswise and
  separated into rings
2 large cloves garlic, minced (2 teaspoons)
1 tablespoon olive oil
1 3-pound broiler-fryer, skinned and cut into
  serving pieces
Salt, if desired, to taste
Freshly ground black pepper to taste
1 16-ounce can tomatoes, coarsely chopped,
  with their juice
3 large carrots, cut into 1-inch lengths
2 large stalks celery, cut into 1-inch lengths
1 medium turnip *or* ¼ of a large rutabaga,
  peeled and cut into ½-inch cubes
½ teaspoon cinnamon
½ teaspoon ground cumin
¼ teaspoon turmeric
Several dashes cayenne to taste
A few strands saffron (optional)
2 teaspoons honey
½ pound zucchini, *unpeeled* and cut into ½-inch
  pieces
2 to 4 ounces chopped pimientos
½ cup raisins
1 to 1⅔ cups cooked chickpeas, drained
  (optional)
1¾ cups quick-cooking couscous, cooked
  according to package directions
¼ cup minced fresh parsley

1. In a large deep skillet with a cover or a Dutch oven, sauté the onions and garlic in the oil over medium heat for about 3 minutes. Remove the onions and garlic from the pan with a slotted spoon, leaving the oil behind.

2. Sprinkle the chicken pieces with salt and pepper, and brown them in the leftover oil on all sides over medium heat, adding a little more oil if necessary.

3. Return the onion mixture to the pan. Add the tomatoes and their liquid, the carrots, celery, turnip or rutabaga, cinnamon, cumin, turmeric, cayenne, saffron, and honey. Add more salt and pepper, if desired. Stir the ingredients gently to combine them, but leave the chicken pieces at the bottom of the pan. Bring the liquid in the pan to a boil, cover the pan, reduce the heat, and simmer the chicken for about 25 minutes.

4. Add the zucchini, pimientos, raisins, and chickpeas, if desired. Cover the pan, and simmer the chicken for another 15 minutes or until the zucchini is tender.

5. Place the warm couscous in the bottom of a serving bowl (or place a portion of couscous on each person's plate), and top the couscous with the chicken-and-vegetable stew. Sprinkle the bowl or plates with parsley.

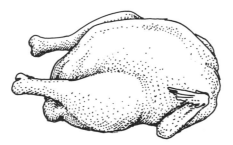

LEMON CHICKEN WITH BULGUR   *6 servings*

This recipe is one of my favorite company dishes, both easy and tasty. *Preparation tip:* You can make it with kasha (buckwheat groats) instead of bulgur. If you prepare it in advance, reduce the baking time to 45 minutes so that it does not get overcooked and dry when reheated.

    2 teaspoons butter or margarine
    2 teaspoons vegetable oil
    1 broiler-fryer (about 3½ pounds), skinned and
        cut into serving pieces
Salt, if desired, to taste
Freshly ground black pepper to taste
    3 medium onions, chopped (1½ to 2 cups)
    2 cloves garlic, minced (2 teaspoons)
1½ cups bulgur
    ½ teaspoon ground cardamom
    ½ teaspoon ground coriander
    ½ teaspoon ground cumin
Grated rind and juice of 1 lemon
    3 cups boiling chicken broth

1. In a large skillet, heat the butter or margarine and the oil, add the chicken, and brown the pieces on all sides. Season the chicken with salt and pepper, and remove it to a large casserole.
2. Add the onions and garlic to the skillet, and cook the vegetables, stirring them, until the onions are translucent.
3. Add the bulgur to the skillet, stirring to coat it and brown it lightly.
4. Add the cardamom, coriander, cumin, and lemon rind and juice to the bulgur mixture, mixing the ingredients well. Spoon the bulgur on top of the reserved chicken.
5. Pour the boiling broth over the chicken and bulgur. Cover the casserole, and place it in a preheated 350° oven for 1 hour or until the chicken is tender.

GINGER CHICKEN AND CHICKPEAS *6 servings*

This dish, derived from a *Gourmet* magazine recipe, is not for delicate stomachs, although it is far from being as hot as East Asians might eat it. *Preparation tip:* If you like very spicy food, you can always increase the amount of red pepper flakes. I prepare this dish without any added salt, especially if I use canned broth. It is very good served over brown rice or egg noodles (regular or spinach). If you do not use a nonstick pan, add 1 teaspoon of oil in step 3 to cook the onions.

    1 broiler-fryer (3 to 3½ pounds), skinned and
      cut into serving pieces
    ⅓ cup lemon juice
    Cold water
    Salt, if desired, to taste
    Freshly ground black pepper to taste
    1 tablespoon butter, margarine, or vegetable oil
    2 large onions, chopped (2 cups)
    ¼ cup minced fresh ginger
    1 teaspoon ground cumin
    1 teaspoon ground cardamom
    1 teaspoon ground coriander
    Generous pinch hot red pepper flakes
    2 cups cooked chickpeas (if you use canned
      chickpeas, drain and rinse them)
    2 cups chicken broth (homemade or canned)

1. Soak the chicken in the lemon juice and water to cover for 15 minutes. Drain the chicken, and pat dry. Season it with salt and pepper.
2. In a Dutch oven or wide-bottomed saucepan, heat the butter, margarine, or oil, and brown the chicken in it on both sides. Remove the chicken from the pan.
3. Add the onions to the pan, and cook them, stirring them, over low heat until they are soft.
4. Add the ginger, cumin, cardamom, coriander, and pepper flakes, and cook the mixture, stirring it, a few minutes longer.
5. Return the chicken to the pan, add the chickpeas, broth, and additional salt and pepper to taste. Bring the liquid to a boil, reduce the heat, cover the pan, and simmer the mixture for 30 minutes or until the chicken is tender.

40-CLOVE GARLIC CHICKEN   *8 servings*

Some people may find it hard to believe that *anything* made with 40 cloves of garlic would be edible, but this dish is delicious and delicately flavored. The long, slow cooking tames the garlic into a vegetable while preserving its flavor and most of its health benefits (see p. 149). Because the dish is fairly juicy when done, it goes well served over cooked millet or barley and/or with a whole-wheat French bread to mop up the juices and to act as a foil for the garlic.

  8 chicken legs and thighs, skinned and
     separated
  2 tablespoons oil
  1 large onion, coarsely chopped (1 cup)
  4 ribs celery, sliced into ¼-inches pieces (1½
     to 2 cups)
  2 tablespoons minced fresh parsley *or*
  2 teaspoons dried parsley flakes
  1 teaspoon dried tarragon
  ½ cup dry vermouth
  ½ teaspoon salt, if desired
  ¼ teaspoon freshly ground black pepper
Dash nutmeg
 40 cloves garlic, separated but not peeled

1. Brush the chicken pieces on all sides with the oil.
2. In a large casserole or heavy Dutch oven (5 to 6 quarts), combine the onion, celery, parsley, and tarragon. Lay the chicken pieces over the vegetables and herbs, and pour the vermouth over the chicken. Sprinkle the chicken with salt, pepper, and nutmeg. Distribute the unpeeled garlic cloves throughout the casserole, tucking them under the chicken pieces. Cover the casserole tightly (you might fit a piece of foil around the top under the lid).
3. Bake the chicken in a preheated 325° oven for 1½ hours. *Do not uncover the casserole* until after this time has elapsed.
4. Serve the chicken with the garlic, advising the diners to squeeze the flesh from its papery coat. The garlic is especially tasty when eaten on crusty bread.

CABBAGE-STUFFED CORNISH HENS   *4 servings*

Cornish game hens have become almost commonplace in American supermarkets in recent years (although in many markets, they can only be obtained frozen), and that's good news. For Cornish hens are low in fat and elegant enough for the finest company. The hens are roasted with their skin, but you don't have to eat the skin if you're trying to control fat and calorie intake. *Preparation tip:* Only about half the stuffing will fit into two hens, so bake the rest in a covered dish. Or make 4 hens to serve 8.

HENS
2 Cornish game hens, preferably fresh (defrost if frozen)
Salt, if desired, to taste
Freshly ground black pepper to taste
Vegetable-oil spray (optional)

STUFFING
1 tablespoon butter or margarine
2 cups chopped green cabbage (½ pound)
1 medium onion, chopped (½ cup)
¼ cup broth
3 tablespoons dry white wine
½ teaspoon caraway seeds
4 slices bread (white or whole-wheat), cut into ½-inch cubes
Freshly ground black pepper to taste
Salt, if desired, to taste

1. Remove all visible fat from inside the cavity of the hens. Sprinkle the hens with salt and pepper.
2. To prepare the stuffing, in a large skillet, melt the butter or margarine, add the cabbage and onion, tossing the vegetables to coat them with the fat, and sauté them for a minute or so. Then add the broth, and cook the vegetables for another 3 minutes or until they are limp. Add the wine, and cook the vegetables 1 minute longer.
3. Remove the pan from the heat, stir in the caraway seeds and bread cubes, and season the stuffing with pepper and salt.
4. Place about ¼ of the stuffing into the cavity of each bird. Close the cavities with skewers or by tying the legs together. Place the leftover stuffing in a small oven-proof dish, cover it, and set it aside. Fold the wings of the hens back, and place the birds legs up in a shallow greased baking dish. Spray the hens with vegetable oil, if desired.
5. Roast the hens in a preheated 400° oven for 50 minutes. Place the extra stuffing in the oven about 25 minutes into the roasting time. To serve, cut the hens in half lengthwise, and place each half on a plate stuffing side down.

CORNISH HENS MANDARIN   *8 servings*

Here rice is the stuffing. Mandarin oranges add color, elegance, and a lovely fruity contrast. *Preparation tip:* Sake is Japanese rice wine. If you have none, you can substitute dry sherry, dry vermouth, or white wine.

    4 Cornish game hens, with livers reserved
    1 tablespoon butter or margarine
    1 cup minced onion (1 large), divided
    2 cups cooked rice (white or brown)
    ½ teaspoon salt, if desired
    ¼ teaspoon freshly ground black pepper
    ½ teaspoon dried sage, crumbled, or seasoning of
        your choice
    1 11-ounce can mandarin oranges, drained and
        juice reserved, divided
    Vegetable oil (about 1 tablespoon) or
        vegetable-oil spray
    ¼ cup sake

1. Remove the livers from the hens, and chop the livers.
2. In a small skillet, melt the butter or margarine, and sauté the livers and ½ cup of onion until livers have lost their pink color.
3. Place the rice in a medium bowl, and combine it well with the cooked livers and cooked onions, salt, pepper, sage, and ½ cup of the oranges. Use ¼ of the rice mixture to stuff each hen, enclosing stuffing by tying the feet together or closing the cavities with skewers.
4. Place the stuffed birds legs up in a shallow greased roasting pan, brush or spray the hens with vegetable oil, sprinkle them with additional salt and pepper, if desired, and the remaining ½ cup of onion.
5. Roast the hens in a preheated 350° oven for 1 hour. Remove the pan from the oven, pour the reserved orange juice and the sake over the hens, and return the pan to the oven. Turn the heat up to 400°, and roast the hens for another 15 minutes. Remove the pan from the oven again, add the remaining orange segments, and return the pan to the oven for 5 minutes longer.
6. To serve, cut the hens in half lengthwise, place each half on a plate stuffing side down, and spoon the pan juices over it.

TURKEY MEATBALLS   *about 20 meatballs*

Ground turkey is lower in fat than ground beef and deserves a more prominent place in American cooking. It can be found in supermarkets throughout the country, usually in 1-pound rolls. Sometimes it is sold frozen or in thick slices from a large roll. The following turkey balls are wonderful for dinner. They also make tasty hors d'oeuvres (you can omit the sauce). Since the sauce contains soy sauce, this is not a low-sodium recipe. *Preparation tip:* The meatballs can be made ahead and frozen, to be reheated later in the cooking broth. The sauce should be made at the last minute. For a main dish, try serving them on a bed of rice surrounded by peas (snow peas or sugar snaps are superb) and mandarin orange sections.

MEATBALLS
1 pound ground turkey
1 tablespoon chopped pimiento or roasted pepper
1 tablespoon imported soy sauce (preferably reduced-sodium)
1 tablespoon minced onion
1 teaspoon minced garlic
1 egg

COOKING BROTH
4 cups water
2 tablespoons imported soy sauce (preferably reduced-sodium)
1 tablespoon minced fresh ginger

SAUCE
1 teaspoon cornstarch
1 tablespoon cold water
1 cup reserved broth

1. In a medium bowl, combine all the meatball ingredients, stirring them to mix thoroughly.
2. Shape the mixture into balls about 1½ inches in diameter. (Periodically wet your hands to make the shaping of the meatballs easier.) Place the meatballs on a tray or platter so that they don't touch.
3. In a wide saucepan, combine all the cooking broth ingredients, and bring the broth to a boil. Add all the meatballs one at a time, reduce the heat, cover the pan, and simmer the meatballs for about 30 minutes. Remove the meatballs from the pan with a slotted spoon. Place the meatballs in a serving dish and keep them warm.
4. Strain the cooking broth, and save 1 cup of the liquid.
5. To make the sauce, in a small saucepan combine the cornstarch with the cold water, and then stir in the reserved broth. Bring the sauce to a boil, and cook it, stirring it, until it thickens, about 1 minute. Pour the sauce over the meatballs.

TURKEY BURGERS

6 servings

These well-seasoned, low-fat burgers can be "fried" in a pan or grilled on a barbecue. They have a unique flavor. Just don't think of them as beef (which they are not), and you'll really enjoy them. I like them in whole-wheat pita bread with lettuce and tomato slices.

    1 pound ground turkey
    ½ cup dried bread crumbs, preferably
       whole-grain
    3 tablespoons finely chopped onion
    2 tablespoons ketchup
    1 tablespoon lemon juice
    1 teaspoon Worcestershire sauce
    1 teaspoon soy sauce
    ½ teaspoon paprika
    ¼ teaspoon hot pepper sauce (Tabasco)
    Freshly ground black pepper to taste

1. Combine all ingredients, and shape the mixture into 6 patties.
2. Fry, broil, or grill the burgers until they are done, about 5 minutes a side.

TERRIFIC TURKEY LOAF

6 servings

This rich-tasting but low-fat loaf is delicious and pretty enough to serve to company. Few would even guess it is based on the lowly bird! It can be served hot like meat loaf or cold like pâté, surrounded by salad vegetables. It can also be sliced for sandwiches. *Preparation tip:* The loaf can be made ahead and refrigerated overnight. If you reheat it, cover it to keep it from drying out.

    1 tablespoon vegetable oil
    2 teaspoons minced garlic (2 large cloves)
    1 cup finely chopped celery (2 large stalks)
    1 cup thinly sliced leeks (white and pale green
       parts) *or* ½ cup chopped onion
    1½ cups diced red sweet pepper (2 medium) *or* 2
       roasted red peppers, diced
    2½ cups thinly sliced mushrooms (½ pound)
    1¼ pounds ground turkey
    1 egg white *or* 1 whole egg, lightly beaten
    ½ teaspoon salt, if desired
    ½ teaspoon freshly ground black pepper
    Dash nutmeg

½ cup fresh bread crumbs (1 slice)
½ cup minced fresh parsley

1. In a large skillet, preferably nonstick, heat the oil briefly, and sauté the garlic, celery, leeks or onions, and red pepper, stirring the vegetables until they are slightly softened (do not let them burn), about 3 to 5 minutes.
2. Meanwhile, boil a kettle of water, and preheat the oven to 375°.
3. Stir the mushrooms into the red pepper mixture, cover the pan for a few minutes until the mushrooms start to give up their liquid, then remove the cover, and sauté the vegetables, stirring them, until all the liquid has evaporated. Remove the vegetables from the heat and set them aside.
4. In a large bowl, combine the turkey, egg white or whole egg, salt, pepper, nutmeg, bread crumbs, and parsley. Add the sautéed vegetables, and combine the ingredients well. Transfer the turkey mixture to a lightly greased loaf pan (approximately 8 × 4 inches), and set the pan in a large, shallow baking dish.
5. Place the pans in the preheated oven, pour the boiling water into the *outer* pan to a depth of about one inch, and bake the loaf for 1 hour 15 minutes. Remove the loaf pan from the outer pan and from the oven. Let the loaf rest for 15 minutes, then remove it from its pan for slicing.

ROAST STUFFED TURKEY   *about 12 servings*

Even though this is traditional Thanksgiving fare, a roast stuffed turkey is wonderful during any of the cooler months of the year. It may entail more than the usual preparation, but it gives you at least two family meals as is, and if you roast a big bird, the leftovers are an excellent start for a variety of nutritious dishes, including main-course salads, soups, and sandwiches (see, for example, pp. 348, 363, and 494). And while stuffing has traditionally been made from white bread and fatty ingredients like sausage or butter, there are far more nourishing yet delicious stuffings you can try, like those listed here. Figure on ¾ to 1 cup for each pound of poultry. If you have extra, bake it in a covered oven-proof dish when the turkey is about 40 minutes from done, and treat it as the starchy vegetable in your meal.

1 12-pound turkey, fresh or defrosted
Salt, if desired, to taste
Freshly ground black pepper to taste
12 cups stuffing (approximately, see pp. 442–443)

1 tablespoon vegetable oil
2 tablespoons broth or water
2 large cloves garlic, mashed (2 teaspoons)
2 teaspoons paprika
1 cup water (optional)
1 onion, sliced (optional)

1. Wash the bird, and dry it with paper towels. Sprinkle the cavity with salt, if desired, and pepper.
2. Spoon in the stuffing (do not pack tightly), leaving a little space at the end for expansion. If the neck skin is available, stuff that, too. Sew up the open ends (try dental floss instead of thread), or close with skewers and cord.
3. In a small bowl, make a paste of the vegetable oil, broth or water, garlic, and paprika. Smear this on the skin of the bird with a pastry brush or with your fingers (do the underside of the bird first).
4. Place the turkey breast side up on a rack in a roasting pan big enough to hold it without squeezing it. Pour the water into the bottom of the pan, if desired (you will end up with more gravy, and the turkey will be moister), and sprinkle the onion around the edges. Cover the turkey with a tent of foil, and roast the bird in a preheated 325° oven for approximately 4½ to 5 hours (or until a thermometer inserted in the bird's thigh registers 180° to 185°), removing the foil and basting the turkey with the pan juices several times during the last 30 to 60 minutes. For an unstuffed turkey, reduce the roasting time by about 30 minutes.
5. To serve, remove the stuffing to a separate bowl before carving the turkey. Serve the turkey without the skin, if possible.

APPLE-RAISIN WHOLE-WHEAT STUFFING   *stuffing for a 12-pound turkey*
1 1-pound loaf *stale* whole-wheat raisin bread *or*
   plain whole-wheat bread and ¾ cup raisins
2 large apples, unpeeled, chopped
2 large onions, chopped (2 cups)
3 stalks celery, diced (about 1½ cups)
1 egg white and 1 whole egg, lightly beaten
½ cup chopped walnuts or pecans
2 tablespoons butter or margarine, melted
1¼ cups broth (chicken or vegetable)
Freshly ground black pepper to taste

1. If you are starting with a loaf of fresh bread, spread the slices out on a rack for half a day to dry them out. Or you can toast them lightly to speed the drying process. Then cut the slices into small cubes.
2. Combine the bread cubes with the remaining ingredients.

BULGUR-RAISIN STUFFING   *about 12 cups*

  1 cup golden raisins
Hot water for plumping raisins
  1 large onion, chopped (1 cup)
  1 cup chopped celery (2 large stalks)
  2 tablespoons butter or margarine
  4 cups bulgur (raw), preferably coarsely cut
  7 cups chicken broth
  2 teaspoons thyme leaves
  2 teaspoons dried sage
½ teaspoon freshly ground black pepper
Salt, if desired, to taste (omit if broth is salty)
⅔ cup chopped walnuts

1. Place the raisins in a bowl, cover them with hot water, and set them aside.
2. In a large skillet with a tight-fitting cover or in a Dutch oven, sauté the onion and celery in the butter or margarine until the vegetables are soft. Stir in the bulgur, and cook it, stirring it, for about 5 minutes.
3. Add the broth, thyme, sage, pepper, and salt. Mix the ingredients well. Bring the mixture to a boil, reduce the heat, cover the pan, and simmer the bulgur for 15 to 20 minutes or until all the liquid is absorbed.
4. Drain the raisins, and add them with the nuts to the cooked bulgur.

POTATO STUFFING   *stuffing for a 12-pound turkey*

  2 pounds potatoes, whole and unpeeled
  4 cups whole-wheat bread cubes (8 slices)
  2 tablespoons butter, margarine, or vegetable oil
  2 medium onions, chopped (1⅓ cups)
  3 cups chopped green cabbage (¾ pound)
  3 medium red apples, unpeeled, diced
½ cup raisins
  1 egg white and 1 whole egg, lightly beaten
  1 tablespoon caraway seeds
¼ teaspoon salt, if desired
¼ teaspoon freshly ground black pepper

1. In a medium saucepan, boil the potatoes in water to cover for 30 to 40 minutes or until they are soft. When they are cool enough to handle, peel them, and mash them in a large bowl (this works best with a potato ricer).
2. While the potatoes cook, toast the bread cubes in a 400° oven until they are crisp, turning them once.
3. Meanwhile, in a medium skillet, heat the butter, margarine, or oil, and sauté the onions and cabbage, stirring them often, until they begin to turn golden, about 10 minutes (do not let them brown or burn).
4. Combine the mashed potatoes with the cooked vegetables, bread cubes, diced apples, raisins, beaten eggs, caraway seeds, salt, and pepper.

Main-Dish Fish

Fish is an excellent source of protein in a wholesome diet. It is usually low in fat (and those fish that are not low-fat contain a kind of fat that helps to prevent heart disease [see p. 11]), and it can be cooked into tasty dishes without the need to add a lot of fat. At one time it was thought that shellfish were high in cholesterol, but a recent reanalysis of their cholesterol content showed that this is not so for most shellfish. Only shrimp remains relatively high in cholesterol (90 milligrams in 3 ounces). Still, a serving of shrimp contains only a third the cholesterol in one egg yolk. Shellfish also have the advantage of being extremely low in fat and, therefore, low in calories. I guess the main problem with fish is that it has become too expensive to be a frequent main dish in most American households, including my own. My advice is to shop for the specials in fresh fish, and try some of the lesser known and less expensive kinds, including shark and monkfish, when available.

The secret to well-cooked fish is timing: overcooking toughens and dries it. Your best guide is the one used by professional cooks, the so-called 10-minute rule: for each inch of thickness, cook for 10 minutes. As fish cooks, it turns from translucent white (or pink) to opaque white, like egg whites. To be certain it is done, test it with a fork at its thickest point: if the fish is opaque, it is done; if it flakes easily when tested, you probably overcooked it. Fish that is enclosed in foil or simmered or baked in a sauce takes longer to cook than fish that is broiled, poached, or fried in the usual way. In this case, apply a "15-minute rule" instead.

STIR-FRIED STRIPED BASS

4 servings

Firm-fleshed fish are wonderful in stir-fries. *Preparation tip:* As with all other such dishes, the ingredients can be prepared in advance, but cook them at the last minute, after you turn off the rice.

    2 tablespoons vegetable oil, divided
    1 pound striped bass (or other firm fish) fillets,
      cut into ½-inch strips
    ¼ cup finely chopped scallions
    ½ cup sliced bamboo shoots
    ½ cup celery, diagonally sliced into ¼-inch
      pieces (1 medium stalk)
    ½ cup sliced water chestnuts
    ½ cup sliced mushrooms
    ⅓ cup stock (fish, vegetable, or chicken)
    2 teaspoons reduced-sodium soy sauce
    1 teaspoon cornstarch
    1 tablespoon cold water

1. Heat 1 tablespoon of the oil in a wok or heavy skillet. Add the fish, and, over high heat, fry it rapidly, turning the fish carefully to cook it about 1 minute per side. Remove the fish from the pan, and keep it warm.
2. Add the remaining oil to the pan, and, over heat high, stir-fry the scallions, bamboo shoots, celery, water chestnuts, and mushrooms for about 1 minute.
3. Add the stock and soy sauce, cover the pan, and let the mixture boil for 5 minutes.
4. Meanwhile, mix the cornstarch and the water. When the vegetables are done, add this mixture to them along with the reserved fish. Stir-fry the mixture until the sauce is thickened. Serve the stir-fry immediately with the rice or grain of your choice.

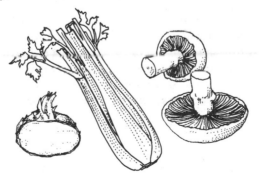

COLD POACHED STRIPED BASS

4 servings

These tasty fillets for a fine make-ahead feast were suggested by the late James Beard, who avoided salt for health reasons. Two sauces are offered, both low-cal and low-sodium, but still with plenty of zip. *Preparation tip:* You can use the same recipe for fillets of cod, red snapper, monkfish, pompano, haddock, or steaks of salmon or halibut. Poach according to the rule of 10 minutes for each inch of maximum thickness. You can save the strained poaching liquid (refrigerate or freeze it) for making fish stock or another poached fish dish.

FISH
Water
1 medium onion, peeled and quartered
12 whole black peppercorns
1 bay leaf
3 slices lemon
1½ pounds striped bass fillets (or one large fillet,
    cut into 4 pieces)

SAUCE I
1 cup plain low-fat yogurt
¼ cup finely snipped fresh dill
¼ cup grated horseradish, fresh if
    available
White pepper to taste
1 teaspoon lemon juice

SAUCE II
½ cup plain low-fat yogurt
1 tablespoon drained, bottled
    horseradish
¾ teaspoon Dijon mustard
2 tablespoons snipped fresh dill
White pepper to taste

1. In a deep sauté pan or poacher with a tight-fitting cover and large enough to hold the fish in a single layer, add water to a depth of 2 inches. Add the onion, peppercorns, bay leaf, and lemon. Cover the pan, bring the liquid to a boil, and boil it for 5 minutes.
2. Reduce the heat, but keep the liquid simmering. Add the fish gently, cover the pan, and poach the fish over low heat for about 5 minutes (if ½-inch thick—longer if the fillets are thicker). The fish is done when it is opaque all the way through. Remove the fish from the liquid, and set it aside to cool.
3. Prepare the sauce of your choice by combining all the ingredients in a small bowl. Refrigerate the sauce until serving time.

COLD BLUEFISH IN WHITE WINE

4 servings

Here is a *Craig Claiborne's Gourmet Diet* no-salt masterpiece with three added virtues: it is made from a fish with heart-protecting fat (see p. 11); it contains fewer than 200 calories per serving; and it is amenable to preparation one or more days in advance. The lemon takes the edge of "fishiness" from the bluefish and turns it into elegant fare.

- 1 pound boneless bluefish fillets, with skin
- 1 lemon, cut into 8 to 10 slices
- ½ cup water
- ¼ cup dry white wine
- 2 tablespoons white vinegar
- 1 teaspoon sugar
- 1 medium-large onion, cut in half and thinly sliced (about 1 cup)
- 1 bay leaf
- 3 whole cloves
- ⅛ teaspoon hot red pepper flakes
- 12 black peppercorns
- ½ teaspoon thyme

1. Arrange the fillets skin side down in a shallow baking dish (if they are large, you may have to cut the fillets into pieces). Spread the lemon slices over the fish.
2. In a small saucepan, combine the rest of the ingredients, bring them to a boil, reduce the heat, and simmer them for 10 minutes.
3. Pour the boiling hot sauce over the fish. Place the fish in a preheated 400° oven, and bake it for 15 minutes. Remove the baking dish from the oven, and let the fish remain in the marinade until cool. Chill the fish, and serve it cold.

SPAGHETTI SQUASH WITH
CLAM SAUCE

4 servings

A low-fat winner, said my tasters. This recipe, derived from one in *Gourmet* magazine, is my favorite way to serve spaghetti squash as a main dish for family and company. *Preparation tip:* Both the squash and the sauce can be prepared as much as a day ahead and reheated separately just before serving time. The canned clams are sufficiently salty; do not add more salt before you've tasted the completed dish.

  1 medium spaghetti squash, about 3 to 3½
    pounds
13 ounces canned minced clams
  1 tablespoon oil, preferably olive
  1 large onion, minced (1 cup)
  2 teaspoons minced garlic
Freshly ground black pepper to taste
½ cup dry white wine
½ teaspoon hot red pepper flakes
⅓ cup minced fresh parsley
  1 tablespoon lemon juice
  1 tablespoon butter or margarine for reheating
    the squash (optional)

1. Set the squash on a steamer rack in a large pot over a few inches of boiling water. Cover the pot, and steam the squash for 35 to 40 minutes or until the squash is tender when pressed or when pierced with a fork. Set the squash aside to cool.
2. Drain the clams, and save the juice. Set the clams aside.
3. Heat the oil in a skillet, and sauté the onion and garlic for 3 to 5 minutes, or until they are soft. Season the vegetables with pepper, add the wine, and cook the mixture over moderately high heat to reduce the liquid by half.
4. Add the reserved clam juice and the red pepper flakes, and cook the mixture to reduce the liquid to about ⅓ cup.
5. Add the clams, parsley, lemon juice, and more pepper, if desired.
6. Split the spaghetti squash lengthwise, and scrape out and discard the seeds and dark orange pulp around them. With a fork, "comb" out the pale yellow flesh, working from the cut edges toward the center to produce long spaghetti-like strands.
7. Reheat the squash either in the oven in a covered, heat-proof bowl or pan or on top of the stove, stirring the strands gently in a saucepan with 1 tablespoon of butter or margarine. Simultaneously heat the clam sauce, but do not boil it. To serve, combine the hot squash with the sauce.

TOMATO-CROWNED COD

4 to 6 servings

This low-sodium recipe, developed by the American Heart Association, is one of the most popular recipes in *Jane Brody's Nutrition Book.* In addition to having no added salt, it is very low in calories—under 200 per serving. *Preparation tip:* The dish can be prepared in advance through step 3 and refrigerated.

1½ pounds cod fillets
 2 tablespoons lemon juice
 ⅛ teaspoon freshly ground black pepper
 2 large tomatoes, sliced ¼ inch thick
 ½ medium green pepper, finely chopped
 2 tablespoons chopped onion
 ¼ cup dry bread crumbs
 ½ teaspoon dried basil, crumbled, *or* 1
    tablespoon chopped fresh basil
 1 tablespoon oil

1. Place the fish in an oiled baking dish. Season it with lemon juice and pepper.
2. Place the tomato slices on the fish, and sprinkle the fillets with the green pepper and onion.
3. In a small bowl, combine the bread crumbs, basil, and oil. Spread the crumb mixture evenly over the tomatoes.
4. Bake the fish, uncovered, in a preheated 350° oven for 25 minutes.

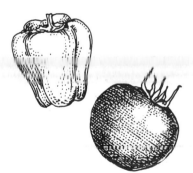

FISH FILLETS WITH RATATOUILLE   *6 servings*

Ratatouille is one of the most versatile of foods: it can be eaten as a hot vegetable, cold salad, condiment, stuffing, or seasoning. If you make plenty of it when the vegetables are in season (late summer), it stores very well in the freezer all year and can be used to make a gourmet meal in minutes. Try this, for example.

1 tablespoon olive oil, divided
2 tablespoons bread crumbs, divided
2 pounds fish fillets (flounder, scrod, striped bass, etc.)
3 tablespoons lemon juice
Salt, if desired, to taste
Freshly ground black pepper to taste
4 cups ratatouille, coarsely chopped (see p. 520)

1. On the bottom of a baking dish big enough to hold the fish in a single layer, smear a teaspoon of the olive oil, and sprinkle on half of the bread crumbs.
2. Spread the fillets over the crumbs, and sprinkle the fish with the lemon juice, salt, and pepper.
3. Spread the ratatouille over the fish, and sprinkle on the remaining crumbs and the rest of the oil.
4. Bake the fish in a preheated 400° oven for 25 minutes. Serve the fish hot or at room temperature.

BROILED FILLETS WITH MUSTARD   *4 servings*

This tasty, low-fat way of preparing fish could hardly be simpler, and I thank *Pierre Franey's Low-Calorie Gourmet* for the suggestion. *Preparation tip:* Although Franey recommends flounder (skinless and boneless), I have also successfully prepared sole and slender fillets of scrod this way. Adjust the cooking time according to the thickness of the fillet. In place of fresh chives, you can use snipped dill or minced scallions or parsley.

1¼ pounds thin, skinless fish fillets
2 teaspoons olive oil
1 or 2 tablespoons Dijon mustard, to taste
⅛ teaspoon freshly ground black pepper
2 tablespoons snipped fresh chives
1 lime, cut in wedges

1. Preheat the broiler.
2. Arrange the fillets on a greased baking sheet. Then brush them with olive oil, and spread the mustard evenly over them. Sprinkle the fillets with pepper.
3. Place the fish in the broiler, about 3 or 4 inches from the heat. Broil the fish for 2 or 3 minutes or until it is golden brown. Do not overcook it; the fish is ready when it turns opaque. Serve the fish sprinkled with chives and with a wedge of lime on each plate.

DRESSED BAKED FLOUNDER

6 servings

Here is an unusual but simple and delicious way to prepare flounder or other white fish fillets. It is an ideal supper for a working family (have the kids make the crumbs while you do the rest) that comes complete with the starch (bread) and needs only a vegetable and/or salad to make a full meal.

1½ pounds flounder fillets
  4 cups fresh bread crumbs, preferably whole-wheat (8 slices)
½ medium onion, minced (¼ cup)
  1 tablespoon lemon juice
½ teaspoon marjoram
¼ teaspoon salt, if desired, or to taste
¼ teaspoon freshly ground black pepper
  2 tablespoons butter or margarine, melted
  1 medium tomato, coarsely chopped
Grated Parmesan

1. Arrange the fish in a single layer in a greased shallow baking dish.
2. In a bowl, combine the bread crumbs, onion, lemon juice, marjoram, salt, pepper, and butter or margarine. Spread this mixture over the fish. Then spread the tomato over the crumb mixture, and sprinkle the entire dish with Parmesan.
3. Bake the fish in a preheated 400° oven for about 15 minutes or until the fish is opaque.

ASPARAGUS-STUFFED FLOUNDER   *6 servings*

When asparagus is in season, try this attractive and delicious way to serve flounder.

     1 medium onion, chopped (½ cup)
     3 teaspoons butter or margarine, divided
     6 flounder or sole fillets, 4 to 6 ounces each
    18 spears asparagus, steamed tender-crisp (about
         5 minutes)
     2 teaspoons flour
     1 cup skim or low-fat milk
     ½ cup shredded sharp Cheddar (2 ounces)
     Salt, to taste, if desired
     ⅛ teaspoon freshly ground black pepper
     Few dashes cayenne
     Dash nutmeg

1. In a nonstick skillet, sauté the onion in 1 teaspoon of the butter or margarine until the onion is tender. Sprinkle the onion evenly over the 6 fillets.
2. Lay 3 asparagus spears crosswise on each fillet, and roll the fillet around them. Secure the rolls with skewers or toothpicks, and arrange them in a single layer in a greased shallow baking dish.
3. In a small saucepan, melt the remaining 2 teaspoons of butter or margarine, stir in the flour, cook the roux, stirring it, for a minute, and then gradually add the milk. Continue cooking the sauce, stirring it, until it begins to thicken. Stir in the cheese, salt, black pepper, and cayenne. Pour the sauce over the fish rolls, and sprinkle them with the nutmeg.
4. Bake the fish in a preheated 350° oven for about 20 minutes.

FLOUNDER WITH MEXICAN HOT SAUCE

4 servings

Few would disagree that flounder is a mildly flavored fish. Thus, the addition of a spicy salsa—as suggested by *Gourmet* magazine—does it a world of good and, to my mind, eliminates the need for salt. It also looks beautiful. *Preparation tip:* To keep the fat content minimal, the fish is best prepared in a nonstick skillet. An alternative method would be to broil it. The flounder can be cooked and the salsa made hours ahead; just don't combine them until serving time. The dish is best served at room temperature, and its 2-minute cooking time makes it an ideal summer entrée or appetizer.

FISH

- 4 flounder fillets, about 6 ounces each
- Oil for brushing fish and pan
- Freshly ground black pepper to taste
- Salt, if desired, to taste
- 1 tablespoon white wine vinegar

SALSA

- 2 large tomatoes (1 pound), seeded and chopped
- ½ cup minced scallions
- 1 clove garlic, minced
- 1 tablespoon minced fresh parsley
- 1 teaspoon oil, preferably olive
- 2 teaspoons fresh lemon juice
- ¼ teaspoon sugar
- Freshly ground black pepper to taste
- Salt, if desired, to taste

1. Dry the fillets well, and brush them with oil on both sides. Then sprinkle them with pepper and salt, if desired. Brush the pan surface with oil, and heat the pan for 30 seconds over moderately high heat. Add the fillets, leaving room between each for turning. Cook the fish fillets on one side for 1 minute, then turn them carefully and cook them on the other side for 1 minute or less, or until the fish is opaque but not flaky. Arrange the cooked fish in a single layer on a serving platter. Sprinkle the vinegar over the fillets, cover them, and chill them for 20 minutes or longer.

2. Meanwhile, in a bowl combine all the salsa ingredients. If the fish is to be served soon, let the salsa stand at room temperature until the fish has been cooled for 20 minutes. Otherwise, refrigerate the salsa.

3. If the dish has been prepared in advance, remove the fish and the salsa from the refrigerator about 20 minutes before serving time. To serve, pour the sauce over the fish, and let the dish come to room temperature.

CHINESE-STYLE STEAMED MACKEREL   *4 servings*

Though not low in sodium (very little Oriental cooking is), this easy-to-prepare recipe makes use of an inexpensive fish that is a good source of heart-protecting fat (see p. 11). *Preparation tip:* While the fish steams, you can cook the rice and a vegetable and end up with an impressive meal that took only about 40 minutes to prepare.

    1 cup chopped celery (2 medium stalks)
    ¼ cup scallions, with tops, cut in 1-inch pieces
    1 large clove garlic, minced (1 teaspoon)
    2 tablespoons reduced-sodium soy sauce
    1 tablespoon oil, preferably peanut
    1 tablespoon sherry
    1 teaspoon finely minced fresh ginger
    ⅛ teaspoon sugar
    1 2-pound whole mackerel, cleaned

1. In a bowl, combine the celery, scallions, garlic, soy sauce, oil, sherry, ginger, and sugar. Set the mixture aside.
2. Score both sides of the fish with a knife (about 3 or 4 slits per side), and place the fish in a shallow baking dish. Spoon the vegetable mixture over the fish.
3. In a wok or roasting pan large enough to hold the dish, place four inverted custard cups or small cans that have had both lids removed. Set the baking dish on them, add very hot water to the pan an inch deep, cover the pan, and bring the water to a boil over high heat. Reduce the heat, and steam the fish gently for 25 minutes.

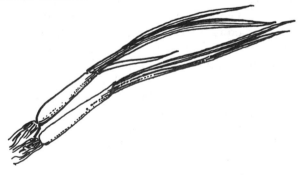

MUSSELS PROVENÇAL

4 main-course servings

If you have the patience to clean them (or a kitchen helper who will do it for you), mussels are an ideal food for fat-conscious diners: mussels are packed with quality protein, are extremely low in fat, are low in cholesterol and calories (this recipe comes in at under 200 calories per serving), and are quick to cook. *Preparation tip:* Leftovers can be eaten cold or used for a pasta sauce. They can also be served as a first course for 8. The dish can be prepared ahead through step 3, and the sauce reheated and mussels cooked at serving time. Be sure to clean the mussels before cooking time.

- 1 tablespoon oil, preferably olive
- 1 large onion, chopped (1 cup)
- 2 *tablespoons* minced garlic (6 large cloves)
- 1 16-ounce can peeled tomatoes, drained
- ½ cup minced fresh parsley, divided
- ¼ teaspoon freshly ground black pepper, or to taste
- 1 strip orange peel (about a 2-inch strip removed with a potato peeler)
- 1 cup dry white wine
- 4 to 5 pounds fresh mussels, cleaned (see note, below)

1. In a large broad-bottomed saucepan or Dutch oven, heat the oil, and cook the onion and garlic for a minute.
2. Add the tomatoes, chopping them up with a spatula or wooden spoon. Stir in all but 2 tablespoons of the parsley, and add the pepper and orange peel. Turn up the heat, and cook the mixture for about 2 minutes.
3. Add the wine, and cook the mixture for another 2 minutes.
4. Add the cleaned mussels, tossing them well to coat them with the sauce. Cover the pan, and, shaking the pan occasionally, cook the mussels for 2 or 3 minutes or until the mussels have opened, discarding any that have not opened. Serve the mussels sprinkled with the remaining 2 tablespoons of parsley.

NOTE: To clean mussels, discard any that are already opened or that have cracked shells. With a paring knife, scrape off the beards. Place the mussels in a large bowl or pot covered with very cold water. Drain them, and rinse them before use.

DIETER'S DELIGHT SALMON MOUSSE   *8 servings*

A tangy, light, refreshing dish that is simple to prepare as a main course at lunch or supper or as a first course at an elegant dinner. Prepared in a fish mold, the mousse is a beautiful addition to a buffet table. *Preparation tip:* For a smaller mousse, simply reduce all the ingredients by half.

    2 envelopes (2 tablespoons) unflavored gelatin
 1¼ cups cold water
    2 16-ounce cans salmon, drained, skin removed,
       bones crushed
    2 cups plain low-fat yogurt
    2 tablespoons mayonnaise (optional)
    2 tablespoon fresh snipped dill *or* 1 teaspoon
       dried dillweed
    2 tablespoons grated onion
    2 tablespoons lemon juice
    2 tablespoons minced fresh parsley
    1 teaspoon snipped fresh chives (optional)
Several dashes cayenne
White or black pepper to taste

1. Sprinkle the gelatin on the cold water in a small saucepan. Let the gelatin stand for 5 minutes to soften it. Then heat the water until the gelatin melts.
2. While the gelatin softens, purée 1 can of salmon with 1 cup of yogurt and 1 tablespoon mayonnaise in a blender. Transfer the purée to a large bowl, and repeat the process with the remaining salmon, yogurt, and mayonnaise. Combine the two purées.
3. When the gelatin has completely dissolved, pour it into the salmon purée, and add the dill, onion, lemon juice, parsley, chives, cayenne, and white or black pepper. Combine all the ingredients thoroughly. Place the bowl in the refrigerator until the mousse is partially set (the mixture should form a heap when dropped from a spoon).
4. Lightly oil or grease a 6-cup mold with vegetable-oil spray. Pour in the partly gelled mixture. Chill the mousse until it is firm, about 3 hours. At serving time, unmold the mousse by inverting it onto a platter. It should not be necessary to dip the mold in hot water, but if it does not unmold, hold the mold in a bowl of lukewarm water for 10 seconds.

SEAFOOD PILAF   *6 servings*

Gourmet magazine was the inspiration for this tasty dish, which is suitable for a company dinner, party buffet, or family meal. I modified the original recipe by reducing the amount of oil and salt and by using long-grain brown rice in lieu of white. *Preparation tip:* The seafood can be cooked ahead, stored in the refrigerator in a heatproof bowl for a day, and reheated in a steamer (in the bowl) just before serving. Or on a hot day you might serve the dish at room temperature.

```
  2 tablespoons olive oil
  8 scallions, thinly sliced, including green tops
  1 small onion, minced (⅓ cup)
  1 large clove garlic, finely minced (1 teaspoon)
  ½ pound bay scallops
  ½ pound cleaned shrimp (can use frozen)
  1 or more cups dry white wine
  ⅔ cup bottled clam juice
  2 teaspoons tomato paste
1½ pounds mussels, scrubbed and beards removed
1½ cups long-grain brown rice
  1 tablespoon minced fresh mint or 1 teaspoon
      dried mint (optional)
  ½ cup minced fresh parsley, divided
Freshly ground black pepper to taste
Lemon wedges
```

1. In a large saucepan, heat the oil, and cook the scallions, onion, and garlic over moderate heat until they are soft. Transfer the mixture to a bowl with a slotted spoon, leaving in the pan as much oil as possible.
2. To the remaining oil in the saucepan, add the scallops and shrimp (if you're using frozen shrimp, add them first, and add the scallops as soon as the shrimp defrost), and cook them, stirring, for a few minutes or until the shrimp turn pink. Transfer the seafood to the bowl with the cooked-scallion mixture.
3. Add 1 cup of wine, the clam juice, and the tomato paste to the pan, stirring to combine the ingredients. Add the cleaned mussels, cover the pan, and bring the liquid to a boil over high heat. Shaking the pan occasionally, cook the mussels for about 5 minutes or until they have opened. With a slotted spoon, remove the mussels from the pan, reserving all the liquid. When they are cool enough to handle, remove the meat from the mussels, and discard the shells. Add the meat to the bowl containing the seafood-scallion mixture.
4. Measure the liquid in the pan, and add wine, if needed, to make 3 cups. Return the liquid to the pan, bring the liquid to a boil, add the rice, stir it, cover the pan, reduce the heat to low, and cook the rice for 30 to 40 minutes or until all the liquid is absorbed and the rice is tender.
5. To serve, add the seafood mixture, mint (if desired), 2 tablespoons of the parsley, and pepper to the cooked rice. Fluff the rice with a fork, and (if necessary) reheat, covered, over low heat for a few minutes. Sprinkle the remaining parsley on top of the dish, and serve the pilaf with lemon wedges.

Meat Main Dishes

A wholesome diet does not necessarily mean you have to eliminate red meat. In fact, meat is an excellent source of top-quality protein, vitamins, and minerals, especially the B vitamins and iron. Rather, the idea is to take advantage of what meat has to offer while minimizing its primary nutritional disadvantage—its high fat content—and its high cost. In most of the following recipes, approximately ½ pound of meat is used to prepare four adult servings. In a few recipes, 1 pound of meat serves six. Either way, that's a lot less meat than most people eat if they have a steak, chop, or burger. The meat not only provides protein itself, it also completes the protein in the starchy food that is either a part of the recipe or served along with it. Once you get accustomed to thinking of meat as an ingredient rather than the featured item in a dish, and you realize that you can be satisfied with a meal that is low in meat but high in vegetables and wholesome starches, you may find, as we have, that you hardly ever think about basing a meal around a hunk of meat.

In the following recipes, the meat used is lean, well-trimmed beef or pork. Veal, although naturally lean, is very expensive and no lower in cholesterol than beef or pork. Organ meats, which are also lean, are very high in cholesterol. And good fresh lamb is very hard to come by in most parts of the country.

BULGUR-BEEF BALLS
about 8 servings

This tasty combination of beef and bulgur was devised for Fisher's Ala cracked wheat (bulgur). The meatballs need no other adornment than a hearty appetite. *Preparation tip:* The same combination of ingredients can also be formed into a tasty meat loaf. Combine all the ingredients, including the juice, place the mixture in a greased loaf pan, and bake the loaf in a 350° oven for 1½ hours.

1½ pounds lean ground beef
  1 cup uncooked bulgur (fine or medium)
¼ cup finely chopped onion
  1 egg
Salt, if desired, to taste
¼ teaspoon freshly ground black pepper
  1 teaspoon Worcestershire sauce
½ teaspoon orégano
  1 13-ounce can (about 1⅔ cups) tomato juice

1. Combine thoroughly the beef, bulgur, onion, egg, salt, pepper, Worcestershire sauce, and orégano. Shape the mixture into balls of desired size (smaller ones tend to hold together better).
2. Grease a nonstick or heavy skillet that has a tight cover, and in it brown

the meatballs on all sides. Add the juice to the skillet, bring it to a boil, reduce the heat, cover the pan, and simmer the meatballs for 1 hour.

GREEN-AND-GRAIN MEATBALLS
4 to 6 servings

These meatballs (the recipe is compliments of Kretschmer's wheat germ) have a great flavor, a light texture, and are a cinch to make, even for a crowd. Other sauces should also work well, such as a garlicky tomato sauce or a light cheese sauce. The meatballs and sauce can be served over hollowed-out French bread or long rolls, spaghetti or egg noodles, rice or some other grain. *Preparation tip:* The meatballs can be frozen for later use, as can the sauce. For the sake of efficiency, prepare the sauce while the meatballs bake.

MEATBALLS
- ¾ pound lean ground beef
- ½ cup wheat germ (regular)
- ⅓ cup minced fresh parsley
- ⅓ cup minced scallions
- 3 tablespoons grated Parmesan
- 2 tablespoons milk
- 1 egg *or* 1 egg white
- ¼ teaspoon salt, if desired
- ¼ teaspoon freshly ground black pepper

SAUCE
- 1 cup chopped zucchini
- ½ cup chopped mushrooms (fresh or use a 4-ounce can)
- 1 medium onion, chopped (½ cup)
- 2 teaspoons cooking oil (more if pan is not nonstick)
- 1 8-ounce can tomato sauce
- 1 teaspoon chili powder (can use some hot chili powder)
- 1 teaspoon ground cumin
- A few dashes hot pepper sauce (Tabasco) (optional)
- Salt, if desired, to taste

1. Prepare the meatballs by thoroughly mixing all the ingredients together in a medium bowl. Shape the mixture into 24 balls.
2. Place the meatballs in a shallow baking pan (oil the pan lightly if it is not nonstick). Bake the meatballs in a preheated 400° oven for 8 to 10 minutes.
3. Meanwhile, prepare the sauce in a skillet by sautéeing the zucchini, mushrooms, and onion in the oil for 3 to 5 minutes. Stir in the tomato sauce, chili powder, cumin, hot pepper sauce, and salt, and heat the sauce thoroughly.
4. To serve, pour the sauce over the meatballs, and combine the two well.

MEAT LOAF WITH SHREDDED VEGETABLES

4 servings

I love this moist, low-fat loaf, adapted from a recipe published in *Family Circle* magazine. The leftovers make a tasty sandwich for lunch the next day.

    4 cups packed finely shredded cabbage (about 1
      pound)
    1 medium onion, finely chopped (½ cup)
 1½ tablespoons oil
    1 cup packed shredded carrots (2 medium)
    1 very large clove garlic, minced (1 heaping
      teaspoon)
   ½ pound ground round or lean ground beef
    1 egg white
    1 whole egg
   ⅓ cup bread crumbs, preferably whole-wheat
    1 teaspoon dried basil, crumbled
   ¼ teaspoon orégano, crumbled
   ½ teaspoon salt, if desired, or to taste
   ¼ to ½ teaspoon freshly ground black pepper, to
      taste
   ¼ cup water
    2 tablespoons vinegar
    1 cup packed shredded potato (2 medium)

1. Sauté the cabbage and onion in the oil in a large skillet over medium heat, stirring them often, for about 5 minutes. Reduce the heat to medium-low, and sauté the vegetables 5 to 10 minutes longer or until the cabbage begins to turn golden.
2. Add the carrots and garlic, and sauté the vegetables for another 5 minutes. Remove the vegetables from the heat, and let them cool to room temperature.
3. In a large bowl, combine the beef with the egg white and whole egg, bread crumbs, basil, orégano, salt, pepper, water, and vinegar. Add to the beef mixture the cooked vegetables and the shredded potatoes, and mix the ingredients well. In a shallow baking pan, shape the meat-and-vegetable mixture into a loaf about 8 inches long. Cover the pan tightly with aluminum foil.
4. Bake the meat loaf in a preheated 350° oven for 30 minutes. Uncover the meat loaf, and bake it 30 minutes longer. Let the meat loaf rest for about 15 minutes before slicing it.

BEEF AND TOFU LOAF

4 or more servings

Tofu is an excellent low-calorie protein food that gives lightness to a meat loaf made with just half the beef you'd ordinarily use. The grated potato and carrot help to keep it moist. *Preparation tip:* The vegetables are easy to prepare in a food processor. Don't expect the loaf to hold together well when sliced.

½ pound very lean ground beef
¼ pound firm-style tofu, finely chopped
1 medium potato, finely grated
1 large carrot, finely grated
1 large onion, finely chopped (or coarsely
   grated)
1 large clove garlic, minced (1 teaspoon)
2 tablespoons tomato paste
1 tablespoon fresh chopped basil *or* 1 teaspoon
   dried basil, crumbled
1 teaspoon orégano, crumbled
1 teaspoon finely minced hot pepper (optional)
½ teaspoon salt, if desired
Freshly ground black pepper to taste

1. In a large bowl, combine all the ingredients well.
2. Press the mixture into a lightly greased loaf pan (9 × 5 × 3 inches), and bake the loaf in a preheated 350° oven for 1 hour.

CHILI POT PIE

6 to 8 servings

Here's another meal in a dish that is especially good on a cold winter day. *Preparation tip:* The filling can be prepared ahead and frozen for later use. I have even frozen it in the baking dish with the uncooked corn-meal batter on top. You can use your own favorite chili recipe, or the one below, for the filling. Or you can use a vegetarian chili (see p. 386). The corn-bread topping can be made tangier with the addition of grated sharp Cheddar and chopped jalapeño or green chili peppers.

FILLING

- 1 pound lean ground beef
- 1 large onion, finely chopped (1 cup)
- 1 tablespoon finely minced garlic (3 large cloves)
- 1 medium-sized green pepper, coarsely chopped
- 1 medium-sized red pepper, coarsely chopped
- 1 stalk celery, diced
- 2 cups tomato sauce (homemade or canned)
- 1 cup corn kernels (frozen, fresh, or canned)
- 2 cups cooked beans (e.g., small red, pinto, or pink)
- 1 tablespoon mild chili powder, or to taste
- 2 teaspoons hot chili powder *or* ½ teaspoon hot pepper sauce (Tabasco), or to taste

Freshly ground black pepper to taste
- ½ teaspoon orégano leaves, crushed, *or* ¼ teaspoon ground orégano
- ¼ teaspoon ground cumin
- ¼ teaspoon coriander
- ⅛ teaspoon allspice

CRUST

- 1 egg white
- 1 whole egg
- 1 tablespoon vegetable oil
- ½ cup buttermilk
- ¾ cup yellow corn meal, preferably stone-ground
- 1 tablespoon flour
- 1 teaspoon baking soda
- ¼ teaspoon salt, if desired
- ½ cup grated sharp Cheddar (optional)
- 1 4-ounce can jalapeño or green chili peppers, chopped (optional)

1. Brown the beef in a large nonstick skillet or Dutch oven. Drain off the fat.
2. Add the onion and garlic to the beef, and sauté the mixture for a few minutes until the onion is soft.
3. Add all the remaining filling ingredients to the beef mixture, stirring to

combine them well. Bring the mixture to a boil, reduce the heat, cover the pan, and simmer the mixture for about 15 minutes. Transfer the filling to a 10-inch deep-dish pie plate or shallow casserole of similar size.

4. In a medium bowl, beat together the egg white and whole egg, oil, and buttermilk for 1 minute. Add the corn meal, flour, baking soda, and salt, beating the ingredients until they are well blended.

5. Stir the cheese and chopped peppers, if desired, into the batter, and spoon the batter over the prepared filling.

6. Bake the pie in a preheated 350° oven for about 30 minutes or until the crust is done.

VEGETABLE CHILI CON CARNE   *6 to 8 servings*

I've made this recipe in five times the quantity for big parties and found it was gobbled up. The seasonings, suggested by *New York Times* food writer Marian Burros, are superb, and the vegetables turn the chili into a complete meal that needs only a salad. The flavor of chili improves upon standing, so this is an excellent make-ahead dish. *Preparation tip:* You can prepare this dish well in advance and freeze it. If desired, serve the chili accompanied by cold plain yogurt.

CHILI BASE

1 large onion, finely chopped (about 1 cup)
2 large cloves garlic, minced (2 teaspoons)
2 teaspoons vegetable oil
1 pound very lean ground beef
1 28-ounce can tomatoes in purée, coarsely chopped, purée reserved (if tomatoes are packed in water, add 2 to 3 tablespoons of tomato paste)
1¼ cups dried kidney beans, cooked (see p. 103), or 2½ cups cooked beans, drained and rinsed
1 or more jalapeño peppers, finely chopped (wear rubber gloves), to taste
1 cup diced green peppers
1 cup sliced carrots
1 cup diced celery
1 cup corn kernels, fresh or frozen (optional)

SEASONINGS

5 teaspoons brown sugar (or more, to taste)
5 teaspoons mild chili powder
1 tablespoon ground cumin
1 tablespoon orégano leaves, crumbled
½ teaspoon salt, if desired, or to taste
½ teaspoon coriander
¼ teaspoon whole cloves *or* ⅛ teaspoon ground cloves
¼ teaspoon whole allspice berries *or* ⅛ teaspoon ground allspice

1. In a large, deep, heavy skillet or Dutch oven, sauté the onion and garlic in the oil until the vegetables are softened.
2. Add the meat, browning it and stirring it to break up the pieces. Drain off any fat that accumulates in the pan.
3. Add the tomatoes and their purée (or liquid and tomato paste) and all the seasonings. Heat the mixture until it is bubbly, reduce the heat, cover the pan, and simmer the chili for about 30 minutes.
4. Add the kidney beans, jalapeño peppers, green peppers, carrots, and celery. Simmer the chili, covered, about 20 minutes longer or until the carrots are softened. If desired, add corn kernels to the pot after 10 minutes.

HALF-THE-BEEF TACOS

4 to 6 servings

Tacos—crisp corn tortillas stuffed with seasoned meat, cheese, and salad vegetables—are a make-your-own-meal-in-a-shell. But most recipes for 4 or 6 servings suggest using a pound of beef, which—along with the cheese—represents a protein overload. Here is a very tasty version that replaces half the beef with the all-American potato. *Preparation tip:* You can buy ready-made taco sauce in a jar or can. Taco shells are also readily available in supermarkets, or you can make your own by toasting or frying corn or flour tortillas according to package directions.

FILLING

- ½ pound lean ground beef
- ½ pound new potatoes
- 2 teaspoons vegetable oil
- 1 medium onion, finely chopped (½ cup)
- 2 teaspoons minced garlic (2 large cloves)
- ½ teaspoon ground cumin
- 3 tablespoons taco sauce (mild or hot)

- 12 taco shells, sprinkled with water, wrapped in foil, and heated in the oven

TOPPINGS

- 1 cup shredded cheese (e.g., Cheddar or Monterey Jack) (about 4 ounces)
- ¼ to ⅓ cup finely chopped onion, to taste
- 1½ cups finely diced tomato
- 1½ cups finely shredded lettuce
- ⅓ cup taco sauce

1. In a nonstick or cast-iron skillet, brown the meat over medium heat, crumbling it with a spatula. Pour off all the accumulated fat, and transfer the beef to a plate lined with a paper towel. Set the beef aside. When the skillet is cool enough to handle, wipe it with a paper towel, or wash and dry it.
2. Peel and coarsely shred the potatoes.
3. Heat the oil in the skillet, and add the potatoes, spreading them out and pressing them into a cake. Fry them over medium-high heat until the cake is lightly browned on one side. Then divide the cake in half with the spatula, and flip the halves over to brown the other side. When browned, break up the potato cake with the spatula.
4. Add the onion, garlic, and cumin, and sauté the mixture for about 3 minutes. Stir in the reserved cooked beef and 3 tablespoons of taco sauce. Cook the mixture, stirring to combine it thoroughly, 2 minutes longer to heat it through.
5. To serve, distribute the meat-and-potato mixture among the taco shells. Provide diners with separate bowls of the cheese, onion, tomato, lettuce, and taco sauce to add to their tacos according to taste.

GROUND BEEF AND GREEN BEANS   *4 servings*

A quick, low-calorie "stir-fry" that is delicious with rice or noodles. *Preparation tip:* The beef mixture (step 3) can be prepared in advance, then reheated at serving time and combined with the freshly cooked beans. If you do this, you'll need an extra teaspoon of oil to sauté the ginger and garlic.

SAUCE
- 2 teaspoons cornstarch
- ⅓ cup cooled broth
- 1 tablespoon reduced-sodium soy sauce
- 1 tablespoon dry sherry
- 1 teaspoon cider vinegar

MAIN INGREDIENTS
- 1 tablespoon oil
- 1 pound green beans, trimmed and sliced diagonally into 2-inch lengths
- 2 teaspoons finely minced fresh ginger
- 2 teaspoons finely minced garlic (2 large cloves)
- ¼ teaspoon hot red pepper flakes (optional)
- ½ pound lean ground beef

1. In a small bowl, combine all the sauce ingredients. Make sure the cornstarch is completely dissolved. Set the mixture aside.
2. In a wok or large skillet, heat the oil for 30 seconds over high heat, and add the green beans. Stir-fry the green beans for about 4 minutes—the beans should be tender-crisp and lightly charred in spots. Remove the green beans with a slotted spoon, and set them aside.
3. Add the ginger and garlic to the pan, cook them for 30 seconds, and then add the pepper flakes and beef, crumbling the meat with a spatula. Stir-fry the mixture just until the beef loses its pinkness. Drain off all the excess fat from the pan.
4. Stir the reserved sauce once more, and add it to the meat. Cook the mixture, stirring it, for a few minutes until the sauce thickens. Fold in the reserved green beans, heat the mixture for 1 minute, and serve.

BEEF LO MEIN   *4 generous servings*

Norman Weinstein, Brooklyn's best Chinese cook (and sole instructor for The Hot Wok cooking school), taught me the joys of preparing and eating lo mein, a noodle-based dish loaded with luscious vegetables and seasoned with lots of garlic and the smoky flavor of sesame oil. Like most Chinese dishes, this is not a low-sodium recipe, even though I use less of the sodium-containing ingredients than Weinstein suggests. *Preparation tip:* Lo mein can also be made with shrimp, chicken, turkey, tofu, roast pork, or nearly any leftover cooked meat. If using cooked meat, omit step 3, and add the meat after stir-frying the vegetables in step 4. The best noodles to use are fresh Chinese egg noodles (lo mein noodles), which are available in many Oriental markets, as are the vegetables in this dish. The noodles can be purchased in quantity, divided into ½-pound packages, and stored in the freezer for up to a year. Light soy sauce, also called thin soy sauce, is available in most Oriental markets. It is not less salty, but rather lighter in consistency and better suited for a noodle dish.

SAUCE
- 3 tablespoons light (thin) soy sauce or reduced-sodium soy sauce
- 2 tablespoons oyster sauce
- 1 tablespoon Oriental sesame oil, or more, if desired
- ½ teaspoon sugar

MAIN INGREDIENTS
- ½ pound fresh thin Chinese egg noodles or any thin dry noodle
- 3 to 4 quarts boiling water
- ½ pound lean, tender beef (e.g., flank steak)
- 1 tablespoon oil, preferably peanut, divided
- 6 large cloves garlic, minced (2 tablespoons)
- 1 cup julienned celery
- ½ cup julienned bamboo shoots
- 1 cup shredded Chinese cabbage
- 1 cup julienned bok choy
- 1 cup bean sprouts
- 3 to 4 cups fresh, well-washed spinach, coarsely chopped

1. Combine all the sauce ingredients, stirring them well. Set the sauce aside.
2. Cut or break the noodles in half, and cook them in the boiling water for 3 to 4 minutes (longer if starting with dry noodles). Drain the noodles, rinse them under cold water, drain them again, and set them aside.
3. Slice the beef across the grain into thin strips.
4. Heat a wok or large skillet, and add about 1½ teaspoons oil, heating it for 15 seconds. Add the beef, and stir-fry the meat over high heat until it has just lost its pink color. Remove the meat to a platter, and set it aside.
5. Add the remaining 1½ teaspoons oil, and heat it for 15 seconds. Add the garlic, and immediately add the celery and bamboo shoots. Stir-fry the vegetables for 30 seconds, and then add the Chinese cabbage, bok choy, and bean sprouts. Stir-fry the mixture, tossing it constantly, for 1 minute, and then add the reserved cooked beef and cooked noodles. Mix the ingredients well, and then add the chopped spinach.
6. Stir the sauce, add it all at once to the stir-fry, mixing it thoroughly with the other ingredients, and heat through or chill and serve cold.

SWEET-AND-SOUR
STUFFED CABBAGE

12 to 18 medium-sized
rolls

I include this relatively complicated recipe for several reasons: it is a beloved remnant from my family's eastern European origins; it contains lots of cancer-preventing cabbage and a moderate amount of beef; and it can be prepared weeks ahead and frozen (reheating actually improves the flavor). I have often made it in double, triple, even quadruple the quantity to serve at parties. It goes well with mashed potatoes, noodles, or rice. *Preparation tip:* The size of the cabbage rolls can be varied; if you prefer small ones, buy two or more small heads of cabbage and use the smaller leaves for rolling. If made ahead, prepare the complete recipe before refrigerating or freezing it, and simply reheat the stuffed cabbage in a covered pot in the oven before serving it.

1 large head cabbage (2 or 3 pounds)
2 tablespoons butter or margarine
2 large onions, sliced
1 16-ounce can tomatoes with their juice,
   coarsely chopped
Salt, if desired, to taste
½ teaspoon freshly ground black pepper, divided
Beef bones, about 1 pound (optional)
1 pound very lean ground beef
¼ cup grated onion
3 tablespoons uncooked rice (white or brown)
3 tablespoons water
1 egg
2 cups (approximately) boiling broth
⅓ cup raisins
¼ cup fresh lemon juice
¼ to ½ cup honey, to taste

1. Boil the whole cabbage in a large pot of water for 5 to 10 minutes to soften the leaves. When the cabbage is cool enough to handle, gently remove the leaves, taking care not to tear them. As you get down into the cabbage, you may have to reboil it for a few minutes to soften the inner leaves. Use only the more tender, whitish leaves for rolling, and shred the tough outer leaves and the very small inner ones for the sauce.

2. Melt the butter or margarine in a deep, heavy saucepan, Dutch oven, or roasting pan. Add the onions, and brown them lightly. Add the tomatoes with their juice, about ½ teaspoon of salt, if desired, ¼ teaspoon of the pepper, the beef bones, if desired, and the shredded cabbage. Bring the mixture to a boil, reduce the heat to low, and cook the mixture, uncovered, for about 30 minutes.

3. Meanwhile, prepare the cabbage rolls. In a medium bowl, combine the beef, grated onion, rice, water, egg, another ½ teaspoon of salt, and the remaining ¼ teaspoon of pepper. Depending on the size roll desired, place from 1½ to 3 tablespoons of the meat mixture toward the stem end of each cabbage leaf. Fold in the shorter sides of the leaf, then roll from the stem end to the outer edge, enclosing the meat and the short ends of the leaf to form a fairly tight, compact roll or "ball."

4. Add the broth to the sauce, mixing well. Then add the cabbage rolls to the sauce, arranging them so that they are surrounded by the sauce. Cover the pan, and cook the stuffed cabbage slowly over low heat for 1½ hours.

5. Add the raisins, lemon juice, and honey (start with ¼ cup, and taste the sauce before adding more), distributing these ingredients as evenly as possible. Cook the cabbage, uncovered, 30 minutes longer.

YEMEN FATAH

4 servings

The origins of this dish should be obvious. I devised the combination after feasting on a dish so named at a Middle Eastern restaurant. It is more authentic made with lamb, but beef will do. *Preparation tip:* Cook the couscous (or rice or millet) while the meat is being prepared.

1 tablespoon oil
1 large onion, halved lengthwise and sliced
   crosswise (1 heaping cup)
1 large clove garlic, minced (1 teaspoon)
¾ pound lean lamb or beef, cut into thin 2-inch
   strips
½ cup broth (beef, preferably)
¼ teaspoon ground orégano
¼ teaspoon ground cumin
¼ teaspoon coriander
⅛ teaspoon allspice
Salt, if desired, to taste
Freshly ground black pepper to taste
1 cup couscous (or rice or millet), cooked
   according to package directions
2 tablespoons minced fresh parsley

1. In a medium skillet, heat the oil, and sauté the onion and garlic until the onion is translucent.

2. Add the lamb or beef, and sauté the meat, stirring it often, just to brown the strips on all sides. Stir in the broth, orégano, cumin, coriander, allspice, salt, and pepper, and cook the mixture a few minutes longer.

3. Serve the meat mixture, sprinkled with parsley, over the hot couscous.

STIR-FRIED PORK WITH GREEN BEANS

4 servings

I concocted this stir-fry one day when a colleague gave me part of his bumper crop of green beans and hot peppers. As written, this is not a low-sodium recipe; you can reduce the sodium by using low-salt broth and omitting (or reducing) the oyster sauce. *Preparation tip:* Start cooking the rice or noodle accompaniment before you start preparing this recipe. If desired, you can add 1 or more cloves of minced garlic, with or without fresh ginger, in step 2 along with the pork.

    1 tablespoon cornstarch
    2 tablespoons soy sauce (preferably
      reduced-sodium)
    ½ teaspoon dry mustard
    ½ pound lean boneless pork, trimmed well and
      cut into thin strips
    2 teaspoons oil, preferably peanut
 1½ cups chicken broth
    1 tablespoon oyster sauce
    ¾ pound green beans, cut into 2-inch lengths
    4 to 6 stalks celery, sliced diagonally
    ½ cup bamboo shoots, sliced into strips
    4 hot peppers (or to taste), seeded and sliced
      (wear rubber gloves)

1. In a small bowl, combine the cornstarch, soy sauce, and mustard. Add the slivered pork, and toss it to coat it well with the soy-sauce mixture.
2. Heat a large skillet or wok for 1 minute. Add the oil, and heat it 30 seconds longer. Add the pork, and stir-fry it until the meat has lost its pink color.
3. Combine the chicken broth with the oyster sauce, and gradually add the mixture to the pan, pouring it down the side of the pan to heat it. Stir-fry until the sauce begins to thicken.
4. Add the green beans, celery, bamboo shoots, and hot peppers. Toss the ingredients to combine them well. Cover the pan, and simmer the stir-fry for about 5 minutes or until the green beans are tender-crisp.

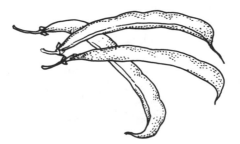

ZUCCHINI STUFFED WITH MEAT AND RICE

6 to 8 servings

Large zucchinis are ideal containers for all kinds of stuffings, both for side dishes and entrées. This wholesome recipe gives you a meal-in-a-zucchini-boat—meat, vegetable, and starch rolled into one. *Preparation tip:* The filling can be prepared and the zucchini stuffed in advance, to be baked prior to serving.

3 pounds zucchini (1 very large or 2 medium-large)
10 ounces (approximately) ground meat, including at least ¼ pound pork
2 teaspoons oil
1 large onion, chopped (about 1 cup)
2 large cloves garlic, minced (2 teaspoons)
3 cups cooked brown rice (1 cup raw)
½ teaspoon salt, if desired
½ teaspoon hot paprika *or* sweet paprika plus dash cayenne
Freshly ground black pepper to taste
⅜ cup finely chopped fresh parsley, divided
2 tablespoons finely snipped fresh dill *or* 1 teaspoon dried dillweed
6 tablespoons grated Parmesan

1. Trim the ends of the zucchini, and then cut it in half lengthwise. Using a melon baller or grapefruit spoon, scoop out the center of the zucchini, leaving a shell about ⅓ inch thick. Chop the zucchini pulp, and reserve it (you should have about 2½ cups). If the zucchini is large and tough, parboil the shull for 3 minutes (a roasting pan works well).
2. Brown the meat in a large saucepan or deep skillet, breaking up the pieces until the meat is crumbly and has lost its pink color. Drain off the fat. Remove the meat to a paper towel, and set it aside. Wipe out the pan.
3. Heat the oil in the pan, and sauté the onion and garlic until they wilt. Add the reserved meat and the reserved zucchini pulp. Cook the mixture for several minutes, stirring it.
4. Add the cooked brown rice, salt, paprika, and pepper. Stir in ¼ cup (all but 2 tablespoons) of the parsley and the dill, and heat the mixture through.
5. Sprinkle the insides of the zucchini with pepper (and salt, if desired). Pack in the stuffing mixture, smoothing the top (it can be rounded).
6. Combine the Parmesan with the remaining 2 tablespoons of parsley, and sprinkle this over the top of the stuffed zucchini. Place the zucchini on a cookie sheet or in a baking pan.
7. Bake the zucchini in a preheated 425° oven for 30 minutes.

Pizza

I was once told with some authority that pizza was an American invention not to be found in Italy. I'd like to believe Americans had the culinary wit to devise something almost universally loved that is also nourishing, but my source was mistaken. The earliest examples of pizza date back 2,000 years to Pompeii, and Neapolitans are acknowledged to be the originators of modern pizzas.

Too many pizza lovers indulge with a fair measure of guilt over their "fast food" foray. But, in fact, a properly prepared pizza almost precisely meets the Dietary Goals of the Senate Select Committee on Nutrition and Human Needs in terms of its protein, fat, and carbohydrate content. An analysis by Consumers Union showed that a 3½-ounce slice of pizza would provide the following proportions of a teen-aged boy's recommended daily intake of nutrients: 26 percent of the protein, 28 percent of the calcium, 19 percent of the riboflavin, 14 percent of niacin and thiamin, and 10 percent of the vitamin A. Fat accounts for 32 percent of the total calories (246), which, although a bit high to my taste, is at least within generally recommended guidelines. And, I believe, you can prepare your own pizza with a lower fat content, with virtually all the fat coming from the cheese. Pizza's main nutritional failing is its tendency to be high in salt. The salt content can be controlled if you prepare your own tomato sauce with little or no added salt (or buy a no-salt sauce) and avoid salty toppings like anchovies, pepperoni, and sausage.

The traditional ungarnished Italian-style pizza consisting of a crust, tomato sauce, and melted cheese has in recent years undergone some radical transformations that are decidedly American. There are now broccoli, spinach, bean, zucchini, onion, mushroom, eggplant, shrimp, and tuna pizzas, as well as those made with meatballs and sausage meats. In other words, almost anything but sweets and starches will do as the topping for a pizza crust if it can withstand baking at temperatures in excess of 400 degrees.

The crust, too, can be varied. Many potential pizza cooks are intimidated by the need to prepare a yeast dough, knead it, roll it, and fit it into the pan. For those of you willing to try it, I offer a few excellent crust recipes. I can tell you that it is similar to, but easier than, baking a yeast bread (only one rising is needed, and the dough can be prepared in advance and refrigerated or frozen), and it is much easier to roll than a pie crust because it's not crumbly. But you do have a choice. You can buy a prepared bread dough and roll it out to form a crust. You can use pitas of varying sizes as the base of a pizza if the top does not require long baking (see, for example, Pita Pizzas on p. 475). You can use tortillas, as in the Mexican Pizza on page 473. Or you can make a vegetable or grain-based crust, as in the Zucchini-Crust Pizza on page 481 or the Rice-Crust Pizza on page 480. While to some pizza aficionados, doughless pizzas "are not really pizzas" but more like deep-dish pies, I see no point in such culinary rigidity. If they're prepared and eaten like pizza, why not call them pizza?

MEXICAN PIZZA WITH TORTILLA CRUST

8 servings

Here's one that spares you the trouble of making a crust. I served it as an hors d'oeuvre at a party, and it was consumed in minutes. It could just as easily be a main dish for lunch or supper (or breakfast, if you adhere to my reversed meal scheme). *Preparation tip:* If you are starting with raw beans, cook ½ pound of picked-over, rinsed, and soaked beans in 6 cups of water for 1 hour. You can set up the pizza in advance and bake it just before serving time.

- 6 8-inch flour tortillas
- 2 tablespoons oil, divided
- 3 cups cooked kidney beans, drained and mashed, with ¼ cup liquid reserved
- Salt, if desired, to taste (omit if beans are canned)
- ¼ cup finely minced onion
- 2 to 4 ounces chopped canned green chilies, to taste, divided
- ½ cup taco sauce, mild or hot, to taste
- 1 cup shredded Monterey Jack (3 to 4 ounces)

1. Preheat the oven to 375°. Lightly brush the tortillas with oil (1 tablespoon or less should do it), prick them in several places with a fork, and bake them directly on the oven rack for 5 minutes. Arrange the crisped tortillas in a pizza pan or large baking pan, overlapping them so that no holes are left.
2. Heat the remaining 1 tablespoon of oil in a skillet, and add the mashed beans, reserved liquid, and salt. Cook the beans until all the liquid is absorbed. Remove the beans from the heat, and stir in the onion and half the chopped chilies.
3. Spread the bean mixture over the tortillas. Spread the taco sauce over the beans, and sprinkle the pizza with cheese and the remaining chopped chilies.
4. Raise the oven temperature to broil, and place the pizza under the broiler for 1 to 2 minutes or until the cheese melts. Cut the pizza into eight wedges with a sharp, heavy, or serrated knife.

ONION AND CHEESE PIZZA   *4 main-course servings*

Although it was the last of six different pizzas tried in one meal, my tasters all raved about this one. My recipe is a slightly modified version of one devised by Florence Fabricant, an excellent food writer who keeps an close eye on nutrition as well as flavor. The crust, the "wheatiest" that I have tried with success, comes from Horn of the Moon, a café in Montpelier, Vermont. *Preparation tip:* The crust recipe is large enough to prepare two 12-inch pizzas; you can freeze half of it for later use. You can also divide it into smaller pieces and prepare 9-inch pizzas for one or two people. This is a very cheesy pizza. If you are watching calories or cholesterol, use the lesser amount of cheese indicated.

CRUST
- 1 cup warm water (105° to 115°)
- 1 package (1 scant tablespoon) active dry yeast
- 1 teaspoon honey or sugar
- 1 tablespoon oil
- ½ teaspoon salt, if desired
- 1½ cups whole-wheat flour
- 1 to 1½ cups (approximately) all-purpose flour

TOPPING
- 1 tablespoon butter or margarine
- 3 large onions, thinly sliced (3 cups)
- 2 tablespoons grainy mustard
- 8 to 12 ounces Fontina or Fontal, coarsely shredded
- 1 tablespoon minced fresh parsley
- ½ teaspoon dried thyme

TO PREPARE THE CRUST

1. Place the warm water in a large bowl. Add the yeast and honey or sugar, stirring to dissolve the ingredients. Let the mixture stand 5 to 15 minutes or until it is bubbly.
2. Add the oil, salt, whole-wheat flour, and about 1 cup of the all-purpose flour, or enough to form a ball of dough that pulls away from the sides of the bowl.
3. Turn the dough out onto a floured surface, and knead the dough for about 5 minutes, adding more all-purpose flour as needed to make a firm, smooth dough that is not sticky.
4. Place the dough in a greased bowl, turning the dough to grease the top, cover the bowl lightly with plastic wrap, and set the dough aside in a warm, draft-free place to rise until it has doubled in bulk.

TO ASSEMBLE THE PIZZA

5. While the dough is rising, melt the butter or margarine in a heavy skillet (preferably nonstick), add the onions, cover the skillet, and cook the onions over low heat for about 10 minutes or until the onions are translucent. Uncover the skillet, turn the heat up to medium, and continue to cook the onions, stirring them, for about 10 minutes longer or until they are golden. Remove them from the heat.

6. When the dough has risen, set the rack of your oven on the lowest rung, and preheat the oven to 475°.
7. Punch down the dough, divide it in half, and roll out half the dough (save the other half for another time or double the topping recipe given here) on a lightly floured surface into a 13-inch round, or 1 inch wider than your pan. Place the dough in a lightly oiled 12-inch round pan with a slightly raised edge or on a flat baking sheet and form a raised edge with the dough.
8. Spread the mustard on the dough, scatter the onions evenly over it, sprinkle the cheese over the onions, and top with the parsley and thyme. Place the pie in the preheated oven for about 20 minutes.

PITA PIZZAS

4 servings

Though good at any meal, in our house these are a breakfast favorite. When the boys are late for school, the pizzas can be eaten en route. *Preparation tip:* The pizzas take only 5 minutes to prepare and can be set up the night before, for quick heating in the toaster oven or broiler at serving time. If you prefer less bread, split two pitas (instead of using four whole ones), and use one round side for each pizza (put the smooth side down). Or the pizzas can be made on English muffins that have been split and lightly toasted or, for that matter, on any lightly toasted bread of substance. You can also skip the sauce and instead sprinkle the tomato slices with your favorite pizza spices (e.g., orégano, garlic, pepper).

4 sandwich-sized pitas (whole-wheat or white)
¼ to ½ cup tomato sauce, to taste
4 slices cooked turkey or chicken breast or ham
8 slices tomato (optional)
4 thin slices cheese (e.g., muenster, American, Gouda, Jarlsberg)

1. Smear one side of each pita with some tomato sauce. Add 1 slice of turkey, chicken, or ham, 2 slices of tomato, and 1 slice of cheese, in that order.
2. Heat the pitas in a toaster oven or under the broiler for a few minutes or until the cheese melts and the pizzas are heated through.

SHRIMP AND FETA PIZZA

8 servings

Gourmet magazine is the origin of this delicious pizza. I made two basic changes: I cut the salt by soaking the feta, and I used less oil in the sauce and on the pizza. The results were still wonderful. *Preparation tip:* Prepare the dough first, and while that is rising, make the tomato sauce. While the tomato sauce cooks, soak the feta. The sauce is runny, so this pizza is best made in a pan with an edge.

CRUST
- ¾ cup warm water (105° to 115°), divided
- 1 package (1 scant tablespoon) active dry yeast
- Pinch sugar
- 1 cup all-purpose flour
- ¾ cup whole-wheat flour
- ½ teaspoon salt, if desired
- 2 tablespoons olive oil
- 1 tablespoon corn meal (for pan)

SAUCE
- 1 35-ounce can Italian plum tomatoes with their juice
- 1 tablespoon olive oil
- 1 6-ounce can tomato paste
- 1 large onion, halved lengthwise
- 1 bay leaf
- 1 teaspoon sugar
- ½ teaspoon salt, if desired
- ¾ teaspoon dried orégano, or to taste
- Freshly ground black pepper to taste

TOPPING
- 2 cups shredded part-skim mozzarella (about 8 ounces)
- 1 pound medium shrimp, shelled and deveined (can use frozen)
- 8 ounces feta, soaked for 30 minutes in cold water, drained, and crumbled
- 1 teaspoon rosemary, crushed
- Several dashes olive oil

TO PREPARE THE CRUST

1. Place ¼ cup of the warm water in a small bowl, add the yeast and sugar, stirring to dissolve them, and set the yeast mixture in a warm place until it is bubbly.
2. In a large bowl, combine the all-purpose flour, whole-wheat flour, and salt. Stir in the remaining ½ cup warm water, the oil, and the yeast mixture. Form the dough into a ball, and turn it out onto a floured surface. Knead the dough for about 8 minutes or until it is smooth and satiny, adding as little flour as needed to keep the dough from sticking (it is softer than most pizza doughs).
3. Place the dough in a greased bowl, cover it with greased plastic wrap, and set it in a warm, draft-free place to rise until it has doubled in bulk, about 1 to 1½ hours. The dough can also be prepared well in advance and allowed to rise in the refrigerator overnight.

TO PREPARE THE SAUCE

4. Place the tomatoes and their juice in a food mill or sieve set over a large saucepan, and purée them, discarding the seeds.
5. Add to the purée the oil, tomato paste, onion, bay leaf, sugar, salt, and orégano. Bring the sauce to a boil over medium-high heat, stirring it occasionally. Reduce the heat to low, and simmer the sauce, uncovered, for about 1 hour, stirring it occasionally. Remove and discard the onion (eat it, if you wish—it's delicious) and the bay leaf. Add the pepper. You should have about 2¾ cups of sauce.

TO ASSEMBLE THE PIZZA

6. Place the oven rack on the lowest rung of the oven, and preheat the oven to 500°.
7. Punch down the dough, turn it out onto a lightly floured surface, and roll it out into a 15-inch circle, or 1 inch larger than your pan. Sprinkle a 14-inch round pan with the corn meal, and place the dough in it, forming a double-thickness edge.
8. Sprinkle the mozzarella evenly on the dough, and spoon the tomato sauce over the cheese, spreading it evenly up to the raised edge. Arrange the shrimp on top of the sauce in an attractive pattern. Sprinkle the feta over the shrimp and the rosemary over all. Sprinkle the pizza with oil.
9. Bake the pizza for about 15 minutes or until the crust is golden.

DEEP-DISH SPINACH PIZZA

6 servings

This may be my favorite pizza. I first had it at Pizzapiazza, a fabulous pizza palace in Lower Manhattan where each person can order an individual pizza and taste a portion of everyone else's. I chose the deep-dish spinach pizza and, after one taste, refused to give any of mine away! My recipe tasters agreed: this one is more than good enough to justify the effort involved in its preparation. *Preparation tip:* The dough can be prepared in a food processor, if desired, with half reserved for another use. Or you can use any other pizza crust made with about 1½ cups of flour (the amount for a 12-inch pie). You can use a 10-ounce package of frozen chopped spinach, drained, and skip step 8.

CRUST
1 cup warm water (105° to 115°)
1 package (1 scant tablespoon) active dry yeast
Pinch sugar
2 to 2¼ cups all-purpose flour
1 cup whole-wheat flour
1 teaspoon salt, if desired
2 tablespoons olive oil
Corn meal for sprinkling pan

SAUCE
1 tablespoon olive oil
1 medium onion, sliced (⅔ cup)
1 teaspoon finely minced garlic
1 16-ounce can plum tomatoes with their juice
¼ teaspoon salt, if desired
¼ teaspoon sugar
Freshly ground black pepper to taste
Pinch hot red pepper flakes

TOPPING
1 pound fresh spinach, washed but not dried, stems trimmed
1 tablespoon olive oil
1 teaspoon finely minced garlic (1 large clove)
1½ cups shredded part-skim mozzarella (6 ounces)
¾ cup shredded Swiss cheese (about 3 ounces)
⅓ cup grated Parmesan
2 or 3 ripe plum or small round tomatoes, sliced thinly lengthwise
16 fresh basil leaves, if available
1 small green pepper, sliced into ¼-inch strips
1 small red sweet pepper, sliced into ¼-inch strips

TO PREPARE THE CRUST
1. Place the water in a small bowl, add the yeast and sugar, stirring to dissolve the ingredients. Let the mixture stand in a warm place until it is bubbly.
2. In a large bowl (or in the bowl of a food processor), combine 2 cups of the all-purpose flour, the whole-wheat flour, and the salt, stirring or processing to blend the ingredients.
3. Add the oil to the bubbly yeast mixture, and stir this into the flour mixture

(or add it gradually through the tube of the food processor) until a dough is formed that pulls away from the sides of the bowl.

4. Transfer the dough to a floured surface, and knead it until it is smooth and elastic (or process it until a firm, elastic dough forms), using up to ¼ cup more flour, if needed, to keep the dough from sticking.

5. Place the dough in a greased bowl, turning the dough to grease the top, cover the bowl with plastic wrap, and place the dough in a warm, draft-free place to rise until it has doubled in bulk. Punch the dough down, wrap it well, and refrigerate it until it is needed.

TO PREPARE THE SAUCE

6. Heat the oil over medium-low heat in a large skillet, and sauté the onion and garlic until they are soft but not brown. Turn the heat to low.

7. Add the tomatoes and their liquid (breaking up the tomatoes slightly), salt, sugar, pepper, and pepper flakes. Simmer the sauce, uncovered, stirring it occasionally, until it is very thick, about 30 minutes.

TO PREPARE THE TOPPING

8. Cook the wet spinach in a covered saucepan for 3 minutes or until it wilts. Remove it to a colander, rinse it under cold water, and squeeze it with your hands to extract as much water as possible. Chop the spinach coarsely.

9. Heat the oil in a small skillet, add the garlic, and sauté it for 15 seconds (do not let it brown). Add the spinach, and cook the mixture, stirring it, for another minute. Remove the mixture from the heat.

TO ASSEMBLE THE PIZZA

10. Place the oven rack on the lowest rung, and preheat the oven to 475°.

11. Using half the prepared dough, roll it out on a lightly floured surface into a 12-inch circle. Lightly grease a 9 × 1½-inch round baking pan (preferably one with removable sides), then sprinkle the bottom of the pan with corn meal. Line the bottom and sides of the pan with the dough, but do not let any dough hang over the edge.

12. In a small bowl, combine the mozzarella, Swiss, and Parmesan cheeses, and spread 1½ cups of the mixture over the bottom of the crust. Spread the tomato sauce evenly over the cheeses, then spread the cooked spinach over the tomato sauce.

13. Arrange the tomato slices along the outer edge of the pie, interspersing the slices with the basil leaves. Place the remaining tomato slices in a circle in the center. Then arrange the pepper slices in similar fashion, alternating red and green strips.

14. Bake the pizza in the preheated oven for 25 minutes or until crust is golden and the filling bubbly. Let it stand for 5 minutes before cutting. (If you used a pan with removable sides, you could remove the pizza to simplify serving it.)

RICE-CRUST PIZZA

8 wedges

A swift (if the rice is already cooked) and easily varied pizza uses rice as the crust. It can be eaten for lunch or supper (or breakfast or brunch, for that matter). You can use either white or brown rice.

    3 cups cooked rice (1 cup raw)
    1 egg white and 1 whole egg, lightly beaten
    2 cups grated part-skim mozzarella (about 8
        ounces), divided
    1 cup tomato sauce (1 8-ounce can)
    2 cloves garlic, minced
    ½ teaspoon dried basil
    ½ teaspoon orégano
    Optional toppings: sliced mushrooms, onion,
        peppers, turkey, chopped shrimp, etc.
    2 tablespoons grated Parmesan

1. In a medium bowl, combine the rice, beaten egg white and whole egg, and 1 cup of the mozzarella. Spread the mixture evenly on the bottom and sides of a greased 12- or 13-inch pizza pan or two 9-inch pie plates, pressing the mixture firmly to form a "crust."
2. Bake the crust in a preheated 450° oven for 20 minutes.
3. In a small bowl, combine the tomato sauce, garlic, basil, and orégano. Spread the sauce evenly over the baked crust.
4. Add the toppings of your choice. Sprinkle the pizza with the remaining cup of mozzarella and the Parmesan. Return the pizza to the oven for another 10 minutes.

ZUCCHINI-CRUST PIZZA

6 to 8 servings

Here's another quick and nutritious crust for a pizza that is best eaten with a fork. *Preparation tip:* The more water you manage to squeeze from the zucchini, the crispier the crust will be. The crust can be prepared hours ahead, as can the toppings ingredients, and the pizza can be assembled and baked just before serving.

CRUST

- 2 pounds zucchini, trimmed but unpeeled, shredded (about 6 cups)
- 1 egg white and 2 whole eggs, lightly beaten
- 1 large onion, finely chopped (1 cup)
- ⅓ cup whole-wheat flour
- ½ cup finely grated part-skim mozzarella (2 ounces)
- ½ cup grated Parmesan
- ½ teaspoon dried basil *or* 1 tablespoon chopped fresh basil
- ¼ teaspoon salt, if desired
- Freshly ground black pepper to taste

TOPPING

- 1 cup cooked shredded chicken breast (about ½ pound) *or* 1 7-ounce can tuna, drained
- 1 cup finely diced sweet pepper (red or green)
- 1 cup sliced pitted black olives
- 2 cups tomato sauce, canned or homemade
- 1 cup grated Gruyère or similar cheese (4 ounces)
- ½ teaspoon orégano, crumbled

TO PREPARE THE CRUST

1. Place the grated zucchini in a kitchen cloth or several thicknesses of cheesecloth, and squeeze out all the moisture you can (you should be able to reduce the amount by about half).
2. In a large bowl, combine the squeezed zucchini with all the remaining crust ingredients. Press the mixture on the bottom and sides of a greased 12- or 13-inch pan with a shallow rim.
3. Bake the crust in a preheated 350° oven for 25 to 30 minutes or until the crust is firm. Remove the crust from the oven.

TO ASSEMBLE THE PIZZA

4. Sprinkle the chicken, pepper, and olives evenly over the surface of the prebaked crust. Spoon the tomato sauce over all, spreading it evenly with the back of a spoon.
5. Sprinkle the sauce with the grated cheese and orégano.
6. Bake the pizza in a preheated 350° oven for 25 to 30 minutes.

Egg-based Main Courses

You may be surprised to find egg recipes in a healthful cookbook. But I am not one to throw out the baby with the bathwater. Eggs are an inexpensive source of protein, vitamins, and minerals; they have a long shelf life; and they are easy to prepare. Their primary drawback is the extremely high cholesterol content of the yolk; the yolk of a single large egg contains nearly all the cholesterol an adult should be consuming in an entire day. The yolk also contains a fair amount of saturated fat (80 percent of the calories in the yolk come from fat), which exacerbates the harmful effects of cholesterol. However, *there is no cholesterol in egg white,* which is, for all intents and purposes, pure fat-free protein.

Unless you are on a very strict low-cholesterol diet, there is no reason why you cannot occasionally indulge in a meal that contains egg yolks. My approach is (1) not to have egg-based dishes too often, and (2) to reduce the cholesterol content of the dishes by eliminating, on average, one yolk from every two eggs. If you have a dog, feed the yolks you discard to your pet; it will make his coat shiny without clogging his blood vessels (dogs are true carnivores and handle cholesterol differently than people do). Or you can save the yolks in the freezer and donate them periodically to a neighbor's dog. Another option is to hard-cook the yolks and crumble them among the offerings on your bird feeder.

The recipes that follow contain no more than one egg yolk per serving and usually less. On a day you eat eggs, it would be wise to avoid other high-cholesterol fare, such as fatty meats and organ meats (like liver), as well as other foods made with egg yolks. If you must avoid all yolks, you could substitute a cholesterol-free product like Eggbeaters.

HOME-STYLE CORN PUDDING   *6 servings*

My husband devised this recipe based on the dish he enjoyed as a child in the Midwest.

    2 tablespoons butter or margarine
    3 tablespoons flour
1¼ cups skim or low-fat milk
    1 cup grated cheese (sharp Cheddar, for
        example) (about 4 ounces)
    2 15-ounce cans corn niblets, drained, *or* 3 cups
        fresh or frozen corn kernels
    1 cup soft fresh bread crumbs (2 slices)
Salt, if desired, to taste (I use ½ teaspoon)
    1 teaspoon dry mustard
    ½ teaspoon sugar
    ½ teaspoon freshly ground black pepper

2 egg whites and 3 whole eggs, beaten
1 cup diced cooked ham (optional)

1. In a 3-quart saucepan, melt the butter or margarine, and stir in the flour. Cook the roux for a minute or so, and gradually add the milk, stirring the sauce constantly over low heat until it is slightly thickened.
2. Remove the pan from the heat, and stir in the rest of the ingredients. Mix the ingredients well, and pour the mixture into a greased 2-quart casserole.
3. Set the casserole in a pan of hot water, and bake the pudding in a preheated 325° oven for 1¼ hours or until a knife inserted in the center of the pudding comes out clean.

FRITTATA WITH BROCCOLI AND POTATOES

4 servings

Most frittatas (Italian omelets) are too high in cholesterol to be served as a main course. However, I've found that many can be made with only half the yolks (1 per serving) and still be tasty. Here's one that was enjoyed by tasters of all ages.

1¼ pounds potatoes (3 medium-large), peeled and
    finely diced
2 tablespoons vegetable oil
10 ounces chopped broccoli (fresh or frozen)
6 scallions, cut diagonally into ¼-inch slices
4 egg whites
4 whole eggs
¼ cup grated Parmesan
2 tablespoons minced fresh parsley *or* 2
    teaspoons dried parsley flakes
½ teaspoon salt, if desired
¼ teaspoon freshly ground black pepper

1. In a large, covered oven-proof skillet (preferably nonstick), cook the potatoes in the oil over medium heat, stirring them once or twice, for about 10 minutes, or until they are tender and lightly browned.
2. Add the broccoli and scallions, cover the skillet, and cook the mixture for another 5 minutes (the broccoli should be tender-crisp).
3. Preheat the oven to 350°.
4. Meanwhile, in a medium bowl, beat the egg whites and whole eggs with the Parmesan, parsley, salt, and pepper. Pour this over the vegetable mixture, and cook the frittata for about 5 minutes, pushing the ingredients occasionally with a spatula to allow any uncooked egg to make contact with the skillet. Place the skillet in the preheated oven for 5 minutes or until the eggs are set on top.

SPINACH FRITTATA

9 servings

Matilda Cuomo, wife of New York governor Mario Cuomo, says this recipe is a favorite of their large family. My tasters agreed that it is delicious. I eliminated one yolk so that there is less than half a yolk per serving. *Preparation tip:* Cuomo uses frozen chopped spinach. I made it with 2 pounds of fresh spinach, chopped and cooked until it wilted, and got good results.

    2 10-ounce packages frozen chopped spinach,
      defrosted
    3 cups low-fat cottage cheese
    1 cup plain bread crumbs, divided
    ½ cup grated Romano or Parmesan
    1 egg white
    4 whole eggs, divided
    Paprika

1. Preheat the oven to 350°.
2. Drain the spinach well. In a large bowl, combine the spinach with the cottage cheese, ¾ cup of the bread crumbs, and the grated cheese.
3. In a separate bowl, beat the egg white and 2 of the whole eggs, and add them to the spinach mixture, stirring the mixture to combine the ingredients thoroughly.
4. Lightly oil the bottom of a 9-inch square baking pan, and sprinkle it with the remaining bread crumbs. Place the pan in the oven for 3 to 5 minutes to lightly brown the crumbs.
5. Carefully spread the spinach mixture over the baked crumbs. Beat the remaining 2 eggs, and pour them over the spinach mixture. Sprinkle the frittata with paprika.
6. Bake the frittata for 45 minutes in the preheated oven. Let it cool for about 10 minutes before cutting it into thirds in both directions (you will end up with 3-inch squares).

ZUCCHINI FRITTATA

6 to 8 servings

Here's a long-time family favorite that I have served often to company at brunch, always to loud acclaim. It's especially handy when the zucchini crop comes in, since it uses up a lot of it. It's also one of the few ways in which my children will eat zucchini (even though they can see the green specks and they know it's there, the flavor and texture are well disguised). *Preparation tip:* It can be served hot or at room temperature, so it is also a handy make-ahead and buffet dish. Garnish individual servings with fresh tomato slices or cherry tomatoes and black olives, if desired.

8 cups shredded unpeeled zucchini (about 3 pounds)
1 tablespoon olive oil
1 teaspoon butter or margarine
2 tablespoons finely chopped onion
1 clove garlic, finely minced or crushed
4 egg whites
4 whole eggs
2 tablespoons milk
½ teaspoon orégano, crumbled
½ teaspoon dried basil, crumbled
½ teaspoon salt, if desired
½ teaspoon freshly ground black pepper, or to taste
Dash hot pepper sauce (Tabasco) *or* pinch cayenne
½ cup grated Parmesan, divided

1. Place the shredded zucchini in a dish towel or several layers of cheesecloth, and squeeze out as much liquid as possible (gather the ends of the towel and twist hard).
2. Heat the oil and the butter or margarine in a large oven-proof skillet (preferably nonstick), and sauté the onion and garlic for 30 seconds. Add the zucchini, and cook the vegetables over moderately low heat, stirring often, until the zucchini is just tender. If any liquid collects in the pan, pour it off.
3. Meanwhile, in a medium bowl, beat the egg whites, whole eggs, milk, orégano, basil, salt, black pepper, pepper sauce or cayenne, and 2 tablespoons of the Parmesan. Add this to the zucchini mixture, and cook the ingredients, stirring them often, until the eggs begin to set.
4. Sprinkle the frittata with the remaining Parmesan, and place the pan under the broiler (if it fits) or in a very hot oven (500°) until the top of the frittata is lightly browned (this just takes a few minutes, so stay with it to be sure the cheese does not burn). Let the frittata stand for a few minutes before slicing it into wedges.

ASPARAGUS QUICHE

4 to 6 servings

Preparation tip: I originally prepared this quiche using 2 slices of bacon cooked crisp and crumbled onto the prepared crust before adding the filling. This adds a nice crunch and contrasting flavor and texture. However, the bacon can be omitted entirely, or you can substitute 2 tablespoons of minced ham or Canadian bacon (both are low in fat), smoked pork, or, to keep to the vegetarian theme, imitation bacon bits, which are made from soybeans.

1 9-inch pie crust (see, for example, p. 632)
2 strips bacon, cooked crisp, drained, and
   crumbled (optional)
½ pound asparagus, cooked tender-crisp and cut
   into 1-inch pieces (2 cups)
1 cup shredded Swiss cheese or Gruyère (4
   ounces)
1 cup whole milk *or* ½ cup low-fat milk and ½
   cup evaporated skim milk
2 egg whites
2 whole eggs
1 teaspoon tarragon, crumbled
⅛ to ¼ teaspoon nutmeg, to taste
½ teaspoon salt, if desired, or to taste
⅛ teaspoon freshly ground black pepper

1. Line a 9-inch pie plate with the crust. Prick the crust in several places with a fork. Bake the crust in a preheated 450° oven for 7 minutes. Set the crust aside to cool. Lower the oven temperature to 350°.
2. Sprinkle the crust with the bacon, if desired. Add the asparagus pieces, then the shredded cheese.
3. In a small bowl, beat together the milk, egg whites, whole eggs, tarragon, nutmeg, salt, and pepper. Pour this mixture carefully over the cheese.
4. Bake the quiche for 30 minutes or until the custard has set (a knife inserted in the center of the quiche should come out clean).

ZUCCHINI-RICE "QUICHE"

6 main-dish servings

The word *quiche* is in quotes in the recipe title because this is really a crustless pie made of vegetables and rice held together by a low-fat custard. The net effect, however, is that of a quiche. The three egg yolks are divided among 6 servings, so each person consumes only half a yolk.

1 tablespoon butter or margarine
1 large onion, chopped (1 cup)
2 cloves garlic, minced or crushed
1 cup coarsely chopped mushrooms
2 cups chopped, unpeeled zucchinis (about 1½ medium ones)
1 peeled tomato, chopped (about ½ cup)
2 cups cooked rice (white or brown)
½ teaspoon dried basil
½ teaspoon orégano
Freshly ground black pepper to taste
Several dashes cayenne, or to taste
2 egg whites
3 whole eggs
⅔ cup low-fat cottage cheese
¼ cup skim or low-fat milk
⅓ cup grated Parmesan, divided

1. In a medium saucepan, melt the butter or margarine, and sauté the onion and garlic for 1 minute. Then add the mushrooms and zucchinis, and cook them, stirring them occasionally, until the vegetables are soft.
2. Remove the pan from the heat, and stir in the tomato, rice, basil, orégano, pepper, and cayenne.
3. In a small bowl, beat the egg whites and whole eggs, and mix in the cottage cheese, milk, and 2 tablespoons of the Parmesan. Add to this to the vegetable-rice mixture.
4. Pour the mixture into a 9-inch deep-dish or 10-inch greased pie plate. Sprinkle the quiche with the remaining Parmesan.
5. Bake the quiche in a preheated 350° oven for 25 to 30 minutes or until the custard has set (a knife inserted in center of the quiche should come out clean). Let the quiche stand for about 10 minutes before serving it.

BROCCOLI-RICOTTA SOUFFLÉ

4 servings

This recipe from *Gourmet* magazine required no changes except for a reduction in oil and butter.

¼ cup dried bread crumbs
½ cup minced onion
2 teaspoons olive oil
2 teaspoons butter or margarine
1 cup chopped cooked broccoli
1 15-ounce container part-skim ricotta
3 large eggs, lightly beaten
½ cup Parmesan, preferably freshly grated
Salt, if desired, to taste
Freshly ground black pepper to taste
4 egg whites
Pinch cream of tartar
Pinch salt

1. Grease a 1½-quart soufflé dish, and sprinkle it with the bread crumbs, shaking out the excess. Chill the dish until you are ready to fill it.
2. Preheat the oven to 375°.
3. In a skillet, preferably nonstick, sauté the onion in the oil and the butter or margarine, stirring the onion, until it is softened. Stir in the broccoli, and transfer the mixture to a large bowl.
4. Add the ricotta, 3 beaten eggs, Parmesan, salt, and pepper, and combine the ingredients thoroughly.
5. In a separate bowl with an electric mixer, beat the egg whites with the cream of tartar and salt until the whites form stiff peaks. Stir one-third of the beaten whites into the ricotta mixture, then fold in the rest of the beaten whites gently but thoroughly.
6. Transfer the mixture to the prepared chilled dish, and bake it in the pre-heated oven for 35 to 40 minutes or until the soufflé is puffed and golden-brown. Serve the soufflé immediately.

POTATO SOUFFLÉ

4 main-course servings

I got the idea for trying a potato soufflé from a little paperback cookbook. Although I suspected potatoes would result in a leaden soufflé, I was delighted to be proved wrong. In fact, this dish is a wonderful treat, akin to a fluffy potato pudding. *Preparation tip:* To speed preparation, do step 2 while the potatoes cook in step 1.

1½ pounds potatoes, peeled and cubed
  2 tablespoons unsalted butter or margarine, divided
  1 medium onion, chopped (about ½ cup)
 ¼ pound mushrooms, chopped (about 1 cup)
 ¼ cup grated Parmesan, divided
 ¼ teaspoon salt, if desired
Freshly ground black pepper to taste
  4 egg yolks
  6 egg whites

1. Cook the potato cubes in water to cover until they are soft, about 10 minutes. Drain the potatoes, and mash them with a ricer or process them through a food mill into a large bowl. Stir in 1 tablespoon of the butter or margarine.
2. While the potatoes are cooking, melt the remaining 1 tablespoon butter or margarine in a small skillet. Add the onion, and sauté it for 2 minutes. Add the mushrooms, and sauté them until they give off their liquid and begin to dry.
3. Preheat the oven to 325°. Grease a 2-quart soufflé dish with butter or vegetable-oil spray. Sprinkle 1 tablespoon of the Parmesan on the bottom and sides of the dish. Set the dish aside.
4. Add the sautéed vegetables to the mashed potatoes along with the remaining Parmesan, the salt, and pepper. Beat the egg yolks, one at a time, into the mixture.
5. In a clean medium bowl, beat the egg whites with a pinch of salt, if desired, until they are stiff but not dry. Fold one-third of the beaten whites into the potato mixture, mixing gently but well. Fold in the remaining whites. Immediately transfer the mixture to the prepared soufflé dish.
6. Bake the soufflé in the preheated oven for 45 to 50 minutes. Serve the soufflé immediately.

NO-YOLK SOUFFLÉ

4 servings

Gourmet magazine, which has been offering more and more delicious, health-conscious recipes in recent years, came up with this one for a cheese soufflé without the high-cholesterol contribution of egg yolks. I substituted a little hot chili powder for salt, and the result was wonderful.

⅔ cup freshly grated Parmesan, divided
3 tablespoons unsalted butter or margarine
¼ cup white flour
1 cup skim or low-fat milk
Nutmeg to taste
Cayenne to taste
¼ teaspoon hot chili powder, or to taste
Freshly ground black pepper to taste
Egg whites from 6 large eggs (¾ cup)
¼ teaspoon cream of tartar
4 ounces Gruyère, grated (about 1¼ cups)

1. Grease a 1-quart soufflé dish, and fit it with a 3-inch-high band of foil, doubled and greased, to form a collar that extends 2 inches above the rim of the dish. Sprinkle the dish and collar with 2 tablespoons of the Parmesan.
2. In a small, heavy saucepan, melt the butter or margarine over moderately low heat, stir in the flour, and cook the roux, stirring it, for 3 minutes. Gradually add the milk, whisking the sauce constantly. Continue whisking the sauce while you bring the mixture to a boil, reduce the heat, and simmer the sauce for 2 minutes. Add the nutmeg, cayenne, chili powder, and pepper.
3. Remove the pan from the heat, stir in ½ cup of the Parmesan, and transfer the sauce to a large bowl.
4. Preheat the oven to 375°.
5. In another large bowl, beat the egg whites until they are frothy, add the cream of tartar, and continue beating the whites until they hold stiff peaks.
6. Stir one-fourth of the whites into the sauce. Fold in the remaining whites and the Gruyère. Spoon the mixture into the prepared soufflé dish, and sprinkle the soufflé with the remaining Parmesan.
7. Bake the soufflé in the preheated oven for 30 to 35 minutes, or until the soufflé is puffed and golden. Serve the soufflé immediately.

Sandwiches

If there is one type of food that every American is sure to have eaten, it's the sandwich. The English may have invented sandwiches (Lord Sandwich, a fanatical card player, had his servants bring two pieces of bread with meat between them so he wouldn't have to leave the card table to eat), but it was on-the-go Americans who honed the sandwich into a high art. While the English may be content with such delicate sandwiches as watercress or cucumber on crustless white bread, Americans go for much heartier fare: from the peanut butter and jelly of childhood to the famous BLT (bacon, lettuce, and tomato), chicken salad, and hefty hero (also called grinder, submarine, hoagie, and so forth, depending on the region) stuffed with cold cuts, cheese, hot peppers, and a host of other miscellaneous ingredients.

It's time, though, to expand your notion of a sandwich to include some foods you wouldn't ordinarily think of putting between two slices of bread. I'm fond of sandwiches made from various leftovers, such as croquettes, pieces of chicken or turkey topped with ratatouille (see p. 520), and so forth. The proliferation of pita, or pocket bread—that Middle Eastern invention that forms a sealed circle of two thin but firm layers that separate in the middle—has permitted a major expansion of sandwich fillings because the pockets can hold ingredients that are looser or more liquid than you'd usually find in a sandwich. Pita is also widely available in whole-wheat form. Here are a few pita and other sandwiches I think you'll enjoy.

FELAFEL FOR SANDWICHES

4 servings

When these spicy chickpea patties are made properly, they absorb very little of the oil in which they are fried. Although they are often made into balls and served as an appetizer with a dipping sauce, I prefer them in a pita sandwich with a tahini (sesame paste) or a yogurt dressing (see pp. 641 and 645), lettuce and tomato, and possibly also alfalfa sprouts. This recipe, from *Medical Self-Care* magazine, starts with cooked chickpeas (you can use canned peas, but rinse and drain them first) processed in a blender, and adds wheat germ, which, along with the sandwich bread, completes the pea and seed protein. The result is a quick, easy, and tasty pancake. *Preparation tip:* The batter can be prepared in advance through step 2 and refrigerated before frying.

     1 egg
     1 tablespoon water
     1 teaspoon lemon juice
     2 tablespoons minced fresh parsley *or* 2
        teaspoons dried parsley flakes
     2 cloves garlic, minced or crushed
     1 tablespoon reduced-sodium soy sauce
     ¼ cup tahini (sesame paste)
     2 cups cooked chickpeas (garbanzos), drained
     1 teaspoon ground cumin
     1 teaspoon ground coriander
     ½ teaspoon chili powder
     ⅓ cup wheat germ

1. In a blender or food processor, combine the egg, water, lemon juice, parsley, garlic, soy sauce, and tahini. Process the ingredients until they form a smooth mixture.
2. Add the chickpeas, cumin, coriander, and chili powder, and blend the mixture again. Transfer the mixture to a bowl, and stir in the wheat germ.
3. Form the mixture into patties (6 or more), and fry the patties on a lightly oiled griddle or in a skillet until they are lightly browned on both sides. Serve the felafel with Yogurt-Tahini Sauce (p. 645).

LENTIL-AND-BULGUR PATTY SANDWICHES

6 servings

Once the lentils are cooked, the patties are easy to prepare. The combination of lentils and bulgur (and bread) makes a complete protein. The parsley adds a great deal of vegetable-derived vitamins and minerals. *Preparation tip:* Serve the patties in pitas with lettuce and sliced tomato and cucumber.

1½ cups lentils
  1 large onion, chopped (1 cup)
  2 large cloves garlic, crushed
  4 cups water
  1 cup bulgur (cracked wheat)
1¼ cups minced fresh parsley, divided
  2 tablespoons oil
  ½ teaspoon salt, if desired
  1 teaspoon paprika (hot or sweet)
  ¼ teaspoon freshly ground black pepper
  1 cup finely chopped scallions with tops (about
     8 scallions)
  6 pitas

1. In a medium saucepan, combine the lentils, onion, garlic, and water. Bring the liquid to a boil, reduce the heat, cover the pan, and cook the lentils for 20 to 25 minutes or until they are very tender.

2. Add the bulgur, ¼ cup of the parsley, the oil, salt, paprika, and pepper. Stir the mixture to combine the ingredients well, cover the pan, and cook the mixture over low heat for 2 minutes. Let the mixture cool to lukewarm in the covered pan.

3. When the mixture is lukewarm, shape it into 12 patties. Combine the remaining parsley and the scallions on a dish, and press the patties into this mixture on both sides. Serve the patties cool or chilled in the pitas.

MOROCCAN POCKETS

8 servings

This recipe was devised by Cornelius, the chef for Corning Glassware. It is suitable for a company buffet or a family lunch or supper.

> 1 pound lean ground beef
> 1 large onion, chopped (1 cup)
> 1 cup chopped green pepper
> 1 clove garlic, crushed
> 1 16-ounce can tomatoes, with their juice
> 2 *tablespoons* chili powder
> 1 teaspoon ground cumin
> 1 teaspoon orégano
> 1 cup barley
> 1¾ cups hot water
> 1 cup raisins
> ¼ teaspoon salt, if desired
> ¼ teaspoon freshly ground black pepper
> 4 large pitas, cut in half crosswise to form 8 pockets
> 2 cups plain low-fat yogurt
> ¼ cup minced fresh parsley

1. In a 10-inch skillet, brown the beef. Add the onion, green pepper, and garlic, and cook the mixture until the onion is softened. Drain off the fat, and transfer the meat mixture to a medium saucepan.
2. Add to the saucepan the tomatoes with their juice, chili powder, cumin, orégano, barley, and hot water. Bring the mixture to a boil, reduce the heat, cover the pan, and simmer the mixture for about 30 minutes or until the barley is tender (check after 20 minutes, and add more water if needed).
3. Stir in the raisins, and season the mixture with salt and pepper. Spoon the mixture into pita pockets.
4. Combine the yogurt and parsley to use as a topping.

TURKEY POCKETS

2 sandwiches
(4 large halves)

This sandwich filling could be made with chicken and could also be eaten as a salad.

> ½ pound cooked turkey, diced
> ½ cup diced celery
> ¼ cup diced red onion
> ½ sweet red pepper, diced

2 teaspoons mayonnaise
1 teaspoon lemon or lime juice
⅛ teaspoon salt, if desired
⅛ teaspoon freshly ground black pepper
Pinch cayenne
2 pitas
Alfalfa sprouts for garnish

1. Combine the turkey, celery, onion, sweet pepper, mayonnaise, lemon or lime juice, salt, pepper, and cayenne. Refrigerate the mixture for ½ hour.
2. Slice the pitas in half crosswise to form 4 pockets. Fill the pockets with the turkey mixture, and top them with some alfalfa sprouts.

TEMPEH BURGERS

10 patties (5 servings)

Protein-rich and naturally sweet tempeh (a product of fermented soybeans—see p. 101) is the basis for these tasty croquettes. *Preparation tip:* The burgers are especially good in whole-wheat pita with lettuce, tomato, and a yogurt-based sauce (see pp. 641 and 645).

8 ounces tempeh, very finely chopped (2 cups)
1 small onion, finely chopped (⅓ cup)
2 teaspoons finely minced garlic (2 large cloves)
1 cup finely shredded carrot (1 large)
2 egg whites and 1 whole egg, lightly beaten
¼ cup low-fat or skim milk
¾ cup toasted wheat germ
½ cup cooked brown rice
¼ teaspoon dried dillweed
¼ teaspoon dried basil
¼ teaspoon salt, if desired
Freshly ground black pepper to taste

1. In a medium bowl, combine all the ingredients well. Shape the mixture into 10 patties, using about ⅓ cup of the mixture for each patty.
2. Lightly grease a griddle (preferably one with a nonstick surface), and cook the patties, several at a time, until they are golden brown on the bottom. Turn the patties over carefully with a spatula, and brown the other side.

OTHER POSSIBLE SANDWICH FILLINGS

Try some of these variations on the sandwich theme for nutrition-packed meals and snacks:

- Peanut butter (the natural unsalted kind) and sliced banana.
- Chunky peanut butter mixed with chopped apple and a little cinnamon.
- Low-fat cottage cheese mixed with raisins, chopped apple, and a sprinkling of cinnamon-sugar, stuffed at eating time into whole-wheat pita.
- Low-fat cottage cheese mixed with sunflower seeds and raisins.
- Tuna (packed in water and drained) mixed with low-fat cottage cheese, finely chopped celery, scallions, and radishes.
- Sardines (low-sodium, packed in water), flaked and mixed with low-fat cottage cheese and topped with thinly sliced onion.
- Diced cooked chicken mixed with diced apple and pineapple and dressed with a mixture of mayonnaise and yogurt seasoned with curry powder.
- Unsalted peanuts, coarsely chopped, mixed with shredded carrots and raisins and dressed lightly with mayonnaise and yogurt.
- Curried lentils, tomato, and alfalfa sprouts in pita with a yogurt-based dressing.
- Smear whole-grain bread with mustard, sprinkle on chopped watercress, and fill with sliced turkey breast.
- Chili with or without meat (works best in pita).
- A "hash" of cooked lean ground beef, chopped boiled potato, chopped onion, and green pepper, sautéed until the vegetables are softened (in pita).
- Scrambled egg (or 2 egg whites) topped with sautéed green peppers and onions.
- Hummus (see p. 292) with lettuce and tomato.

Pancakes and Crêpes

Too many Americans associate pancakes only with Sunday breakfast, especially if it's eaten out. And those who do bother to make pancakes at home more often than not start with a packaged mix to which they add milk and eggs and sometimes oil or butter. Still others avoid pancakes altogether because they think of them as "so fattening." But pancakes need not be a "production number" that you only have time for on weekends. Nor do you have to be limited by the flour and flavoring combinations in packaged mixes. Nor are pancakes necessarily a high-calorie, low-nutrient treat. The way I make them—even on days I'm racing out to catch a plane—they are fast, loaded with foods that are good for your body, and low in fats and sugars. Nor do we eat them drowning in syrup. Rather, sautéed apple or pear slices or fruit purées and fruit butters often supply the sweetening. Sometimes fruit, either fresh or dried, is included in the batter, resulting in a naturally sweetened pancake that needs no further adornment. If syrup is used, it's dribbled on, not poured.

There are two tricks to making pancakes efficiently from scratch: one is to have all the basic dry ingredients handy, either on easily reached open shelves or in one spot in the pantry; the other is to mix up a big batch of the dry ingredients and store it in a tightly closed container for convenient use. You can even mix the dry ingredients and liquid ingredients separately hours ahead or the night before and combine them in a moment in the morning.

Furthermore, pancakes are far more than just breakfast food. Crêpes, which are very thin unleavened pancakes devised by the French, are superb wrappers for all kinds of main-course and dessert fillings. They can even be made up ahead and frozen. The Russian buckwheat pancake, called a blini, is an excellent base for a main dish for supper or lunch. Eastern European Jews are familiar with the blintz, a pancake stuffed with, among other things, a lightly sweetened curd cheese (like dry cottage cheese) or fruit. Asians are also fond of pancakes; you may be familiar with the meat-and-vegetable stir-fry that's stuffed into pancakes to make mu shu pork.

In addition, a number of vegetables (for example, zucchini, potatoes, corn) can be used as the main ingredient in pancakes that are more like croquettes. These pancakes can be used as a main course or vegetable side dish.

Your imagination is the limit. Once you appreciate the balance of basic ingredients and cooking technique, it's hard to ruin a pancake. Almost any kind of flour or combination of flours will work. Pancakes are also another perfect way to unload bits and pieces of leftovers, fruits that are getting too soft, or dairy products that have turned sour in the refrigerator. (If you use a sweetened yogurt, be sure to omit the sugar or other sweetener in the recipe.) All you need to do to counteract a sour or acidic ingredient is to add baking soda to the dry ingredients in the right proportions. According to Arthur E. Grosser, author of *The Cookbook Decoder,* ½ teaspoon of baking soda (bicarbonate of soda) will neutralize the acidity of the following foods:

1 cup sour milk	1 cup mashed banana
1 cup yogurt	½ cup molasses
1 cup buttermilk	1 tablespoon vinegar
1 cup applesauce	1 tablespoon lemon juice

Sodium watchers can try two approaches: use low-sodium baking powder (check the dietetic section of the supermarket or a health-food store) in about twice the amount called for in the recipe; and omit all added salt.

It is important when cooking pancakes to heat the pan before it is greased and not to let the grease burn. If you use a pan with a nonstick surface, you may not need to worry about greasing it at all. For making most pancakes, a griddle is the best kind of pan to use because it is easier to flip the pancakes when they are on a flat surface without much of a ledge. For crêpes and other pancakes that are thin and meant for stuffing, a small (7- or 8-inch) slope-sided skillet is ideal. If you have two similar skillets, you can work two at once and get the job done twice as fast.

BASIC MULTIGRAIN PANCAKES
4 to 6 servings

These are the pancakes I often whip up for before-school breakfasts. *Preparation tip:* Serve them as is with syrup or topped with sliced apples or pears sautéed in a teaspoon or two of butter with a generous sprinkling of cinnamon or cinnamon-sugar. Or you can try one of the fruit additions listed in the "Variations," below. If you do not have oat flour or an alternative, simply add another ¼ cup of whole-wheat flour to the dry-ingredients mixture.

DRY INGREDIENTS
- ⅔ cup whole-wheat flour, preferably stone-ground
- ⅓ cup all-purpose flour
- ¼ cup oat or other flour (e.g., corn meal, barley, buckwheat, millet)
- 2 tablespoons wheat germ
- 2 teaspoons sugar
- 1 teaspoon baking powder
- ½ teaspoon baking soda
- ¼ teaspoon salt, if desired

WET INGREDIENTS
- 1 cup buttermilk
- ¼ cup or more skim milk
- 1 egg white
- 1 whole egg
- 1 tablespoon vegetable oil
- ¼ teaspoon vanilla extract (optional)

1. Mix together all the dry ingredients in a medium bowl.
2. In a second bowl, combine all the wet ingredients, whipping them enough to beat the egg white and whole egg lightly. Add these to the dry ingredients, stirring just to combine them. The batter can stand for about 10 minutes out of the refrigerator, or for an hour or more refrigerated.
3. Heat a griddle over medium heat. Grease it lightly if not nonstick, and immediately pour sufficient batter to make pancakes of the size you desire (don't let them get too big, or they will be hard to flip). Try to leave some space between the pancakes to keep them from sticking together. Turn the heat down to moderately low, and cook the pancakes until the bottoms are golden brown and the tops begin to bubble. Flip them over, and cook them until the undersides are golden brown. Serve them immediately.

VARIATIONS: You can add a variety of fruits to these pancakes after step 2. Among my favorites are cranberries, blueberries, raisins, apples, pears, and bananas. In the case of cranberries, which lend a tart counterpoint to the slightly sweet batter, slice the raw berries in half, and gently stir them into the batter. Blueberries (cleaned, of course) can just be stirred in. Apples and pears can be peeled and cut into thin strips or coarsely chopped and added to the batter. For bananas, a slightly different technique is needed: pour slightly less than the usual amount of batter on the heated griddle, spread a single layer of banana slices on top of the batter, and dribble some batter over each slice (this works best with a spoon) to keep the fruit from sticking to the pan when you flip the pancakes. For apple, pear, and banana pancakes, a sprinkle of cinnamon-sugar on the top before the pancake cooks is a nice touch.

CORN GRIDDLE CAKES

about 10 4-inch pancakes

These are good for breakfast, brunch, lunch, or even a late-night snack.

DRY INGREDIENTS
⅔ cup all-purpose flour
⅓ cup whole-wheat flour
1 tablespoon sugar
2 teaspoons baking powder
¼ teaspoon salt, if desired

WET INGREDIENTS
¾ cup milk (skim or low-fat)
1 egg
2 tablespoons vegetable oil
1⅓ cups corn kernels (either frozen, canned, or fresh cooked)

1. In a medium bowl, stir together the dry ingredients.
2. In another bowl, whisk together the milk, egg, and oil. Stir in the corn, and add the wet ingredients to the dry ingredients, mixing them just to blend (don't worry about lumps).
3. For each pancake, spread ¼ cup of batter on a hot, greased griddle. Cook the pancakes over moderate heat until they are golden brown on the bottom and the tops begin to bubble. Then flip them over, and cook them until the undersides are golden brown.

COTTAGE CHEESE PANCAKES

about 12 4-inch pancakes

These pancakes get an added protein boost from cottage cheese. They're a good way to use up cottage cheese that's begun to turn and no longer is desirable as a separate food.

WET INGREDIENTS
1 cup low-fat cottage cheese
1 egg white
1 whole egg
1 cup buttermilk *or* ½ cup buttermilk and ½ cup skim or low-fat milk
2 teaspoons honey

DRY INGREDIENTS
½ cup whole wheat flour
½ cup all-purpose flour
2 tablespoons wheat germ
1 teaspoon baking powder
½ teaspoon baking soda
¼ teaspoon salt, if desired

1. In a blender or in a bowl with an electric mixer, blend together all the wet ingredients.
2. In a medium bowl, combine all the dry ingredients. Pour in the liquid mixture, and stir the ingredients just enough to blend them.
3. For each pancake, spread ¼ cup of batter on a hot, greased griddle. Cook the pancakes over moderate heat until they are golden brown on the bottom and the tops begin to bubble. Then flip them over, and cook them until the undersides are golden brown.

SUSAN'S OATMEAL PANCAKES

12 to 14 large pancakes

My friend Susan Oakley is an ingenious pancake cook. She never seems to make the same ones twice. That's partly because she uses whatever ingredients are at hand. Once or twice, I've managed to extract a recipe from her for one of her more winning combinations, such as this one that she serves to the lucky patrons of Sweet Sue's, her wonderful restaurant and bakery in Phoenicia, New York.

DRY INGREDIENTS
1¼ cups whole-wheat flour
1 cup rolled oats (regular or quick)
¼ cup wheat germ
2 tablespoons sunflower seeds or finely chopped walnuts
4 teaspoons baking powder
1 tablespoon sugar
¼ teaspoon baking soda
¼ teaspoon salt, if desired
⅛ teaspoon cinnamon
⅛ teaspoon ground cloves
⅛ teaspoon nutmeg

WET INGREDIENTS
1 cup low-fat milk
½ cup buttermilk
2 eggs *or* 1 egg white and 1 whole egg
1 tablespoon oil
½ banana, mashed
1 medium apple, finely chopped
2 tablespoons raisins or currants
1 teaspoon grated lemon peel (optional)
1 teaspoon vanilla extract

1. In a medium bowl, combine all the dry ingredients.
2. In a second bowl, whisk together the milks, eggs, and oil. Stir in the banana, apple, raisins or currants, lemon peel, and vanilla. Combine the wet ingredients well, and add them to the dry ingredients, stirring them just to blend them. The batter will be thick.
3. On a hot, lightly greased griddle, use about 3 tablespoons of batter for each pancake, flattening the batter with the back of a spoon. Cook the pancakes over moderately low heat until they are golden brown on the bottom. Then flip them over, and cook them until the undersides are golden brown.

PUMPKIN-OAT PANCAKES

4 servings

You can add a little color, flavor, and vitamin A to your pancakes by substituting puréed pumpkin for some of the milk.

"WET" INGREDIENTS
½ cup rolled oats (quick or regular)
1 cup buttermilk
1 egg white

DRY INGREDIENTS
½ cup whole-wheat flour
⅓ cup all-purpose flour
2 tablespoons wheat germ
1 tablespoon sugar, or to taste

"WET" INGREDIENTS (CONT'D)
1 whole egg
1 tablespoon oil
½ cup pumpkin purée
⅓ cup (approximately) skim or
  low-fat milk

DRY INGREDIENTS (CONT'D)
1 teaspoon baking powder
½ teaspoon baking soda
¼ teaspoon cinnamon

1. In a large bowl, combine the oats and buttermilk, and let the mixture stand for about 15 minutes or longer to soften.
2. Add the remaining wet ingredients, blending them well.
3. In a small bowl, combine all the dry ingredients. Stir them into the wet ingredients, mixing them until the batter is fairly smooth. Add more milk if the batter is too thick.
4. For each pancake, place about 3 tablespoons batter on a hot, lightly greased griddle. Flip the pancakes when their undersides are golden brown and the tops begin to bubble.

QUICK BLINIS

4 servings (with accompaniments)

Blinis are a Russian pancake specialty made from buckwheat flour, found in health food and specialty food stores. The pancakes are traditionally served with melted butter, sour cream, caviar, chopped onion, and chopped egg—heart-attack heaven! I still prepare them in the traditional manner perhaps once a year as a special treat (when I can get some reasonably priced caviar, that is). But blinis can also be eaten with other "fillings"—sardines with a mustard-dill-yogurt sauce or chopped herring, for example, or even with sweet fruit–and–cottage-cheese toppings. Blinis are also traditionally made with yeast and lots of eggs, but I've used the following one-egg–baking-powder recipe with much success.

DRY INGREDIENTS
1 cup buckwheat flour
1 teaspoon baking powder
1 teaspoon sugar
⅛ teaspoon salt, if desired

WET INGREDIENTS
1 egg
2 tablespoons sour cream or plain
  yogurt
1 tablespoon melted butter or
  margarine
¾ cup lukewarm milk (skim or
  low-fat)

1. In a medium bowl, sift or stir together the dry ingredients.
2. In a small bowl, lightly beat the egg, and mix it with the remaining wet ingredients. Stir the mixture into the dry ingredients until the batter is smooth.
3. Drop the batter by the tablespoonful onto a hot greased griddle to form 2-inch cakes (or larger ones, if desired). Flip the blinis when they are lightly browned, and cook them for 30 to 60 seconds on the other side.

BASIC CRÊPES

8 or 9 crêpes

Crêpes can be stuffed with a number of fillings for a make-ahead main course, a dessert, or even an appetizer. *Preparation tip:* Crêpe batter is best made ahead and refrigerated for at least 1 hour before baking. Leftover batter will keep in the refrigerator for several days, or it can be frozen for longer periods. In cooking crêpes, it is important to start with a hot pan. *Unfilled* crêpes can be stacked with pieces of wax paper placed between them, wrapped airtight in heavy foil, and frozen for up to three months. Crêpes will also keep in the refrigerator for about three days (be sure they are well wrapped to keep them from drying out). For larger batches, this recipe can be increased fourfold (to make 32 to 36 crêpes), but do not use more than ¼ teaspoon salt and ¼ cup melted butter in the batter.

  1 egg
Pinch salt, if desired (omit for dessert crêpes)
½ cup all-purpose flour
⅝ cup (½ cup plus 2 tablespoons) milk
  1 teaspoon sugar (for dessert crêpes only)
¼ teaspoon vanilla (for dessert crêpes only)
  2 tablespoons melted butter or margarine
    (approximately), divided

1. In a mixing bowl, combine the egg and salt. While beating the egg with a whisk or electric mixer, gradually add the flour alternatively with the milk. *For dessert crêpes only* add the sugar and vanilla. Add 1 tablespoon of the melted butter or margarine. Mix the ingredients to eliminate lumps. *Or* combine all the ingredients in a blender jar, and blend them for about 1 minute. Scrape down the sides of the jar, and blend the ingredients for another 15 seconds.
2. Heat a 7- or 8-inch crêpe pan or nonstick skillet with sloping sides. Add about 1 teaspoon of butter or margarine to the pan, tipping the pan to distribute the fat all over the bottom (try not to burn the fat). Add 2 tablespoons of batter to the hot pan, and swirl the batter around the pan by tipping the pan gently so that the batter completely covers the bottom. Cook the crêpe over moderately high heat for about 30 to 40 seconds or until the bottom of the crêpe is lightly browned. Flip the crêpe, and cook the other side for 15 seconds. Turn the crêpe out onto wax paper.
3. Repeat the cooking procedure with the remaining batter, brushing the pan lightly with butter or margarine as needed to keep the crêpes from sticking to it (with a nonstick pan, little if any fat will be needed).

HERB CRÊPES

These are delicious main-course crêpes, good for any mildly flavored filling, such as chicken or shrimp. *Preparation tip:* Note that the batter should be refrigerated for at least 2 hours before baking. The herbs can be varied to taste.

½ cup unbleached white flour
½ cup whole-wheat *pastry* flour
2 teaspoons orégano leaves, crushed
1 tablespoon minced fresh parsley *or* 1 teaspoon
  dried parsley flakes, crushed
1 teaspoon snipped chives
2 eggs
¼ teaspoon salt, if desired
1 cup skim or low-fat milk
1 tablespoon melted butter or margarine, plus
  extra for cooking the crêpes

1. In a small bowl, combine the white flour, whole-wheat flour, orégano, parsley, and chives.
2. In a medium bowl, combine the eggs, salt, and milk.
3. Add the flour mixture to the milk mixture, whisking the ingredients until the batter is smooth. *Or* place the milk mixture in a blender jar, and add the flour mixture while the motor runs on low, blending the ingredients until the batter is smooth.
4. Stir in the melted butter. Cover and refrigerate batter for *2 hours* or longer.
5. Cook the crêpes as in Basic Crêpes on page 502.

RATATOUILLE CRÊPES

8 crêpes (4 servings)

For those who keep ratatouille on hand, this is a quick yet impressive dish.

   1 cup part-skim ricotta
   ¼ cup grated Parmesan
   8 Basic (no sugar) or Herb Crêpes (see pp. 502
     and 503)
1½ cups ratatouille (see p. 504)

1. In a small bowl, combine the ricotta and Parmesan.
2. Spread all (or half) the crêpes out on a work surface, and divide the cheese
   mixture among them, placing the cheese in an off-center strip that ends
   about ½ inch from the edges of each crêpe. Top the cheese with the
   ratatouille, and fold the crêpe over, starting with the shorter side.
3. Place the filled crêpes in a shallow baking pan, seam side down. Cover them
   lightly with foil, and bake them in a moderate oven (about 350°) for about
   10 to 15 minutes or until they are heated through.

CHICKEN AND VEGETABLE CRÊPES

*8 crêpes
(4 servings)*

Crêpes are handy meal starters when there are cooked leftovers in the refrigera-
tor. You can also use parts of vegetables that are less desirable when served
otherwise, such as broccoli stems. *Preparation tip:* These crêpes can be made with
the vegetables of your choice, and you can use turkey or ham in place of the
chicken.

   1 cup cooked finely diced chicken (1 whole
     breast, approximately)
   1 cup cooked chopped broccoli stems
   1 cup cooked finely diced carrots
   2 teaspoons butter or margarine
   1 tablespoon flour
   1 cup skim milk
   ¼ cup grated Parmesan or Romano
   8 Basic (no sugar) or Herb Crêpes (see pp. 502
     and 503)

1. In a medium bowl, combine the chicken, broccoli, and carrots. Set the bowl
   aside.

2. In a medium saucepan, melt the butter or margarine, whisk in the flour, and cook the roux, stirring it, for 1 or 2 minutes. Gradually add the milk, stirring the sauce constantly over moderate heat. When the sauce is hot and has begun to thicken, stir in the grated cheese, and cook the sauce a few moments longer to melt the cheese.
3. Remove the sauce from heat, and reserve about ⅓ cup of it for later use.
4. Add the chicken-vegetable mixture to the remaining sauce in the pan, stirring the ingredients just to combine them.
5. Fill the crêpes as described in step 2 of Ratatouille Crêpes (p. 504). Place the crêpes in a baking pan, and pour the reserved sauce over them. Bake the crêpes in a moderate oven (about 350°) until they are heated through, about 10 minutes.

CURRIED SHRIMP CRÊPES

10 crêpes (5 servings)

Four generations of tasters loved these crêpes. *Preparation tip:* You can use frozen shrimp (be sure to cook them). Or you can substitute a firm-fleshed white fish or even cooked diced chicken. (If you use chicken, omit the lemon juice.)

¼ cup finely chopped onion
¼ cup finely chopped celery
2 teaspoons butter or margarine
1 large clove garlic, finely minced (1 teaspoon)
1½ tablespoons flour
¾ teaspoon curry powder, or to taste
1½ cups low-fat milk
1 teaspoon lemon juice (omit if using chicken)
¼ teaspoon salt, if desired
Dash ground ginger
½ pound shrimp, cooked and diced if large
10 Basic Crêpes (see p. 502)

1. In a medium skillet or small saucepan, sauté the onion and celery in the butter or margarine until the vegetables are just tender, about 3 minutes. Add the garlic, flour, and curry powder, and heat the mixture, stirring it, until it is very hot.
2. Stir in the milk, lemon juice, salt, and ginger, and cook the sauce, stirring it, over low heat until it has thickened.
3. Remove the sauce from the heat, and stir in the shrimp.
4. Fill the crêpes as described in step 2 of Ratatouille Crêpes (p. 504). Place the crêpes in a shallow baking pan or on an oven-proof serving platter. Cover them lightly with foil, and warm them in a moderate oven (about 350°) for about 5 to 10 minutes.

MILLET CAKES

6 servings

It's always a thrill for me to see people "turn on" to a food they've never tasted before. So it was with these croquette-like cakes, adapted from *Sharon Cadwallader's Complete Cookbook. Preparation tip:* The cakes can be prepared for frying hours ahead, to be cooked just before serving. You can keep the cooked ones warm in the oven, loosely covered, while the rest are frying.

PANCAKE
2 cups cooked millet (see p. 71)
⅔ cup grated Swiss cheese
¼ cup grated Parmesan
½ cup fresh bread crumbs (1 slice)
1 small onion, minced (¼ cup)
2 cloves garlic, mashed
1 teaspoon orégano
Salt, if desired, to taste
Freshly ground black pepper to
    taste

COATING
1 cup fresh bread crumbs (2
    slices)
½ cup minced fresh parsley

Oil for frying (about 2
    tablespoons)
Lemon wedges for garnish
    (optional)

1. In a medium bowl, thoroughly combine all the pancake ingredients. With your hands, form the mixture into 12 small cakes (they will be moist).

2. In a shallow bowl, stir together the coating ingredients. Press the millet cakes into the bread-crumb mixture, coating the cakes on both sides.

3. Heat 1 tablespoon oil (or less) in a shallow skillet, or grease a griddle, preferably a nonstick one. Fry the cakes over medium heat until they are golden brown, turning them once. Add more oil, as needed, to fry the remaining cakes. Serve the cakes with lemon wedges, if desired.

POTATO PANCAKES   *12 to 15 pancakes*

Better known by their Yiddish name *latkes* (lot'kis), these pancakes are tradi-
tionally served during Hanukkah, the festival of lights. But they are good almost
any time of the year (except perhaps in hot summer). There are as many
different versions of potato pancakes as there are cooks who make them. This
one is as good as any I've tried. *Preparation tip:* Potato pancakes are fried in oil
and can be very greasy if not done properly. Be sure the oil is hot before you
add the batter. Also, drain the cooked pancakes by placing them on paper
toweling. The amount of milk and flour you'll need depends on how moist the
potatoes are. Potato pancakes are usually served with applesauce and sour
cream. However, I've found low-fat yogurt to be a refreshing substitute for its
fatty cousin.

    2 pounds potatoes (6 medium), peeled or
      unpeeled and coarsely grated
    1 large onion, coarsely grated
    ¼ cup milk
    1 carrot, finely grated
    1 egg white and 1 whole egg, lightly beaten
    ½ cup white flour *or* ¼ cup matzo meal
    1 teaspoon salt, if desired, or to taste
    Freshly ground black pepper to taste
    Oil for frying

1. Place the grated potatoes and onion in a colander set over a large bowl, and
   press the vegetables to squeeze out the excess liquid. Let the vegetables
   stand for about 5 minutes, and press them again. Pour off the liquid, but
   leave in the bowl any starch that may have collected at the bottom.
2. Add the potato mixture to the bowl along with the milk, carrot, beaten egg
   white and whole egg, flour or matzo meal, salt, and pepper. Stir the ingredi-
   ents to combine them thoroughly.
3. In a large, heavy skillet or nonstick pan, heat enough oil to cover the
   bottom. Using about ¼ cup batter for each pancake, fry the pancakes a few
   at a time, turning them when they are golden brown on the bottom. As the
   pancakes cook, set them on paper towels, preferably laid over a rack, and
   keep them warm in a preheated very low oven.

Breakfast Specials

Although I strongly adhere to the "anything goes" principle for breakfast (see p. 191), for those of you who are wedded to more traditional fare, I offer the following specialties of the house. Of course, if you do reverse your meal pattern and have supper for breakfast, you can have any of the following for supper! (See also the pancake recipes on pp. 498–501, Spaghetti Pancake on p. 355, and Pita Pizzas on p. 475 for other Brody breakfast favorites.)

GREAT GRANOLA   *about 6 cups*

Most supermarket varieties of granola are sickeningly sweet and laced with a fair amount of an undesirable fat, like coconut or palm oil. It is *very easy* to make your own granola. Placed in a jar with a tight-fitting lid, it will last for weeks in your cupboard (longer in the refrigerator), if you haven't devoured it long before then. You can also make half a recipe at a time, which might be best since even homemade granola is sufficiently rich to restrict it to the status of a garnish on cereal or yogurt rather than using it as the main cereal in your bowl. The ingredients should be available in your supermarket. If not, try a health or natural food store. For strict low-cholesterol diets, use margarine and leave out the coconut.

  ¼ cup butter or margarine, or a combination
  ¼ cup honey
  3 cups rolled oats (regular or quick)
  1 cup shredded or flaked coconut (I use
    unsweetened) (optional)
  1 cup sunflower seeds (untoasted)
1½ teaspoons cinnamon
  ½ cup wheat germ (optional)
  ⅔ cup raisins

1. In a large oven-proof skillet or 9 × 13-inch baking pan, melt the butter, and stir in the honey.
2. Add the remaining ingredients *except the wheat germ and raisins,* and bake the mixture in a preheated 350° oven for about 15 minutes, stirring it several times. Stir in the wheat germ, if desired, and bake 10 minutes longer, or until the mixture is lightly browned.
3. Remove the granola from the oven, stir in the raisins, and cool the granola completely before transferring it to a storage container.

HEARTY OATMEAL

4 servings

Although originally devised to provide a stick-to-the ribs, bone-warming, pre-ski breakfast, this nutrient-packed version of oatmeal is good anytime for any body and soul.

    4 cups skim milk *or* 2 cups low-fat or skim milk
      and 2 cups water or apple juice
    2 cups rolled oats (regular or quick, not instant)
    ¼ teaspoon salt, if desired
    ½ cup raisins
    2 apples, peeled and chopped
    ¼ cup sunflower seeds
    1 teaspoon cinnamon-sugar *or* ½ teaspoon
      cinnamon and 1 teaspoon sugar (optional)

1. In a heavy saucepan, combine the milk, oats, salt, raisins, and apples. Bring the oatmeal to a boil, reduce the heat, cover the pan, and simmer the cereal, stirring it often, for about 5 minutes.
2. Add the sunflower seeds, and cook the oatmeal for another 5 minutes or until it reaches the desired consistency. Serve the oatmeal sprinkled with cinnamon-sugar, if desired.

RICE PUDDING CEREAL

3 to 4 servings

A great breakfast treat that I usually make whenever I have leftover cooked rice, white or brown (as long as it was cooked in water, not broth). Actually, the dish is good enough to warrant cooking the rice especially for it.

    3 cups cooked rice (1 cup raw)
    2 cups skim or low-fat milk
    1 egg white and 1 whole egg, lightly beaten
    1 tablespoon sugar (optional)
    ¼ cup raisins
    ¼ teaspoon cinnamon

Combine all the ingredients in a medium saucepan, and mix them well. Cook the rice over moderate heat, stirring it now and then, until it has thickened (about 5 minutes after the milk reaches a boil).

BRODY'S MILE-HIGH PANCAKES   *1 serving*

Here is a tasty, nutritious, and very attractive way to serve any breakfast-type pancake.

    1 or 2 large multigrain or other pancakes
    1 teaspoon apple butter or fruit purée *or* ½
        teaspoon jelly, jam, or preserves
    ½ cup or more plain low-fat yogurt
    Fresh fruit (e.g., banana, mango, pear, peach,
        pineapple, strawberries, blueberries), sliced, or
        fruit salad

    1. Place the hot pancake on a warm plate, and smear it with the apple butter or alternative spread.
    2. Spoon the yogurt over the pancake, and top it with the fresh fruit.

CHOLESTEROL-CONTROLLED FRENCH TOAST   *4 servings*

By discarding one of every two yolks (or feeding them to your dog), you can keep foods like French toast in a wholesome diet. The nutritive value of the meal would be enhanced by replacing syrup with fruit purée or with yogurt and sliced fruit for a topping. *Preparation tip:* The bread slices can be soaked in the batter the night before and refrigerated, covered, until morning, when they take just a few minutes to cook.

    2 egg whites
    2 whole eggs
    ¼ cup skim or low-fat milk
    2 teaspoons sugar
    ¼ teaspoon cinnamon
    ¼ teaspoon vanilla
    8 slices bread, preferably whole-wheat, halved

    1. In a shallow bowl or pie plate, whisk together the egg whites, whole eggs, milk, sugar, cinnamon, and vanilla.
    2. Dip the half slices of bread into the egg mixture one by one, turning to coat both sides of the bread.
    3. Heat a griddle that has been lightly greased with butter, margarine, or oil, and fry the bread over moderate heat. When the bread is golden brown on the bottom, flip it and brown the other side.

COTTAGE CHEESE TOASTIES

2 to 4 servings

A quick, nutritious, satisfying breakfast, the flavoring of which can be varied according to taste and what you have in the house.

1 cup low-fat cottage cheese
4 slices bread, preferably whole-wheat, toasted
Cinnamon-sugar
Sliced fruit (e.g., banana, peaches, apples,
    raisins, dates)

1. Divide the cottage cheese among the 4 pieces of toast, spreading it evenly. Sprinkle the cheese with the cinnamon-sugar, and top the toasties with sliced fruit.
2. Place the toasties on a tray, and heat them through in a toaster oven or under the broiler for a few minutes.

BREAKFAST SHAKE

1 serving

Here's a refreshing way to start a hot summer day.

1 cup buttermilk *or* ¾ cup plain low-fat yogurt
    and ¼ cup low-fat milk
1 cup of fresh fruit, cut up (e.g., banana,
    pineapple, mango—the riper the better)
1 teaspoon sugar (optional)
½ teaspoon vanilla
3 ice cubes or ⅓ cup crushed ice

Place all the ingredients in a blender, and process them until they are well combined and frothy.

VEGETABLE SIDE DISHES

I had a hard time coming up with recipes that were "just vegetables" to be served along with something else, because at home we almost never treat vegetables as side dishes. They are nearly always part of the main dish. Or, if we do eat a vegetable side dish, the vegetable is nearly always a fresh one that in our view warrants little or no adornment. However, now and again you'll want to eat a more traditional American meal, with a hunk of chicken or turkey, fish, or meat on your plate accompanied by a wonderful vegetable side dish or two. Vegetable side dishes also go well with simple pasta dishes, croquettes, and crêpes. Or perhaps you'll make a meal of two or more side dishes that offer complementary nutrients, such as a bean dish with rice, or use a vegetable dish like ratatouille as a "topping" for a nutritious starchy food like potatoes or pasta. Here are some suggestions for dressing up vegetables without robbing them of their nutritional virtues by adding too much fat.

CHILLED ASPARAGUS WITH YOGURT SAUCE

4 to 6 servings

It's a toss-up as to whether this is a vegetable side dish or a salad. Either way, the taste is divine and the appearance equally lovely. It is an excellent accompaniment to a main-dish mold or a sandwich.

MAIN INGREDIENTS
1½ pounds fresh asparagus, bottoms trimmed
Leaf lettuce, parsley, and cherry tomatoes for garnish (optional)

SAUCE
1 cup plain low-fat yogurt
2 teaspoons minced fresh parsley
1 teaspoon prepared mustard (I prefer Dijon)
1 teaspoon snipped fresh chives
½ teaspoon dried tarragon leaves, crumbled
½ teaspoon sugar
¼ teaspoon salt, if desired
¼ teaspoon paprika
Dash cayenne

1. Steam the asparagus tender-crisp, about 5 to 7 minutes, depending on their thickness. Cut the asparagus into 2-inch pieces, cover them, and refrigerate them.
2. In a small bowl, combine all the sauce ingredients. Mix the ingredients thoroughly, and refrigerate the sauce for at least 1 hour.
3. Just before serving, toss the asparagus with the yogurt sauce. Serve the asparagus on a bed of lettuce, garnished with parsley and cherry tomatoes, if desired.

HAITIAN BLACK BEANS
6 to 8 servings

Although most often eaten in soup from (see, for example, p. 313), black beans also can be a delicious and nourishing side dish, even without a ham hock for flavoring. Alex D. Hawke's *The World of Vegetable Cookery* is the source of this fine recipe. *Preparation tip:* Although the recipe calls for nearly 2 hours of cooking time, it can be prepared in advance through step 3. If served with rice or any grain, the beans can be turned into a main course.

2 cups dried black beans, picked over, rinsed,
  and soaked (see p. 103)
4 cups water (approximately)
2 large onions, chopped (2 cups)
1 cup chopped green pepper (1 large or 2 small)
1 tablespoon minced garlic
2 bay leaves
½ teaspoon salt, if desired
¼ teaspoon freshly ground black pepper
¼ teaspoon orégano
¼ teaspoon thyme
3 tablespoons cider vinegar
1 4-ounce jar pimientos, drained and chopped

1. Drain the soaked beans, and add them to the water in a medium saucepan. Bring the water to a boil, reduce the heat, cover the pan, and simmer the beans for 30 minutes.
2. Add the onions, green pepper, garlic, bay leaves, salt, pepper, orégano, and thyme, and simmer the ingredients 1 hour longer. Check after 40 minutes, and add more water if necessary.
3. Stir in the vinegar, and simmer the beans for another minute.
4. Five minutes before serving the beans, remove the bay leaves, stir in the pimiento, and heat the beans, stirring them often to avoid scorching.

GARLICKY GREEN BEANS

4 servings

This dish is delicious enough to set before a king but requires the preparation time available to a servant (i.e., tired working cook). •

  1 pound green beans, trimmed
  1 small onion, chopped (⅓ cup)
  2 teaspoons minced garlic (2 large cloves)
  2 teaspoons oil
  1 tablespoon flour
  1 teaspoon paprika
  1 16-ounce can whole tomatoes, drained (save
     the liquid) and coarsely chopped

  1. Steam the green beans for 5 minutes, then quickly chill them under cold water. Set them aside.
  2. In a medium saucepan, sauté the onion and garlic in the oil for about 3 minutes. Stir in the flour and paprika, cook the mixture for 1 minute, and then stir in the reserved liquid from the tomatoes. Cook the mixture, stirring it, until it is slightly thickened.
  3. Add the tomatoes and the reserved green beans, mixing the ingredients well. Cook the mixture, stirring it, over medium heat for about 2 minutes or until it is heated through and the beans are tender-crisp.

BRUSSELS SPROUTS WITH LEMON-MUSTARD SAUCE

4 servings

Too many people have tried Brussels sprouts in years past and have dismissed them as adorable but disappointing. That's because few people knew how to prepare them without producing a mushy vegetable with an unpleasantly bitter flavor. When young sprouts are cooked until just tender-crisp, they are wonderful. And they are a member of the cancer-fighting cabbage family to boot. The best way to prepare them is by steaming. Noted food writer Marian Burros put me onto the delightful combination of lemon and mustard to enhance this vegetable. The same sauce also suits broccoli, cauliflower, green beans, asparagus, and carrots.

  1 pound Brussels sprouts
  2 teaspoons butter or margarine
  1 tablespoon fresh lemon juice
1½ teaspoons coarse-grained mustard

1. Rinse the sprouts, and trim off the stems. Cut an X about ¼-inch deep into the remaining base of each sprout. Steam the sprouts for 7 to 10 minutes or until they are barely tender.
2. In a butter-melter or small saucepan, melt the butter or margarine, and stir in the lemon juice and mustard. To serve, toss the sauce with the hot sprouts.

BASIC BULGUR PILAF

4 servings

Bulgur, or cracked wheat, is the staple grain of eastern Mediterranean countries and well worth knowing everywhere. My college roommate, Dr. Linda Himot, picked up this fundamental recipe while living in Turkey and got my whole family hooked on it when she returned home.

2 teaspoons butter or margarine
1 small onion, finely minced (¼ to ⅓ cup)
1 cup bulgur
2 cups boiling broth
¼ teaspoon freshly ground black pepper
Salt, if desired, to taste (omit if the broth is
    salted)

1. Melt the butter or margarine in a medium saucepan. Sauté the onion for about 5 minutes or until it just begins to turn golden.
2. Stir in the bulgur, and cook the mixture for another 1 to 2 minutes.
3. Add the broth, pepper, and salt. Stir the ingredients to mix them well. Cover the pan, reduce the heat to low, and simmer the pilaf for about 15 minutes or until all the liquid is absorbed.

BRASED CABBAGE WITH CARAWAY   *6 servings*

I am especially pleased when my tasters ask for seconds (or for the recipe) for a vegetable like cabbage, traditionally the lowest of the low in prestige, though a delight to a nutritious diet (low in calories and high in nutrients, cancer blockers, and fiber). This recipe, from the *American Heart Association Cookbook,* is one of my favorites, and it has only about 30 calories a serving.

> 1 1½-pound head of green cabbage
> 1 teaspoon butter or margarine
> 1 tablespoon minced fresh parsley
> 1 teaspoon sugar
> Freshly ground black pepper to taste
> ½ cup chicken broth
> ½ teaspoon caraway seeds, or to taste

1. With a sharp knife, cut out most of the core of the cabbage, leaving just enough to hold the head together. Slice the head into wedges about 1½ inches thick.
2. In a large skillet, melt the butter or margarine, and add the cabbage, parsley, sugar, pepper, and broth. Cover the skillet, and cook the cabbage over moderate heat for about 12 minutes, basting it several times with the pan juices.
3. When the cabbage is nearly done, sprinkle it with caraway seeds. Serve the cabbage with a little of the pan juices.

BRASED RED CABBAGE   *6 servings*

Pierre Franey's Low-Calorie Gourmet is the happy source of this wonderful vegetable side dish, which can be eaten hot or cold.

> 1 tablespoon butter or margarine
> 1 large onion, chopped (1 cup)
> 1¼ pounds red cabbage (1 small head), cored and
>   thinly sliced
> 1 Golden Delicious apple, peeled, quartered,
>   cored, and thinly sliced
> ½ teaspoon salt, if desired
> ⅛ teaspoon freshly ground black pepper
> 1 tablespoon dark brown sugar
> 1 cup warm water
> 1 tablespoon red wine vinegar

1. Melt the butter or margarine in a large skillet, preferably nonstick, and add the onion. Sauté the onion for 1 minute.
2. Add the cabbage and apple, and cook the ingredients, stirring them occasionally, for another 5 minutes.
3. Meanwhile, combine the salt, pepper, brown sugar, water, and vinegar. Add this mixture to the sautéed cabbage mixture, and cook the cabbage, covered, over low heat for 30 minutes.
   Serve the cabbage hot or cold.

CARROT AND BROCCOLI STIR-FRY
4 servings

This dish, suggested by Nancy Jenkins, food writer for *The New York Times,* tastes as elegant as it looks, yet is deceptively simple to prepare. It goes especially well with broiled or baked chicken or fish and rice, but I'd like it any time, even with a sandwich. *Preparation tip:* Since this is a quick-cooking stir-fry, be sure to have all your ingredients ready before you turn on the stove. If leeks are not available, you can substitute ½ cup of sliced mild onion.

    1 tablespoon oil, preferably peanut
    1 teaspoon finely minced garlic
    1 teaspoon finely minced fresh ginger
    1 head broccoli, cut into flowerets (save the
      stems for another use)
    3 medium carrots, sliced thin
    3 medium leeks (white part only), sliced thin
    2 tablespoons broth
    1 teaspoon soy sauce (preferably
      reduced-sodium)
    1 tablespoon sesame seeds, toasted (see p. 412)
    1 teaspoon Oriental sesame oil

1. In a wok or large skillet, heat the oil briefly. Add the garlic and ginger, and stir-fry the ingredients for 15 seconds.
2. Add the broccoli, carrots, and leeks, tossing the vegetables to mix them well. Add the broth, cover the pan, and cook the vegetables for 3 minutes over medium heat.
3. Remove the cover, turn the heat up to high, and cook the vegetables, stirring them, 5 minutes longer or until the vegetables are tender-crisp.
4. When the vegetables are cooked, mix in the soy sauce. Remove the pan from the heat, and sprinkle the stir-fry with sesame seeds and sesame oil.

PINEAPPLE-POACHED CARROTS
3 servings

A slightly different way to prepare a common vegetable can turn it into a gourmet treat. This salt-free carrot recipe is simple, delicious, and likely to appeal to people of all ages.

 2 cups julienned carrots
¾ cup (6 ounces) pineapple juice
¾ teaspoon cinnamon
⅛ teaspoon nutmeg (optional)
Freshly ground black pepper to taste (a few
     turns of the peppermill)

In a medium saucepan, combine all the ingredients. Bring the mixture to a boil, reduce the heat, cover the pan, and simmer the carrots for about 10 minutes or until they are tender-crisp.

SAUTÉED COLLARD GREENS
3 to 4 servings

Although popular with American blacks, collards are practically unknown to most of us. Too bad, because this dark-green leafy vegetable is not only a terrific low-calorie source of calcium, beta-carotene (vitamin A), and dietary fiber, it is delicious even when cooked without a ham hock.

 1 pound fresh collard greens, washed, stems
     removed, cut into shreds
 2 quarts boiling water, salted if desired
 2 teaspoons butter or margarine
 1 teaspoon minced garlic
 2 tablespoons broth or water

1. Plunge the shredded greens into the boiling water for 3 minutes. Drain them immediately.
2. In a skillet, heat the butter or margarine, and cook the garlic, stirring it, for 30 seconds. Then add the blanched greens and the broth or water, tossing the ingredients well. Cover the pan, and cook the greens over low heat for 15 minutes, stirring them occasionally.

MEXICAN SUCCOTASH

4 to 6 servings

Here's a superb dish for any time of year, but especially when these vegetables are freshly harvested in mid- and late summer and the delicate flavors are too exquisite to disguise with salt. *Preparation tip:* In addition to using this recipe as a side dish, you might mix in ¼ cup of grated Parmesan after the dish is cooked and serve it over cooked pasta. If you use a high-protein pasta, with or without the cheese you've got a complete meal.

    1 large onion, very finely chopped (1 cup)
    1 tablespoon butter or margarine
1½ cups corn kernels, fresh (cut from about 3
      ears), or frozen
    1 pound zucchini, unpeeled, quartered
      lengthwise, and cut crosswise into ½-inch
      slices
    1 pint cherry tomatoes, halved (if small) or
      quartered *or* 1 28-ounce can plum tomatoes,
      drained and quartered
    1 teaspoon orégano, crumbled
Freshly ground black pepper to taste

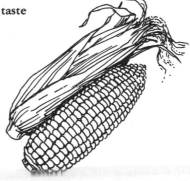

1. In a large skillet (preferably nonstick) that has a cover, sauté the onion in the butter or margarine until it is soft.
2. Add the corn, zucchini, tomatoes, orégano, and pepper, tossing the ingredients lightly to combine them. Cover the skillet, and cook the succotash over moderately low heat for 15 minutes, stirring it gently a few times.

MEXICAN-STYLE HOMINY

6 servings

The large white corn kernels of hominy are a visual and gustatory complement to the red tomatoes and green zucchini in this casserole-type vegetable dish, based on a recipe in *Betty Crocker's Mexican Cookbook.*

    1 medium onion, chopped (½ cup)
    1 teaspoon butter or margarine
    1 teaspoon oil
 1½ pounds zucchini (remove seeds if the squash is
        large), cut into chunks or slices ½ inch thick
    1 20-ounce can whole hominy, drained
    2 tomatoes, cored and diced
    2 tablespoons lime juice
    3 or more teaspoons chili powder (mild or hot
        or a combination), to taste
Salt, if desired, to taste
Freshly ground black pepper to taste

1. In a large, deep skillet or wide saucepan, sauté the onion in the butter or margarine and the oil until it is soft.
2. Add the remaining ingredients. Heat the ingredients over medium heat until they bubble, and cook them, uncovered, stirring several times, until the zucchini is barely tender, about 10 minutes.

THE BEST RATATOUILLE

about 2½ quarts

Ratatouille—a well-seasoned vegetable "stew" of eggplant, zucchini, onions, peppers, and tomatoes—is a versatile dish that should be part of every cook's repertoire. In addition to its time-honored service as a side dish, it can be used as a hot topping for chicken breasts, fish fillets, pita (as in Ratatouille Pizza) or a filling for crêpes (see pp. 305 and 450), or a cold dip or an appetizer or a salad accompaniment to cottage cheese or a sandwich. I've tried many versions, but this is the one I like the best. *Preparation tip:* Ratatouille freezes well, so when you find a recipe you like, it pays to make a double batch and store the extra in containers of varying sizes (from ½ cup to 3 cups) for later use. But since seasonings tend to lose their zip during freezer storage, consider adding them when you reheat a frozen batch or adding more to an already seasoned recipe. The salt sprinkled on the eggplant is needed to extract the bitter juices. To keep salt to a minimum, the eggplant is rinsed after it has drained. For a Middle Eastern version, substitute 1 teaspoon of ground cumin, 1 teaspoon of turmeric and ½ teaspoon of coriander for the thyme, orégano, and basil.

1½ pounds eggplant (if possible, use 2 small
   eggplants), unpeeled
Salt
¼ cup olive oil, divided
2 large onions, thickly sliced
1 large green pepper, seeded and cut into 2-inch
   strips ¼ inch thick
1 large sweet red pepper, seeded and cut into
   2-inch strips ¼ inch thick
1 tablespoon finely minced garlic (3 large
   cloves)
2½ pounds ripe tomatoes, peeled, seeded, and
   coarsely chopped
1½ pounds zucchini (small or seeded, if large),
   halved lengthwise and cut crosswise into
   ½-inch slices
½ teaspoon thyme
½ teaspoon orégano
2 teaspoons minced fresh basil, *or* ½ teaspoon
   dried basil
½ teaspoon freshly ground black pepper
¼ teaspoon salt, if desired
⅛ teaspoon cayenne
2 tablespoons minced fresh parsley

1. Cut the eggplant into ¾-inch cubes. Place the diced eggplant in a colander,
   sprinkle the eggplant well with salt, weight the pieces down with a plate or
   bowl, and let the eggplant drain for 30 minutes.
2. Heat 1 tablespoon of the oil in a large, heavy skillet or Dutch oven. Add
   the onions and green and red peppers, and sauté them until the onions are
   translucent. Add the garlic and tomatoes. Cook the vegetables, stirring
   them, for about 3 minutes. Transfer the mixture to a bowl, and wipe out
   the pan.
3. Heat another tablespoon of oil in the pan, and sauté the zucchini for about
   10 minutes. Add the zucchini to the other vegetables in the bowl, leaving
   behind as much oil as possible.
4. Rinse, drain, and dry the diced eggplant with paper towels. Add the remain-
   ing 2 tablespoons oil to the pan, and sauté the eggplant for about 10
   minutes.
5. Return the reserved vegetables to the pan, and mix them well with the
   eggplant. Heat the ratatouille, and cook it for about 5 minutes. Stir in the
   thyme, orégano, basil, pepper, salt, cayenne, and parsley.

STEAMED KALE

4 servings

Here is a cancer-protecting, vitamin-packed vegetable that deserves to be better known in this country. Half a cup of cooked kale provides nearly the entire day's recommended vitamin C intake plus twice the vitamin A and a fair amount of calcium—all for only 22 calories! This garlicky recipe adds only a bit of fat to each serving.

  1 pound kale
  2 teaspoons olive oil
  2 large cloves garlic, minced (2 teaspoons)
  ¼ teaspoon salt, if desired
  ¼ cup water

  1. Wash the kale well, but do not dry it. Cut off and discard the tough stems (or chop them and use them), slice the leaves once down the middle, and then cut them crosswise into 1-inch-wide strips.
  2. Heat the oil briefly in a pot that is large enough to accommodate the kale. Add the garlic, and cook it, stirring it, for 15 seconds (do not let it brown). Add the salt and water, and bring the mixture to a boil. Add the kale, and toss it to mix it well.
  3. Cover the pot, and steam the kale for about 6 minutes or until the kale is just tender but still bright green.

BRAISED KOHLRABI

4 to 6 servings

This little-known but worth-knowing member of the cabbage family can be prepared simply and flavorfully in broth.

  1 tablespoon butter or margarine
  1½ pounds small kohlrabies, peeled and cut into
      ¼-inch julienne strips
  2 cups chicken broth, preferably homemade
Freshly ground black pepper to taste

  1. In a saucepan, heat the butter or margarine, and sauté the kohlrabi strips over medium-high heat, stirring them often, until they are slightly golden (about 5 minutes).
  2. Add the broth, bring the mixture to a boil, reduce the heat, and simmer the vegetable, partially covered, for about 15 or 20 minutes, or until it is just tender. Serve the kohlrabi as is, sprinkled with pepper, or uncover the pot and cook the vegetable at high heat for another 5 minutes or until the liquid has evaporated.

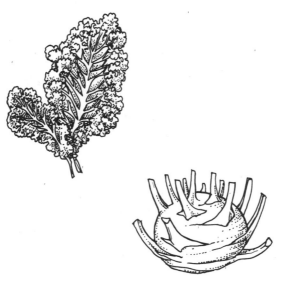

CURRIED LENTILS

6 servings

This is one of my favorite "bean" dishes. I usually make enough to freeze 1-serving portions, which I eat for lunch whenever I have some leftover cooked rice. The combination is a complete protein and a meal that really sticks to the ribs. *Preparation tip:* Try serving this with cooked white or brown rice and sliced lemon for garnish.

1 cup lentils
3 cups broth or water
2 large onions, chopped fine (2 cups), divided
Salt, if desired, to taste (omit if using salted
    broth)
1 tablespoon oil, preferably olive
1 clove garlic, minced (1 teaspoon)
1 teaspoon curry powder

1. In a medium saucepan, combine the lentils, broth or water, half the onions, and salt. Bring the ingredients to a boil, reduce the heat, cover the pan, and simmer the lentils until they are tender, about 30 to 40 minutes. Drain the lentils.
2. While the lentils are cooking, heat the oil in a skillet, add the remaining onions and the garlic, and sauté the vegetables until they begin to brown. Add them to the cooked lentils along with the curry, combining the ingredients well. Cover the pan, and heat the lentils a few minutes longer.

MILLET SUPREME

4 servings

A plethora of vegetables turns millet into a hearty side dish with a delicate curry flavor. The recipe is derived from *The Great Garlic Cookbook* by Barbara Friedlander and Bob Cato. Friedlander is a creative nutrition specialist for the New York City public school lunch program. *Preparation tip:* If you like hot foods, add more curry. You can also turn this dish into a complete meal by adding some cooked cubed chicken or shrimp just before the end of step 3.

   1 tablespoon olive oil
   1 medium onion, halved lengthwise and sliced
     fine crosswise
   2 stalks celery, diced (1 cup)
   1 green pepper, cored and sliced thin
   2 carrots, sliced fine
   2 small zucchinis, cut into ⅓-inch slices
   1 tomato, cored and chopped
   1 cup millet
   3 cloves garlic, minced (1 tablespoon)
   1 teaspoon minced fresh ginger
   2 cups boiling broth
   1 teaspoon curry powder, or more, to taste
   ¼ teaspoon salt, if desired (omit if the broth is
     salted)
   ⅛ teaspoon freshly ground black pepper

1. Heat the oil briefly in a large skillet that has a tight cover. Add the onion, celery, green pepper, carrots, zucchinis, and tomato. Sauté the vegetables, stirring them often, for about 5 minutes.
2. Meanwhile, in a dry skillet over medium-low heat, toast the millet lightly, stirring it constantly so that it does not burn.
3. Add the garlic and ginger to the skillet containing the vegetables, stir the mixture, and cook it for another minute. Add the toasted millet, broth, curry, salt, and pepper. Stir the ingredients to mix them well. Cover the pan, and simmer the mixture over low heat for about 15 minutes or until all the liquid is absorbed.

OAT GROAT PILAF

4 servings

A crunchy and tasty change of pace from rice, oat groats (available in most natural foods stores) are also more nutritious. And they help to lower choles-terol. *Preparation tip:* Canned broth is too salty. If you have no homemade or salt-free commercial broth, dilute the canned broth with an equal amount of water.

2 teaspoons oil
1 cup oat groats, washed and drained
2 teaspoons butter or margarine
1 medium onion, minced (½ cup)
1 cup sliced mushrooms (about ¼ pound)
2 cups chicken or vegetable broth
¼ teaspoon freshly ground black pepper
Salt, if desired, to taste
2 tablespoons minced fresh parsley

1. Heat the oil in a heavy, medium saucepan, and stir in the groats. Cook the groats, stirring them, for about 3 minutes to toast them.
2. Add the butter or margarine and the onion, and sauté the mixture for about 3 minutes, until the onion is soft. Add the mushrooms, and cook the mixture for another 5 minutes or so, until the mushrooms are wilted.
3. Add the broth, pepper, and salt (but only if the broth is salt-free). Bring the mixture to a boil, reduce the heat, cover the pan, and simmer the pilaf for about 40 minutes, stirring it occasionally.
4. Remove the pilaf from the heat, and stir in the parsley.

PEPERONATA

6 to 8 servings

Here's a colorful Italian vegetable dish, especially ideal for the days of Indian summer, that can be served hot or cold as a vegetable side dish. *Preparation tip:* The recipe can be made with sweet peppers of any persuasion: red, green, or yellow (I use all three when I can get them—I consider the red ones essential for maximum natural sweetness). You can also omit the hot peppers or use more or less of them, to taste.

    1 tablespoon olive oil
    4 teaspoons minced garlic (about 4 large cloves)
    2 large onions, chopped (about 2 cups)
    2 fresh chili peppers (red or green), halved
        lengthwise, seeded and sliced crosswise (wear
        rubber gloves)
    6 sweet peppers, cut into strips ½ inch wide
    3 tomatoes, cored and coarsely chopped
    ¼ teaspoon salt, if desired, or to taste
    Freshly ground black pepper to taste

1. In a large, deep skillet that has a cover, heat the oil for 10 seconds, and add the garlic and then the onions and chili peppers. Sauté the vegetables for 1 minute.
2. Add the sweet pepper strips, stir the vegetables, cover the pan, and simmer the vegetables over low heat, stirring them occasionally, for about 10 minutes or until the peppers are soft but not brown.
3. Add the tomatoes, and cook the mixture, stirring it often, over moderately low heat, without covering the pan, for another 5 minutes. Season the peperonata with salt and pepper to taste. Serve the peperonata hot, chilled, or at room temperature.

PUMPKIN AND "PEAS"

6 servings

The "peas" in this dish are lentils, a high-protein, quick-cooking, tasty food. For a complete vegetarian meal, try it with pilaf (rice cooked in a light broth) and yogurt.

    1 tablespoon butter or margarine
    1 medium onion, finely chopped (½ cup)
    1 cup lentils
    3 cups water
    ¾ pound pumpkin, peeled and cut into 1-inch
        cubes (about 3 cups)

1 tablespoon lemon juice
1 tablespoon minced fresh parsley
½ teaspoon ground ginger
¼ teaspoon salt, if desired, or to taste
⅛ teaspoon freshly ground black pepper
Generous pinch ground cumin
⅓ cup sliced scallion tops

1. In a large saucepan, melt the butter or margarine, and sauté the onion over medium heat until it is soft.
2. Add the lentils, stirring to combine them with the onion, and pour in the water (it should cover the lentils). Bring the mixture to a boil, reduce the heat, cover the pan, and simmer the lentils, stirring them occasionally, for 20 minutes.
3. Add the pumpkin, lemon juice, parsley, ginger, salt, pepper, and cumin, stirring to combine the ingredients well. Cover the pan, and cook the mixture for another 15 minutes or until the pumpkin is tender. Before serving, toss the mixture with the scallion tops.

PUMPKIN AND PARMESAN
4 servings

Try this colorful and nutritious vegetable dish as a side dish with cottage cheese, as well as with any simple fish, fowl, or meat entrée. Or sprinkle it with several tablespoons of toasted sunflower seeds, and eat it as a luncheon or light supper entrée. *Preparation tip:* Winter squash can substitute for the pumpkin.

1 tablespoon olive oil
1 tablespoon minced garlic (3 large cloves)
4 cups peeled, diced pumpkin (½-inch cubes)
1 tablespoon flour
½ cup grated Parmesan
Salt, if desired, to taste (omit if cheese is salty)
¼ teaspoon freshly ground black pepper
¼ cup minced fresh parsley

1. Heat the oil in a skillet, and sauté the garlic over low heat, stirring it, for 30 seconds. Transfer the garlic to a medium bowl.
2. Add the pumpkin, flour, cheese, salt, and pepper to the garlic, and toss the ingredients to combine them well. Transfer the mixture to a greased shallow 1½-quart casserole dish.
3. Bake the pumpkin uncovered in a 325° for 1½ hours. Sprinkle the pumpkin with parsley before serving it.

RICE WITH COLLARDS

4 servings

This recipe from *The Victory Garden Cookbook,* is a tasty way to add nutrients to a rice side dish. By combining the rice and greens, you can get two vegetables for the work of one.

2 cups broth (chicken or vegetable)
1 cup long-grain rice (white or brown)
1 teaspoon butter or margarine
3 cups chopped fresh collard greens
Freshly ground black pepper to taste
Salt, if desired, to taste (omit if the broth has
      salt)

1. Bring the broth to a boil in a medium saucepan. Add the rice and the butter or margarine, stir the rice, and add the collards in three batches, stirring the mixture after each addition.
2. Return the mixture to a boil, reduce the heat, cover the pan, and simmer the mixture for 20 minutes (35 minutes for brown rice) or until the rice is done. Add pepper and salt, if needed.

WILD RICE WITH INDIAN NUTS

6 to 8 servings

Although the ingredients are costly, this is a scrumptious side dish, elegant enough for holiday fare. Wild rice expands tremendously (to about 4 times its original volume), so this recipe will go far. *Preparation tip:* Indian nuts are simply a larger version of pine nuts, with which they can be interchanged.

2 cups beef broth
1½ cups water (or more)
1⅓ cups wild rice (½ pound)
½ cup currants
Freshly ground black pepper to taste
½ cup Indian or pine nuts (pignoli)
1 tablespoon butter or margarine
1 medium onion, finely chopped (½ cup)

1. Bring the broth and water to a boil in a large saucepan (3 quarts or larger). Add the wild rice, currants, and pepper. Reduce the heat to low, cover the pan, and simmer the ingredients for 1 hour or longer, or until the liquid is absorbed and the rice is tender. Add more water, if needed, to cook the rice fully.

2. Meanwhile, in a small skillet, toast the Indian nuts, tossing them constantly, until they turn golden. Remove the nuts from the pan, and set them aside.
3. In the same skillet, melt the butter or margarine, and sauté the onion for about 3 minutes or until it is soft. When the rice is done, toss the onion and nuts with it, and serve.

MASHED RUTABAGA

6 servings

Rutabaga, sometimes called a "swede" or yellow turnip, is nearly always sold with a waxy coating to prevent spoilage during prolonged storage. It is a tasty and nutritious vegetable that is not well known to most Americans. Here's a good way to get acquainted.

1 2-pound rutabaga, peeled, cut into 1-inch cubes
1 cup skim or low-fat milk
2 teaspoons butter or margarine (optional)
Nutmeg to taste

1. Place the cubes of rutabaga in a medium saucepan, and add cold water to cover. Bring the water to a boil, reduce the heat, and cook the rutabaga for about 20 minutes or until it is tender. Drain the rutabaga.
2. Purée the cooked rutabaga in a food processor, blender, or food mill.
3. Heat the milk and the butter or margarine, if desired, in the saucepan. Stir in the rutabaga and nutmeg, and heat the vegetable, stirring it, for 1 to 2 minutes.

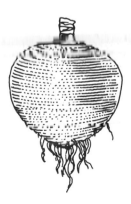

SWEET POTATOES WITH APPLES   *6 servings*

This product of the fall harvest is good any time of the year except during the heat of summer. It is almost sweet enough (thanks to the fruit and juice) to be a dessert. It would be lovely with that Thanksgiving turkey, decorated perhaps with a string of cranberries. Or serve it as a side dish with cottage cheese.

   3 Delicious apples, peeled, halved, cored, and
     very thinly sliced
   1 tablespoon lemon juice
1½ pounds sweet potatoes or yams, peeled, halved
     lengthwise, and very thinly sliced
   ¼ cup apple juice or cider
   1 tablespoon butter or margarine, melted

1. Toss the apple slices with the lemon juice.
2. In a 1½-quart baking dish or casserole, arrange layers of the potatoes and apples. Save the most attractive potato slices for the top layer, arranging them in a pinwheel design.
3. Pour the apple juice or cider and the melted butter or margarine over all. Cover the casserole, and bake it in a preheated 350° oven for 1 hour. Uncover it, and bake it for another 15 minutes.

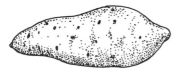

SWISS CHARD SAUTÉ

3 to 4 servings

If you have a little patch of garden, Swiss chard is one of the most satisfying vegetables to grow. Rich in nutrients and flavor, it can be used as a substitute for spinach in many dishes. But it is also good on its own, as follows.

> 2 teaspoons oil
> 1 to 2 teaspoons minced garlic, to taste
> ½ cup sliced leeks (white part) *or* 1 very small
>   onion, halved lengthwise and thinly sliced
> ⅔ cup sliced celery
> 1 tablespoon broth or water
> 4 cups coarsely chopped Swiss chard
> Freshly ground black pepper to taste
> Salt, if desired, to taste

1. Heat the oil in a large skillet (preferably nonstick), and add the garlic, leeks or onion, and celery. Sauté the vegetables, stirring them, for about 3 minutes.
2. Add the broth or water and the Swiss chard. Season the mixture with pepper and salt, stirring the ingredients to combine them well. Cover the pan, and simmer the mixture, stirring it occasionally, over low heat for about 5 minutes or until the chard is wilted and tender.

PEPPERY TURNIP TREAT

4 servings

I'm one of those odd people with a passion for turnips. This recipe, compliments of Bert Greene in *Greene on Greens,* could make turnip lovers of us all. I cut the fat and omitted salt, and the result was still fabulous. *Preparation tip.* You can adjust the hotness of the dish by using more or less pepper.

> 2 teaspoons butter or margarine
> 2 tablespoons honey
> 1 pound turnips, peeled, finely diced (¼-inch
>   cubes)
> ¼ to ½ teaspoon freshly ground black pepper
> 1 tablespoon minced fresh parsley (optional)

In a medium saucepan, melt the butter or margarine and honey over moderately low heat. Add the turnips and pepper. Cover the pan, and cook the turnips until they are tender, stirring them once, about 12 minutes (the turnips should brown lightly). Sprinkle the turnips with parsley.

PURÉED TURNIPS AND POTATOES   *4 to 6 servings*

Bert Greene of *Greene on Greens* has done it again. A delicate orange-and-ginger seasoning brings out the best in the turnips. *Preparation tip:* The purée can be prepared in advance through step 1 and reheated at serving time with the seasonings.

  1 pound turnips, peeled, cubed
½ pound potatoes, peeled, cubed
¼ cup orange juice
  1 tablespoon dark brown sugar
⅛ teaspoon ground ginger
  1 tablespoon butter or margarine
¼ teaspoon salt, if desired
Freshly ground black pepper, to taste

1. In a medium saucepan, cook the turnips and potatoes in boiling water (lightly salted, if desired) until they are tender, about 15 minutes. Drain the vegetables, transfer them to a food processor or food mill, and purée them.
2. Return the purée to the saucepan. Add the juice, sugar, ginger, and butter or margarine. Cook the purée, stirring it often, over moderately low heat until the purée is heated through (about 5 minutes if the purée was warm to start with). Add salt and pepper to taste.

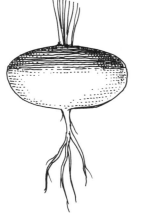

SIDE-DISH SALADS

Salads, whether served as main dishes (see pp. 402–417) or side dishes, are ideal foods for health- and weight-conscious people. Most salads are what I call "slow foods"—like soup, they take a while to eat, giving your body a chance to register its satisfaction before you have a chance to overeat. In addition, salads usually require a lot of chewing, which adds to their satiety value. Unfortunately, too many salads are "spoiled" from a nutritional and caloric perspective by being drowned in fatty (and often salty) dressings. In traditional salads, a single serving may have as much as 200 calories worth of fat in the dressing and as much as 500 milligrams of sodium. Thus, all the salads you'll find in this book are dressed with low-fat mixtures, and most, except where noted, are also low in salt. Once you get used to using only 1 or 2 tablespoons of oil in a dressing that serves four, you may find it hard to go back to the ⅓ to ½ cup you once enjoyed. You'll resent salads that are too greasy or so overdressed that the flavor of the main ingredients is disguised.

APPLE SALAD

4 1-cup servings

If and when you should ever tire of traditional salads, this fruit salad, based on one devised by Cornell University's Division of Nutritional Sciences, is a delightful change of pace.

SALAD
- 2 large Red Delicious apples, cored but unpeeled and cut into chunks
- ⅔ cup crushed pineapple, drained (or fresh pineapple, minced), juice reserved
- ⅓ cup celery, diced
- 2 tablespoons raisins

DRESSING
- 3 tablespoons plain low-fat yogurt
- 2 teaspoons mayonnaise
- 1 tablespoon pineapple juice (reserved from pineapple)
- ⅛ teaspoon cinnamon

1. In a medium bowl, combine the salad ingredients.
2. In a small bowl, combine the dressing ingredients, and blend the dressing with the fruit mixture.

NUTTY ASPARAGUS SALAD

4 servings

Aptly named, this salad not only has nuts in it, but it should appeal to those who are nuts about asparagus. *Preparation tip:* Any type of salad green or combination of greens will do, but my favorite for this salad is Boston lettuce.

SALAD
1 pound fresh asparagus, steamed for about 5 minutes (until tender-crisp) and chilled
½ cup chopped walnuts
2 grapefruits, peeled and separated into sections
3 cups salad greens

DRESSING
2 tablespoons olive or salad oil
2 tablespoons raspberry vinegar or wine vinegar
2 tablespoons fresh lemon juice
1½ teaspoons brown sugar
Freshly ground black pepper to taste

1. Cut the cooked asparagus into 1-inch lengths. Place them in a salad bowl, and add the walnuts, grapefruit sections, and greens.
2. In a small bowl, combine all the dressing ingredients. Add the dressing to the salad just before serving.

AVOCADO SALSA

4 servings

A cocktail salsa, a Spanish/Mexican delight, has already been offered (see p. 295). Here is a slightly richer version (the avocado is fatty) you can serve as a salad course on a lettuce leaf or a bed of greens.

SALAD
1 ripe avocado, peeled and diced
4 small tomatoes, diced
1 small red onion, diced
1 green pepper, seeded and diced
1 fresh or canned jalapeño pepper or green chili, finely diced (wear rubber gloves) (optional)

DRESSING
1 clove garlic, minced
Salt, if desired, to taste
2 tablespoons red wine vinegar
1 tablespoon olive or salad oil
4 drops hot pepper sauce (Tabasco)

1. In a medium bowl, combine the salad ingredients.
2. In a cup or small bowl, mash the garlic with salt. Add the vinegar, oil, and pepper sauce. Pour the dressing over the salad, and toss the salad to combine the ingredients. Serve the salad chilled or at room temperature.

CRUNCHY BARLEY SALAD

4 to 8 servings
(4 cups)

I love this salad so much that I have actually gotten a bellyache from eating too much of it! *Preparation tip:* Though described here to be served chilled, it can also be eaten warm: mix the vegetables with the barley while the grain is still warm, and serve the salad immediately.

SALAD
1⅔ cups chicken broth (canned or homemade)
1⅓ cups water
1 cup barley, rinsed

1 cup diced green pepper (1 large)
1 cup thinly sliced carrot (1 large)
½ cup diced red onion (1 medium)
½ cup thinly sliced radishes
¼ cup chopped fresh dill *or* 1 tablespoon dried dillweed
¼ cup chopped fresh parsley (optional)

DRESSING
1 large clove garlic, peeled and flattened
½ teaspoon salt, if desired
¼ teaspoon freshly ground black pepper
2 tablespoons olive or salad oil
3 tablespoons red wine vinegar

1. In a heavy, medium saucepan, bring the broth and water to a boil, and add the barley. When the boiling resumes, reduce the heat to low, cover the pan, and simmer the barley for 40 to 45 minutes or until it is tender (check after about 30 minutes, and add more water if the barley is dry).
2. While the barley cooks, in a large bowl whisk together all the dressing ingredients.
3. When the barley is done, remove the garlic from the dressing, and add the barley to the dressing while the barley is still hot. Toss the ingredients to mix them well. Cover the mixture, and refrigerate it for 1 hour or longer.
4. Before serving, add the green pepper, carrot, onion, radishes, dill, and parsley. Toss the salad well.

GREEN BEAN AND CHICKPEA SALAD

6 to 8 servings

As well as being a delicious and unusual combination of ingredients, this salad easy to prepare and high in protein.

SALAD
1 pound green beans, trimmed and cut into 2-inch lengths
1 16-ounce can chickpeas (garbanzos), drained and rinsed
¼ cup chopped onion

DRESSING
2 tablespoons red wine vinegar
1 tablespoon chopped fresh basil *or* 1 teaspoon dried basil
¼ teaspoon salt, if desired
¼ teaspoon freshly ground black pepper
1 large clove garlic, crushed
1½ tablespoons olive or salad oil

1. Steam the green beans until they are tender-crisp, about 5 minutes.
2. Place the beans, chickpeas, and onion in a large bowl.
3. In a small bowl, combine all the dressing ingredients. Add the dressing to the bean mixture, tossing the ingredients well. Chill the salad for 1 hour or longer before serving.

CHINESE BEAN SALAD

6 servings

Faced with an August bumper crop of green beans and a pot-luck lunch to attend, I threw together this simple salad. It drew raves and requests for the recipe, which luckily I had written down.

SALAD
1 pound green beans, trimmed and cut into 2-inch lengths

2 tablespoons lightly toasted sesame seeds (see p. 412)

DRESSING
1 *tablespoon* finely minced fresh ginger
1 teaspoon finely minced garlic (1 large clove)
1 tablespoon salad oil
1 tablespoon mild vinegar (e.g., rice or berry vinegar)
1 teaspoon Oriental sesame oil
1 to 2 teaspoons reduced-sodium soy sauce, to taste
¼ teaspoon sugar
⅛ teaspoon freshly ground black or white pepper

1. Steam the beans over boiling water for 4 to 5 minutes, or blanch them in boiling water for 2 to 3 minutes (the beans should be crunchy but not hard), and cool them immediately under cold water to stop the cooking. Transfer them to a serving bowl.
2. In a small bowl, combine all the dressing ingredients. Pour the dressing over the beans, and toss to coat them well. Chill the beans until serving time.
3. Just before serving the beans, stir in the sesame seeds.

DILLY BEAN SALAD

4 servings

All I can say is "Yum"! I love beans and I love dill. And when you can get both garden-fresh, this is the salad to prepare.

SALAD
- 1 pound small green beans, steamed tender-crisp (about 5 minutes)
- 2 tablespoons snipped fresh dill
- 6 scallions, sliced, with some tops

DRESSING
- 2 tablespoons olive or salad oil
- 1 tablespoon red wine vinegar
- 1 teaspoon Dijon mustard
- Salt, if desired, to taste
- Freshly ground black pepper, to taste

1. In a medium serving bowl, combine the cooked beans, dill, and scallions.
2. In a small bowl, whisk together all the dressing ingredients. Add the dressing to the bean mixture, and mix the ingredients well. Serve the salad at room temperature.

BLACK-EYED PEA SALAD   *6 servings*

If you're having trouble convincing some family members to eat dried beans and peas, perhaps black-eyed peas are the place to start. They are adorable; you might even be able to convince small children that the beans are looking at them! While this salad may be a bit too snappy for little ones, adult appeal is fairly certain. It is adapted from a recipe devised by Alabama farm wife Janie Carpenter, who says it can be turned into a main course simply by adding ¾ cup each of cubed cooked ham and cubed cheese. *Preparation tip:* Note that the beans should marinate overnight.

DRESSING
  2 tablespoons olive or salad oil
  3 tablespoons red wine vinegar
  1 medium onion, chopped (½ cup)
  ½ cup minced fresh parsley
  1 large clove garlic, crushed
  1 teaspoon dried basil, crumbled
  ½ teaspoon orégano, crumbled
  ¼ teaspoon dry mustard
  ¼ teaspoon freshly ground black pepper
  ⅛ teaspoon hot red pepper flakes, or to taste

SALAD
  ½ pound black-eyed peas, cleaned, rinsed, and cooked without salt until tender but firm (see p. 103)
  Green pepper rings for garnish

1. In a bowl, combine all the dressing ingredients. Pour the dressing over the warm cooked peas, which have been placed in a large bowl, and toss the salad gently. Cover the peas, and refrigerate them for at least 8 hours or overnight, tossing them once.
2. To serve, line the edge of a large platter with the pepper rings, and heap the beans in the middle.

MUNG BEAN SPROUT SALAD   *6 to 8 servings*

This great-tasting salad is a sight for sore eyes as well as a treat for dulled taste buds. I have often served it at a buffet supper, Oriental or otherwise. Try it with the kind of sandwiches you might usually serve with coleslaw. *Preparation tip:* Mung bean sprouts are the type usually sold as "bean sprouts" in produce markets. You can also sprout your own (see p. 110).

SALAD

4 cups fresh bean sprouts
1 red sweet pepper, slivered
2 scallions, with tops, chopped

2 tablespoons sesame seeds,
lightly toasted (see p. 412)

DRESSING

3 tablespoons rice or wine vinegar
1 tablespoon soy sauce (preferably
reduced-sodium)
2 tablespoons salad oil
1 teaspoon Oriental sesame oil
(optional)
Freshly ground black pepper to
taste

1. Combine the sprouts, sweet pepper, and scallions in a medium bowl.
2. In a small bowl, mix the dressing ingredients, and combine the dressing
with the vegetable mixture, tossing the salad to mix the ingredients well.
3. Before serving, add the sesame seeds and toss again.

MUSTARDY BEET SALAD

4 servings

I was a peculiar child who loved beets and spinach but loathed peas and carrots.
Though my tastes in vegetables have broadened considerably, beets, hot or
cold, still rank among my favorites. Hence, I offer you two beet salads, one
seasoned with mustard and the other with horseradish.

SALAD

4 medium beets, unpeeled, *or* 1
16-ounce can sliced beets,
drained

DRESSING

2 tablespoons lemon juice
2 tablespoons Dijon mustard
1 tablespoon cider vinegar
1 tablespoon salad oil
1 teaspoon sugar
2 tablespoons chopped fresh dill
or 2 teaspoons dried dillweed
1 tablespoon chopped fresh
parsley (optional)
Dash freshly ground black pepper

1. Cook the beets in water to cover until they are just tender (about 1 hour),
peel them, and slice them crosswise.
2. Combine all the dressing ingredients in a medium bowl.
3. Add the beets to the bowl and stir them gently to coat them with the
dressing. Chill the beets for about 1 hour before serving them.

BEET SALAD IN HORSERADISH DRESSING

6 or more servings

In addition to the usual way to eat salads, this oil-free one can be used as the garnish on a green salad. For me, it sometimes takes the place of salad dressing, perhaps with a little of the beet marinade as added dressing.

SALAD
3 pounds beets, unpeeled, cooked until tender

DRESSING
¼ cup cider vinegar
¼ cup sugar
2 tablespoons drained bottled horseradish
¼ teaspoon caraway seeds
Salt, if desired, to taste

1. When the beets are cool enough to handle, peel them, slice them, and then cut them into julienne strips about ¼ inch wide.
2. In a medium bowl (not metal), combine all the dressing ingredients. Add the beet strips to the dressing, cover the bowl, and marinate the beets in the refrigerator for several hours or overnight.

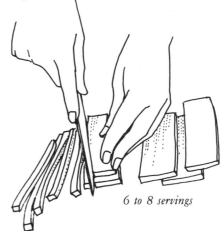

JANE'S TABBOULI

(Bulgur Salad)

6 to 8 servings

When asked to bring something to a picnic or cocktail party, my first choice is tabbouli, a bulgur and parsley salad from the Mideast. My name is on this one because I use unique seasonings to give the tabbouli a little kick. It is usually eaten on pieces of pita, but can also be scooped up with a vegetable like celery or pieces of sweet pepper as well as eaten with a fork like ordinary salads. *Preparation tip:* Bulgur can be found in supermarkets (check near the rice or hot cereals) as well as in natural food and specialty stores. Both the salad ingredients and the dressing can be prepared ahead separately and mixed together about an hour before serving.

SALAD
- 1 cup bulgur (cracked fine or medium)
- 2 cups boiling water
- 2 tomatoes, finely diced
- 1 bunch scallions (about 6), with tops, finely chopped
- 1 cup finely chopped fresh parsley, or more, to taste
- 3 tablespoons chopped fresh mint leaves *or* 2 teaspoons dried mint

DRESSING
- ¼ cup lemon juice
- 2 tablespoons olive or salad oil
- ½ teaspoon salt, if desired
- ¼ teaspoon (or more) freshly ground black pepper
- ¼ teaspoon orégano (ground or crumbled leaves)
- ¼ teaspoon ground cumin
- Dash allspice (optional)
- Dash coriander (optional)

1. In a medium bowl, soak the bulgur in the boiling water for 1 hour. Drain the bulgur well, pressing out the excess water through a fine strainer or cloth.
2. Add the tomatoes, scallions, parsley, and mint to the bulgur. Combine the ingredients well.
3. Mix all the dressing ingredients in a small bowl. About 1 hour or less before serving, add the dressing to the bulgur mixture, and toss the salad to coat the ingredients thoroughly.

FRUITED SLAW

8 to 10 servings

Cabbage is one of the most versatile and underrated salad ingredients. This nutrient-rich, low-fat salad from *Gourmet* magazine is surprisingly delicious, even to people who say they don't like cabbage. The tart yogurt is a nice contrast to the sweet fruit and spares you the high-fat content of mayonnaise. *Preparation tip:* Be sure to grate the lemon rind before you squeeze out the juice.

SALAD
- 4 firm ripe pears (e.g., Bosc), peeled and diced
- 2 firm tart apples (e.g., Granny Smith), peeled and diced
- 2 tablespoons lemon juice
- 3 cups shredded green cabbage
- ½ cup raisins or currants

DRESSING
- 1 cup plain low-fat yogurt
- 1 teaspoon grated lemon rind
- 1 teaspoon lemon juice
- 1 teaspoon honey

1. In a large bowl, toss the diced pears and apples with the lemon juice.
2. Add the cabbage and raisins or currants, and combine the ingredients well.
3. In a small bowl, whisk together all the dressing ingredients, and add the dressing to the slaw. Toss the slaw, and chill it for about 1 hour.

CURRIED COLESLAW

4 to 6 servings

Several people who tried this slaw at a recipe-tasting party asked for doggie bags. To their chagrin, none of the coleslaw was left at the end of the meal. It is a simple low-fat, high-flavor twist on traditional coleslaw and takes no longer to prepare.

SALAD

4 cups shredded green cabbage
   (about 10 ounces)
½ cup shredded carrot (1 medium)
½ cup finely slivered green pepper
   (½ large pepper)

DRESSING

¼ cup cider vinegar
4 teaspoons mayonnaise
1 tablespoon minced onion
2 teaspoons lemon juice
2 teaspoons sugar
½ teaspoon curry powder, or
   more, to taste
¼ teaspoon celery seed
⅛ teaspoon salt, if desired
Freshly ground black pepper to
   taste

1. In a medium bowl, combine the cabbage, carrot, and green pepper.
2. In a small bowl, combine all the dressing ingredients, mixing them well, and pour the dressing over the cabbage mixture. Toss the slaw, and chill it for at least 2 hours, tossing it again just before serving.

CRANBERRY SALAD MOLD

8 to 12 servings

An Ocean Spray promotion was the inspiration for this beautiful, delicious, fruited salad, which for years has been a frequent contribution from me to pot-luck parties as well as an accompaniment to home meals of roasted fowl. It is a great dish to serve at Thanksgiving and Christmas dinners, for example. It is wonderful with a turkey sandwich. Or with cottage cheese or yogurt, it makes a nutritionally complete breakfast or lunch. *Preparation tip:* If you're thinking about cutting back on the sugar, remember that cranberries have no natural sweetness. I never use a dressing, but if you wish, you can make one by combining plain yogurt with lemon juice, sugar, salt, pepper, and a little oil.

3 cups fresh cranberries, rinsed and drained
   (1 12-ounce package)
1 cup water
1 cup sugar
3 envelopes (3 scant tablespoons) unflavored
   gelatin

2 cups orange juice
1 cup diced celery
1 cup shredded carrots
½ cup raisins or currants
1 cup chopped peeled apples

1. In a large saucepan, combine the cranberries, water, and sugar. Bring the mixture to a boil, reduce the heat, and simmer the cranberries for 5 minutes.
2. In a small bowl, sprinkle the gelatin onto the orange juice to soften it, and then add the gelatin-juice mixture to the hot cranberry mixture. Cool the mixture, and then chill it until it becomes syrupy.
3. Fold in the celery, carrots, raisins or currants, and apples. Pour the mixture into an oiled 6-cup ring mold. Chill the mold until the salad is firm.
4. To serve, unmold the salad by dipping the mold into lukewarm (not hot) water for about 10 seconds. Tap the mold to loosen its contents, and invert the salad onto a platter.

EGYPTIAN FÊTE SALAD

6 to 8 servings

I have my friend Margaret Shryer of Minneapolis to thank for this one. It is especially lovely on a hot summer day, when the local cucumber crop is in. *Preparation tip:* To reduce the salt content of the feta, cut the cheese into chunks, and soak them in cold water for 1 hour.

SALAD
2 large cucumbers, peeled
Salt

2 tablespoons chopped fresh mint

DRESSING
6 ounces feta
¼ cup finely chopped scallions
1 tablespoons lemon juice or white wine vinegar
1 tablespoon olive oil
Freshly ground black pepper to taste

1. Score the cucumbers with the tines of a fork, and cut the cucumbers in half lengthwise. Remove the seeds (a grapefruit spoon or melon baller does this efficiently). Sprinkle the cucumbers with salt, and let them stand for about ½ hour. Then rinse, pat dry, and slice the cucumbers into ½-inch chunks.
2. In a medium serving bowl, crush the feta with a fork, and mix it with the scallions, lemon juice, oil, and pepper.
3. Combine the cucumber chunks with the cheese mixture. Sprinkle the salad with the mint.

GREEK EGGPLANT SALAD

4 servings

Even my husband, who does not count eggplant among his preferred foods, had to admit that this salad was delicious. Bert Greene of *Greene on Greens* is the inspiration. This could also be served as a first course.

SALAD
- 1 medium eggplant (about 1 pound)
- 1 large tomato, peeled, seeded, and chopped
- 1 green pepper, finely chopped
- 1 small onion, grated
- 1 large clove garlic, crushed

DRESSING
- ½ teaspoon salt, if desired
- ¼ teaspoon freshly ground black pepper
- 3 tablespoons red wine vinegar
- 1 or 2 tablespoons olive oil

Minced fresh parsley for garnish

1. Place the eggplant under the broiler, turning it often, until its skin blackens. Let the eggplant cool, and rub off the skin with damp paper towels. Chop the eggplant pulp, and transfer it to a medium bowl.
2. Add the tomato, green pepper, onion, and garlic to the eggplant.
3. In a small bowl, combine all the dressing ingredients. Pour the dressing over the eggplant mixture, and combine them thoroughly. Chill the salad well. Serve the salad sprinkled with parsley.

KOHLRABI SALAD

6 to 8 servings

This simple, oil-free salad was my first taste of kohlrabi, and I knew immediately it wouldn't be my last. My tasters were amazed to learn of the vegetable's humble origins—it is a member of the cabbage family. I have Bert Greene, author of *Greene on Greens,* to thank for this recipe. *Preparation tip:* Select small kohlrabies for tenderness and flavor. If you can get them, try the recipe with shallots instead of onions. If you do not have tarragon wine vinegar, use white wine vinegar and add a pinch of crumbled tarragon to the dressing.

SALAD
- 2½ pounds kohlrabi bulbs (about 4 small)
- 2 small white onions, thinly sliced

DRESSING
- ½ cup tarragon wine vinegar
- ¼ cup sugar
- 2 teaspoons sesame seeds
- ½ teaspoon minced fresh ginger
- ½ teaspoon hot red pepper flakes, or to taste
- ½ teaspoon freshly ground black pepper
- ¼ teaspoon salt, if desired

1. Trim and peel the kohlrabi bulbs, and cut them into strips about ¼ inch thick and 2 inches long. Drop the strips into boiling water for 1 minute. Rinse them under cold water, and drain them.
2. Put the kohlrabi strips into a bowl, and add the onions, tossing the two vegetables to mix them.
3. In a small bowl, combine all the dressing ingredients. Pour the dressing over the kohlrabi mixture, and toss the salad. Chill the salad, covered, for 2 hours or longer before serving.

POTATO AND GREEN BEAN SALAD   *6 servings*

This potato salad is my favorite. It not only tastes wonderful (despite its low-fat dressing), it also looks great and is easy to prepare. It's the one I'm most inclined to make for company.

SALAD
- 1 pound green beans, cut into 2 inch lengths, steamed tender-crisp, and kept warm
- 4 large potatoes, cooked until just soft, peeled, cubed, and kept warm (about 4 cups cubes)
- 2 scallions, sliced

DRESSING
- 2 tablespoons olive or salad oil
- 2 tablespoons white wine vinegar
- 1 large clove garlic, crushed, or more, to taste
- 1 small red onion, thinly sliced into rings
- ½ teaspoon orégano
- ½ teaspoon salt, if desired
- ⅛ teaspoon freshly ground black pepper, or more, to taste

1. Place the beans, potatoes, and scallions in a medium bowl. Set the bowl aside.
2. In a jar, combine all the dressing ingredients. Shake the dressing, and pour it over the vegetables. Toss the salad gently to mix the ingredients well.
3. Cover the salad, and chill it for several hours or overnight.

"CARRIED AWAY" POTATO SALAD   *6 servings*

My husband, who is fond of making plays on words, named this potato salad for its prominent caraway seasoning and for the fact that he found it hard to stop eating it. It is a fine picnic salad (no quick-spoiling ingredients) and barbecue accompaniment. But I could enjoy it any time. *Preparation tip:* This salad's flavor develops as it stands, so make it the day before or at least a few hours in advance. For expedience, prepare the dressing and the remaining ingredients while the potatoes cook. Don't expect to smash the caraway seeds; simply press them in a mortar with a pestle or with the back of a heavy wooden handle to enhance their flavor.

DRESSING
- 1½ teaspoons caraway seeds, lightly crushed
- ¼ cup cider vinegar
- 2 tablespoons vegetable oil
- ½ teaspoon salt, if desired
- ¼ teaspoon freshly ground black pepper, or more, to taste

SALAD
- 2½ pounds potatoes, cooked, peeled, cubed, and kept warm
- 1 cup coarsely shredded carrots
- ⅓ cup chopped sweet onion or shallots
- ¼ cup minced fresh parsley

1. Combine all the dressing ingredients in a large bowl.
2. Add the potatoes, carrots, onion, and parsley. Toss the salad gently to combine all the ingredients. Cover the salad with plastic wrap, and chill it.

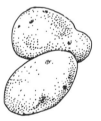

MIDEAST POTATO SALAD   *about 6 servings*

I doubt that the peoples of the Mideast include potato salad in their cuisine, but traditional Middle Eastern seasonings certainly do justice to the potato. Since the dressing is based on yogurt, the calories are about as low as one could get, too. *Preparation tip:* The trick in making potato salad is not to overcook the potatoes; when done, they should yield to a fork but still feel firm.

SALAD
- 2 pounds medium to large potatoes, unpeeled, steamed or boiled in lightly salted water

- 1 small red onion, sliced thin crosswise and separated into rings
- 2 tablespoons minced fresh parsley
- 2 tablespoons chopped fresh mint leaves *or,* if unavailable, 2 more tablespoons parsley

Paprika for garnish (optional)

DRESSING
- 1 cup plain low-fat yogurt
- ½ teaspoon salt, if desired
- ½ teaspoon ground cumin
- ½ teaspoon ground coriander
- ⅛ teaspoon freshly ground black pepper

1. As soon as they are cool enough to handle, peel and cut the potatoes into ¾-inch cubes.
2. In a medium bowl, combine all the dressing ingredients. Add the potatoes to the dressing, and toss them gently to coat them with the yogurt mixture. Transfer the potatoes to a serving platter.
3. Place the onion rings on top of the potato mixture, and sprinkle the salad with the parsley, mint, and paprika.
4. Cover the salad, and refrigerate it for at least 30 minutes before serving it.

CHINESE RADISH SALAD

6 servings

There's hardly a salad that's easier to prepare that can equal this one in flavor. It looks pretty, too.

SALAD
- 20 radishes, ends trimmed, sliced very thin
- 1 green pepper, finely slivered

DRESSING
- 2 tablespoons vinegar
- 4 teaspoons soy sauce (preferably reduced-sodium)
- 1 tablespoon sugar

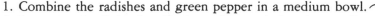

1. Combine the radishes and green pepper in a medium bowl.
2. In a cup, mix all the dressing ingredients, stirring them well to dissolve the sugar. Add the dressing to the vegetables, and toss the salad to mix the ingredients thoroughly.

CITRUS AND SPINACH SALAD

4 servings

This is a fine winter and spring salad, when citrus fruits are luscious and inexpensive. *Preparation tip:* Note that the recipe makes extra dressing, which should be prepared in advance so that the flavors can blend.

DRESSING
- ½ cup grapefruit juice
- 2 tablespoons prepared mustard
- ¼ cup olive oil
- ¼ cup honey
- 2 tablespoons poppy seeds
- 2 tablespoons grated onion
- ¼ teaspoon salt, if desired
- Freshly ground black pepper to taste

SALAD
- 4 cups packed spinach leaves, well washed
- 1 cup orange sections
- 1 cup grapefruit sections
- ½ cup red onion rings

1. In a small bowl, combine all the dressing ingredients. Chill the dressing.
2. At serving time, place the salad ingredients in a salad bowl, and toss them with about ¼ cup of the chilled dressing.

RED AND GREEN WATERCRESS SALAD

4 servings

A Pierre Franey special that I changed not at all except to reduce the amount of oil in the dressing. The first time I tried it, I scrawled "SUPER!!" across the recipe.

SALAD
- 1 bunch watercress, tough stems removed
- 1 head Boston lettuce, cored and leaves separated
- 1 ripe tomato, cored and cut into eighths
- 6 radishes, trimmed and thinly sliced

DRESSING
- 2 tablespoons tarragon vinegar, or white wine vinegar and pinch tarragon
- 1 clove garlic, finely minced
- 1 tablespoon Dijon mustard
- 2 tablespoons olive oil
- Salt, if desired, to taste
- Freshly ground black pepper to taste

1. Put the watercress and lettuce in a salad bowl. Add the tomato and radishes.
2. In a small bowl, combine the vinegar, garlic, and mustard. Gradually add the oil, whisking or stirring the mixture constantly. Add salt and pepper to taste. At serving time, pour the dressing over the salad, and toss the salad gently to coat the ingredients well.

Salad Dressings

Too often, the most nutritious and low-calorie salad is "spoiled" by a fatty, high-calorie dressing. Just 2 tablespoons of an ordinary dressing based on oil or mayonnaise can increase a salad's caloric value by 150 calories and make fat by far the largest source of calories in the dish. And many people use a lot more dressing than 2 tablespoons! In recent years, a number of low- or no-fat commercial dressings have been marketed, and some of these are good. Unfortunately, nearly all those I've examined have a fair amount of salt in them, and all those I've tasted have a decidedly artificial flavor or consistency (largely because gummy liquids must be used to give the dressing the desired thickness and shelf life when oil is reduced or omitted).

The goal of my dressing recipes is (1) to keep fat as low as possible and (2) to keep down the salt and other high-sodium ingredients. I've found that buttermilk, low-fat yogurt, part-skim ricotta, and low-fat cottage cheese are the best substitutes for the usual high-fat ingredients. However, for those who cannot use dairy products, a few dressings are included that do not depend on them. In addition to the dressings included in this section, you might want to try some of the dressings used in the main-dish and side-dish salads on pages 402–410 and 533–548. In nearly every case, the dressing is best made a few hours ahead and allowed to chill so that flavors can meld. Most will keep in the refrigerator for a week or longer. After years of using low-fat dressings, I've come to dislike "oily" and overly dressed salads. I bet you will, too.

BLEU CHEESE DRESSING   *1 cup*

½ cup plain low-fat yogurt
¼ cup low-fat cottage cheese
2 ounces (¼ cup) bleu cheese
4 teaspoons white wine vinegar
1 scallion, finely chopped
½ teaspoon Worcestershire sauce
¼ teaspoon salt, if desired
Freshly ground black pepper to taste

In a blender or food processor, blend well all the dressing ingredients.

BUTTERMILK DRESSING

about 1¼ cups

The Golden Door, a California health spa, devised this low-fat, low-salt dressing.

  1 cup buttermilk
  ¼ cup grated cucumber
  2 tablespoons minced scallions
  1 tablespoon Dijon mustard
  2 teaspoons minced fresh parsley
  2 teaspoons lemon juice
  ¼ teaspoon dried dillweed
  ¼ teaspoon freshly ground black pepper

Combine all the dressing ingredients in a screw-top jar, and shake the dressing well. Chill the dressing.

CURRY SAUCE FOR PASTA SALAD

3 tablespoons

This recipe contains less than 130 calories *in total,* to be divided among 2 or more servings. Most of the calories come from the mayonnaise, which is mainly polyunsaturated fat. There should be enough dressing for 4 cups of salad.

  ¾ teaspoon vinegar
  ½ teaspoon curry powder, or more, to taste
  2 tablespoons low-fat plain yogurt
  1 tablespoon mayonnaise

In a small bowl, combine all the dressing ingredients well, and chill the dressing. Just before serving the salad, add the dressing, and toss the salad well.

CREAMY FRENCH DRESSING

about 1 cup

  ½ cup plain low-fat yogurt
2½ tablespoons ketchup
  2 tablespoons water
1½ tablespoons cider vinegar
  1 tablespoon mayonnaise
  1 clove garlic, crushed
  ¼ teaspoon sugar
Freshly ground black pepper to taste

In a bowl or jar, mix all the dressing ingredients thoroughly.

FRUIT SALAD DRESSING

about 1¼ cups

1 cup plain low-fat yogurt
2 tablespoons orange juice
1 or 2 tablespoons honey, to taste
1 tablespoon fresh lemon juice
1 teaspoon poppy seeds *and/or* ½ teaspoon
  celery seeds
Salt, if desired, to taste
Freshly ground black pepper to taste

Combine all the dressing ingredients in a small bowl or jar, and whisk or shake them well.

HORSERADISH DRESSING

about ¾ cup

For stimulating your taste buds without adding salt, try this dressing. *Preparation tip:* For a lower-fat dressing, you could substitute ⅔ cup plain low-fat yogurt for the mayonnaise and buttermilk.

⅓ cup mayonnaise
⅓ cup buttermilk
2 tablespoons drained bottled horseradish
2 tablespoons snipped fresh dill
½ teaspoon crushed garlic
1 teaspoon Worcestershire sauce

Combine all the dressing ingredients, and chill the dressing.

LOW-CAL MAYONNAISE

about 1⅓ cups

Although there are 2 egg yolks in this recipe, the amount of cholesterol per serving (1 or 2 tablespoons) is low.

1 cup low-fat cottage cheese or part-skim ricotta
2 tablespoons fresh lemon juice
2 egg yolks
½ teaspoon prepared mustard
½ teaspoon AHA herb mix (see p. 182)
¼ teaspoon salt, if desired

Blend all the dressing ingredients in a blender until they are smooth.

NO-CAL DRESSING

about ½ cup

When you think you're ready to go the no-oil route, you might try this vinegar-and-herb dressing, which is for all intents and purposes nearly calorie-free.

  ½ cup wine or white vinegar
  4 sage leaves, crushed
  ¼ teaspoon tarragon
  1 pinch savory
  1 tablespoon minced fresh parsley *or* 1 teaspoon
    dried parsley flakes, crushed
  ½ clove garlic, crushed
  1 teaspoon snipped fresh dill *or* ¼ teaspoon
    dried dillweed
  ½ teaspoon salt, if desired
  Freshly ground black pepper to taste

Combine all the dressing ingredients in a jar, and mix them thoroughly.

DILLED RICOTTA DRESSING

about ¾ cup

  ⅓ cup buttermilk
  ¼ cup part-skim ricotta
  4 teaspoons mayonnaise
  2 tablespoons snipped fresh dill
  1 tablespoon minced fresh parsley
  ¼ teaspoon dry mustard
  ¼ teaspoon AHA herb mix (see p. 182) *or* 1½
    teaspoons dried minced onion
  ⅛ teaspoon salt, if desired
  ⅛ teaspoon freshly ground black pepper

Blend well all the dressing ingredients in a blender or food processor.

TOMATO-HERB DRESSING

about 1 ⅓ cups

6 ounces (1 small can) tomato or V-8 juice
¼ cup apple cider vinegar
2 tablespoons olive oil
1 tablespoon fresh lemon juice
1 tablespoon Dijon mustard
1 tablespoon fresh chopped chives
1 tablespoon fresh minced parsley
1 large clove garlic, crushed
½ teaspoon dried basil *or* 1 tablespoon fresh minced basil
⅛ teaspoon cayenne, or to taste

In a bowl or jar, combine all the dressing ingredients, whisking or shaking them to blend them well.

VARIATION: For a thicker dressing, try adding about 4 ounces of tofu (soybean curd), creaming the ingredients together in a blender or food processor. This would increase the yield to about 2 cups.

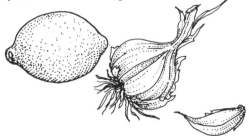

CREAMY VINAIGRETTE

about 1¼ cups

⅔ cup plain low-fat yogurt
⅓ cup apple cider vinegar
2 tablespoons olive oil
1 tablespoon Dijon mustard
1 tablespoon fresh lemon juice
1 very large clove garlic, crushed
1 tablespoon reduced-sodium soy sauce (optional)
¼ teaspoon dried dillweed

Combine all the vinaigrette ingredients in a bowl or jar with a tight-fitting lid, whisking or shaking them to blend them well.

BREADS AND ROLLS

Bread Baking for Beginners (and Old Pros)

The day I started writing this book I baked my first yeast-leavened bread—my first *successful* one, that is. Many years earlier, I had twice tried to make bread from scratch, but on both occasions the outcome resembled the unleavened loaves that the ancient Israelites carried on their backs in their haste to escape from Egyptian slavery. (The flat bread called matzo is the modern-day equivalent.) I was convinced that yeast died when it looked at me, and I wasn't going to give it a chance to reject me a third time. *Jane Brody's Nutrition Book* included a recipe for my husband Richard's Best Bread; *he* never failed at it, and he never even followed a recipe (I had to stand over his shoulder while he made it to write down what he did). But if I was going to write a book on preparing wholesome food, I clearly had to master the ancient art of baking yeast-leavened bread.

I am delighted to report that after about two awkward tries, which resulted in delicious breads despite my clumsiness and uncertainty, I became hooked on home bread baking. It is a delight to all the senses: it *feels* good to knead the dough; it *smells* good throughout the house for hours; it *looks* good to see the golden-brown loaves on the cooling rack and later on the bread board at the table; it *tastes* better than almost any store-bought bread; and it *sounds* good to hear the satisfied "mmms" of fellow diners.

Like any new skill, bread baking is a learning experience. But you don't need a college degree to master it. With a few basic principles and helpful hints to guide you, you, too, can become a master baker. I *would* recommend, however, that the first few breads be made for family or close friends (they'll love them no matter what the breads look like) and that you make them when you are not hurried or otherwise under pressure. Here are some facts and tips every newcomer to bread baking should know (and every experienced bread baker should already know).

YEAST My husband insists that yeast knows when you're afraid of it. If you think of yeast as a bunch of mindless microorganisms (which, of course, is what it is), you'll have an easier time establishing your superiority. Seriously, though, yeast is a living organism and as such demands some care and respect. It is sold in two forms: compressed in cakes (sometimes called fresh yeast) or active dry in packages (either individual packets each containing a scant table-spoon of yeast or in bulk packages from which you measure out each scant tablespoon). Active dry yeast is easier to buy and easier to work with. (If you use compressed yeast, ½ ounce equals one packet of active dry yeast.) There is now available a quick-rising active yeast that may appeal to time-pressured cooks.

Active dry yeast must be dissolved in warm liquid and given a chance to start growing and producing bubbles of carbon dioxide that allows bread to rise. *The temperature of the liquid is very important:* too cold and the yeast will just sit there doing nothing; too hot and it will be scalded to death. Lukewarm (the temperature to which baby bottles used to be heated) is just right: to be exact, *between 105 and 115 degrees Fahrenheit.* (Compressed yeast should be dissolved in liquid no hotter than 95 degrees.) I find it best to use a thermometer, since what feels lukewarm to me can vary greatly with the seasons and my mood. If you have no kitchen thermometer, you can achieve the proper temperature by mixing equal parts of boiling water and ice water.

It is a good idea to "proof" active dry yeast (establish its viability) before you mix it with the rest of the more expensive ingredients. Simply mix the yeast first with warm liquid and a bit of sugar for the yeast to feed on. If you add a pinch of powdered ginger, it will speed the action of the yeast. In 5 to 15 minutes, you should see the yeast start to foam. (Nearly every recipe in this book instructs you to proof the yeast first, and you can adapt other recipes accordingly.) Then you're sure you're starting with live yeast. As long as you don't overheat it before baking time, the yeast will remain viable and produce a well-leavened loaf.

If you double a yeast-bread recipe, *don't* double the yeast—add only about 1 extra teaspoon.

FLOURS You'll notice that most bread recipes are indefinite about the amount of flour needed to produce a dough that can be handled. This is because the amount varies with the type of flour, how it was ground, how long it has been stored, the temperature and humidity of the air, and, I've come to think, a certain arbitrary independence that likes to keep bread bakers guessing. It is a good idea, when you come down to the last cup of flour, to add it slowly, mixing as you go and stopping when you think the dough can be kneaded without becoming glued to your hands. I often find it easiest to flour my hands and work in the last cup of flour by hand; additional flour can be worked in during kneading if the dough is still too sticky. If too much flour is added, you may end up with a dry bread. Most recipes indicate whether the dough should feel stiff or soft (after some experience, you'll know the difference) and whether you can expect it to feel sticky at first. Sticky dough usually firms up during the first rising.

Unless otherwise specified, these are my preferences in flour:

- Whole-wheat flour—stone-ground regular or graham (this is a coarser grind). Although stone-ground flours cost more, the flavor and nutritive value are decidedly superior. If you're going to the trouble to make your own bread, it pays to invest in the best ingredients.
- All-purpose or white flour—unbleached white flour.
- Rye flour—whole-grain rye (but the refined supermarket variety called medium rye will do if you can't get whole-grain).
- Cornmeal—whole-grain or stone-ground meal, usually available in supermarkets.

For a bread dough to rise, it must contain an elastic protein called gluten that traps the bubbles of carbon dioxide given off by the yeast. Of all the flours used in bread baking, only wheat flour contains substantial amounts of gluten-making protein (the gluten is developed during the kneading of the dough). Therefore, virtually every yeast-bread recipe contains wheat flour. If not, gluten flour may be added (this is an extract of wheat flour). So-called bread flour contains an extra amount of gluten; it is often used in breads made in food processors, which aren't kneaded very long.

SALT Many people who are trying to cut down on salt (or who have to for health reasons) want to know if good yeast bread can be made salt-free. The answer is a qualified yes. Salt-free doughs rise quickly, sometimes too quickly, resulting in air holes and incomplete development of flavors. There is also less time for the flours to absorb liquid, so the dough may be quite moist. To compensate for the shorter rising time, use less yeast if you omit the salt in a recipe, and watch the risings carefully (they will go faster than the recipe indicates). If the dough is too wet after the first rising, knead in some extra flour. You might also reduce the amount of salt, rather than eliminating it entirely. I never use more than 1 teaspoon of salt per loaf (if the loaf is sliced into 16 pieces, this would mean 134 milligrams of sodium per slice), and for many recipes—especially those on the sweet side—I use only ½ teaspoon per loaf.

SWEETENERS These help to make a more tender and flavorful bread. They also create a darker crust and prolong freshness. Honey and molasses are my favorites from a flavor standpoint. Molasses, especially blackstrap, also adds some nutrients besides calories. If you substitute honey or molasses for sugar in a recipe, you will probably need to increase the flour to balance out the added liquid.

FATS Fats help to keep breads from drying out quickly because they hang on to moisture (that's why the fatless French bread stales in a day). Fat also retards the development of gluten, keeping the bread from rising too fast. Oils can be used in place of hard fats like butter or margarine. Omitting fat is likely to result in a chewier bread that has more air holes in it.

LIQUIDS Many different ones make an excellent bread. Water is the most common liquid used in breads. Milk or buttermilk adds protein and calcium to a loaf and produces a more delicate texture and darker crust; fruit juices add sweetness and color; vegetable cooking water adds nutrients and flavor; tomato juice adds color, flavor, and salt; potato water adds starch that helps to condition the dough; beer provides food for the yeast and results in a heartier flavor. Other "liquids" can also be used, such as fruit purées like applesauce and cooked cereals.

KNEADING Some would-be bread bakers are put off by the need to knead bread dough. They think of it as endless hard work. Actually, it's a brief exercise that's great fun and very therapeutic. You can think of every push on the dough as an acceptable expression of aggression, a tension reliever, an upper-body strengthener, or a calorie-burning activity (it is all of these). It certainly gets my blood going on cold winter mornings. Breads rarely need more than 8 to 10 minutes of kneading (my husband says he never kneads dough longer than 5 minutes, and his breads always turn out great). (See "Note" on p. 560.) As far as I'm concerned, you miss all the fun if you prepare the dough in an electric mixer or food processor; besides, it's harder to tell if you've added the right amount of flour. But if using a motorized device gets you to make your own nutritious, tasty bread, far be it from me to say don't use it. Homemade bread in a food processor is still bound to be better than what comes out of a package.

Kneading is necessary to develop the gluten in the dough, which allows the dough to rise properly. Dough is best kneaded on a firm surface that has been lightly floured. You can add flour as needed to keep the dough from sticking to it. Knead by repeatedly pressing the heels of your hands into the dough and folding the dough over. Lean into the job, using the weight of your upper body to put pressure on the dough (1). The dough has been adequately kneaded when it appears smooth and bounces back after you press it in with a fingertip (this indicates that the elastic gluten has been well developed).

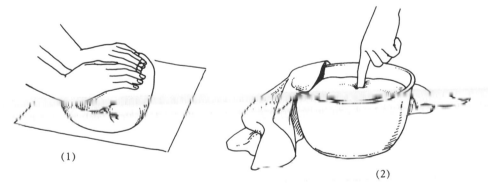

(1)

(2)

(3)

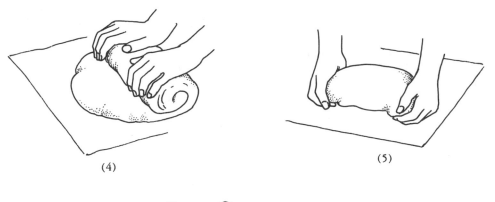

(4)   (5)

(6)   (7)

RISING Yeast goes about its work best when the dough is placed in a warm (about 85 degrees), draft-free place to rise. If you have a gas oven with a pilot light on, that's an ideal place for raising bread. In an electric or gas oven without a pilot light, you can heat the oven to low (about 120 degrees), then turn it off before you put the dough in. Or try the top of your refrigerator, if it's warm up there. To prevent excessive drying, the dough should be covered with plastic wrap or with a cloth (usually a damp one) such as a linen dishtowel. Dough should rise until it has doubled in bulk; when pressed with a fingertip, the indentation should remain (2). The amount of time needed for risings will vary with the temperature and the contents and consistency of the dough. Regardless of the times indicated in recipes, check on your dough about ½ hour before it's supposed to be finished rising. If the dough rises too much, punch it down and let it rise again to double the bulk. Dough is punched down by pushing your fist into the center (3). After the dough has risen, it is formed into a loaf (4) and (5) and allowed to rise a second time (6) before baking (7).

Dough that has been prepared to the point of rising (or even after the first rising) can be stored in the refrigerator for a day or two (be careful, though, because some aggressive doughs will rise even at refrigerator temperatures and may need an occasional punching down). Before baking a refrigerated dough, allow it to come to room temperature and rise once or twice.

PANS Most breads are baked in aluminum or glass loaf pans that measure approximately 9 × 5 × 3 inches. The baking temperatures here are usually geared for aluminum pans; if you use glass pans, reduce the oven temperature by 25 degrees to prevent the crust from scorching before the middle is done. Breads can also be baked free-form on baking sheets or tiles. My favorite is unglazed ceramic loaf pans. When properly tempered, these require no washing, and they result in a superior product because they distribute the temperature more evenly than other pans.

Most pans should be greased before the dough is placed in them. You can use oil, butter, or margarine. I prefer vegetable-oil spray (sold in spray-top cans in the supermarket), which evenly distributes a thin, nonstick coating. Sometimes, you will be told to flour the pan or sprinkle it with corn meal after greasing.

CRUST TYPES For a softer crust, brush melted fat on the top of the bread just before the last rising or while the loaf is baking. For a crisp crust, brush the bread with cold water just before or while it's baking. For a hard crust on rolls, put a pan of boiling water on the oven bottom during baking. For a shiny crust, brush the bread with a beaten mixture of 1 egg and 1 tablespoon of water. For a softer glaze, use just the egg white beaten with 1 tablespoon of water.

BAKING Most breads bake best in the middle of the oven. If you bake bread near the top, you may have to place a piece of foil loosely over the loaf toward the end of the baking to prevent excessive browning before the inside is done. The oven should always be preheated to the proper temperature before you put the bread in. Breads are done when they begin to pull away from the sides of the pan and sound hollow when rapped on the bottom with your knuckles (obviously, the bread must be removed from the pan to find this out). Overbaking results in a dry bread.

COOLING AND STORING As soon as they're done (unless otherwise specified), breads should be removed from the pan and placed on a wire rack to cool. If you don't have a cooling rack, improvise, perhaps using a cool oven rack or the rack of a toaster oven, roasting pan, or pressure cooker.

Cooled bread should be wrapped in plastic wrap or placed in a plastic bag and closed with a wire twist. It is best stored at room temperature, as long as it will be eaten within a week (or within 4 or 5 days in hot, humid weather). Breads get stale fastest in the refrigerator, although refrigeration delays spoilage. However, breads freeze very well; tightly wrapped in plastic, they keep for months. Thaw bread at room temperature or in the oven (wrap the loaf in foil, and place it in a 350-degree oven for about 30 minutes). If you use a microwave, follow the instructions that came with your oven.

EATING Home-baked bread, especially whole-grain bread, tends to be more crumbly than packaged bread. It is best sliced with a long, straight knife that has a serrated or scalloped edge.

The real trick with home-baked bread is to keep from devouring an entire loaf the first day (just in case, I always bake at least two loaves at a time). Not only are these breads wonderful with meals and for sandwiches, they're also great as snacks—for example, with coffee, tea, or milk. To me, home-baked bread is delicious enough as is—no butter or margarine needed. If you prefer some fat on your bread, smear it thinly to keep calories low and nutrient density high.

NOTE After months of experience in baking whole-grain breads, I discovered something that has both reduced kneading time and improved the texture of my breads. And after reading a dozen bread cookbooks, I was delighted finally to find one, *Whole Grain Baking* by Diana Scesny Greene (Trumansburg, N.Y.: The Crossing Press, 1984), that substantiated my discovery—the fact that whole-grain flours are slower to absorb moisture than refined white flours; therefore, to avoid adding more flour than is really needed to produce a manageable dough (which can result in too dry a bread), it is best to let the dough sit for ½ hour or so *before* kneading it. Greene recommends letting the covered dough rest for a total of 90 minutes: 30 at room temperature; 30 in a warm spot, after which the dough is punched down; and another 30 in a warm spot, after which the dough is kneaded for only 2 to 5 minutes. At this point, proceed with two risings, about 45 minutes in the bowl for the first and 30 minutes in the pans for the second or until the dough doubles in bulk.

OTHER RECIPE SOURCES The recipes in this book represent a mere smattering of the wonderful, nutritious possibilities. If you get serious about bread baking, you may want to invest in a cookbook devoted to breads. In my experience, one of the least expensive books is also the best: *Betty Crocker's Breads,* a Golden Press 8½ × 11–inch illustrated paperback. Another excellent one is *Beard on Bread* (Knopf, 1974; now a Ballantine paperback) by food expert James Beard. Devotees of whole-grain breads might also consult *The Laurel's Kitchen Bread Book* by Laurel Robertson with Carol Flinders and Bronwen Godfrey (Random House, 1984) and *Bread Winners* (Rodale Press, 1979) and *Bread Winners Too* (Rodale Press, 1984), both by Mel London.

BEARD'S RAISIN-WHEAT BREAD

2 loaves

This bread, adapted from *Beard on Bread* by James Beard, is delicious, and the dough is easy to handle. *Preparation tip:* If you would rather not use alcohol, you can soak the raisins in warm water or apple juice.

⅓ cup raisins
Brandy or sherry for soaking raisins
1½ cups warm water (105° to 115°), divided
  2 packages (2 scant tablespoons) active dry yeast
  2 tablespoons sugar
  4 cups whole-wheat flour, preferably
    stone-ground
1¾ to 2 cups white flour
  2 teaspoons salt, if desired
¾ cup skim or low-fat milk
½ cup honey
  2 tablespoons melted butter or margarine or oil

1. Place the raisins in a small bowl, add the brandy or sherry just to cover, and soak the raisins until they soften and swell.
2. Meanwhile, place ½ cup of the warm water in another small bowl, add the yeast and sugar, stir them to dissolve, and let the mixture stand until it is bubbly.
3. In a large bowl, combine the whole-wheat flour, 1½ cups of the white flour, and the salt. Add the yeast mixture to the flour mixture.
4. In a small bowl, combine the remaining 1 cup of warm water, milk, honey, and butter. Make a well in the flour mixture, and add the milk mixture, blending the ingredients well. Add more white flour if necessary to make a manageable dough.
5. Turn the dough out onto a floured board, and knead it for about 10 minutes or until it is smooth and elastic. Place the dough in an oiled bowl, turning the dough to grease the top. Cover the bowl, and let the dough rise in a warm, draft-free place until it has doubled in bulk, for about 1 to 1½ hours.
6. Punch down the dough, turn it out, and divide it in two. Drain the soaked raisins, press them into the dough, and shape the dough into two loaves. Place the loaves in greased 9 × 5 × 3-inch bread pans, cover the loaves, and let them rise again until they have doubled in bulk, about 45 minutes.
7. Bake the loaves in a preheated 425° oven for 10 minutes. Then reduce the heat to 350°, and bake the loaves for another 30 minutes or so, or until the loaves sound hollow when tapped on the bottom.

BRAN CEREAL BREAD   *2 loaves*

The Kellogg Company developed this tasty and simple bread recipe to promote the use of its bran cereals All-Bran and Bran Buds. *Preparation tip:* You can, of course, make it with other 100-percent bran cereals (but not 40% Bran Flakes), as long as they have some sweetening in them. Or you could use unprocessed bran and add another 2 tablespoons of molasses or honey to the recipe. Either way, the result is a dense bread that freezes well. Note that the recipe does not involve proofing the yeast, so be sure to use yeast you know is good. The dough can also be shaped into round loaves and baked on a greased baking sheet.

2 cups all-purpose flour
2 cups whole-wheat flour, preferably
    stone-ground
2 cups ready-to-eat bran cereal
1 to 2 teaspoons salt, if desired, to taste
2 packages (2 scant tablespoons) active dry yeast
1½ cups skim or low-fat milk
¼ cup light molasses
⅓ cup butter or margarine
2 eggs

1. In a medium bowl, combine the all-purpose and whole-wheat flours.
2. Place the bran cereal in a large mixing bowl. Add 1 cup of the flour mixture, the salt, and the yeast. Set the mixture aside.
3. In a small saucepan, combine the milk, molasses, and butter or margarine, and heat the liquid until it is very warm, about 120° (do not let the milk get too hot or it will kill the yeast). Gradually add this to the cereal mixture, beating the ingredients with an electric mixer at medium speed for 2 minutes.
4. Add the eggs and another ½ cup of the flour mixture, and beat the mixture for another 2 minutes. Stir in enough of the remaining flour by hand to make a stiff dough.
5. Turn the dough out onto a lightly floured surface, and knead it for about 5 minutes or until it is smooth and elastic. Place the dough in a greased bowl, turning the dough to coat it on all sides. Cover the bowl loosely with a damp towel or greased plastic wrap, and let the dough rise in a warm, draft-free place until it has doubled in volume, about 1½ hours.
6. Punch down the dough. Divide it in half, and shape it into two loaves, placing each loaf in a bread pan (about 9 × 5 × 3 inches). Cover the loaves, and let them rise until they have doubled in bulk, about 1½ hours.
7. Bake the loaves in a preheated 375° oven for about 25 minutes or until the breads are golden-brown and sound hollow when tapped on the bottom.

BUTTERMILK-OAT-POTATO BREAD   *3 loaves*

Even though this bread is made mainly with white flour, the potato, oat flour (available in health food stores), and wheat germ give it a nutritional boost without detracting from its lightness. It is fairly moist and a good dinner and sandwich bread that freezes well. *Preparation tip:* If desired, add raisins, currants, or your choice of herbs when forming the loaves. Simply flatten the dough pieces into rectangles about 8 inches wide, sprinkle on the desired seasonings, and roll the dough up into loaves.

¾ cup warm water (105° to 115°)
 2 packages (2 scant tablespoons) active dry yeast
½ teaspoon sugar
Dash ground ginger (optional)
1½ cups mashed potatoes
1½ cups buttermilk
¼ cup butter or margarine, melted or finely diced
½ cup honey
2½ teaspoons salt, if desired
2½ cups oat flour
½ cup wheat germ
3½ to 4 cups unbleached white flour

1. Place the warm water in a small bowl, and dissolve the yeast, sugar, and ginger in it. Set the yeast mixture aside until it becomes bubbly.
2. In a very large mixing bowl, combine the mashed potatoes, buttermilk, butter or margarine, honey, and salt. Stir the ingredients well, or beat them for 1 to 2 minutes.
3. Stir the proofed yeast mixture into the potato mixture.
4. Add the oat flour, wheat germ, and about 2½ cups of the white flour to the potato yeast mixture, mixing to combine the ingredients thoroughly. Gradually add as much of the remaining white flour as needed to make a manageable dough. When not too sticky to knead, turn the dough out onto a floured board. Knead the dough until it is smooth, about 8 minutes, adding more flour as needed to keep the dough from sticking.
5. Place the dough in a large greased bowl, turning the dough to coat it on all sides with grease. Cover the bowl with plastic wrap, and place the dough in a warm, draft-free place to rise until it has doubled, about 1½ hours.
6. Punch down the dough, remove it from the bowl, and divide it in thirds, and form each third into a loaf. Place each loaf in a greased loaf pan (about 9 × 5 × 3 inches). Cover the pans with greased plastic wrap (use vegetable-oil spray or brush with oil), and let the breads rise again until they have doubled in bulk, about 1½ hours.
7. Bake the bread in a preheated 375° oven for about 30 to 35 minutes or until the loaves sound hollow when tapped on the bottom.

CORNELL BREAD

3 loaves

In the 1930s, Dr. Clive M. McCay, a Cornell University scientist concerned about improving nutrition and longevity, devised a basic bread recipe that could enhance health at a low monetary and caloric cost. It includes two protein-rich ingredients—milk and soy flour (available in health food stores)—and still produces a fine-textured and delicious bread. Although Dr. McCay is now dead, his legacy, the Cornell Formula, lives on. His basic Cornell bread is the foundation for the following recipe, which I have changed from white to whole-wheat and sweetened somewhat by doubling the honey. *Preparation tip:* Note that there are three risings and a brief resting period needed for this bread. You can also use this recipe to prepare rolls (or both loaves and rolls). Simply form one or more of the dough balls in step 7 into 9 balls and place them, just touching, into a round or square 8-inch baking pan. Or, if you prefer separate rolls, space the balls 2 inches apart on a baking sheet or in muffin tins. The rolls will bake in about 30 minutes.

3 cups warm water (105° to 115°)
2 packages (2 scant tablespoons) active dry yeast
¼ cup honey
2 teaspoons salt, if desired
2 tablespoons vegetable oil
3 cups whole-wheat flour, preferably
  stone-ground
2½ to 3½ cups unbleached white flour
  (approximately)
3 tablespoons wheat germ
1 cup soy flour
¾ cup nonfat dry milk

1. Place the warm water in a large bowl, and sprinkle in the yeast, stirring to dissolve it. Stir in the honey, and let the mixture stand until the yeast is bubbly.
2. Add the salt and oil to the yeast mixture.
3. In a medium bowl, stir together the whole-wheat flour, 2½ cups of the white flour, wheat germ, soy flour, and dry milk. Add three-fourths of the flour mixture to the yeast mixture, beating the dough with a hand mixer or an electric mixer. Work in the rest of the flour mixture, using a strong wooden spoon or your hands, mixing the dough until it firms up.
4. Turn the dough out onto a floured board, and knead it, using ½ to 1 cup more white flour, as needed, to produce a manageable dough. When the dough is smooth and elastic, place it in an oiled bowl, turning the dough to grease the top. Cover the bowl lightly, and place the dough in a warm, draft-free place until it has doubled in bulk, about 1 hour.

5. Punch down the dough, fold in the edges, and turn it upside down. Cover the dough, and let it rise in the bowl, covered, for another 20 minutes or until it has doubled in bulk again.

6. Turn the dough out onto a board, and divide it into three equal portions. Form each piece into a smooth, tight ball, and let the balls stand for 10 minutes.

7. Shape each ball into a loaf, and place the loaves into greased loaf pans (9 × 5 × 3 inches). Let the dough rise again, covered, for 45 minutes.

8. Bake the breads in a preheated 350° oven for about 50 minutes or until the loaves sound hollow when tapped on the bottom.

CURRANT EVENT BREAD

3 loaves

This slightly sweet, cinnamon-flavored oat-and-wheat bread can also serve as a tea bread. The recipe is large (it makes 3 loaves), but the bread is so good you'll want extras for the freezer. *Preparation tip:* The dough is sticky and soft and may require more flour than the recipe indicates, especially in warm weather. Note that this bread requires three risings, and so is best made when you'll be around the house for about 6 hours altogether.

   3 cups skim or low-fat milk, scalded
1½ cups rolled oats (quick or regular)
 ½ cup wheat germ
 ¾ cup sugar, divided
   1 *tablespoon* salt, if desired
 ½ cup vegetable oil
   1 cup dried currants
 ½ cup warm water (105° to 115°)
   1 teaspoon sugar
   2 packages (2 scant tablespoons) active dry yeast
   3 cups (approximately) whole-wheat flour
   3 to 4 cups white flour
   2 eggs, beaten
   3 *tablespoons* cinnamon
   1 tablespoon butter or margarine, melted

1. In a very large bowl, combine the hot milk with the oats, wheat germ, ½ cup of the sugar, salt, oil, and currants. Mix the ingredients well, and set the mixture aside to cool to lukewarm.
2. When the milk mixture has cooled somewhat, place the warm water in a small bowl, and add the 1 teaspoon sugar and the yeast, stirring to dissolve. Let this mixture stand for about 10 minutes or until the yeast starts to foam.
3. In a separate medium bowl, combine the whole-wheat flour and 3 cups of the white flour. Add about 4 cups of the flour mixture to the milk mixture, blending the ingredients well.
4. Add the yeast mixture and the beaten eggs to the dough. Stir in enough of the remaining flour to form a stiff dough.
5. Lightly flour a board, and turn out the dough. Using as much of the remaining white flour as needed, knead the dough for about 10 minutes or until it is smooth and elastic.
6. Form the dough in a ball, and place the ball in a very large oiled bowl, turning the dough to coat it on all sides with the oil. Cover the dough, and let it rise in a warm, draft-free place for about 2 hours or until it has doubled in bulk.

7. Punch down the dough, turn it over, cover it, and let it rise again for about 1 hour.

8. Punch down the dough again, and divide the dough into three equal parts. Form each part into a ball, and let the balls rest for about 10 minutes, lightly covered.

9. Meanwhile, mix the cinnamon with the remaining ¼ cup sugar, and set the mixture aside. Working with one ball of dough at a time, flatten it into a long rectangle about 7 inches wide and 15 to 18 inches long. Spread one third of the cinnamon-sugar on the rectangle of dough. Starting from the short end, roll up the dough tightly, sealing the ends with your fingers. Set the loaf into a greased loaf pan, 9 × 5 × 3 inches. Repeat the procedure with the other two balls of dough.

10. Brush each loaf with the melted butter or margarine. Cover the loaves lightly, and let them rise again for about 1 hour or until they have doubled in bulk.

11. Bake the bread in a preheated 375° oven for about 40 to 50 minutes or until the loaves start to leave the sides of the pans.

EVERYTHING-BUT-THE-KITCHEN-SINK BREAD
3 loaves

This nutrition-packed bread is delicious enough to be treated like a cake. *Preparation tip:* If you would like a sweeter bread to serve as a coffee, tea, or dessert bread, increase the honey to ⅔ cup.

  2 cups low-fat or skim milk
  3 tablespoons butter or margarine, preferably
    unsalted
  2 teaspoons salt, if desired
  ⅓ cup honey
  1 or 2 tablespoons molasses, to taste
  ½ cup warm water (105° to 115°)
  2 packages (2 scant tablespoons) active dry yeast
  ½ teaspoon sugar
  3 cups whole-wheat flour, preferably stone-ground
2½ to 3 cups unbleached white flour (approximately)
  ½ cup rye flour
  ½ cup sunflower seeds
  ¼ cup wheat germ
  ¼ cup bran flakes
  2 tablespoons melted butter or margarine, for
    brushing loaves (optional)

1. In a medium saucepan, heat the milk, 3 tablespoons of butter or margarine, salt, honey, and molasses until the butter or margarine melts. Remove the mixture from the heat, and let it cool to lukewarm.
2. While the milk mixture cools, place the warm water in a large bowl, and add the yeast and the sugar, stirring to dissolve them. Let this mixture stand until the yeast is bubbly.
3. Stir the cooled milk mixture into the yeast, add the whole-wheat flour, 2 cups of the white flour, the rye flour, sunflower seeds, wheat germ, and bran flakes. Stir the mixture to combine the ingredients well, adding additional white flour, as needed, to make a manageable dough. If you have time, cover the bowl loosely, and let the dough rest for about ½ hour.
4. Turn the dough out onto a floured board, and knead it for 5 minutes or longer, adding white flour as needed to prevent sticking. When the dough is smooth and elastic, place it in a large greased bowl, turning the dough to grease it on all sides. Cover it lightly, and set it in a warm, draft-free place to rise until it has doubled in bulk, about 1½ hours.
5. Punch down the dough, divide it in thirds, and shape each third into a loaf. Place each loaf in a greased bread pan (about 9 × 5 × 3 inches or slightly smaller), cover the pans loosely, and set them in a warm place until the loaves have doubled in size, about 1 hour.

6. Bake the bread in a preheated 350° oven for about 40 minutes or until the loaves sound hollow when tapped on the bottom. If desired, brush the loaves with the melted butter about 20 minutes into the baking.

HIGH-PROTEIN THREE-GRAIN BREAD   *2 loaves*

This is the best whole-grain bread I've tasted, and it's practically a complete meal in itself. The protein in the oats and wheat complement that in the soy flour, and the milk adds a further boost. The loaves are dense and well textured, slicing easily and holding together for sandwiches even when thinly sliced.

2½ cups boiling water
 1 cup rolled oats (regular or quick)
 ¾ cup nonfat dry milk
 ½ cup soy flour
 ¼ cup wheat germ
 ¼ cup brown sugar (firmly packed)
 ¼ cup honey
 2 teaspoons salt, if desired
 3 tablespoons vegetable oil
 ½ cup warm water (105° to 115°)
 2 packages (2 scant tablespoons) active dry yeast
 1 teaspoon sugar
5½ to 6 cups whole-wheat flour, preferably stone-ground

1. In a very large bowl, combine the boiling water, oats, dry milk, soy flour, wheat germ, brown sugar, honey, salt, and oil. Cool the mixture to warm.
2. Place the warm water in a small bowl, and add the yeast and 1 teaspoon of sugar, stirring to dissolve them. Let the mixture stand for about 10 minutes or until the yeast starts to bubble.
3. Add the yeast mixture and 2½ cups of the whole wheat flour to the oats mixture. Beat this for 2 minutes, and then add enough of the remaining flour to form a dough that is easy to handle.
4. Turn the dough out onto a lightly floured board, and knead it for about 10 minutes or until it is smooth and elastic. Place the dough in a large greased bowl, turning the dough to coat the top. Cover the bowl, and let the dough rise in a warm, draft-free place until it has doubled in bulk, about 1½ hours.
5. Punch down the dough, and divide it in half. Flatten each half into a rectangle about 18 inches long and 8 inches wide. Starting from the short end, roll up each rectangle, pressing with your fingertips to seal the loaf as you go. Seal the ends, and place each loaf in a greased loaf pan, about 9 × 5 × 3 inches. Cover the pans, and let the loaves rise until they have doubled in bulk, about 1 hour.
6. Bake the bread in a preheated 375° oven for about 35 to 40 minutes or until the loaves sound hollow when tapped.

NANA'S OAT-WHEAT BREAD

3 loaves

"Nana" is Nellie Kelder, an upstate New York grandmother in her mid-80s who whips up this wonderful bread at the slightest provocation. It is a real winner of a health bread that gets most of its sweetness from nutritious molasses.

½ cup warm water (105° to 115°)
1½ packages (4 teaspoons) active dry yeast
1 teaspoon sugar
¼ teaspoon ginger
3 cups quick-cooking rolled oats
3½ cups boiling water
4 tablespoons butter or margarine
½ cup light molasses
1 *tablespoon* salt, or as desired
1 cup All-Bran or 100% Bran cereal
2 cups whole-wheat flour
4 to 5 cups white flour

1. Place the warm water in a small bowl, and stir in the yeast, sugar, and ginger. Set the mixture aside until the yeast starts to bubble.
2. Place the oats into a large bowl, and pour the boiling water over them. Add the butter or margarine, molasses, and salt, stirring to dissolve the ingredients and combine them well.
3. Add the bran cereal, whole-wheat flour, and proofed yeast mixture. Combine the ingredients well, and start adding the white flour until the dough pulls away from the sides of the bowl and can be handled easily.
4. Turn out the dough on a floured board, and knead it for 8 to 10 minutes or until it is smooth and elastic. The dough will be soft rather than stiff. Place the dough in a greased bowl, turning the dough to coat it with grease. Cover the bowl with plastic wrap or a damp cloth, and set the dough in a warm, draft-free place to rise until it has doubled in bulk, about 1½ hours.
5. Punch down the dough, divide it into thirds, and form each third into a loaf. Place each loaf in a bread pan (9 × 5 × 3 inches or smaller), cover the pans lightly, and set them in a warm place to let the loaves rise until they have doubled in bulk, about 1 to 1½ hours.
6. Bake the bread in a preheated 350° oven for about 40 minutes or until the loaves sound hollow when tapped on the bottom.

ORANGE-CARROT BREAD

2 loaves

This moist loaf was devised from a recipe in Marian Morash's *The Victory Garden Cookbook. Preparation tip:* The dough is quite soft and does not require much kneading.

> 2 cups orange juice
> 2 teaspoons sugar
> 1 package (1 scant tablespoon) active dry yeast
> ¼ cup honey
> ¼ cup oil
> 2 teaspoons grated orange rind
> 2 teaspoons salt, if desired
> 4½ cups unbleached white flour, divided
> 2 cups *finely* grated carrots (4 medium-large)
> 2 eggs
> 3 cups whole-wheat flour, preferably
>   stone-ground

1. Heat the orange juice to lukewarm (105° to 115°). Sprinkle in the sugar and yeast, stirring to dissolve them. Set the mixture aside for about 10 minutes or until it is bubbly.

2. In a large mixing bowl, beat the honey, oil, orange rind, salt, and 1 cup of the white flour. Add the yeast mixture, carrots, and eggs, and mix the ingredients thoroughly.

3. Beat in the whole-wheat flour and 3 cups of the white flour. Spread the remaining white flour on a board or work surface, turn out the dough, and knead it, working in the flour, until the dough is smooth and elastic, about 5 to 8 minutes.

4. Place the dough in a greased bowl, turning the dough to coat all sides with the grease. Cover the bowl lightly with plastic wrap, and set the dough in a warm, draft-free place until it has doubled in bulk, about 1½ hours.

5. Punch down the dough, and divide it in half. Form each half into a loaf (the dough will feel loose and somewhat amorphous), and place the loaves in greased bread pans (9 × 5 × 3 inches). Cover the pans loosely with plastic wrap, and place them in a warm place for another 30 to 40 minutes, or until the loaves have doubled in bulk.

6. Bake the bread in a preheated 350° oven for 45 minutes or until the loaves sound hollow when tapped on the bottom.

RICHARD'S BEST BREAD   *3 loaves*

This recipe was originally published in *Jane Brody's Nutrition Book* as the one my husband usually makes to the great delight of family and friends. Hundreds of readers have told me it has become their favorite as well. It is a large recipe because it disappears fast. *Preparation tip:* Flavorings, if desired, are added just before the loaves are formed so that each loaf can be seasoned differently.

    2 cups skim or low-fat milk, scalded
    ⅓ cup vegetable oil
    ⅓ cup sweetener (any combination of honey,
        sugar, brown sugar, molasses, or corn syrup)
    2 teaspoons salt, if desired
    ½ cup warm water (105° to 115°)
    2 packages (2 scant tablespoons) active dry yeast
    ½ teaspoon sugar
    2 well-beaten eggs
    1 cup rolled oats (regular or quick)
    ½ cup bran flakes (unprocessed bran)
    3 cups whole-grain flour (any combination of
        whole wheat, rye, or buckwheat)
    3 cups (approximately) unbleached white flour
    Flavorings to taste (for example, orégano, basil,
        thyme, sesame seeds, caraway seeds, anise seeds,
        poppy seeds, fennel seeds, etc.) *or* raisins
    1 tablespoon melted butter or margarine
    Cinnamon or nutmeg (optional)

1. In a large mixing bowl, combine the hot milk, oil, sweetener, and salt. Set the mixture aside to cool.
2. Place the warm water in a small bowl, and dissolve the yeast and ½ teaspoon of sugar.
3. When the yeast is bubbly and the milk mixture has cooled to lukewarm, combine the two and add the beaten eggs. Then add the oats and bran flakes, and mix the ingredients well.
4. Add all the whole-grain flour and as much of the white flour as needed to make the dough easy to handle (it should be slightly moist but not sticky).
5. Turn the dough out on a floured board, and knead it for 6 to 8 minutes, adding more white flour if necessary. Place the dough in a greased bowl, turning the dough to coat it with the grease. Cover the bowl with a damp towel or some plastic wrap, and set the dough in a warm, draft-free place to rise until it has doubled in bulk, about 1½ hours.
6. Punch down the dough, and divide it into three equal parts. Knead into each part the desired flavorings, and form the parts into loaves. Place the

loaves in greased bread pans (9 × 5 × 3 inches), cover the pans, and set the loaves in a warm place to rise until they have doubled in bulk, about 1½ to 2 hours.

7. Brush the tops of the loaves with melted butter or margarine, and sprinkle them with cinnamon or nutmeg, if desired. Preheat the oven to 350°. Put the loaves in the oven, and turn the oven down to 325°. Bake the bread for 35 to 40 minutes or until the loaves sound hollow when tapped on the bottom.

TOMATO JUICE BREAD

2 large loaves

I was trying to use up an opened can of tomato juice when I stumbled on a recipe for tomato juice bread in *The New Book of Favorite Breads from Rose Lane Farm* by Ada Lou Roberts. This is my adaptation. The tomato juice gives the bread an attractive pale-orange hue. It is a light loaf that may be a little soft for sandwiches, but the seasonings make it wonderful with soups and entrées.

½ cup warm water (105° to 115°)
1 teaspoon sugar
¼ teaspoon ginger
2 packages (2 scant tablespoons) active dry yeast
1½ cups warm tomato juice
¼ cup sugar
2 cups whole-wheat flour
4 tablespoons (½ stick) butter or margarine, softened
1½ teaspoons salt, if desired
½ teaspoon AHA herb mix (see p. 182) or other
　no-salt seasoning
½ teaspoon crushed celery flakes or celery
　powder or crushed celery seeds
3½ to 4 cups white flour
Melted butter for brushing loaves (optional)

1. Put the warm water in a small bowl, and dissolve the 1 teaspoon of sugar, ginger, and yeast. Set the mixture aside until the yeast starts to bubble, about 5 to 10 minutes.
2. In a large bowl, combine the tomato juice, ¼ cup sugar, and whole-wheat flour, beating the ingredients well. Add the proofed yeast mixture, and combine it well with the other ingredients.
3. Add the softened butter or margarine, salt, herb mix, celery flakes, and 3 cups of the white flour, stirring the mixture until the dough pulls away from the sides of the bowl.
4. Sprinkle ½ cup of the remaining white flour on a work surface, turn out the dough, and knead it thoroughly (about 8 minutes), adding more flour if needed to make a satiny smooth dough. Place the dough in a greased bowl, turning the dough to coat it with the grease on all sides. Cover the bowl, and set the dough in a warm place to rise until doubled, about 1½ hours.
5. Punch down the dough, and turn it out onto a board. Knead the dough lightly, divide it in half, and form each half into a loaf. Place the loaves in greased bread pans about 9 × 5 × 3 inches, brush the tops with butter, if desired, and let the loaves rise again until they have doubled, about 1 hour.
6. Bake the bread in a preheated 350° oven for 45 minutes, checking halfway through to be sure the tops are not browning too quickly (if they are, reduce the oven temperature to 325°).

PUMPERNICKEL SUPREME

2 large loaves

Not only is this dark rye bread delicious, it is also easy to make. *Preparation tip:* Instead of using both molasses and honey, you can use ½ cup of light molasses and omit the honey, which will produce a less sweet bread.

1½ cups warm water (105° to 115°)
  3 packages (3 scant tablespoons) active dry yeast
  1 teaspoon sugar
1¼ cups skim or low-fat milk, heated to
    lukewarm
 ⅓ cup light molasses
  2 tablespoons honey
  2 tablespoons sugar
  3 tablespoon butter or margarine, melted
  2 tablespoons caraway seeds
  2 teaspoons salt, if desired
  3 cups rye flour
1½ cups whole-wheat flour, preferably
    stone-ground
  3 cups (approximately) all-purpose flour
Corn meal for sprinkling pan

1. Place the warm water in a small bowl, and dissolve the yeast and 1 teaspoon sugar. Let the mixture stand for about 10 minutes or until the yeast starts to foam.
2. In a large bowl, combine the milk, molasses, honey, sugar, butter or margarine, caraway seeds, and salt. Stir the mixture well.
3. Add the yeast mixture to the milk mixture. Stir in the rye and whole-wheat flours, beating the mixture well. Add enough of the all-purpose flour to make a somewhat stiff dough.
4. Turn the dough out onto a lightly floured board, and knead it for about 10 minutes or until it becomes smooth and elastic.
5. Place the dough in an oiled bowl, turning the dough to oil the top. Cover the bowl, and let the dough rise in a warm, draft-free place for about 1½ to 2 hours or until the dough has doubled in bulk.
6. Punch down the dough, and turn it out onto a lightly floured board. Divide the dough in half, and shape each half into a loaf, either long (about 14 inches) or round. Place each loaf on a greased baking sheet that has been lightly sprinkled with corn meal.
7. Cover the loaves, and let them rise again until they have doubled in bulk, about 1 to 1½ hours. With a very sharp knife, cut about three slashes ½ inch deep in the tops of the loaves.
8. Bake the bread in a preheated 375° oven for about 30 to 35 minutes, or until they sound hollow when tapped on the bottom.

SUNFLOWER LOAF

1 large loaf

Here's another protein-packed flavorful whole-grain bread that is well worth the extra trouble it takes to prepare. The friend who gave me the original recipe said she had clipped it from a newspaper in which it appeared under the name of Max's Loaf. Max, whoever you are, I'm delighted to pass your wonderful bread along.

1¼ cups warm water (105° to 115°)
  1 package (1 scant tablespoon) active dry yeast
  1 teaspoon sugar
  ¼ cup honey
  ½ cup buttermilk
1½ teaspoons salt, if desired
  4 cups whole-wheat flour, preferably
    stone-ground
  ½ cup toasted sunflower seeds
  1 egg yolk
  1 tablespoon milk
  ½ cup *untoasted* sunflower seeds

1. Place the warm water in a large bowl, and dissolve the yeast and sugar. Let the mixture stand about 10 minutes until the yeast starts to foam.
2. Add the honey, buttermilk, and salt, stirring to dissolve the honey.
3. Add the flour and toasted sunflower seeds, mixing the ingredients well. The dough will be sticky until after it rises.
4. Turn the dough out onto a lightly floured board, and knead it for about 10 minutes. Shape it into a ball. Coat the dough lightly with flour, and place it on a baking sheet. Cover it with plastic wrap, and let it rise in a warm, draft-free place for 20 minutes.
5. Knead the dough again briefly, and form it into a ball. Let the dough rise, covered, a second time for about 40 minutes. Shape the dough into a loaf.
6. Mix the egg yolk with the milk, and brush the top of the loaf with the mixture. Sprinkle the untoasted sunflower seeds on a work surface, and roll the top of the loaf in them. Place the loaf in a greased 1½-quart loaf pan. Cover the pan with plastic wrap, and let it rise for 45 minutes or until the loaf is about 1 inch over the top of pan.
7. Bake the bread in a preheated 375° oven for about 40 minutes or until the bread sounds hollow when tapped on the bottom.

WHEAT GERM CASSEROLE BREAD   *2 loaves*

There's no need to knead this easy, tasty, crusty, nutritious bread, the recipe for which was developed by the producers of Kretschmer wheat germ. *Preparation tip:* If you prefer a bread that's not as sweet, reduce the amount of molasses and/or honey. I have already reduced the salt, but you may want to cut back even further if sodium content is a special concern.

2½ cups stone-ground whole-wheat flour or
    graham flour (or a combination of
    whole-wheat, buckwheat, and/or whole-rye
    flour)
1½ cups wheat germ
  2 packages (2 scant tablespoons) active dry yeast
  2 teaspoons salt, if desired
2½ cups buttermilk
  ¼ cup light molasses
  ¼ cup honey
  ¼ cup butter or margarine
  2 eggs
2½ cups all-purpose flour

1. Combine the whole-wheat or graham flour, wheat germ, *undissolved* yeast, and salt in a large bowl. Stir the ingredients to blend them well.
2. Heat the buttermilk, molasses, honey, and butter or margarine together until the mixture is warm (105° to 115°).
3. Add the warm liquid and the eggs to the dry ingredients in the bowl, blend the ingredients with an electric mixer at low speed for about 30 seconds, and then beat the mixture at high speed for 3 minutes, scraping the sides of the bowl occasionally.
4. Stir in the all-purpose flour with a wooden spoon.
5. Cover the dough, and let it rise in a warm, draft-free place for about 1 hour or until it has doubled in bulk.
6. Punch down the dough, divide it in half, and place the halves into two greased 1½-quart casseroles or oven-proof bowls. Brush the tops of the dough with oil or spray it with vegetable-oil spray, and cover the casseroles loosely with plastic wrap. Let the dough rise 45 minutes or until the loaves have doubled in bulk.
7. Bake the loaves in a preheated 375° oven for 35 to 40 minutes or until they are done. If the crust starts to brown too quickly, cover the loaves loosely with foil during the last 5 to 10 minutes of baking.

WHOLE WHEAT–CARROT PITAS

12 pitas

I thank Jeanette B. McCay and her late husband Dr. Clive M. McCay of Cornell University for putting together the ingredients in this nutrient-packed, delicious recipe, published in *The Cornell Bread Book.* I love making pitas. It's fun to form the balls of dough and roll them out into rounds, a step that is just slightly more time-consuming than forming loaves in an ordinary bread recipe. It's even more fun to watch the pitas puff up toward the end of their baking time. *Preparation tip:* If you want your pitas to puff, it's important to follow carefully the baking instructions described below. However, these breads are so tasty that you shouldn't worry much if you don't succeed in creating the pocket. They can always be cut in half sideways to form two slices. Or you can cut them in half crosswise and, with a sharp knife, cut a pocket into the two halves. It helps to have a wooden paddle or large spatula to handle these breads before and after baking. They freeze very well. The sesame seeds—which are my addition—contribute protein, fat, and much flavor.

2½ cups warm water (105° to 115°)
 1 package (1 scant tablespoon) active dry yeast
 1 teaspoon sugar
 2 cups *finely* grated carrots (4 medium-large)
 2 teaspoons salt, if desired
 3 tablespoons wheat germ
 ½ cup soy flour
 ¾ cup nonfat dry milk
 5 to 6 cups whole-wheat flour, preferably
   stone-ground
 ⅓ cup (approximately) corn meal
 ¼ cup sesame seeds, lightly toasted (see p. 412)
   (optional)

1. Place the warm water in a large mixing bowl. Add the yeast and sugar, stirring to dissolve them. Let the mixture stand for about 5 to 10 minutes until the yeast foams.
2. Add the carrots and salt to the proofed yeast, and stir in the wheat germ, soy flour, dry milk, and about 5 cups of the whole-wheat flour or enough to make a dough that pulls from the sides of the bowl.
3. Turn the dough out onto a floured board, and knead it for 5 minutes or until it becomes smooth, adding more flour as needed to make a dough that can be handled. The dough will be sticky; it's important not to add too much flour or the pitas will be too dry.
4. Place the dough in a greased bowl, turning it to coat all the sides. Cover the bowl lightly with plastic wrap, and place the dough in a warm, draft-free place to rise until it has doubled in bulk, about 1 hour.

5. Punch down the dough, and return it to the work surface. Form the dough into a 1-foot-long roll. Cut the roll into 12 1-inch slices, and roll each piece into a ball (about the size of a large lemon). Cover the balls lightly, and let them rest for 5 to 10 minutes.

6. Place the corn meal in a shallow bowl, and, before flattening the balls, dip each ball in the corn meal to lightly coat all sides. Sprinkle the work surface with ½ teaspoon of the sesame seeds, if desired, and roll out each ball with a rolling pin into a circle about 6 inches in diameter, sprinkling another ½ teaspoon of sesame seeds on the top as you roll. Place the flattened pieces of dough on a board or cookie sheet that has been generously sprinkled with corn meal. Cover the pieces with wax paper and then with a light cloth. Place the pitas in a warm, draft-free place for about 30 minutes or until they rise slightly.

7. Meanwhile, place the oven rack in the bottom third of the oven, and heat the oven very hot, to 500° or 550°. Place a baking sheet (or for puffier breads use unglazed, ungreased baking tiles) into the oven to heat for about 8 minutes. Then oil the sheet (but not the tiles). Using a wooden paddle or very wide spatula, carefully transfer to the hot baking sheet or tiles as many of the circles of dough as will fit comfortably, and bake the pitas for about 4 or 5 minutes or until they just begin to brown (they should puff after about 3 minutes). Remove the baked rounds from the oven, and place them on a sheet of wax paper, covering them with additional wax paper and a towel (this holds in the steam which creates the pockets and keeps the breads soft). Repeat the procedure with the remaining circles.

BRAN PRETZEL ROLLS

24 rolls

These no-knead, slightly sweet rolls are unquestionable winners. They can be made into any shape. As figure-eight pretzels, they make a wonderful party roll and an appealing snack for children. They are delicious with tea or coffee. They can also be made with less sugar for a dinner roll.

¼ cup warm water (105° to 115°)
1 package (1 scant tablespoon) active dry yeast
¾ cup boiling water
½ cup butter or margarine, softened
1 cup whole-bran cereal (e.g., All-Bran)
⅓ cup sugar
1 teaspoon salt, if desired
1¼ cups whole-wheat flour, preferably
    stone-ground
1 egg, slightly beaten
1¾ cups white flour
½ teaspoon oil

1. Place the warm water in a small bowl, dissolve yeast in it, and set the yeast aside for about 10 minutes until it gets bubbly.
2. In a large bowl, pour the boiling water over the butter or margarine, cereal, sugar, and salt, and stir the mixture until the butter or margarine melts.
3. Beat in the whole-wheat flour, then stir in the yeast mixture and the egg. Add 1 cup of the white flour, and beat the mixture well. Stir in the rest of white flour, using your hands to mix the ingredients into a stiff dough.
4. Brush the dough with the oil, wrap the dough with plastic wrap, and refrigerate it for 2 or more hours (it can be refrigerated for up to 4 days).
5. Punch down the dough if it has risen, shape it into a 12 × 6-inch rectangle, and cut the rectangle into 24 equal pieces. Roll each piece with your hands into a strip about 12 inches long. Shape the strip into a figure 8.
6. Place the rolls about 2 inches apart on a greased baking sheet. Cover them with plastic wrap, and let them rise in a warm, draft-free place for about 2 hours or until they have doubled in bulk.
7. Bake the rolls in the middle of a preheated 400° oven for about 12 minutes or until they are lightly browned. Remove the rolls from the sheet to a rack to cool. They are delicious warm or at room temperature.

EASY WHEAT BISCUITS

24 biscuits

These tear-off biscuits are a favorite for informal family dinners. Eat one panful now, save the other in the freezer for a rainy day.

  1 cup warm water (105° to 115°)
  1 package (1 scant tablespoon) active dry yeast
  1 teaspoon sugar
 ¼ cup brown sugar (firmly packed)
 ¾ teaspoon salt, if desired
 ½ cup wheat germ
  1 egg
  3 tablespoons butter or margarine, melted
1½ cups whole-wheat flour
1¼ to 1¾ cups white flour

1. Place the warm water in a large bowl, and dissolve the yeast and 1 teaspoon of sugar. Let the mixture stand until the yeast starts to bubble.
2. Add the brown sugar, salt, wheat germ, egg, butter or margarine, and whole-wheat flour, beating the ingredients until they are smooth. Stir in enough of the white flour to make a dough that is easy to handle.
3. Place the dough in a greased bowl, turning the dough to grease the top. Cover the bowl, and let the dough rise in a warm, draft-free place until it has doubled in bulk, about 1½ hours.
4. Punch down the dough. With greased hands, pinch off bits of dough, and shape them into balls 1½ inches in diameter. You should have about 24 balls. Arrange the balls in two well-greased round cake pans (about 9 × 1½ inches), cover the pans, and let the dough rise until it has doubled in bulk, about 45 minutes.
5. Bake the biscuits in a preheated 375° oven until they are brown, about 20 to 25 minutes.

QUICK COTTAGE-OAT BISCUITS   *18 large biscuits*

These protein-rich baking-powder biscuits are a snap to prepare and good at any meal or for between-meal snacks. *Preparation tip:* If you do not have access to oat flour, you can grind up rolled oats in the blender or food processor, or substitute 1 cup of whole-wheat flour for the oat flour. The biscuits freeze well.

```
   2 cups unbleached white flour
   1 cup oat flour
   2 teaspoons sugar
   1 teaspoon salt, if desired
   4 teaspoons baking powder
  ½ teaspoon baking soda
  ½ teaspoon cream of tartar
  ¼ cup butter or margarine
   2 eggs, beaten well
1½ cups low-fat cottage cheese
Corn meal for sprinkling pans
```

1. In a large bowl, combine the white flour, oat flour, sugar, salt, baking powder, baking soda, and cream of tartar.
2. With a pastry blender or fork, work the butter or margarine into the flour mixture.
3. Combine the beaten eggs and cottage cheese, and add this to the flour mixture. Use your hands to blend the ingredients well.
4. Turn the dough out onto a lightly floured board, and knead the dough for 1 to 2 minutes or until it is smooth.
5. Divide the dough into three parts. Working with one part at a time, form it into a fat roll about 3 inches long. With a thin, sharp knife or cheese wire, cut the roll into 6 slices, each ½ inch thick. *Or* roll the dough out on a lightly floured board to a thickness of about ½ inch, and, with a knife or cookie cutter, cut the dough into 6 pieces (or more, if you want small biscuits) of any shape you desire. Repeat this procedure with the other two parts.
6. Sprinkle two cookie sheets with the corn meal, and place the cut dough on them, allowing space between the biscuits for the dough to rise. Bake the biscuits in a preheated 425° oven for 10 to 12 minutes.

Quick Breads

Instead of yeast, quick breads are leavened with baking powder and or soda, which are activated to release harmless gases in two ways: when they are mixed with wet ingredients and when they are heated during the baking process. Therefore, there is no need to knead them or to allow time for them to rise. As a result, they are just about the simplest baked goods to prepare, even easier than muffins or cookies, which rise the same way but have a more complicated distribution of batter before baking. Some quick breads closely resemble yeast breads in texture and flavor. But most are heavier than yeast breads and sweet enough to be a snack or dessert bread. If wrapped airtight, they will keep in the freezer for months. I nearly always have some frozen loaves on hand for expected and unexpected guests and for instant treats for the family. They make precious gifts, too, at holiday time or when you visit friends and relatives. They can be made in pans of various sizes, from tiny 4×2-inch pans to full-sized 9×5-inch pans (of course, the baking time must be reduced when smaller pans are used).

Unfortunately, quick breads have the nutritional disadvantage of being higher in sodium than breads leavened with yeast (assuming not much salt is added to the yeast breads). This is because both baking powder and baking soda contain sodium compounds. If sodium is of particular concern to you, you can buy sodium-free baking powder in many health and natural foods stores. Because it is not a double-acting baking powder, use twice as much of it as the recipe calls for. Also, many quick breads contain more fat than yeast breads do (usually a polyunsaturated vegetable oil) and thus should not be devoured with the same abandon you might apply to (unbuttered) yeast bread. In our household, we treat them more like cake or cookies than bread (although they are a lot more wholesome than cake and cookies). On the following pages, you'll find several family favorites. Note that the recipes tell you to combine the wet and dry ingredients *until the dry ingredients are just moistened.* This is important to prevent gluten development (see "Bread Baking," p. 556), which would result in a tough product with air holes—undesirable characteristics in quick breads.

APPLESAUCE-OAT BREAD

1 loaf

Since I prepare and preserve applesauce in quart-sized canning jars each fall from a bushel of apples, I'm always on the lookout for good applesauce recipes. This low-fat, nutritious quick bread resembles a spice cake in flavor.

⅓ cup raisins
Hot water to cover
1 cup whole-wheat flour
1 cup all-purpose flour
1 cup rolled oats (quick preferably)
4 teaspoons baking powder
½ teaspoon cinnamon
½ teaspoon ground ginger
½ teaspoon ground cloves
¼ teaspoon baking soda
¼ teaspoon salt, if desired
1 egg
½ cup packed brown sugar
¾ cup applesauce, preferably unsweetened
½ cup water
2 tablespoons oil

1. Place the raisins in a small bowl. Add the hot water to cover, and let the raisins soak while you prepare the remaining ingredients.
2. In a large bowl, combine the whole-wheat flour, all-purpose flour, oats, baking powder, cinnamon, ginger, cloves, baking soda, and salt.
3. In a medium bowl, beat together the egg, brown sugar, applesauce, water, and oil until they are well blended.
4. Drain the raisins, stir them into the appplesauce mixture, and then add this mixture to the flour mixture, stirring the ingredients just to moisten them. Pour the batter into a greased 9 × 5 × 3-inch loaf pan.
5. Bake the bread in a preheated 350° oven for 50 to 60 minutes or until a pick inserted in the center of the loaf comes out clean. Let the bread cool in the pan for 10 minutes, and then turn it out onto a rack to cool completely.

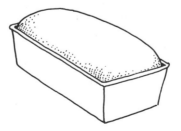

BANANA BREAD

1 loaf

This bread gets its crunch from Grape-Nuts cereal instead of nuts. *Preparation tip:* If desired, omit one egg yolk and add in its place 1 tablespoon of oil.

    ¾ cup whole-wheat flour
    ¾ cup all-purpose flour
    ⅓ cup sugar
    ½ cup nonfat dry milk
  2¼ teaspoons baking powder
    ¼ teaspoon salt, if desired
    ¾ cup Grape-Nuts cereal
    ½ cup raisins
    2 eggs
    1 cup mashed bananas (2 to 3 medium bananas)
    ¼ cup butter or margarine, melted
    ¼ cup water

1. In a large bowl, combine the whole-wheat and all-purpose flours, sugar, dry milk, baking powder, and salt. Stir in the cereal and raisins.
2. In another bowl, beat the eggs, and combine them with the bananas, butter or margarine, and water. Add this mixture to the flour mixture, stirring the two until the dry ingredients are just moistened.
3. Grease and flour a 9 × 5 × 3-inch loaf pan. Pour in the batter.
4. Bake the bread in a preheated 350° oven for 50 to 55 minutes or until a tester inserted in the center of the bread comes out clean. Let the bread cool in the pan for about 15 minutes, then turn it out to finish cooling on a rack. Wrap the bread tightly in plastic wrap or foil, and, if possible, let it stand for at least 8 hours before slicing it.

BRAN CAKE BREAD

1 loaf (16 servings)

Moist and sweet—but not too sweet—are the outstanding characteristics of this quick bread, which resembles a good bran muffin in taste and texture. *Preparation tip:* If you like bran muffins, I'd suggest doubling the recipe, since the bread freezes well for months if tightly wrapped. If you prefer a less sweet loaf, omit the sugar.

  1 cup bran flakes (not cereal, but whole
     unprocessed bran)
1½ cups skim or low-fat milk
 ⅓ cup light unsulphured molasses
  1 cup whole-wheat flour, preferably
     stone-ground
  1 cup white flour
  2 tablespoons sugar
  1 *tablespoon* baking powder
 ½ teaspoon baking soda
 ¼ teaspoon salt, if desired
 ¼ cup finely chopped nuts (e.g., pecans or
     walnuts)
 ¼ cup currants or chopped raisins (optional)
  1 egg, lightly beaten
  3 tablespoons vegetable oil

1. In a medium bowl, combine the bran flakes, milk, and molasses, and let the mixture stand until the bran is softened.
2. In a large bowl, combine the whole-wheat and white flours, sugar, baking powder, baking soda, salt, nuts, and currants or raisins (if desired). Set this mixture aside.
3. Add the egg and oil to the bran mixture, and then add this to the flour mixture, stirring the mixture just to moisten the dry ingredients. Pour the batter into a greased 9 × 5 × 3-inch loaf pan.
4. Bake the bread in a preheated 350° oven for 50 to 55 minutes or until a pick inserted in the center of the bread comes out clean. Cool the bread in the pan for 10 minutes, then turn it out onto a rack to cool completely.

CARROT CAKE

2 loaves

Garneta Baurle, author of *Country Cooking,* was the inspiration for this great carrot cake, which I make with less sugar and half whole-wheat flour. Unlike other carrot cakes, this one has only 1 tablespoon of added fat, yet it is moist and tasty. *Preparation tip:* Note that the first set of ingredients should rest for 12 hours after cooking before the cake is made. If desired, this recipe can be baked (also at 275°) like a cake in a single tube pan instead of two loaf pans.

¾ cup sugar
1¼ cups water
1 cup raisins
2 cups *finely* grated carrots (4 medium-large)
1 tablespoon butter or margarine
1 teaspoon ground cloves
1 teaspoon cinnamon
½ teaspoon nutmeg
1 cup chopped nuts (walnuts or pecans)
1¼ cups whole-wheat flour
1⅛ cups all-purpose flour
2 teaspoons baking powder
1 teaspoon baking soda
½ teaspoon salt, if desired

1. In a medium saucepan, combine the sugar, water, raisins, carrots, butter or margarine, cloves, cinnamon, and nutmeg. Bring the mixture to a boil over moderately high heat, reduce the heat, and simmer the mixture for 5 minutes. Cover the pan, and let the mixture rest for 12 hours (refrigeration is not necessary).
2. In a medium bowl, combine the nuts, whole-wheat and all-purpose flours, baking powder, baking soda, and salt. Add this to the carrot mixture *after* the carrot mixture has rested, stirring just to combine the ingredients. Divide the batter between two oiled loaf pans (9 × 5 × 3 inches).
3. Bake the cake in a preheated *275°* oven for 1 hour 10 minutes.

MEXICAN CORN BREAD

8 to 16 servings

This tasty and moist corn bread is an excellent accompaniment not only for traditional Mexican dishes but for a variety of American standards as well, such as soup and salads. I have also used it to prepare a delicious turkey stuffing.

1 cup yellow corn meal, preferably
   stone-ground
¾ cup all-purpose flour
2 teaspoons baking powder
1 teaspoon baking soda
½ teaspoon salt, if desired
1 egg white
2 whole eggs
1 17-ounce can cream-style corn
1 cup buttermilk
2 tablespoons butter or margarine, melted and
   cooled
1 cup grated Cheddar (4 ounces)
¼ cup seeded and chopped jalapeño peppers
   (wear rubber gloves) *or* 1 4-ounce can
   jalapeño or green chili peppers, seeded and
   chopped

1. In a large bowl, combine the corn meal, flour, baking powder, baking soda, and salt. Set the bowl aside.
2. In a medium bowl, lightly beat the egg white and whole eggs, and combine them with the corn, buttermilk, butter or margarine, cheese, and peppers. Stir this mixture into the reserved corn-meal mixture, until the ingredients are just combined.
3. Grease a 9-inch square or round baking pan or 9-inch cast-iron skillet, and heat it for several minutes in a preheated 400° oven. Remove the pan from the oven, and pour the batter into it. Return the pan to the oven, and bake the bread for about 25 minutes or until a tester inserted in the center of the bread comes out clean.

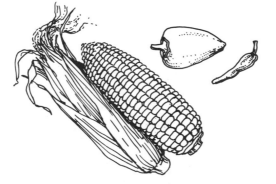

CRANBERRY BREAD BRODY

1 loaf

I adore cranberries. Their tang and color and juiciness add verve to many baked goods. This recipe has been an annual hit among those on my holiday gift list. *Preparation tip:* Cranberries freeze well in their original bags (unwashed) for year-round use, so you can stock up in the fall if you have the freezer space. Also, this bread freezes well, so feel free to make a double batch. The bread is much easier to slice if first wrapped and allowed to rest overnight.

    1 cup whole-wheat flour
    1 cup all-purpose flour
    ½ to ⅔ cup sugar, to taste
 1½ teaspoons baking powder
    ½ teaspoon baking soda
    ½ teaspoon salt, if desired
    3 tablespoons vegetable oil
    4 teaspoons grated orange peel
    ¾ cup orange juice
    1 egg
 1⅓ cups fresh cranberries, sliced in half or
      coarsely chopped
    ½ cup chopped nuts (e.g., walnuts or pecans)

1. In a large bowl, stir together the whole-wheat and all-purpose flours, sugar, baking powder, baking soda, and salt.
2. In a small bowl, whisk together the oil, orange peel, orange juice, and egg. Add this mixture to the flour mixture, stirring the two mixtures just to moisten the dry ingredients. Fold in the cranberries and nuts, and pour the batter into a greased 9 × 5 × 3-inch pan or two miniloaf pans.
3. Bake the bread in a preheated 350° oven for 1 hour (about 50 minutes for the small pans). Set the pan on a rack for about 10 minutes before turning out the loaf to cool completely. Wrap the bread well, and let it stand overnight before slicing it.

HONEY HEALTH BREAD

1 loaf (16 servings)

There are some people who think that all health breads are, by definition, dry and uninteresting. Here is the exception. Not only does this bread taste good enough to substitute for cake, it is so simple that a child could prepare it. *Preparation tip:* The bread freezes well, so consider preparing a double recipe.

2½ cups whole-wheat flour, preferably
    stone-ground
½ cup plus 2 tablespoons soy or rye flour
2 teaspoons baking soda
½ teaspoon salt, if desired
2 cups buttermilk
¼ cup honey
2 tablespoons vegetable oil

1. In a large bowl, stir together the whole-wheat and soy or rye flours, baking soda, and salt.
2. In a small bowl, combine the buttermilk, honey, and vegetable oil. Add the liquid ingredients to the dry ingredients, stirring until the ingredients are just combined. Pour the batter into a well-greased 9 × 5 × 3-inch loaf pan or 2 miniloaf pans.
3. Bake the bread in a preheated 325° oven for 1 hour (45 to 50 minutes for small loaves).

PUMPKIN BREAD

1 loaf

This recipe has a little more fat than I would ordinarily use, but it is unsaturated vegetable oil and the result is a moist, cakelike bread. *Preparation tip:* You can double the recipe and bake it in a 10-inch tube pan, if desired.

½ cup sugar
½ cup vegetable oil
¾ cup pumpkin purée
2 eggs *or* 1 egg white and 1 whole egg
1 cup all-purpose flour
½ cup whole-wheat flour
1 teaspoon baking powder
1 teaspoon baking soda
1 teaspoon cinnamon
¼ teaspoon salt, if desired
¼ cup dark raisins
¼ cup golden raisins
½ cup chopped walnuts or pecans

1. In a large bowl, beat together the sugar, oil, pumpkin, and eggs.
2. In a medium bowl, stir together the all-purpose and whole-wheat flours, baking powder, baking soda, cinnamon, and salt. Fold this into the pumpkin mixture, stirring the two mixtures just to moisten the dry ingredients. Stir in the dark raisins, golden raisins, and nuts. Pour the batter into a greased 9 × 5 × 3-inch loaf pan (or two miniloaf pans).
3. Bake the bread in a preheated 350° oven for about 1 hour or until a pick inserted in the center of the bread comes out clean (check after 50 minutes if using miniloaf pans). Set the pan on a rack for 10 minutes, then turn out the loaf to cool completely.

RHUBARB BREAD

2 loaves

Every rhubarb-containing recipe I tested was rated a winner. This spice cake is a cousin to the rhubarb cake on page 619, but it is baked as a loaf and slices like one, too. *Preparation tip:* Diced fresh rhubarb can be frozen in season for later use.

  2 cups all-purpose flour
1¼ cups whole-wheat flour
  2 teaspoons baking soda
  1 teaspoon baking powder
  ½ teaspoon salt, if desired
  2 teaspoons cinnamon
  ½ teaspoon allspice
  ¼ teaspoon nutmeg
  1 egg white
  2 whole eggs
  1 cup vegetable oil
1¼ cups packed dark-brown sugar
  2 teaspoons vanilla
  2½ cups diced rhubarb (about ½ pound)
  ¾ cup chopped walnuts

1. In a medium bowl, combine the all-purpose and whole-wheat flours, baking soda, baking powder, salt, cinnamon, allspice, and nutmeg.
2. In a large mixing bowl, combine the egg white, whole eggs, oil, brown sugar, and vanilla. Beat the mixture with an electric mixer on high speed until it is fluffy. Stir in the flour mixture until it is just moistened. Stir in the rhubarb and walnuts.
3. Divide the batter between two greased 9 × 5 × 3-inch loaf pans. Bake the breads in a preheated 350° oven for about 50 minutes or until a pick inserted in the center of the breads comes out clean. Set the pans on a rack for about 10 minutes, then turn out the loaves to cool completely.

WHOLE WHEAT IRISH SODA BREAD

1 large loaf
(24 servings)

Gourmet magazine is the source of this low-fat, high-nutrient, easy-to-make soda bread. I simply reduced the salt. It is wonderful fresh or toasted and looks especially lovely on a buffet table. *Preparation tip:* Caraway fans might want to use an extra tablespoon of these flavorful seeds. Ordinary raisins can be substituted for golden; you might also soak the raisins for 5 to 10 minutes in hot water, drain and cool them, and add them along with the wet ingredients.

2½ cups unbleached white flour, divided
  2 cups whole-wheat flour, preferably
    stone-ground
1½ tablespoons sugar
2½ teaspoons baking soda
  1 teaspoon salt, if desired
  2 tablespoons unsalted butter or margarine, cut
    into bits
  1 cup golden raisins
  2 tablespoons caraway seeds
1½ cups buttermilk
  2 large eggs, lightly beaten
Melted butter for brushing loaf, if desired

1. In a large bowl, combine thoroughly 2 cups of the white flour, the whole-wheat flour, sugar, baking soda, and salt. Add the butter or margarine, and work it in with a pastry blender or fork until it is well mixed (the flour mixture should resemble fine meal). Stir in the raisins and caraway seeds.
2. In a small bowl, combine the buttermilk and eggs. Stir this into the flour mixture, beating the ingredients with a wooden spoon until the dough forms a ball. Turn the dough out onto a floured surface, and work in as much of the remaining white flour as needed to make a soft but not sticky dough. Knead the dough for 1 to 2 minutes or until it is smooth.
3. Shape the dough into a fat 8-inch pancake. Place the dough on a greased baking sheet. Using a floured knife, cut an "X" ¼ inch deep across the top.
4. Bake the bread in the center of a preheated 350° oven for 45 to 55 minutes or until the loaf sounds hollow when tapped on the bottom. Remove the bread from the oven to a board, and brush the top with melted butter, if desired. Serve the bread warm, at room temperature, or toasted.

ZUCCHINI-PARMESAN BREAD

1 loaf (16 servings)

I first served this bread at a party about 10 years ago, and half the guests requested the recipe. By now I suspect it's been distributed to hundreds of people. But in case it has not yet gotten to you, here it is. *Preparation tip:* This bread does not hold up as well in the freezer as some others. Rather than making more than we're likely to eat within a few weeks, I freeze packages of grated, squeezed zucchini to make the bread fresh each time.

1½ cups whole-wheat flour
1½ cups white flour
⅓ cup sugar
3 tablespoons grated Parmesan
5 teaspoons baking powder
½ teaspoon baking soda
¼ teaspoon salt, if desired
1 cup shredded unpeeled zucchini, squeezed dry
⅓ cup butter or margarine, melted and cooled
1 cup buttermilk
2 eggs *or* 2 egg whites and 1 whole egg, lightly beaten
2 tablespoons grated onion

1. In a large bowl, mix together the whole-wheat and white flours, sugar, Parmesan, baking powder, baking soda, and salt. Mix in the zucchini.
2. In a small bowl, combine the butter or margarine, buttermilk, eggs, and onion. Add this to the flour mixture, stirring the ingredients to combine them well. Pour the batter into a greased 9 × 5 × 3-inch pan.
3. Bake the bread in a preheated 350° oven for 55 to 60 minutes or until a pick inserted in the center of the bread comes out clean.

"GRATE" ZUCCHINI BREAD

1 loaf (16 servings)

This version of the ever-popular zucchini bread is lower in sugar and fat than you're likely to find elsewhere. We think it's *great* (hence the punnish name).

¾ cup whole-wheat flour
¾ cup unbleached white flour
½ cup sugar
1 teaspoon baking powder
½ teaspoon baking soda
¼ teaspoon salt, if desired
1 teaspoon cinnamon
¼ teaspoon nutmeg
¼ teaspoon ground cloves
1 egg white
1 whole egg
⅜ cup (6 tablespoons) vegetable oil
1¼ cups packed, finely grated unpeeled zucchini
  (about 1 medium zucchini)
1 teaspoon vanilla
½ cup finely chopped nuts (optional)
⅓ cup raisins (optional)

1. In a large bowl, combine the whole-wheat and white flours, sugar, baking powder, baking soda, salt, cinnamon, nutmeg, and cloves.
2. In a medium bowl, mix together the egg white, whole egg, oil, zucchini, and vanilla. Add this mixture to the flour mixture, stirring the ingredients to combine them well. Stir in the nuts and/or raisins, if desired. Pour the batter into a greased 9 × 5 × 3-inch loaf pan.
3. Bake the bread in a preheated 350° oven for 50 to 60 minutes or until a pick inserted in the center of the bread comes out clean.

Muffins

Minimally sweet muffins, loaded with nourishing as well as delicious ingredients, are a mainstay at my house. They are quicker and easier to make than cookies, and they generally contain much less fat and sugar. They are excellent for dessert as well as for a snack. I often prepare a batch in the morning to serve for breakfast. If you mix the wet ingredients and dry ingredients in separate bowls the night before and refrigerate the wet ones, all you have to do in the morning is turn on the oven, combine the two mixtures, and spoon out the batter into a muffin tin. Or, for real ease of preparation, try the Refrigerator Bran Muffins on page 598—the ready-to-bake batter can sit for 3 weeks in the refrigerator. Most muffins bake in about 20 minutes—while you shower, shave, or set your hair.

Unlike yeast-leavened baked goods, muffins are raised with baking powder and/or baking soda, both of which contain quite a bit of sodium. Low-sodium baking powder can be purchased in many health food stores and in special diet sections of some supermarkets and can be used in place of double-acting baking powder (especially if you double the amount), but I've yet to find low-sodium baking soda. Baking soda is needed when a recipe contains acidic ingredients like buttermilk or citrus juice. The salt in the recipes that follow can be omitted if necessary (I have already reduced it to the minimum I consider desirable). Nonetheless, those people on strict low-sodium diets should be moderate in their consumption of muffins and other "quick" baked goods.

Take care not to overbake muffins, or they will be dry and hard. They usually start to pull away from the sides of the cups when done. Or use a toothpick or cake tester to determine when they are fully baked. For the sake of time and convenience, I strongly recommend using a vegetable-oil spray (e.g., Mazola No Stick or PAM) to grease muffin tins. And if you have reason to believe you will like the recipe, I also recommend preparing a double batch and setting 1 dozen aside in the freezer. They tend to go fast, especially if there are children in the house.

APPLESAUCE MUFFINS   *12 muffins*

Applesauce makes these muffins delectably moist without overloading them with fat.

1¼ cups unsweetened applesauce
1 large egg
2 tablespoons oil
¼ cup honey
1 cup whole-wheat flour (regular or pastry)
1 cup white flour
2 teaspoons baking powder
¾ teaspoon baking soda
½ teaspoon cinnamon
¼ teaspoon nutmeg
¾ cup raisins

1. In a large bowl, beat together the applesauce, egg, oil, and honey. Set the bowl aside.
2. In a medium bowl, combine the whole-wheat and white flours, baking powder, baking soda, cinnamon, and nutmeg. Add this to the applesauce mixture, stirring just to moisten the dry ingredients. Stir in the raisins, and divide the batter among 12 greased muffin cups.
3. Bake the muffins in a preheated 375° oven for 20 minutes.

BEST-OF-BRAN MUFFINS

24 muffins

I've tasted probably a hundred different kinds of bran muffins in my life, but these are my favorites, especially prized because they are moist but not greasy. In fact, they are so delicious, I won't even bother to give you a recipe for 1 dozen. (If you insist on making only 12, cut each ingredient in half.)

3 cups shredded bran cereal (e.g., All-Bran,
   100% Bran, etc.)
½ cup vegetable oil
1 cup raisins
1 cup boiling water
2 eggs, lightly beaten
2 cups buttermilk
¼ cup molasses
2¼ cups whole-wheat flour
4 teaspoons sugar
2½ teaspoons baking soda
½ teaspoon salt, if desired

1. In a large bowl, combine the cereal, oil, and raisins, and pour the boiling water over them. Set the mixture aside to cool slightly.
2. In a small bowl, combine the eggs, buttermilk, and molasses. Add this to the partly cooled cereal mixture.
3. In another small bowl, combine the flour, sugar, baking soda, and salt. Add the flour mixture to the cereal mixture, stirring just enough to moisten the dry ingredients. Cover the batter with plastic wrap, wax paper, or a damp towel, and let it stand for at least 15 minutes, preferably for 1 hour.
4. Preheat the oven to 400°. Grease 24 muffin cups, and divide the batter among them, filling each cup about three-fourths full. Bake the muffins for 20 to 25 minutes. Remove the muffins from the oven, and, when they are slightly cooled, take them out of the tin and place them on a rack to cool completely.

BUTTERMILK–BRAN FLAKE MUFFINS *12 muffins*

These are made with unprocessed bran flakes rather than prepared cereal, which contains a fair amount of sweetener. Although low in fat, they are delicious. You can omit the salt entirely, and if you use low-sodium baking powder (4 teaspoons), these are ideal for those on a low-sodium diet.

       1 cup bran flakes
       1 cup whole-wheat flour
       1 cup all-purpose flour
       2 teaspoons baking powder
    ½ teaspoon baking soda
    ¼ teaspoon salt, if desired
       1 egg, beaten
       2 tablespoons vegetable oil
    ¼ cup molasses
       2 teaspoons honey
  1½ cups buttermilk
    ⅓ cup raisins

1. In a large bowl, combine the bran flakes, whole-wheat and all-purpose flours, baking powder, baking soda, and salt.
2. In a separate bowl, combine the egg, oil, molasses, honey, and buttermilk. Add this mixture to the dry ingredients. Stir in the raisins.
3. Spoon the batter into 12 well-greased muffin cups. Bake the muffins in a preheated 400° oven for 15 to 20 minutes.

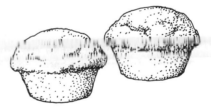

REFRIGERATOR BRAN MUFFINS   *24 to 36 muffins*

If you want to save time and effort when you're trying to get a meal on the table, these muffins are for you. You can prepare the batter as much as 3 weeks in advance and store it in a tightly covered container in the refrigerator until you want to bake it. *Preparation tip:* The following recipe makes batter for about 3 dozen small muffins. But if you have the refrigerator space, you could easily increase it.

    3 cups whole-bran cereal (e.g., All-Bran or Bran
      Buds)
    1 cup boiling water
    2 cups buttermilk
    ½ cup butter or margarine
    ¾ cup sugar
    2 eggs
    2 cups all-purpose flour
    1 cup whole-wheat flour, preferably
      stone-ground
  2½ teaspoons baking soda
    ½ teaspoon salt, if desired
    ½ cup raisins or other chopped dried fruit
      (optional)

1. In a medium bowl, soak the cereal in the boiling water. Set the cereal aside to cool, and then stir in the buttermilk.
2. In a large mixing bowl, beat the butter or margarine and the sugar until they are well blended. Beat in the eggs, and then mix in the bran-buttermilk mixture.
3. Sift or stir together the all-purpose and whole-wheat flours, baking soda, and salt. Add this mixture to the bran mixture, stirring the ingredients just enough to combine them. Add the raisins or other dried fruit, if desired.
4. Either refrigerate the batter in a tightly closed container for later use, or divide it among 36 well-greased small muffin cups, about 2½ × 1¼ inches, or 24 large muffin cups, filling each cup about two-thirds full.
5. Bake the muffins in a preheated 400° oven for 15 to 18 minutes. Remove them to a rack to cool down to warm (they are best when eaten that way).

BLUEBERRY MUFFINS

18 to 24 muffins

For cake lovers, these are great blueberry muffins—light and just sweet enough to satisfy that tooth. *Preparation tip:* You can use maple-flavored pancake syrup if you don't have (or would rather not "waste") the real thing. Frozen blueberries that have not been sweetened can also be used.

   2 eggs
 ⅓ cup vegetable oil
 ⅓ cup sugar
 ¼ cup maple syrup
1½ cups skim or low-fat milk
   2 cups all-purpose flour
   1 *tablespoon* baking powder
 ½ teaspoon salt, if desired
 ½ cup bran flakes (unprocessed bran)
1½ cups blueberries, picked over and rinsed

1. In a large bowl, beat the eggs, and add the oil, sugar, syrup, and milk, mixing the ingredients well.
2. In a medium bowl, stir together the flour, baking powder, and salt. Add the flour mixture to the liquid mixture, stirring the ingredients until they are just blended.
3. Fold in the bran flakes and blueberries. Divide the batter among 18 to 24 well-greased muffin cups, filling each about two-thirds full.
4. Bake the muffins in a preheated 375° oven for about 25 minutes or until they are lightly browned. Remove the muffins from the tins to a wire rack to cool.

SUGARLESS BLUEBERRY MUFFINS   *12 to 18 muffins*

If you are as crazy about blueberries as I am, you don't want their luscious natural sweetness overwhelmed by added sugar. In this recipe, all the sweetening comes from the berries and orange juice. The calorie count is also admirably low (less than 100 calories for a large muffin). *Preparation tip:* For best results, let all the ingredients come to room temperature before you start this recipe. Once the dry and liquid ingredients are mixed, the muffins should be baked as soon as possible.

    1¾ cups all-purpose flour
    ½ teaspoon salt, if desired
     1 *tablespoon* baking powder
    ¼ teaspoon cinnamon
    ¼ teaspoon nutmeg
     2 eggs
    ¼ cup vegetable oil
    ¾ cup orange juice
     1 teaspoon grated orange or lemon rind
     1 cup blueberries, picked over, rinsed, drained,
        and lightly tossed with 2 teaspoons flour

1. In a large mixing bowl, sift or stir together the flour, salt, baking powder, cinnamon, and nutmeg.
2. Preheat the oven to 400°.
3. In a small bowl, beat the eggs lightly, add the oil, orange juice, and grated rind, and add this mixture to the flour mixture. Before the flour and liquid ingredients are fully combined, fold in the blueberries, stirring gently.
4. Fill 12 or more well-greased muffin tins about two-thirds full with the batter. Bake the muffins for 20 to 25 minutes.

CORNY CORN MUFFINS   *12 muffins*

For corn lovers, these easy muffins are a double treat that combines both corn meal and kernels. *Preparation tip:* If you don't have cream-style canned corn or prefer not to use it, you can use corn kernels combined with ¼ cup of either milk, buttermilk, or yogurt, and add a pinch of baking soda in step 1.

    1 cup whole-wheat flour
    1 cup yellow corn meal, preferably whole meal
    4 teaspoons baking powder
    ½ teaspoon salt, if desired

¼ cup sugar
2 eggs, lightly beaten
1 cup skim or low-fat milk
3 tablespoons butter or margarine, melted
1 cup cream-style corn

1. In a large bowl, combine the flour, corn meal, baking powder, salt, and sugar.
2. In a medium bowl, combine the eggs, milk, butter or margarine, and corn. Add this mixture to the flour mixture, stirring them just until the dry ingredients are moistened.
3. Spoon the batter into 12 greased muffin cups. Bake the muffins in a preheated 425° oven for 20 to 25 minutes or until the tops are golden.

OATMEAL-RAISIN MUFFINS　　*12 muffins*

Oats give muffins a lovely texture as well as important nutrients. These are my family's favorite oatmeal muffins.

1 cup buttermilk
1 cup rolled oats (regular or quick)
½ cup raisins
1 cup flour (either half whole-wheat and half white, or all white)
1 teaspoon baking powder
½ teaspoon baking soda
¼ teaspoon salt, if desired
3 tablespoons wheat germ
⅓ cup butter or margarine, softened
¼ cup packed light-brown sugar
1 tablespoon honey
1 egg

1. In a small bowl, combine the buttermilk, oats, and raisins, and let the mixture stand until the liquid is absorbed, about ½ hour.
2. In another bowl, combine the flour, baking powder, baking soda, salt, and wheat germ.
3. In a large mixing bowl, beat the butter or margarine and the sugar until the mixture is light. Beat in the honey and the egg.
4. In alternating batches, add the flour mixture and the oat mixture to the butter mixture, stirring to moisten the dry ingredients after each addition.
5. Divide the batter among 12 well-greased muffin cups. Bake the muffins in a preheated 400° oven for 25 to 30 minutes.

ORANGE-WHEAT MUFFINS   *12 muffins*

These are great for breakfast and can be put together with only one eye open while the coffee is brewing.

    2 cups whole-wheat flour
    2 teaspoons baking powder
    ½ teaspoon baking soda
    ¼ teaspoon salt, if desired
    1 egg, beaten
    ¼ cup vegetable oil
    1½ cups orange juice
    ½ cup raisins

1. In a large bowl, combine the flour, baking powder, baking soda, and salt.
2. In a small bowl, combine the egg, oil, and orange juice, and add them to the flour mixture, stirring the mixture until the flour is just moistened.
3. Mix in the raisins, and divide the batter among 12 greased muffin cups. Bake the muffins at 400° for about 20 minutes.

WHEAT-AND-WALNUT MUFFINS   *12 muffins*

I'm especially fond of the crunchiness of these whole-wheat muffins, which derive their only fat from the nuts and egg and contain just 1 tablespoon of sweetener. They could double as dinner rolls.

    1½ cups whole-wheat flour
    2½ teaspoons baking powder
    ½ teaspoon salt, if desired
    3 tablespoons wheat germ
    1 large egg, lightly beaten
    1 cup skim or low-fat milk
    1 tablespoon honey
    1 cup chopped walnuts

1. In a large bowl, combine the flour, baking powder, salt, and wheat germ.
2. In a small bowl, beat together the egg, milk, and honey. Add this to the flour mixture.
3. Stir in the nuts, and let the batter stand for a few minutes.
4. Spoon the batter into 12 greased muffin cups. Bake the muffins in the middle of a preheated 400° oven for 15 to 18 minutes (do not overbake or the muffins will be too dry). Remove the muffins from the tin to cool on a rack.

COOKIES FOR THE HEALTH-CONSCIOUS

My objection to the nutrition advice offered by some health enthusiasts is that it is far too rigid. A cookie now and then won't kill you—not even a high-fat, high-sugar cookie. Some people, however, like to eat cookies more often than "now and then." Or they have children who wonder why there are never cookies in the house or who clamor for the packaged cookies that are made without a nod to nutrition. Cookies are so easy to make that I can't understand why anyone who cooks would resort to the commercial varieties, most of which are laden with highly saturated coconut or palm oil (to prolong shelf life) and far too much sugar to allow the taste of much else to come through. However, I must admit that finding and devising decent cookie recipes that are not loaded with one or another fat and sweetener was one of the most difficult cooking challenge I'd ever faced. I don't think it's enough simply to toss in some whole-wheat flour, or grated carrots or apples, or raisins and nuts and declare that the product is nutritious when there are 100 calories of fat and sugar in every mouthful. Here are recipes for some cookies that were given a passing grade by the most critical of taste testers—my children and their friends. Keep in mind, though, that all cookies—even "healthy" ones—are relatively high in sodium (from the baking powder, baking soda, and salt) as well as in fat.

"WHOLESOME" BROWNIES

25 brownies

The sinfulness of brownies is a bit softened by some nutritious ingredients in this recipe, in which fat contributes about half the calories. If you cut them into small portions, as indicated, there are only about 85 calories in each, which is good for a brownie.

    1 6-ounce package (1 cup) semisweet
      chocolate chips
 1/3 cup butter or margarine
    1 scant cup quick-cooking rolled oats
 1/4 cup wheat germ
 1/3 cup nonfat dry milk
 1/2 teaspoon baking powder
 1/4 teaspoon salt, if desired
 1/2 cup chopped walnuts
    2 eggs
 1/4 cup packed brown sugar
    2 tablespoons white sugar
    1 teaspoon vanilla

1. In the top of a double boiler or in a small heavy saucepan over very low heat, melt the chocolate chips and the butter or margarine. Remove the pan from the heat, and stir the mixture until it is smooth. Set it aside.
2. In a medium bowl, combine the oats, wheat germ, dry milk, baking powder, salt, and nuts. Set the mixture aside.
3. In a large mixing bowl, beat the eggs, and mix in the brown and white sugars and the vanilla until the mixture is thick. Stir in the melted-chocolate mixture. Fold in the oats mixture until it is just blended. Pour the batter in a greased 8-inch square baking pan.
4. Bake the brownies in a preheated 350° oven for 20 to 25 minutes or until the top is crisp but a toothpick inserted in the center of the pan comes out slightly moist. Set the pan on a rack to cool completely before cutting the cake into 5 strips in each direction.

CARROT-OATMEAL COOKIES

3 to 4 dozen cookies

Jean Hewitt's *The New York Times Natural Foods Cookbook* is the source of this excellent recipe for cookies that equal in taste their nutritive value. *Preparation tip:* I cut the salt in half but did not touch the sugar; if less sweetening is desired, you could reduce the brown sugar and molasses to ¼ cup of each and still produce an acceptable cookie.

⅓ cup vegetable oil
⅓ cup brown sugar
⅓ cup unsulphured light molasses
1 egg
1 cup unbleached white flour
½ teaspoon baking powder
½ teaspoon baking soda
¼ teaspoon nutmeg
¼ cup nonfat dry milk
½ teaspoon salt, if desired
¼ teaspoon cinnamon
1 cup grated carrots (2 medium-large)
½ cup raisins
1¼ cups quick rolled oats

1. In a large bowl, beat together the oil, brown sugar, molasses, and egg.
2. In another bowl, sift together the flour, baking powder, baking soda, nutmeg, dry milk, salt, and cinnamon. Add the flour mixture to the oil mixture.
3. Preheat the oven to 400°.
4. Add the carrots, raisins, and oats to the flour-and-oil mixture, and stir the ingredients to mix them well. Drop the dough by the rounded teaspoonful about 2 inches apart onto lightly oiled baking sheets.
5. Bake the cookies for 10 minutes or until they are lightly browned around the edges. Remove the cookies to a rack to cool.

COTTAGE CHEESE COOKIES   *about 36 cookies*

These are soft, cake-like cookies that are packed with nutritious ingredients and yet are not high in fat.

    1 cup whole-wheat flour
    ¼ cup bran flakes (unprocessed bran)
    ¼ cup nonfat dry milk
    ¼ cup toasted wheat germ
    2 teaspoons baking powder
    1 teaspoon cinnamon
    ¼ teaspoon nutmeg
    ¼ teaspoon salt, if desired
    ½ cup raisins
    ¼ cup butter or margarine, softened
    ½ cup low-fat creamed cottage cheese
    ¼ cup sugar
    2 tablespoons honey
    1 egg
    1 teaspoon vanilla

1. In a small bowl, combine the flour, bran flakes, dry milk, wheat germ, baking powder, cinnamon, nutmeg, salt, and raisins. Set the mixture aside.
2. In a large mixing bowl, beat the butter or margarine and the cottage cheese until they are smooth. Add the sugar and honey, and beat the mixture until it is fluffy. Add the egg and vanilla, and beat the mixture again.
3. Gradually stir the reserved flour mixture into the cottage-cheese mixture until they are just blended. Place rounded teaspoonfuls of batter about 2 inches apart on greased cookie sheets.
4. Bake the cookies in a preheated 350° oven for 8 to 10 minutes or until the edges of the cookies turn golden. Remove the cookies from the pan to a rack to cool.

CRANBERRY-NUT TURNOVERS   *18 small turnovers*

Here's a treat that's fit for the finest company. The turnovers take a little more effort to prepare than cookies, but they are worth it. If you should end up with extra filling, freeze it and use it another time, or smear it on pancakes or French toast instead of syrup.

FILLING
- ⅓ sugar
- ⅓ cup water
- 1½ cups (6 ounces) cranberries, fresh or frozen
- ¼ cup golden raisins, chopped
- ¼ cup finely chopped pecans

DOUGH
- 1 cup all-purpose flour
- ½ cup whole-wheat *pastry* flour
- 2 tablespoons sugar
- ½ teaspoon baking powder
- ⅛ teaspoon salt, if desired
- ½ cup vegetable shortening
- ¼ cup milk
- 1 egg mixed with 1½ teaspoons water

1. In a medium saucepan, combine the ⅓ cup sugar, water, and cranberries. Bring the mixture to a boil, and cook it, stirring it often, for 10 minutes or until the sauce thickens.
2. Stir in the raisins, and cook the filling over medium heat for 2 minutes longer, stirring it. Remove the filling from the heat, and stir in the nuts. Set the filling aside to cool while you make the dough.
3. In a large bowl, combine the all-purpose and whole-wheat flours, the 2 tablespoons sugar, baking powder, and salt. With a pastry blender or two knives worked in crisscross fashion, cut in the shortening until the dry ingredients are crumbly. Add the milk, and stir the mixture with a fork until the dough can be formed into a ball. Turn out the dough on a lightly floured work surface, and knead the dough a few times to make a smooth ball.
4. On a lightly floured surface, roll out the dough to a thickness of ⅛ inch to ¼ inch. Using an inverted glass or a cookie cutter, cut out 3-inch circles, and place them on ungreased cookie sheets.
5. Place a teaspoon of filling in the center of each circle. With your finger brush the edges of the circles with the egg-water mixture, and fold the circles in half, pressing the edges together to make a tight seal. (Do one circle at a time to prevent the egg mixture from drying before you seal the dough.) When all the circles are sealed, with a pastry brush, brush the remaining egg mixture on top of the turnovers.
6. Bake the turnovers in a preheated 375° oven for 18 minutes or until the crust is a light golden-brown.

PEANUT BUTTER ROUNDS   *about 3 dozen cookies*

These cookies are a little rich, given their butter and peanut-butter content, but they are also nourishing and fun to make. Get the kids to help form the balls and roll them in wheat germ.

⅓ cup butter or margarine
½ cup peanut butter, smooth or chunky
½ cup packed dark-brown sugar
1 egg
½ teaspoon vanilla
1¼ cups white flour
¾ teaspoon baking soda
½ teaspoon nutmeg
2 tablespoons sesame seeds
1 egg white, lightly beaten
½ cup wheat germ

1. In a medium bowl, with an electric mixer beat the butter or margarine, peanut butter, brown sugar, egg, and vanilla until the mixture is light and fluffy.
2. Sift the flour, baking soda, and nutmeg into the peanut-butter mixture. Add the sesame seeds, and stir the mixture until the ingredients are just combined.
3. With your hands, form 1-inch balls of dough. Dip each ball into the beaten egg white, and then roll it in the wheat germ. Place the balls on lightly greased cookie sheets about 1 to 2 inches apart.
4. Bake the rounds in a preheated 375° oven for 10 to 12 minutes. Remove them to a rack to cool.

PUMPKIN COOKIES

about 6 dozen cookies

The sweetness of the dates and raisins more than makes up for the relatively little added sugar in these cookies.

½ cup butter or margarine
⅔ cup sugar
2 eggs
1 cup fresh cooked or canned pumpkin purée
1½ cups white flour (or a little more if you use homemade pumpkin)
2 teaspoons baking powder
½ teaspoon baking soda
1 teaspoon cinnamon
½ teaspoon nutmeg
⅛ teaspoon ground cloves
1¼ cups rolled oats (regular or quick)
½ cup chopped dates
¾ cup raisins
½ cup chopped walnuts

1. In a large mixing bowl, cream the butter or margarine and the sugar together. Beat in the eggs, and add the pumpkin.
2. In another bowl, combine the flour, baking powder, baking soda, cinnamon, nutmeg, and cloves. Stir this mixture into the pumpkin mixture.
3. Add the oats, dates, raisins, and walnuts, and combine the ingredients well. Drop the dough by rounded teaspoonfuls about 2 inches apart on greased baking sheets.
4. Bake the cookies in a preheated 375° oven for about 12 minutes. Remove the cookies to a rack to cool.

WHOLE WHEAT–RAISIN COOKIES   *8 dozen cookies*

This recipe, donated by a friend, has more oil than I usually use. But note that it makes 8 dozen cookies, so the 1 cup of fat is well distributed, as long as you don't eat all 8 dozen yourself!

    1 cup water
    2 cups raisins
    1 cup oil
    ½ cup honey
    3 large eggs
    1 teaspoon vanilla
    4 cups whole-wheat *pastry* flour
    1 teaspoon baking powder
    1 teaspoon baking soda
    2 teaspoons cinnamon
    ¼ teaspoon nutmeg
    ¼ teaspoon allspice
    ¼ teaspoon ground cloves
    ½ teaspoon salt, if desired
    1 cup chopped nuts
    ½ cup wheat germ (approximately)

1. In a small saucepan, bring the water to a boil, add the raisins, reduce the heat, and simmer the raisins for 5 minutes. Remove the raisins from the heat, drain them, and let them cool.
2. In a large bowl, beat together the oil, honey, eggs, and vanilla. Add the cooled raisins.
3. In another bowl, sift together the flour, baking powder, baking soda, cinnamon, nutmeg, allspice, cloves, and salt. Add this mixture to the raisin mixture, and stir them to combine the ingredients well. Stir in the nuts, and add enough wheat germ to make a thick batter that can be dropped from a spoon.
3. Drop the batter by the teaspoonful onto oiled baking sheets. Bake the cookies in a preheated 400° oven for 10 minutes. Remove the cookies to a rack to cool.

DESSERTS

Some readers may be surprised to find so many desserts included in a book promoting good health. But let's face facts: along with weight-loss diets, desserts are the most popular items among the readers of the nation's leading service magazines. Although my family does not make a habit of eating dessert after meals, millions of Americans are hooked on them. Thus, I thought it wise to help those who wish "to have their cake and eat it too" do so without compromising their health and in many cases maybe even helping to promote their health. Thus, you shouldn't be surprised to find that most of my desserts are fruit-based. All are as low in fat and sugar as they can be and still turn out properly and taste good. I see no point in using so little sugar that a dessert no longer tastes like dessert. Better to have something that tastes good and eat less of it, if necessary. Where corners could be cut without serious consequence, I cut them. Thus, milk and evaporated skim milk are often used in place of cream; yogurt, low-fat cottage cheese, and part-skim ricotta stand in for sour cream, ice cream, whipped cream, and cream cheese; fruit purées and fruit-juice concentrates replace some of the sugar; fresh fruit and fruit canned in unsweetened juice are used instead of fruit canned in heavy syrup; beaten egg whites substitute for whipped cream; small amounts of liqueurs and extra vanilla (be sure to use pure extract) are sometimes used to enhance flavor without adding much sugar or calories; crumb crusts are used wherever possible because dough crusts have twice the fat. I will admit that I experimented with modified dough crusts until my family practically refused to taste them, and I never found one "healthy" crust any of us really liked. They were either tough or strange-tasting or both. I have decided that when you want to make a pie with a dough crust, use a normal recipe, despite its high-fat content. Just don't make pies too often, and/or eat smaller servings when you do.

Although I do not give precise calorie counts, I can tell you that when divided according to the number of servings listed, virtually every one of the desserts offered here contains fewer than 200 calories per serving, and some are a lot lower than that. That's pretty good when you realize that a standard serving of a regular pie has between 400 and 600 calories and most puddings are in the range of 300 calories or more per serving.

After reading the recipes here, you may want to try modifying some of your own family favorites according to the principles I've applied.

BLUEBERRIES AND PEACHES
IN MINT SAUCE

4 servings

This refreshing, simple summer dessert, adapted from a recipe in *Gourmet* magazine, may be prepared several hours before serving time.

4 peaches, peeled, halved, pitted, and sliced
½ pint blueberries, picked over, rinsed, and drained
3 tablespoons fresh lemon juice
¼ cup loosely packed fresh mint leaves, chopped
4 teaspoons sugar

1. Combine the peaches and blueberries in a serving bowl.
2. In a blender, food processor, or large mortar with pestle, blend the lemon juice, mint, and sugar. Pour the sauce over the fruit, toss the ingredients gently, cover the bowl, and chill the dessert before serving it.

DRUNKEN ORANGES

4 to 6 servings

This simple and simply heavenly dessert was inspired by a recipe in *Gourmet* magazine. If you're lucky enough to have leftovers, you can have "a hair of the dog" for breakfast the next day. *Preparation tip:* The oranges should be prepared ½ day in advance so they have time to "marinate" in the rum.

4 navel oranges, peeled and cut into ⅓-inch
    crosswise slices
¼ cup finely chopped dates
¼ cup dark rum
2 tablespoons pine nuts, lightly toasted

1. Arrange the orange slices on a serving dish, and sprinkle them with the chopped dates and rum. Cover the dish, and chill the oranges for at least 4 hours, preferably overnight.
2. At serving time, sprinkle the oranges with the toasted pine nuts.

POACHED PEARS WITH
PEACH SAUCE

4 or 8 servings

This low-calorie dessert looks and tastes elegant (some tasters thought the pears were poached in port). The only added sugar is already in the cranberry juice. I thank *Health* magazine for the suggestion.

4 large ripe pears, peeled, halved lengthwise,
  and cored
4 cups cranberry juice
2 teaspoons vanilla
1 16-ounce can peaches (slices or halves) in juice
  or extra-light syrup
½ teaspoon almond extract
Fresh mint leaves for garnish (optional)

1. Place the pears, cranberry juice, and vanilla in a large saucepan. Bring the ingredients to a boil over medium heat, reduce the heat to low, cover the pan, and simmer the pears for 15 to 20 minutes or until the pears are tender but not mushy.
2. Transfer the pears and juice to a bowl, setting aside ¼ cup of the liquid. Let the pears cool, then chill them in the refrigerator for at least 2 hours.
3. Meanwhile, drain the peaches (the juice can be used for another purpose), and place them in a blender or food processor. Add the almond extract and the reserved ¼ cup of the poaching liquid. Blend the ingredients at high speed until the peaches are puréed. Refrigerate the sauce for at least 1 hour.
4. To serve, remove the pear halves with a slotted spoon from the poaching liquid, place 1 or 2 halves in each dish, and top each half with the peach sauce. Garnish each serving with mint, if desired.

SPICY POACHED PEARS

4 to 8 servings

This slightly sweeter, spicier version of poached pears serves equally well as an accompaniment for fowl or meat or as a dessert or snack.

4 ripe pears, peeled, halved lengthwise, and
  cored
2 cups cranberry juice
2 tablespoons sugar
¼ teaspoon cinnamon
¼ teaspoon ground cloves
1 teaspoon grated orange rind
½ teaspoon grated lemon rind

Combine all the ingredients in a saucepan. Bring the liquid to a boil, reduce the heat, cover the pan, and simmer the pears for about 15 minutes or until they are just tender. Serve the pears warm, at room temperature, or chilled.

STRAWBERRIES 'N' PURÉE

4 servings
(8 as topping)

This simple dessert is delicious by itself or as a topping for sorbet or sherbet. The sweetness or tartness can be adjusted according to taste.

   2 pints strawberries, washed, dried, hulled, and
      halved, divided
   ⅓ cup fresh lemon juice
   ⅓ cup sugar

1. Place 1 cup of the strawberries into a blender or food processor. Add the lemon juice and sugar, and purée the mixture.
2. Place the remaining berries in an attractive bowl. Pour the purée over them, and toss the berries to coat them with the purée. Chill the strawberries, covered, for 1 hour or longer.

FLOURLESS APPLE "CAKE"

6 servings

This moist, no-bake apple dessert was devised by Carol Cutler, author of *The Woman's Day Low-Calorie Dessert Book,* a source of many low-fat, low-sugar, delicious desserts made with real ingredients used in imaginative, low-calorie ways. This "cake" seems much richer than its 165 calories per serving. It can be enjoyed by all, from kids to company.

   2 tablespoons butter or margarine
   2 pounds apples, peeled, cored, and thinly sliced
   ¼ cup packed brown sugar
   ½ teaspoon nutmeg
   3 tablespoons rum (dark preferred)
   ½ recipe Creamy Dessert Sauce, heated (see the
      recipe on p. 647)

1. Melt the butter or margarine in a wide skillet, add the apple slices, and sprinkle them with the sugar, nutmeg, and rum.
2. Cook the apples, uncovered, over medium heat until they are soft, about 15 minutes, turning them occasionally without crushing them. Remove the pan from the heat, and cool the apples.
3. When the apples are lukewarm, lightly oil a 6-cup soufflé dish. Arrange the apple slices in an attractive pattern along the bottom of the dish. Add the remaining slices, and press them down firmly. Refrigerate the "cake" for 3 hours or longer.

4. About ½ hour before serving, remove the dish from the refrigerator. Loosen the edges of the "cake" with a knife, dip the dish into a bowl of hot water for about 30 seconds, and invert the "cake" onto a serving platter.

5. Serve the apple "cake" with the hot dessert sauce (if the sauce is made in advance, heat it in the top of a double boiler).

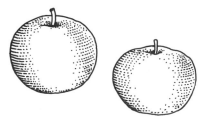

APPLESAUCE-CARROT CAKE

16 servings

What a treat to eat an almost guilt-free cake, well under 200 calories a slice and rich in vitamin A and other nutrients. And it takes only 10 to 15 minutes to throw together. With a cake recipe that's so easy, there's no reason to have to rely on packaged mixes. *Preparation tip:* This is a great make-ahead cake. If you wrap it well in foil, it will keep in the refrigerator for a week or in the freezer for months.

1½ cups white flour
½ cup whole-wheat *pastry* flour
⅔ cup sugar
2 teaspoons baking soda
1½ teaspoons cinnamon
½ teaspoon nutmeg
½ teaspoon salt, if desired
¾ cup unsweetened applesauce
¼ cup oil
3 large eggs *or* 2 egg whites and 2 whole eggs
3 cups coarsely grated carrots (about ¾ pound)

1. In a large mixing bowl, combine the white and whole-wheat flours, sugar, baking soda, cinnamon, nutmeg, and salt.

2. In a small bowl, combine the applesauce, oil, and eggs, and add them to the flour mixture, stirring until the ingredients are well blended. Add the carrots, and mix again. Pour the batter into a greased 9-inch tube pan.

3. Bake the cake in a preheated 350° oven for about 1 hour 10 minutes or until a toothpick inserted in thickest part of the cake comes out clean. Set the cake pan on a wire rack for 5 minutes. Then run a knife around the edges of the pan to loosen the cake, and turn the cake out onto the rack to cool.

LEMON CHEESECAKE

10 to 12 servings

Cheesecake in a low-fat, health-conscious cookbook? You bet. Here's a light cheesecake you can eat with a minimum of guilt, since each serving has very little fat and fewer calories than half a sandwich.

CRUST
1 cup graham cracker crumbs
2 tablespoons butter or
    margarine, melted

FILLING
1 pound (2 cups) low-fat creamed
    cottage cheese
2 egg whites
2 whole eggs
½ cup evaporated skim milk
⅓ cup sugar
1 tablespoon grated lemon rind
⅓ cup fresh lemon juice
¼ cup flour
Lemon slices for garnish

1. In a small bowl, combine the crumbs and the butter or margarine, and press the mixture into the bottom of a greased 9-inch loose-bottomed or spring-form pan. Place the pan in the freezer while you prepare the filling.
2. Preheat the oven to 300°.
3. In a blender or food processor, combine the cottage cheese, egg whites, whole eggs, evaporated milk, sugar, lemon rind, and lemon juice. Process the ingredients until they are smooth. Add the flour, and process the mixture a few seconds longer to blend the ingredients thoroughly. Pour the filling into the prepared chilled crust.
4. Bake the cake for 1 hour or until the filling has set. Cool the cake in the pan on a rack. Loosen the edges of the cake with a thin knife before removing the sides (but not the bottom) of the pan from the cake. Place the cake on a serving platter, and garnish it with lemon slices.

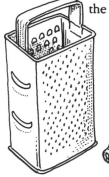

COCONUT COFFEE CAKE

9 to 12 servings

This is a moist cake that would be excellent as a snack or picnic cake, as well as a not-too-sweet dessert. It has a mild chocolate-like flavor without the calories of chocolate. If cut into 12 portions, it contains 165 calories per serving, which is very good for a cake. *Preparation tip:* Kellogg's devised the recipe as yet another way to use its bran cereals, but you can, of course, substitute any other all-bran ready-to-eat cereal. I prefer it less sweet (you can reduce the sugar to ½ cup), but my tasters said they like it as is. I prepare the cake with unsweetened coconut, which is available in natural food stores if it is not in your supermarket.

½ cup All-Bran or Bran Buds cereal
1 cup cold, strong coffee
1½ cups white flour
1 teaspoon baking soda
½ teaspoon salt (I use ¼ teaspoon), if desired
1 teaspoon cinnamon
¾ cup sugar
¼ cup oil
1 tablespoon vinegar
½ teaspoon almond extract
½ cup flaked coconut, divided

1. In a large mixing bowl, combine the bran cereal and coffee, and set the mixture aside.
2. In a small bowl, stir together the flour, baking soda, salt, cinnamon, and sugar. Set the mixture aside.
3. Into the bran mixture, stir the oil, vinegar, almond extract, and all but 2 tablespoons of the coconut. Add the reserved flour mixture, and stir the ingredients to combine them thoroughly. Pour the batter into a greased 8-inch square baking pan. Sprinkle the reserved coconut on top.
4. Bake the cake in a preheated 350° oven for about 25 minutes or until a tester inserted in the center of the cake comes out clean. Serve the cake warm or at room temperature.

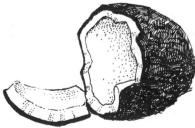

STEAMED CRANBERRY-NUT CAKE   *12 servings*

This refreshingly tart dessert bread is made like steamed pudding, which results in a moist texture even though the recipe contains no fat other than what is in the nuts. It can be served, if desired, with Creamy Dessert Sauce (see the recipe on p. 647) and is good warm or at room temperature.

1⅓ cups all-purpose flour
½ cup sugar
1 teaspoon baking soda
¼ teaspoon salt, if desired
¾ cup orange juice
2 cups cranberries
½ cup chopped walnuts

1. In a medium bowl, combine the flour, sugar, soda, and salt.
2. Stir in the juice just until the ingredients are combined.
3. Stir in cranberries and nuts.
4. Pack the stiff dough into a well-greased 6-cup mold. Cover the mold with a greased lid or with heavy foil (if you use foil, tie it on with a string so that it fits tightly).
5. Place the mold on a rack in a deep kettle. Add boiling water to the kettle until it reaches halfway up the sides of the mold, cover the kettle, and simmer the cake for 2 hours, adding more water if necessary.
6. Remove the mold from the kettle, and let it cool for about 20 minutes before inverting the cake onto a serving plate. Serve the cake plain or with Creamy Dessert Sauce (see p. 647), if desired.

DOLORES'S RHUBARB CAKE

12 or more servings

This luscious, moist cake with a texture and taste reminiscent of cheese-filled pastry was served to me by Dolores Peterson, a special friend and wonderful cook from Scandia, Minnesota. I made only a few small changes in the recipe, to increase the nutrients and decrease the sugar and calories, without any ill effect on the outcome that I could discern.

CAKE
- 1¼ cups white flour
- ¾ cup whole-wheat flour
- 1 teaspoon baking powder
- ½ teaspoon baking soda
- ¼ teaspoon cinnamon
- ⅛ teaspoon salt, if desired
- ½ cup butter or margarine
- ½ cup packed dark-brown sugar
- ¼ cup white sugar
- 1 egg
- 1 teaspoon vanilla
- 1 cup buttermilk
- ½ pound fresh or frozen rhubarb, finely diced (2 cups)

TOPPING
- ¼ cup brown sugar
- 1½ teaspoons cinnamon
- ½ cup chopped walnuts

1. In a small bowl, combine the white and whole-wheat flours with the baking powder, baking soda, ¼ teaspoon of cinnamon, and salt. Set the mixture aside.
2. In a large mixing bowl, beat the butter or margarine with the ½ cup of brown sugar and the white sugar. Add the egg and vanilla, and beat the mixture until it is fluffy. To this mixture alternately add the flour mixture and the buttermilk, and beat the ingredients until they are mixed well.
3. Stir in the rhubarb, and pour the batter into a greased 9 x 13-inch baking pan.
4. Mix together the topping ingredients, and sprinkle the topping evenly over the batter.
5. Bake the cake in a preheated 350° oven for 35 to 45 minutes or until a toothpick inserted in the center of the cake comes out clean.

BLUEBERRY COBBLER

8 servings

I am so fond of blueberries straight from the box that I hate to use them for cooking. However, this easy dessert, which takes only about 10 minutes to prepare for baking, is so delicious and universally adored that I am more than willing to donate a pint of berries to it.

⅔ cup all-purpose flour
½ cup sugar
1½ teaspoons baking powder
¼ teaspoon salt, if desired
⅔ cup skim milk
2 tablespoons butter or margarine, melted
2 cups blueberries, cleaned and washed

1. In a medium bowl, combine the flour, sugar, baking powder, and salt. Stir in the milk, and mix the batter until it is smooth.
2. Pour the melted butter or margarine into a 1- or 1½-quart casserole-type baking dish. Pour in the batter, and sprinkle the blueberries on top.
3. Bake the cobbler in a preheated 350° oven for 40 to 45 minutes or until it is lightly browned. Spoon out the cobbler onto individual dishes to serve.

IDEAL APPLE CRISP

6 to 8 servings

Apple crisps are quick, easy, and popular desserts, good any night of the week or with tea or coffee. This recipe was adapted from one provided by the manufacturers of Ideal Flat Bread. (See other options on pp. 621 and 622.)

6 apples, *unpeeled,* cored, and sliced (about 4 cups)
2 tablespoons lemon juice
1 tablespoon water
18 rectangles of Ideal Flat Bread, crushed (1¼ cups crumbs)
¼ cup packed brown sugar
½ teaspoon cinnamon
⅛ teaspoon nutmeg
3 tablespoons butter or margarine, melted

1. Arrange the apple slices on the bottom of a greased 8-inch square baking pan.
2. Combine the lemon juice and water, and sprinkle this over the apples.

3. In small bowl, combine the flat-bread crumbs, brown sugar, cinnamon, nutmeg, and butter or margarine. Spread the mixture over the apples.

4. Bake the crisp in a preheated 350° oven for about 35 minutes.

BANANA-RHUBARB CRISP
6 servings

Banana and rhubarb may seem an unlikely combination, but in fact the sweetness of the banana sets off the tartness of the rhubarb without the need for much added sugar. This fast and easy recipe is adapted from one originally published in *Woman's Day* magazine.

     2 medium-to-large bananas, sliced crosswise into
        rounds ¼ inch thick
  2½ cups diced rhubarb (about 10 ounces, thawed
        if frozen)
     4 tablespoons sugar, divided
   ¼ teaspoon cinnamon
Generous dash nutmeg
   ½ cup flour (white or whole-wheat pastry)
   ½ cup graham cracker crumbs (about 6 squares)
  1½ teaspoons baking powder
   ¼ cup butter, margarine, or diet margarine
     1 egg, lightly beaten
   ¼ cup skim milk

1. In a medium bowl, combine the bananas, rhubarb, 2 tablespoons of the sugar, cinnamon, and nutmeg. Spoon the mixture into a well-greased 9-inch pie plate or shallow baking dish (preferably glass or ceramic).

2. In a medium bowl, combine the flour, graham cracker crumbs, and baking powder. With a pastry blender or two knives worked in crisscross fashion, cut in the butter or margarine until the mixture is crumbly.

3. Combine the egg and milk, and stir this into the flour mixture. Spoon the batter as evenly as possible over the fruit mixture (the batter is hard to spread, so don't try). Sprinkle the top of the crisp with the remaining 2 tablespoons of sugar.

4. Bake the crisp in a preheated 400° oven for 25 to 30 minutes. Serve the crisp warm or at room temperature.

CRANBERRY-APPLE CRISP

8 servings

The tartness of cranberries is a wonderful contrast to sweet apples, and the color is irresistible. This simple yet crowd-pleasing dessert messes up only one bowl. *Preparation tip:* If you prefer a higher ratio of fruit to crust, use 4 cups of cranberries, 3 apples, and ⅔ cup of sugar.

    3 cups cranberries (1 12-ounce package)
    2 large apples, *unpeeled,* cored, and sliced thin
    ½ cup sugar
    1 teaspoon cinnamon
    ¼ cup all-purpose flour, divided
    2 tablespoons packed brown sugar
    ¾ cup rolled oats (regular or quick)
    ½ cup chopped walnuts (optional)
    3 tablespoons butter or margarine, melted

1. In a large bowl, combine the cranberries, apples, sugar, cinnamon, and 1 tablespoon of flour. Transfer the mixture to a greased 6-cup shallow baking dish.
2. In the same bowl (no need to wash it), combine the remaining flour, brown sugar, oats, and nuts, if desired. Stir in the melted butter or margarine, and mix the ingredients well (the mixture should be crumbly). Sprinkle the oat mixture over the fruit mixture.
3. Bake the crisp in a preheated 375° oven for 40 minutes or until the crisp is lightly browned. Let the crisp stand for 10 minutes before serving it.

PEAR CRISP

9 servings

Ready-to-eat pears have a short life span, and crisps are a good way to use up a surfeit of fresh fruits that are bruised or beginning to go bad. *Preparation tip:* This recipe can be made with pears alone or with a mixture of pears and apples. It can be served warm or at room temperature, so you can make it well ahead, if desired.

FRUIT
4½ cups thinly sliced, peeled, cored
    pears (2 to 3 pounds)
 1 teaspoon grated lemon rind
 1 tablespoon lemon juice
 2 tablespoons sugar
 ¼ teaspoon cinnamon

TOPPING
 ½ cup quick-cooking rolled oats
 ¼ cup whole-wheat *pastry* flour or
    white flour
 ¼ cup packed brown sugar
 ½ teaspoon cinnamon
 3 tablespoons butter or margarine

1. In a medium bowl, combine the pears, lemon rind, lemon juice, sugar, and ¼ teaspoon of cinnamon. Transfer the mixture to a lightly greased 8-inch square baking pan.
2. In a small bowl, combine the oats, flour, brown sugar, and ½ teaspoon of cinnamon. With a pastry blender or two knives worked in crisscross fashion, cut in the butter or margarine until the mixture is uniformly crumbly. Sprinkle the topping over the pear mixture.
3. Bake the crisp in a preheated 350° oven for 45 minutes.

PUFFED APPLE PANCAKE   *6 servings*

An easy but impressive as well as delicious dessert that tastes much naughtier than it really is. *Preparation tip:* The two main mixtures—the apples and the batter—can be prepared in advance, but the final pancake must be baked just before serving. I find that if I put it in the oven just as I'm serving the main course, the pancake is ready to eat when the diners are ready for it. Incidentally, there is nothing sacred about apples. Many other fruits will work: firm pears (such as Anjous), canned pineapple or cherries, blueberries, and even bananas.

FRUIT	BATTER
4 medium apples (a sweet type like Red Delicious)	1 cup white flour
1 tablespoon butter or margarine	1 cup milk (can be low-fat)
2 tablespoons sugar	2 egg whites
1 teaspoon vanilla	2 large eggs
A few dashes cinnamon	1 tablespoon sugar
	¼ teaspoon salt, if desired
	Confectioners' sugar

1. Peel and core the apples, cutting them into narrow wedges the long way.
2. Melt the butter or margarine in an oven-proof (preferably nonstick) skillet. Add the apple slices, and sprinkle them with the 2 tablespoons of sugar. Cook the slices over medium heat, stirring them gently now and then, until the apples have softened and the liquid has mostly evaporated. Mix in the vanilla, and sprinkle the apples with cinnamon. You can bake the pancake in the skillet if the pan has a heat-proof handle. Otherwise, transfer the apples to a deep-dish pie plate or a small shallow baking dish.
3. In a medium bowl, combine the flour, milk, egg whites, eggs, 1 tablespoon of sugar, and salt. Beat the batter until the ingredients are well blended.
4. About 45 minutes before serving time, preheat the oven to 425° for 10 minutes. Pour the batter over the hot fruit (if you have prepared the fruit in advance, heat it before adding the batter), and bake the pancake for 20 minutes. Reduce the heat to 350°, and bake the pancake for another 10 to 15 minutes or until it is puffed and browned.
5. Before serving the pancake, sprinkle it with confectioners' sugar. Cut the pancake into wedges, and serve it immediately.

FRUITED BUCKWHEAT CRÊPES   *6 servings*

By now you must know that I'm crazy about pancakes in almost any form. As a nutritious grain with a distinctive nutty flavor, buckwheat makes an especially good flour for a dessert crêpe. *Preparation tip:* This recipe is particularly appealing for company meals because it can be set up in advance and baked for 10 minutes as you near the end of dinner. Note that the crêpe batter should stand for 30 minutes before you cook the pancakes.

CRÊPES
½ cup buckwheat flour
½ cup white flour
1½ cups low-fat or skim milk
1 egg, lightly beaten
2 tablespoons sugar
¼ teaspoon salt, if desired

FILLING
2 tablespoons butter or margarine
6 pears, peeled, cored, and sliced
2 tablespoons maple syrup or
   brown sugar
Several dashes nutmeg

Confectioners' sugar for garnish,
   if desired

1. Prepare the crêpe batter by combining all the crêpe ingredients in a medium bowl. Cover the bowl, and let the batter stand for about 30 minutes.
2. Heat a 7- or 8-inch skillet (preferably a nonstick one with slanted sides) or a crêpe pan over moderately high heat. Brush the pan with oil, and remove it from the heat. Pour ⅛ cup of batter into the pan, tilting the pan in all directions so that the batter covers the entire bottom in a thin layer. Place the pan back on the heat, and cook the crêpe for about 1 minute until its underside is lightly browned. Loosen the edges of the crêpe with a spatula and flip the crêpe over. Cook it another 30 seconds or so to brown the other side. Transfer the crêpe to a plate, and cover it with a damp linen or cotton towel or wax paper. Repeat the procedure with the remaining batter. You should end up with 12 crêpes.
3. Prepare the filling by melting the butter or margarine in a large skillet. Add the pear slices, and sauté them for a few minutes over moderately high heat. Add the maple syrup or brown sugar and the nutmeg, and cook the filling for another 2 minutes.
4. Divide the filling among the 12 crêpes, placing a small amount in a strip in the middle of each crêpe and rolling the crêpe. Arrange the crêpes seam side down in a single layer in a shallow baking dish.
5. Bake the crêpes in a preheated 350° oven for 10 minutes. Serve the crêpes sprinkled with confectioners' sugar, if desired.

APPLE-RICOTTA PIE   *8 servings*

This pie saves hundreds of calories by doing without a real crust. The Grape-Nuts cereal provides the necessary crunch to set off the smooth apples and creamy topping.

  ¾ cup Grape-Nuts cereal
  2 large apples (e.g., Rome Beauty), peeled,
    cored, and sliced thin
  1 teaspoon grated lemon rind
  1 teaspoon lemon juice
  ½ teaspoon cinnamon
1½ cups part-skim ricotta
  ⅓ cup sugar
  1 egg white and 1 whole egg, lightly beaten
  1 cup plain low-fat yogurt

1. Sprinkle the cereal on the bottom of a greased 8-inch springform cake pan.
2. Arrange the apple slices over the cereal, and sprinkle them with the lemon rind, lemon juice, and cinnamon.
3. In a medium bowl, combine the ricotta, sugar, egg white and whole egg, and yogurt, mixing the ingredients with a spoon until they are smooth. Pour the mixture evenly over the apples.
4. Bake the pie in a preheated 350° oven for 45 minutes. When it is cool, go around the circumference of the pan with a knife before removing the side.

OPEN-FACED BLUEBERRY PIE WITH BRAN CRUST

8 servings

This dessert will not only stimulate your taste buds but your gut as well! It's loaded with fiber (from the blueberries as well as the bran), and it has the lowest fat content of any pie I've ever made and liked. *Preparation tip:* The crust can be used for a variety of unbaked pies, such as those with pudding- or gelatin-based fillings. And the filling can be adapted to any kind of berry that would taste good fresh as well as cooked. Or you can make a filling that is fully cooked and simply pour it in.

CRUST

1½ cups Bran Buds (or any all-bran cereal)
¼ cup all-purpose flour
2 tablespoons butter or margarine, melted
½ cup apple juice

FILLING

4 cups fresh blueberries, cleaned and washed, divided
6 tablespoons sugar, or to taste
2 tablespoons all-purpose flour
1 tablespoon lemon juice
⅛ teaspoon nutmeg, or to taste
2 teaspoons confectioners' sugar (optional)

1. Combine the crust ingredients in a medium bowl. Blend the ingredients until they are well mixed and the cereal is partially softened. Press the mixture onto the bottom and sides of a greased 9-inch pie plate, leaving no holes.
2. Bake the crust in a preheated 375° oven for about 12 minutes or until edges of the crust begin to brown. Let the crust cool on a rack before filling it.
3. To make the filling, in a medium saucepan with a tight cover, combine 2 cups of the blueberries with the sugar, flour, lemon juice, and nutmeg. Cover the pan, and cook the filling, stirring it occasionally, over moderately low heat for about 15 minutes or until the sugar is melted and the berries have begun to burst. Remove the filling from the heat.
4. Stir in remaining berries, and mix the filling well. Pour the filling into the prepared crust. Let the pie cool on a rack. If desired, sprinkle the top with the confectioners' sugar just before serving.

CHOCOLATE–ALMOND RICOTTA PIE

8 to 12 servings

This pie tastes so rich it could easily provide 12 servings at under 200 calories apiece. It was a winner among my tasters.

CRUST
- 1 cup graham cracker crumbs (about 12 squares)
- 1 tablespoon sugar
- ½ teaspoon cinnamon
- 1 tablespoon butter or margarine, melted and cooled
- 1 egg, lightly beaten

FILLING
- ½ envelope (1½ teaspoons) unflavored gelatin
- 1 cup milk (skim or 1-percent), divided
- ½ cup semisweet chocolate bits
- ½ cup blanched almonds
- 1 15-ounce container part-skim ricotta
- ½ teaspoon almond extract
- Chocolate bits and almonds for garnish (optional)

TO PREPARE THE CRUST

1. Combine the crumbs, sugar, and cinnamon in a small bowl.
2. Combine the butter or margarine and the egg, and add this to the crumb mixture, mixing the ingredients well.
3. Press the mixture onto the bottom and sides of a 9-inch pie plate. Bake the crust in a preheated 350° oven for 10 minutes. Set the crust aside to cool.

TO PREPARE THE FILLING

4. In a medium bowl, sprinkle the gelatin over ¼ cup of the milk, and let the mixture stand for 5 minutes. Heat the rest of the milk (but do not boil it), and add it to the gelatin mixture, stirring the liquid until the gelatin dissolves. Cool the mixture, and chill it until the mixture thickens to the consistency of yogurt.
5. In a blender or food processor, whirl the ½ cup chocolate bits and ½ cup almonds for 1 to 2 minutes. Add the ricotta and almond extract, and process the mixture again. (You will probably have to scrape down the sides of the container and redistribute the contents to get the ingredients evenly mixed. Just be sure to turn off the machine when you do this.) Transfer the mixture to a large bowl.
6. Beat the milk-gelatin mixture with an electric beater until it is light and fluffy. Fold this into the ricotta mixture, combining the ingredients well. Pour the filling into the prepared crust, and chill the pie for 2 hours or more. Garnish the pie with chocolate bits and almonds, if desired.

FRESH-FRUIT LAYER PIE

8 servings

With a crust of whole-wheat cereal topped by a stack of luscious fruits held in place by a nectar glaze, you get top nutrition as well as a refreshing dessert. With a scoop of cottage cheese, it could almost be breakfast or lunch. *Preparation tip:* The fruits used can be varied according to taste and availability—just avoid crunchy fruits like apples. Good possibilities include banana, pear, strawberries, blueberries, raspberries, seedless grapes, peach, mango, kiwi, cantaloupe, honeydew, seedless orange, and tangerine.

CRUST
- 4½ cups **Wheaties** or other whole-grain flaked cereal
- ¼ cup **wheat germ**
- 2 tablespoons sugar
- 4 tablespoons butter or margarine, melted
- 1 egg white, lightly beaten

FILLING
- 1 12-ounce can peach, apricot, or pear nectar
- 1 tablespoon cornstarch
- 1 teaspoon vanilla
- 2 tablespoons lemon juice
- 1 tablespoon water
- Approximately 7 cups of various sliced fruits (for example, 1 large banana; 2 cups sliced strawberries; 2 cups sliced pears; 1 mango, sliced; 1 kiwi, sliced crosswise)

TO PREPARE THE CRUST

1. In a food processor or blender, process the cereal into fine crumbs. *Or* place the cereal in a strong plastic bag, and crush it with a rolling pin. You should have about 1 cup of crumbs.
2. In a medium bowl, combine the crumbs, wheat germ, and sugar. Add the melted butter or margarine and the egg white, and mix the ingredients well.
3. Press the mixture into a 9-inch pie plate to form an even crust. Bake the crust in a preheated 375° oven for 10 minutes. Cool the crust on a rack.

TO PREPARE THE PIE

4. In a small saucepan, stir the nectar into the cornstarch, and cook the mixture, stirring it, over medium heat until the glaze is thick and bubbly. Cook the glaze for another 2 minutes, and stir in the vanilla.
5. Combine the lemon juice and water in a small bowl, and into the lemon-water dip in fruits such as banana, pear, and mango that darken upon exposure to air.
6. Pour ¼ cup of the glaze over the prepared crust. Place a layer of one kind of fruit over it. Add another ¼ cup of the glaze, a second layer of fruit, another ¼ cup of glaze, a third layer of fruit, topped with the remainder of the glaze. Arrange the top layer of fruit in an attractive pattern—for example, in a wheel of alternating slices of pear and mango with kiwi slices for the hub and perhaps with a whole strawberry in the center.
7. Chill the pie for several hours before serving it.

LIME-YOGURT PIE

8 servings

A no-bake, low-calorie dessert that guests described as refreshingly tart and cool and much preferred to the high-calorie whipped-cream version they had tried at a party just a few days before. *Preparation tip:* This recipe has a crumb crust that is deliberately crumbly. If you prefer a firmer baked crust, bake the unfilled crust at 350° for 10 to 12 minutes, and let it cool completely before filling it. You can, of course, substitute a regular baked pie crust, but keep in mind that the fat content will be considerably higher.

CRUST
- 1¼ cups graham cracker crumbs (about 14 squares)
- 2 tablespoons butter or margarine, melted

FILLING
- ½ cup frozen apple-juice concentrate, defrosted
- 1 envelope (1 scant tablespoon) unflavored gelatin
- ⅓ cup sugar
- 1 tablespoon grated lime rind, divided
- ⅓ cup fresh lime juice
- ¼ teaspoon vanilla
- 1½ cups (12 ounces) plain low-fat yogurt

1. In a small bowl, combine the crumbs and butter or margarine, and press the mixture into the bottom and sides of a greased 9-inch loose-bottomed or springform pan or a pie plate. Place the pan in the freezer while you prepare the filling.
2. Place the apple-juice concentrate in a small saucepan, sprinkle in the gelatin, and let the mixture stand for a few minutes to soften the gelatin. Then add the sugar, and heat the mixture gently until the gelatin and sugar dissolve. Transfer the mixture to a medium bowl. Stir in 2 teaspoons of the rind, the lime juice, and the vanilla, and set the mixture in the refrigerator or freezer until it has chilled to the consistency of raw egg whites.
3. With an eggbeater or electric mixer, whip the lime mixture until it is fluffy. Stir in the yogurt, and whip the mixture again. Pour the mixture into the partially frozen prepared crust. Sprinkle the pie with the reserved lime rind, and chill the pie until it is firm.
4. At serving time, run a thin knife around edge of the springform pan, push up from the bottom, and place the pie on a platter. (Disregard this step if you use a regular pie plate.)

NO-BAKE PEACH PIE

8 servings

Though low in calories (less than 200 per slice), fat, and sugar, this easy-to-prepare pie is high in flavor and essential nutrients. It is a joy to make on a hot day since you needn't use the oven. *Preparation tip:* You may use any other crumb crust or a regular baked pie shell, if desired.

CRUST
1¼ cups ginger-snap crumbs
2 tablespoons butter or
    margarine, melted

FILLING
6 ounces peach nectar
1 envelope (1 scant tablespoon)
    unflavored gelatin
⅓ cup frozen orange-juice
    concentrate (can be frozen)
¼ teaspoon vanilla
Drop almond extract
1 cup plain low-fat yogurt
1 pound peaches, peeled, pitted,
    and sliced (save a few slices for
    garnish)

1. In a small bowl, combine the crumbs and the butter or margarine well, and press the mixture into a 9-inch pie plate. Place the plate in the freezer while you prepare the filling.
2. Place the nectar in a small saucepan, and sprinkle in the gelatin. Let the gelatin soften for a few minutes, then heat the mixture, stirring it, until the gelatin is dissolved.
3. Stir in the orange-juice concentrate, vanilla, and almond extract. Chill the mixture until it is the consistency of raw egg whites, then whip the mixture with an eggbeater or electric mixer until it is fluffy.
4. Fold in the yogurt, and whip the mixture again.
5. Remove the crust from the freezer, and arrange half the peach slices on the bottom of the crust. Pour in two-thirds of the yogurt mixture. Arrange another layer of peaches on top of this, and pour in the rest of the yogurt mixture. Chill the pie until it has set. If desired, garnish the pie with the reserved peach slices when the pie has nearly set.

PUMPKIN-ORANGE CHIFFON PIE   *8 servings*

Pumpkin pie need not be high-calorie fare. Try this light, easy version that requires no baking. As written, the pie comes in at just under 200 calories per serving. *Preparation tip:* Note that the pie should be chilled for at least 4 hours. It can also be made a day ahead. If you can take the extra fat and calories, before serving garnish with whipped cream and orange sections, halved lengthwise.

CRUST

1¼ cups graham cracker crumbs
   (about 14 squares)
 3 tablespoons butter or
   margarine, melted

FILLING

 2 eggs, separated
⅔ cup water
 1 envelope (1 scant tablespoon)
   unflavored gelatin
½ cup packed brown sugar,
   divided
½ teaspoon cinnamon
¼ teaspoon nutmeg
⅛ teaspoon ground ginger
 1 tablespoon grated orange peel
 1 cup orange juice
 1 cup puréed pumpkin

TO PREPARE THE CRUST

 1. In a small bowl, combine the cracker crumbs and the butter or margarine thoroughly. Press the mixture onto the bottom and sides of a 9-inch pie plate. Chill the crust in the refrigerator or freezer.

TO PREPARE THE FILLING

 2. In a small saucepan, combine the egg *yolks* and water. Sprinkle in the gelatin, and let the mixture stand for 5 minutes to soften the gelatin.
 3. Add ½ cup of the brown sugar, cinnamon, nutmeg, and ginger, stirring the ingredients to blend them thoroughly. Cook the mixture over a very low heat, *stirring constantly,* for several minutes until the gelatin melts. Take care not to let the yolks cook into a solid mass.
 4. Transfer the mixture to a medium-large bowl. Stir in the orange peel, orange juice, and pumpkin, blending the ingredients thoroughly. Chill the mixture, stirring it occasionally, until it begins to set (the mixture should form soft mounds when dropped from a spoon).
 5. In a clean bowl, beat the egg *whites* until they form soft peaks. Beat in the remaining ¼ cup of brown sugar until the mixture forms stiff, shiny peaks. Gently fold the egg whites into the pumpkin mixture, blending the ingredients well. Pour the filling into the chilled crust.
 6. Chill the pie in the refrigerator until the filling is firm, for at least 4 hours.

PUMPKIN PIE

8 to 10 servings

Although more caloric than the Pumpkin-Orange Chiffon Pie on page 631, this more traditional version still is considerably lower in fat and calories than the standard fare, but it retains the delicious flavoring and texture of a good pumpkin pie.

CRUST

1¼ cups all-purpose flour
 1 teaspoon sugar
 ½ teaspoon salt, if desired
 ¼ cup vegetable shortening
 1 tablespoon butter or margarine
 4 tablespoons (approximately) ice water

FILLING

1½ cups pumpkin purée
 2 tablespoons butter or margarine, melted
 ¼ cup maple syrup
 ¼ cup sugar
 ¾ teaspoon cinnamon
 ½ teaspoon mace
 ¼ teaspoon ground cloves
 ¾ cup evaporated skim milk
 2 egg yolks
 4 egg whites

TO PREPARE THE CRUST

1. In a medium bowl, combine the flour, sugar, and salt. With a pastry blender or two knives worked in crisscross fashion, cut in the shortening and the butter or margarine until the mixture is uniformly crumbly.
2. Add the ice water 1 tablespoon at a time, mixing the ingredients with a fork to moisten them evenly and adding just enough water to permit the dough to be formed into a ball. Flatten the ball slightly, wrap it in plastic wrap, and chill it for 15 minutes or longer. (Meanwhile, the filling can be prepared through step 4.)
3. On a floured surface, roll out the dough into a circle 11 or 12 inches wide (the dough can be rolled between sheets of floured wax paper). Fit the dough into a 10-inch pie plate *or* a deep 9-inch pie dish.

TO PREPARE THE FILLING

4. In a large bowl, combine the pumpkin, butter or margarine, syrup, sugar, cinnamon, mace, cloves, evaporated milk, and egg yolks, beating the ingredients well to blend them thoroughly.
5. Preheat the oven to 350°.
6. In a separate clean bowl, beat the egg whites until they are stiff. Gently but thoroughly fold them into the pumpkin mixture.
7. Pour the filling into the prepared pie shell, and bake the pie for 50 to 60 minutes or until a tester inserted in the center of the pie comes out clean.

APRICOT CRÈME

6 servings

This creamy, refreshing dessert was inspired by a much richer version I tasted at a party. By using yogurt instead of ice cream, I greatly reduced both the fat and calorie content but retained the delicate apricot flavor and luscious color, especially beautiful when served with blueberries and/or strawberries. *Preparation tip:* If you use apricots canned in heavy syrup, you should use less sugar, if any.

  1 pound fresh apricots (about 8), unpeeled, *or* 1
     1-pound can apricots, drained and syrup
     reserved
Water to cover
  ½ cup cold water *or* ½ cup of the reserved
     apricot syrup
  2 envelopes (2 scant tablespoons) unflavored
     gelatin
  6 tablespoons sugar, or to taste (eliminate or
     reduce the amount if using the syrup from the
     canned fruit)
  ½ cup hot milk *or* use the remaining syrup,
     heated with enough milk to measure ½ cup
1¼ cups plain low-fat yogurt
Fresh blueberries and/or strawberries for garnish
     (optional)

1. If you are using fresh apricots, poach the fruit for about 5 minutes in water to cover. Remove the fruit with a slotted spoon, and, when the fruit is cool enough to handle, remove and discard the pits.
2. Place the pitted unpeeled apricots in a blender or food processor, and process the fruit until it is smooth.
3. Place the ½ cup of cold water or syrup in a small bowl, and sprinkle the gelatin on top to soften. Add the sugar and the hot milk or syrup-milk mixture. Stir the mixture to dissolve the sugar and gelatin.
4. Add the gelatin mixture and the yogurt to the purée in the blender or food processor. Blend the mixture until it is thoroughly mixed. Pour the mixture into a mold, and chill it until the crème is firm.
5. To serve, unmold the apricot crème, and surround it with berries, if desired.

COUSCOUS PUDDING

16 servings

A simple and tasty variation on the rice-pudding theme, this dessert can also serve as a between-meal snack or as a breakfast main course. *Preparation tip:* Couscous cooks so quickly that you need not worry about preparing it in advance. The pudding can be baked ahead and served at room temperature or reheated before serving (cover the dish with buttered foil to prevent the pudding from drying out). Note that this is a large recipe. For a small family or gathering, you can cut it in half.

    4 cups water
    2 cups couscous
    2 tablespoons butter or margarine
 1½ cups skim or low-fat milk
    5 tablespoons sugar
  ½ teaspoon salt, if desired
  ¼ teaspoon ground cinnamon
    1 teaspoon vanilla
  ½ teaspoon grated lemon rind
    1 teaspoon lemon juice
    2 egg whites
    2 whole eggs
  ½ cup raisins
    2 tablespoons coconut flakes (optional)
Cinnamon for garnish (optional)

1. In a medium saucepan, bring the water to a boil, stir in the couscous, reduce the heat, cover the pan, and simmer the couscous until the water is absorbed (less than 5 minutes). Transfer the couscous to a large bowl, and stir in the butter or margarine until it melts and is well distributed.
2. In a medium bowl, beat together the milk, sugar, salt, the ¼ teaspoon of cinnamon, vanilla, lemon rind, lemon juice, egg whites, and eggs. Add this to the couscous, stirring the ingredients to combine them well.
3. Stir in the raisins, and transfer the mixture to a greased 3-quart baking dish. Sprinkle the pudding with coconut and additional cinnamon, if desired.
4. Bake the pudding in a preheated 325° oven for about 45 minutes or until the pudding is set. Serve the pudding warm or at room temperature.

FRUITED BROWN RICE PUDDING   *6 to 8 servings*

This pudding is as nutritious as it is tasty. It is especially easy to prepare if you've got leftover cooked rice. Eat it hot or cold, as a dessert or snack. *Preparation tip:* The dried fruits can be varied according to taste.

½ cup nonfat dry milk
⅓ cup sugar
¼ teaspoon salt, if desired
2½ cups low-fat or skim milk
2 eggs *or* 2 egg whites and 1 whole egg
¾ teaspoon vanilla
2 cups cooked brown rice (⅔ cup raw rice cooked in 1⅔ cups water)
½ cup raisins
½ cup coarsely chopped dried apricots (optional)
Sprinkle nutmeg

1. In a large bowl, combine the dry milk, sugar, and salt.
2. Add the milk, eggs, and vanilla, mixing the ingredients well with a fork.
3. Stir in the rice, raisins, and apricots.
4. Pour the mixture into a greased 6-cup casserole. Sprinkle the mixture with nutmeg.
5. Bake the pudding in a preheated 325° oven for 15 minutes. Stir the pudding, and then bake the pudding for another 35 minutes or longer until the milk is absorbed. Serve the pudding warm or chilled.

CREAMY PEACH SHERBET   *8 ½-cup servings*

Another no-fat, low-sugar dessert that tastes rich and creamy and yet is very refreshing, especially at the conclusion of a spicy or heavy dinner. *Preparation tip:* It is an extra-special treat when served with strawberry purée (see p. 614) or another fruit sauce. The sherbet can also be made in an ice-cream freezer according to manufacturer's directions.

> 2 1-pound cans sliced peaches in fruit juice or
>   extra-light syrup
> Water
> ¼ cup sugar
> 1 envelope (1 scant tablespoon) unflavored
>   gelatin
> 2 tablespoons lemon juice
> ¼ teaspoon almond extract
> ⅔ cup nonfat dry milk
> Mint sprigs for garnish (optional)

1. Drain the peaches, and reserve liquid in a large measuring cup. Add water to the reserved liquid to make 1¾ cups.
2. In a small saucepan, combine ½ cup of the peach liquid mixture with the sugar and gelatin. Stir the mixture, and heat it just to dissolve the gelatin. Set it aside to cool.
3. In a blender or food processor, combine the peaches, remaining peach liquid mixture, lemon juice, almond extract, and dry milk. Process the ingredients until they are smooth. Add the cooled gelatin mixture, and blend the ingredients at low speed to combine them thoroughly.
4. Pour the mixture into a large bowl (preferably a metal one that has been chilled in the freezer), cover the bowl with plastic wrap, and freeze the mixture until it is nearly firm.
5. With an electric hand mixer or in a blender or food processor, beat the partially frozen sherbet at high speed. Pour the sherbet into a 4-cup container, or divide the sherbet among 8 serving dishes, and return it to the freezer for several hours or until it is firm.
6. Remove the sherbet from the freezer about 10 minutes before serving it. Garnish the sherbet with mint if desired, or serve it with a fruit sauce.

PINEAPPLE SHERBET

8 to 10 servings

A creamy yet nearly fat-free dessert that is both sweet and refreshing, this sherbet was a universal favorite among my tasters on both the Atlantic and Pacific coasts. It makes a wonderful party dessert because it can be prepared a day ahead and comes in a beautiful serving tray—the pineapple shell itself. *Preparation tip:* The sweeter the pineapple, the less sugar you need to add. The sherbet also could be made with 2 cups of canned unsweetened pineapple chunks and served in a bowl. The sherbet can be prepared in an ice-cream freezer according to manufacturer's directions.

½ cup orange juice
½ cup (or less) sugar
 1 large ripe pineapple (about 4 pounds)
 1 cup buttermilk
Mint sprigs for garnish (optional)

1. Combine the orange juice and sugar in a small saucepan, and warm the mixture, stirring it, over low heat until the sugar dissolves. Set the mixture aside to cool.
2. Cut the pineapple in half lengthwise, including the crown. Using a grapefruit knife, pineapple knife, or small paring knife, carefully cut the flesh from the skin, leaving shells that are about ½ inch thick. Use a spoon to scrape out loose flesh from skin, taking care not to cut through the skin. Save any juice that collects. Place the shells in a plastic bag or a bowl, and refrigerate them.
3. Quarter and core the flesh, discarding the hard core. Then cut the flesh into small pieces, saving the juice in a separate container. Measure 2 cups of flesh and ½ cup of juice.
4. In a blender or food processor, combine the flesh, juice, orange-sugar mixture, and buttermilk, and process the ingredients until they are pureed.
5. Pour the purée into an 8-inch metal baking pan, and place the pan in the freezer for about 3 hours.
6. Transfer the partially frozen purée to a bowl, and beat the purée with an eggbeater or an electric mixer to break up the ice crystals. Then spoon the sherbet into the reserved pineapple shells. Set the shells on a tray or serving platter, and return them to the freezer for several more hours or until the sherbet is completely frozen. Remove the sherbet from the freezer about 10 minutes before serving it. Garnish the sherbet with mint, if desired.

CHOCOLATE SOUFFLÉ

6 to 8 servings

Chocolate lovers can indulge guiltlessly in this light, almost fat-free and choles-terol-free dessert devised by Carol Cutler, author of *The Woman's Day Low-Calorie Dessert Cookbook.* Cutler has raised the soufflé to new nutritious heights. *Preparation tip:* Like all soufflés, this one must be prepared at the last minute, with diners ready to eat it right after it emerges from the oven. Be sure to take the eggs out of the refrigerator and separate the whites about an hour before you plan to prepare the soufflé.

1½ teaspoons soft butter or margarine
  4 tablespoons sugar, divided
  2 tablespoons cornstarch
  ¼ cup unsweetened cocoa
Pinch salt
  1 teaspoon instant coffee (regular or
     decaffeinated)
  1 cup evaporated skim milk
1½ teaspoons vanilla
  1 teaspoon orange liqueur
  6 egg whites, at room temperature
  ½ teaspoon cream of tartar

1. Smear the bottom and sides of an 8-cup soufflé dish or oven-proof mold with the butter or margarine, and sprinkle the dish with 1 tablespoon of the sugar. Set the dish aside.
2. Preheat the oven to 425°.
3. In a heavy saucepan, stir together the cornstarch, cocoa, salt, coffee, and remaining 3 tablespoons of sugar. Slowly stir in the evaporated milk, va-nilla, and liqueur.
4. Place the pan over medium heat, and cook the mixture, stirring it con-stantly, until the sauce thickens. Transfer the hot sauce to a large mixing bowl. Proceed immediately with step 5.
5. With an electric mixer at high speed, in a clean bowl beat the egg whites with the cream of tartar. When the egg whites form stiff peaks, add one-third of the beaten whites to the hot sauce, folding them in thoroughly. Add the rest of the beaten whites to the sauce, and fold them in gently. Be sure to work with the sauce while it is still hot.
6. Transfer the mixture to the prepared soufflé dish, smoothing the surface. With your finger, remove about ¼ inch of batter from around the edge of the dish (this helps the soufflé to rise evenly).
7. Place the soufflé in the preheated oven, and immediately turn the heat down to 375°. Bake the soufflé for 15 to 20 minutes or until the puffed top has darkened a little and has begun to crack slightly. Serve the soufflé immedi-ately.

SAUCES, MARINADES, AND MISCELLANY

A sauce or marinade does not have to be high in fat or calories to enhance a dish. And if fat is an essential part of the sauce, as in mayonnaise or pesto, at the least the fat can be a kind that does not damage blood vessels. In addition, a little bit of the sauce should go a long way. Here are some I have used successfully for various purposes. See if you can think of other uses for them. (See the index for other sauces, such as salsa, and see pp. 549–553 for salad dressings.)

BARBECUE SAUCE FOR BAKED CHICKEN

about 1¼ cups

This tangy sauce turns low-fat chicken into a taste delight, both hot and cold. *Preparation tip:* To bake the chicken, arrange skinned, defatted pieces from 2 chickens in a shallow baking dish. Top the chicken with the sauce, coating the surfaces of all the pieces, and bake the chicken, uncovered, for about 1½ hours at 325 degrees.

¼ cup cider vinegar
½ cup water
2 tablespoons brown sugar
1 tablespoon prepared mustard
¼ teaspoon salt, if desired
¼ teaspoon freshly ground black pepper
Juice 1 lemon (about ¼ cup)
 1 medium onion, halved lengthwise and sliced
  thin crosswise (about ⅔ cup)
 1 tablespoon butter or margarine (optional)
 2 *tablespoons* Worcestershire sauce
½ cup ketchup

1. In a medium saucepan, combine all the ingredients *except* the ketchup. Bring the mixture to a boil, and cook it over moderately low heat for 20 minutes. The sauce should be thick.
2. Stir in the ketchup, and remove the sauce from the heat.

BROCCOLI AND FRESH TOMATO SAUCE

6 servings
(1 pound pasta)

This simple sauce is excellent with spaghetti or linguine. *Preparation tip:* Do not overcook the broccoli; it should be tender-crisp in the finished dish. Fresh basil really makes a difference. If you don't have any, I would vote for leaving out the basil entirely.

    1 bunch broccoli (about 1¼ pounds), cut into
        bite-sized flowerets and stems sliced (6 cups
        all together)
    2 tablespoons oil, preferably olive
    1 *tablespoon* finely minced garlic (3 large cloves)
    ½ pound fresh tomatoes, cored and diced (about
        1½ cups)
    ½ cup chicken broth
    ¼ to ½ teaspoon hot red pepper flakes to taste
    2 to 4 tablespoons chopped fresh basil to taste
        or 2 teaspoons dried basil
Freshly ground black pepper to taste
Freshly grated Parmesan for garnish

1. Steam the broccoli for 3 minutes, remove it from the heat, and chill it quickly under cold running water. Drain the broccoli, and set it aside.
2. In a large skillet, heat the oil briefly, and sauté the garlic for about 15 seconds. Add the broccoli, and cook the mixture, stirring it, for 3 minutes. Then add the tomatoes, broth, red pepper flakes, basil, and black pepper; bring the sauce to a boil.
3. Remove the sauce from the heat, and toss the sauce immediately with hot pasta. Serve the pasta with Parmesan.

CREAMY COTTAGE SAUCE

about 1½ cups
(12 ounces pasta)

This is an excellent sauce to use either as is for a pasta side dish or to combine with high-protein pasta or with chunks of cooked chicken, turkey, or tuna for a pasta main meal. The basic sauce recipe was originally published in *Self* magazine. *Preparation tip:* The sauce is best prepared a little ahead of the pasta and allowed to reach room temperature before being mixed with the hot pasta. If you prefer to heat it, do so in a double boiler *or* over a very low flame, taking care not to let it boil. Herbs other than dill can be used.

1 cup low-fat cottage cheese
¼ cup skim milk
2 tablespoons grated Parmesan
2 tablespoons snipped fresh dill *or* 2 teaspoons
  dried dillweed
Generous dash nutmeg
Freshly ground black pepper to taste

1. Combine all the ingredients in a blender or food processor, and purée them until the sauce is smooth.
2. Toss the sauce with hot pasta. *Or* combine the sauce with 1 to 2 cups diced cooked chicken, turkey, or chunks of tuna, and heat it gently before spooning it over pasta.

CUCUMBER-YOGURT SAUCE

about 2½ cups

This is an excellent topping for many vegetarian and Middle Eastern dishes as well as for salad vegetables. *Preparation tip:* You can make this sauce quite thick by first draining 4 cups of yogurt in a colander lined with several layers of cheesecloth or a cotton kitchen towel. Gather together the ends of the cloth, and hang it overnight on a faucet over a bowl so that the yogurt will lose its excess moisture and be reduced to about 1½ cups of yogurt "cheese." The nutritious liquid in the bowl can be used in soups or baked goods.

1½ cups plain low-fat yogurt (*or* 4 cups yogurt, drained)
 1 cup seeded, finely diced cucumber
 1 teaspoon finely minced garlic (1 large clove)
 2 tablespoons finely snipped fresh dill *or* 2 teaspoons dried dillweed
 1 tablespoon olive oil
 2 teaspoons white vinegar
Salt, if desired, to taste

Combine all the ingredients, and chill the sauce.

MARINARA SAUCE

about 3 ¼ cups

This is a versatile low-fat tomato sauce with a distinct garlic flavor, good with fish, shellfish, chicken, and veal, among other foods. It freezes well.

    1 28-ounce can peeled Italian plum tomatoes
    2 teaspoons olive oil
    4 teaspoons finely minced garlic (4 large cloves)
    1 6-ounce can tomato paste
 1¼ teaspoons orégano, crumbled
Salt, if desired, to taste
Freshly ground black pepper to taste
    ⅓ cup minced fresh parsley

1. Purée the tomatoes in a food mill, blender, or food processor.
2. In a medium saucepan, heat the oil briefly, and add the garlic. Sauté the garlic, stirring it, for 15 seconds (do not let it brown), and add the puréed tomatoes, tomato paste, orégano, salt, and pepper. Bring the sauce to a boil, reduce the heat, and simmer the sauce for 20 minutes.
3. Remove the sauce from the heat, and stir in the parsley.

PESTO

about 1 ¼ cups

Another traditional sauce for pasta that has proved extraordinarily versatile as a condiment, filling, or what-have-you for main courses, hors d'oeuvres, and salads. The oil is olive, a beneficial fat as far as blood vessels are concerned, and I use about half of what you'll find in a traditional recipe. Keep in mind that a little of this rich, potent sauce goes a long way. *Preparation tip:* If you want a thinner sauce or have difficulty processing it, you can add some chicken or vegetable broth in step 2. Pine nuts (pignoli) are traditionally used, but if they are too expensive for your budget or hard to obtain, you can substitute walnuts. Pesto can be frozen in ½-cup or 1-cup containers or by the tablespoon in ice-cube trays.

    3 cloves garlic, chopped (1 tablespoon)
 ¼ teaspoon salt, if desired
 ¼ cup olive oil
    2 cups firmly packed fresh basil leaves
 ¼ cup pine nuts or walnuts
 ½ cup grated Parmesan

1. In a blender or food processor, combine the garlic, salt, and oil. Process the ingredients until they are smooth.

2. Add the basil and pine nuts, and blend the mixture until it is smooth. (You may have to stop the machine once or twice to scrape down the sides of the container and redistribute the ingredients.)
3. Transfer the mixture to a bowl, and stir in the Parmesan. Serve the pesto at room temperature.

CREAMY TOMATO SAUCE

about 1¼ cups

Another low-fat gem from *Self* magazine. *Preparation tip:* The sauce requires gentle heating to keep it from boiling. The addition of 1 cup of cooked baby shrimp or the use of a high-protein pasta would make this a main dish.

½ cup low-fat plain yogurt
½ cup tomato sauce (canned or homemade)
2 tablespoons grated Parmesan
1 tablespoon minced fresh basil or parsley, or
  both (optional)

In a small saucepan, combine all the ingredients, and warm them over low heat. *Or* heat the ingredients in the top of a double boiler. Toss the sauce with hot pasta.

FRESH TOMATO AND BASIL SAUCE

1 cup

Although traditionally used for pasta, this uncooked sauce is also delicious as a seasoning for cold steamed vegetables, such as green beans, or for cold cooked chicken cubes, or for tuna chunks, or spooned over hot rice or bulgur.

2 large cloves garlic, finely minced (2 teaspoons)
1 cup peeled, seeded, and chopped tomato
3 tablespoons minced fresh basil leaves
2 teaspoons olive oil
½ teaspoon salt, if desired
Several dashes cayenne

1. In a blender, purée the garlic and tomato. Transfer the mixture to a bowl (nonmetal).
2. Stir in the basil, oil, salt, and cayenne. Serve the sauce at room temperature.

LONG-SIMMERING TOMATO SAUCE   *4 quarts*

This is a great sauce to have on hand. It can be made any time of year since it does not depend on fresh ingredients, although late summer, when you can get fresh plum tomatoes and basil, is the ideal time to prepare it. I usually make this whole batch and freeze or "can" most of it in 1- or 2-cup containers for year-round use.

    2 pounds onions, chopped
    6 large cloves garlic, minced (2 tablespoons)
    ¼ cup olive oil
    10 pounds ripe plum tomatoes, quartered, *or* 10
        28-ounce cans Italian plum tomatoes with
        their juice
    2 cups fresh chopped basil *or* 3 tablespoons
        dried basil
    3 tablespoons dried thyme leaves
    1 *tablespoon* salt, if desired
    1 tablespoon sugar
    1 teaspoon freshly ground black pepper

1. In a large stock pot or kettle, sauté the onions and garlic in the oil until they are just soft. Add all the remaining ingredients, bring the sauce to a boil, reduce the heat, partially cover the pot, and let the sauce simmer for 2½ to 3 hours, stirring it occasionally.
2. Strain the sauce through a food mill to remove the tomato seeds and skins. If you prefer a thicker sauce, put the strained purée back in the pot, and simmer the sauce, uncovered, for another ½ hour, stirring it occasionally.

SESAME-PARSLEY SAUCE

about 2 cups

Delicious is an understatement in describing this nutrient-rich dip, which I found in *The Herb Book* by Arabella Boxer and Philippa Back (London: Octopus/Mayflower, 1980). It is good with crudités but also wonderful when served with fried fish, broiled meat, or the Pita Meat Pies on page 304. *Preparation tip:* See page 293 for instructions on making tahini if you are unable to obtain it already prepared. Do not substitute dried parsley flakes.

⅔ cup tahini (Middle Eastern sesame paste)
3 cloves garlic, crushed
⅔ cup fresh lemon juice
¼ cup water
Pinch salt, if desired
1 cup finely chopped parsley

1. In a medium bowl, beat the tahini smooth. Add the garlic, lemon juice, water, and salt, and beat the sauce until its texture becomes thick and creamlike. If necessary, thin the sauce with additional water.
2. Stir in the chopped parsley.

YOGURT-TAHINI SAUCE

1¼ cups

This is a delicious topping for a variety of grain and bean dishes such as felafel sandwiches (p. 492). It will keep for a week or longer in the refrigerator.

1 cup plain low-fat yogurt
2 tablespoons tahini (Middle Eastern sesame paste, see p. 293)
2 tablespoons fresh lemon juice
1 small clove garlic, crushed
¼ teaspoon ground cumin

Combine all the ingredients in a small bowl, cover the bowl with plastic wrap, and refrigerate the sauce until serving time.

COTTAGE CREAM

about 1¼ cups

Some call it "mock sour cream." But since I'm not a fan of imitation anything, I call it what it really is: cottage cheese that is made tart and creamed. It is a very effective substitute in many dishes for its high-fat cousin, sour cream, especially as an herb-flavored topping on baked potatoes. It takes less than 5 minutes to prepare.

> 3 tablespoons milk or buttermilk
> 1 tablespoon lemon juice
> 1 cup low-fat cottage cheese

1. In a blender, combine the milk and lemon juice. With the blender on low speed, gradually add the cottage cheese. Increase the speed to high, and blend the mixture for about 2 minutes.
2. Transfer the cream to a jar, cover it, and refrigerate it. If the cream becomes too thick, thin it by stirring in a little milk or buttermilk.

CRANBERRY RELISH TO REMEMBER

2½ cups

This is a wonderful fresh cranberry relish that uses surprisingly little sugar. Don't wait for Thanksgiving; if you freeze fresh cranberries in season, you can serve it any time of year (it's even good on toast).

> 2 cups (½ pound) fresh (or frozen and defrosted) cranberries, cleaned
> 1 unpeeled orange, cut in eighths and seeded
> 3 tablespoons sugar
> Pinch salt
> 2 to 3 tablespoons orange-flavored liqueur

1. Chop the cranberries and oranges together by hand or in a food processor (don't let them get mushy) or by forcing them through the coarse blade of a meat grinder.
2. Transfer the fruit to a bowl, and stir in the sugar, salt, and liqueur.

CREAMY DESSERT SAUCE

1¾ cups

Carol Cutler *(The Woman's Day Low-Calorie Dessert Cookbook)* devised this pud-dinglike sauce that complements many desserts (especially those made from fruit) at only 20 calories per tablespoon. The liqueur and brandy add flavor and richness without many calories.

  1 13-ounce can evaporated skim milk
  3 tablespoons sugar
  2 tablespoons cornstarch
  ⅓ cup skim milk
  1 teaspoon vanilla
  2 teaspoons orange liqueur
  1 teaspoon brandy

1. In a small saucepan, combine the evaporated milk and sugar, and place the pan over low heat.
2. Place the cornstarch in a cup, and add the skim milk, stirring the ingredients into a smooth paste. Slowly add this to the heated milk and sugar, stirring the mixture with a whisk. Continue cooking the mixture and whisking it until the sauce thickens.
3. Add the vanilla, liqueur, and brandy. Simmer the sauce 1 minute longer. Chill the sauce, covered with plastic wrap, until serving time. To reheat the sauce, place it in the top of a double boiler, and warm it over boiling water.

20 ·
PUTTING IT ALL TOGETHER: A MENU GUIDE

By now I'm sure you realize that there is no one "right way" to eat. The possible selections in a healthful, good-tasting diet are numerous and varied and can be put together in many different nutritionally sound patterns to suit various life styles. What I offer here are just suggested combinations to give you some ideas about how to construct wholesome menus that do not turn you into a galley slave. You can modify these menus to suit your own or your family's tastes and needs. Just be sure to eat a variety of foods that include representatives of the Basic Four food groups. Strive in your daily eating plan to include 4 servings of vegetables and fruits; 4 servings of breads and cereals; 2 servings of a high-protein food like meat, poultry, fish, or beans; and 2 to 4 servings (depending on your age and circumstances) of a dairy food like low-fat milk, yogurt, or cottage cheese (see Table 16 on p. 649). No one is expected to eat a perfectly "balanced" menu every single day; rather, nutrient intake should be balanced over the course of several days to a week.

Nor are people expected to cook three-course dinners—or even one-course dinners—everyday. Under normal circumstances, my husband and I cook main meals (other than breakfast) only about three or four times a week. Much of this cooking is done on weekends (or after supper on weekday evenings). And wherever the recipe and our tastes permit, we make double recipes so that there are leftovers for an instant meal another day. Other times, leftovers of various meals are combined to make a quickly prepared meal that is as good or better than the individual ingredients were the first time around. For example, leftover spaghetti sauce might be combined with leftover chicken and served over freshly cooked rice; with a salad and bread, we've got a supper that requires little thought and is ready to eat in about 20 minutes. The same with soups from leftovers: starting with refrigerated or frozen broth, we might add various bits and pieces of leftover vegetables, some frozen shrimp or cooked (usually canned) chickpeas or other beans, and rice or potatoes or tiny pasta and serve it with grated Parmesan cheese and whole-grain bread and salad. If you have a microwave oven, dining deliciously on leftovers is even easier since you don't even have to remember to take things out of the freezer before you leave for work. And with a microwave, it's easy to add a fresh ingredient to your meal such as a baked potato. Cooking this way, we rarely need to rely on packaged

Table 16   THE BASIC FOUR

Food	Amount per serving*	Servings per day
BREAD, GRAIN, AND CEREAL GROUP		
Bread	1 slice	4, whole-grain or enriched only, includ-
Cooked cereal	½ to ¾ cup	ing at least 1 serving of whole-grain
Pasta	½ to ¾ cup	
Rice	½ to ¾ cup	
Dry cereal	1 ounce	
VEGETABLE AND FRUIT GROUP		
Vegetables, cut up	½ cup	4, including one good vitamin C source
Fruits, cut up	½ cup	like oranges or orange juice and one
Grapefruit	½ medium	deep-yellow or dark-green vegetable
Melon	½ medium	
Orange	1 medium	
Potato	1 medium	
Salad	1 bowl	
Lettuce	1 wedge	
PROTEIN GROUP		
Meat, lean	2 to 3 ounces	2, can be eaten as mixtures of animal and
Poultry	2 to 3 ounces	vegetable foods or as a combination of
Fish	2 to 3 ounces	complementary vegetable proteins
Hard cheese	2 to 3 ounces	
Eggs	2 to 3	
Cottage cheese	½ cup	
Dry beans and peas	1 to 1½ cups	
Nuts and seeds	½ to ¾ cup	
Peanut butter	4 tablespoons	
DAIRY GROUP		
Milk	8 ounces (1 cup)	Children 0–9: 2 to 3; children 9–12: 3;
Yogurt, plain	1 cup	teens: 4; men: 2; women: 3; pregnant and
Hard cheese	1¼ ounces	nursing women: 4
Cheese spread	2 ounces	
Ice cream	1½ cups	
Cottage cheese	2 cups	

*Amounts are chosen to meet specific nutritional needs. For the protein group, serving size is determined by the food's protein content. For the dairy group, serving size is based on the calcium content of 1 cup of milk.

precooked foods as the centerpiece of our meals. Nor do we eat out often. At worst, we sometimes bake a frozen pizza (or buy one from a take-out restaurant) or frozen pasta stuffed with cheese, to which we add our own sauce.

As a cook who resists following other people's menus, I don't expect you to adhere to mine, rigidly or otherwise. I offer them primarily to stimulate your thinking and to help you start planning meals that focus around starchy foods and vegetables rather than meat and other animal protein foods. For those who need more structure than I provide, there are several excellent cookbooks to help you establish a "game plan" by which to shop and cook. Two of the best are by Marian Burros, *The New York Times* food writer: *Keep It Simple* and *You've Got It Made,* both published by William Morrow.

But be wary of cookbooks that promise you meals in 15 minutes. True, an experienced and well-organized cook can often prepare individual dishes that quickly, but those dishes are only one part of the meal. Good cooking from scratch takes time—not hours necessarily, but usually more than 15 minutes. Also watch out for cookbooks that rely heavily on prepared foods as ingredients. These rarely meet the nutritional guidelines I have outlined since most are high in saturated fats and/or salt. I admit, however, that I am no purist. I do use processed ingredients like ketchup and mustard, canned tomatoes and beans, frozen spinach, corn, and peas, and an occasional can of bouillon or even a bouillon cube. But in most recipes, the emphasis is clearly on cooking with basic foods as they come from farm and field rather than processing plant.

The menus that follow were devised to meet a variety of common circumstances: weekday and weekend meals at different times of the year as well as meals for holiday weekends. Included are meal plans for households in which all adults work away from home, meals for folks who eat most or all of their meals at home, as well as meals for brown-baggers. (For wholesome dining-out suggestions, see pp. 204–215.)

In the menus that follow, I sometimes encourage you to make recipes big enough to feed your family for two or more meals. The leftovers can be stored in the refrigerator for several days and can often be frozen for months. Then you can prepare "instant" meals during the week when you come home tired and hungry and anxious to get supper cooked and eaten as quickly and simply as possible. Recipes for the dishes marked with asterisks can be found in this book. Of course, you may substitute a similar low-fat alternative from your own recipe collection or from other recipes contained here.

You'll notice that I include snacks in my menu plans. These can be eaten at any time of the day, whenever you feel hungry between meals. Or, if you cannot afford the extra calories, you can save mealtime desserts, salads, or bread to eat as snacks. Most of our meals include bread in one form or another, even when not specifically stated in the menu. And most of our breads are homemade (see the many wholesome choices on pp. 561–582), although you should be able to buy 100-percent whole-grain bread or close to it in your supermarket. As for beverages, acceptable choices include low-fat or skim milk, fruit juices (not "drinks"), club soda or seltzer (plain or flavored but not soda pop, with or without sugar), plain water or mineral water, coffee or tea (mostly decaffeinated), beer or wine (limit to once a day), hot cocoa or low-fat chocolate milk (if you can handle the extra calories).

Feeding Children

When the household includes small children who are fussy eaters, some modifications and imagination may be necessary. For example, instead of trying to feed a 3 year old a pasta salad for supper, it may make more sense to cook some extra pasta for the child and heat it at mealtime in a sauce of low-fat milk and grated cheese. Or, when dining on a main-dish soup, you may want to purée some of the vegetables or beans to disguise their presence but preserve their nutrient contribution. As parents who raised two normally picky eaters, my husband and I are well aware of the need to modify recipes so that the kids will eat them. We also know that adults can tire quickly of the kinds of foods that appeal day in, day out to young children. Few adults would want to spend a decade dining mainly on burgers and macaroni and cheese! Two tactics can help you preserve dining diversity despite the presence of young children in the household. One is occasionally to make two different meals for the adults and children that use the same basic ingredients but differ in specifics and level of culinary sophistication. The other is to periodically introduce your children to grown-up fare, insisting only that they taste the food. If they then refuse to eat it, offer them cereal or a sandwich and fruit as an alternative. Eventually, most children expand their taste horizons and learn to enjoy the foods that they once refused to let pass their lips (see also "How to Get Kids to Eat Vegetables" on p. 131).

A Week in Winter (NOTE: *Recipes are provided for asterisked entries.*)

	SATURDAY	SUNDAY	MONDAY

Breakfast	Citrus juice
	*Brody's Mile-High
	   Pancakes
	Beverage
		(*See brunch below*)	Citrus juice or fruit
			*Rice Pudding Cereal
			   (from leftover rice)
			Whole-wheat toast
			Beverage

Lunch
*(Brunch on
Sunday)*
	*Chili without Carne
	   (2 meals)
	Rice (2 meals)
	Salad (e.g., *Citrus and
	   Spinach)
	Bread
	Beverage
		Fruit Salad
		*No-Yolk Soufflé
		Muffin
		Beverage
			Soup (e.g., *Potato and
			   Turnip Soup)
			Sardine sandwich
			Fruit
			Beverage

Supper
*(Dinner on
Sunday)*
	*Fine Fish Chowder
	   (2 meals)
	Bread (e.g., *Buttermilk-
	   Oat-Potato)
	*Couscous Pudding (2 or
	   more meals)
	Beverage
		½ grapefruit
		*Meat Loaf with Shredded
		   Vegetables (2 meals)
		Baked potatoes (2 meals)
		Bread (e.g., *Quick
		   Cottage-Oat Biscuits)
		Salad
		*Poached Pears with Peach
		   Sauce (2 meals)
		Beverage
			*Fine Fish Chowder
			   (leftover)
			Bread
			Salad (e.g., *Green Bean
			   and Chickpea)
			Beverage

Snacks	Fruit
	*Carrot Cake
	Milk
		Hot cocoa
		Fruit
		*Couscous Pudding
		   (leftover)
			*Poached Pears with Peach
			   Sauce (leftover)
			*Carrot Cake (leftover)
			Milk

A Week in Spring (NOTE: *Recipes are provided for asterisked entries.*)

	SATURDAY	SUNDAY	MONDAY

Breakfast	Citrus juice or fruit
	*Corn Griddle Cakes
	Beverage
		(*See brunch below*)	Citrus juice or fruit
			Whole-grain ready-to-eat
			   cereal with sliced fruit
			   or raisins
			Beverage

Lunch
*(Brunch on
Sunday)*
	*Pasta and Peanut Salad
	   (2 meals)
	Muffin (e.g.,
	   *Orange-Wheat)
	Beverage
		Citrus juice or fruit
		*Spinach Frittata (2 meals)
		Whole-wheat toast
		Beverage
			Soup
			*Pasta and Peanut Salad
			   (leftover)
			Beverage

Supper
*(Dinner on
Sunday)*
	*Chicken with Carrots and
	   Cabbage (2 meals)
	Rice *or* bulgur
	Salad (e.g., *Apple Salad)
	Bread
	*Dolores's Rhubarb Cake
	Beverage
		*Sweet-and-Sour Stuffed
		   Cabbage (2 or more
		   meals, freeze some)
		Mashed potatoes
		   (2 meals)
		Bread
		*Fresh-Fruit Layer Pie
		Beverage
			*Asparagus-stuffed
			   Flounder
			Pasta with *Creamy
			   Tomato Sauce
			Salad
			Bread
			Beverage

Snacks	Fruit Milk	Fruit Muffin Milk	Fruit *Carrot-Oatmeal Cookies Milk

TUESDAY	WEDNESDAY	THURSDAY	FRIDAY
Citrus juice or fruit *Pita Pizzas Beverage	Citrus juice or fruit *Hearty Oatmeal Toast Beverage	Citrus juice or fruit *Cholesterol-controlled French Toast with unsweetened apple butter and yogurt Beverage	Citrus juice or fruit *Spaghetti Pancake (from leftover spaghetti) Beverage
Soup (e.g., *Cream of Squash) *Chili without Carne (leftover) Bread Beverage	*Stuffed Baked Potatoes (from leftover) Salad *or* fruit Bread Beverage	Soup (e.g., *Curried Cream of Broccoli) Chicken-salad sandwich Beverage	Soup (e.g., *Puréed Split Pea) Sandwich (e.g., tuna and cottage cheese) Beverage
*Meat Loaf with Shredded Vegetables (leftover) *Basic Bulgur Pilaf or Rice Salad (e.g., *Red and Green Watercress) Beverage	*Turkey Burgers Whole-wheat pita Salad (e.g., *Mung Bean Sprout) Beverage	*Chickpea Sauce and Spaghetti (spaghetti for 2 meals) Bread Mixed green salad Beverage	*Tomato-crowned Cod *Brussels Sprouts with Lemon-Mustard Sauce Couscous *or* rice Salad Bread Beverage
Fruit *Couscous Pudding (leftover) Hot cocoa	Fruit Muffin (e.g., *Best-of-Bran) Milk	Fruit Hot cocoa	Fruit Muffin

Citrus juice or fruit *Cottage Cheese Toasties Beverage	Citrus juice or fruit *Cottage Cheese Pancakes with yogurt and sliced fruit Beverage	Citrus juice or fruit Sandwich: turkey breast and Swiss on whole-wheat pita Beverage	Citrus juice or fruit Oatmeal with raisins and cinnamon Beverage
*Spinach Frittata (leftover) Salad (e.g., *Beet Salad in Horseradish Dressing) Bread Beverage	*Potato-Bean Patties (use leftover mashed potatoes) Salad Bread Beverage	*Broccoli and Crab Bisque (can prepare night before) Bread Salad (e.g., *Fruited Slaw) Beverage	Soup Peanut butter and apple butter sandwich Fruit Beverage
*Chicken with Carrots and Cabbage (leftover) Millet Salad Bread Beverage	*Sweet-and-Sour Stuffed Cabbage (leftover) Egg noodles Salad Bread Beverage	*Kasha Varnishkas *Pineapple-poached Carrots *Mustardy Beet Salad Bread Beverage	*Potato-Salmon Croquettes *Braised Kohlrabi *or* *Braised Cabbage with Caraway Salad (e.g., *Nutty Asparagus) Bread Beverage
Fruit Milk Muffin	Fruit Muffin Milk	Fruit Muffin Milk	Fruit Whole-wheat toast Milk

A Week in Summer (NOTE: Recipes are provided for asterisked entries.)

	SATURDAY	SUNDAY	MONDAY

Breakfast	Citrus juice or fruit
	*Basic Multigrain Pancakes
	  with blueberries and
	  yogurt
	Beverage
		(See brunch below)	Citrus juice or fruit
			Whole-grain ready-to-eat
			  cereal with fruit
			Beverage

Lunch
(Brunch on
Sunday)
	*Sardine Salad with
	  Broccoli (2 meals)
	Bread
	Fruit
		Fruit salad (2 meals)
		*Marlys's Zucchini and
		  Cheese Casserole
		  (2 meals)
		Bread
		Beverage
			*Gazpacho Grande
			  (leftover)
			*Marlys's Zucchini and
			  Cheese Casserole
			  (leftover)
			Tortilla or bread
			Beverage

Supper
(Dinner on
Sunday)
	*Gazpacho Grande
	  (2 meals)
	*Tortilla Chips
	*Meatless Tamale Pie
	  (2 meals)
	*Drunken Oranges
	  (2 meals)
	Beverage
		*Cold Cucumber and
		  Yogurt Soup (2 meals)
		*Cold Poached Striped Bass
		  (2 meals)
		*Jane's Tabbouli (2 meals)
		Bread
		*Blueberry Cobbler
		Beverage
			*Meatless Tamale Pie
			  (leftover)
			*Dilly Bean Salad or
			  *Jane's Tabbouli
			  (leftover)
			Bread
			*Drunken Oranges
			  (leftover)
			Beverage

Snacks	Chocolate milk Muffin or quick bread	Plain yogurt with fruit Muffin or toast	Fruit salad (leftover) Milk Muffin or cookie

A Week in Fall (NOTE: Recipes are provided for asterisked entries.)

	SATURDAY	SUNDAY	MONDAY

Breakfast	Citrus juice or fruit
	Egg noodles and cottage
	  cheese
	Beverage
		(See brunch below)	Citrus juice or fruit
			*Black Bean Soup with
			  Cumin (leftover)
			Pita
			Beverage

Lunch
(Brunch on
Sunday)
	*Lentil-and-Bulgur Patty
	  Sandwiches (2 meals)
	Salad (e.g., *Curried
	  Coleslaw or *Greek
	  Eggplant)
	Bread
	Beverage
		Fruit Salad
		*Potato Soufflé (2 meals)
		Bread
		Beverage
			Burger on roll (plain)
			Salad
			Beverage

Supper
(Dinner on
Sunday)
	*Hot and Sour Chinese
	  Soup (2 meals)
	*Beef Lo Mein (2 meals)
	Salad (e.g., *Chinese
	  Radish)
	Beverage
		*Black Bean Soup with
		  Cumin (2 meals)
		*Tortilla Casserole (2 or
		  more meals, can freeze)
		Salad (e.g., *Avocado
		  Salsa)
		Tortilla or pita
		*Spicy Poached Pears
		  (2 meals)
		Beverage
			*Lentil-and-Bulgur Patty
			  Sandwiches
			*Carrot and Broccoli
			  Stir-Fry
			Salad
			Beverage

Snacks	Fruit Muffin Milk	Hot cocoa Fruit Muffin	Fruit Milk Muffin or cookie

NOTE: Saturday or Sunday, prepare a large batch of
*The Best Ratatouille and freeze for year-round use.

TUESDAY	WEDNESDAY	THURSDAY	FRIDAY

Citrus juice or fruit
Peanut butter and
  apple butter sandwich
Beverage
	Citrus juice or fruit
	Yogurt with
	  blueberries and
	  strawberries
	Muffin (e.g., *Corny
	  Corn)
	Beverage
		Citrus juice or fruit
		Whole-grain
		  ready-to-eat cereal
		  with fruit
		Beverage
			Citrus juice or fruit
			Sliced turkey sandwich
			Beverage

Soup
*Sardine Salad with
  Broccoli (leftover)
Bread
Fruit
Beverage
	*Cold Cucumber and
	  Yogurt Soup
	  (leftover)
	*Tricolor Chickpea
	  Salad (can prepare
	  night before)
	Bread
	Fruit
	Beverage
		Pizza
		Salad
		Beverage
			Yogurt and fruit
			*Corny corn muffin
			  (leftover)
			Beverage

*Cold Poached Striped
  Bass (leftover)
*Potato and Green
  Bean Salad
Bread
Beverage
	*Zucchini Lasagne (can
	  prepare night
	  before)
	Mixed green salad
	Garlic bread
	Beverage
		*Scandinavian Salmon
		  Salad
		*Mexican Succotash
		Bread
		Beverage
			*Flounder with Mexican
			  Hot Sauce
			*Peperonata
			Rice
			Bread
			Beverage

*Pineapple Sherbet Muffin or cookie	Fruit Frozen yogurt	*Corny Corn Muffin Fruit Milk	Fruit *Pineapple Sherbet (leftover) Milk

Citrus juice or fruit
*Pumpkin-Oat Pancakes
*Spicy Poached Pears
  (leftover)
Beverage
	Citrus juice or fruit
	Whole-grain
	  ready-to-eat cereal
	  with banana
	Beverage
		Citrus juice or fruit
		*Spaghetti Pancake (use
		  leftover spaghetti)
		Beverage
			Citrus juice or fruit
			*Hearty Oatmeal
			Toast
			Beverage

*Potato Soup
  (leftover)
Salad
Bread
Beverage
	*Tortilla Cantoful
	  (leftover)
	Salad
	Fruit
	Beverage
		Soup
		Sandwich
		Fruit
		Beverage
			Soup
			Tuna and cottage
			  cheese salad
			Bread
			Beverage

*Hot and Sour Chinese
  Soup (leftover)
*Beef Lo Mein
  (leftover)
Beverage
	Spaghetti (for 2 meals)
	  with *White Clam
	  Sauce
	Salad (e.g., *Green
	  Bean and Chickpea)
	Garlic or Parmesan
	  bread
	Beverage
		*Chicken Cacciatore
		  with Noodles
		  (2 meals)
		*Swiss Chard Sauté
		Bread
		Beverage
			*Fish Fillets with
			  Ratatouille
			Spaghetti with grated
			  Parmesan
			Salad
			Bread
			Beverage

Fruit Muffin or quick bread Milk	Fruit Hot cocoa	Fruit Milk Muffin or quick bread	Fruit Muffin Milk

Thanksgiving Weekend (NOTE: *Recipes are provided for asterisked entries.*)

	THURSDAY	FRIDAY	SATURDAY
Breakfast	Citrus juice or fruit Hot cereal Beverage	Citrus juice or fruit *Potato Stuffing (leftover) Yogurt Beverage	Citrus juice or fruit *Cottage Cheese Toasties Beverage

Lunch
(Brunch on
Sunday)
	(See dinner below)	*Turkey Pockets
		*Cranberry Relish to
		  Remember (leftover)
		Beverage
			*Turkey Carcass Soup
			  (leftover)
			Salad
			Bread
			Beverage

Supper
(Dinner on
Thursday
and
Sunday)
	*Cranberry-Wine Punch
	*Roast Turkey (plan on
	  half leftover)
	*Potato Stuffing (make
	  extra)
	*Cranberry Relish to
	  Remember
	*Steamed Kale *or*
	  *Broccoli Chinoise
	*Wheat Germ Casserole
	  Bread
	*Pumpkin-Orange Chiffon
	  Pie
	Beverage
		*Turkey Carcass Soup
		  (2 meals)
		Bread
		Salad
		Beverage
			*Turkey and Rice Salad
			  (1 or 2 meals)
			Bread
			*Cranberry-Apple Crisp
			Beverage

Snacks	Hot cocoa NOTE: *Tonight prepare* *turkey broth from carcass* *and giblets (see *Turkey* *Carcass Soup).*	*Pumpkin-Orange Chiffon Pie (leftover) Fruit Milk	Fruit Hot cocoa

Parties and Picnics (NOTE: *Recipes are provided for asterisked entries.*)

SUNDAY	SUMMER BUFFET	WINTER BUFFET	FOURTH OF JULY
(See brunch below)	*Mango Cocktail	*Mulled Cider	*Jane's Tabbouli
	*Strawberry Daiquiri	*Vegetable Platter	*Salsa Dip
	*Vegetable Platter	*Tortilla Chips	Pita toasts *or* *Tortilla
Citrus juice or fruit	*Dips:	*Dips	Chips
*Basic Multigrain	Salsa	Chilied Bean	*Cold Sesame Noodles
Pancakes with	Curried Yogurt	Guacamole	*Cold Poached Striped
cranberries, topped	Indian Peanut	Sesame-Parsley	Bass
with yogurt and	*Bulgur-stuffed Cherry	Sauce	*Chinese Bean Salad
sautéed pears	Tomatoes	*Cocktail Knishes	*Chilled Asparagus with
Beverage	*Egyptian Fête Salad	*Ratatouille Pita Pizza	Yogurt Sauce
*Turkey Tetrazzini	*Hummus	*Polish Potato Casserole	*Blueberries and
(2 meals)	*Baba Ghanoush	*Bulgur-Beef Balls	Peaches in Mint
Salad	Pita toasts	Rice *or* *Wild Rice	Sauce
Bread	*Tomato-Seafood Aspic	with Indian Nuts	*Strawberries 'n' Purée
*Fruited Brown Rice	*Tricolor Chickpea	*Curried Coleslaw	Beverage
Pudding	Salad	*Cranberry Salad Mold	
Beverage	*Intercontinental	*Drunken Oranges	
	"Ravioli"	*Flourless Apple	
	*No-Bake Peach Pie	"Cake"	
	*Lime-Yogurt Pie	*Applesauce-Carrot	
	Beverages	Cake	
		Beverages	
Fruit			
*Cranberry Bread			
Brody			
Milk			

Cake," which appears on page 587, is adapted with the permission of Garneta Baurle. The recipe for "Puréed Peanut Butter and Vegetable Soup," which appears on page 319, is reprinted with permission from *Environmental Nutrition,* Vol. 5, No. 10, October 1982 issue. The recipe for "Tomato Juice Bread," which appears on page 574, is adapted from *The New Book of Favorite Breads from Rose Lane Farm* with the permission of Dover Publications, Inc. The recipes for "Cornell Bread" and "Whole Wheat–Carrot Pitas," which appear on pages 564 and 578, are adapted from *The Cornell Bread Book* with the permission of Dover Publications, Inc. The recipes for "Millet Cakes" and "Meatless Tamale Pie," which appear on pages 506 and 389, are adapted with the permission of Sharon Cadwallader. The recipe for "Deep-Dish Spinach Pie," which appears on page 478, is adapted with the permission of Pizzapiazza, 785 Broadway, New York, New York.

INDEX

Page numbers in **boldface** refer to recipes.

Page numbers in **boldface** refer to recipes.

Page numbers in **boldface** refer to recipes.

Page numbers in **boldface** refer to recipes.

Page numbers in **boldface** refer to recipes.

Page numbers in **boldface** refer to recipes.

Page numbers in **boldface** refer to recipes.

Page numbers in **boldface** refer to recipes.

Page numbers in **boldface** refer to recipes.

Page numbers in **boldface** refer to recipes.

Page numbers in **boldface** refer to recipes.

Page numbers in **boldface** refer to recipes.

Page numbers in **boldface** refer to recipes.